Social
Problems

HARPER & ROW, PUBLISHERS, New York
Cambridge, Hagerstown, Philadelphia, San Francisco,
London, Mexico City, São Paulo, Sydney

1817

Social Problems

JAMES WILLIAM COLEMAN
California Polytechnic State University, San Luis Obispo

DONALD R. CRESSEY
University of California, Santa Barbara

Sponsoring Editor: Alan Spiegel
Project Editor: Claudia Kohner
Designer: Emily Harste
Senior Production Manager: Kewal K. Sharma
Photo Researcher: Myra Schachne
Compositor: Ruttle, Shaw & Wetherill, Inc.
Printer and Binder: The Murray Printing Company
Art Studio: J & R Technical Services Inc.
Cover Photo: Christian Irgens

Social Problems

Library of Congress Cataloging in Publication Data

Coleman, James William, Date-
   Social problems.

   Includes bibliographical references and indexes.
   1. Sociology. 2. Social problems. 3. Social institu-
tions. 4. United States—Social conditions. I. Cressey,
Donald Ray, 1919–   joint author.
II. Title.
HM51.C593   301   79-23645
ISBN 0-06-041326-3

To Jack and Nema Coleman
and
To Myrtle Prentiss Cressey Nelson

Contents

Preface

We wrote this book for students. Our objective is to familiarize under-
graduates with some of the most trying problems of their times. We have
tried to get students to think about the social issues with which they are
already familiar, and we have tried to challenge the half-truths and pat answers that many people accept simply because they have heard them
repeated so often. By pointing out the disagreements among authorities
and by including strongly worded debates arguing both sides of controversial issues, we hope to stimulate students to question these common assumptions and to think for themselves.

Professors who are looking for a new theory of social problems will not
find it here. Many textbooks devote long sections to promoting or defending a particular theoretical position without telling the readers about other
theories. Others try to resolve long-standing sociological controversies involving complicated theoretical paradigms and niceties of research. Our
book tries only to prepare students for later reading and discussions about
such issues. By analogy, this is a book on how to listen to music rather
than a book on harmony or the structure of the fugue.

We have not neglected theory, and we have not avoided controversy.
One of the distinctive features of this book is its presentation of social
problems from the theoretical perspectives of functionalism, conflict
theory, and social psychology. Each of these broad frameworks is used at
some place in every chapter, and each chapter closes with a simple statement about what a functionalist, a conflict theorist, and a social psychologist might say about the problem just discussed. After reading eighteen
presentations of this kind, every student will have an appreciation of the
similarities and differences between these theories, but without having
waded through long treatises on exactly what Parsons and Merton said,
what Durkheim, Marx, and Weber had in mind, or what George Herbert
Mead really meant. Moreover, the students will be able to see that controversy is the stuff of which social problems are made, no matter what
the various authorities may say about them.

Although we are both Americans, we have tried to avoid the insular
view of social problems so common in other American texts. Every

problem in the book is shared by people in all parts of the world, and we have tried to show how North America's social problems are affected by international social forces. The exclusion of Canadian materials from texts designed for the American market is a particularly troubling omission. We believe there is much to be learned by comparing the different policies pursued in the United States and Canada, and we have done so wherever possible.

Writing in simple language about complex and controversial issues is not easy. We have tried to do so without "writing down" to the readers. In order to avoid the distracting changes in style and tone so common in books with multiple authors, we did not follow the usual procedure of dividing up the chapters between the authors. Instead, Coleman wrote the rough drafts of every chapter. Cressey then revised these pieces, making them into first drafts. Then, for subsequent drafts, the two of us worked together to sandpaper, polish, and otherwise smooth out these writings. Maureen Harrington de Vivas assisted in these revisions by collecting and inserting some of the Canadian data. Our students helped us clarify almost every page, and they noted dozens of instances where a little word could be used as effectively as a big one.

We thank the following people for their insightful reviews of the entire manuscript: James P. Driscoll, Sonoma State College; Rollie E. Dorsett, Austin Community College; Peter Kassebaum, College of Marin; Carl C. Jorgenson, University of California, Davis; Victoria L. Swigert, College of the Holy Cross; and Julie C. Wolfe-Petrusky, University of Utah. Dozens of changes suggested by these reviewers have been made, and we are deeply indebted to them. We also thank the hundreds of freshmen and sophomores who, over the years, have read and criticized one draft or another. Our special thanks goes to Fred Simon. Our wives, Theo Coleman and Elaine Cressey, showed amazing tolerance and patience during the three years it took us to write this book, and we are grateful. Finally, we thank Cathy Jarosz and Miye Narkis who, fortunately for us, edited as they typed.

James William Coleman
Donald R. Cressey

Acknowledgments

Photo Credits (The numbers in italics preceding each credit are page numbers in this text.)

1 George Gardner; *5* Karlin, DeWys; *9* DeWys; *16* © Tracy Ecclesine; *24* Forsyth, Monkmeyer; *30–31* Malave, Stock, Boston; *33* Rogers, Monkmeyer; *38* Miller, Monkmeyer; *42* Maytree, Monkmeyer; *47* Whitaker, DeWys; *51* Conklin, Monkmeyer; *62* Sherman, Nancy Palmer; *66* Forsyth, Monkmeyer; *81* Müller, Peter Arnold; *83* Hoops, DeWys; *92* Conklin, Monkmeyer; *95* DeWys; *102* Murray, Nancy Palmer; *107* Karales, Peter Arnold; *118* Campbell, Taurus; *121* Consilvio, Stock, Boston; *123* Franken, Stock, Boston; *134* Vandermark, Stock, Boston; *139* Zeiberg, Taurus; *146–147* Menzel, Stock, Boston; *149* Rogers, Monkmeyer; *151 top* Joel Gordon; *151 bottom* Murray, Nancy Palmer; *165* Sacks, Editorial Photocolor Archives; *167* Joel Gordon; *172* Forsyth, Monkmeyer; *178* Kroll, Taurus; *189* UPI; *196* Charles Gatewood; *200* UPI; *210* Wolinsky, Stock, Boston; *217 top* Pfeffer, Peter Arnold; *217 bottom* Mezey, DPI; *223* Karales, Peter Arnold; *227* Weldon, DeWys; *236* Miller, Nancy Palmer; *246* Eagan, Woodfin Camp; *248* DeWys; *251* Eagle, Nancy Palmer; *253* Marjorie Pickens; *255* Albertson, Stock, Boston; *259* Charles Gatewood; *266* Muller, Woodfin Camp; *269 top* Vivienne, DPI; *269 bottom* Kaplan, DPI; *280* Leinwand, Monkmeyer; *286–287* Charles Gatewood; *289* Weldon, DeWys; *291* Bodin, Stock, Boston; *295* UPI; *298 left* Wolinsky, Stock, Boston; *298 right* Kroll, Taurus; *304 top* Baker, Nancy Palmer; *304 bottom* Karales, Peter Arnold; *306* Johnson, DeWys; *313* Beckwith Studios; *318* Charles Gatewood; *327* Park, Monkmeyer; *329* DPI; *331* Kroll, Taurus; *343* Tress, Woodfin Camp; *346* DeWys; *360* Forsyth, Monkmeyer; *364* Anderson, Woodfin Camp; *366* Weldon, DeWys; *373* Kroll, Taurus; *391* Sydney, DeWys; *395* DeWys; *401* Magee, Editorial Photocolor Archives; *405* UPI; *407* Kroll, Taurus; *412* Berndt, Stock, Boston; *416* Wilks, DeWys; *420* Marjorie Pickens; *426* Reininger, DeWys; *429,* DeWys; *434–435* Weldon, DeWys; *437* US Air Force; *441* UPI; *445* UPI; *450* DeWys; *457* Charles Gatewood; *460* Finch, Stock, Boston; *470* Hollander, Stock, Boston; *478* Lovering, Stock, Boston; *483* Hopker, Woodfin Camp; *484* DeWys; *489 top* Reininger/Contact, DeWys; *489 bottom* Griffiths, DPI; *494* Gazdar, Woodfin Camp; *502* Botts, Nancy Palmer; *504* Mentzel, Nancy Palmer; *509* Charles Gatewood; *513* DeWys; *517 top* Gsheidle, Peter Arnold; *517 bottom* Franken, Stock, Boston; *520* Wide World; *522* Reininger, DeWys; *531* Johnson, DeWys.

Figure Permissions

Figure 1.1, adapted from Robert H. Lauer, "Defining Social Problems: Public Opinion and Text Book Practice," *Social Problems,* 24 (October 1976): 25, is used by permission of The Society for the Study of Social Problems and the author. *Figure 2.1,* from Daniel R. Fusfeld, *Economics,* 2d ed. (Lexington, Mass.: D.C. Heath, 1976), pp. 521, 522, is used by permission of the publisher and the author. *Figure 4.2* is used by the permission of the Los Angeles Times. Copyright, 1976, Los Angeles Times. *Figure 17.1* is reprinted from "From Suburb to Urban Place" by David Birth, in Volume 422 of *The Annals* of the American Academy of Political Science. © 1975, by the American Academy of Political and Social Science.

Text Permissions (The numbers in italics preceding each credit are page numbers in this text.)

20–21 Cartwright quotation is from Dorwin Cartwright, "Achieving Change in People: Some Applications of Group Dynamics Theory," *Human Relations* 4 (1951): 381–392. Used by permission of the publisher. *36* Zwerdling quotation is from Zwerdling's "The Food Monopolies" reprinted by permission from *The Progressive,* 408 West Gorham Street, Madison, Wisconsin 53703. Copyright © 1974, The Progressive, Inc. *75* Nader quotation is excerpted from the introduction by Ralph Nader from the book *America, Inc.* by Morton Mintz and Jerry S. Cohen. Introduction Copyright © 1971 by The Dial Press. Reprinted by permission of The Dial Press. *77* Mills quotation is from "The Structure of Power in American Society" from *Power, Politics and People: The Collected Papers of C. Wright Mills,* published by the Oxford University Press. *124* Mirande quotation is from Alfred M. Mirande, "The Isolated Nuclear Family Hypothesis: A Reanalysis," in Mildred W. Weil, ed., *Sociological Perspectives in Marriage and the Family* (Danville, Illinois: The Interstate, 1972), p. 40. Used by permission of the publisher. *139* O'Neill quotation is from "Open Marriage: The Conceptual Framework" in James R. Smith and Lynn G. Smith, eds., *Beyond Monogamy* (Baltimore: The Johns Hopkins University Press, 1974) p. 64 © 1974, The Johns Hopkins University Press. Used by permission of the publisher. *155* Rainwater quotation is excerpted from Lee Rainwater's "The Problems of Lower Class Culture" in *On Understanding Poverty* edited by Daniel Moynihan, © 1968, 1969 by the American Academy of Arts and Sciences, Basic Books, Inc., Publishers, New York. *188–189* Lurie quotation is from Nancy O. Lurie and Stuart Levine, *The American Indian Today,* Everett/Edwards, Inc., Deland, Florida, 1968. Reprinted by permission of the publisher. *192* Cash quotation is from *Viewpoints: Red & Yellow, Black & Brown* by the Editors of Winston Press. Copyright © 1972 by Winston Press. Reprinted by permission of Holt, Rinehart and Winston. *228* Blumenthal and Fallows quotation is from "Health: The Care We Want and Need" by Blumenthal and Fallows. Reprinted with permission from The Washington Monthly, October 1976. *268* Hartley quotation is reprinted with permission of author and publisher from R. E. Hartley's "Sex-Role Pressures and the Socialization of the Male Child," *Psychological Reports,* 1959, 5, 548. *269–270* Bardwick and Douvan quotation is from Chapter 9, "Ambivalence: The Socialization of Women" by Judith M. Bardwick and Elizabeth Douvan, in *Woman in Sexist Society: Studies in Power and Powerlessness,* edited by Vivian Gornick and Barbara K. Moran, © Basic Books Inc., Publishers, New York. *271–272* Komisar quotation is from Chapter 13, "The Image of Woman in Advertising" by Lucy Komisar, in *Woman in Sexist Society: Studies in Power and Powerlessness,* edited by Vivian Gornick and Barbara K. Moran, © Basic Books Inc., Publishers, New York. *350* Ball and Urbaitis quotation is from John Ball and John Urbaitis, "Absence of Major Complications Among Chronic Opiate Users," in John Ball and Carl Chambers, eds., *The Epidemiology of Opiate Addiction in the United States,* 1970. Reprinted courtesy of Charles C Thomas, Publisher, Springfield, Illinois. *396* Petersen quotation is from David M. Petersen, "The Police Officer's Conception of Proper Police Work" in *The Police Journal* (England) 47 (1974): 102–108. Reprinted by permission of the publisher. *446* Finsterbusch and Greisman quote is from Kurt Finsterbusch and H. C. Greisman, "The Unprofitability of Warfare: A Historical-Quantitative Approach," *Social Problems,* 22:3 (February 1975), p. 451. Used by permission of The Society for the Study of Social Problems and the authors. *501* Ehrlich and Ehrlich quotation is excerpted from "What Happened to the Population Bomb?" by Dr. Paul R. Ehrlich and Dr. Anne M. Ehrlich in *Human Nature,* January 1979. Copyright © 1978 by Human Nature, Inc. Reprinted by permission of the publisher. *504* Notestein quotation is from Frank W. Notestein, "The Population Crisis: Reasons for Hope." Quoted by permission from *Foreign Affairs,* October 1967. Copyright 1967 by Council on Foreign Relations, Inc.

Social
Problems

1
Sociology and Social Problems

Poverty, racism, war, violence, mental disorders, pollution—the list of our social problems is depressingly long, so long that many people throw up their hands in despair. Though a picture of a starving Asian baby or the sight of a lonely old man may stir our concern, most of us quietly decide that there is nothing we can do to help. But is this true? Can we do nothing? The sociological study of social problems is founded on the belief that something can indeed be done if we first make the effort to study our problems and then act on our understanding.

But understanding people's conflicts and problems does not mean that change will come easily. Medical scientists have sharply reduced many dread diseases by applying the knowledge they have built up over the years. But most social problems are woven into the fabric of social relationships in ways that diseases are not, and effective action to deal with them is almost always painful and difficult. However, failure to act is likely to lead to more devastating consequences, as history has repeatedly shown.

Politicians, statesmen, and other officials spend their lives trying to solve social problems, often with the "help" of conflicting advice from experts. Citizens vote for officials who promise to do something about problems ranging from crime and poverty to sexual inequality. But voters' ideas about these and other important issues are often distorted and confused.

While serious study of social problems will clear up much confusion and misunderstanding, beginning students often have the uncomfortable feeling that the more they read, the less they understand. There are many conflicting viewpoints. One group with certain interests views a social problem one way, and another group with conflicting interests sees it another way. Even the results of objective, scientific research may appear to be contradictory.

Sociology is a framework for sorting out this mass of facts, ideas, and beliefs. It provides the perspective and the tools needed to make sense of our social problems. The use of the sociological perspective helps reduce confusion in the minds of those who wish to participate intelligently in public discussions of these important issues. With this perspective we can develop solutions to problems and evaluate their results once they have been put into effect.

This is not to say, or course, that sociologists agree on just what a social problem is or how it can be explained. But fortunately such disagreements often result in a richer understanding for the student who is willing to examine all sides of the issues involved.

WHAT IS A SOCIAL PROBLEM?

Most people probably would define a social problem as something that is harmful to society. But the matter is not so simple, for the meaning of such everyday terms as *harm* and *society* are not really clear. Conditions that some people would see as social problems harm some segments of society but are beneficial to others. Consider air pollution. An automobile manufacturer may argue that government regulation of free enterprise is a social problem because laws requiring antipollution devices on all new cars do harm by raising the cost of a new car, decreasing gasoline mileage, and stimulating inflation. On the other hand, residents of a city with heavy air pollution will argue that the government's failure to regulate automobile emissions effectively is a social problem because the smog created by automobiles harms their health and well-being. One person's social problem is another person's solution. Clearly, most people define social problems as conditions that harm or seem to harm their own interests.

A more precise sociological definition holds that a social problem exists when there is a sizable difference between the ideals of a society and its actual achievements.[1] Social problems are created by failure to close the gap between the way people believe things should be and the way things really are. For example, according to this definition racial discrimination is a social problem because we believe that everyone should receive fair and equal treatment, yet certain groups are still denied equal access to education, employment, and housing. Before this definition can be applied, we must first examine the ideals and values of society and then decide whether these standards are being achieved. This definition permits sociologists and other experts to decide what is or is not a problem, because they are the ones with the skills necessary for measuring the desires and achievements of society.

Critics of this approach note that no contemporary society has a single, unified set of values and ideals. Instead, there are many conflicting and contradictory beliefs. Thus, sociologists must decide which ideals will serve as standards for judging whether a certain condition is a social problem. Critics charge that the ideals and values that the sociologists select as standards are not outcomes of objective analysis but, rather, reflections of their personal opinions and prejudices.

A different sociological definition holds that a social problem exists when a significant number of people believe that a certain condition is in fact a problem.[2] Here "the public" — not a sociologist — decides what is or is not a social problem. The sociologist's job is to determine which problems are of concern to substantial numbers of people. Thus, pollution did not become a social problem until environmental activists were able to convince others to show concern about conditions that had actually existed for some time.

The advantage of this definition is that it does not require a value judgment by sociologists who try to decide what conditions are social problems. Such decisions are made by "the public." However, a serious shortcoming of this approach arises because the public often is uninformed or misguided. If thousands of people did not know they were being poisoned

[margin note: belief – reality]

[margin note: Public decides]

by radiation leaking from a nuclear-power plant, wouldn't radiation pollution still be a social problem?

All the topics we will cover in the chapters that follow qualify as social problems according to both sociological definitions. Each problem involves conditions that conflict with strongly held ideals and values, and all are considered social problems by significant groups of people. We have tried to discuss every problem fairly and objectively. However, it is important to understand that the selection of the problems to be considered requires a value judgment, whether by social scientists or by concerned citizens. As a result honest disagreements about the importance of the various issues competing for public attention cannot be avoided.

SOCIAL PROBLEMS AND SOCIAL MOVEMENTS

The social issues that concern the public change from time to time, and an examination of the Gallup poll's surveys of opinion on major social problems will reveal some interesting trends. War and peace and various economic issues have consistently ranked high on the public's list of social concerns. Interest in other problems seems to move in cycles. Thus, concern over taxes, foreign policy, and lack of religion and morality is high in some years and low in others. Other social problems are like fads, attracting a great deal of interest for a few years before dropping from public attention. For instance, concern about the atom bomb was frequently expressed in the 1950s but has not appeared in public-opinion polls since then.[3] (See Figure 1.1.)

Changes in the problems that receive the most attention have many dif-

**FIGURE 1.1
SOCIAL PROBLEMS AS IDENTIFIED BY PUBLIC-OPINION POLLS**

PROBLEM	1935	1939	1945	1947	1949	1951	1956	1959	1963	1965	1967	1969	1971	1973	1975
1. War and Peace (including neutrality)	X	X	X	X	X	X	X	X	X	X	X	X	X	X	X
2. The Economy, Including Unemployment	X	X	X		X	X	X	X	X				X	X	X
3. High Cost of Living Including Inflation				X	X	X	X	X	X	X	X	X	X	X	X
4. Taxes	X	X	X		X	X		X							
5. Government Spending	X	X				X	X								
6. Labor Problems	X	X	X	X	X			X							
7. Foreign Policy						X	X	X		X	X		X	X	X
8. Communism						X	X		X		X				
9. Crime and Delinquency								X	X		X		X	X	X
10. Civil Rights and Race								X	X	X	X	X	X	X	X
11. Farm Problems	X							X							
12. The Atomic Bomb				X	X										
13. Lack of Religion and Morality	X	X				X			X				X		X
14. Poverty										X			X	X	X

Source: Adapted from Robert H. Lauer, "Defining Social Problems: Public Opinion and Text Book Practice," *Social Problems,* 24 (October 1976): 125.

Social movements help create public awareness and concern about social problems. Most social movements push for specific government action to help resolve those problems.

ferent causes—changes in ideals and values, the solution of an old problem, the creation of new ones. But the most important forces affecting changes in public opinion are social movements that focus attention on a certain social problem. For example, none of the Gallup polls in the 1930s and 1940s showed civil rights and race relations to be significant problems, even though racial discrimination was widespread and openly practiced. It was not until the civil-rights movement began in the late 1950s that the polls began to reflect an interest in this problem. It is quite likely that the civil-rights issue would have remained buried if a powerful social movement had not developed.

Such movements begin with a group objecting to social conditions of which they disapprove. The group may be composed of people who believe they have been victimized, such as black victims of racial discrimination or female victims of sexual discrimination. Or it may be made up of concerned outsiders such as opponents of alcohol use or those favoring the death penalty. As people with a common interest in an issue begin to talk with each other and express their feelings about the problem, moral crusaders step forward to lead the developing movement.[4] Martin Luther King, Jr., was such a leader for the civil-rights movement, as Ralph Nader has been for the consumer movement. The moral crusader's first job is to mold separate groups of dissatisfied people into an organized political movement. The success of the movement depends on publicity, for it is only through publicity that the general public can be made aware of the problem and encouraged to do something about it. In other words, it is through publicity that the problem of a particular group becomes a social problem.

Three factors help a social movement gain public support and favorable action by government. The most important is the political power of the movement and its supporters. If the movement's supporters are numerous, highly organized, wealthy, or in key positions of power, it is much more likely to be successful. Such support made the anticommunist crusades of the 1950s enormously successful, while similar efforts to protect the civil rights of political dissidents have been unsuccessful.

A second factor is the strength of the movement's appeal to people's values and prejudices. A movement to protect children from sexual abuse by adults is much more likely to gain widespread support than an effort to protect the civil liberties of child molesters.

The strength of the opposition to a movement is a third element in its success or failure. The money available for attempts to solve social problems is limited, and the advocates of various social programs must compete with each other for funds. For example, few people object to the proposition that elderly citizens deserve greater government assistance. However, a variety of opponents quickly emerge when someone suggests raising taxes to pay for such improvements. Opposition to social movements also comes from people whose special interests are threatened by the proposed change. Thus, a proposal to raise the minimum wage for farm workers is bound to be opposed by farm owners.

A principal goal of many social movements is to create a social problem and then mobilize government action to resolve it. But even when a movement achieves these objectives government action may be ineffective. A new government agency is often the means chosen to deal with a problem, and governments all over the world have created huge bureaucracies to deal with poverty (departments of welfare), health care (medicare and medicaid), pollution (the Environmental Protection Agency), and crime (police, courts, and prisons). Like all bureaucracies, these agencies are clumsy and slow moving, and are often more concerned with their own survival than with the social problems they are designed to solve. After all, if narcotics enforcement agencies stopped all drug use, if police departments prevented all crime, or if mental hospitals quickly cured all disturbed people, the employees of these agencies would soon be out of work. Occasionally, it appears that agencies that are set up to deal with a particular social problem are not actually expected to solve it. Politicians have been known to approve funds for a social program just to silence troublesome protesters, creating new agencies with impressive titles but no real power.

THE SOCIOLOGICAL APPROACH: BASIC IDEAS

Using standards and methods developed in other fields, sociologists try to study society scientifically. But they have found that human behavior is more complex and more difficult to understand than the topics studied by physicists, chemists, and biologists. Despite these handicaps, sociologists have developed a body of knowledge, theories, and methods which guides their research and forms the heart of sociology. Like other sciences, sociology has its own terms to describe what it studies, often words taken from everyday language. But because precision is necessary, sociologists give special meanings to common terms such as *role, group,* and *culture.*

Roles

A role is a set of expectations and behavior associated with a social position. All positions — daughter, son, student, automobile driver, and countless others — have a set of expectations for the person who occupies that position. These can be divided into two parts — the *rights* a person has because of his or her position, and the *duties* that go with these rights. For instance, the traditional father has a right to make important family decisions, to direct and supervise his children, and to wield considerable authority within the family. But he also has a duty to provide for and protect the family. When a man becomes a father and accepts these rights and duties, he takes the *role* of father.

Every individual plays many roles. A person may be a wife, mother, sister, worker, consumer, student, and criminal — all at the same time. Some people experience role strain because what is expected of them in one role conflicts with what is expected in another. For instance, the roles of student and employee may each require large amounts of time and energy; the individual who attempts to fulfill both is likely to experience considerable role strain.

Roles are one of the basic building blocks of our social world, and every society has countless positions with roles attached. Roles are interwoven in complex ways, so it is often impossible to understand a particular role unless related roles are also understood. For example, it is not possible to define the role of wife without reference to the roles of husband, daughter, son, mother, and father. This interdependence stems from the fact that the rights of one position — wife, for example — are interlaced with the duties of another position — husband, daughter, son. Each of us is judged by our performance as we fill our roles, and the negligent mother, the abusive father, the incompetent professor, and the disruptive student who fail to meet role expectations will be judged harshly.

Norms

A norm is a social rule that tells us what behavior is acceptable in a certain situation and what is not. Every human group, be it a small circle of friends or an entire society, generates norms that govern its members' conduct. Like roles, the norms of various groups may conflict. But individuals who violate norms are often labeled deviants and given some kind of formal or informal punishment. A person who violates norms against taking the lives of others may be tried and formally punished with a prison term, while a person who violates the trust of his or her friends will be informally punished by exclusion from the group.

It should be obvious that not all social norms are of equal importance. Norms that are merely customary procedures and are not strongly held by the group involved are called folkways. The Western custom of eating with a knife and fork, not fingers, is a good example. Those who eat with their fingers at a formal dinner are not sent to jail. They might not even be shunned by their friends, yet they certainly would be considered odd, crude, or unsophisticated. On the other hand, norms that a group considers very important are called mores. People who violate our mores, such as the prohibition of murder and rape, are punished severely. Many ancient mores have been absorbed into criminal law.

Groups

In the sociological sense a group is not just a gathering of people in the same place at the same time. Instead, it is a number of individuals with organized and recurrent relationships with each other. Within the group, members quickly develop expectations about the roles and norms that define their behavior and relationships. Groups have boundaries, and most group members share some common purpose or goal, even if it is only to enjoy each other's company.

To take a simple example, there is a great difference between students who sit quietly in a college library reading their sociology books and a similar number of students who have formed a study group. The group has norms. All members are expected to come prepared to discuss and criticize what they have read and to be helpful rather than competitive. No member is to waste time discussing the weather or last week's football game. In time the group develops specialized roles such as "the brain," "the joker," and "the plodder." A few students may even make their contribution to the group by looking intelligent and dignified while saying little or nothing. The group thus has a division of labor whereby various individuals help achieve the group's goal, each in his or her own particular way.

Socialization

Socialization is the process by which individuals learn the proper ways of behaving in their culture. In fact, it is often called the process of becoming human. Roles, norms, customs, values, how to speak, even how to think — all these are learned in the process of socialization. Aside from a few basic impulses, almost everything humans think or do is learned from others around them.

Most of our basic socialization occurs in the early years of life. The rare child who has been hidden away with little contact with the world at large has limited speech and appears to be mentally defective. But socialization is not confined to the childhood years; it continues throughout our lives. As we enter new social groups, we begin new processes of socialization by acquiring new attitudes, perspectives, and other behavior patterns.

In the process of socialization, children learn to play adult roles by imitating their parents and other adults.

Institutions

Social institutions are relatively stable patterns of thought and action centered on the performance of important social tasks. All societies have institutions for producing children and giving them guidance and support (family), relating to the supernatural (religion), producing and distributing food and other goods and services (economics), socializing children (education), and making and enforcing rules (politics). Social institutions thus are organized around one or more of the necessities of social life. But sometimes the norms of one institution conflict with those of another, as when the norms of an economic institution that stresses free competition and the accumulation of individual wealth clashes with the norms of a family institution stressing cooperation, mutual care, and sharing.

Classes

A social class is a category of people with similar shares of the things that are valued in a society. They have common life chances—the chance to get a good education, to get good health care, to obtain goods, to gain a position in life, to find inner satisfaction, and so on. Karl Marx and other nineteenth-century writers defined class basically in economic terms. Most modern sociologists use a broader conception of class taken from the work of the German sociologist Max Weber. According to Weber, the valuables a society distributes include social status and power as well as money. Status rests on a claim to social prestige, inherited from one's family or derived from occupation and life style. Power is the ability to force

[Handwritten margin notes: Marx - economic; Max Weber - Status, Power, $]

others to do something whether they want to or not. Power is often associated with political institutions, though it may have other sources. In order to assess the class positions of individuals and groups, we must know their social and political standing as well as their income.

Culture

In everyday speech culture refers to the refinements of civilization, such as art, music, and literature. But to sociologists culture is the way of life of the people in a certain geographic area, particularly their ideas, beliefs, values, patterns of thought, and symbols. A culture provides a way of understanding the world and making it meaningful to individuals. A related concept is that of subculture — a culture within a culture. Shared by people who participate in the larger culture, a subculture has its own unique ideas and beliefs yet is influenced by the larger culture. In the United States and Canada it is proper to speak of a working-class subculture, a youth subculture, a criminal subculture, and so on, despite the fact that working-class people, youths, and criminals all share the same overall culture.

Social Structure

Although culture and social structure cannot be separated, sociologists sometimes distinguish between the two for analytical purposes. In such studies social structure refers to organized patterns of human *behavior* in a society while culture emphasizes the *symbolic* aspects of that society. Social structure is composed of positions, roles, classes, and institutions, while culture is made up of norms, values, ideas, and beliefs.

SOCIOLOGICAL PERSPECTIVES ON SOCIAL PROBLEMS

Over the years sociologists have developed and refined several broad theories to account for the nature of society and its problems. An understanding of these theoretical perspectives is essential to the study of social problems because they are designed to make sense of the conflicting claims that are so often made about social issues. There has been a great deal of debate about the superiority of one theoretical perspective over another, and the strengths and weaknesses of each theory have been carefully examined from many different viewpoints.

Different sociological theories are designed to serve different purposes. Some try to make sense of the behavior of large groups of people and the workings of entire societies. These are called macro theories. Other theories are concerned primarily with the behavior of individuals and small groups. They are called micro theories. Functionalist theory and conflict theory are the two most widely used macro theories. Sociologists who are guided by functionalist theory say that social problems arise when societies are disorganized or unorganized. Conflict theorists, on the other hand, point to the exploitation and oppression of one group by another as the principal source of social problems. There are also many different micro theories for making sense of the effects of group life on individuals. These are social-psychological theories. We will consider only the four most important of these—the biosocial, personality, behaviorist, and interactionist theories. (See Figures 1.2 and 1.3.)

**FIGURE 1.2
THEORIES OF SOCIETY
(MACRO LEVEL)**

BASIC ISSUES	FUNCTIONALISM	CONFLICT THEORY
What holds society together?	Agreement on basic norms and values	Power, authority, and coercion
What is the basic nature of modern society?	A balance among various institutions, each performing different functions necessary to the survival of society	A competitive struggle for dominance among various social groups
Is society normally static or dynamic?	Static—when significant changes occur, a healthy society quickly readjusts and returns to a stable equilibrium	Dynamic—society is in a continual state of flux as it adjusts to the shifting balance of power among its competing groups
What is the major cause of social problems?	Social disorganization caused by rapid social change	The exploitation and oppression of some groups by others

**FIGURE 1.3
SOCIAL-PSYCHOLOGICAL
THEORIES (MICRO LEVEL)**

BASIC ISSUES	BIOSOCIAL THEORY	PERSONALITY THEORY	BEHAVIORIST THEORY	INTERACTIONIST THEORY
What is the most fruitful area for research?	The physical human organism and its hereditary makeup	Individual personality	Behavior	Social interaction
What is the principal source of human behavior?	Human biology	Individual personality	Reinforcements from the environment (human and physical)	Interaction with people and groups through symbols and shared meaning
What is the major cause of social problems?	Innate human characteristics; biological defects in certain individuals	Personality disorders	The reinforcement of inappropriate behavior	Social support for deviant or dysfunctional behavior

The supporters of these various theories often disagree with each other, but none of the theories can be said to be "right" or "wrong." Some theories, however, are more effective than others in analyzing a particular social problem, and more than one theory can be applied to the same problem. In fact, the greatest understanding of our social problems comes when the insights gained from different theoretical perspectives are combined.

The Functionalist Perspective

Durkheim

In recent times the functionalists have been among the most influential schools of social thought. Starting with the work of the French sociologist Emile Durkheim, functionalist theory has been refined by Talcott Parsons, Robert K. Merton, and many others. Functionalists see society as a well-organized system in which most members agree on common norms and values. Roles, groups, and institutions fit together in a unified whole. People do what is necessary to maintain a stable society because they accept its rules and regulations.

According to functionalist theory, the various parts of society are in delicate balance, and a change in one part affects the others. Each part has a function in maintaining the balanced order. For instance, the function of economic institutions is to provide the food, shelter, and clothing that people need in order to survive, while the function of the educational institution is to train individuals in the skills needed to keep society operating.

But societies, like automobiles and biological organisms, do not always work the way they are supposed to work. Things get out of whack. Changes introduced to correct a particular imbalance may produce other imbalances, even when things are going well. When the actions of institutions interfere with the effort to carry out essential social tasks, they are said to be dysfunctional. For example, educators may train more people for certain jobs than society can use. Those who cannot find jobs in their special line of work may become resentful, rebelling against the society that has treated them unfairly. Thus, "overeducation" may be said to be a dysfunction of modern education.

Some of the functions and dysfunctions of an organization are *manifest,* that is, obvious to everyone. A manifest function of police departments, for example, is to keep crime rates low. Other functions and dysfunctions are *latent*—hidden and unintended. A latent function of police departments is to assist people in distress. Sociologists who study social problems have placed particular emphasis on exposing *latent dysfunctions* that are unknown to the general public. For instance, sociologists who have studied police departments have noted that these agencies burden the people they arrest with stigmatizing labels ("criminal," "delinquent," "outlaw," "hoodlum," etc.) and that those who are thus labeled may actually commit more crimes than would have been the case *breakdown in org.*

if they had been left alone. By trying to stop crime, criminal-justice agencies unintentionally contribute to its increase. (See Chapter 14.)

According to functionalists, social problems arise when society or some part of it becomes disorganized. This *social disorganization* involves a breakdown of social structure, so that its various parts no longer work together and norms lose their influence on particular groups or individuals.

Functionalists see many causes of social disorganization. Norms may be violated because of inadequate socialization, or the society may fail to control the individual tensions produced in its members. A society's relationship to its environment may be disrupted, so that it no longer has sufficient food, oil, building materials, or other resources. However, underlying all of these causes is rapid social change, which disrupts the balance of society, producing social disorganization. Society responds well to change only if it occurs slowly.

Modern industrial societies have been harmed by social disorganization because more change has occurred in less time than in any other era in human history. Basic institutions have undergone revolutionary changes, with technology advancing at such a speed that other parts of the culture have failed to keep pace. This *cultural lag* between technological changes and our adaptation to them is one of the major sources of social disorganization. For instance, refrigeration, knowledge of nutrition, and modern medical technology began spreading throughout the world in the nineteenth century, thus saving many lives, especially those of the newly born. Yet in many cultures traditional attitudes toward the family have not been adjusted to deal with the fact that more children survive to adulthood. The result has been a worldwide population explosion.

Although functionalism has been a standard theoretical approach to social problems, it has a growing number of critics. Despite its claims of objectivity, many sociologists see functionalism as a politically conservative philosophy, arguing that it takes for granted the idea that society as it is (the status quo) should be preserved. Functionalism blames social problems on individual deviance or temporary social disorganization while seeming to ignore the basic injustices of society. The critics of functionalism claim that it is impossible to separate the functions of the various segments of society. They also argue that one person's disorganization is another person's organization, and that what functionalists really mean when they say something is functional is that it works for the benefit of the privileged social classes.

The Conflict Perspective

The major alternative to the functionalist approach is conflict theory. This perspective is based on a different set of assumptions about the nature of society and comes to different conclusions about the causes of social problems. As the name implies, conflict theory sees society as a struggle for power among various social groups. Conflict is believed to be inevitable and in many cases actually beneficial to society. For instance, many needed social changes arose from such conflicts as the French Revolution and the American War Between the States.

Conflict theory can best be understood by contrasting it with functionalist theory. Functionalists assume that society is held together primarily by the agreement of its members on a common set of values, attitudes, and norms. For example, they say that most people obey the law because they believe the law is fair and just. On the other hand, conflict theorists insist that social order is maintained by authority backed by the use of force. One or more groups hold power legally, using it to force others to obey their will. To this way of thinking, most people obey the law because they are afraid of being arrested, jailed, or even killed if they do not obey. Another important difference between functionalism and conflict theory may be seen in their assumptions about social change. Functionalists tend to view society in relatively static terms, asserting that too much change is disruptive and that society has a natural tendency to regain its balance whenever it is disturbed. But conflict theorists see society in more dynamic terms. Because people are constantly struggling with each other to gain power, change is inevitable. One individual or group is bound to gain the upper hand, only to be defeated in a later struggle.

Of course, there are many different interpretations of these theories. The differences are particularly pronounced among conflict theorists. Some of them are concerned mainly with value conflict, which includes the differences in attitudes among different social groups, while others focus on class conflict, which involves differences in power, wealth, and prestige.

Value Conflict   Sociologists who emphasize value conflict disagree with the functionalist assumption that most people in society share the same set of norms and values. They point out that modern societies are composed of many different groups with different attitudes, values, and norms, and that conflicts are bound to arise. For instance, consider the abortion issue. Traditional Catholics believe that the human fetus at any stage of its development is a complete, living human being and that aborting a pregnancy is a form of murder. Feminists and other proabortionists hold that an unborn child is not yet a human being because it is unable to survive outside the womb. They assert that if the state forbids a woman to obtain an operation that she desires, the state is violating her right to control her own life. Conflict theorists argue that the clash between these two groups is a result of value conflict and does not reflect social disorganization.

There are numerous value conflicts in the United States and Canada. One reason for those conflicts is certainly the great size and diversity of

North American societies. The continent of North America is the home of hundreds of ethnic groups: white Anglo-Saxon Protestants, French Canadians, Germans, Ukrainians, Italians, Irish, Navahos, Mexicans, and Africans, to name only a few. Each of these groups has its own set of cultural values and norms. In addition, all the world's major religions are represented, not to mention thousands of cults and splinter groups. There is also a rich diversity of subcultures within the dominant cultures, including hippies, physicians, organized criminals, and hundreds of other groups who have developed their own perspectives on the world.

However, value conflicts may arise from other sources. Values shared by the members of the same group or society may be inconsistent or even directly opposed to each other. For example, the values of freedom and equality often come into conflict. The individual who values equality may believe that only an unjust system could allow the children of a Rockefeller or a DuPont to inherit tremendous wealth while many others receive nothing. However, another person may feel that any attempt to change this system violates the freedom of those who possess inherited wealth. Freedom itself can be interpreted in conflicting ways. To some, affirmative-action laws requiring factory owners to hire members of a minority group violate the owners' freedom to run their businesses as they see fit. To others, repeal of such laws would violate the freedom of factory workers to work where they choose.

Class Conflict

Not all conflicts stem from disagreement over values and their interpretation. Some conflicts arise in part *because* people share the same values. If two groups of people place a high value on wealth and power and only one group has access to them, conflict is likely to result. Such conflicts are called class conflicts. Many sociologists believe that class conflict over wealth, power, and status is the basic cause of most social problems.

One of the first theorists to focus on class conflict as the underlying cause of social problems was Karl Marx, who wrote in the 1800s. For Marx, the position a person holds in the system of production determines his or her class position. In a capitalist society a person may be in one of two different positions. Some people are in the position of owning capital and capital-producing property (e.g., factory owners, landlords, and merchants). This class Marx called the bourgeoisie. Other people work for wages as producers of capital (e.g., factory workers, miners, and laborers of all kinds). Marx called this class the proletariat. Marx asserted that these two classes have directly opposing economic interests because the wealth of the bourgeoisie is based on exploitation of the proletariat.

Class conflict, according to Marx, is a result of an inevitable historical process. He thought the workers (proletariat) would develop a growing awareness of their exploitation by the bourgeoisie, and predicted that their growing political organization would eventually lead to violent class

Those who use the class conflict perspective feel that the origins of social problems are found in the unequal distribution of wealth, power, and prestige in contemporary society.

conflict. A revolution won by workers over their masters would, Marx contended, lead to a classless society. Private property and inheritance would be abolished; steeply graduated income taxes would be introduced; education and training would be free; and production would be organized for use, not profit.

Marxist theory is an activist approach to social problems and social change. It guides the actions of people throughout the world. However, not everyone who sees class conflict as a cause of social problems is a Marxist. All sociologists know that modern industrial society has a class system, and most agree that the classes have competing interests that may generate conflict. But most sociologists do not believe that a classless society is possible under present conditions, or that a violent social revolution must come. In fact, many sociologists study social stratification in order to refute Marx's ideas about the nature of class society. Many social scientists who use the class conflict approach believe that society can best be changed through gradual reforms rather than violent revolution.

A conflict theorist need not focus only on class or value conflict. Indeed, most sociologists recognize that conflict can arise both from differences in values and from differences in the distribution of wealth, power, and status. Some emphasize one type of conflict, while others argue that the two are equally important.

Just as functionalism has been criticized for being too conservative, conflict theory has been criticized for being too radical. Critics say that conflict theorists overemphasize the role of conflict, arguing that if there were as much conflict as these theorists claim, society would have collapsed long ago. Functionalists do not agree that the maintenance of a capitalist society benefits only the bourgeoisie. Finally, many conflict theorists, particularly Marxists, are criticized for judging capitalist society too harshly. Critics argue that the classless utopia that Marx envisioned is impossible to achieve, and that capitalist societies do a good job of dealing with their social problems.

Functionalism and conflict theory are the two principal macro-level approaches to social problems. While some sociologists claim that one or the other is the only valid approach, most use whatever theory seems to work best for the problem being studied. The use of both functional and conflict approaches often sheds more light on a problem than either approach used alone. For instance, crime can usefully be studied as a product of social disorganization, of class conflict between the poor and the other classes, and of value conflict between those who respect the law and those who don't. Obviously, all of these perspectives are useful if we are to understand social problems.

The Social-Psychological Perspective

Social-psychological theories operate on a different level of analysis from functionalist and conflict theories. Social psychology is concerned primarily with the behavior of single individuals and small groups, their relationships with each other and with the larger society. Socialization and the part that group interactions play in the individual's psychological development have been among the central concerns of social psychology. A second major concern is to explain why some individuals conform to various norms and expectations while others become deviant. Most contemporary explanations of crime, mental illness, and sex role behavior are based on the findings of social psychology.

Even social problems that seem to stem from social disorganization or conflict, such as warfare and economic inequality, have a social-psychological aspect. Therefore, while the functionalist and conflict perspectives offer competing explanations of social problems, micro social-psychological theories can supplement both of these macro theories. However, the supporters of various social-psychological theories are often at odds with each other too. Of the many micro theories, the following are most commonly applied to the study of social problems: biosocial theories, personality theories, behavioral theories, and interactionist theories.

Biosocial Theories

For generations, scholars have tried to explain social behavior by pointing to the biological traits of the human species. At one time such explanations were quite influential in economics, political science, psychology, and sociology. A host of different behaviors were said to be instinctual. Warfare was seen as stemming from an "aggressive instinct," cooperation from a "social instinct," crime from a "criminal instinct," and so on. Critics of these instinct theories charged that they added nothing to the understanding of human behavior and had little factual support. They argued that even if there were, for instance, an instinct of aggression, this biological fact would help very little in the understanding of the complex economic, political, religious, and social conflicts that lead to wars. Most social scientists eventually lost confidence in instinct theory and turned instead to explaining human behavior almost entirely in terms of social and cultural conditions. "To explain a social fact," Emile Durkheim said, "seek other social facts." However, biosocial theories of human behavior have recently begun to receive new attention.

Some of the new biosocial theories seem to imply that virtually all human behavior is inherited. It is argued that even such values as altruism (unselfishness), which appear to be entirely cultural, have actually been built into our genetic structure in the process of evolution.[5] After studying the incredible diversity of behavior in human societies, few anthropologists or sociologists can accept the idea that most human behavior is genetically determined. Nevertheless, social scientists are beginning to recognize that biological influences on human behavior have been neglected in the years since instinct theory was discredited. Certainly, the structure of the human body and its biological needs have enormous influences on both individual and social behavior. After all, the most basic task of any society is to provide for the biological needs of its members. Imagine how different human society would be if we reproduced without sexual intercourse, as some plants do, or if human beings matured into adults in a few weeks, as some animals do.

Although no single, broad biological theory is accepted by all social scientists, dozens of specific theories are relevant to discussions of specific social problems. These theories advance a biological cause for everything from sex role differences to warfare. While some are very convincing, others are based on little more than myth and prejudice. Sociologists have traditionally avoided biological explanations of social problems, in part because the social-policy implications of these theories are quite pessimistic. If a social problem is believed to be biologically caused, policy makers have little incentive to try to solve it. Obviously, they cannot change human biology. For example, if people live in poverty only because they are biologically inferior (a proposition that virtually no social scientist would support), there is very little that policy makers could do to eliminate poverty. Even more disturbing is the blatant racism of some biosocial theories. In the past many reputable scientists believed that blacks and other minorities were poor because they were racially inferior. But the obvious errors in this theory should not be taken as evidence that all biosocial theories are in error. On the contrary, many sociologists believe that the biosocial perspective will make an increasingly important contribution to the understanding of human behavior in the years ahead.

Personality Theories

Personality is one of the most widely used words in psychology. It refers to the relatively stable characteristics and traits that distinguish one person from another, and that account for differences in individual social behavior. For example, criminals are said to break the law because they have "sociopathic personalities" (impulsive, unstable, and immature). Racial prejudice is said to stem from an "authoritarian personality" (rigid, insecure, with repressed feelings of guilt and hostility).

Although there are many different personality theories, the one developed by Sigmund Freud has been the most influential. Freud asserted that an individual's **personality** is formed during the early years of childhood and that for this reason the family is the major force in personality development. If children have conflicts with their parents, and if these conflicts cause trauma (injury), the children are likely to have psychological difficulties in later life. For example, traumas caused by the parents' reaction to infantile sexual behavior may create an unconscious conflict that emerges later in the form of impotence, frigidity, or other psychological problems.

Freud divided the personality into three parts. The most basic is the **id** — the instinctual drives, particularly sex, which motivate all human behavior. The second part of the personality to develop is the **ego** — the individual's conscious, reality-oriented experience. The last part of the personality to develop is the **superego** — the individual's conscience, or sense of morality. Freudians assume that these three parts of the personality are balanced in normal people and that personality disorders arise from imbalances. Freudians also place much importance on the unconscious mental life that is presumed to go on without the individual's awareness.

Freud's theory has been attacked because of its overemphasis of the sex drive, its neglect and misunderstanding of females, and its departure from standard scientific procedure. As a result few sociologists or psychologists apply Freud's theory in its original form. However, many psychologists have used Freud's ideas as a basis for new personality theories, which in turn have been criticized because of their vagueness and lack of supporting factual evidence.

A different approach focuses on *personality traits* rather than on the structure and dynamics of personality. Trait theories classify people according to basic personality characteristics, such as dominance–submissiveness, impulsiveness–self-control, and introversion–extraversion.

Many tests have been developed to determine the presence of such traits in particular individuals, and attempts have been made to link specific traits with specific types of deviant behavior. However, so far this line of research has produced few satisfactory results.

Critics of this approach note the great differences among the traits that various psychologists claim to have found with their tests, arguing that personality is not composed of the simple, distinct traits that the tests are said to measure. Instead, the critics assert, personality can be understood only as a unified whole.

Behavioral Theory

Some social psychologists are convinced that it is a waste of time to try to figure out what is going on inside people's heads. They argue that because the psychological traits that are said to determine behavior cannot be observed, such efforts ultimately reflect the subjective judgments of the theorist. Because these social psychologists confine their studies exclusively to observable behavior, this theoretical perspective, originally led by J. B. Watson and more recently developed by B. F. Skinner, is known as behaviorism.

Behavior, from this perspective, depends on the reinforcements the actor receives from its performance. If an individual receives positive reinforcement (reward) for a certain behavior in a certain situation, he or she is likely to repeat the behavior when the situation recurs. On the other hand, if negative reinforcement (punishment) is given, the behavior is less likely to be repeated. For instance, if parents respond to their daughter's temper tantrum with concern and attention, she is likely to repeat that behavior the next time she wants attention. But if the girl's tantrum is ignored she will use a different means to attract attention. Thus, behavioral theory explains human action primarily in terms of the individual's environment. Of course, the process of learning is not nearly as simple as our illustration implies; behaviorists have developed an elaborate set of principles about the many kinds of reinforcements that encourage or discourage the learning of specific behaviors.

Critics of behavioral theory object to its exclusion of mental processes and the subjective outlooks of individuals, arguing that it is impossible to understand human behavior without understanding the way people think and feel, or the structure of their personalities. They agree that it is difficult to study personality directly but assert that this is hardly enough reason to conclude that personality has no influence on human behavior.

Interactionist Theory

Interactionist theory sees behavior as a product of each individual's social relationships. As one interactionist has said,

> How aggressive or cooperative a person is, how much self-respect or self-confidence he has, how energetic and productive his work is, what he aspires to, what he believes to be true and good, whom he loves or hates,

personality's (margin note)

*George Mead
— communication* (margin note)

and what beliefs or prejudices he holds—all these characteristics are highly determined by the individual's group memberships. In a real sense, they are properties of groups and of the relationships between people.[6]

Because the socialization process forms the foundation for human interaction, interactionists study it in detail. Their theory holds that individuals are products of the kinds of social relationships and the culture in which they participate. People develop their outlook on life from participation in the symbolic universe that is their culture. They develop their conceptions of themselves, learn to talk, and even learn how to think as they interact, early in life, with family and friends. But unlike the Freudians, interactionists believe that an individual's personality continues to change throughout life in response to changing social environments.

The work of the American philosopher George Herbert Mead has been the driving force behind interactionist theories of social psychology. Mead noted that the ability to communicate in symbols (principally words and combinations of words) is the important feature that distinguishes humans from other animals. Individuals develop the ability to think and to use symbols in the process of socialization. At first children blindly imitate the behavior of their parents, but eventually they learn to "take the role of the other," pretending to be "Mommy" or "Daddy." And from such role taking children learn to understand the interrelationships among different roles and to see themselves as they imagine others see them. Eventually, Mead said, children begin to take the role of a generalized other. In doing so, they adopt a system of values and standards that reflect the expectations of people in general, not just those in the immediate present. In this way reference groups as well as actual membership groups come to determine how the individual behaves.

After Mead's death in 1931, his ideas continued to gain stature among sociologists and social psychologists. Those who adhered most closely to Mead's original ideas became known as symbolic interactionists.[7] They have been very active in the study of social problems and have contributed a great deal to our understanding of critical social issues. For example, differential-association theory, a leading explanation of delinquency and crime, is a direct offshoot of Mead's theories. (See Chapter 14.) But despite his enormous influence Mead has many critics. The most common criticism of interactionist theory is similar to the criticism of Freudian theory—it is difficult to substantiate. In fact, some critics have charged that symbolic-interactionist theory is so abstract and vaguely worded that it is virtually impossible either to prove or disprove it.

RESEARCH METHODS

The theoretical perspectives that we have discussed serve as guides and points of reference for the student of social problems. However, theories are of little value unless they deal with facts. Unfortunately, showing how a theoretical process actually works to produce its effects is much more difficult for social scientists than it is for other scientists. In the study of controversial social problems, people rarely agree on what "the facts" are. Many sociologists long for the simplicity of sciences like physics because it is much easier to study the movement of inanimate objects than to predict or explain our own behavior.

Because their task is so difficult, sociologists give a great deal of attention to determining the best ways of doing social research. Volumes have been written on the subject, yet there is no widespread agreement about the most effective methods. The selection of research techniques must be based on the particular problem that is under study. Among the many available research methods, the case study, the survey, and the experiment are those most commonly used by sociologists.

The Case Study

A detailed examination of specific individuals, groups, and situations is known as a case study. There are many different ways of making such investigations, including using official records, biographies, and newspaper reports. More common are personal interviews and participant observation.

Suppose you were interested in studying juvenile delinquency. You might locate a gang of delinquent boys and interview them, asking each boy why he became involved in the gang, what he does with other gang members, what his plans for the future are, and so on. You would then study the replies, put them together in some meaningful way, and draw your conclusions. On the other hand, in a participant observation study you would attempt to take part in gang activities. You might disguise yourself and work your way into the gang as a regular member, or you might tell the boys your purpose and ask their permission to watch their activities. One problem with the interview technique is that we can never be sure that the subjects are telling the truth, even if they think they are. Although the participant observation technique avoids this problem, it is difficult and sometimes even dangerous to study people in this way, for they often resent the intrusion of nosy outsiders. An additional objection is that accuracy of the results is difficult to check.

When compared to other research methods, the case study has the advantage of allowing researchers to come into close contact with the object of their study. Interviews and direct observation can provide rich insights that cannot be obtained from statistics. But the case study method has its limitations, especially when the cases selected for study are not typical. For instance, a researcher might unknowingly select for study a group of delinquents who are strongly opposed to drug use, while all the other gang members in the same area are heavy drug users. Another common criticism of the case study method is that it relies too heavily on the ability and insights of the person doing the study. While this problem is common to all research methods, it is especially troublesome in case studies because all the "facts" that are disclosed for examination are filtered by the researcher.

The Survey

Rather than concentrating on an in-depth study of a few cases, the survey asks more limited questions of a much larger number of people. Because it is seldom possible to question everyone concerned with a certain social problem, a sample is used. For instance, suppose you were interested in the relationship between age and attitudes toward the abortion issue. You might select an appropriate city for your study and randomly select a sample of 100 names from a city directory. If the sample is properly drawn, it will be representative of all the people in the city. Each person in the sample would then be interviewed to determine his or her age and attitudes toward abortion. You would then analyze the responses statistically to determine the relationship between these two variables.

The survey is an invaluable tool for measuring the attitudes and behaviors of large numbers of people. The famous Gallup poll is a good example of how the survey method can be used effectively. However, because this method simply reports what people say they think or do, it is not as effective as the case study approach in developing new ideas and insights. One defect is that people do not always answer the questions honestly, particularly if they deal with sensitive issues such as sexual behavior or crime. Another problem arises because surveys are expensive. But a survey that is conducted properly ensures that the people studied are not misleading exceptions. Even the best case study cannot provide this assurance.

The Experiment

In social science, as in the physical and biological sciences, the experiment provides an opportunity for the most carefully controlled type of research. Although there are many types of experimental designs, experimenters usually divide their subjects into an experimental group and a control group. Then, under controlled conditions, the experimental group is given information or shown material that is withheld from the control group. By comparing the two groups at the end of the experiment, researchers try to discover the effects of what was done to the experimental group. To illustrate, suppose you were interested in the effects of violent programs on television viewers. You might select two groups of people and show one, the experimental group, a number of violent television programs and the other, the control group, nonviolent programs. You would then test the two groups to see whether the violent programs caused any increase in violent behavior or attitudes.

A major problem arises because most experimental studies of human behavior must be conducted in laboratory settings. Watching violent television programs in a laboratory is likely to have different effects than

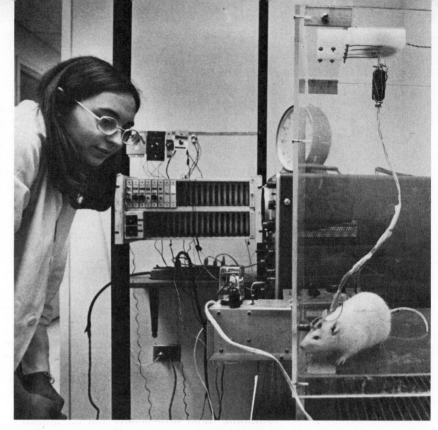

The experiment permits more carefully controlled research than any other technique. But it is extremely difficult to re-create everyday social conditions in laboratories when using human subjects.

watching the same programs at home because the conditions in the two settings differ so greatly. True "social experiments," in which a social change is introduced to determine its effect on a social problem, are very rare indeed. Because control is difficult or impossible in many settings, true experiments are few and far between.

INTERPRETING CLAIMS ABOUT SOCIAL PROBLEMS

Even those who never do research on social problems will at some time have to interpret the claims made about them. Politicians, journalists, and sociologists, as well as an assortment of cranks and oddballs, constantly bombard the citizenry with opinions and "facts" about these problems. Each citizen must decide whether to believe or disregard these assertions. Many of the claims are patently false, but some are presented with impressive arguments. Reasonable skepticism is an important scientific tool. It should be practiced, at least on an elementary level, by anyone who is interested in knowing how social problems arise, persist, and change.

Some people find it easy to believe almost anything they see in print; they even accept the exaggerated claims of TV commercials. The ability to speak well may be taken as a sign that the speaker is trustworthy and honest. The belief that those who lie in public are usually sued or even put in jail adds to the credibility of public speakers. But there are many ways of telling lies without risking trouble with the law. One technique is to lie about groups rather than individuals. While a speaker could not say that John Jones is a narcotics addict without some proof, the speaker could say that college students or musicians are addicts. Another technique is to imply guilt by association. A speaker might charge that Judge Mary Jones is "frequently seen in the company of thugs, degenerates, and narcotics addicts." Consider the difference between these two statements:

> Mary Jones, the Communist party, and student revolutionaries agree that there are great injustices in the American economic system.

> Mary Jones, the National Council of Churches, and Supreme Court judges agree that there are great injustices in the American economic system.

Another way of conveying a misleading impression is to quote out of context. This sort of misrepresentation has been brought to the level of a fine art by the merchandisers of paperback books. For example, a reviewer in *The New York Times* might say something like this: "This book is somewhat interesting, but certainly not one of the greatest books of the decade." And it might end up being quoted like this: "Interesting . . . one of the greatest books of the decade. — *The New York Times*."

It is essential to read claims about social problems and their solutions carefully. Wild propaganda and intentional distortions usually are self-revealing. However, most people who are concerned about social issues do not intentionally lie or distort the truth. They may merely be vague, using phrases such as "many people believe" and "it is widely thought" because their knowledge is incomplete. But sometimes they are biased, and misleading statements are hardest to detect when the speaker is sincere. There are a number of standards that can be used to measure the validity of a statement, but they are by no means foolproof.

The Author One of the best places to begin evaluating an article or speech is with the author. What are his or her qualifications? Why should the speaker or writer know anything more about the problem than the audience? Titles and academic degrees in themselves do not mean very much unless they have some clear relation to the problem under consideration. For instance, a professor of physics might be qualified to talk about nuclear power, but her opinion about the influence of international politics on our oil supplies would be of little value. A professor of sociology might be well qualified to comment on the causes of crime but unqualified to recommend how police departments should be organized. An impressive title does not guarantee authority or expertise.

It is also helpful, when possible, to know an author's biases. This will usually become clear if one looks at the author's published work. For example, suppose that an economist who has always supported the social-security system publishes a study concluding that the system has been a failure. These findings should be given more weight than the same conclusions published by a long-time opponent of social security. The same is true of articles published by people with special interests. An article concluding that criminals have been mistreated by police officers is more persuasive if it is written by a police officer than if it is written by a burglar.

The Support Scientific research projects are expensive. If authors say their assertions are based on research, it is important to know who paid for the research and what, if anything, its supporters stand to gain or lose from its conclusions. Few organizations, including federal agencies, will fund a study that is likely to arrive at conclusions harmful to their interests. It is not very surprising to find a study funded by an oil company that asserts that oil drilling will produce little environmental damage, or to find a study funded by a tobacco company that says that smoking cigarettes is as safe as playing badminton. However, a study funded by an oil company that concludes that oil drilling will cause serious damage to the environment merits attention.

The Distribution Where an article is published or a speech is given can be another important guide to the reliability of the statements made. One can usually assume that articles published in recognized professional journals such as the *American Sociological Review* or *Social Problems* meet some minimal professional standards. But an article on communism published in a journal of the John Birch Society, an article on minimum wages published in a trade union weekly, or a speech on gun control before the National Rifle Association is likely to contain few surprises.

The Content There are no firm rules for judging which conclusions are reasonable and which are not. Some research papers are so technical that only experts can judge their contributions. But most books, magazine articles, and speeches about social problems are directed to nonexpert audiences, so that readers and listeners need no special qualifications when they make a judgment about the accuracy of what is said. The following questions should be asked when rating the value of an article or speech.

Does the Article or Speech Make Sense? It is important to get involved with what is being said rather than just passively accepting it. Are the author's arguments logical? If a person says that drug addiction is widespread because enemy agents are trying to weaken the country by enslaving its youth, ask yourself whether it is reasonable to claim that such methods could be used in secret. It also is logical to ask why those who are being enslaved by drugs are the least powerful people in the population. Do the author's conclusions seem to follow from the evidence presented? There is good reason to reject an argument that, for example, asserts that college students who smoke pot do so because of poverty. Subtler gaps in logic can also be detected by the attentive listener.

Why Does the Writer or Speaker Use a Particular Style?

A book or speech need not be boring to be accurate. Nevertheless, there is a difference between a calm, thoughtful analysis and windy talk. Skillful speakers who give emotion-packed examples of human suffering may only be trying to get an audience's attention, or they may use such examples to cloud the issue. Most articles, speeches, and books necessarily contain some vague claims or assertions. One should always ask whether the vagueness is necessary because some facts are unknown or because the author is trying to conceal information. On the other hand, a collection of numbers and statistics does not guarantee that conclusions are valid. An old saying holds that figures don't lie but liars figure.

Do an Author's Claims Fit in with What Others Say About the Subject?

The truth of a proposition is not decided by democratic vote. Majorities can be wrong and minorities right. Even an individual who strays far from what most people — including experts — accept as true is not necessarily wrong. In scientific work especially, a successful experiment by a lone researcher can change truths that have long been accepted as gospel. But if an author's claims differ greatly from those of others who know something about the subject, there is reason to be skeptical. The question to be asked is whether the author presents enough evidence to justify rejection of the old ideas.

SUMMARY

There are two major sociological definitions of the term *social problem*. One says that social problems are created by gaps between a society's ideals and actual conditions in that society. The other defines social problems as conditions that a significant number of people consider to be problems.

The public's perceptions of social problems change from time to time. The major forces influencing these changes in attitude are social movements that try to introduce changes. These movements are usually led by moral crusaders who dedicate themselves to finding a solution to the problem. If the supporters of a social movement are powerful, or if they can appeal to a population's values and prejudices, the movement has a much greater chance of success. On the other hand, if the opponents of the social movement have more influence, the desired action is less likely to be taken. Further, even if the government takes official action, the agencies that are supposed to deal with the problem may still do little or nothing to change it.

Over the years sociologists have developed a body of knowledge, theories, and methods that aid in the study of social problems. Eight basic sociological terms essential to the understanding of the sociological approach are: *roles, norms, groups, socialization, institutions, classes, culture,* and *social structure.*

Sociologists approach the study of social problems from different theoretical perspectives. The two major theories dealing with large groups and entire societies are the functionalist perspective and the conflict perspective. Functionalists see a society as a delicate balance among its basic components: every society has a set of basic needs that must be fulfilled if it is to survive. All the components of a society have functions that they perform to meet these needs. But some parts also have dysfunctions or harmful consequences for society. Social problems occur when a society becomes disorganized so that its basic functions cannot be performed as well as they should. Conflict theorists, on the other hand, see social order as a set of power relationships. Coercion, not shared values and beliefs, is the cement that holds a society together. Some conflict theorists emphasize conflicts among values (value conflict); others emphasize conflicts among people with different amounts of wealth, power, and prestige (class conflict).

The social-psychological perspective focuses on individuals and small groups rather than entire societies. Biosocial theories emphasize the role of heredity in human behavior. Personality theories focus on the traits that an individual develops in early socialization. Behavioral theories ignore internal mental processes and concern themselves only with observable behavior and the ways in which it is learned. Interactionist theories note the important effects of social interaction on behavior.

Theory is an important guide, but becomes effective only when it is applied to facts. Social scientists use three main methods to test theories. The case study is a detailed examination of specific individuals, groups, or situations. Surveys put questions to cross-sections of the population. Experiments usually try to duplicate the social world in a laboratory so that the various factors being studied can be carefully controlled.

Even those who never do research on social problems should be able to interpret and judge the claims of others. There are at least four common-sense methods for evaluating speeches, books, and articles about social problems: (1) Check the qualifications and biases of the author. (2) Check the biases of the people who pay the bills of the speaker or author. (3) Check the publishers of magazine articles and the special interests of the audience listening to a speech. (4) Check the content of the speech or article and the logic of the arguments the author uses to support a point.

KEY TERMS	behaviorist theory	case study
	biosocial theory	class conflict
	bourgeoisie	conflict theory

culture
deviant
dysfunctional
ego
experiment
folkway
function
functionalist theory
generalized other
group
id
institution
interactionist theory
macro theory
membership group
micro theory
moral crusader
mores
norm
participant observation
personal interview
personality

personality theory
power
proletariat
reference group
reinforcement
role
role strain
sample
social class
socialization
social movement
social problem
social-psychological theory
social stratification
social structure
sociology
status
subculture
superego
survey
symbol
value conflict

Part I
Troubled Institutions

2
Problems of the Economy

Do large corporations restrict competition?
Who controls corporations?
Is the "work ethic" dead?
What should the government do to solve economic
    problems?

Everyone must have food and shelter to survive. It is the job of the economic institution to provide for these two basic needs. But our economic system does much much more as well, and there is virtually no part of our lives that it does not touch. Where we work, where we live, the food we eat, the things we own—all are influenced by economic concerns. But the economic system has subtler effects that often pass unnoticed. The anxieties of competition, the pride of ownership, the constant yearning for a newer car, a bigger house, and finer clothes are not part of "human nature," as we so often assume. They are the results of our particular cultural and economic systems. Life in societies that discourage economic competition or the accumulation of wealth is profoundly different from the day-to-day life most of us know.

Because economic relationships are so fundamental to human affairs, it is no wonder that all social problems have an economic side to them. Problems of inequality, health care, ethnic relations, and environmental pollution—even problems of mental disorder, drug addiction, crime, and violence—are partly economic problems as well. In the first place, it is easy to suggest solutions to most social problems if the question of money is ignored. But in reality the money has to come from somewhere, and the first critical question about any proposed reform is often "How much will it cost?" Governments, like most individuals, do not have enough money to do everything. They must make choices. Second, many economic relationships create social problems. Why isn't there enough money to satisfy everyone's needs? Why aren't there enough jobs for all who want them? Why are there poor people in an affluent society? These and similar questions suggest that solving social problems is not just a matter of spending money wisely. There are basic problems in the economic system itself.

MYTHS AND REALITIES

Almost everyone will agree that the United States, Canada, and many European countries have capitalist economies. But exactly what does this mean? There are great differences among the economic systems of the countries that are considered capitalist. All share a common problem: the systems for producing, distributing, and consuming never seem to work the way planners and theorists predict. Therefore, the capitalist model is modified and adjusted in various ways. The way a system actually works is not revealed by its label, be it capitalism, socialism, or something else. It is important to understand the realities of capitalism as well as its general principles.

The Characteristics of Capitalism

Although it is not possible to define capitalism precisely, pure capitalist economic systems display three essential characteristics. First, there is private property. Commodities are owned by specific individuals or corporations, as are the means of production—land, factories, mines, refineries, machines, and so on. Second, there is an exchange of commodities and capital—a market. The market controls the production and distribution of valuable commodities. Third, the market for both goods and labor is unregulated or "free." Workers sell the only commodity they own, their labor power. Businesspeople sell commodities produced by their property and the labor of their workers. Each business competes in the free market with others that produce similar commodities, and each aims to make the greatest possible profit.

The classic statement of the principles of free-market capitalism was set forth in Adam Smith's book *The Wealth of Nations*, first published in 1776.[1] Smith argued that each individual will work hard and produce as much as possible if he or she is allowed to work for personal profit. Private greed will be transformed into public good through the workings of the free market, regulated only by supply and demand. The profit motive will drive manufacturers to supply goods that the public demands, and competition will ensure that the goods are reasonably priced. The market will regulate itself in the most efficient possible way—as though guided by an "invisible hand"—if the government does not interfere with the free play of economic forces.

The Modern Economy

Adam Smith's revolutionary ideas won great international acceptance. And because of their popularity, many people continue to believe that our economy operates the way Smith said it should. However, there have been drastic changes since the early days of capitalism.

Competition simply did not remain free, for it soon became obvious to businesspeople that special advantages could be secured with the help of the government. Individuals and industries obtained tariffs, franchises, patents, and other special privileges, thus reducing the free competition that Smith had hoped for. Many producers banded together to limit the supply of goods so that prices would rise. Trade associations, chambers of commerce, and many other organizations were formed with the objective of cooperating rather than competing. Even Adam Smith himself recognized the problem: "People of the same trade seldom meet together, even for merriment and diversion, but the conversation ends in a conspiracy against the public, or in some contrivance to raise prices."[2]

But Smith did not foresee another development that would reduce competition even more: the rise of corporations. Huge banks, multinational corporations, newspaper chains, and broadcasting companies all represent the merging of competing interests. In some industries a single corporation was able to take over complete control of the market and create a monopoly. Great companies like Standard Oil and United States Steel drove their competition out of business and then could charge virtually any price they wanted for their products. In response, the government tried to restore competition by breaking up the monopolies and regulating the giant companies. However, such regulation was only partially successful. There are few outright monopolies today, but they have been replaced by oligopolies — industries dominated by a few large companies.

In addition, government intervention in the economy transfered competition from the marketplace to the offices of regulatory agencies, where businesspeople compete for favorable rules and regulations. The government is deeply involved in the modern economy, sometimes intervening in the public interest, sometimes in the interests of manufacturers or other special-interest groups, but always involved.

THE CORPORATIONS

Although huge corporations are relatively recent arrivals on the economic scene, they have quickly come to dominate it. Unlike businesses owned by single individuals or partners, corporations are owned by their stockholders. Most large corporations have thousands of owners, although some are controlled by a few major stockholders. Because it would be impractical for all stockholders to be involved in important corporate decisions, they elect a board of directors to set general policies and oversee the running of the corporation. Executives and managers who are full-time employees make the day-to-day decisions and carry on the work of the corporation. Many of these executives have worked their way up the "corporate ladder" from the lower levels of management.

Business Giants

If all the world's largest enterprises, including governments, were listed in order of size, half would be corporations. Such American giants as General Motors and Exxon have huge assets, estimated at $18 and $21 *billion*, respectively. Antitrust laws now prohibit single corporate giants from monopolizing an entire industry. But to get around these laws some corporations have expanded into related fields, buying out suppliers and distributors. Others have become conglomerates — large firms that own businesses in many areas of production and distribution. Consider the following description of the Safeway corporation:

> At Safeway's latest count this $7 billion food empire owned more than 2,400 supermarkets, 109 manufacturing and processing plants, 16 produce packaging plants, 4 soft drink bottlers, 3 meat processors, 3 coffee roasting plants, a soap and peanut butter and salad oil factory, plus a fleet of 2,100 tractor-trailers shuttling among Safeway's 60 distributor warehouses.[3]

Another distinctive characteristic of today's corporations is their market control. The markets for many important products, ranging from automobiles and gasoline to aspirin and broadcasting, are dominated by just three or four giant firms. About 60 percent of all the goods and services produced in the United States (not counting those produced by the government) are made in industries dominated by such oligopolies. (See Figure 2.1.)

Source: Daniel R. Fusfeld, *Economics*,
2d ed. (Lexington, Mass.: D.C. Heath,
1976), pp. 521, 522.

FIGURE 2.1
CORPORATE MARKET
CONTROL IN THE
AMERICAN ECONOMY

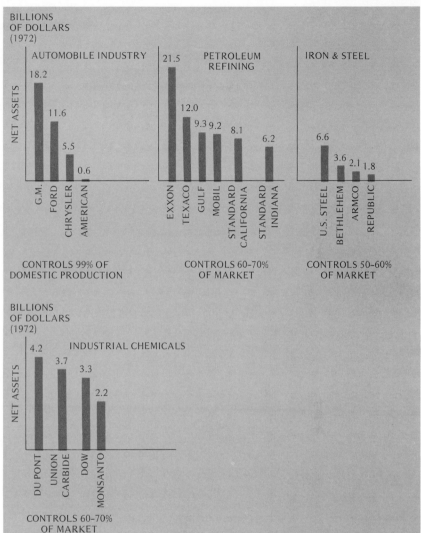

Even in these restricted markets there is usually one giant that is larger and stronger than any other. For instance, General Motors produces more cars than all other American car manufacturers combined. But this pattern of oligopoly is not limited to the United States. In Canada, for example, about two-thirds of all manufactured goods comes from oligopolies, and the concentration is even higher in some nonmanufacturing industries such as mining.[4]

The growth of oligopolies has shattered the "free competitive market." Because there are so few major corporations in some important markets,

Because the same individuals serve on the board of directors of many different corporations, most giant firms are said to have *interlocking directorates*. These interlocking directorates create channels of communication between the major corporations and encourage them to cooperate to advance their mutual interests.

it is easy for them to restrict competition. The largest corporation in an industry often becomes the price leader. It sets the prices for the merchandise it sells, and other corporations set theirs at the same level, ignoring the principles of competition. The business giants also communicate and cooperate through interlocking directorates. While it is illegal for a member of the board of directors of one large firm to sit on the board of a competing firm, it is not illegal for directors of competing firms to be on the board of a third firm in a different industry. Accordingly, powerful individuals sit on the boards of directors of several giant corporations, exchanging views and ideas and plans with other corporate leaders.

Some business giants are linked together as corporate interest groups based on common family holdings or controlled by the same giant banks. For instance, when Richard K. Mellon died (in 1970) his obituary indicated that the Mellon family still held dominating interests in six companies with total assets of over $15 billion (Gulf Oil, Aluminum Corporation of America, Mellon National Bank, Koppers, Carborundum, and General Reinsurance).[5] The enormous power of the major banks comes not only from the control of loans and other essential financial services but also from the control of pension funds and trust accounts that own huge blocks of corporate stock. Obviously, corporations that are controlled by the same financial interests are more likely to cooperate than to compete.

These new realities have created a basic change in our economic system. According to the principles of an open market, when demand drops and supply remains constant, prices will drop as well. However, in a market controlled by an oligopoly the opposite often occurs. For example, during a recent sales slump American automobile companies raised their prices to keep their profits up. The noted American economist

**DEBATE
Should the Giant
Corporations
Be Broken Up?**

PRO

The growth of the giant corporation poses a threat to Western society. One by one corporate giants are driving small farmers and businesspeople into bankruptcy and buying up the firms they cannot crush. The inevitable result will be economic domination by a handful of corporations that are so tightly bound together by economic and social ties that competition will be a thing of the past. All essential goods and services will be controlled by these firms, leaving the public to pay whatever price they demand. Large stockholders and managers will become wealthier as the common people become more and more deprived.

Yet the threat of economic damage posed by unchecked corporate growth is overshadowed by the threat that such growth poses to our freedom. Corporate leaders already exercise inordinate power over all levels of government; unless drastic action is taken, the situation can only grow worse. As corporations expand, their wealth will be used to buy more and more elections, and their power will force government officials to serve their ends. As independent businesspeople and farmers are replaced by corporate bureaucrats, fear and conformism will spread across the nation. Who will speak out against corporate power when such conduct becomes a ticket to unemployment and poverty? Multinational corporate power already supports dictatorial governments in Chile, Brazil, and other Third World countries. The same fate awaits the industrialized nations unless this frightening power is broken.

CON

It is ridiculous to picture modern corporations as sinister "bad guys" plotting to destroy our economic and political freedoms. Corporations did not set out to ruin small businesses and farmers. Their growth resulted from the natural development of our capitalist economy. The best and most efficient organizations grew while the weaker firms failed. We all benefit from the efficiencies generated by the large size of corporations.

Breaking up the large corporations would bring economic disaster. Many of the new smaller companies would fail, thereby creating massive unemployment. American corporations would suffer an enormous disadvantage in competition against foreign corporations that remained large and efficient. The instability and uncertainty resulting from such drastic action could lead to another depression like that of the 1930s.

Fears about the political power of the corporations are as unfounded as fears about their economic impact. Like most people, the managers of today's corporations are committed to the ideals of democracy. Although multinational corporations have been attacked for their involvement in less developed countries, they have in fact made substantial contributions to the economic prosperity of these nations and have shunned any major role in their internal politics. The growth of the modern corporation was basic to the development of an economic system that has produced more wealth than was even dreamed of in earlier centuries. Why change now?

John Kenneth Galbraith argues that the big corporations are so rich and powerful that they can no longer afford to compete vigorously or take major risks.[6] He notes that if professional corporate managers make a bad decision and the corporation loses money, they are likely to be fired. By cooperating with their competitors they achieve the corporate aim of maintaining a steady flow of profits with a minimum of risk.

Who Runs the Corporations?

The modern corporation is a vast financial network. The relationships between a given corporation and its competitors, banks, subcontractors, and suppliers, its stockholders, directors, and managers, the workers, unions, and various local and national governments are extremely complex and may change without warning. Researchers who try to determine who, or what, controls this network rarely have the cooperation of corporations. Because they must rely on secondhand data, their conclusions often appear to contradict each other.

Supporters of the corporate system often claim that corporations are democratic institutions owned by many different people, and point to the fact that over 30 million citizens own stock in American corporations. However, those who are more critical of the power of the corporate system note that although many people own some stock, most stock is owned by a small group of wealthy individuals. The best available information on stock ownership is a survey conducted by the U.S. Federal Reserve system in the 1960s. This survey found that the wealthiest 1 percent of American families owned 61 percent of all corporate stock.[7] Three researchers from the University of Pennsylvania reached a similar conclusion for the year 1971. Working with income rather than wealth, they concluded that the highest-paid 1 percent of American families owned 51 percent of all stock.[8]

Institutional stockholders such as banks, insurance companies, and investment companies also hold major blocks of stock. More than half of all public trading on the New York Stock Exchange is conducted by institutional stockholders.[9] While the stock in these corporations is held by individual investors, the directors nevertheless have considerable influence on the affairs of the corporations whose stock is purchased.

Most economists agree that there is some degree of separation between ownership and control in most modern corporations. Because there are so many stockholders, most of them simply vote for or against the current management. The technical complexity of modern business is so great that stockholders lack the knowledge and expertise to influence important decisions. Galbraith calls the group of managers who make the important decisions the corporate technostructure. He points out that most national and international corporations are no longer run by a single powerful person like Andrew Carnegie or John D. Rockefeller. Decisions are made by anonymous executives and managers who spend their entire careers gaining the technical skills and knowledge needed to manage a modern corporation.

Considering the huge size of the modern corporation and the interlocking of corporate directorships, the top business leaders in the United States are a relatively small group—perhaps 5,000 to 10,000 people.[10] C. Wright Mills argued that these managers are part of a unified power elite that includes other very wealthy people and pursues its own interests at the expense of the average person.[11] Proving or disproving Mills' thesis is very difficult and rests largely on conflicting interpretations of inconclusive data. Perhaps Mills' most telling argument is that corporate managers, regardless of their backgrounds, must accept the ideology of the corporation and perform like elitists if they are to be successful. As Mills put it, "In personal manner and political view, in social ways and business style, he [the new manager] must be like those who are already in, and upon whose judgments his own success rests."

The Multinationals

In recent years large corporations have expanded across national boundaries, becoming conglomerates of production and distribution facilities, employees, and stockholders in many nations. Sixty-two of the top 100 American firms have production facilities in at least six nations. About 60 percent of the world's largest corporations are American, but other nations have also produced giant multinationals, such as the Swiss Nestlé Company and the Royal Dutch Shell Petroleum Company.

The existence of these powerful multinational corporations has generated tremendous controversy. Some people see their growth as the first step toward world unity. They are convinced that corporations are slowly linking together the economies of the world's nations, laying the foundations for a global economy and world government that will usher in a new era of peace and prosperity. Critics of the multinationals, on the other hand, see them as lawless international bandits who exploit small countries and play large ones off against each other.

Most of the expansion of multinational corporations has been in industrialized countries with advanced capitalist economic systems—the United States, Canada, Britain, Japan, Germany, France. This growth has created problems of international control and regulation that have yet to be solved. Concern has been mounting in Canada, for instance, over the transmission of U.S. laws and policies to the Canadian branches and affiliates of American companies. The economic power of American multinationals in Canada has grown steadily, despite repeated efforts by the Canadian government to promote economic independence. Sixty percent of Canada's manufacturing, 75 percent of its petroleum and natural-gas industry, and 60 percent of its mining and smelting industries are now controlled by foreign corporations, mostly American. These figures contrast with those of just 25 years ago, when 38 percent of Canada's manufac-

The growth of multinational corporations has made many brand names familiar around the world. However, the expansion of powerful corporations into weak and impoverished nations brings with it the threat of foreign domination of these firms.

turing and 42 percent of its mining and smelting were under foreign control. Many Canadians have come to see foreign economic domination as a grave threat to their national sovereignty and independence.[12]

Many of the worst abuses of the multinational corporations have resulted from their expansion into the poor countries of Africa, Asia, and Latin America. While the multinationals bring in advanced technology and encourage certain types of economic development, developing nations must pay a heavy price. Reliance on foreign technology decreases economic and political independence even in wealthy countries like Canada, and in small undeveloped nations foreign corporations may wield tremendous political and economic power. Too often the critical economic decisions in small nations are made by foreign corporate executives. In addition, the multinationals often remain in a poor country only as long as they make large profits, which are returned to their home country.

One of the clearest recent examples of political interference was International Telephone and Telegraph's involvement in Chile. ITT, one of the largest and richest corporations in the world, used its international financial influence in an effort to stop Salvatore Allende, a Marxist, from coming to power. After he had been elected—democratically—ITT and the CIA did all they could to create economic havoc and overturn Allende's government. Their aim was finally achieved when Allende and many of his supporters were killed in a military coup. Allende's government was replaced by a military dictatorship that soon became notorious for its brutality and intolerance.[13]

Corporate Crimes

The business world is sometimes described as a lawless jungle where profits rule and those who let honesty and ethics stand in their way are considered fools. Although this is certainly an exaggeration, there is ample evidence that the crime rate is high in the business world.

Everyone has had the experience of buying an article of clothing or an appliance that seemed to fall apart after the slightest use. Although the manufacture and sale of such merchandise is not a violation of the law, selling an inferior product while making false claims for it is fraud. Such illegal deception was recently discovered in the meatpacking industry, where a number of companies were detected selling cheap cuts of meat to the U.S. Army as "top sirloin" or other high grades of beef, while offering special favors to meat inspectors to look the other way.[14] Some fraudulent claims about products endanger the health or even the life of the consumer. In one recent case a drug company marketed a drug that would lower cholesterol levels in the blood. It was tested and approved by the Food and Drug Administration before being marketed. But it was soon found that people using the drug suffered severe side effects, including inflammation of the skin, loss of hair, and loss of sex drive. The fraud in this case was silence. The company had in fact discovered these side effects during its own early tests but had concealed them from the government.[15]

Price fixing (collusion by several companies to cut competition and set uniformly high prices) takes many forms. Though all of them are illegal, price fixing is widespread. A recent survey of the heads of the 1000 largest manufacturing corporations asked whether "many" corporations engaged in price fixing. Among those heading the 500 largest corporations, a surprising 47 percent agreed that price fixing is a common practice. An overwhelming 70 percent of the heads of the remaining 500 corporations also agreed.[16] It is quite possible that violations of the laws outlawing price fixing cost consumers more than any other single crime.

The most famous price-fixing case was a conspiracy in the heavy electrical equipment industry that came to light in 1960. Highly placed executives of such companies as General Electric, Westinghouse, and McGraw-Edison admitted that they had been meeting secretly for years to fix prices. The executives did not associate in public, used only public telephones, and even had a secret code. This conspiracy alone is estimated to have cost the public over $1 billion.[17]

Consumers are not the only victims of corporate crimes. Companies steal from each other as well. Industrial espionage is a thriving industry in which investigators are hired to "bug" the offices and telephones of competing companies. Valuable data stored in the computers owned by one company are stolen by the use of computers belonging to another company. Employees of competing companies are bribed to cheat their own companies or governments by paying more for a product than it is worth. A few years ago Lockheed Aircraft Corporation admitted bribing dozens of different foreign officials to buy Lockheed planes. Lockheed officials claimed that this was a common practice among international businesses, and the claim was soon supported by a rash of bribery scandals in other companies.

Many companies have used illegal practices to drive their competitors out of business. One technique is for a big company to sell certain products at a loss in order to bankrupt a small competitor. The loss is recovered and profits increased by selling products at much higher prices after the competition has been eliminated. Another technique is to sell at a low price to an affiliated company and at a high price to independent companies, eventually driving the latter out of business. Still a third technique is for a giant corporation to cut off supplies of raw materials to its small competitors.[18]

A number of consumer groups have been formed to combat these abuses. Some of them try to inform the public about unsafe or inferior products. Others engage in political action aimed at promoting tougher government regulation of business and better antitrust legislation and enforcement. But whatever tactics these groups adopt, they face an uphill battle against enormous corporate power and a largely indifferent and unaware public.

THE GOVERNMENT

According to Adam Smith and his followers, the government should avoid all interference in the economy, allowing the free market to regulate itself. In the United States the government's involvement with the economy was minimal until the early twentieth century, when efforts were made to break up monopolies and regulate a few industries. But it was the Great Depression of the 1930s that spurred the government into its current economic role. The collapse of the stock market, falling incomes, and rising unemployment in the early days of the Depression created something close to panic. President Franklin D. Roosevelt took office in the midst of widespread social unrest. He launched the "New Deal"—a variety of new economic programs, including public-works projects, public-welfare programs for the unemployed, and social security for the employed. While these new government programs did not cure the Depression, their administrators demanded economic planning and streamlined bureaucratic procedures. By 1945, when World War II ended, the federal government had acquired its current position as regulator and manager of the economy.

In contrast to the situation in the United States, the Canadian government played a central economic role from the beginning of national confederation (1876). The first prime minister of Canada, John A. MacDonald, set up a national policy based on agricultural expansion and settlement of the Canadian West. The government lavishly subsidized the building of the transcontinental railway and protected manufacturers with a high tariff against imported American goods. The objective of the policy was to prevent absorption by the United States and set an independent course for Canada's economic destiny. But the Canadian economy lost what measure of independence it had achieved through the government's policy after World War I, when Britain's strength declined and the United States rose to power on the world stage.

Governments in the United States, Canada, and other Western nations use many different techniques to regulate their economies. Government officials control the amount of buying by manipulating the amount of money in circulation and the interest rates on loans. By increasing the money supply the government can give a boost to the economy. As we will see, however, this is done at the risk of increasing inflation. Restricting the money supply helps reduce inflation but also is likely to reduce economic growth and increase unemployment. Tax policies also have a tremendous impact on the economy. Taxation influences the general rate of economic growth and can give special benefits or problems to specific industries. The federal budget, and particularly the size of the budget deficit (the amount the government spends in excess of the money it takes in), is also used to regulate the economy. A large deficit is likely to stimulate buying, while a reduction in the deficit will do the opposite. The average citizen now expects the government to do everything possible to ensure economic prosperity, whether it uses these techniques or others. When the economy is bad, the government is blamed and politicians have a difficult time getting reelected. On the other hand, a prosperous economy is a great asset to officeholders.

One of the most common economic myths is the idea that big business and big government are bitter rivals competing for economic power. In fact, government and business cooperate more often than they conflict. As Galbraith put it, "The industrial system, in fact, is inextricably associated with the state. In notable respects the mature corporation is an arm of the state. And the state in important matters, is an instrument of the industrial system."[19] Of course, this does not mean that corporation executives wouldn't like lower taxes and less government control, or that government officials wouldn't like the corporations to show more concern for the welfare of citizens. Businesspeople are antagonistic toward government, but they nevertheless look to the government when they are in economic trouble. Further, the government's basic economic strategy in the United States and many other capitalist countries has been to achieve general prosperity by ensuring the prosperity of the big corporations. Many of today's corporations are so large and important that the government cannot afford to let them fail. For example, in 1971, when the Lockheed Corporation found itself on the brink of bankruptcy, the American government stepped in to guarantee a $250 million loan to that "private" company.

Government regulatory agencies such as the Federal Trade Commission and the Food and Drug Administration have come under increasing attack by consumer groups in recent years. Although these agencies were set up to control certain industries in the public interest, they often end up helping the industries rather than the public:

> The regulated industries—transportation, communication, power, natural resources, and financial—now account for about 15 percent of the nation's income. Yet the regulatory agencies have become the natural allies of the industries they are supposed to regulate. They conceive their primary task to be to protect insiders from new competition—in many cases, from any competition.[20]

One problem is that the directors of these agencies often come from the industries they are supposed to regulate and return to those same industries when they leave the government. In such circumstances the regulators are unlikely to sacrifice their future by offending powerful corporations. Another common problem is that the power of the corporations is so great that small government agencies with a few hundred employees are too weak to get the job done.

THE UNIONS

The early period of industrialization created misery among workers. Entire families labored in mines and factories. Industrialists paid the barest subsistence wages, claiming that workers were lazy and would stop working if they were better paid. Working conditions were terrible, and deaths from occupational accidents were common. Working days were long, often fourteen hours or more, and holidays were few and far between. Conditions were so bad that Karl Marx proclaimed that the workers would soon destroy capitalism in a violent revolution. But the workers did not respond with revolution. They responded with unionization.

The early unions faced bitter struggles with employers and even with government. In many places unions were outlawed and organizers jailed; even when unionization became legal, organizers found themselves harassed at every turn. But the unions gradually gained official recognition and acceptance, and as they won power the conditions of the average worker improved.

Today trade unions are a major economic and political force. Union endorsements are sometimes critical to the success of political candidates, and corporation executives no longer denounce union leadership. Union membership in the United States peaked in the late 1950s, when 32 percent of nonagricultural workers were members of a union. This figure has since declined to 28 percent.[21] In contrast, union membership in Canada has remained at about 33 percent.[22]

Unions tend to be concentrated in certain sectors of the economy, particularly manufacturing and blue-collar jobs. Some of the decline in union membership in the United States was caused by a decline in the importance of these occupations to the economy. Unions are now directing more efforts toward organizing government workers and white-collar employees.

The signs in the photograph read:

Higher Pay for the Work Day

FOOD STAMPS FEDERAL AID HELL! IT'S OUR MONEY!

WE DON'T WANT OUR DADS ON A SPLIT WORK WEEK

DON'T LET ALCOA DO THIS TO THE UNION

ALL THE POOR PEOPLE ARE NOT IN WASHINGTON

I'M NOT GETTING FAT ON MY DADS PAY

BACK MY HUSBAND 05%

ALCOA IS UNFAIR TO Organized Labor

The strike has been the unions' most effective technique to win official recognition and to increase pay and fringe benefits for the workers.

Like giant corporations, unions have become larger and more concentrated. About 42 percent of all union members in the United States are in eight unions, and most of the smaller unions are part of the gigantic American Federation of Labor–Congress of Industrial Organizations (AFL–CIO). The very size of modern unions creates problems for their members, who often feel lost and unimportant in such huge organizations. As their power and importance grows, union leaders often become unresponsive to the needs of members. Gangsterism and violence have also plagued American unions. For example, James Hoffa, former president of the Teamsters Union, apparently was murdered in 1975 by political opponents, and it was alleged that organized criminals had taken over control of the union's pension funds.

Like similar ideas about corporations and the government, the assumption that unions and corporations are always bitter enemies is not true. Unions and corporations perform many services for each other. Obviously, unions rely on corporations to employ their members. If the corporation goes out of business, the workers are unemployed. Good relationships with management permit union leaders to deliver better contracts without strikes, thus winning favor with the membership. On the other side of the coin, unions perform some valuable services for corporations. If wage differences among the various companies in an industry are eliminated, the most powerful firms can control prices more easily. The big unions also help eliminate unauthorized ("wildcat") strikes and work stoppages. Union contracts give stability to an industry and ensure that if a strike comes, it will occur only at a predictable time. Yet despite these cooperative relationships there are still bitter union-management conflicts. Thus, the relations between unions and corporations range between competition and cooperation.

THE WORKERS

The difference between thinking of oneself as an unemployed street sweeper or an outstanding surgeon is enormous. People's self-concepts—their ideas of who and what they are—are profoundly affected by their occupations. Not only are workers the heart of the economic system, but an individual's work is often a central focus of his or her life. Workers' occupations bring them into contact with specific social worlds and specific groups of people. If we consider, for example, the differences between the social world of a police officer and that of a ballet dancer, it becomes obvious that people are deeply influenced by their work.

Attitudes Toward Work

To the citizen–philosophers of ancient Greece, work was a curse on humanity, fit only for slaves and barbarians. In their view work took the mind away from higher pursuits—art and philosophy—and made it impossible for workers to attain true virtue. The ancient Hebrews had a more favorable attitude toward work, regarding it as sheer drudgery, but drudgery that might help them atone for Adam's original sin. The early Christians generally accepted the Hebrew idea of work as a punishment for original sin with little value in itself. It was the Protestant reformers, particularly the Puritans, who transformed the meaning of work. To John Calvin and his followers, work was the sacred duty of every person and economic success was a sign of divine favor. However, Calvinists were forbidden to enjoy the fruits of their labor and admonished to value work for its own sake.

This "work ethic" remains a potent force, and it has spread to people of all religious backgrounds. One study found that 80 percent of those surveyed said that they would continue working even if they had enough money to live comfortably without doing so.[23] The workers gave a variety of reasons for continuing to work, ranging from the positive idea that work is fun to the negative notion that not working would make them feel lost or nervous. Despite such evidence, many people seem convinced that the work ethic is dying out. Some feel that the "hippie movement" encouraged people to ignore the value of honest labor. Others argue that we are drifting toward a "consumer culture" oriented toward leisure and personal pleasure rather than production. However, the desire for more personal wealth continues to be a powerful motivation for hard work. For instance, because of recent increases in the productivity of workers, some employers have offered the choice between a bonus in the form of higher wages or more leisure. In the past 20 years about 90 percent of the rewards for increased productivity have been taken in the form of increased wages and only 10 percent in the form of increased leisure.[24]

The Work Force

The types of jobs available as well as the kinds of people in the work force have changed radically in this century. Three significant trends are apparent in the job market. First, farm workers, owners, and managers—once the largest job category — have declined steadily. They now make up only 3.5 percent of the work force in the United States and 5.9 percent in Canada.[25] Mechanization and modern technology have enabled a handful of workers to feed millions. Second, there has been a great decline in the number of self-employed workers. Small farmers, businesspeople, and independent craftspeople have found it increasingly difficult to survive in competition against the corporate giants. The late C. Wright Mills viewed this trend with alarm. He feared that the traditional independence of the self-employed worker that formed the basis of American democracy would be replaced by the obedience and conformity of faceless bureaucrats. Third, there has been a shift of workers away from manufacturing and other blue-collar jobs and into white-collar and service occupations. By the 1950s the majority of American workers was no longer in manufacturing. White-collar and service workers now make up over two-thirds of the work force.

Perhaps the two most significant trends in the work force have been (1) a marked increase in the participation of women and (2) an accompanying decrease in the participation of younger and older males. Particularly important changes are occurring in the role of married women, who are entering the work force in unprecedented numbers. In 1900 only one out of twenty married women participated in the work force; today one out of three holds a job. Young males, on the other hand, now are more likely to remain in school until they are well past adolescence. The work force participation of men between the ages of 20 and 24 has dropped steadily, while the participation of women in this age group has continued to rise. There has also been a significant decline in the percentage of older men who work. Of all the American men who are 65 or older, only one out of every five is now in the work force.[26]

The Occupational Hierarchy

People rank each other on the basis of their occupations. The work people do helps define their place in society as well as their personal options. It also has a profound influence on their psychological state. Although some people try to separate their personal identity from their work, this is extremely difficult to do. A sense of inferiority or inadequacy is common among people with low status jobs.

Occupational rankings are based on two separate factors: prestige and income. While most jobs with high prestige also provide high incomes, this is not always true. Most people will agree that schoolteachers have higher standing in the community than cocktail waitresses, but many waitresses make more money than teachers.

At the bottom of the heap both in terms of prestige and income are unskilled workers such as day laborers and migratory farm workers. Blue-collar workers and "hard hats" employed in manufacturing and construction jobs demanding greater skill are generally considered the next step up in occupation ratings. But blue-collar jobs are usually low in prestige. Television shows tend to portray such workers as crude and socially unappealing, even though blue-collar workers receive higher incomes than many white-collar workers. A recent survey showed that the average blue-collar production worker in the United States makes about $25 more per week than the average clerical worker.[27] Individual service and white-collar workers may or may not have higher incomes than individual blue-collar workers, but they almost always have greater prestige. Although the reasons for this are not entirely clear, three factors seem to be involved: (1) white-collar workers deal with people more than with objects and are not required to perform dirty or physically demanding jobs— "brains" are valued more highly than "brawn." (2) White-collar workers often possess such status symbols as a desk or an office and wear more formal dress (a "white collar"). (3) White-collar employees usually work in closer association with top management than blue-collar workers, and some of the managers' prestige reflects on them. At the top of the occupational hierarchy are doctors, lawyers, and high-level managers, people who hold challenging jobs and have great individual autonomy. They are rewarded with high incomes and great prestige.

Worker Alienation

The mechanization of the work place during the industrial revolution dehumanized workers, who came to resemble cogs in a machine. Even today, many factory workers find their jobs dull and trivial, a situation that gives rise to what has become known as "blue-collar blues." It is hardly surprising that some workers who perform the same repetitive tasks hundreds of times a day, year in and year out, become dissatisfied. A recent study by the Survey Research Center of the University of Michigan asked a large sample of workers which of twenty-five aspects of work they considered most important. The top eight were (1) interesting work, (2) enough help and equipment to get the job done, (3) enough information to get the job done, (4) enough authority to get the job done, (5) good pay, (6) opportunities to develop special abilities, (7) job security, and (8) seeing the results of one's work.[28] Another study found occupational self-direction—the ability to use initiative, thought, and independent judgment in one's work—to have the most significant psychological benefits.[29]

By these standards professionals, upper-level managers, and self-employed individuals are most likely to be satisfied with their work. Programs to help blue-collar workers gain greater satisfaction have generally attempted to broaden the task that a single worker performs, making the work less repetitive and enabling the worker to see the finished product. A similar approach has been used with groups of workers, giving them responsibility for assembling a finished product rather than one small part of it. Other companies encourage workers to rotate from one job to another in order to vary their tasks. Some managers allow employees to set up

The repetitive work so common for industrial laborers creates alienation and boredom, often called the "blue-collar blues."

their own working procedures and schedule their own hours. Allowing workers to participate in management decisions that affect their jobs also reduces alienation.

Not all of these experiments have been successful. Some workers seem happier in simple repetitive jobs than in jobs requiring decision making, and a few observers have charged that job enrichment programs are just a fad that will soon blow over.[30] Others argue that worker alienation will not be reduced significantly until workers receive a greater share of the profits of the companies using their labor.

UNEMPLOYMENT, INFLATION, AND THE BUSINESS CYCLE

Unemployment and inflation are the two economic problems that the public is most concerned about. They remain chronic despite numerous attempts to eliminate them, persisting like bulges on a toy balloon filled with water. Attempts to solve one problem always seem to make the other worse. To complicate matters, both unemployment and inflation are affected by cyclical changes in the state of the economy. Like the balloon with its bulges, these three conditions are really one problem.

Unemployment

To be unemployed in today's industrial society is to be excluded from the mainstream of social life. While most unemployed people suffer severe financial difficulties, despite unemployment insurance and welfare programs, their difficulties go far beyond money. The unemployed lose some of their self-respect along with their jobs, and thus may tend to avoid old social groups and employed friends. In the absence of daily contact and companionship with their fellow workers, their lives become increasingly empty, leading to feelings of helplessness and inadequacy. Unemployment may even affect health. A recent study showed an increase in physical complaints after a group of workers had been notified that their plant

NINETEENTH CENTURY SOCIAL PROBLEMS*

Poverty and no work caused August Schultz of Appleton to shoot himself in the head while sitting in his little home with his wife and 5 children.
September 24, 1891

was closing down, another increase after the plant closed, and a third increase after a prolonged period of unemployment.[31] Of course, severe strains are placed on the family of the unemployed worker as well. An unemployed husband often feels that he has failed in his duty to his wife and children, and if he is unemployed for a long period his wife may come to share these feelings.

Unemployment statistics supplied by government agencies have been widely criticized for concealing the real extent of the problem. But even if the official figures are accepted at face value, the picture they paint is not a bright one. Both the United States and Canada consistently have higher rates of unemployment than do most other industrialized nations. (See Figure 2.2.) In addition, unemployment rates showed substantial increases in the 1970s. The unemployment rate in the United States today is roughly double what it was in the late 1960s, and similar increases have occurred in Canada. Some of this increase has been caused by the growing number of women competing for jobs. But some groups of workers have even greater employment problems. The unemployment rate of black teenagers in the United States increased from 16 percent forty years ago to over 40 percent today.[32]

Economists have identified several different types of unemployment. Among these, structural and cyclical unemployment are the most serious. Structural unemployment often results from long-term changes in the economy. For instance, when technological changes make certain occupations obsolete—blacksmiths, buggy whip makers, milk bottle molders—structural unemployment results. Cyclical unemployment arises from changes in the demand for labor, which in turn is caused by changes in the business cycle. Thus, when the economy goes into a recession cyclical unemployment occurs.

While cyclical unemployment may be reduced by keeping the economy growing, this is becoming increasingly difficult in an era of depleted resources and growing international competition. Structural unemployment is even more difficult to deal with. One proposed solution is government support for programs to retrain unemployed workers for jobs that are in high demand. But it is difficult to determine which kinds of skills

*These "Nineteenth Century Social Problems" throughout the text are excerpts from the *Badger State Banner* published in Black River Falls, Wisconsin.

FIGURE 2.2
UNEMPLOYMENT RATES—
AN INTERNATIONAL
COMPARISON, 1959–1975

Source: U.S. Department of Commerce,
Social Indicators 1976 (Washington, D.C.:
GPO, 1976), p. 362.

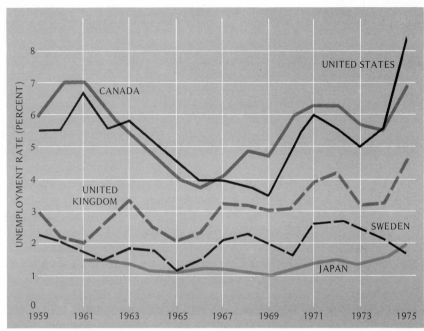

will be in demand in the future, so some people remain unemployed even after the training. The hard fact is that there are simply not enough jobs for everyone, no matter what sort of training the unemployed may have.

A different approach is job sharing to spread the available work among more people. This type of program would, of course, create an "underemployment problem" while easing the unemployment problem. Finally, many people have suggested that the government become an "employer of last resort," providing a job for anyone who wants to work and cannot find other employment. Critics claim that this program would be too expensive, but it is not clear whether the cost of such a program would be greater than the cost of the current loss of human potential due to unemployment.

Inflation Everyone is aware that things keep getting more and more expensive. Since World War II the United States and Canada have experienced three bursts of high inflation. The first occurred with the lifting of tight economic controls at the end of World War II. The Korean and Vietnam Wars contributed to the next two rounds of inflation in the United States, which spread to Canada.[33]

It is obvious that massive wartime demands for military goods eventually drive up prices. Another important factor in recent inflation has been the giant corporations, which control the major markets and do not have to respond to competition. As noted earlier, when demand slackens, prices do not go down and may even be raised to keep profits high. A related factor is organized labor. When big unions demand large wage increases, the corporations may avoid costly strikes by granting the demands and then raising the prices of their products to cover the costs. Inflation follows. When corporations raise prices, the workers' real income goes down. Another wage increase is then called for, resulting in the vicious circle known as the wage–price spiral. Those who are hurt most by such spirals are workers who lack powerful unions to demand cost-of-living wage increases, and the poor and elderly living on low fixed incomes.

Government officials fuel this inflationary fire when they try to spur economic growth by deficit spending (spending more money than is coming in). International shortages of basic resources also contribute to the problem. For example, when we use all the oil that is easy to extract, the price of the remaining oil rises because it costs more to produce. Countries with surpluses of scarce resources also are beginning to understand their importance and are demanding higher prices on the world market, thus contributing to inflation.

The Business Cycle

The economies of capitalistic countries go through cycles of "boom and bust," alternating between periods of economic growth and periods of economic stagnation or recession. The economies of North America and Western Europe always seem to be expanding or contracting and are rarely stable over extended periods. During years of growth and prosperity, wages, profits, and employment all go up. In a recession, the reverse occurs. Such trends have a tremendous social impact. The Great Depression of the 1930s was an especially low and prolonged dip in the business cycle.

Inflation generally accompanies business booms. When the economy improves, the demand for products goes up and inflation increases. When the economy declines and demand goes down, inflation is reduced. But in recent years the world has witnessed something new—stagflation. This is inflation that occurs during periods of economic stagnation or recession. Prices continue to rise despite economic recession because today's markets are dominated by large corporations that are extremely resistant to anti-inflationary pressures.

Unemployment rates also follow the business cycle. Generally, when business is good, unemployment is low and inflation is high. When the economy slows down, workers are laid off and inflation goes down. In periods of stagflation, however, both unemployment and inflation are high. (See Figure 2.3.)

Everything from sunspots to fluctuations in gold mining has been blamed for the business cycle. The most widely accepted explanation relates changes in the cycle to changes in the general outlook of businesspeople and consumers. When optimism prevails, merchants and manu-

FIGURE 2.3
UNEMPLOYMENT AND
INFLATION RATES IN THE
UNITED STATES, 1948–1976

Source: U.S. Department of Commerce,
Social Indicators 1976 (Washington, D.C.:
GPO, 1976), p. 340.

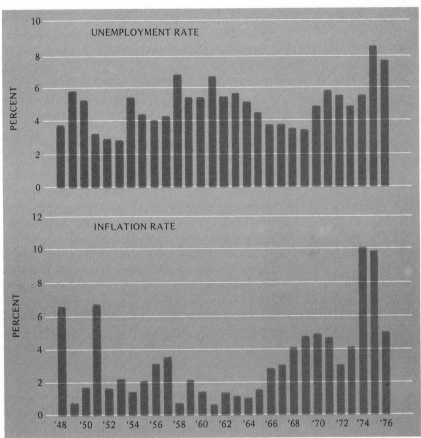

facturers build up their inventories of merchandise and invest in plant expansion; consumers buy more; and employment increases. When pessimism is the rule, inventories are sold off; production is cut back; and consumers reduce their spending; unemployment increases; and the rate of economic growth begins to decline. So changes in the business cycle seem to feed on themselves, aggravating whatever trend develops.

Governmental Action

At first glance it seems obvious that the government should always encourage as much economic growth as possible. At least in the short run, such a policy would reduce unemployment and increase general prosperity. But three complications stand in the way. First, rapid economic growth is likely to produce rapid inflation. Second, when the economy grows too rapidly the recession that eventually follows is likely to be severe. Many economists believe that the boom of the 1920s was a major cause of the disastrous depression of the 1930s. Third, there are limits to growth. Sooner or later, when the earth's resources are used up, the crunch will come.

For these reasons most modern governments try to promote steady but moderate growth. As noted earlier, this is done by manipulating monetary policies, taxes, and the federal budget to counteract harmful economic trends. If the economy grows too rapidly, the government acts to slow it down; if it does not grow rapidly enough, the government tries to introduce some economic stimulus. Democratic governments often find it impossible to resist the temptation to induce rapid economic growth and a false prosperity just before an important election, even if the long-term consequences are harmful.

Price and wage controls are one of the few government policies that can be used to combat both inflation and unemployment at the same time. Under this system the government restricts increases in prices and wages to some fixed percentage. It is hoped that such controls will limit inflation, making it unnecessary to restrict the economic growth that keeps unemployment low. The record of price and wage controls in North America is a mixed one. The Nixon administration's halfhearted attempts at such controls in the early 1970s met with little success. Canada's more recent controls have apparently been much more effective.[34]

RESPONDING TO PROBLEMS OF THE ECONOMY

Most of the economic programs that we have discussed are limited responses to specific economic problems. However, some more basic and far-reaching changes have been suggested. It seems clear that we have a choice among three economic roads: (1) We can maintain our present system, perhaps with minor changes; (2) we can move toward much greater government control and ownership of key industries; or (3) we can break up the big corporations, reduce government, and return "free" competition to the marketplace. All three courses have their advantages, but none is easy or without risk.

The first option—letting things go on as they are—seems to be the easiest and most familiar. After all, our present economic system has produced a tremendous amount of wealth and most people seem reasonably satisfied with it. Despite its faults, the present system, which is in fact a combination of free enterprise and government regulation, does a good job of providing the necessities of life and some luxuries for most people. The real question is whether the system can be improved. It is possible that ill-conceived attempts at change may backfire and produce serious harm; but it is also possible that if the system remains unchanged things will get worse. While many people argue that it would be foolish to tamper with such a successful system, others are convinced that the system is producing an authoritarian society controlled by a handful of economic elites.

The second alternative is to move toward increasing government control and socialism. But there are as many different types of socialism as there are countries that practice it. Our options range from the nationalization of a few major industries to government ownership of all the means of production. Although there are tremendous differences between moderate and radical socialism, all forms have some common advantages and disadvantages. The proponents of this system argue that only government control will allow the people to determine their economic destiny. The people have no voice in the selection of corporate leaders, but they do elect legislators and government executives. Advocates of the socialist alternative believe this system will bring greater economic equality, primarily by producing goods for use and not for profit. Critics of socialism point to the flaws of communist nations and argue that the system is wasteful and inefficient because it destroys individual initiative and puts economic decisions in the hands of bumbling bureaucrats. To some critics, socialism and totalitarianism are virtually inseparable.

The third alternative is to return to a free-enterprise system without giant corporations and big government. This end could be achieved by taxing huge corporations out of existence or by using stronger antitrust laws to break them up. After their goal is achieved, the size of government could be reduced. The proponents of this approach argue that such actions would restore the freedom and innovation of private enterprise, thus decentralizing economic power and promoting greater economic equality. Critics of this proposal make two main points: First, it is not likely that the corporations can be dismantled, and second, they believe that giant corporations and big government are more efficient than smaller organizations and therefore should not be broken up.

Our economic system is an incredibly complex network of interdependent forces, and there are no easy solutions to our economic problems. Every option is likely to have unintended and undesirable consequences, and must be carefully weighed before being put into effect. Yet inactions may be equally dangerous, producing just as many unexpected and undesirable results.

SOCIOLOGICAL PERSPECTIVES on Problems of the Economy

The rising cost of living, the control of prices by corporations, the hardships of unemployment, and similar difficulties seem to be matters for economists to consider. Indeed, some economists devote their lives to the study and solution of these problems. But sociologists are involved too. The three perspectives sketched out in Chapter 1 are used by sociologists and others to understand our persistent economic problems. To the sociologist, economic problems can be understood only in their social context. It makes no more sense to study economic problems apart from their social background than it does to try to solve social problems without understanding their economic basis.

The Functionalist Perspective

Functionalists see the economic system as a machine that produces and distributes the commodities a society needs. If the system functions efficiently to give the society what it wants, there are no economic problems. But sometimes the machine balks or strains. One part may run faster or slower than others, throwing the whole machine out of balance. For example, distribution may not keep up with production, or the production machinery may produce too many goods of one kind and not enough of another. Such maladjustments may correct themselves (free enterprise) or may be corrected by officials (government intervention). Economic crises occur when the whole machine becomes disorganized and coordination throughout the system falters.

Functionalists blame contemporary economic problems on rapid changes that have thrown the traditional system out of balance. It took hundreds of years for Western society to develop and perfect an economic system based on open competition among private individuals in a free market. But as the system became larger and more complex, its problems multiplied. As we have seen, huge corporations sprang up and gained control of many vital markets; the government stepped in to regulate the overall economy; and powerful unions began to control the labor market. Thus, three new cogs—corporations, government, and unions— threw the old machinery out of balance. Under these conditions old economic ideas were no longer effective and dysfunctional economic decisions followed. In addition, the economy has continued to change so rapidly that it has been unable to achieve a new and stable balance, with serious economic problems remaining unresolved while new ones continue to arise.

Most functionalists shy away from radical, far-reaching proposals for solving our economic problems, principally because they know that change brings problems as well as solutions. Disruptive change in an unbalanced system makes a new balance even more difficult to achieve. Functionalists favor specific, limited cures for specific, limited problems. Education and training for the unemployed and better law enforcement to deter corporate crime are functionalist solutions to economic problems. The basic goal of the functionalist is to reduce the disorganization in our economic institutions and improve the coordination between them and other social institutions. Only when this goal has been reached will the economic system function smoothly and efficiently.

The Conflict Perspective

Conflict theorists take a very different view of the economic system. Unlike functionalists, they do not consider society a unified whole based on a consensus about norms and values. Consequently, they do not say that the economic system performs either well or badly for the entire society; rather, they believe that it benefits certain groups at the expense of others, and that who benefits, and to what degree, changes from time to time.

From the conflict perspective, society is composed of many different groups, each trying to advance its economic interests at the expense of the others. Most economic problems arise because one group — or a coalition of groups — seizes economic power and acts in ways that advance its own interests at the expense of the rest of society. Thus, conflict theorists say that recent changes in the economic system reflect free competition among different groups. Each works for its own selfish interests as Adam Smith said they should. But conflict theorists do not, like Smith, assert that this competition brings advantages to everyone. They say it benefits only the most powerful competitive groups. Conflict theorists charge that ever since businesspeople and industrialists seized power from the landed nobility, they have busily enlarged their power and their affluence.

According to conflict theory, the underlying cause of most of our economic problems is the exploitation of workers by employers and the powerful elites of which the employers are usually a part. If these problems are to be solved, the workers must somehow gain enough power to make the elites give up their advantages and create a more just economic order. The first step, according to some theorists, is for oppressed workers to develop "class consciousness," a sense of unity based on the realization that they are being exploited. Then the workers must organize themselves for political action and achieve change either through peaceful conflicts — elections, protests, and strikes — or if need be through violent conflicts.

The Social-Psychological Perspective

Because social psychologists are concerned mainly with individuals, they rarely address large-scale economic problems. Instead, they are more interested in the impact of the economic system on an individual's psychological makeup, attitudes, and behavior patterns. They also examine the impact of these ways of behaving on the larger economic system.

According to social psychologists, our open, competitive economic system encourages a strong achievement orientation that often leads to dissatisfaction and anxiety. When a large percentage of a population is oriented toward individual competition, the culture they share is likely to show many forms of innovation and creativity. But this system also creates a considerable amount of insecurity, anxiety, and hostility.

Social psychologists have observed, however, that the economic system's norms are not equally shared by everyone in a society. Those who are upwardly mobile or are dropping in occupational standing are likely to be more oriented toward competitiveness and conflict than those in secure economic positions. The unskilled, the unemployed, and the downwardly mobile have more personal and psychological problems than other people. They also are more likely to be hostile, aggressive, and anxious.

Effective solutions to the psychological problems created by our economic system are not easy to find. One possible solution would be to deemphasize the values of competition and achievement and to emphasize instead cooperation and mutual support. But despite the fact that a noncompetitive orientation has long been stressed in family and religious institutions, its application to society at large meets with strong resistance. This opposition seems to be based on fear that reducing competitiveness will destroy initiative and creativity. Perhaps this is why stress is placed on clinical treatment of psychological disorders rather than on changing the economic and other social conditions that seem to produce them. But many social psychologists continue to argue that reducing economic insecurity, even in a competitive society, would improve the mental health of our entire population.

SUMMARY

Change has come so rapidly to our economic system that many people have difficulty seeing things as they are. The Scottish philosopher Adam Smith was one of the first people to advocate free open markets and a minimum of government interference in economic processes. Smith's ideas became part of the theoretical foundation of capitalism, and they remain very popular. However, the economy has changed tremendously from the early days of capitalism, and Smith's theories represent the ideal more than the reality.

The corporation is a major force in the modern economic system. Some corporations have grown so large that they control dozens of different companies in many countries. Although the government no longer permits most markets to be controlled by a monopoly (one corporation), many industries are controlled by an oligopoly (a few large corporations). Corporations work together in a variety of legal and illegal ways to exercise market control. Accordingly, prices are often determined by the corporations and not by changes in supply and demand.

There is considerable debate over who runs the corporations. Some people see small stockholders as the owners and controllers, while others claim that a few large stockholders dominate most corporations. The most widely accepted idea is that control rests with corporate managers, who have the special technical skills needed to make decisions that will increase profits. Some sociologists argue that high-level corporate decision makers represent the interests of a "power elite" that dominates the economic and the political system. Other studies suggest that the decision makers represent a wide variety of conflicting interests.

More and more large corporations are becoming multinational. Although most of the big multinationals are American, many other countries are represented as well. Some authorities think the multinationals are laying the foundation for a new and benevolent world government, but others see them as exploiters of the poor and powerless nations.

Corporate crime, whether it is committed against the consumer or against other business, is a serious problem. Proposed solutions include increasing government intervention and regulation, as well as consumer education and political awareness.

Like the corporation, government and labor unions have come to play important parts in the economic system. The government is deeply involved in managing the economy. When the economy is growing too fast, government officials try to slow it down; when it is growing too slowly, they try to speed it up.

Workers are at the heart of any industrial economy. Recent years have seen a sharp decline in the number of unskilled workers, but white-collar and service jobs have been on the increase. Women have been entering the work force in increasing numbers, while the participation of both older and younger males has been declining.

The economy of a capitalist country generally alternates between periods of rapid economic growth and periods of stagnation or recession. When economic conditions are good, unemployment is usually low while inflation is high, and in periods of depression the opposite is usually true. However, in the recession of the 1970s inflation as well as unemployment increased, a condition called stagflation. Governments try to control the economy, thus reducing the peaks and valleys of the cycles.

Many proposals for reorganization of our economic system have been made. The three major options are to (1) leave the present economic system pretty much as it is, (2) move toward greater government control and socialism, or (3) keep the private-enterprise system but break up the giant corporations, reduce big government, and restore free competition.

Personal responses to economic problems depend in part on which of the three main sociological perspectives is applied. Functionalists see economic problems as products of poor organization. Conflict theorists see them as a result of struggles between competing groups. Social psychologists note that personality problems are closely linked with economic problems.

KEY TERMS		
	capitalism	oligopoly
	conglomerate	power elite
	corporate technostructure	price fixing
	cyclical unemployment	price leader
	industrial espionage	stagflation
	interlocking directorate	structural unemployment
	market control	wage–price spiral
	monopoly	

3
Problems of Government

Are bureaucrats and bureaucracies necessary?
Do special-interest groups serve a useful purpose?
Is there a power elite?
Can government be made more responsive to social
   problems?

The essence of politics is power — the power to determine what is a criminal act and what is not, the power to start or avoid wars, the power to collect vast sums of money and spend them on everything from ball point pens to atom bombs. Those with political power regulate thousands of aspects of our daily lives, from issuing birth certificates to demanding burial licenses. The list is almost endless. Clearly, the political institution is of crucial importance to any society. Problems of government quickly spread to other social institutions. Therefore, when government fails to function properly, it is the whole society's problem.

Governments are also crucial in the solution of social problems. Even such personal problems as divorce, mental disorders, and drug addiction have their political side. In modern societies such problems are given to the government to solve, usually by passing new laws or spending tax dollars in ways that are expected to help. As government has grown in size and influence, it has become the principal institution for dealing with social problems. It is hard to imagine effective solutions to such diverse problems as crime, poverty, environmental pollution, or urban decay without effective political action.

Many problems of government stem from conflicts in basic values. Freedom and liberty are highly valued in our culture, but so are respect for authority and economic security. These two sets of values are often in conflict, and people sometimes seem to trade one for the other. For example, in times of war or severe economic depression, people seem willing to give up their freedoms to political leaders who promise to restore order or bring back prosperity. The government is also the principal agency for handling class and group conflicts. Indeed, our current class system would be impossible without governmental support and protection. Societies without organized government have no social classes as we know them.

Problems *in* government often arise from disorganization, which makes it difficult for the government to provide necessary services. Some parts of government seem to have a life of their own. There is a tendency for individual agencies and bureaus to set their own goals, which may be unrelated or even in opposition to the official goals of the government as a whole.

THE GROWTH OF GOVERNMENT BUREAUCRACY

Governments throughout the world have been expanding rapidly in recent times. In the United States government expenses have grown much faster than the total economy. In 1973 the economy was about 20 times larger than it was in 1902, but government expenditures were 65 times larger. In the same period civilian employment in the U.S. Government increased from 1 million to over 12 million. There has been a similar expansion in Canada. In 1947, government employment accounted for 13

DEBATE
Is Government
Too Big?

PRO

Growth in the size and power of government has gotten out of hand and must be curbed. Productive businesspeople are being replaced by government bureaucrats who do little more than shuffle the piles of paper created by their own rules and regulations. Competition keeps private business efficient; the absence of competition has made government fat and wasteful. Despite the inefficiency of government, more and more critical economic decisions are being made by bureaucrats who ignore the demands of the marketplace. The complex maze of government rules and regulations costs business billions of dollars each year, driving up the prices of virtually all goods and services. In addition, the taxes required to support an army of government employees place a crushing burden on the average citizen.

But the damage done by big government goes far beyond the economic system. The government's almost limitless power has enabled it to regulate and dominate citizens as never before. After paying for necessities—food, shelter, and clothing—most of the average person's income goes to the government as taxes to be spent as politicians see fit. Thus, the incentive and drive that made this country great are being replaced by the mindless conformity of the welfare state. The government has convinced many people that society owes them a living, so it is hardly surprising that they refuse to work. Clearly, big government must be cut down to size before it is too late to repair the damage it has done.

CON

Proposals to make slashing cuts in government are naïve, unworkable, and dangerous. We can no more go back to an old style of government than we can go back to the days of the horse and buggy. It was not government but private corporations that led the way to today's huge, impersonal bureaucracies. The federal government remained quite small until well into the twentieth century. It was finally forced to take responsibility for the economy during the Great Depression, when private enterprise failed. If the effort to shrink the government were successful, we would soon experience another economic disaster.

Those who continually attack government waste and corruption feed the public distorted and misleading information. Of course, a few dramatic examples of mismanagement can be found in any organization as large as the federal government, but on the whole the government serves the public interest well. Indeed, the corporations are clearly more wasteful and corrupt than government. Corporations squander billions of dollars in lavish salaries and fringe benefits for management, while government officials earn only a fraction of the income of their counterparts in private business. Hundreds of millions are wasted promoting a particular brand of toothpaste or deodorant. But waste is not the worst abuse of business. Unsafe products, industrial pollution, and hazardous working conditions kill or maim thousands of people every year. Government must not be reduced; rather, it should be made larger and stronger in order to protect the public against such abuses.

percent of the Canadian labor force; by 1965, that figure had risen to 25 percent of total nonfarm employment.[1]

The influence of government on the daily lives of citizens has also grown. In past centuries most centralized governments were distant and ineffective. Important decisions were made locally and were based on custom and tradition. Today governments are much stronger and less tightly bound by traditional restraints. Much of this growth in size and influence has taken place in response to changes in other social institutions in the past fifty years. For example, as the family became smaller and less stable the government had to assume some of the functions that the family once performed, such as educating children and caring for the elderly. The emerging industrial economy also showed considerable instability. Conditions became so bad during the Great Depression that the government was virtually forced to get more involved in the economy.

The Nature of Bureaucracy

Max Weber, one of the founders of sociology, was among the first people to study public and private bureaucracies. He noted that **bureaucracies** have the following five characteristics:

1. A clear-cut *division of labor*. Each office has its own task to perform, and all workers are specialists.
2. A *hierarchy of authority*. Each office worker is under the control and supervision of a person with higher rank.
3. A set of *formal rules* that guide the workers and supervisors and the operations of the organization as a whole.
4. *Impersonal enforcement of rules*. Officials treat all people impersonally, applying the rules to specific cases without feelings for or against the person involved.
5. *Job security*. Employment in a bureaucracy is based on technical qualifications; the employee who does his or her duty is protected against arbitrary dismissal. Promotion is made according to objective standards and rules.[2]

Everyone complains about bureaucratic inefficiency, yet Weber saw bureaucracies as the most rational and efficient form of social organization. Although some bureaucracies are inefficient, the alternatives are, on the whole, even more inefficient. Organizations based on personal loyalty and allegiance without formal rules have many advantages, but efficiency is not one of them. As Weber pointed out,

> Experience tends universally to show that the purely bureaucratic type of administrative organization . . . is, from a purely technical point of view, capable of attaining the highest degree of efficiency. . . . It is superior to any other form in precision, in stability, in the stringency of its discipline, and in its reliability.[3]

Both public and private bureaucracies have grown rapidly in the twentieth century.

More recent studies reveal that bureaucratic employees do much more than follow formal rules. Bureaucracy has another face—the informal activities and procedures that develop among the employees. For example, it may turn out that the duties of an official who is incompetent are performed on an informal basis by a lower-status employee. Sometimes rules are so awkward that employees must develop ways of circumventing them if they are going to get the job done. Some worker protests that fall short of outright strikes take the form of "working to the rules"—if all employees do exactly as the rules direct, productivity decreases. Obviously, no matter what the rules say, bureaucratic employees are human beings, not impersonal machines.

The Problems of Bureaucracy

The very strength of a bureaucracy can also be its weakness. The formal rules that permit it to function smoothly can also drown it in a sea of red tape. No system of rules is perfect, and when unusual cases occur it may be necessary to break the rules in order to meet the organization's goals. However, carrying out official policy is not the only concern of most bureaucrats. Holding onto their jobs is often a more important goal, and because they can be fired for breaking rules, the tendency is to play it safe. Employees try at least to give the appearance of following rules to the letter, regardless of the consequences for the organization. For example, a welfare worker may know that a family is needy and deserves government assistance but is ineligible because of some technicality. An employee who is afraid to violate the rules "passes the buck" by sending the applicant to another office. At the next office the applicant may be referred to someone else, and so on through the bureaucratic maze while the family goes hungry. Such displacement of goals is extremely common in bureaucracies both in the government and in private industry.[4] Even Max Weber had nagging doubts about the depersonalizing effects of bureaucratization. He came to fear that our unending drive for bureaucratic efficiency would imprison us in an "iron cage" of reason, with little room for human emotions.

James Q. Wilson, a political scientist and presidential adviser, has listed several basic problems that must be solved if government bureaucracies are to provide the maximum benefit to society.[5] First, each bureaucracy must be made to serve the function for which it was intended. Second, bureaucracies must manage to treat everyone equally under the rules while retaining the ability to cope with special cases. Third, bureaucracies should maximize efficiency in order to provide the most benefits for the least cost. Fourth, financial corruption and favoritism must be avoided.

Solving such problems is no easy task, and even small improvements require intensive thought and effort. Corruption receives public attention because it is shocking and dramatic, but the other problems are often ignored.

THE AMERICAN SYSTEM OF GOVERNMENT

There are many different forms of government, ranging from the vast Communist party bureaucracy in the Soviet Union to feudal Saudi Arabia. Governments that try to carry out the will of their citizens through elections are in the minority. The American system is one of these, as are the parliamentary systems of Canada, Australia, and some European nations. The problems of any government, democratic or dictatorial, are closely associated with its structure and organization.

In the United States (and Canada as well), national affairs are handled by a central government and local affairs are left to semi-independent local governments, each with its own geographic boundaries. The goal of this federal system is to provide overall unity and cohesion while allowing for local autonomy and self direction. It permits smaller local governments to operate on a more human scale and provides for the expression of regional differences in government. But the federal system has certain drawbacks. The overlapping authority and duties of federal, state, county, and city governments is inefficient, and officials at these different levels of government often work at cross-purposes, wasting valuable resources on useless squabbling. Duplication of services is another characteristic of the federal system. For example, in the United States it is possible for a single criminal case to be investigated by a city police officer, a county sheriff, a state police official, and a federal investigator, with each asking the same questions of the same witnesses and suspects. The delicate balance among the various governments in a federal system may also promote inaction. Officials at one level of government who try to deal with a pressing social problem may be opposed by officials at another level because the proposed solution conflicts with their interests.

Geographically, government in the United States is highly decentralized, with authority and power spread among fifty independent states and thousands of local communities. Politically, there has been a trend toward increasing concentration of power in the federal government, particularly the executive branch. This growing dominance can be seen in the pattern of federal spending. At the turn of the century, about two-thirds of all government spending was done by the state and local governments; by the 1970s, the relationship had been reversed. The federal government now accounts for two-thirds of all government spending, while state and local governments dispense the remainder. One cause of this centralization was American involvement in one war after another and the consequent need for centralized control and coordination. The growing involvement of the federal government in economic and social problems has been another factor, since state and local governments cannot manage the national economy or respond effectively to nationwide problems.

The recent financial crisis of New York City typifies the economic problems faced by state and local governments. The employees of these governments have unionized and are demanding wages comparable to those in private industry. At the same time, many groups, especially the poor and underprivileged, are demanding more and better services, while overburdened local taxpayers are protesting the increased costs. The root of the problem, as Thomas Bodenheiman points out, is in the system of taxation.[6] The income of local governments comes from taxes that fall most heavily on low- and middle-income taxpayers, whose ability to pay is reaching its limits. About half of state revenues come from sales and excise taxes, and over 80 percent of local revenues come from property taxes.

Political Parties

American political parties are loosely organized, and national party officials have little control over state and local party activities. This decentralization is so great that it might be said that there are really 50 separate Democratic parties and 50 separate Republican parties. Indeed, there may be even more, since local party officials are quite independent of state officials. American political parties seldom meet until election time draws near. Then they assemble to nominate candidates and plan strategy for the coming contest. Membership in a political party requires no more than claiming a preference when registering to vote. Few party members actively involve themselves in party activities, and the parties have little control over candidates after they are elected or appointed to office.

The two major parties in the United States do not have distinct political ideologies. Republicans tend to be conservative and Democrats incline to liberalism, but both parties are broadly based, and each has a conservative wing and a liberal wing. Indeed, both parties have tended to move toward the middle of the ideological road, where most of the voters are presumed to be. The parties seem to be held together mainly by the members' desire to elect their candidates, but there is little unity even in elections. Many Republicans vote for Democrats, and many members of the Democratic Party vote Republican.

Despite their lack of concern for ideology, American political parties do reflect class differences. The Republicans have closer ties with business, the Democrats with lower-paid workers and minorities. The two parties consistently take different positions on important political issues. Studies show that Democrats favor government regulation of business, social-welfare spending, and higher taxes for the wealthy, while Republicans favor minimal government controls on business, low expenditures for social welfare, and weak government generally.[7] Democrats receive larger contributions from organized labor, while Republicans receive more money from business. One study of the political contributions of twelve of America's most prominent and wealthy families found that they gave over four times as much money to the Republicans as they did to the Democrats.[8]

Separation of Powers

In addition to dividing power geographically, the nation's founders partitioned the federal government into separate branches in the hope that each branch would check and balance the powers of the others. The legislative branch was designed to enact laws, the executive branch to carry out the laws, and the judicial branch to interpret the laws and decide on their constitutionality. The theory was that a balance of power would develop among these three branches of the federal government and prevent any one of them from gaining dictatorial power.

The Legislative Branch

The U.S. Constitution gave Congress broad legislative powers, and for about 150 years it dominated the other two branches. However, in the twentieth century Congress became more of a reactive force than an active force in American government. It still exercises great power, but this power tends to take the form of approving, modifying, or rejecting presidential proposals. Rather than trying to tell the executive branch what it should do, Congress tries to tell it what it should not do.

Congress can restrain the executive branch by means of the budget. It can simply refuse to grant presidential requests for money. But its own cumbersome bureaucratic form of organization prevents it from doing this very effectively:

> Congress has shackled itself with inadequate political campaign laws, archaic rules, the seniority system, secrecy, understaffing, and grossly deficient ways to obtain crucial information. . . . It is a Congress which does not

FIGURE 3.1
CONFIDENCE IN SELECTED
INSTITUTIONS, 1976

Source: U.S. Department of Commerce,
Social Indicators 1976 (Washington, D.C.:
GPO, 1976), p. xlvii.

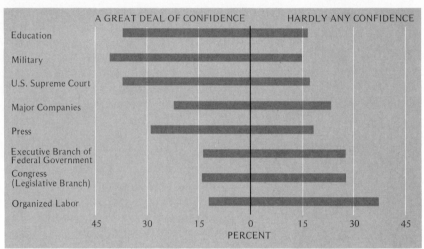

lead but is led, and which continues to relinquish its constitutional authority
and leadership role in government. Crushed by the burden of checking and
balancing the executive branch, Congress operates nonetheless on a yearly
budget equivalent to less than three days' expenditure of the Pentagon.[9]

Congress does most of its work in committees. The Senate currently
has 17 standing committees and the House 21. In addition, there are almost 250 subcommittees specializing in issues ranging from agriculture to
foreign affairs. Congress could not function efficiently without specialized
committees to consider specialized matters. However, the committee
members, who must pass on legislation before it goes to the entire body,
usually get their jobs on the basis of seniority. In most cases, the chairperson of a committee is the member who has been in Congress the longest.
This means that legislators from "safe" districts, who are reelected year
after year, end up with the lion's share of power. Some of these older
members are firmly opposed to the innovation and experimentation
proposed by younger members. Ten years ago the average age of the ten
most powerful committee chairpersons in the House was 74, and three of
them were in their 80s. At that time the average age of the presidents of
America's largest corporations was 57.[10] In early 1975 a post-Watergate
revolt in the House of Representatives removed several of the oldest and
most powerful committee chairpersons, but it remains to be seen whether
the seniority system has undergone permanent change.

Another reason that Congress is ineffective is that many legislators are
afraid to make any move that might arouse controversy. Even trying to restrain the executive branch through budgetary controls is likely to be politically dangerous, especially if the executive branch proposes to spend
money in ways that the taxpayers think are in their immediate interests.

As Republican Representative Paul McCloskey has put it, "The penalties in the profession of politics are applied to those who attempt to lead, take controversial positions and, most of all, allow those controversial positions to become known to constituents."[11] McCloskey noted that Congress has three informal rules that function to restrict its power: (1) Never take a position on a controversial issue unless you have to. (2) When you do take a position, try to be as vague as possible. (3) Try to keep your votes secret or unrecorded. To put it bluntly, members of Congress do not exercise strong national leadership on social issues because they do not care to take the political risk of doing so.

The Executive Branch

In recent years the executive branch has gained power at the expense of the legislature. The President is the only federal official elected by all the people, and as the symbol of the American nation he has tremendous moral authority, which can be translated into political power in many ways. The President is now a major initiator of congressional legislation. In addition, he has the power to veto legislation and is the commander-in-chief of the armed forces. Even though the Constitution requires a declaration of war by Congress before the nation can enter into deadly international combat, this provision has been ignored. The Korean and Vietnam Wars were initiated entirely by the President, and in both instances war was never declared.

Another source of presidential power is control of the federal bureaucracy. Not only can the President reward supporters with federal jobs; he can muster the massive resources of the federal bureaucracy in conflicts with the other two branches of the government. The President has generally proven more effective than Congress in making and carrying out important decisions. While congressional decisions require extensive debate and slow progress through various committees, the President is much freer to act quickly.

The growth of executive power poses some troubling questions. The fact that the President can arrive at important decisions more quickly than the legislature does not mean that presidential policies are better than those created in Congress. Continuing erosion of the system of checks and balances may create an executive branch so powerful that Congress will not be able to restrain it.

The Judicial Branch

The federal judicial system consists of 89 district courts, 10 circuit courts of appeal, and the Supreme Court. Because the Supreme Court is at the top of this hierarchy, it has the greatest political impact. Whether the Court is liberal, conservative, or somewhere in between, it does much more than interpret laws. In its decisions it makes social policy as well. In recent decades the Court has been one of the most effective forces for social change in America, in contrast to the earlier years of this century, when it was an obstacle to social reform. For example, the Court once held that corporations have all the rights guaranteed to individual citizens by the Fourteenth Amendment, and it prohibited all sorts of federal regulation, even restrictions on child labor. But more recently, under the leadership of Chief Justice Earl Warren, the Court was extremely active in dealing with important social problems. It attacked racial segregation, demanded that state legislators be elected in ways that give more equal representation to all voters, restrained zealous police officers, and held that all criminals are entitled to be represented by lawyers.

Throughout its history the Supreme Court has been the focus of political storms. Debate has raged about whether an appointive body should have such great power in a democracy. On one side of the debate are those who argue that "nine old men" should not have the power to block the will of the entire nation. On the other side are those who assert that the Court's insulation allows it to protect the rights of minorities who are being abused by majority rule. For better or worse, the Court is not as immune from the political currents of its time as many people suppose. The justices are informed men who understand their political environment and respond to it. If there is sufficient opposition to a decision, it is often modified in later rulings.[12]

THE PARLIAMENTARY SYSTEM OF GOVERNMENT

The British parliamentary system is used in one form or another by most of the democratic governments in the world. It differs from the American system in that the American executive has much more power than the executive in a parliamentary system. In Great Britain, Canada, and other nations with parliamentary governments, the prime minister is not directly elected by the people. A political party's objective is to elect a majority to the House of Commons; the House, in turn, elects a prime minister. The parties also have a strong voice in the selection of the members of the prime minister's cabinet. If the party in power (called "the government") loses an election, the prime minister resigns. Indeed, if the party in power cannot muster enough votes in the House to carry out its policies, the House is dissolved and a new election called.

There also is an upper house, called the House of Lords in Britain and the Senate in Canada. In Britain, most lords inherit their titles and are therefore eligible to sit in the House of Lords. In Canada, members of the Senate are not called lords or ladies but are appointed for life.

Canada, like the United States, is a federal system. Its ten provinces would be called states in America. The national parliament, like the federal government in the United States, has jurisdiction over foreign relations, national defense, the postal system, transportation and communication between provinces, trade with other countries, and other national affairs. The remaining areas of legislation—education, administration of justice, the administration of public lands, and so on—are in the hands of the provincial governments. Unlike the United States, however, Canada has only one set of criminal laws, those made by the federal government. In America, each state has its own criminal laws, as does the federal government.

The principal advantage of the parliamentary system over the American system is its flexibility. In the United States, the chief executive officer (president) is elected for four years, so the people are stuck with him for that period even if he leads them in directions they dislike. In Canada or England, a chief executive officer (prime minister) who antagonized the voters would be replaced much more quickly. The Watergate scandal, for example, would not have caused as great a furor in Great Britain or Canada as it did in the United States. Shortly after the first crimes were discovered, new elections would have been called and a new government probably would have been elected.

The main advantage of the American system is its stability. In times of political crisis parliamentary systems can become extremely unstable. Prime ministers are elected with weak parliamentary support and are sometimes thrown out of office before they have a chance to take effective action. If the parliament is divided among many small parties, it is often difficult for any candidate to get the votes needed to be elected prime minister. In the American system the President is in a much more secure position, for he knows he will be in office for at least four years. Thus, it is easier for a President to take unpopular actions that he believes are in the public interest.

WHO RUNS THE GOVERNMENT?

Many governments claim to be democratic, but few actually are. Even the claims of such countries as England, the United States, and Canada that "the people" hold the political power are open to question. Does power really reside in the people, or is it in the hands of special-interest groups or an exclusive "power elite"? As in the case of the giant corporations, there is no simple answer. An enormous number of factors influence important government decisions—decisions that are not restricted to lawmaking alone. Court rulings and other determinations about policies and programs are involved as well. Exactly how these decisions are made, or by whom, has been the subject of much research, but the results are open to many different interpretations.

The Citizens

In an ideal democracy political power is shared by all citizens. But today's nation-states are too large for direct participation by everyone, making elected representatives a special power group in and of themselves. This is not to say that elected representatives never express the interests of the majority of their constituents. Majority rule is certainly possible, but there are sizable obstacles in its way.

One of the major problems of any democracy is the apathy and indifference of its citizens. Only 60 to 70 percent of the registered voters actually participate in the presidential elections in the United States, and the turnout for lesser offices is much smaller. And because many eligible voters never register, these figures actually overestimate public interest. Other forms of political participation, such as working in a political campaign or participating in a political rally, are even less common than voting. This fact is not lost on our political representatives, as may be seen in the following comment by Representative McCloskey:

> It is indeed difficult to obtain his [the citizen's] enthusiastic commitment to political involvement. To obtain the attention of a sufficient percentage of the electorate, the candidate is stimulated either to espouse sensational causes, or to campaign eighteen hours a day for many months.[13]

It is not necessary for all of the citizens in a democracy to participate if those who do are representative of those who do not. But this is not the case. Studies of citizen participation reveal a strange paradox. Those who most need the government's help are least likely to participate in the political process. People with higher incomes and many years of schooling— usually white males—are much more likely to participate. Minorities, the poor, and females are less likely to get involved in politics. Thus, it seems that wealth and education create the interest and the resources necessary for political participation.[14] (See Figure 3.2.)

FIGURE 3.2
VOTERS AS A PERCENT OF
THE VOTING-AGE
POPULATION, BY ETHNIC
GROUP, 1964–1976

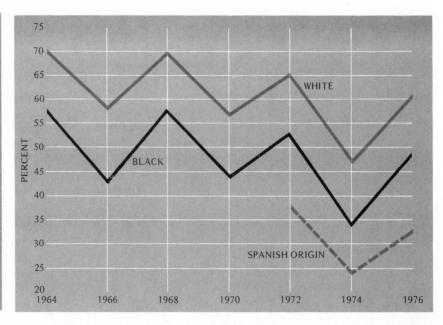

Source: U.S. Department of Commerce, *Social Indicators 1976* (Washington, D.C.: GPO, 1976), p. 527.

Even the citizen who is interested in politics often finds it difficult to decide where a particular politician really stands on the issues. As pointed out earlier, politicians often try to conceal their opinions about controversial issues. In addition, the voters seldom get a chance to talk directly with candidates, relying instead on the mass media for their information. Effective campaigners try to project a positive image in their advertising and television speeches, which often have little to do with the issues. Advertising agencies sell candidates like soaps and deodorants. In a 30-second television commercial there is little time for serious consideration of political issues.

Another source of voter apathy is distrust of the government and a feeling of powerlessness. Many people do not think their votes or opinions count for much against the powerful special-interest groups and the huge number of other voters. A single vote is almost never decisive, even in the closest elections.

Special-Interest Groups

Legislators and other government officials are influenced by special-interest groups with a particular stake in specific legislation. Physicians, realtors, women, small businesses, big businesses, labor unions, and ethnic minorities, among others, are special-interest groups. Such groups are concerned about the laws and policies that affect their economic well-being. Other groups come together because of their feeling about a certain issue. Examples include antiabortion groups, civil-liberties groups, and patriotic groups. The influence of these groups depends to a large extent on their size, their degree of organization, and the money at their disposal. Big business is the most powerful of all interest groups because it has more of these resources. As Ralph Nadar puts it,

> Much of what passes as governmental power is derivative of corporate power whose advocacy or sufferance defines much of the direction and deployment of government activity. The federal government is replete with supportive programs — subsidies, research, promotional contracts, tax privileges, protections from competition — which flow regularly into the corporate mission of profit and sales maximization. So much of government resources is allocated and so much government authority is utilized to transfer public wealth into corporate coffers that Washington can be fairly described as a bustling bazaar of accounts receivable for industry — commerce.[15]

Lobbying various legislative bodies is the principal activity of most special-interest groups. Lobbyists try to convince lawmakers to pass the kind of legislation they desire. One of their most effective tools is information. Because individual legislators are seldom well informed on all the bills they must consider, and because legislative bodies lack the funds to make independent investigations, the facts and figures supplied by lobbyists are quite influential. Lobbyists also try to influence legislation by cultivating the friendship of individual legislators. A lobbyist's promise of political support from a powerful special interest often determines an elected official's decision. Threats by a special interest can be effective too. Opposition by a powerful labor union or an important corporation has resulted in the defeat of many politicians.

Money is one of the special-interest groups' main tools. Modern political campaigns require large sums of money, and some groups are very generous in their contributions to legislators who support their interests. Several cases from the Watergate era suggest that corporations buy political influence with campaign contributions. For example, several years ago International Telephone and Telegraph was blocked from merging with the Hartford Fire Insurance Company by a federal antitrust suit. ITT subsequently promised a $400,000 contribution to help underwrite the Republican National Convention, and the suit was dropped. In another case the Secretary of Agriculture announced that there would be no increase in the price support for milk, but two weeks later the price supports were raised by 6 percent. Although the full story may never be known, the milk lobby did give $322,500 in contributions to various Republican committees working to reelect President Nixon immediately after the Secretary made his announcement.[16]

In response to such abuses Congress passed a campaign reform bill that limits the amount of money an individual or organization may donate to a political candidate, and provides federal financing for presidental elections. But abuses will continue to occur.

Many political scientists have noted that, despite such abuses, lobbyists and special-interest groups are important to a political democracy. They, like political parties, provide a channel of communication between citizens and their government. Moreover, interest groups compete with each other, and out of this conflict comes a reasonable compromise. But interest groups do not have equal power. The poor, the uneducated, and the deprived lack the resources to create an effective interest group and are therefore left out of the governmental process. Critics argue that the most powerful lobbyists represent the interests of only the affluent and influential and do great harm to the interests of the majority of the people.

Is There a Power Elite?

As noted in Chapter 2, one of the most heated debates in the social sciences concerns the existence of what C. Wright Mills called a power elite — a small unified ruling class.[17] Supporters of the idea that the United States and other capitalist nations are ruled by a small upper class are called elitists. Those who believe that political decisions are made by changing coalitions of many political forces are called pluralists.

The Elitists

Although radicals have long argued that America is dominated by a small group of powerful men, it was Mills' book *The Power Elite*, published in the 1950s, that started the current debate. According to Mills, the power elite is a coalition of people in the highest ranks of the economy, the government, and the military who together form a unified and self-conscious social class:

> There is no longer, on the one hand, an economy and, on the other hand, a political world, containing a military establishment unimportant to politics and to money-making. There is a political economy numerously linked with military order and decision. This triangle of power is now a structural fact, and it is the key to any understanding of the higher circles in America today. For as each of these domains has coincided with the others, as decisions in each have become broader, the leading men of each—the high military, the corporation executive, the political directorate—have tended to come together to form the power elite of America.[18]

According to Mills, one of the major sources of the unity of the power elite is its members' common social background. They come from upper-class and upper-middle-class white families living in urban areas. They attend the same Ivy League colleges and, by and large, share the same attitudes toward the world and their positions in it. In addition, the social networks that they represent are closely interconnected, with many common interests. Finally, although the power elite does not represent some great conspiracy, its members do meet both socially and professionally and often coordinate their activities.

Below the power elite Mills saw two other levels of power in American society. At the bottom of the heap are the great masses of people—unorganized, ill informed, and virtually powerless. Between these masses and the elite are the "middle levels" of power, where some true competition between interest groups still exists. Mills saw the U.S. Congress as a reflection of these middle levels of power. Although Congress decides some minor issues, the power elite ensures that no serious challenge to its control is tolerated in the political arena.

More recent writings of the elitist school accept Mills' conclusion that power is concentrated and centralized but question his inclusion of the military leadership in the power elite.[19] Although they recognize the importance of the military, they are convinced that the most critical decisions, even in the field of international relations, are made by an economic-political elite.

The Pluralists   In contrast, pluralists believe that democratic societies are indeed democratic. Although they recognize that there is a large apolitical mass with little power, they argue that critical political decisions are not made by a single group but are decided in a contest among many competing groups. David Riesman, a pluralist writing at about the same time as Mills, arrived at some very different conclusions. He called interest groups "veto groups" because he thought their main objective was merely to block policies that might threaten their interests.[20] Where Mills saw common interests among powerful groups, Riesman saw divergence; where Mills saw growing concentration of power, Riesman saw growing dispersion of power.[21]

Current pluralist thought runs along the lines taken by Riesman. However, his idea that interest groups are concerned mainly with stopping unacceptable proposals is no longer widely accepted. For example, the late Arnold M. Rose, a distinguished sociologist who was also a state legislator, concluded that interest groups take action on their own behalf:

> [The pluralist] conceives of society as consisting of many elites, each relatively small numerically, and operating in different spheres of life, and of the bulk of the population classifiable into organized groups and publics as well as masses. Among the elites are several that have their power through economic controls, several others that have power through political controls, and still others that have power through military, associational, religious, and other controls. While it is true that there are inert masses of undifferentiated individuals without access to each other (except in the most trivial respects) and therefore without influence, the bulk of the population consists not of the mass but of integrated groups and publics, stratified with varying degrees of power.[22]

The debate between the elitists and the pluralists is not likely to be resolved quickly. As G. William Domhoff points out, "These disagreements often reflect differences in style, temperament and degree of satisfaction with the status quo as well as more intellectual differences concerning the structure and distribution of political power."[23] Indeed, both sides seem to agree on more than they are willing to admit. Most elitists will grant that conflicting interest groups play a political role at some level of power, and most pluralists will grant that some power is held by elites. The real question is a factual one: How unified or competitive are the elites?

An Iron Law of Oligarchy?

The influence of powerful interest groups in the democratic process has made some experts doubt the very possibility of a truly democratic government. One of the most famous doubters is Robert Michels, a political sociologist who did his major work between World Wars I and II.[24] Michels was a socialist who became disillusioned when he discovered that European socialist parties that claimed to stand for freedom, equality, and democracy actually were controlled by elites just like other political parties. He concluded that all large organizations, including governments, are inevitably ruled by a few powerful people at the top. Michels called this conclusion the iron law of oligarchy.

Michels' studies convinced him that the administration of any political party or government requires delegation of power to an individual or a small group. The entire membership simply cannot make all the day-to-day decisions. The leaders, who are talented and capable, gain access to information and facilities that are not available to the average member, enabling them to improve and refine their skills. The leaders then become interested in keeping their positions, and use their growing power to do so. Further, Michels said, the masses have a natural respect, even reverence, for people in positions of power and may often follow their leaders almost automatically. Even if they do not, they lack the knowledge and skills to understand the technicalities of modern organizations and their administration. Even if the leaders have a commitment to democracy, the structural and psychological demands of the organization still create an oligarchy. "Thus the majority of human beings, in a condition of eternal tutelage, are predestined by tragic necessity to submit to the dominion of a small minority, and must be content to constitute the pedestal of an oligarchy."[25]

Most social scientists are not as pessimistic as Michels. They note that even the strongest elites do not have unlimited power but are restricted by the political structure and expectations of their society. Pluralists argue that because there are many competing elites in democratic societies, the masses can wield great influence by shifting their support from one elite to another. Elitists deny that such a system exists in modern-day democracies, but they do not deny its possibility. Indeed, elitists call attention to a "power elite" at least in part because they hope that doing so will stimulate action toward a more democratic system.

The Military

The military poses a dilemma for democratic societies. It is essential but at the same time extremely dangerous. With its traditions of command, authority, and unquestioning obedience, the military often responds when disorganization and confusion paralyze a democratic government.

The list of struggling democracies that have been taken over by their military powers is a long one, particularly in the underdeveloped nations of Asia, Africa, and Latin America. In fact, there are more military governments than democratic governments in the world today. However, developed countries with long democratic traditions—such as Great Britain, Canada, the United States, and Switzerland—are in little danger of a direct military takeover because the tradition of civilian control of the military is too well established. But even in these nations there is the danger of growing too dependent on the military, both politically and economically. Thus, some people have charged that the United States is a "garrison society" in which military, civilian, and economic powers work together to further their mutual interests.[26]

Because a military force is generally considered necessary for defense, the critical question is how much of the national budget should be spent for this purpose. (See Figure 3.3.) Different nations answer this question in different ways. The United States spends a high percentage of its income on its military, while Japan and Germany, with similar economic

FIGURE 3.3
PUBLIC SATISFACTION
WITH FEDERAL
PRIORITIES, 1976

Source: U.S. Department of Commerce,
Social Indicators 1976 (Washington, D.C.:
GPO, 1976), p. xlviii.

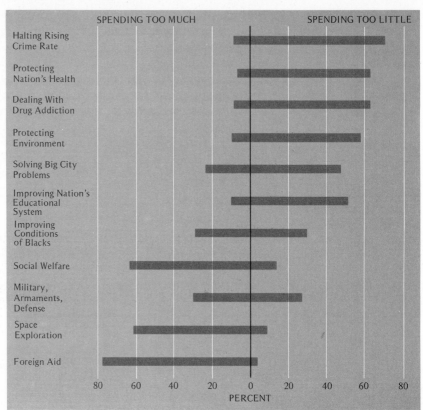

and political systems, spend comparatively little. Though American military forces help protect these nations, the basic question remains unanswered.

One point is clear, however. Although military spending can give a boost to a lagging economy, little long-range economic benefit results. Most military products have no practical use unless there is a war—you can't eat them, wear them, or live in them. Moreover, military research and development take scientific talent away from more productive civilian research. It has been estimated that more than 60 percent of those engaged in research and development in the United States work for the military.[27]

The prolonged warfare of World War II, closely followed by the cold war with the Soviet Union and the Korean and Vietnam conflicts, left the United States with a military establishment of enormous proportions. At the peak of the Vietnam War, the United States had over 3.5 million men and women in the armed forces. The current *peacetime* figure remains

The military poses a dilemma for democratic societies. It is essential to national defense, yet it may become a threat to civil liberties and the democratic process.

over 2 million. Workers in defense industries and civilian employees of the Air Force, Army, and Navy swell the number of defense personnel to almost 5 million, not counting those who depend indirectly on military spending. The current military budget is well over $100 billion. But a considerable portion of all military expenses is hidden in other government budgets, so the total actually is much higher than this figure. Probably about 30 percent of all government money goes to the military, making it the single largest customer of American business.[28]

Given the enormous size and economic strength of the American military, it is not surprising that many observers have expressed concern about its influence in a democratic society. One of the most unexpected warnings came from President Dwight D. Eisenhower, a career Army officer. In his farewell address President Eisenhower warned against the influence of the "military–industrial complex," and the growing interdependence between the military and giant corporations. Such companies as General Dynamics, Lockheed, and North American Rockwell are not owned by the military, but their profits come largely from military contracts. Hundreds of other companies also sell a substantial percentage of their products to the military, with the result that corporations and the armed forces have many interests in common. President Eisenhower feared that this "complex" could dominate the nation.

The military has its own lobbyists, who wield tremendous influence in Washington. They are assisted by lobbyists for organized labor, which see military spending as an important source of jobs, and by lobbyists for corporations, which see military spending as good business. Even if there were no military lobbyists, senators and representatives from states with high concentrations of military bases or defense industries would still be vigorous supporters of military appropriations. While all this does not add up to military control of the American government, the military–industrial complex obviously has enormous influence and power.

No nation has infinite resources, no matter how great its wealth. At some point every government must choose between guns (military spending) and butter (social-welfare spending). Some politicians have tried to avoid this decision, but the results are usually disastrous. President Johnson tried to fight a peaceful war on poverty and a shooting war in Vietnam at the same time. Both efforts failed, and Johnson's policies generated economic problems that are still with us today.

FREEDOM OR OPPRESSION?

Of all the problems and dilemmas confronting democratic government, none strikes closer to home than the issue of how to maximize personal freedom and protect civil rights while maintaining social order. The belief that governments try to regulate every aspect of our lives is shared by people in all walks of life. The nightmare that could come from a fusion of technology and totalitarianism, depicted in such books as George Orwell's *1984* and Aldous Huxley's *Brave New World,* has haunted the Western world for decades.

Lists of "human rights" usually include freedom of speech, assembly, and movement and the right to privacy, autonomy, and political expression. But the ideas embodied in these noble generalizations are difficult to apply in practice. The expression of one person's rights may interfere with those of another person, and there is always someone to claim that "the common good" or "the general welfare" requires the suppression of individual freedom.

The list of systematic violations of individual liberties is tragically long, even in democratic countries. One example was the anticommunist "witch hunts" that took place in the United States in the 1950s. The hysterical search for communist subversives led to the "blacklisting" and disgrace of many people whose only offense was belonging to the wrong political organization or holding an unpopular opinion. A more recent example comes from Canada, a country born of a long democratic tradition. Ten years ago two prominent Canadians were kidnaped by members of a group seeking independence for the province of Quebec. In the wave of

The growing sophistication of computer technology has made it possible to store and retrieve detailed records of citizens' private lives. The creation of such a centralized data bank would pose an obvious threat to individual freedom.

shock and indignation that followed, the government invoked the War Measures Act, thereby suspending civil liberties. Membership in or support for the group responsible for the kidnaping was forbidden and about 490 "separatist sympathizers" were rounded up and jailed. Of these, 435 were eventually released without ever being charged with a crime. Polls indicated that the Canadian people clearly approved the use of the War Measures Act, just as the American people approved of the anticommunist crusades.[29]

"Watergate," the greatest political scandal in American history, involved a different sort of violation of civil liberties. President Nixon's White House was not riding a wave of popular fear and resentment but, rather, working behind a cloak of official secrecy. The scandal first broke when several White House employees were caught breaking into the headquarters of the Democratic National Committee. These arrests led to the uncovering of dozens of felonies, misdemeanors, and undemocratic practices. An "enemies list" of the President's political opponents had been drawn up, and many people had been placed under the surveillance of wiretaps and other electronic eavesdropping equipment. The Internal Revenue Service had been pressured to harass the President's political opponents with tax audits. White House operatives had attacked Democratic candidates with a variety of "dirty tricks" such as false accusations of homosexuality or drunken driving. A number of attempts were made to silence or control the press.

As these and other misdeeds came to light, the President's assistants resorted to bribery and destruction of evidence in a bold attempt to deceive the public and maintain their hold on power, using tactics resembling those commonly used by dictatorships. Defenders of democracy can take comfort from the fact that these tactics failed, the President was driven from office, and many of his associates were jailed. But if one lesson is to be learned from Watergate, it is that constant public vigilance is essential in a democratic society. Arthur Waskow was close to the truth when he wrote, "To put it bluntly, Watergate was an attempt to create a Presidential dictatorship."[30]

It should not be assumed, however, that all threats to civil liberties will disappear if bad people are kept out of political office. The momentum of cultural and technological change is almost irresistible. Modern technology has provided the means for establishing a more powerful totalitarian state than has ever existed before. Even democratic nations are now using sophisticated electronic eavesdropping and wiretapping techniques and assembling computerized files on large numbers of individual citizens. People of all political persuasions are becoming concerned about the threat that the use of these new technologies may pose to civil liberties. As the American Civil Liberties Union put it,

> The wedding of sophisticated information storage and dissemination systems has created, for the first time, a very real danger that the sense of privacy which as traditionally insulated Americans against the fear of state encroachment will be destroyed and be replaced, instead, by a pervasive sense of being watched. The emergence of such a police state mentality could mean the destruction of our libertarian heritage.[31]

The federal government maintains dozens of different files of information about its citizens. They range from files on "subversives" and criminals kept by investigative agencies such as the FBI, the CIA, and Military Intelligence to the massive record-keeping systems of the Internal Revenue Service and the Social Security Administration. The Department of Justice alone maintains at least ten major files, including lists of persons involved in civil disturbances, organized criminals, narcotics addicts, criminal defendants, individuals wanted by the police, passers of forged checks, and aliens. The Justice Department has been attempting to computerize a number of these systems. There have been repeated battles over the FBI's attempt to establish a "Computerized Criminal History File" that would centralize information that is now in various state and local files.

Clearly, government agencies need many of these files if they are to do their work efficiently. But is such efficiency dangerous? The prospect that hundreds of files might be centralized frightens civil libertarians. It is now technologically possible to establish a system that could, at the punching of a single identification number, reveal all the significant events in an individual's entire life history. The power available to the controller of such a system would be immense.

An additional concern is the fact that some of the information in these data files is false or misleading. People have lost their jobs, or been unable to find new ones, because false information was included in one of their files. But even if all of the information were accurate, the prospect of hapless individuals being followed forever by a single mistake is not a pleasant one. As former Senator Sam J. Ervin has warned,

> The new technology has made it literally impossible for a man to start again in our society. It has removed the quality of mercy from our institutions by making it impossible to forget, to forgive, to understand, to tolerate. When it is used to intimidate and to inhibit the individual in his freedom of movement, associations, or expressions of ideas within the law, the new technology provides the means for the worst sort of tyranny.[32]

Clearly, the nightmares of Orwell and Huxley are now technologically possible. The problem facing all free people is to prevent them from coming true.

RESPONDING TO PROBLEMS OF GOVERNMENT

Practically all social problems are in part government problems. But "the" problem of government is the problem of democracy itself—creating and maintaining political systems that are truly a government "of the people, by the people, and for the people." In recent years there have been three principal responses to the challenge of getting people involved in the affairs of their own government.

Decentralization

Many social scientists believe that the sheer growth of modern nations has made the government more distant and less responsive to the will of their citizens. Many people do not even know the names of major local officials, let alone the name of their prime minister or president. Many citizens see government policies as decisions made in a distant place by officials who are not aware of or concerned with their interests. And too often they are right. In response to this problem, it has been suggested that governmental power be decentralized. Advocates of decentralization claim that local governments are closer to the people and therefore more responsive to their needs. Further, they are convinced that if local governments were given self-determination in vital issues many more citizens would become involved in the political process.

However, there is another side to this issue. Some political scientists argue that local governments are too close to the people to be given unrestricted power, contending that local passions and prejudices often lead to the oppression of defenseless minorities. For example, the federal government had to force unwilling southern states to abandon racial segregation. A strong central government is also needed to cope with problems that cross local boundaries, such as air pollution, sewage disposal, and air traffic management. But much doubt remains about how effective central governments have been in responding to such problems as poverty, ethnic and sexual inequality, and urban decay.

Limiting Government Secrecy

There are good reasons for government secrets. National governments must keep military and sometimes economic information from potential enemies. Local governments must not let speculators know that a certain piece of land is about to be purchased for public use. But the "secret" stamp used for these purposes can also be used to cover up official mistakes and incompetence and, worse yet, crimes and violations of civil liberties. The cold light of publicity can do a great deal to restrain over-zealous government officials. For this reason the Constitution prohibited Congress from making any law that abridges the freedom of the press. In effect, the press was given the duty of uncovering government secrets.

Making sure government bureaucrats inform the public about their behavior is not easy. In 1966 the Freedom of Information Act was passed and signed into law. This act requires U.S. government agencies to hand over any information they have about an individual citizen at the request of that person. However, many government bureaucracies responded to requests with months of stalling, and some charged fees for the information they furnished. Other agencies were able to protect information they did not want the public to see by classifying it as secret. In response Congress added tough new amendments to the bill, providing a deadline for responding to requests for information, limiting the fees that could be charged, and providing for judicial review of classified material. This new legislation gave the public much greater access to government records, but the bureaucracies continue to put up a determined resistance. However, there are signs that elected officials are becoming more responsive to the public's need to be informed about the government's activities. For example, "sunshine laws" now require more government activity to be conducted in public instead of behind closed doors.

Political Involvement

Despite the range of complex and difficult political problems facing modern democracies, there is one response that can help resolve them all: increased involvement of ordinary citizens in the process of government. Despite special interests and powerful elites, the common people wield tremendous power when they become involved in the political process. But apathy is the custom in modern democracies. Some sociologists have noted that, in politics as in sports, the mass media have transformed the average citizen into a passive spectator rather than an active participant.

There are grounds for optimism. One of the most promising recent developments has been the growth of lobbies representing consumers and other ordinary citizens against the formidable power of special-interest groups. Good examples are Common Cause and the Ralph Nader organization, both of which fight for the rights of the consumer against giant corporations. Many hope that the publicity generated by these and other "people's lobbies" will stimulate more citizens to stand up and be counted, to take an interest in politics, and to organize themselves for effective action for or against specific issues.

SOCIOLOGICAL PERSPECTIVES on Problems of Government

Practically everyone agrees that the government has serious shortcomings. Pointing out these weaknesses has become a career for some public figures. Yet there is considerable disagreement over exactly what the problems are. Conservatives are usually concerned about government inefficiency and waste, maintenance of military preparedness, and what they consider excessive interference with the economy. Those of a more liberal persuasion are more often concerned about violations of civil liberties, protection of minority rights, and the government's effectiveness in dealing with society's other problems. The basic sociological perspectives help make sense of these differences and provide insights into the causes of governmental problems and possible solutions.

The Functionalist Perspective

The government performs at least four basic functions that are essential to modern society. First, government is a system for using force to ensure conformity to society's norms and values when other means of control have failed. Police departments and other criminal-justice agencies enforce the norms that have been made into law. Second, government maintains order by serving as the final arbiter of disputes arising between individuals and groups, as illustrated by the thousands of lawsuits settled by the courts every year. Third, government is responsible for the overall planning and direction of society and the coordination of other social institutions. While this function is more obvious in communist countries, it is just as critical in modern democracies. Fourth, government is responsible for handling international relations and, if necessary, warfare.

According to functionalists, the rapid social changes of the past century have made it very difficult for many governments to perform these functions effectively. Government has accepted more and more responsibilities but has been ill prepared for its new tasks. Many governments are saddled with old-fashioned systems of organization that were adequate in the eighteenth and nineteenth centuries but are ineffectual today. Government officials often fail to understand their duties, or they pursue their own interests rather than the public's. Technological changes have taken place so rapidly that government officials are unable to control their applications. As a result government fails to function effectively.

Functionalists suggest that steps be taken to reduce this disorganization by reshaping governments. The tasks of government bureaucracies should be spelled out in detail, and each bureau should be rationally organized to achieve them. The decision-making machinery should be revamped to remove the awkward traditional structures that impede efficiency. For example, the U.S. Congress should reform its committee system so that more effective laws can be drafted and passed. Tougher laws that reduce unnecessary secrecy and protect our civil liberties should also be enacted.

The Conflict Perspective

Conflict theorists see the government as a source of tremendous political power, which is used to advance the interests of those who control it. Government works to repress conflict rather than to resolve it. That is, the groups in control of the government (usually the upper class) use its power to smother their opposition. For example, vagrancy laws have been used to force the poor to work in unpleasant low-paying jobs. Tax laws with loopholes that benefit the rich are another example of the expression of class interests through legislation. When value conflicts produce tension, opposing groups often go to the government asking for favorable legislation. For instance, those who believe homosexuality, drug use, or abortion to be immoral often seek to outlaw such behavior. When successful, such efforts result in the use of the power of the state to oppress those who think or act in unpopular ways.

According to conflict theory, control of the government is a prize that is won through political conflict. Once a group gains such control, it uses the power of the government to maintain its position, and thus the group becomes difficult to dislodge. The law and its administration become tools of special interests, and the result usually is the exploitation of the masses. The solution to this problem is political and economic equality, that is, giving a greater voice to the "common" man or woman. Such measures as limiting the size of contributions to political campaigns, restricting lobbying, and requiring full disclosure of all government deliberations and proceedings are steps in this direction. But conflict theorists believe that greater economic equality is necessary before we can have true democracy. The key to a more equal distribution of wealth and power is greater political involvement and concern by those who are not now represented in government.

The Social-Psychological Perspective

Social psychologists focus on relationships between political systems and individual personality. Some suggest that the character of a nation's people affects its political system; others assert that political systems affect personality just as economic systems do. The citizens of some nations seem to accept their leaders with almost unquestioning obedience, while other cultures breed rebellious individualists who are suspicious of all higher authority. One study of fascism concluded that many of the followers of totalitarian leaders have "authoritarian personalities."[33] The person with such a personality is said to be rigid, extremely conformist, and uncomfortable with ambiguity and uncertainty. As a result this type of individual favors strong leadership that provides order and conformity at the expense of individual liberty. It could well be, however, that fascism generates authoritarian personalities rather than the reverse.

Another concern of social psychologists is political socialization—the ways in which people learn their political values and perspectives, whether authoritarian or democratic. Children learn most of their political attitudes from their parents, and early in life develop attachments to such symbols as the flag, patriotic slogans, and well-known public figures. As they grow older their views are affected by their peer groups, teachers, and others. A democratic society can do little to change the home environment of its children because to do so would threaten basic civil liberties. However, schools can teach children to respect the rights of others, to understand the principles of democratic government, to be knowledgeable about how governments actually operate, and to work for the equality of all people.

SUMMARY   In recent times governments and their bureaucracies have been expanding rapidly. Although both public and private bureaucracies are often criticized for waste and inefficiency, they remain more efficient than other forms of organization. However, today's huge government bureaucracies are not without problems. Employees sometimes become more concerned with protecting and enhancing their jobs than with the efficiency of the organization. And for the same reason they resist attempts to reduce the size of their organization, even if some of its functions could be performed more efficiently elsewhere.

The American government is a federal system with three distinct levels —local, state, and federal. The federal government is divided into three separate branches—executive, legislative, and judicial—so that each branch counterbalances the others. The legislative branch, consisting of the Senate and the House of Representatives, has been declining in power and influence because of problems in its organizational structure and in the politics of its members. The executive branch, headed by the President, contains most of the huge federal bureaucracy. With the growth of the federal bureaucracy has come an increase in presidential power. Although a powerful President has the means to provide effective leadership and take quick, decisive action, some people fear that excessive presidential power may pose a threat to democratic government. The judicial branch is the federal court system. It is headed by the Supreme Court, which has tremendous political power. Indeed, some authorities are convinced that the Court has more power than any nonelected body in a democratic government should have.

American political parties tend to be broadly based and nonideological. The Republican and Democratic parties both have liberal and conservative wings; nevertheless, there are significant differences between them. The Democrats receive greater support from the poor, minority groups, and organized labor, while the Republicans receive more support from the wealthy and business interests.

The American system of government has its roots in the parliamentary system found in most of the world's democratic governments, including Canada and Britain. In the parliamentary system the executive branch is not distinctly separated from the legislative branch. Members of the House of Commons are elected by the people, and the majority of the members of that body select one of their members as the prime minister. If the party in power cannot get enough votes to carry out its policies, the House of Commons is dissolved and a new election is called.

Social scientists have tried to determine who really controls democratic governments. Theoretically, the power of the vote should give control to the citizenry. But citizens are often apathetic, and occasionally they are misled. The richest and most highly educated citizens are most active in expressing their opinions to government.

Special-interest groups wield tremendous power through their lobbying activities and by giving large sums of money to candidates they like and using their influence to defeat those who oppose them. Some social scientists, known as elitists, believe that the government is controlled by a small, unified power elite. Others, the pluralists, see many different groups competing for power and are not convinced that a single ruling class exists. According to believers in the iron law of oligarchy, every large organization is ruled by a small group of individuals no matter how great its efforts to be democratic.

The military poses a basic dilemma in a democratic society. Its traditions of unquestioning obedience and authoritarianism can be a real threat to democratic institutions, yet its power seems essential to national survival.

Protection of civil liberties is a critical task in every democracy. There are many recent examples of governments violating individual rights and interfering with democratic processes. The growing use of modern technology to collect, store, and retrieve information about individual citizens is a growing threat to civil liberties. Many different responses to these problems have been proposed, including decentralizing government powers, limiting government secrecy, and maximizing political participation by citizens.

Functionalists see governmental problems as signs of failure—the political institution has failed to work correctly and must be adjusted so it runs smoothly again. Conflict theorists are more likely to note that the political system itself, not just parts of it, produces the conditions that we call social problems. Value and class conflicts are part of the political system, but the balance of power now favors elites, and special interests rather than the poor and the deprived. If political problems are to be resolved, this dominance must be ended. Social psychologists note that there is a relationship between political systems and personality; they have found that people's political behavior is learned just as other behavior is learned.

KEY TERMS

bureaucracy
displacement of goals
elitist
executive branch
federal system
iron law of oligarchy
judicial branch
legislative branch

lobbying
parliamentary system
pluralist
political party
political socialization
power
special-interest group

4
Problems of Education

How does school integration affect students?
What is the nature of the crisis in education?
What is the cause of declining student achievement?
Does more money mean better schools?

North Americans place tremendous faith in education. It is expected to provide a "guiding light" for the young and a way for average people to "make something of themselves." Education is seen as a path out of the slums for new immigrants, and out of poverty for the sons and daughters of the disadvantaged. But these ideals are now being shaken as never before. Education is in a crisis of controversy and indecision. The poor and minorities who were excluded for so long are demanding their share of the educational dream. Critics are charging that the educational system has failed to reduce social inequality. They argue that, rather than helping the disadvantaged improve their lives, our educational system helps maintain the pattern of oppression. For example, by channeling the poor into occupationally oriented high school courses rather than into college preparatory courses, the educational system ensures that those who get ahead in life are mostly the sons and daughters of well-to-do parents.

In addition to its other problems, our educational system does not seem to be educating very well. Students' scores on achievement tests have been dropping rapidly in recent years, indicating that the basic skills of reading, writing, and arithmetic are not being taught adequately. Disgruntled teachers have charged that some inner-city schools are so torn by violence that students and teachers alike are concerned more with survival than with education. But the picture is not really so bleak, for North Americans are the most educated and best-informed people in the world. The educational system is a "failure" only because the goals set for it are so high.

EDUCATION IN MODERN SOCIETY

In small traditional societies education takes place in the home and in children's informal day-to-day association with adults. Training for the few specialized occupations that exist is the responsibility of those who hold the jobs, usually members of the same family. Customs and traditions are passed along from one generation to the next without the assistance of schools or professional teachers.

In more complex societies specialized organizations for the transmission of knowledge by highly educated teachers have developed. In the beginning, these schools were mostly for the training of priests and other religious officials, but secular education soon followed. Until the second half of the nineteenth century, education was reserved for aristocrats and a few of their important servants. The masses had little need to read or write, and some aristocrats saw any attempt to develop these skills in the lower classes as a threat to their power. Only 200 years ago the governor of the colony of Virginia viewed ignorance as bliss: "Thank God there are no free schools or printing; . . . for learning has brought disobedience and heresy into the world, and printing has divulged them . . . God keep us from both."[1]

It was not until the end of the eighteenth century, when democratic revolutions took place in America and France, that the idea of education for the common people began to catch on. Education for the lower classes became more important as the masses began to share in important governmental decisions and processes. The ability to read the Bible became important as well. Yet progress toward equality has been slow, and the children of the wealthy continue to receive more and better education than the children of the poor.

A high school education is now the rule, not the exception. In 1890 only 7 percent of children of high school age in the United States were actually in school; today this figure is almost 94 percent.[2] Because of this growth, education has become a big business. Virtually every American receives some formal education, and most people spend a good portion of their lives in schools and classrooms. There are about 1.3 million primary-school teachers and 1 million secondary-school teachers in the United States at present.[3] Another 270,000 people teach at the college and university level, making the total number of teachers about 2.5 million.

Some Functions of Education

Despite the fact that most teachers are public employees, there is much confusion about what they are supposed to do. It is clear that radicals, liberals, conservatives, and reactionaries disagree on what the goals of the educational system should be. Although sociologists are unable to resolve these value conflicts, they can define the functions that schools actually perform in our society.

The most obvious job of the school system is to teach young people the skills they will need when they become adults. The "three R's"—reading, writing, and arithmetic—are basic, but schools also teach many other skills, ranging from sewing and automobile mechanics to elementary engineering. A second task is that of grading students on how well they have mastered their studies. The educational system thus performs a kind of "sorting service" for the rest of society by directing the most talented and motivated students toward the most important and highest-paying jobs. Education then becomes a channel for the upward mobility of capable people from the lower classes, as well as a downward conduit for upper-class people with little talent or motivation.

It would be a mistake to assume that the schools teach only knowledge and skills, however. They also transmit culture: values, attitudes, roles and patterns of behavior. Much socialization still takes place in the family, but schools also try to inspire children to behave according to accepted customs. Students are instructed to respect property, avoid violence, obey the law, and generally behave like "decent" and "respectable" citizens. A recent Gallup poll found that 79 percent of all Americans favor special moral instruction in the schools.[4] However, not all of the socialization that occurs in the schools is beneficial. Many

Studies of the effects of individual desegregation programs on academic achievement have led to contradictory conclusions and often to bitter debates.[12] After carefully reviewing over 120 studies, Nancy St. John drew the following conclusion:

> In sum, adequate data have not yet been gathered to determine a causal relationship between school racial composition and academic achievement. More than a decade of considerable research effort has produced no definitive positive findings. In view of the political, moral, and technical difficulties of investigation on this question, it is doubtful that all the canons of scientific method will ever be met or a causal relationship ever established.[13]

Studies of the impact of school integration on racial prejudice are also inconclusive. Some show a reduction in prejudice, but others show that it remains the same or may even increase.[14] The explanation for these contradictory conclusions probably lies in the enormous differences in environment and circumstances under which integration occurs. Integration carried out under a court order with mobs of protesters demonstrating in the streets is hardly likely to reduce prejudice. On the other hand, when integration takes place in an atmosphere of good will, much better results are likely.

SOCIAL CLASS AND ACHIEVEMENT

Grade school teachers and university professors alike can easily see that the daughters and sons of middle- and upper-class parents do better in school than the children of the poor. In fact, as noted earlier, the Coleman Report and a variety of other surveys have found social class to be the single most effective predictor of achievement in school.[15] Students from the middle and upper classes get higher scores on standardized achievement tests, do better in class, and stay in school longer than other students. There are two principal explanations for this difference. One focuses on the advantages higher-status children have because they come from home environments in which books, informed discussions, and emphasis on achievement are common. The other notes that the schools themselves are organized and operated in ways that fail to meet the educational needs of the poor.

Family Background

Lower-class children live in a very different world from that of middle-class children. The homes of the poor have fewer books, newspapers, and magazines, and the parents have less education. Recent Gallup polls show that people with low incomes are less inclined than others to read for entertainment and thus children in low-income homes are less likely to be encouraged to learn that important skill.[16] Further, lower-class families are larger and are more likely to be headed by only one adult. Children in such families are less likely to receive parental contact, guidance, and ed-

Source: U.S. Department of Commerce,
Social Indicators 1976 (Washington, D.C.:
GPO, 1976), p. 272.

FIGURE 4.1
ENROLLMENT IN HIGHER
EDUCATION, BY RACE AND
FAMILY INCOME,
OCTOBER 1973

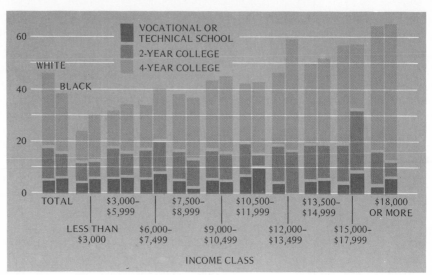

ucational encouragement. Another factor is health; poor children are more likely to be undernourished than their middle-class counterparts, and unhealthy children do not learn as well as healthy children.

More positively, the academic success of children from wealthier homes stems from the value their parents place on education. A number of surveys have shown that children from wealthy families want more education than children from poorer backgrounds. (See Figure 4.1.) After extensive study Christopher Jencks and his associates concluded that "perceived pressure from home seems to explain most of the difference between working-class and middle-class students' educational aspirations."[17] Differences in such pressures, in turn, can be explained by cultural differences—middle-class homes place a higher value on education and long-range planning. But some of these differences may merely reflect a realistic adjustment to the fact that poor children have less chance of getting a good education.

Children who speak only Spanish or some other language foreign to the schools are obviously handicaped. But language also makes an important difference to the educational achievements of the various social classes in the *same* ethnic group. Standard English is more commonly spoken by middle-class blacks, while lower-class blacks are more likely to speak "black English" dialects. Because schoolwork is done in standard English, lower-class blacks are handicaped. Similar language differences are found among whites. Basil Bernstein has noted that people from the lower class tend to use short, simple sentences while middle-class people use longer, more complex sentences containing more abstract concepts.[18]

These differences give middle-class students a substantial head start in their schoolwork and also make it easier for them to understand their teachers.

The Schools   In addition to handicaps in the home environment of lower-class students, the school system itself favors the education of middle- and upper-class students. This fact is obvious, first of all, in the way schools are financed. Even a brief examination of the American system of school finance reveals glaring inequities both in how taxes are levied and in how they are spent. Thus, students who live in wealthy tax districts have much more money spent on their education than students who live in poorer districts. About 55 percent of the funds for American public schools come from local school district taxes, 39 percent from state taxes, and 7 percent from federal taxes.

There are great differences among the various states in the importance placed on education and in the state's ability to pay for it. Alaska spends almost three times as much money per pupil as Alabama.[19] But the differences between school districts within the same state are often even greater. Because most of the money for schools comes from property taxes, school districts containing many expensive homes receive much more revenue for their schools.

Even more unjust is the way school taxes are assessed. Those who live in rich school districts often pay a lower percentage of the assessed value of their property in taxes than people who live in poor districts. For example, Beverly Hills, California, recently had a property tax rate of $2.38 per $100 of assessed valuation and spent about $1231 per student. In neighboring Baldwin Park the tax rate was more than twice this amount, but the district spent only $577 per pupil.[20] The explanation of this inequality is simply that the value of all the property in Beverly Hills was 13 times the value of all the property in Baldwin Park. A study of education in the state of New York concluded that "it is unconscionable that a poor man in a poor district must often pay local taxes at higher rates for the inferior education of his child than the man of means in a rich district pays for the superior education of his child. Yet, incredibly, that is the situation today in most of the 50 states."[21]

Defenders of the present system of financing may point to studies that conclude that the amount of money spent per student has little effect on educational achievement.[22] But such findings, even if they are accurate, do not justify the practice of making the poor pay higher property taxes than the rich. Further, it is not certain that the affluence of the school environment has no important effect on the students. As Jencks points out,

> There is no evidence that building a school playground, for example, will affect the students' chances of learning to read, getting into college, or making $50,000 a year when they are 50. Building a playground may, however,

The current system of school finance is grossly unequal. The poor often pay a larger proportion of their income in school taxes and receive an inferior education for their children in return. Much more money is spent on the education of children from wealthy districts than on the education of children from poor districts.

have a considerable effect on the students' chances of having a good time during recess when they are 8. The same thing is probably true of small classes, competent teachers, and a dozen other things that distinguish adequately from inadequately financed schools.[23]

Family finances clearly affect educational achievement, for despite the fact that education itself is often free, students from poor families simply cannot afford as much education as students from wealthier backgrounds. Students from poor homes are more likely to drop out of school and go to work. At the college and university level, the costs of tuition fees, books, and transportation put extra pressure on poor students. Many highly qualified lower-class students must attend local community colleges, which lead to technical careers, while less qualified upper- and middle-class students go to expensive private universities to prepare for professional careers.

Achievement in school is also affected by the way the schools are operated. There is considerable evidence that teachers expect less from lower-class students, in terms of both academic achievement and behavior, than is expected from others.[24] Students respond to such expectations by underachieving and misbehaving. The expectation of low achievement thus acts as a self-fulfilling prophecy: Students become what they are expected to become. Robert Rosenthal and Lenore Jacobson performed an interesting experiment to demonstrate this fact.[25] Experimenters gave a standard IQ test to pupils in 18 classrooms in a neighborhood elementary school. However, teachers were told that the instrument was the "Harvard Test of Inflected Acquisition" (which does not exist). Next the experimenters arbitrarily selected 20 percent of the students' names and told their teachers that the test showed that these students would make remarkable progress in the coming year. When the students were retested eight months later, those who had been singled out as intellectual bloomers showed a significantly greater increase in IQ than the others. Rosenthal and Jacobson concluded that the increase was due to the higher expectations of the teachers and to the communication of these expectations to the students. Many similar studies have since been made, with mixed results. Some found that the teachers' prophecy was self-fulfilling while others did not. If teachers' expectations do indeed affect student achievement, minority and lower-class students are clearly at a disadvantage even if they share classrooms with more affluent students.

The chances are, however, that lower-class students will not be in the same high school classes as middle-class students. Most high school students are placed in one of several different "tracks" or "ability groups." The "most promising" are put into college preparatory courses, while others go into vocational or "basic" classes. There is considerable evidence that lower-class students are much more likely to be placed in the vocational or basic track. For instance, Cicourel and Kitsuse found that in the high school they studied, incoming freshmen from the lowest classes were much less likely to be placed in the college preparatory track than those from the higher classes.[26] Although tracking is based on such criteria as academic record, performance on standardized tests, and the student's own feelings about college, a serious problem remains. Once students have been placed in a lower track, they will be exposed to less challenging material and teachers will have lower expectations for them. Because they are isolated from college-bound students, even the best students in the lower tracks are less likely to aspire to a college education.

EDUCATION IN CRISIS

Educators and social scientists have been talking about a "crisis in education" for some time. Much of the talk is about the unequal treatment of children from different ethnic groups and social classes, which we have just discussed. Severe attacks have also been made on authoritarian administrative structures and teachers' demands for unquestioning obedience by students. Another aspect of the "crisis" is seen in students' falling scores on tests of achievement. In addition, increasing concern is being expressed about "overeducation" — training more people for prestigious and high-paying occupations than there are jobs for them to fill.

But beneath these visible problems lies a crisis of confidence. Educators are seeing some of their most cherished beliefs challenged as the public, for the first time in memory, questions the value of formal education. Traditionally, schools have been considered a means for achieving success and upward mobility. Now that their effectiveness is being questioned, educators fear that there may be a weakening of the time-honored belief in the importance of education.

Authority and Obedience

Despite all the talk about teaching children the principles and practices of democracy, most schools are authoritarian systems demanding strict obedience. Our primary and secondary schools have even been compared to prisons, with principals as wardens and teachers as guards. The very nature of our school system both reflects and requires authoritarianism. Students are required by law to go to school, where they are compelled to spend large amounts of time in classrooms; truancy is considered a form of delinquency. In addition, elaborate rules and regulations are necessary to coordinate the activities of large numbers of students. School life would quickly degenerate into chaos without such rules. However, many observers believe that the schools have gone beyond the enforcement of mere orderliness, carrying the emphasis on authority and obedience to harmful extremes. Silberman, for example, argues that the primary goal of many schools has become order and efficiency rather than education:

> This preoccupation with efficiency, which is to say with order and control, turns the teacher into a disciplinarian as well as a time keeper and traffic manager. In the interest of efficiency, moreover, discipline is defined in simple but rigid terms: the absence of noise and of movement. . . . But no justification is offered or expected. Indeed, there is no more firmly rooted school tradition than the one that holds that children must sit still at their desks without conversing at all, both during periods of waiting, when they have nothing to do, and during activities that almost demand conversation.[27]

NINETEENTH CENTURY SOCIAL PROBLEMS

Miss Mary Jeffrey, a teacher in one of the schools of Centerville, was badly beaten by one of her pupils, a 14 year old girl. The teacher, for some offense committed by the girl's brother, proceeded to punish him, when the sister interfered and struck the teacher in the face. The teacher, in attempting to avoid the blow, dodged, throwing back her head, with the result that her hair caught on a hook in a hat rack and held her. While in this position, the girl rained blow after blow on the face of the defenseless teacher who was not a match for the strong, husky country girl. . . . She had just been pounded into unconsciousness when people attracted by the teacher's screams ran in and released her.
June 1, 1899

Such authoritarian control extends beyond the classroom. In most schools students cannot leave a classroom without written permission from the teacher, and the hallways of junior and senior high schools are patrolled by students or teachers on "guard duty." Jonathan Kozol, a former Boston schoolteacher, argues that "the whole concept of respect for unearned and undeserved authority is bitter and brittle and backbreaking to children. . . . There is too much respect for authority in the Boston school and too little respect for truth." Kozol goes on to say that the Boston schools today have "the atmosphere of a crumbling dictatorship in time of martial law."[28] Although most teachers probably would not consider their schools dictatorships, many recognize the conflict between the "teacher as teacher" and the "teacher as guard and disciplinarian." Most parents apparently are not disturbed by the authoritarian atmosphere of the schools. When a recent Gallup poll asked a sample of Americans what they thought was the biggest problem in the public schools, the most common response was "lack of discipline."[29]

Declining Achievement

A growing body of evidence suggests that American students' competence in reading, writing, and arithmetic is declining rapidly. Scores on a variety of tests, including the Scholastic Aptitude Test (SAT) and the Graduate Record Examination (GRE), were rising until the mid-1960s. Since then they have shown a steady decline that has been particularly steep since 1970. For instance, the average score on the SAT's measure of verbal ability dropped from 478 to 434 in the 12 years between 1963 and 1975. (See Figure 4.2.) Some educators have tried to explain these changes by claiming that a larger percentage of poor and minority students (who traditionally have lower scores) began taking the tests in the 1960s. However, the records do not bear out this claim. The percentage of minority students taking the SAT between 1971 and 1975, a period of sharp decline, remained constant at 13 percent. During the same period the average family income of all students taking the test rose slightly.[30]

There are two additional explanations for the decline in student achievement, the first holding the schools responsible and the second blaming the decline on changes in students' social environment. In response to the protests of the 1960s, many schools reduced the number of required courses and gave students more freedom in course selection. As a result, enrollments in basic academic courses declined. For instance, enrollments in English composition classes in California's junior and senior high schools declined an amazing 77 percent between 1971 and 1975. During the same period enrollments in basic English classes dropped 19 percent.[31] It seems reasonable to expect that achievement scores will decline if students do not enroll in courses designed to teach basic skills. It can also be expected that scores will go down even more if the content of basic courses is watered down. Such softening of the school

FIGURE 4.2
DECLINING ACADEMIC
ACHIEVEMENT, 1957–1976

Source: Los Angeles *Times*, August 16,
1976, September 12, 1976. © 1976 *Los
Angeles Times*. Used by permission.

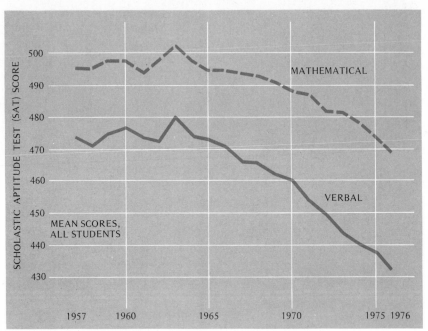

curriculum has often been covered up by the practice of grade inflation—
assigning grades of A or B to students who have barely learned to read
and write.

There also have been major changes in the home environment of
students. For example, most students spend more time watching television than in any other activity except sleep. Obviously, children who sit in
front of television sets instead of playing basketball will not become good
basketball players. Just as obviously, children who watch television instead of reading books will not become good readers and, consequently,
will not learn to write very well either. However, there have been no
carefully controlled studies to determine how great an effect television
has had on the ability to read and write.

Teachers also complain that their students have been growing more
rebellious and less interested in their studies. Such changes are often
blamed on growing permissiveness in child-rearing practices. However, it
is very difficult to determine whether students really are less interested in
their studies than they used to be. One of the few solid pieces of evidence
indicating reduced interest is the increase in absenteeism in recent years.
At one time the daily attendance in California schools was 97.3 percent of
total enrollment, but today it is 93.5 percent.[32] While this seems to in-

The growing number of college graduates has made it increasingly difficult for them to find the kinds of jobs for which they are trained.

dicate that interest in school has declined, it could also mean that uninterested students are not coerced into attending school as efficiently as they once were.

Overeducation

If the goal of education is to help people understand the world in which they live, it is hard to imagine how someone could be "overeducated." However, if the goal is to teach occupational skills, as is so often the case, the concept of overeducation makes a great deal of sense. More and more students are finishing high school, college, and even postgraduate work only to find that there are no jobs to fit their training and education.

Nevertheless, formal education still helps people get better, higher-paying jobs. In the United States each additional year of college is associated with a 12 percent increase in average income; but about 40 percent of this increase seems to be due to class background rather than to education.[33] Statistics from Canada show that university graduates earn almost twice as much on the average as people who have only completed secondary school.[34]

Such figures are little consolation to an unemployed or underemployed college graduate. It seems that many years of schooling no longer ensure that students will get good jobs but that, statistically speaking, lack of a good education ensures that they will not get good jobs. There are two obvious solutions to the problem of unemployment and underemployment among the educated: One is to provide less education in general; the other is to provide more jobs for educated people. David Saxon, president of the University of California, argues persuasively for the second solution, pointing out the tragic loss of human potential that would result from any limitation of education and learning. Instead, Saxon proposes that we expend greater effort to utilize the full potential of all our citizens.[35]

Despite the attractiveness of this argument, the creation of more employment opportunities for the educated requires money and the will to make significant changes in our society. The most likely response — if anything at all is done — is that there will be a reduction in the number of people who receive a higher education.

Contributing to Delinquency

In recent years schools have been expected to take an increasing role in the socialization process rather than merely teaching skills and knowledge. Like the family, the school is supposed to teach juveniles certain moral values and provide interesting activities that keep them off the labor market and out of trouble. It is believed that these efforts will prevent delinquency and other juvenile problems. However, recent studies have shown that the school actually contributes to delinquency rather than preventing it.

Although the schools try to teach moral values and keep children "off the streets," these efforts are offset by processes within the school that generate delinquency. The way the school handles its academic work, the way it structures relationships between teachers and students, and the way it determines relationships among the students themselves all promote delinquency. After following a group of schoolchildren for eleven years, Feldhusen, Thurston, and Benning concluded that school relationships are the third most important contributors to delinquency, following only the family and the peer group.[36] Another study found the school itself, not the family or "the streets," to be the critical social context for the generation of delinquent behavior.[37]

Sutherland and Cressey show that schools generate delinquency because they inadvertently promote association with delinquent subcultures. They note that many students are unable to meet the demands of their teachers because of lack of ability or a lower-class background. Such students, in turn, are rejected by teachers and other students. This "locking-out" process produces alienation, truancy, and rebellion, and its victims often drift into association with the delinquent subculture.[38] Elliott and Voss have shown that most of the original contact with delinquent subcultures occurs *within* the school at the same time that the "locking-out" process is occurring. For four years they followed 2600 junior high school students. Surprisingly, they found that the delinquency rate was significantly *lower* among those who dropped out than it was among those who remained in school.[39] There was also considerable evidence that the dropouts' involvement in delinquency began while they were still in school and was primarily a response to experiences in school. Departure from school reduced the dropouts' delinquent behavior and the likelihood of police contact. This finding is consistent with the well-known fact that there is a temporary decline in delinquency rates during the summer months and on weekends, when school is not in session.

RESPONDING TO PROBLEMS OF EDUCATION

The problems of education are primarily economic and political problems. Some proposals for change call for modification of the entire structure of our society, including the educational institution. But educational problems are also bureaucratic problems, and other proposals for change call for improved efficiency in the existing school system and its teaching methods. Some of these suggestions have already been implemented in private schools, with varying degrees of success. Responses to educational problems usually fall into two broad categories: proposals for providing more equal educational opportunities for all citizens and proposals for improving the quality of education.

Toward Equal Educational Opportunity

Almost everyone agrees with the idea that there should be equal educational opportunity for all. But there is great disagreement about what this means and how it can be achieved. Integration of students from different ethnic backgrounds into the same schools is often proposed as a solution to educational inequality, as we have already noted. A second approach to this problem is to set up special compensatory-education programs to help disadvantaged students. A third and widely accepted idea for how to remedy educational inequality is to spend an equal amount of money on each student's education.

Effective Integration

For years the American government, particularly the judicial branch, has been trying to achieve racial integration in the schools. Despite many advances, this goal still has not been achieved. Following integration, unofficial resegregation often occurs as whites move to the suburbs or enroll their children in private schools. It has been suggested that resegregation can be reduced by fusing suburban school districts with inner-city school districts and then busing children within each district. One difficulty with this proposal is distance. Some suburban communities are so far from city centers that students would have to spend a large part of their school day on a bus. Another difficulty is prejudice. The proposal does nothing to discourage white parents from putting their children in private schools, and in fact would encourage them to do so.

Coleman has proposed a voluntary desegregation plan as an alternative.[40] Mandatory busing would be abolished and students would have the right to be bused to any school they wished, provided that the school selected does not have a higher percentage of students of that child's race than his or her neighborhood school. Thus, students could attend their neighborhood school if they wished to do so. They would not be forced to take a bus to a distant school that they did not care to attend. This plan would reduce "white flight" into private and suburban schools while still allowing minority and lower-class students to attend integrated middle-class schools if they wished. Critics of this plan point out that it is not likely to reduce segregation significantly, for most students would choose to attend their neighborhood school.

Another possibility would be to encourage the integration of residential areas so that neighborhood schools would be integrated automatically. In many ways this is the most appealing solution, for it would provide the broadest possible opportunity for development of interracial friendships and cooperation. However, this proposal really does not solve the problem of school segregation; it merely turns it into a housing problem. People from different ethnic groups often have no desire to live together in the same neighborhood. Also, members of minority groups frequently cannot afford to live in affluent neighborhoods, and white residents of such districts have stubbornly resisted governmental attempts to build low-cost housing near them.

Compensatory Education

It is widely believed that educational achievement of the poor and minorities would be improved if they were provided with special programs and extra assistance. The most popular and widely known compensatory program of this kind was Project Head Start, which gave preschool instruction to disadvantaged children. At first the results of the project seemed quite promising, but follow-up studies found that most of the early gains made by those in the program faded away by the time the children reached the second or third grade. Researchers charged that the program had failed, and it was sharply reduced. Supporters of compensatory-education programs, on the other hand, continue to point out that what is needed is longer-range efforts that provide assistance to disadvantaged students throughout their school years.

On the college level a variety of Education Opportunity Programs have been established. Generally, these programs make special provisions for the admission of disadvantaged students, especially minority students, who do not meet standard admission requirements. They also provide tutoring and special assistance to help these students stay in school. Although these programs also have their critics, they have become an accepted part of most colleges and universities. The greatest conflicts have arisen over special admissions programs for graduate and professional schools. Competition for places in these schools is intense, and white students complain that they are the victims of blatant discrimination because some whites are being rejected in favor of less qualified minority students. Supporters of this practice argue that minorities have already been subjected to a great deal of discrimination and that affirmative-action programs merely attempt to compensate for some small part of it.

In the 1978 *Bakke* decision the Supreme Court took a position between those two extremes. While upholding the legality of affirmative action in general, it ruled that Bakke (an Anglo) was a victim of illegal discrimination when he was denied entrance to a medical school because the school reserved a fixed percentage of its places for minorities. Unfortunately, this famous case raised as many questions as it answered, and the legal status of affirmative action in the United States is still not clearly defined.

Reforming School Finance

As we pointed out earlier, schools in rich districts receive much more money per student than schools in poor districts. Such inequality could be erased if the federal government paid for all primary and secondary education, giving equal financial support to each school. However, in the United States there is a strong tradition of local control of the schools. Many people believe that federal financing would mean federal control and that federal bureaucracies would not be responsive to the needs of local communities. They point to the maze of federal regulations that accompany federal support of colleges and universities. It is estimated that compliance with these regulations costs colleges and universities almost $2 billion a year.[41]

Alternatively, individual states could take on the entire financial burden, eliminating inequality between schools within the same state. In 1971, in *Serrano* v. *Priest,* the California Supreme Court ruled that the state's system of school finance is unconstitutional and ordered the state legislature to establish a more equitable system. However, the legislature has not yet fully implemented this decision.

Improving the Schools

The Coleman study concluded that size of school budget, level of teacher qualifications, and physical facilities have little effect on the educational achievement of students. These findings have been widely interpreted to mean that "schools make no difference." A more accurate interpretation would be that "schools aren't very different." In other words, it appears that most American schools do about the same thing in the same way and get about the same results, regardless of the size of their budgets. However, several proposals to get better results from our schools have been made.

Changing the Curriculum

One of the most common reactions to new educational problems is to change the school curriculum. In response to the protests of the 1960s, a variety of new courses were introduced in an attempt to make schoolwork more relevant to the lives of minority students. In addition, history and social-studies classes began to include discussions of the significant contributions made by blacks and Latinos to the United States. Criticisms of rigidity and authoritarianism in schools have brought increases in the number of electives in high schools and a reduction in the number of required "academic" classes. Now that concern is growing over the decline in scores on achievement tests, it is quite likely that the curriculum will be changed again, probably toward stiffer academic requirements.

Better Educational Techniques

In recent years much concern has been shown for refining and improving teaching methods and the learning environment. Many reformers, unhappy with public schools, have opened their own private schools. Some of these are called free schools because the relationships between students and teachers are relaxed and friendly. The combination of inexperience and underfinancing is too much for most of these schools, and the majority close within a few months. Probably the most notable exception is A. S. Neill's highly successful Summerhill school.[42] Founded on faith in "the goodness of the child," Summerhill was conceived as a place where children were to be granted freedom without repression. Pupils are not ordered to be "nice" or "decent," and they are allowed to use profanity. Because Neill wanted to establish self-confidence and self-discipline in the children, Summerhill is run on a democratic basis. The children vote in weekly "parliamentary" meetings and are not required to attend classes. Learning is based on the child's interests, allowing each pupil to proceed at his or her own speed.

The graduates of Summerhill have generally done quite well in college and in their careers. Their success is not surprising, however, for the cost of attending the school has generally restricted enrollment to the upper and middle classes. Whatever the shortcomings of Summerhill and similar "free schools," these schools have demonstrated that there is a workable alternative to the traditional school setting.

In a different attempt to improve teaching methods, there has been a trend toward organizing schools to give what is called fundamental education. Schools using this approach stress the teaching of basic skills and play down as "frills" such subjects as art, music, home economics, and traffic safety. They also try to teach children to be patriotic, respect authority, and lead moral lives. Many of these schools have strict dress codes and frown on unconventional behavior.

It is difficult to evaluate these attempts to find better educational techniques because the alternative schools do not try to accomplish the same things. The free schools try to develop spontaneity, creativity, and psychologically well-adjusted children. The fundamental schools try to develop academic competence and respect for authority and tradition. The public schools, caught between interest groups with profound differences in basic values and perspectives, try to strike a balance, satisfying neither side.

The Voucher System

It has been suggested that our educational system would improve if schools were required to compete with each other for students the way business firms compete with each other for profits. It is proposed that the parents of each child be given a voucher to cover educational expenses. This would permit them to send their children to the school they prefer, paying for it with the voucher. The school, in turn, would cash the voucher at the state office of education. Schools that performed best — in the sense of giving what parents want for their educational dollars — would receive the most students, while the poor schools would be forced out of business.

Teachers and school administrators have vigorously opposed attempts to experiment with the voucher system. In general, they fear such a radical change in our educational system would endanger their jobs, as well as the whole concept of public education. They also doubt the ability of many parents to tell a good school from a bad one.[43]

SOCIOLOGICAL PERSPECTIVES on Problems of Education

Education has always been an important concern of political leaders. In recent years, however, special interest has been focused on the educational institution because it is seen as a means for dealing with other social problems. The school is expected to improve the mental health of the nation, prevent delinquency and drug abuse, and fight the spread of venereal disease and unwanted teenage pregnancies, as well as eliminating economic, political, and social inequality. These expectations have placed a great burden on our educational system and have made political footballs of school programs.

The Functionalist Perspective

As noted earlier, functionalists see education as a basic institution that is essential to society. In modern times the schools have grown increasingly important in the education of children from all social classes. The school is expected to teach youngsters the basic skills essential to a modern society and to transmit important cultural values. But functionalists note that the educational system is often so disorganized that it does not do these jobs very well, in part because of the increasing demands placed on it. Schools are confronted with so many different tasks that they are not doing any of them very well, and efforts to achieve one goal often conflict with efforts to achieve others. For example, the turmoil caused by some integration programs can interfere with the educational process. Efforts to modify the curriculum and make classes easier so that disadvantaged students will not be discouraged also reduces the achievement levels of more gifted students.

Not all functionalists agree on how to make the schools more effective. One possibility would be to eliminate the new goals and programs that have been introduced in recent years so that schools could concentrate entirely on education. While such changes might well improve fundamental education, they are also likely to disrupt the efforts to deal with other pressing social problems. Proposals for employing more effective teaching methods and techniques are also compatible with the functionalist perspective. But most functionalists argue that such changes can only be effective if they are accompanied by a reorganization of the schools. Teachers must be rewarded for good teaching, rather than for being efficient bureaucrats or for the length of time they have spent on the job. Finally, many functionalists advocate better planning and coordination with other social institutions in order to reduce the problem of unemployment and underemployment among the educated. But such a program must be combined with an effort to reduce the instability of our economic institutions, since it is impossible to train students to meet the manpower needs of an economy that is in a state of rapid and unpredictable flux.

The Conflict Perspective

Conflict theorists are not convinced that providing equal educational opportunity and upward mobility for the poor have ever been goals of our educational system. Rather, they argue that the schools are organized to do the opposite: to keep members of subordinate groups in their place and prevent them from competing with members of the "ruling class." They point to the fact that free public education for all children is a relatively new idea and that many poor children are still forced to drop out of school in order to help support their families. Moreover, expensive private schools still provide a superior education for children from the upper classes, while the public schools that serve the poor are underfunded, understaffed, and growing worse. Conflict theorists also argue that the old system of officially segregated education and the current system of *de facto* segregation are specifically intended to keep blacks and other oppressed minorities at the bottom of the social heap. The general principle is that the social and cultural biases in the educational system are not accidents, but rather are reflections of a social system that favors the powerful.

From the conflict perspective the best and perhaps the only way to change these conditions is for the poor and the minorities to organize, to seize power and reshape the educational system so that it truly provides them with equal opportunity. All children must be given the same quality of education that is now available only in expensive private schools; cash subsidies must be provided for poor students who would otherwise be forced to drop out of school; and special educational programs must be set up to provide extra help for children whose parents have a weak educational background. Nevertheless, most conflict theorists probably agree with Jencks, who concludes that the educational system can do little to reduce inequality without changes in the broader society. Even if there were complete educational equality or if everyone were give a college education, social and economic inequalities would remain. Such changes would not produce more interesting, highly paid professional jobs, nor would they reduce the number of menial, low-paying jobs. Consequently, employment would simply be allocated on same basis other than education.

The Social-Psychological Perspective

Social psychologists are concerned with the impact of the educational system on students' psychological development. Many have commented on the possibility that the authoritarianism so common in our schools impedes learning and encourages undemocratic behavior in later life. Schools also create psychological problems for some of their students. The heavy emphasis on competition and the consequent fear of failure are disturbing to those students who are already anxious and insecure. Students who fail to do well in school are often troubled with feelings of depression and inadequacy. Summerhill and other free-school experiments are attempts to improve the socialization process and, thus, to deal with these problems.

Other social psychologists, however, are not so convinced that the social relationships in most traditional schools are harmful. They note that rational discipline may benefit children by exposing them to the rules and regulations that they will be expected to follow after they leave school. Moreover, some behaviorists have charged that children in free schools are often reinforced for behavior that is unacceptable outside the school. This does not mean that social psychologists necessarily favor the programs of fundamental schools. Some children certainly need a great deal of discipline and an emphasis on obedience to authority, but social relationships of this kind impede the ability of other children to learn and to function effectively. Thus, it seems logical to provide the greatest possible range of educational alternatives so that the unique needs of each student can be met.

SUMMARY

Schools, colleges, and universities were originally reserved for the elite. Today, however, education has become a big business, employing over 2.5 million teachers in the United States alone.

Our schools perform a number of important social tasks. They teach important skills such as reading, writing, and arithmetic. They transmit important values and attitudes. They perform a "sorting service," channeling students into jobs for which they can qualify. The educational system also protects the advantages of dominant social groups by keeping most lower-class people in their "place." Schools serve as agents of social control but also provide a great number of social opportunities for students.

Racial and ethnic discrimination in the American educational system goes back to the days of slavery. Since the Supreme Court's decision outlawing school desegregation (1954), most legal (*de jure*) discrimination has been abolished. However, *de facto* (actual) segregation arising from segregated housing patterns is still widespread. Attempts to eliminate both *de jure* and *de facto* segregation have met with determined and often violent opposition. Current debates over this issue center on programs that attempt to achieve integration by busing students to schools in areas whose ethnic composition differs from that of the students' home neighborhoods.

Children from the lower classes do not do as well in school as children from the middle and upper classes. Poor children usually come to school with a variety of economic and cultural handicaps, and the school system discriminates against these children in a number of ways. Teachers expect lower-class children to do poorly, and their expectations often become self-fulfilling prophecies. The schools attended by working-class children generally have lower budgets than other schools.

The contemporary "crisis" in education consists of four separate problems. First, public schools are accused of placing too much emphasis on authority and obedience. A second serious concern is the declining scores on tests of educational achievement. A third new problem is overeducation — the training of students for jobs that do not exist. Fourth, it has recently been discovered that the school system often generates delinquency rather than preventing it. These problems, taken together, seem to have created a "crisis of confidence" among contemporary educators.

There are many proposals for creating more equal education. These include programs to achieve more effective integration, programs to give special assistance to poor and minority students, and reforms in school finance. Proposals for improving the educational process itself include the use of improved educational techniques such as those used in free schools or fundamental schools; changing the curriculum so the school can do a better job of meeting students' needs; or adopting a voucher system that would allow parents to send their child to any school they wish at state expense.

Functionalists note that the educational system is not running smoothly and that solving problems of education is mostly a matter of reorganizing schools so that they will operate more efficiently. Conflict theorists are prone to look behind the stated goals of the educational system and argue that economic and political elites have an interest in achieving other, unstated goals, including the goal of favoring those in positions of power. Social psychologists are concerned about the harmful effects our educational system may have on individual students and about the best ways to correct these problems.

KEY TERMS   compensatory-education program   grade inflation
de facto segregation   latent function
de jure segregation   overeducation
free school   resegregation
fundamental education

5
Problems of the Family

What are the functions of the family?
Is divorce a social problem?
Are children victims of their parents' problems?
How can the family be made stronger?

The family is found, in one form or another, in every known society. Yet observers have long bemoaned the "decay" of the family, complaining of everything from youthful rebelliousness to a breakdown of traditional moral values. Records of such complaints survive from ancient Greece, centuries before the birth of Christ. But there is convincing evidence that since the time of the industrial revolution the family has grown increasingly unstable. Rates of divorce and illegitimate births have soared, and there is growing confusion about the role the family should play in our daily lives. Traditional beliefs about the family, from the assumption of male dominance to the restriction of sexual relations to one's spouse, are being challenged. Furthermore, there is little agreement about what new attitudes, if any, should replace the old ones.

Despite these signs of trouble, dire warnings of the collapse of the family system are hardly justified. The family is changing, but it shows no signs of disappearing. Almost everyone eventually marries, and most people who divorce marry again. And it is not at all clear that people who lived in different family systems were any happier than people are today. In fact, the opposite may very well be true. In traditional systems marriage partners were pressured to maintain even bitterly unhappy marriages that today would be quickly dissolved. The fact that the divorce rate was lower in the 1870s than it was in the 1970s hardly means that families then were healthier or happier. While the collapse of the traditional family structure has caused serious problems for many people, it has also provided an opportunity to create a new family network that is better suited to the needs and desires of the current age.

THE NATURE OF THE FAMILY

Although some form of family is found in every society, just who is included in "the family" varies greatly from one place to another. In some societies a wide variety of relatives are considered the members of a family, while in others the family consists only of parents and children. Some societies permit only one husband and wife, while others allow more than one husband or wife and occasionally several of each. Murdock's study of 565 different societies found that about one-fourth followed our pattern of monogamy (only one husband and one wife at a time) while over 70 percent allowed polygyny, in which a husband may have more than one wife. Murdock also found four societies in which the wife is allowed more than one husband.[1]

In some societies each parent plays an important role in child rearing, but in others the father has little to do with his children. For instance, among the Nayar of Southern India the mother and her relatives (both male and female) carry the entire responsibility for the children. Some societies allow sexual relations only between married couples, while others permit a broad range of contacts. In some societies marriage is considered permanent and unbreakable, while others allow for easy divorce and remarriage. There are many other variations; the structure of the family is as diverse and varied as culture itself.

Structure Different family types have been classified according to their distinctive structures. One of the most useful classifications divides families into two categories: nuclear and extended. The nuclear family consists of a married couple and their children. Although there are ties between the members of the nuclear family and the relatives of the husband and wife, nuclear families are independent, self-controlled units. When two people marry, the couple and their children become a separate family unit, usually living apart from the families in which the wife and husband were reared. The nuclear family is the dominant family pattern in modern industrialized nations in North America, Europe, and Asia.

Although the nuclear family is the norm in our culture, anthropologists have found that the extended family is the ideal in most cultures. The extended family consists of two or more related nuclear families living together in the same place, usually consisting of several generations living together in the same unit. At the time of marriage the wife becomes a member of the husband's family, which consists of his grandparents, their sons and their wives, and their grandchildren. In some societies, however, the new husband becomes part of his wife's family. In still other societies, the grandparents are excluded and the extended family is based on the tie between brothers and/or sisters of the same generation.

Life in the extended family is very different from the life we know in the nuclear family. For one spouse at least, marriage does not represent a sharp break with the past, as it does in our culture. He or she continues to live with his or her parents as before. Although the adjustment is more difficult for the spouse who must move into a new family, husband and wife both remain under the authority and control of the older generation. They have little chance of controlling their own lives unless they outlive their siblings and, at the time of old age, take control of the entire family. Each child is reared and socialized by many adults, not just by its parents.

Family life in China before the changes of the twentieth century was a classic example of an extended family system. Except in a few coastal cities, control by the older generation affected every aspect of life. Marriages of children were arranged with an eye to public expectations and the family's best interests. Love and compatability between the newly married couple were of little concern, since newlyweds were virtual strangers. Individuals were surrounded by relatives, and this larger family determined each person's career and ambitions. Each person was secure within the group, which cared for its members in case of sickness, accident, old age, or any emergency. Such charity involved no stigma or disgrace, and indeed was accepted as a social duty. The surrounding com-

The contemporary nuclear family consists only of the married couple and their children.

munity, sharing similar values, lent support to the extended family. In societies where the nuclear-family pattern dominates, most people can look forward only to increasing isolation and loneliness as they grow older, but the Chinese could expect their status and authority to increase year by year.[2]

Functions

Most social scientists agree that the family's most important function is to replace those who have died or are disabled.[3] Such replacement has three different aspects. First, the family *provides for reproduction* by creating a stable mating relationship that supports the mother during pregnancy and the children during the critical early months of life. Related to reproduction is the family's regulation of sexual behavior. By limiting the number of permissible partners, the family reduces many possible conflicts, including those related to inheritance from the father; by encouraging sexual relations between husband and wife, it promotes reproduction. Second, the family *socializes the young*. It is in the family that the child learns how to think, talk, and follow the customs, behavior, and values of his or her society. The family, therefore, is an important agency of social control. Third, the family *provides support and protection* for its children, and for its adults as well. A wide range of family members' emotional needs are met, as are their physical needs for food and shelter.

It is not essential that all three of these tasks be performed by the same social unit. The group that physically produces children need not be the group that socializes them, and the group that socializes children need not be the one that supports and protects them. But the fact that all these functions are performed by one group gives the family a peculiar character. Among other things, it must be an intimate group. It must remain together for a period extending at least from the time a child is born until the time that child reaches maturity. Finally, it must be an economic unit that produces and shares wealth among its members. No other basic social institution has such a collection of unrelated functions.

The modern nuclear family is not as efficient as the extended family in performing most of its functions, and many of them are now being carried on elsewhere. In the past the family was the unit of economic production, but in industrialized nations the factory and the corporate farm have replaced the family farm or business. In addition, schools are playing an increasing role in socialization, and family support and protection of the young and the aged is supplemented by government welfare programs. Police, courts, and schools are becoming increasingly important in controlling the young. Nevertheless, the family still contributes to each of these activities.

History Because the nuclear-family system is found in contemporary hunting and gathering societies, it is logical to conclude that it was present in the earliest hunting and gathering societies as well. Hunters and gatherers move from place to place, so it is difficult for them to maintain large family groups. The extended family came into its own only with the development of settled agriculture. As people began to stay in one place and farm single plots of ground, the extended family helped fill the need for a steady supply of labor to work the fields. Also, ownership of land by an extended family often meant that the land would not be cut into smaller and smaller pieces to be divided among the heirs whenever the parents died. Even today most agricultural societies have extended-family systems that provide for the essential needs of their members.

Development of the industrial system created another revolution in family life as the large extended family deteriorated under the impact of changing economic conditions. Because most production took place outside the home, the economic base of the family weakened, causing younger members to leave home to find employment. Like the hunting and gathering economy, industrialization requires a high degree of mobility, forcing workers to move from one place to another as some jobs close and others open. The industrial revolution also had a tremendous impact on traditional culture. As ideals of individualism and "the survival of the fittest" spread, many of the attitudes and values that had supported the extended-family system were abandoned.[4]

THE MODERN As the family's functions have been taken over by other social institu-
FAMILY tions, it has become much easier to live without family support. Marriage has become a matter of individual choice. Couples now marry out of desire for companionship and personal happiness, not out of duty to their family or economic necessity. Romantic love has taken on tremendous importance as the process of mate selection has focused on finding a compati-

Most nuclear families have closer ties to other relatives than is generally recognized. This is particularly true among the very wealthy and the very poor.

ble person and "falling in love." Love is considered a kind of magic potion that can overcome almost any problem. In sharp contrast, traditional societies see romantic love as a frivolous basis for marriage and a threat to the smooth operation of the family system. Without arranged marriages and integration of the young couple into an extended family, the authority of the elder generation collapses.

The emphasis on love and personal happiness in marriage leads to the belief that unhappy marriages should be dissolved. When we say that two people have "fallen" in love, we imply that the matter is beyond their control, a bit like fate. It follows that they can also fall out of love. As a result instability has become a characteristic of the modern family. It should be noted, however, that despite this structured instability most marriages do not end in divorce. The ties between husbands and wives are generally much deeper and longer lasting than those in any other voluntary relationship.

There is considerable debate about the extent to which the modern nuclear family is tied to the families of the husband and wife. Most scholars see the nuclear family as an independent unit relatively isolated from other kinship ties.[5] However, some recent research suggests that the modern family is not so isolated after all. For instance, Sussman and Burchinal found that the American nuclear family is enmeshed in a very significant kinship network.[6] Thus, substantial amounts of financial aid flow from one generation to another, usually from parents to young married couples and later from middle-aged couples to aging parents. Members of kinship networks also provide each other with important services, ranging from

NINETEENTH CENTURY SOCIAL PROBLEMS

John and Leo Koelbel, well-to-do farmers residing in the town of Newton, had a hearing in Manitowoc in the county court before Judge Anderson, having been cited there on the charge of contempt for failing to comply with an order of the court commanding them to pay 60 cents a week each for the support of their aged parents. . . . The 2 sons have positively refused to give a single cent toward the support of their father and mother. The court ordered them both to be committed to the county jail until they saw fit to comply with the order. . . .
June 11, 1900

baby-sitting to emotional and financial support in times of personal distress. Finally, Sussman and Burchinal point out, there are extensive social and recreational contacts between the members of many American kinship networks.

It appears that the members of modern nuclear families have rather extensive contacts with their relatives, despite the fact that they are generally more isolated from kin than are members of extended families. Research in industrial societies indicates that the closest kinship ties are found in the extremes of the status hierarchy—in the upper and lower classes. One study of the nuclear family led to the following conclusions:

> In the middle class there is a strong emphasis on individual achievement and a parallel de-emphasis of extended family obligations. . . . In the upper class, endogamy [the practice of marrying within one's own group] and overall kinship solidarity are effective instruments for maintaining positions of status and power. Family lineage is used to gain access into status groups, and there is enough wealth to maintain a semblance of an extended kinship network with some control of members. Extended family ties are stressed in the lower class for different reasons. Geographical mobility is minimal in the lower class. Lower class persons are isolated, both physically and socially, from the larger society, and they participate in few social activities outside of those which involve relatives.[7]

The overall picture of the modern Western family drawn by social scientists tends to be negative. In comparison with the extended family, the nuclear family is described as isolated, unstable, and weak. There is little doubt that the extended-family system provides for the personal and economic needs of its members more efficiently than the nuclear-family system. On the other hand, the nuclear-family system permits individualism and freedom of choice, encouraging members to pursue individual happiness.

Divorce　Recent years have brought dramatic increases in divorce rates. (See Figure 5.1.) In 1920 there was one divorce for every seven marriages in the United States; fifty years later the rate had climbed to one divorce for every three marriages.[8] Today there are more than four divorces for every

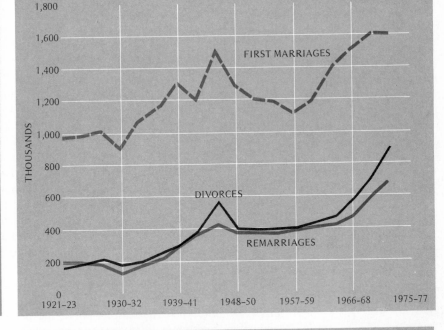

FIGURE 5.1
FIRST MARRIAGES,
DIVORCES, AND
REMARRIAGES OF WOMEN,
THREE-YEAR AVERAGES,
1921–1923 TO 1972–1974

Source: U.S. Department of Commerce, *Social Indicators 1976* (Washington, D.C.: GPO, 1976), p. 53.

FIGURE 5.2
DIVORCES PER 1,000
POPULATION IN
SELECTED COUNTRIES

*Less than .05 thousand.
† Data not available.
‡ Rates for 1910 and 1930 for all Germany, later rates for eastern Germany only.
Source: Based on data from Metropolitan Life Insurance Company, *Statistical Bulletin*, Vol. 33 (June 1952), p. 7. Courtesy of Metropolitan Life Insurance Co. *Demographic Yearbook*, United Nations, various issues.

	1910	1930	1950	1967	1974
United States	1.0	1.50	2.50	2.64	4.58
Canada	.05*	.08	.40	.55	1.66
Mexico	†	.10	.31	.72	.24
England and Wales	.05	.09	.69	.96	2.14
Sweden	.10	.36	1.14	1.36	3.11
Germany‡	.30	.63	2.47	1.55	2.27
France	.30	.49	.58	.75	.95
Japan	1.10	.79	1.01	.83	1.04
Russia	†	†	.40	2.74	2.72

ten marriages, making the divorce rate in the United States among the highest in the world.[9] In Canada fewer than two out of every ten marriages end in divorce, despite the fact that Canada has also seen a rapid rise in its divorce rate. Indeed, divorce rates have been rising more rapidly in Canada and other Western countries than in the United States, an indication that they may eventually reach the U.S. level.[10] (See Figure 5.2.)

Who Gets Divorced? In the nineteenth century divorce was mainly for the wealthy. England and many American states required a special act of the legislature for each divorce, and the poor lacked the influence and money necessary for such decrees. Now divorce is most common among the poor, and the divorce rate declines as education and income increase. In 1975 the Census Bureau surveyed 18.3 million married couples in which the husband was 35 to 54 years old. Of those with incomes under $10,000, 72 percent were in their first marriage; but for couples with incomes of $20,000 or above, 82.6 percent were in their first marriage.

One cause of the higher divorce rate among the poor is the special economic problems they experience. As an old saying puts it, "When poverty comes in the door, love goes out the window." It is possible, too, that divorce is less frequent among the wealthy because dissolution of marriage requires complex arrangements for distributing wealth and income among family members. Also, the availability of travel, entertainment, and servants helps the wealthy adjust more easily to married life. Finally, working-class wives are often less dependent on their husbands for economic support. A woman who is used to working as a waitress, factory hand, or housemaid is not as likely to tolerate an abusive husband as a woman who has never supported herself.

The chances of divorce increase significantly if husband and wife come from different religious, ethnic, or economic groups.[11] Such groups usually have different expectations about the proper behavior of husbands and wives, and when these expectations conflict, marital problems result. A special problem arises from public intolerance of "mixed marriages" between people from different racial backgrounds.

Statistically, age is an important factor in marital instability—the younger the married couple, the greater the chance of divorce. Further, about one-fourth of all divorces occur after less than two years of marriage, and about one-half after less than six years.[12] Considering the length of time it takes to get a divorce in many states, this means that many couples begin divorce proceedings shortly after the wedding.

Why the Upward Trend? The steady increase in the divorce rate has caused considerable alarm among those who consider it a sign of moral decay. Sociologically, this increase is most clearly related to the decline in the extended family. The partners in today's marriages receive considerably less support and assistance from relatives than their great-grandparents did. Thus, when trouble arises they have fewer resources on which to draw. At the same time, unhappy couples are now under much less pressure from their families to stay together and avoid divorce. Even if parents want a married couple to stay together, they no longer have the economic power to enforce their wishes.

The shift from the extended-family system to the nuclear family has made it easier to see marriages as unions that are not permanent. The romanticism on which courtship is now based leads many young people to

DEBATE
Is the Modern
Family Decaying?

PRO

The evidence clearly shows that the family has been eroding throughout the twentieth century. The rates of divorce and illegitimacy have zoomed upward, and more and more people are living alone. Surveys show a shocking decay of sexual morality, with premarital and extramarital affairs at an all-time high. The contemporary family is smaller, weaker, and more unstable than at any other time in our history.

The outlook for the future of the family is dismal. As the children from today's unstable families grow up, they will learn to think of pathological conditions as a normal part of family life. We may thus expect to see increasing family problems in each new generation, until the social fabric of our society finally collapses.

We do not, however, need to look to the future to see the harm created by the decay of the family. The damage is all around us. The most obvious victims are the children of broken homes. Such children are more likely to be poor, unloved, and neglected; they do poorly in school and get into more trouble with the police. But children are not the only victims; adults suffer as well. Today's small, unstable families cannot provide the emotional support that all family members need. As the competition between husbands and wives has grown, the home has become a battleground rather than a refuge from the pressures of the world.

CON

The pessimists who mourn the death of the modern family are confusing change with decay. Today's families are certainly different than they were 100 years ago, but there is every reason to believe that their members are actually happier than their ancestors were. The rise in the divorce rate does not indicate that people are less satisfied with their marriages than they were in the past. Two hundred years ago it was virtually impossible to get a divorce in most Western nations, and as a result couples stayed together no matter how unhappy they were. The increase in divorces is a healthy trend. It reflects the fact that unhappy marital partners are no longer forced to stay together but are striking out on their own and finding new, more compatible partners. Most people who divorce eventually remarry and return to family life.

The critics of the contemporary family conveniently forget the stifling oppression of the nineteenth-century family. Women were denied the most basic political and economic rights and were considered little more than the property of their husbands. Few people were concerned about child abuse, since parents were given unrestricted authority over their children and brutal beatings were considered part of good discipline. Those who were unfortunate enough to be caught violating the rigid standards of Victorian sexual morality were mercilessly condemned and excluded from all "decent" company. It is easy to idealize the past, but few of us actually prefer the rigid and oppressive atmosphere of the traditional family to the free and open atmosphere of today's families.

expect marriage to be a state of perpetual happiness and conflict-free bliss. When they start quarreling about money matters, about how much time they should spend with each other, about recreational or intellectual interests, or about who is supposed to sweep the floor and carry out the garbage, they imagine that love has flown out the window and that they are no longer obligated to continue their relationship.

Changes in the system of economic production have made divorce a much more practical alternative than it was in past years. In the traditional family a man took a wife and had children in order to strengthen the family politically and economically. In agricultural societies husbands and wives were mutually dependent. The man needed a woman to help with the work, and the woman needed a man with access to some land. In time husbands and wives began working outside the home and mutual dependence decreased. Only a generation ago most husbands believed that wives worked only if they "had to work," meaning that they worked only because they had inadequate husbands who could not or would not support their families. A working wife whose husband had a good job was considered a greedy opportunist who was taking a job away from a man who needed it to put food on his family's dinner table. Now our attitudes about the proper roles of men and women are changing. More and more women are demanding economic equality, making them less dependent on their husbands and, thus, less likely to stay married to men whom they dislike.

Attitudes toward divorce have changed too. Only fifty years ago divorce was seen as an immoral act, an affront to "decent" people. The divorced woman was stigmatized as a "grass widow" and her virtue exposed to public question. Public sentiment was so strongly against divorce that it was forbidden in some countries, while many others made it extremely difficult. Today divorce carries less stigma and the consensus seems to be that it is better to separate than to continue in an unhappy marriage.

As attitudes have changed, divorces have become easier to obtain. New York law once required the partner seeking a divorce to prove that the spouse had committed adultery. To satisfy the requirement, one partner would sometimes pose in bed with a person of the opposite sex and have a professional photographer take a picture. Other states required one partner (usually the wife) to show that the other was cruel. As more and more people sought divorces, the courts became more liberal in their interpretation of the laws and the laws finally began to change. In 1969 California became the first state to pass a "no-fault" divorce law, and its example has since been followed by other states. Instead of having to go through the painful process of proving that one partner did not fulfill the conditions of the marriage contract, the "no-fault" law allows for divorce by mutual agreement, substantially reducing the legal costs of a divorce.

**Is Divorce a Social
Problem?**

There is no doubt that a divorce is often the only satisfactory solution to an impossible family situation. Nevertheless, divorce continues to be seen as a sign of failure—an admission by the marriage partners that they lack the ability, trust, or stamina to continue a sacred relationship. Many of the problems confronting divorced people stem from such attitudes, and because the parties to a divorce often share such convictions, they feel guilty and ashamed about the breakup of their marriage. Divorce is still stigmatized in many subtle ways. Those who dissolve their marriages are made to feel that they have failed in their duty to God, country, parents, and children. Despite the high frequency of divorce, we have not developed effective means for helping newly divorced people make the transition to a different life style. When a family member dies, other relatives rally around the widow or widower to provide emotional and financial support. There are also a variety of rituals, such as the funeral service, to help ease the pain of transition. Yet the divorced person, who often is in a similar position, is usually left to face the problems of this transition alone.

However, despite any social support the couple may receive, divorce is bound to cause a measure of personal suffering. The termination of an intimate personal relationship and the accompanying feelings of guilt or foolishness make divorce a painful experience, even if there are no serious clashes. From a social viewpoint the major cost of divorce is the division of families with children into smaller and therefore weaker units. Because of occupational discrimination against women, a family consisting of a mother and children is likely to have a lower income than a two-parent family. And single parents, regardless of their sex, have great difficulty handling both the role of breadwinner and the role of parent.

In a recent study of delinquency, Chilton and Markle found that 40 percent of the children referred to Florida juvenile courts came from broken homes, compared with 17 percent of the children in the general population.[13] There is evidence, also, that the percentage of delinquent girls who come from broken homes is greater than the percentage of delinquent boys who come from such homes. Toby has suggested that control over adolescent boys is so weak that there is little difference in supervision between two-parent and single-parent families. In contrast, the two-parent family gives firm supervision to girls, whereas the one-parent family is unable to do so. Thus, girls from single-parent households are more likely than girls from two-parent families to be exposed to criminal influences.[14]

The fact that delinquency is more common among children from broken homes does not mean, however, that children are better off if an unhappy marriage is preserved. In fact, research shows the opposite to be true. Separate studies by Nye and Landis found that children from broken homes were better adjusted and showed less deviant behavior than children of unhappy parents who stayed together.[15] A divorce often makes it possible for the parents to remarry and create a new family with a better environment for the children.

Illegitimacy

Illegitimate childbirth (usually a child born to an unwed mother) is strongly condemned. But most societies seem more concerned with the illegitimate birth than with the sexual relationships that produce it. In Puritan America, however, it was a crime for a woman to give birth to a child "too soon after the wedding." Illegitimacy is probably condemned because it threatens a basic function of marriage — the creation of a strong unit for the socialization of children. Also, inheritance of wealth and power is doubtful when children cannot identify their fathers. Sadly, illegitimate children are often condemned along with their parents, even though they are clearly innocent.

Illegitimacy Rates

According to official statistics, illegitimacy, like divorce, has shown a remarkable increase in recent years. Less than 4 percent of all babies born in 1950 were illegitimate, but in 1976 almost 15 percent of all births were illegitimate. However, the percentage of single women in their childbearing years has also shown a steady increase. The illegitimacy rate (the number of illegitimate births divided by the number of single women of childbearing age) increased sharply between 1940 and 1970 but has shown a slight decline since then.[16] Thus, the increase in illegitimate births since 1970 has been due to an increasing number of single women rather than a greater tendency for them to have illegitimate children. The statistics also show a substantial difference between blacks and whites in the number of illegitimate births. A single black woman of childbearing age is about seven times more likely to have a child than her white counterpart. Much, though not all, of this difference is explained by the fact that blacks have lower incomes than whites. In general, lower-income people have more illegitimate children than others, regardless of race or ethnic status.

Explaining the Trends

Statistics on unpopular behavior are always open to question, since people are likely to try to disguise it if possible. Some of the increase in the illegitimacy rates may be due to better reporting procedures and greater willingness on the part of young mothers to admit that a child was born out of wedlock. An even more important factor has been the growing unwillingness of young couples to marry simply because the girl is preg-

---

NINETEENTH CENTURY SOCIAL PROBLEMS

Lena Watson of Black River Falls gave birth to an illegitimate child and choked it to death.
October 9, 1890

nant. Studies of births in past centuries, when illegitimacy rates were low, show that about 20 to 25 percent of all marriages occurred after the conception of a child.[17] Today the "shotgun wedding" (in which a pregnant girl's father threatens to kill the young man if he does not marry the virgin he "spoiled") has gone out of style. The parents of an illegitimate child are still condemned, but the stigma has decreased over the years. The recent leveling of the rate of illegitimate births coincides with the wider availability of abortions and other birth control techniques.

The Problem of Illegitimacy

Like divorce, illegitimacy weakens the family unit. The social position of a mother with an illegitimate child is not very different from that of a divorced woman with a child. Yet the illegitimate mother faces some special problems unknown to most divorced women. She often feels deserted by the father of the child and lacks the emotional support she needs during the difficult months of pregnancy. Illegitimacy is more common among teenagers than among older women, so illegitimate mothers often lack the emotional maturity to deal with parenthood. Among the poor the mothers of illegitimate children almost invariably apply for welfare. For most women, giving birth to an illegitimate child creates psychological problems as well; the stigma against illegitimacy may reduce her status in the eyes of friends, creating feelings of guilt and inadequacy.

Illegitimate children also face a hostile world. Children whose fathers will not take responsibility for them are often considered "children without a name." The stigma of illegitimacy may follow them throughout their lives and create feelings of inferiority and shame. Inheriting a father's property can be especially difficult, for in many countries the illegitimate child is given second-class treatment in legal matters. Because most Western nations (Scandinavian countries are exceptions) do not give the illegitimate child and mother enough assistance to compensate for their difficulties, they are unable to cope as well as other families.

Violence

Beatings, slashings, stabbings, burnings, and chokings are common events in many families. Such violence occurs between husbands and wives, between children, and in the abuse of children by parents. Family violence ranges in severity from the spanking of a troublesome child (which, though usually socially acceptable, is still a form of violence) to murder. Until quite recently, much family violence remained hidden because it was considered a private matter. Even now, law enforcement agencies seldom get the cooperation they need to prosecute wife beaters and child abusers.

Violence Between Husband and Wife

Wife beating is by far the most common form of husband–wife violence. However, women are frequently aggressors as well, and a substantial number of men are stabbed, slashed, or shot by their wives every year. The full extent of husband–wife violence is not known, but it is probably the most common form of violence in the United States. More calls to the police involve family disturbances than all other forms of violent behavior combined. In a study of 600 couples who had filed for divorce, George Levinger found that 23 percent of the middle-class couples and 40 percent of the working-class couples gave physical abuse as a major complaint.[18]

Many of the causes of husband–wife violence are similar to those for other kinds of personal violence, and they will be discussed in depth in Chapter 15. In many societies, such as those in the Middle East, husbands have traditionally had the right to punish their wives physically. Although this practice is not approved of in Western culture, it still occurs. In his study of divorce John O'Brien found that violence is most common in families in which the husband is not doing well in his role as provider and in which the status of the wife is in some way superior to that of the husband. O'Brien concluded that violence is often the last resort in the husband's attempt to maintain his dominance.[19]

Because some men react violently when their authority in the family is threatened, Robert Whitehurst concluded that the growing trend toward equality for women may actually increase family violence, at least in the short run. Husbands who are unable to accept their wives' new-found status may well strike out physically.[20] However, in the long run sexual equality will probably produce the opposite result, for as women gain financial and social equality they will also gain greater bargaining power in the home, making it easier for them to leave an abusive husband. At the same time, new generations of men who have been socialized to believe in equality will be less likely to see family problems as a threat requiring a violent response.

Child Abuse

No one knows how many children are seriously injured by their parents each year. For one thing, there is no clear line between "acceptable" punishment and child abuse. It is estimated that at least 93 percent of all American parents spank their children at some time. Certainly, not all these parents are child abusers.[21] Yet severe and repeated spankings can be just as cruel as other forms of violence. In a study of official records David Gil concluded that there are about 9 cases of reported child abuse for every 100,000 children in the United States.[22] However, most child abuse cases go unreported, and Gil estimates that there are actually over 2 million cases of child abuse in the United States every year.[23]

Although such figures make us look bad, we probably do not abuse our children as much as our ancestors did, for the incidence of child abuse seems to have declined substantially over the past few centuries.[24] Traditionally, severe physical punishment was considered essential to the learning process. Many parents believed that "if you spare the rod, you spoil the child." In colonial America a statute even provided for the execution of sons who were "stubborn and rebellious" and failed to follow parental authority. However, there is no record of such an execution actually taking place.[25]

Gil's study of officially reported child abuse cases provides some interesting insights into the type of child who is most likely to be mistreated. Contrary to popular opinion, children of all ages, up to their senior year in high school, are abused. Abused children are much more likely to come from broken homes, and less than half of the abused children in Gil's sample were living with their natural father. Children from large families are also more likely to be abused. Gil found that the usual indicators of social class — income, occupational prestige, and education — are all negatively related to child abuse. In other words, the lower the parents' social and economic status, the more likely they were to hurt their children. The children in Gil's sample were more likely to be abused by their mothers than by their fathers, in part because fathers were not present in many homes. However, these data should not be taken at face value. Since child abuse in single-parent or low-income families is more likely to receive official attention, it is also more likely to show up in the official records that Gil studied.

There are many different explanations of child abuse. Psychologists tend to picture child abusers as people who are mentally ill or at least have severe emotional problems. The typical child abuser is described as impulsive, immature, and depressed, with little control over his or her emotions.[26] Social workers are inclined to see environmental stress as the most important cause of child abuse. They note that an unwanted pregnancy, desertion by the husband, or unemployment and poverty put special pressures on a parent that may result in child abuse. Social psychologists have found strong evidence that most child abusers learned to be abusive when they were children. That is, they were beaten when they were young and they beat their own children. Gil argues that child abuse occurs frequently in American society because physical punishment of children is condoned and even encouraged. He calls for laws that would make it a crime to inflict physical punishment on children. Gil and many others, however, overlook the fact that child abuse can be psychological as well as physical. Countless parents cause severe emotional damage to their children without ever being violent.

Child Rearing

Raising children to replace people who grow old and die is the most critical function of the family. The vitality and even the survival of a society depends on how effectively the family does this job. Thus, every society is only about twenty years from extinction, for if a society fails to socialize its children for that length of time it will cease to exist. Of course, this is not likely to happen. But it is clear that there are many

Child rearing has always been one of the most important and most difficult tasks of the family. The small size of the modern nuclear family has made this task even harder.

"pathological" families in which the relationship between parents and children is warped, and even "healthy" families often fail to socialize their children effectively.

Child rearing has never been an easy task, but in the nuclear family it is particularly difficult. A child's parents have almost exclusive responsibility for the support and upbringing of the child, receiving little assistance from relatives. This means that a single breadwinner, usually the father, must provide for the support of the family, while another person, usually the mother, actually rears the children. There are many variations in this arrangement, but however the responsibilities are shared, the modern nuclear family is quite fragile. If one of the parents is unable to perform family duties, the family is almost automatically plunged into crisis, since there are no relatives in the household to help out.

The growing frequency of single-parent families has made these problems worse. (See Figure 5.3.) Financially most single-parent families are always on thin ice, for the majority of them are headed by women, and women usually earn less money than men. Child support payments from the father sometimes help. However, Kenneth Eckhardt found that less than 40 percent of the fathers he studied paid the full amount of the support payments ordered by the court in the first year the order was effective. Further, compliance with court orders dropped steadily until after 10 years almost 80 percent of the fathers paid no support at all.[27] Another problem in the single-parent family is lack of parental supervision and guidance. Often, single parents do not have time to perform both their breadwinning and their child-rearing roles. This problem is particularly severe for boys reared by their mothers and for girls raised by their fathers because such children must find adult role models outside the home.

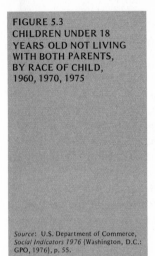

Source: U.S. Department of Commerce,
Social Indicators 1976 (Washington, D.C.:
GPO, 1976), p. 55.

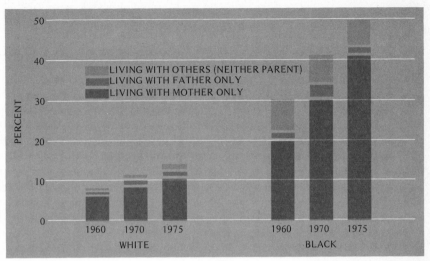

FIGURE 5.3
CHILDREN UNDER 18
YEARS OLD NOT LIVING
WITH BOTH PARENTS,
BY RACE OF CHILD,
1960, 1970, 1975

A great deal of concern has been expressed about the children of working mothers. But while working mothers often bear extra burdens, the fear that maternal employment somehow harms children apparently is unfounded. In reviewing all the available research on this subject, Thomas Taveggia and Ellen Thomas concluded that "there are no substantial differences between the children of working and nonworking mothers," at least in terms of the characteristics that have been tested, such as intelligence, personal development, school achievement, and social adjustment.[28]

Parent–child conflicts pose another set of family problems. Because parents no longer have control over what their children learn, children are exposed to beliefs and customs of which their parents do not approve. Contributing to this problem is the so-called "generation gap." The pace of social change has been so rapid that the world in which children grow up is very different from the one their parents knew, making mutual understanding and communication more difficult than in the past. Parent–child conflicts are typically most acute during adolescence, when children are trying to establish their independence and straining to deal with growing sexual drives. Children who feel they should be independent and "modern" rebel against parents who try to keep them under tight control.

Changing Expectations

Redefinition of the traditional roles of males and females has placed considerable stress on the modern family. In the past each partner in a marriage generally had a clear-cut idea of what to expect from the other. The man's task was to support the family; the woman was expected to keep house and rear the children. While this pattern is still common, there are a growing number of alternatives. A bride and groom can no longer assume that their ideas about the proper roles of a husband and a wife are the same. And if their ideas do not coincide, considerable compromise is required to resolve the differences. More women are working outside the home and demanding an equal share of the decision-making power within the family. Some husbands, socialized to see women as inferiors, consider these demands a threat to their masculinity, particularly if the wives are more successful in their careers than their husbands. Such differences are likely to cause conflicts that are difficult to resolve without damaging the husband's ego or the wife's sense of justice and fair play.

Other problems stem from the family's need to adjust to the demands of two careers. A variety of evidence shows that even in families where both partners work full time, women usually do a disproportionate share of the housework.[29] Even when there is full equality between husband and wife, career conflicts may arise. For example, one partner may be offered an important promotion that requires a move that would be disastrous to the career of the other.

The so-called "sexual revolution" has put pressure on the traditional family from another direction. Premarital sex has become increasingly acceptable, and there has been a remarkable increase in erotic material in the media. Books, movies, advertising, and even television bombard us with erotic stimulation. The ideal of marital fidelity has become increasingly difficult to uphold in the erotically charged atmosphere of twentieth-century life.[30]

RESPONDING TO PROBLEMS OF THE FAMILY

In one sense there are as many responses to family problems as there are families. Because each family is unique, its members respond to family troubles in unique ways. In another sense, however, family problems are institutional, and therefore affect us all. Attempts to improve the family institution usually try to strengthen the nuclear family or expand the kinship network and return to something resembling an extended family.

Strengthening the Nuclear Family

The nuclear-family system is very much in tune with the economic, political, and educational institutions of modern industrial society. Thus, despite its basic weaknesses, most reformers have chosen to direct their efforts toward strengthening the nuclear family rather than trying to establish larger and possibly more durable family units.

Better Preparation

One way of strengthening the nuclear family is to see that people are better prepared for marriage. Perhaps the easiest way to achieve this goal is simply to discourage early marriage so that partners are older and more mature when they do marry. Census Bureau figures show that the average age of couples at the time of their first marriage has increased since the mid-1950s. However, the average increase amounts to only about one year. Publicizing the problems of early marriage might discourage some young couples from marrying, but it is far from certain that such a campaign would be effective.

Another approach is to prepare the young for marriage through educational programs in high schools and colleges. Although such programs encourage realistic expectations about married life and teach techniques for dealing with marital problems, most of them have not been notably successful. Regrettably, a few hours of classroom instruction are not likely to change long-held attitudes and expectations about marriage.

Trial marriage has also been suggested as a means of preparing young people for real marriage. The late Margaret Mead suggested the creation of two legal categories of marriage. The first would be for young couples without children, and it would be easily dissolved. A second, more binding marriage, with children, would follow only for couples who wanted it and who could pass certain psychological and financial tests.[31] However, it is doubtful that the state should be given such power to interfere in people's lives. Moreover, increasing numbers of young couples are living together before deciding on marriage. The results of the marriages that occur after such trial periods may tell us whether this is an effective way of increasing family stability.

Marriage Counseling In recent years there has been a significant increase in the number of people seeking outside help with marital problems and in the number of marriage counselors who offer such help. Some counselors are competent professionals with training in psychology or social work, while others are little more than well-meaning but ineffective busybodies. Because of these variations, the overall effectiveness of marriage counseling is difficult to judge.

Counseling is most helpful for couples with specific, limited problems. When there are serious conflicts between personalities, attitudes, or life styles, even the best professional counseling may prove futile. Sex therapy as pioneered by the famous Masters and Johnson research team has been helpful to many couples because it deals with specific problems, such as impotence or frigidity, that respond to straightforward treatment.[32] But this sort of response is effective for only a limited range of problems. Further, "sex therapy" has been taken up by many frauds, and even some prostitutes now call themselves sex therapists.

Easier Divorces While it may seem strange to advocate divorce as a means of strengthening the family, it is clear that differences between husband and wife are often so great that dissolution of the marriage would be beneficial to both partners. As pointed out earlier, there is considerable evidence that children of parents with persistent marital conflicts are more likely to have psychological problems than children from divorced families.[33] So the argument that marriages should be kept together "for the sake of the children" is not a good one. Thus, it appears that the family as an institution might be strengthened, not weakened, as divorce becomes easier and new nuclear families are formed to replace unhappy ones in which some members are neglected or abused.

Role Changes

Traditional family patterns — in the extended family as well as the nuclear family — have often subordinated women to their husbands' will and deprived them of the power to control their destinies. Further, the traditional division of labor in the family often requires both men and women to do work for which they are poorly suited. Some families clearly would be much better off if the husband stayed home to care for the children while the wife worked. It therefore seems likely that the nuclear-family system will be strengthened by the development of a new pattern of marriage based on sexual equality. In such a system the division of labor would be based on the skills and abilities of each partner rather than on their gender. Decision-making power would be equal. Although many families already function in this manner, our traditional standards lead many people to brand any deviation from the customary patterns as wrong and unnatural, and the entire family system is weakened by this attitude.

Government-supported day care centers for children could contribute to sexual equality by freeing women from some of their traditional child-rearing responsibilities and allowing them to participate more fully in the economic system. Supporters of day care centers argue that they would be particularly helpful to single-parent families and might reduce welfare costs by allowing more mothers to work. However, opposition to this plan has been strong. Critics argue that government agencies are poor substitutes for parents and point to the bureaucratic indifference and coldness that are typical of many orphanages, institutions for delinquents, and schools. They fear that day care centers will harm children by depriving them of motherly love. Advocates of day care centers reply that many children have little contact with their mothers in normal circumstances and that properly run day care centers will enrich, not deprive, these children.

Closely associated with the movement toward sexual equality is the concept of open marriage. Its supporters argue that the nuclear family would be stronger if husbands and wives encouraged each other to grow personally rather than attempting to possess and control each other. This

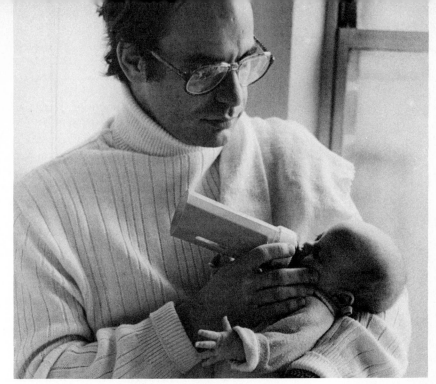

Traditional sex roles are changing. More and more couples are sharing child-rearing responsibilities and allowing each member to perform the tasks they do best regardless of sexual stereotypes.

idea was popularized by Nena and George O'Neill's best-selling book *Open Marriage:*

> [Open marriage is] a relationship in which the partners are committed to their own and each other's growth. It is an honest and open relationship of intimacy and self-disclosure based on the equal freedom and identity of both partners. . . . It is a relationship that is flexible enough to allow for change and that is constantly being renegotiated in the light of changing needs, consensus in decision-making, acceptance and encouragement of individual growth and openness to new possibilities of growth.[34]

Thus, the partners in an open marriage are encouraged by their mates to seek personal fulfillment in a context of full sexual equality.

Discussions of open marriage have unfortunately tended to focus on a single issue: acceptance of sexual relationships outside of marriage. However, open marriages certainly involve much more than the freedom to engage in extramarital sex. Its advocates suggest that couples avoid the temptation to settle into a comfortable routine and instead continue the search for personal growth. Critics and experimenters alike have noted that this is no easy task. Some open marriages are little more than the gradual drifting apart of two people who grow in different directions.

Expanding the Kinship Network

The nuclear-family system is clearly well suited to life in modern industrialized societies. But the fact remains that the nuclear family, no matter how strong, is not as effective as the traditional extended family in performing many of its social functions. For this reason some people long for a return to the extended-family system. But this dream is unrealistic. Any attempt to turn back the clock and reestablish the family system of the past is unlikely to withstand the economic and political forces that originally broke up the extended family.

Nevertheless, as already noted, members of modern nuclear families have more significant contacts with their relatives than is commonly believed. It is quite possible that establishing even closer ties among relatives may provide one of the most practical and effective solutions to the problems of the family. Of course, this solution will not work for people who have no compatible relatives living nearby. A more radical step in the same direction is the attempt to establish what might be called "substitute kinship networks" through group marriages and communal family living.

Group Marriages   A group marriage is basically an expanded nuclear family that includes three or more adults as the marriage partners. Most such marriages are unions of a husband and two or more wives or of a wife and two or more husbands. Group marriages of two or more members of each sex are rare. Although group marriages do occur in our culture, their members are considered deviants, and usually criminals as well. Because of the hostility they face, the members of most group marriages try to keep their relationship secret.

A detailed study by Larry and Joan Constantine found that most people enter group marriage because they want companionship and intimacy with more people than the nuclear family allows.[35] The Constantines also found that the greater number of adults in a group marriage provides several benefits, including greater financial security and a lessening of the burdens of child care. Most of the marriage partners had experienced group sex (involving three or more people) at some time, but it nevertheless was a rare occurrence. Despite the seeming advantages of group marriage, most were rather short-lived. Over half of the group marriages studied by the Constantines lasted less than one year. Although jealousy (but not sex itself) contributed to this high divorce rate, the authors concluded that the basic problem was the clash of personalities. Many married couples are not compatible enough to live together for a long period. By increasing the number of partners, group marriage increases the potential for incompatibility.

Communes   A commune is a close-knit group of people living together in a supportive family environment. A few communes encourage sexual relations among all adult members and may be considered group marriages, but most are merely groups of friends sharing common family tasks. Today's communes are the latest in a series of attempts to establish harmonious communities that goes back as far as 1680 in North America. A number of successful communes were founded in the nineteenth century, and the so-called "hippie" movement of the 1960s inspired renewed interest in the commune. However, most of the new communes are smaller and less closely knit than their successful nineteenth-century counterparts.[36]

Present-day communes can be divided into two categories, urban and rural, each with its special problems. Rural communes often have economic difficulties in their formative years because most of the members come from the cities, have little money, and have no farming experience. Urban communes are easier to start. All that is needed is an old house and a few interested people. But because most members work at outside jobs and are thus in daily contact with the outside world, they are more likely to lose the sense of group identity that is so essential to an ongoing commune.

Both urban and rural communes offer many of the advantages of the extended family. Ideally, they provide love, financial assistance, and emotional support for children and adults alike. But many do not survive. Administrative authority often becomes a critical problem. Democratic communes in which members are encouraged to "do their own thing" often find it difficult to get even the simplest household tasks done. Communes with powerful leaders and a common ideology are more efficient. Things get done. But in such authoritarian settings conflicts are inevitable. Some members eventually come to believe that they are being exploited and either rebel or leave. Another source of problems is the fact that most of the people living in modern communes come from nuclear families that have not socialized them for life in a commune. Finally, many communes disband because of harassment from neighbors who neither understand nor accept their life style. Although some rural communes succeed in isolating themselves from outsiders, most must expend precious economic, psychological, and social resources to protect themselves from the hostility of outsiders.

SOCIOLOGICAL PERSPECTIVES on Problems of the Family

As we have seen, concern for the "decaying" family is nothing new. Because the family is such a basic social institution, it has always been the center of social concern. But the rapid change that the family has undergone since the industrial revolution has created new and difficult problems for sociologists to study.

The Functionalist Perspective

Functionalists see family problems as stemming from the disorganization caused by rapid social change. The extended family is compatible with the traditional cultures in which it is found but ill suited to the modern industrial world. Industrialization broke up the extended family and forced a change to the nuclear-family system. The resultant disorganization made it impossible for the family to perform its functions efficiently. Nor did change cease with the industrial revolution. The increase in the number of women in the work force and the ideal of sexual equality are bringing about another realignment of family structure. From the functionalist perspective the present family system is in trouble because the family system has not had enough time to adapt to these social and economic changes.

Because the family performs so many important social functions, functionalists agree that it should be kept as strong as possible. However, functional analysis does not lead to any single proposal for improvement. One possibility would be for other agencies—such as day care centers and schools—to assume many of the family's functions, permitting the family to handle those that remain more effectively. Strengthening the nuclear family and even returning to the extended family are other possibilities that have already been discussed. Functionalists generally recommend a return to the values associated with the traditional nuclear fmaily, such as a stronger prohibition on divorce and greater restrictions on sexual behavior. However, some functionalists reject these ideas, advocating trial marriage as a test of compatibility as well as easier divorce for marriages that fail.

The Conflict Perspective

Many conflicts of values and attitudes affect the family institution. Traditionalists place great importance on the value of a stable family environment for child rearing and thus reject the idea of divorce; modernists see personal happiness as the most important goal of family life and believe that a child will suffer more from an unhappy home than from a broken one. Traditionalists are convinced that sexual relations should be restricted to one's spouse; modernists advocate greater sexual freedom. Modernists condemn traditional attitudes toward women as exploitive and unjust, and they support full sexual equality. Traditionalists, on the other hand, are likely to believe that male dominance is based on innate differences between the sexes and that any other sort of family relationship is unnatural.

There is no easy way of resolving such fundamental differences of values and opinions. Continued conflict and competition between the two concepts of marriage may eventually produce a new structure about which both sides agree, but this does not seem likely in the immediate future. At present the only practical solution is to cultivate tolerance and understanding for those with whom we disagree, and strive to resolve our disputes in a fair and equitable manner.

Conflict theorists are also concerned with the fact that the poor have higher rates of divorce and illegitimacy and greater overall family instability than other people. They attribute this difference to the special problems of being poor. For instance, some husbands who cannot get decent jobs consider themselves failures, and a variety of problems ranging from alcoholism to wife beating may develop. But conflict theorists assert that such problems are the fault of the economic and political system, not of individuals. Family problems, they maintain, are one of the costs of an industrial state that has allowed powerful individuals and groups to exploit the weak and create conditions of economic and political inequality. A more harmonious family system will develop only when the poor gain power and force the rich to accept a more equalitarian society.

**The Social-
Psychological
Perspective**

Most social psychologists have focused on the family's role in the socialization of children. Social-psychological research has linked faulty socialization to problems ranging from mental disorder to juvenile delinquency. Clearly, some families socialize their children to play conformist roles while in other families the socialization process inspires children to behave in ways that conformists consider indecent and even illegal. For adults the nuclear family's most critical social-psychological function is to provide emotional support and comfort. For some, the family is the only shelter from the relentless demands of modern civilization—the one place where the individual can develop a sense of stability and belonging. But on the other hand, dissension and conflict within the family can have devastating psychological consequences for all of its members.

The social-psychological perspective points to several possible ways to create the kind of stable, emotionally supportive, families that do an effective job socializing their children and provide security and comfort for all of their members. The ideal of romantic love is so heavily emphasized in our culture that young people approach marriage expecting more of each other than either can possibly give. Too often they end up bitter and disappointed when their romantic fantasies fail to come true. More realistic expectations, encouraged by schools and the masss media, may be one way of solving the problem. Another approach to creating more supportive families would be to promote the development of the kinds of alternative family forms discussed earlier, thereby generating a wider network of kin and friends to share the emotional burdens of family life. Such family structures might also do a better job of socializing children. Because more adults would be involved in the socialization of a single child, the harmful effects of an incompetent or vicious parent could be neutralized more easily.

SUMMARY

The institution of the family is found in all societies, but in diverse forms. The two main types of family are the *extended family* and the *nuclear family*. The nuclear family consists of a married couple and their children. The extended family, on the other hand, usually includes several generations of parents, grandparents, and children and is usually found in agricultural societies. The demands of the modern industrial system place tremendous pressure on these large, cumbersome family units. As industrialization has transformed one country after another, the nuclear family has replaced the extended family.

The family provides for the reproduction, socialization, and protection of children to replace the members who are lost to society through death and disability. The family also regulates sexual behavior, provides for economic cooperation and emotional support, and engages in social control. The traditional extended family had the major responsibility for these activities. But in modern society the family's role is being supplemented and even replaced by specialized government agencies such as schools and juvenile courts.

Of all family problems, the rising divorce rate has clearly generated the most public concern. This trend has many causes. As the extended family has deteriorated, married couples have become freer to divorce. At the same time, the stigma against divorce has decreased. Because love and personal happiness are receiving increasing emphasis, there is greater willingness to end marriages that fail to achieve these goals. Both women and men are much more economically independent than in the past, and it is usually easier for them to live independently after a divorce. Many problems are associated with divorce, including personal stress, family instability, and increased difficulty in child rearing. But it is not at all clear that divorce is worse than the alternative of continuing an unhappy marriage.

Like divorce, illegitimacy has increased in recent years. There seems to be a growing reluctance on the part of young couples to marry just because of an unwanted pregnancy. The mother who keeps her illegitimate child has many of the problems experienced by other single-parent families. However, the mother of an illegitimate child, like the child itself, faces some special problems stemming from the stigma of illegitimacy.

Although there are no dependable statistical records, it appears that violence between husband and wife is a common way of settling disputes and leads to a substantial number of injuries and homicides every year. Another form of family violence, child abuse, is even more dangerous because the victims are unable to defend themselves. Studies indicate that child abuse is most likely to occur in large families with low incomes in which the natural father is not present. Many explanations of child abuse have been advanced, including emotional disturbances in the parents and the transmission of child abuse through learning.

Because the modern nuclear family often has little support from its kinship network, child rearing can be difficult. The single-parent family in particular is likely to have economic and behavioral problems because a single adult must play all the roles that are customarily divided between two people.

Another source of strain in the modern family is changing expectations about the behavior of husbands and wives. Because increasing numbers of women have gone to work outside the home, and because there are now a variety of alternatives to traditional sex roles, the expectations of the husband and wife may conflict, creating difficult problems of adjustment.

Many proposals have been made for resolving problems in the family. One approach would strengthen the existing nuclear-family system through education, marriage counseling, and a change in legal procedures that would make it easier to dissolve marriages that have failed. Sexual equality and greater openness to people and opportunities outside the marriage are also frequent suggestions. Many people recommend expansion of the kinship network and a return to something similar to an extended family. Group marriages and communes are among the most radical approaches. Less extreme is the recommendation that the members of nuclear families establish closer ties with relatives, thus creating a more helpful, integrated kinship network.

Sociologists of the functionalist school are convinced that problems of the family are symptoms of the social disorganization caused by rapid social change. Industrialization broke up the extended family but has not produced a strong family system to replace it. Conflict theorists, on the other hand, note the many conflicting values and beliefs about modern family life and point to them as a major source of problems. They also stress the notion that many problems, from divorce to wife beating, arise because modern society allows the powerful to make profits at the expense of the weak. Social psychologists are concerned about the ineffectiveness of the nuclear family as a socializing agency. They encourage the development of stable families that will provide continuity in children's lives and, at the same time, provide more security and emotional support for all family members.

KEY TERMS

commune	monogamy
endogamy	nuclear family
extended family	open marriage
group marriage	polygyny
illegitimacy rate	

Part II
Problems
of Inequality

6
The Poor

Who are the poor?
Are the poor to blame for their poverty?
Is the welfare system fair?
Can poverty be eliminated?

The modern industrial system has produced fantastic wealth. Middle-class Americans have luxuries that were undreamed of in past centuries, and an image of mass luxury and comfort is reflected daily in television dramas, movies, and books. But there is an underside to our industrial affluence—the millions of faceless people who do not share in the abundance. Poverty is a basic characteristic of our industrial society; it is the other face of affluence.

The poor in North America do not look like the starving millions in Far Eastern famine zones, but their misery is just as real. Poverty can be more difficult in a rich country than in a poor one. There is no shame in poverty in India because most people are poor; but the North American poor are constantly confronted by affluence that they do not share.

Although the poor are a minority in every sense of the word, they are a sizable one. When President Lyndon B. Johnson launched his War on Poverty, about 36 million people, or almost 19 percent of the U.S. population, were living below the "poverty line."[1] Twelve years later government estimates placed the number of poor people at 25 million, or about 12 percent of the population.[2] However, it has been noted that the amount of poverty in a nation depends on where the "poverty line" is set.[3] For instance, if we assume that any family that spends 70 percent of its income on basic needs (food, clothing, shelter) is living in poverty, there were 4.7 million poor people in Canada a decade ago. But if it is assumed that a family spending 60 percent of its income on the basics is living in poverty, there were 6.6 million, a staggering 41 percent of the population.[4]

Whatever measure we use, the problem clearly is an enormous one. Despite the widespread appearance of affluence, some of the worst slums in the industrial world may be found in North America. Poor nutrition, nagging hunger, shabby clothing, and a crowded room or two in a deteriorating old building is all that many families can hope for. North Americans' attitude toward the poor is remarkably callous, when compared with those of people in many European countries.

THE RICH AND THE POOR

Poverty and wealth are closely related. In North America and most of the rest of the world, the good things of life are not distributed evenly, and wealth is concentrated in the hands of a few individuals and families. Depriving some of the people creates abundance for others.

There are two ways of determining the extent of economic inequality: by measuring differences in income and by measuring differences in wealth. While these two yardsticks are related, there are some important differences between them. Income refers to the amount of money a person makes in a given year; wealth is a person's total assets—real estate and personal property, stocks, bonds, cash, and so forth. Much more is known about the distribution of income than about the distribution of wealth

Wealth and poverty are two sides of the same coin. The deprivations suffered by some people allow others to live in luxury.

because government officials collect and publish figures on income but seldom collect data on wealth.

The evidence clearly shows that the distribution of income in the United States is extremely unequal. (See Figure 6.1.) In 1976 the richest 20 percent of American families received 41 percent of all income while the poorest 20 percent received only 5.4 percent. The top 5 percent received 15.6 percent of the total income—three times as much as the poorest 20 percent of American families.[5] When these figures are compared with earlier surveys, it can be seen that the distribution of income has changed little in the past three decades.

Examining the distribution of wealth in the United States is more difficult because the government has not systematically collected data on this subject since 1962. There is no evidence, however, of any major changes since that time. Differences in the wealth of individual Americans, as revealed by the 1962 study, are much more striking than the differences in income. The richest 20 percent of the population controlled 76

FIGURE 6.1 DISTRIBUTION OF WEALTH AND INCOME	PERCENTAGE OF TOTAL WEALTH HELD BY EACH FIFTH	PERCENTAGE OF TOTAL INCOME RECEIVED BY EACH FIFTH	
FIFTHS OF POPULATION	1962	1960	1977
Lowest fifth	0.2	5.2	5.4
Second fifth	2.1	12.2	11.8
Middle fifth	0.2	17.8	17.6
Fourth fifth	15.5	23.9	24.1
Highest fifth	76.0	40.9	41.1
Highest 5%		15.5	15.6

Source: Board of Governers of the Federal Reserve System, "Survey of Financial Characteristics of Consumers 1962," as Reported in U.S. Department of Commerce, Social Indicators 1973 (Washington, D.C.: GPO, 1973), and Statistical Abstract of the United States, 1977 (Washington, D.C.: GPO, 1977), p. 443.

percent of the wealth while the poorest 20 percent controlled only two tenths of one percent of the wealth (0.2%).[6] The wealthiest 20 percent of the people in the United States had three times as much wealth as all the rest of the people combined. It is estimated that about one-fourth of the wealth in America is controlled by the richest 1 percent of the population.[7] Much of this wealth must be inherited rather than earned because wealth is distributed so unequally. Edward Kuh has concluded that 57 percent of the total wealth of those making over $100,000 a year in the United States is inherited.[8]

Differences in income and wealth among the rich, the poor, and the middle class have profound effects on life styles, attitudes toward others, and even attitudes toward oneself. The poor lack the freedom and autonomy so prized in our society. They are trapped by their surroundings, living in rundown, crime-ridden neighborhoods that they cannot afford to leave. They are constantly confronted with things they desire but have little chance to own. On the other hand, wealth provides power, freedom, and the ability to direct one's own fate. The wealthy live where they choose and do as they please, with few economic constraints. Because the poor lack education and money for travel, their horizons seldom extend beyond the confines of their neighborhood. In contrast, the world of the wealthy offers the best education, together with the opportunity to visit places that the poor haven't even heard of.

The children of the wealthy receive the best that society has to offer, as well as the assurance that they are valuable and important individuals. Because the children of the poor lack so many of the things everyone is "supposed" to have, it is much harder for them to develop the cool confidence of the rich. In our materialistic society people are judged as much by what they have as by who they are. The poor cannot help but feel inferior and inadequate in such a context.

While the contrast between the very rich and the very poor is most dramatic, the life style of the very wealthy is worlds apart from that of the vast majority of other people as well. Consider the differences between Clay Street, a blue-collar suburb of Washington, D.C., and Kykuit, one of the estates owned by the Rockefeller family:

> An older suburb of Washington, D.C., Clay Street in itself was not a run-down neighborhood. Brick garden apartments occupied one side of the street, duplexes and single-family frame houses with asbestos siding occupied the other. The houses were for the most part two-story structures with small front porches and tiny patches of grass out-front. About half were owner-occupied. Driveways separated each house from its neighbor. Built in the 1920s and 1930s, the houses were showing signs of age, though most were still in adequate condition.[9]

> The Rockefeller estate, Kykuit, [consists] of 4,180 acres at Pocantico Hills, New York, just east of Tarrytown in the fabled Sleepy Hollow country. Such land in the region sells at $5,000 to $10,000 per acre and higher. Until Winthrop left for Arkansas all the brothers had each a large house on this estate, where lived also Rockefellers I and II. The place has many scores of buildings for maintenance and the housing of a large staff, a $1 million playhouse (at cost many years ago) that holds bowling alleys, tennis courts, swimming pool and squash court.
>
> Kykuit is bisected by a public road that affords views of dense forests and open fenced fields on either side for a stretch of many miles. . . .
>
> The main house, Kykuit itself . . . is a fifty-room granite structure in modified Georgian design with spacious views of the surrounding country. . . .
>
> It has four stories with guest rooms on the third and fourth floors. . . . Various price tags have been put on all this by different commentators. . . . When Rockefeller I died, the *New York Times* (May 24, 1947) said the single granite house had cost $2 million to build, while the estate took $500,000 a year at depression prices to maintain. The entire affair required a staff then of 350.[10]

THE NATURE OF POVERTY

Even though everyone has a general idea of what poverty is, it is a difficult term to define precisely. Certainly, the poor lack some of the goods and services that are enjoyed by others. This may mean insufficient food, shelter, clothing, or entertainment, but how much is "insufficient"? Are people poor if they have no means of private transportation at all, no bicycle, no car, only one car? Everyone agrees that some people are poor, but it is extremely difficult to draw a precise line between those who are poor and those who are not.

Poverty may be defined in two ways: relative and absolute. The absolute approach divides the poor from the nonpoor by using some objective standard, such as the lack of money to purchase adequate food, shelter, and clothing. The U.S. government and most other official agencies use the absolute approach, defining poverty on the basis of total income. If the income of a family is below a certain amount (which varies depending on the cost of living), the family is classified as poor. On the other hand, the relative approach holds that people are poor if they have significantly less income and wealth than the average person in their society. For instance, John Kenneth Galbraith holds that "people are poverty stricken when their income, even if adequate for survival, falls markedly behind that of the community."[11]

But whether the absolute or the relative approach to poverty is used, the problem of where to fix the cutoff point between the poor and the non-poor remains. Exactly how much income can a person have and still be "markedly behind the community"? What quality of food, shelter, and clothing is "necessary," and how do you determine whether someone has it? Because these questions cannot be answered objectively, any definition of poverty is arbitrary. Implicit in every division of people into poor and nonpoor is some notion of how big the poverty problem is and who should be helped. As Mollie Orshansky of the Social Security Administration puts it, "There is no particular reason to count the poor unless you are going to do something about them."[12]

The Absolute Approach

Those who see poverty as an absolute lack of the necessities of life tend to use income as the basis for establishing a poverty line. It is assumed that a family needs a certain income in order to secure basic needs, and if its income is less than this amount, the family is poor. However, there has been a great deal of disagreement about exactly how much income a family really needs to be above the "poverty line."

The Economic Council of Canada measured poverty by the portion of income that is spent on food, clothing, and shelter. In the United States the President's Council of Economic Advisers held in 1963 that people living in families with two or more members whose total annual income was less than $3000, as well as single individuals living alone on an income less than $1500, were poor. A major problem with this standard was that it did not divide families into groups on the basis of size. Orshansky notes that this meant that a retired couple with an income of $2900 was considered poor while a family made up of a husband, a wife, and four children with an income of $3000 was not.[13]

To correct this error Orshansky developed a more flexible standard based on the cost of food, and this is now the base for government poverty figures. Concluding that the average poor family spends one-third of its income on food, she calculated the cost of a minimum diet for 124 different types of families and multiplied by three. This new measure yielded about the same number of people as the original $3000 standard, but the "mix" was different. More low-income families with children were counted as poor and fewer two-person retired families were included. Orshansky also developed a measure for the "near-poor" based on a slightly better diet, but it has been largely ignored by government agencies.[14]

When defined in absolute terms, poverty has declined in recent years. In the late 1950s there were about 39 million people below the poverty level. Favorable economic developments between 1962 and 1969 reduced the number of poor people to less than 25 million.[15] Since then the number of poor people has gone up in some years and down in others, generally holding steady at about 25 million. However, because the total population has increased, the percentage of poor people in the population dropped from 12.1 percent in 1969 to 11.9 percent in 1976.[16]

The Relative Approach

Despite widespread acceptance of the absolute approach, there are many experts who claim that the relative position of the poor compared to that of the wealthy is more significant. These authorities see poverty not only in terms of material goods but also in terms of the psychological effects of being worse off than the people around you. As Lee Rainwater has pointed out,

> What causes the various lower-class pathologies that disturb us — "apathy," "poor educational performance," "crime and delinquency," the various forms of striking out at those around you and those who are better off — is not the absolute deprivation of living below some minimum standard, but the relative deprivation of being so far removed from the average American standard that one cannot feel himself part of his society.[17]

In this view people come to need what their society tells them they should have. To the average American, who needs a great deal, the migrant farm workers on the bottom rung of the social ladder lack the essentials for comfortable living. Yet these beliefs obviously are not shared by the hundreds of thousands who enter the United States either legally or illegally to become migrant workers. In the social world of the Mexican villager, these jobs represent affluence, not poverty.

In order to define poverty in relative terms, the "poverty line" must be drawn by comparing the average income in a society with the income of its poorest citizens. Greater inequality in income distribution means greater poverty.

While poverty as measured in absolute terms has declined significantly in the past three decades, poverty measured in relative terms remains virtually unchanged. In 1947, the poorest 20 percent of all Americans received 5.1 percent of all income; in 1974, as already noted, the poorest 20 percent received 5.4 percent, an insignificant difference. It is possible for one measure to show poverty declining while the other shows it remaining the same because the two are concerned with different types of poverty — one economic, the other psychological. Because the past three decades have brought general economic growth and prosperity, in the 1970s rich and poor alike had more economic goods than they had in the 1940s and 1950s. But the *difference* between the rich and the poor has remained the same. In relative, psychological terms the poor have not improved their condition, although they have made some absolute economic gains.

WHO ARE THE POOR?

One of the major reasons for trying to define who is poor and who is not is to discover which segments of our society have the greatest poverty problems. Studies of the distribution of poverty show that many different factors are associated with the chances of being above or below the poverty line. Of particular importance are age, family structure, ethnic background, and area of residence.

Age

The young and the old are much more likely to be poor than people in their middle years. In fact, people under 14 and over 65 years of age account for more than half of the poor.[18] About 12 percent of the total population was below the poverty line in 1976, while 15 percent of all elderly people and almost 17 percent of all young people were poor.[19] The young are over-represented because large families are more likely to be poor and because the young have great difficulty finding jobs even if they are old enough to work. The elderly are poor for many of the same reasons—inability to hold a job or failure to find one if they are able to work.

The elderly poor are receiving increasing national attention. They have few resources, either economic or personal, and little chance of improving their lot. Few employers will hire the aged, and compulsory-retirement rules have forced old men and women who are still capable of productive work into idleness. Because the elderly are excluded from the labor market, they must subsist on savings and retirement benefits and on their social-security payments. In the past old people were supported by their children but today, with the passing of the extended family, few parents live with their children. Significantly, almost one-third of the elderly who live alone are poor, while less than one-tenth of those who live in families are poor.[20]

Family Structure

There has been a steady increase in what the Bureau of the Census terms "female-headed" families, that is, families with no man in the home. (The Census Bureau until recently assumed that the husband heads the family if he is present.) The percentage of female-headed families jumped from 11.5 percent in 1970 to 13.0 percent in 1974.[21]

Female-headed families are much more likely to be below the poverty line than those headed by males. In fact, almost half of all families below the poverty line are headed by women.[22] While there are many reasons why so many female-headed families are poor, the fact that mothers with dependent children find it difficult to hold a full-time job is of primary importance. Even if these mothers get jobs, sex discrimination often confines them to low-paying service, clerical, or sales positions. Welfare is often the only means of survival for these families.

Ethnic Minorities   Contrary to popular stereotypes, most poor people in the United States are white, not black. The latest census figures indicate that two-thirds of all poor people are white. However, the *percentage* of whites below the poverty line is considerably lower than the percentage of minorities below that line. About 9 percent of all whites are poor, compared to 31 percent of all blacks and over 50 percent of all American Indians.

In 1976 the average white family earned $15,540 and the average black family $9,240.[23] Moreover, unemployment is higher for most minorities. The unemployment rate for blacks is usually double the rate for whites, and the rate for American Indians is over 50 percent.[24] To make matters worse, discrimination in housing and various other services often means that minorities must spend more than whites for the same goods and services.

Place of Residence   When we think of the poor, most of us see crowded urban ghettos. But the percentage of rural people below the poverty line is actually greater than the percentage of urban people below that line, despite the fact that most poor people live in the large metropolitan centers. In 1975 over 16 percent of the people who lived on farms in the United States were poor, compared to 12 percent of the rest of the population.[25] Unemployment is high in rural areas, and wages are low. The mechanization of agriculture has left many unskilled rural people with no means of support. What work there is tends to be seasonal, and those who follow the harvest do not fare any better than those who try to hire out at home. Migratory workers make up a considerable portion of the rural poor, as do Native Americans who live on barren reservations where it is impossible for them to make a living.

The urban poor in rundown city slums remain the largest group in terms of numbers, and they share many of the problems of the rural poor. Although there are generally more economic opportunities in the cities, urban slum dwellers often are denied an equal chance to succeed. Lacking adequate transportation, the urban poor are unable to take advantage of opportunities that are available to those who live in more affluent parts of the city.

ATTITUDES TOWARD THE POOR   Rejection of the old European class system plus the availability of a vast new land to conquer helped create a tremendous faith in the value of hard work and competition among North Americans. To this way of thinking, each individual is held responsible for his or her own economic destiny. Even in a period of economic depression and high unemployment, it is believed, any person who puts out enough effort in the right direction can be successful. More generally, it is held that "there is always room at the top" for capable and hardworking people, no matter how humble their origins.

NINETEENTH CENTURY SOCIAL PROBLEMS

Within 5 miles of Milton Junction and in a thickly settled part of Rock County, Mrs. Ira Ames starved and froze to death. The case was reported to the authorities at Janesville and it was found that the father had spent most of his time fishing while his wife and 7 children were in a rickety shanty without fuel or food. The youngest child died a week ago and was buried under the snow by the father in a soap box.
March 16, 1893

Despite its attractiveness, this belief in absolute individual responsibility has a negative side. If the rich are personally responsible for their success, it follows that the poor are to blame for their failure. "Poor folks have poor ways," the old saying goes. Joe Feagin has summarized the principal points in this "ideology of individualism" as follows:

1. Each individual should work hard and strive to succeed in competition with others.
2. Those who work hard should be rewarded with success (seen as wealth, property, prestige, and power).
3. Because of widespread and equal opportunity, those who work hard will in fact be rewarded with success.
4. Economic failure is an individual's own fault and reveals lack of effort and other character defects.[26]

A recent nationwide survey showed that this ideology is still a potent force in American life. When asked about the causes of poverty, the people surveyed usually responded with individualistic explanations that blame the poor themselves, rather than with structural explanations that hold society responsible or with fatalistic explanations that blame such things as bad luck or illness. Fifty-eight percent of the respondents said that lack of thrift and proper money management are significant causes of poverty, and 55 percent said that lack of effort by the poor is a very important cause of poverty.[27]

Because the poor are blamed for their condition, a stigma is attached to poverty, and particularly to those who receive welfare or some other form of government assistance. These prejudices against the poor in general, and against those on the "government dole" in particular, have made it difficult to establish effective programs to help the poor.

THE WELFARE
SYSTEM

The ideology of individualism has had an enormous impact on the response to poverty in both the United States and Canada. Even when individuals are recognized as "legitimately poor," those receiving government assistance continue to be heavily stigmatized. Welfare programs tend to be designed in such a way that obtaining benefits is difficult and

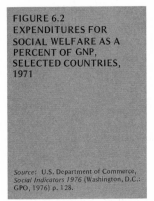

FIGURE 6.2
EXPENDITURES FOR
SOCIAL WELFARE AS A
PERCENT OF GNP,
SELECTED COUNTRIES,
1971

Source: U.S. Department of Commerce,
Social Indicators 1976 (Washington, D.C.:
GPO, 1976) p. 128.

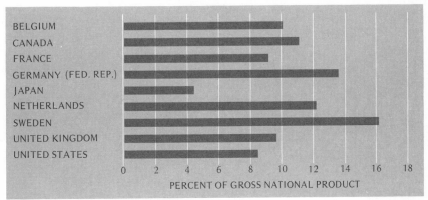

degrading, thus keeping welfare costs down and the poor "in their place."
Piven and Cloward argue that the growth of the modern welfare system
resulted more from an attempt to silence the political discontent of the
poor than from a desire to improve their living conditions.[28] (See Figure
6.2.)

History
In traditional societies many people lived close to the subsistence level,
but poverty did not carry a strong stigma. The extended family had the
primary responsibility for the welfare of its members. However, the industrial revolution fostered the growth of small nuclear families, which
often are too weak and isolated to care for their members in times of
distress. At the same time, industrialization took more and more people
from the land, where most could scratch out enough food to avoid starvation. As a result the government was slowly required to assume an increasing share of the responsibility for the poor.

Modern welfare systems can be traced to sixteenth-century England,
where the effects of the industrial revolution first appeared as thousands
of peasant farmers left the land and migrated to the towns in search of
work and freedom. Political power shifted from the landed aristocracy to
manufacturers and businesspeople. These new elites responded to the
mass migration in two contradictory ways. First, they enacted vagrancy
laws that punished "sturdy beggars" (people who were able but seemingly
unwilling to work). Second, they began giving government assistance to
the "deserving poor." England's sixteenth-century Poor Laws placed the
responsibility for the care of the poor with local officials, requiring them to
establish poorhouses for the sick, disabled, and aged and work programs
for the able-bodied poor and their children.[29]

The North American colonies copied the English Poor Laws, and as in
England, public welfare was made a local responsibility. Outsiders were
not eligible for aid and were forced to leave town if they showed signs of
becoming destitute. Mayors opened fairs and other public meetings by

asking "all idle and evilly disposed persons" to depart. The destitute were publicly stigmatized. In Pennsylvania, for instance, poor people had to wear the letter P on one of their sleeves. Those who were considered idlers or vagrants were punished. Massachusetts, Rhode Island, and Connecticut all had laws calling for the whipping or imprisonment of the able-bodied unemployed.[30]

Urbanization, industrialization, and the steady flow of immigrants produced a growing poverty problem in North America during the eighteenth and nineteenth centuries. But attitudes toward the poor seemed to grow even more hostile. As in England, workhouses were established for the poor. In these institutions employment was furnished for those who were able to work and industrial training was provided for the young. The theory was that workhouses would cure the character defects that the poor were presumed to have, converting them to a life of Christian hard work and sober living. Poorhouses continued to shelter the aged and disabled, and houses of correction were established to compel vagrants and other sturdy beggars to work. Private welfare organizations also grew rapidly.

Few changes were made in this welfare system until the Great Depression of the 1930s, when unemployment rose dramatically and armies of the newly impoverished demanded assistance. As Piven and Cloward have reported, "Groups of men out of work congregated at local relief agencies, cornered and harassed administrators, and took over offices until their demands were met."[31] Despite such determined protests, reforms were made grudgingly. Poor relief was still largely a local matter, but cities and counties proved unable to shoulder the financial burden. The federal government began to give small direct-relief payments to the unemployed, but it soon shifted to work relief programs, which were more in tune with the ideology of individualism. With the coming of President Franklin D. Roosevelt's New Deal, a host of new government agencies were created to make work for unemployed Americans. But public opposition to these and other welfare programs remained strong through the Depression, and the only major New Deal program to survive was Old Age and Survivor's Insurance (social security), which requires workers and their employers to set aside money for the workers' old age and for surviving dependents at the time of the insured person's death.

The 1950s brought only modest increases in welfare support for the poor, but a "welfare explosion" occurred in the 1960s. From December 1960 to February 1969, Aid to Families with Dependent Children (AFDC) increased by 107 percent.[32] Daniel Moynihan laid the blame for this increase on the deteriorating black family and on the sharp rise in female-headed families.[33] Piven and Cloward disagreed, maintaining that family deterioration made only a minor contribution to the growing welfare rolls and that the real cause was increased activism among the poor, who began to demand greater social support.

The 1960s also saw the launching of President Johnson's famous War on Poverty. Most of the programs in this "war" were based on the assumption that people are poor because they lack education and job skills, and not on the more realistic assumption that poverty is a defect in the system for producing and distributing wealth. Such programs as the Job Corps, the Neighborhood Youth Corps, VISTA, Head Start, and family planning clinics were launched to help the poor improve their lot. Most of these programs missed their mark, partly because they were poorly organized and partly because they were aimed primarily at young urban males and neglected females, the rural poor, and the elderly.[34]

Structure   America's current welfare system is a confusing hodgepodge of overlapping programs and agencies. Funding comes from various mixtures of federal, state, and local governments, depending on the program. Benefits vary widely from one state to another and even from one city to the next. The two major programs making direct cash payments to the poor are AFDC and Supplemental Security Income (SSI). SSI was launched in 1974 to replace Aid to the Blind, Aid to the Permanently and Totally Disabled, and Old Age Assistance. The federal government also finances and runs a variety of noncash programs that provide goods or services. For instance, food is supplied through food stamps and surplus commodities, health care through medicaid, and housing through rent subsidies. States, counties, and cities supplement these federal programs, most often with short-term "emergency" payments for people who are waiting for their applications to be processed by federal programs.

Generally speaking, welfare payments cease as soon as recipients become self-supporting. For this reason it has been charged that these programs discourage the poor from working. The rules of AFDC — the major form of direct welfare — recently were revised in the hope that poor people would get jobs if they were allowed to keep some portion of their welfare payments. Lampman has shown, however, that the reduced benefits many poor workers receive from programs such as food stamps, medicaid, and rent subsidies are greater than the wages they earn.[35] Thus, many low-income wage earners are still penalized for working.

Canada has taken a somewhat different approach to public assistance. All Canadians receive government-financed health care, a small family allowance for each child, and an old-age pension at 65. This approach to welfare eliminates the costly bureaucratic red tape necessary to determine who is eligible for welfare payments. And because people are not excluded from these programs on the ground that they earn too much money, work is encouraged rather than discouraged. The Canadian Pension Plan is an important supplement to the Old Age Security Pension, operating like the American social-security system. Citizens are required to contribute a certain percentage of their income and are paid retirement benefits based on their previous earnings. The Canadian Assistance Plan provides 50 percent federal funding for payments to the needy, blind, and disabled, among others. However, Canadian welfare programs often suffer from the same lack of coordination among federal, provincial, and municipal governments that plagues American programs.

Who Receives Welfare?

Most Americans have a distorted picture of the typical welfare recipient. They believe the welfare rolls are full of able-bodied loafers and mothers who have children just to get a government handout, and that people stay on welfare for their entire lives without ever working. These beliefs are false, as are many other common ideas about welfare recipients.

Roughly 15.5 million Americans receive some type of direct welfare assistance; about two-thirds of this number receive AFDC. A comparison of these figures with the total number of people who live below the official poverty line shows that only two-thirds of the poor receive welfare. (These figures do not, however, include people receiving food stamps.)[36]

Contrary to popular belief, less than 1 percent of welfare recipients are able-bodied males; most are over 65 or under 18, and many are blind or disabled. The only substantial group of able-bodied adults on welfare are mothers, usually without husbands, who cannot support their children.

Welfare recipients by no means stay "on the dole" for long periods. About half of the families receiving assistance have been on welfare less than 20 months, and about two-thirds have received assistance for less than three years.[37]

AFDC is probably the most controversial welfare program in the United States. Perhaps this is because it was created with the intention of assisting children whose fathers had died or been disabled, though today only a small percentage of AFDC recipients fit this description. Two-thirds of all the children in families receiving AFDC payments in 1973 lived in female-headed (fatherless) families. Forty-three percent of the mothers had never been married, 18 percent were divorced, and 28 percent were separated. (See Figure 6.3.) These statistics have caused a reaction against AFDC recipients among middle-class Americans, who still place a strong value on the two-parent nuclear family and whose image of a "dependent child" is that of an orphan. Another reason for the reaction against AFDC may be the ethnic composition of the recipients. Blacks comprise 12 percent of the American population, 31 percent of the poor, and about 46 percent of the families receiving AFDC.[38]

Welfare for the Rich

Although welfare programs designed to help the poor are under almost constant public attack, similar programs for the wealthy are largely ignored. These government programs are not called welfare and do not involve direct cash payments. But the effect is the same—to increase the incomes of people whom the government wants to help. Turner and Starnes have called this structure the "wealthfare system."[39] Whatever their

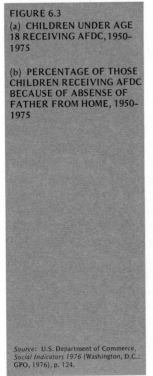

FIGURE 6.3
(a) CHILDREN UNDER AGE
18 RECEIVING AFDC, 1950–
1975

(b) PERCENTAGE OF THOSE
CHILDREN RECEIVING AFDC
BECAUSE OF ABSENSE OF
FATHER FROM HOME, 1950–
1975

Source: U.S. Department of Commerce,
Social Indicators 1976 (Washington, D.C.:
GPO, 1976), p. 124.

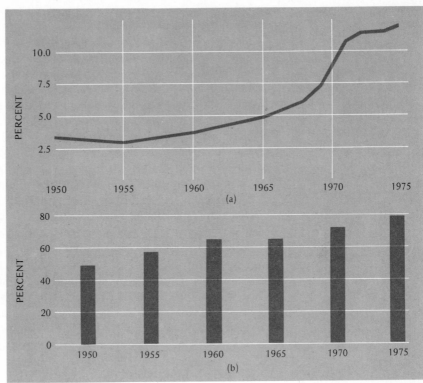

name, government subsidies for the wealthy can be divided into two categories: (1) programs designed to support business and (2) special tax breaks.

Governments in all capitalist countries try to keep their national economies prosperous by assisting key industries. Few people object to such assistance, but the techniques used to achieve this goal tend to help the rich much more than the poor. Government price supports for agricultural products are a good example. The U.S. government has a variety of programs designed to keep the price of farm products high. Farmers are paid not to grow crops, and the government buys huge quantities of grain and livestock if the market price falls below a fixed level. The popular image is that of poor farmers who will go broke if, for example, they must sell their potato crop for less than they paid for the seed, as happened during the Great Depression. But instead of payments to such unfortunate people, most support now goes to agricultural corporations and wealthy owners of huge farms, many of whom grow cotton or tobacco rather than food. Many people believe that welfare payments to families with dependent children are bad because they make the recipients lazy and slovenly. But some of the same people argue that government assistance to the wealthy is good for everyone. For instance, a senator from Mississippi who was a strong opponent of welfare for the poor accepted as much as $150,000 a year in government payments for not growing crops on his land.[40]

The most obvious examples of welfare for the rich can be found in taxation policies and practices. The American income tax system is designed to be graduated or "progressive," meaning that people with higher incomes pay a higher percentage of their income in taxes than people with lower incomes. Nevertheless, the tax laws are full of "loopholes" that permit the wealthy to avoid paying their full share of taxes. Loopholes give tax breaks to the rich, and thus become devices for making welfare payments to those who qualify under the rules. In 1974, 244 Americans with incomes over $200,000 a year paid no income taxes.[41] But it is common knowledge that these people represent only the tip of the iceberg. Many others use tax loopholes merely to reduce their taxes, not to avoid them entirely.

Four major loopholes in the American tax laws benefit the well-to-do: Exclusions allow tax payers to ignore, for tax purposes, the income they receive from some sources, such as municipal bonds. Deductions allow taxpayers to count three-martini lunches and trips to Hawaii as business expenses. Capital gains permits a much lower tax rate on money made from investments than on money received as wages. Tax shelters allow the postponement (sometimes indefinitely) of taxes on income received from certain types of investments.

Although these benefits are permitted on the ground that they stimulate the economy and thus help everyone, the effect is actually to subsidize the wealthy. A Brookings Institution study concluded that $92 million a year in tax breaks goes to the poorest 6 million families in the United States, while 24 times this amount—$2.2 billion—goes to the 3000 families with incomes of more than $1 million a year.[42]

EXPLANATIONS OF POVERTY

The economic base of some societies is so fragile that hunger is a daily experience for most people. Such extreme scarcity of food, clothing, and shelter clearly does not characterize modern industrial societies or even most traditional ones. The poverty problem in these societies is one of distributing wealth rather than one of producing it. From a global viewpoint the fact that some modern nations are poor while others are rich can also be seen as a problem in the distribution of wealth. There are many explanations of economic inequality, but most fall into three overlapping categories—those explanations based on analysis of economic structures, those based on analysis of the culture of the poor, and those based on analysis of political relationships among power groups.

The United States and Canada have persistently high rates of unemployment. Although the unemployment insurance being distributed in this picture provides some temporary relief, it is not a long-term solution.

Economic Explanations

Much of the poverty problem can be traced directly to simple economic causes—low wages and too few jobs. In technological societies like Canada and the United States, people without education and skills find it hard to get any kind of employment, and those who find work are likely to be employed in low-paying jobs. As a result, many of these working people are poor. In 1974, more than half of the poor families in the United States were headed by a worker, and almost 20 percent of the heads of poor families worked full time for the entire year.[43] Their wages simply were not high enough to keep them above the poverty line.

Permanent unemployment is a characteristic of some poor people, and even temporary unemployment may produce poverty. The unemployment rate is consistently higher in the United States than in European countries such as West Germany, France, and the Netherlands.[44] Even more disturbing is the fact that the unemployment rate has soared in recent years. In the late 1960s the rate ranged from 3.5 to 3.8 percent, but in May of 1975 it was over 9 percent. Although the rate has declined since then, it has remained at much higher levels than in the preceding decade. Bad as these official figures are, the reality may be even worse. Because of the way the rates are calculated, many of the poorest of the unemployed are not counted. Those who want jobs but have lost hope and have given up looking are not considered unemployed. Likewise, those who want full-time jobs but are able to find only part-time work are not included in unemployment figures.

Unskilled labor and poverty go together. Unskilled laborers have been particularly hard hit by automation because they are unable to operate the machines that have taken over their jobs. While it is true that automation has not eliminated some lower-level service jobs, such as those of janitors, waitresses, and domestics, these jobs pay poorly and offer few fringe benefits or chances for advancement.

Mass unemployment is common in many areas, for example, the Appalachian coal region of Kentucky and West Virginia. Early in this century thousands of workers left their homes and farms to take jobs in the Appalachian coal mines. Soon the coal industry dominated the area and it became almost impossible to find a job that was not dependent on coal mining. The mines, however, were owned and controlled by outside corporations. After World War II the mines were automated, the work force dropped from a high of 700,000 to about 140,000, and there were no new jobs for the workers who became unemployed. A similar problem can be found in many central cities. The unemployment rate in ghetto areas is about 60 percent higher than in the country as a whole.[45]

To add to the other problems, the poor often get less for their hard-earned dollars than other consumers do. Slum dwellers, for example, may pay more money to rent a rundown apartment than people living in a small town pay to rent a house with a garden. More generally, because the poor are not mobile it is difficult for them to shop around for sales and special values. They are obliged to patronize local merchants, who usually charge higher prices than those in affluent areas. When unexpected expenses occur the poor must borrow money, but because they are not considered good credit risks, bank loans at standard interest rates may be impossible for them to get. Instead, they must go to loan companies, which charge much higher interest rates, or to loan sharks, who charge exorbitant illegal rates. Many stores in slum areas actively solicit sales on credit because the interest charges are more profitable than the sale itself. If the customer cannot meet the installment payments, the merchandise is repossessed and sold to another poor customer.[46]

Cultural Explanations

There are distinct cultural differences between the social classes in modern societies. Some social scientists use these differences to explain poverty. The foremost advocate of this position is Oscar Lewis, who argues that there is a distinct "culture of poverty" among the poor.[47] Lewis does not ignore the economic basis of poverty; his thesis is simply that a separate subculture has developed among the poor as a reaction to economic deprivation and exclusion from the mainstream of society. Once a culture of poverty has taken hold, it is passed down from generation to generation. Children who grow up in poverty acquire values and attitudes that make it very difficult for them to live any other way.

In the culture of poverty the nuclear family is female centered, with the mother performing the basic tasks that keep the family going. The father, if he is present, makes only a slight contribution. Children have sexual relations and marry at an early age. The family unit is weak and unstable,

and there is little community organization beyond the family. Psychologically, those who live in the culture of poverty have weak ego structures, confused sexual identification, and lack self-control.

Lewis studied a number of societies and concluded that the culture of poverty is international. It develops in societies with capitalist economies, persistently high unemployment rates, low wages, and an emphasis on accumulation of wealth and property. However, Lewis found a number of societies that have a considerable amount of poverty but no *culture* of poverty. India and Cuba, for example, have no culture of poverty because the poor are not degraded or isolated. Lewis estimated that in the United States, because of the influence of the mass media and the low level of literacy, only 20 percent of the poor live in a culture of poverty.[48.]

Most social scientists agree that poor people have some of the characteristics described by Lewis, but they are not so sure that their life style is passed from one generation to the next. Rather, it is argued by "situationalists" that each generation of the poor exhibits the same life style because each generation experiences the same conditions—poor housing, crowding, deprivation, and isolation. Charles A. Valentine, for example, argues that the conditions Lewis describes are imposed on the poor from the outside rather than being generated by a "culture of poverty."[49]

Lee Rainwater has pointed out that the debate between the supporters and opponents of the culture-of-poverty thesis is much more than an academic issue.[50] If the situationalists are right, the poor share the same values as the middle class and government assistance need only provide some means of escaping poverty, such as job training and education. However, if a culture of poverty is passed on to children as a way of life, the government must not only provide such economic opportunities but also try to prevent transmission of the traditions of poverty from one generation to the next.

Political Explanations

Poverty is as much a political problem as a problem of economics and culture. This is evident from the fact that industrialized nations that are less wealthy than the United States have been more successful in reducing the gap between the haves and the have-nots. Massive inequality persists in the United States because most Americans are not concerned about the problems of the poor and those who do care are not politically organized. Politicians win votes by promising to eliminate inflation and high taxes, but not many votes are won by promising to eliminate poverty. The ideology of individualism has convinced most Americans that the world is full of opportunities and that the poor deserve to be poor because they are too lazy or incompetent to seize those opportunities. As long as the poor are held responsible for their poverty, political action to change the conditions that cause poverty is unlikely.

Poverty, Herbert Gans has pointed out, is valuable to the wealthy, and many powerful people do not want it eliminated.[51] First, it ensures that society's dirty work gets done, for without poverty few people would be willing to do the low-paying, dirty, dangerous jobs. Second, the low wages the poor receive for their work subsidize the wealthy by keeping the prices of goods and services low. Third, poverty creates jobs for the many people who service the poor (such as welfare workers) or try to control them (such as police officers and prison guards). Fourth, the poor provide merchants with last-ditch profits by buying goods that otherwise would be thrown away—day-old bread, tainted meat, out-of-style clothing, used furniture, and unsafe automobiles. Fifth, the poor guarantee the status of the people above them in the social hierarchy. The poor provide a group of people whom "respectable" people can brand as deviants—examples of what will happen to those who break social rules. Thus, the contribution of poverty to the comfort of the middle and upper classes creates powerful opposition to any program that is likely to reduce it significantly.

RESPONDING TO PROBLEMS OF POVERTY

No one knows whether a classless society in which all people are equal economically can be established in the modern world. Certainly, no such society exists today. What is at issue is whether poverty in an absolute sense can be eliminated, even if some people remain richer than others. Several societies have made great progress toward eliminating the hardships of those at the bottom. For instance, while one of every ten Americans cannot afford a good diet, lives in substandard housing, and is denied decent medical care, almost no Norwegians suffer such a fate. Norway, with a lower per capita income than the United States, spends a much higher percentage of its wealth on education and social-welfare programs. Infant mortality is a full 50 percent lower there than in the United States, and Norway's cities are essentially slum free.[52] Thus, while total equality may not be possible, the degree of inequality can be reduced by government policies and programs.

Tax Reform

The simplest and most effective way of bringing about a more equal distribution of wealth is through the tax system. In theory, federal and state income taxes are sharply progressive—the higher the income, the greater the portion paid in taxes. In practice, as we have seen, tax loopholes give the rich special breaks, and in the end the income tax is only mildly progressive. Many other taxes, including sales taxes, fall most heavily on the poor. When the total tax burden is added up, it is doubtful that the portion of poor people's incomes that goes to taxes is much lower than the portion of rich people's incomes paid in taxes.[53] For years federal and state officials have proposed tax reforms to close the loopholes, but such reforms manage to get transformed into laws that impose new taxes with the same old loopholes for the well-to-do. The creation of a genuinely progressive tax system that was fairly enforced would be a giant step toward economic equality.

Reducing Unemployment

Reducing unemployment is a continuing concern of governments around the world. Despite repeated efforts, most programs to reduce unemployment have met with little long-term success. Providing employment for all who are willing and able to work is not as simple as it may seem. It appears reasonable to assume that if the government takes action to stimulate the economy business will boom and more jobs will open up. However, as noted in Chapter 2, such indirect programs have harmful effects on the poor because they create inflation.

Training, education, and "rehabilitation" of unemployed people are other approaches that have been applied in the effort to reduce the unemployment rate. Indeed, teaching job skills to the "hard-core" unemployed was the major thrust of the War on Poverty. There is considerable disagreement over whether this program was successful. Joan Huber probably came closest to the truth when she observed that the War on Poverty was neither won nor lost: "It just drifted off the political horizon while almost everyone was looking the other way."[54] Training and education programs alone, even if they are efficiently organized, cannot be expected to reduce poverty; something must also be done to increase the number of jobs into which newly trained people can move.

Many governments have attacked unemployment by creating new government jobs. The New Deal took this approach during the Great Depression of the 1930s, and it continues to be used on a reduced scale. It is often suggested that government work programs should be greatly expanded to permit the government to give a job to anyone who is unable to find one in the private sector. Making government an "employer of last resort" could virtually end unemployment, but such a program would be extremely expensive, and this is an expense that most taxpayers have so far been unwilling to bear.

Extending Public Assistance

America's welfare system is a bureaucratic mess. Programs are administered by a patchwork of federal, state, and local agencies. A tremendous amount of time and money that might be used to help poor people is spent on determining who is eligible for assistance. Such administrative waste would be drastically reduced if certain welfare services were provided to all citizens, not just to those who can demonstrate special needs. As mentioned earlier, Canada has taken this approach, providing all citizens with medical care, a small retirement pension, and a family allowance for each dependent child. Many European countries have similar programs. The poor are not discouraged from working by the threat of a reduction in their welfare benefits when they start to earn some money. Welfare fraud and the time and money spent on detecting and apprehending chiselers are greatly reduced.

Opposition to welfare for all is rooted in the ideology of individualism and the belief that people should "stand on their own two feet" and compete with each other without government interference. In the end, it is argued, citizens of socialistic countries lose the incentive to work, and national productivity goes down.

A Guaranteed Annual Income

Absolute poverty could be reduced and the complex maze of welfare programs simplified if the federal government would guarantee everyone a minimum income. Many income guarantee plans have been proposed as solutions to the problem of poverty in the United States, but none has been put into practice. A central feature of these proposals is a "negative income tax." This device was first developed by conservative economist Milton Friedman and incorporated into President Nixon's unsuccessful proposal for a Family Assistance Plan. The basic idea is simple: Families earning less than a certain amount (the poverty line) would receive a government grant called a negative tax. The grant would bring the family's income up to the minimum level. Families with incomes above the poverty line would pay "positive taxes," just as they do now. Most similar proposals provide some incentive to ensure that poor families with working members have more money than the nonworking poor.

A guaranteed minimum annual income for all, properly administered and based on the negative tax idea, could eliminate the worst problems of poverty in the United States. It would also eliminate many of the inefficient programs now in operation. The poor would be helped equally whether they live in Alabama, Missouri, or Wyoming. A gradual reduction in government payments as other family income rises would provide an incentive for working even if the job did not pay well.

These claims are not just wishful thinking. They are among the conclusions of New Jersey's Graduated Work Incentive Experiment, which tested the effectiveness of the negative income tax proposal. The experiment showed that the guaranteed annual income program costs less to administer than more fragmented welfare programs and that more of those receiving negative tax payments go to work than is the case with other welfare programs. The only negative finding was that a guaranteed annual income did not improve family stability as much as the researchers had predicted it would.[55]

Organizing the Poor

Tax reform, reducing unemployment, extending public assistance, and guaranteeing a certain minimum income — all have very high price tags. Americans give much lip service to the ideal of equality, but they appear unwilling to put the ideal into practice with financial support. However, in the 1960s the poor began to realize that they could influence legislation and government policies by organizing and working together.

The National Welfare Rights Organization (NWRO), established in the 1960s, has concentrated on improving administrative practices in the American welfare system. Its lawsuits have directly attacked restrictive eligibility requirements and illegal practices in various welfare agencies. The problem is that Congress has a tendency to set up sweeping programs and then underfund them so that not all eligible individuals can be served. As the executive branch of government tries to make ends meet, three bad administrative practices develop. First, state and local welfare agencies fail to tell poor people about the benefits for which they are eligible. Second, the administrators discourage applicants by treating the poor like loafers and cheats rather than accepting them as honest citizens entitled to their welfare benefits. Third, the administrators illegally deny benefits to some applicants.

NWRO has attacked all three practices. It has informed the poor of their rights and helped them present their claims. By winning a case before the Supreme Court, it put an end to the practice of arbitrarily inspecting the homes of welfare recipients in search of violations of eligibility rules. The Court's decision ended such degrading practices as visiting a welfare mother in the middle of the night to find out whether she is living with a man. NWRO also serves as a watchdog for Congress and for

In the 1960s poor people began to realize that they could improve their economic conditions by organizing themselves and working together to bring changes in government policies. But today greater political efforts will be needed to get effective antipoverty programs passed.

the poor, directing public and judicial attention to illegal practices in welfare agencies.

The United Farm Workers is another organization that has been successful in helping the poor. Under the leadership of César Chávez this labor union has helped to improve the lot of migrant workers despite determined opposition.

Not all of the organizations established to help the poor have been successful. For example, the Poor People's Campaign, an offshoot of Martin Luther King's Southern Christian Leadership Conference, seems to have disappeared without a trace. It appears that the Campaign was too general, attacking too wide a range of problems at one time rather than concentrating on a few key issues.

SOCIOLOGICAL PERSPECTIVES on Problems of the Poor

Poverty has not always been seen as a social problem. Although concern for poor people has a long history, until quite recently poverty was considered the fault of the poor themselves, a lowly status deserved by the lazy and incompetent. But in the past fifty years poverty has increasingly been seen as an institutional problem rather than a personal one. The Great Depression of the 1930s, tragic though it was, made a significant contribution to social science. It helped people see that the conditions of poverty are determined by economic, political, and social processes that are beyond the control of individual citizens. Most social scientists now view poverty as a social problem rather than a collection of personal problems, but they differ among themselves about the causes and solutions to this problem.

The Functionalist Perspective

Functionalists consider the extremes of poverty and wealth common to so many nations to be a result of malfunctions in the economy. In many parts of the world, rapid industrialization has disrupted the economic system, leaving it disorganized and unable to perform many of its basic functions. At first, people who lack skills are forced into menial work at low wages and then, with the coming of automation, find that they are not needed at all. Products produced by industry become outdated (horse carriages, steam engines, milk bottles), and unless rapid adjustments are made, workers lose their jobs. Moreover, training centers and apprenticeship programs may continue to produce graduates whose skills are no longer in demand. Discrimination, whether it is based on sex, age, or ethnic status, wastes the talents of many capable people, and society is the loser.

Functionalists also point out that the welfare system intended to solve the problem of poverty is just as disorganized as the economy. Administrators often show more concern for their own well-being than for that of their clients. Too often the poor go hungry because bureaucrats are afraid to help a deserving family that is technically ineligible for assistance. Legislative bodies establish programs without enough funds for efficient operations. Inadequate communications systems fail to inform the poor about benefits to which they are entitled. Job training and educational programs are not coordinated with the needs of agriculture, commerce, and industry.

The best way to deal with poverty, according to the functionalist perspective, is to reorganize the economic system so that it operates more efficiently. The poor who have been cast out and neglected must be reintegrated into the mainstream of economic life. This so-called "underclass" must be provided with training and jobs so they can resume their role as constructive citizens. But they must also be given a new sense of hope based on knowledge that the rest of society cares about them and is willing to help them overcome their problems. Functionalists also recommend a more stable economic system that will not produce new poor people to replace those who have escaped from poverty.

Generally speaking, functionalists are more concerned about absolute poverty than about relative poverty. They doubt that relative poverty (economic inequality) can or should be eliminated. Davis and Moore, for example, argued long ago that economic inequality is functional (i.e., good for society).[56] Their main point is that desire for more money motivates people to work hard to meet the standards of excellence that are required in many important jobs. Without inequality of reward, the most capable people would not be motivated to train for or perform the demanding jobs that are essential to the economic system. It should not be concluded, however, that functionalists are convinced that the social system should remain unchanged or that the amount of economic inequality should not be reduced. The functionalist conclusion is simply that *some* inequality is necessary for the maintenance of society as we know it.

The Conflict Perspective

Conflict theorists start with the assumption that because there is such enormous wealth in industrialized nations, no one in such societies need be poor. Poverty is present because the middle and upper classes want it to be present. Conflict theorists argue that the working poor are exploited—they are paid low wages so that their employers can make fat profits and live more affluent lives. Conflict theorists also note that wealthy people are more likely than the poor to attribute unemployment and poverty to a lack of effort rather than to social injustice or other circumstances beyond the control of the individual. This application of the ideology of individualism enables the wealthy to be charitable to the poor, giving some assistance freely while ignoring the economic and political foundations of poverty. Charity, including government doles, blunts political protests and social unrest that might threaten the status quo.

Poverty is rooted in value conflicts as well as class conflicts. As already noted, the ideology of individualism that blames poor people for their poverty conflicts with the ideology of cooperation, mutual concern, and equality that demands social concern for the problems of the poor. Further, there seem to be differences between the value systems of the poor and the middle class and even between the values of the poor and the working class. Many poor people have adjusted their values to fit the reality of their poverty by downplaying the importance of competing and achieving in the economic marketplace, and as a result they have reduced their chances of escaping from poverty.

Conflict theorists view these adjustments to poverty as a set of chains that must be broken. They believe the poor should become politically aware and active, organizing themselves to reduce inequality through government action. In other words, political action is recommended as a solution to inequality and, thus, to the poverty problem. Most conflict theorists doubt that economic inequality can be significantly reduced without a concerted effort by poor people that gains at least some support from concerned members of the upper classes.

The Social-Psychological Perspective

Social psychologists study the effects of attitudes and beliefs on behavior, pointing out that poor people learn to behave like poor people. The values of those who live in a culture of poverty are passed on to their children, thus directing them into lives of poverty. Stated differently, socialization practices among the poor develop attitudes and behavior patterns that make upward social mobility difficult. For example, the children of the poor learn to demand immediate gratification. Unlike middle-class achievers, they are not inclined to defer small immediate rewards so that long-run goals, such as a college education, can be reached.

Interactionists emphasize the fact that the main reference group for poor people is their poor neighbors. In many parts of the world, including some places in North America, a successful person is one who knows where the next meal is coming from, and a "big success" may be the assistant manager of a shoe store. People with such attitudes become trapped in their own poverty. More generally, interactionists point to cultural differences in the ways poor people define their world, and they note that even when the real world changes, these differences in definitions function to keep the poor at the bottom of the social ladder.

Social psychologists also study the psychological effects of being poor in a wealthy society. When the poor compare themselves with more fortunate people, many come to believe they are failures. Some attribute their failure to personal shortcomings rather than to social forces that are beyond their control. The outcome may be a variety of personal problems ranging from drug addiction and mental disorders to delinquency and crime.[57]

The social-psychological perspective implies that poverty traps poor people psychologically as well as economically and socially. The trap can be sprung by eliminating absolute poverty (the lack of adequate food, shelter, and clothing) and by opening up more opportunities for the children of the poor, thus reducing overall inequality. Social psychologists also agree that the poor must be encouraged to redefine their social environment. Even if avenues for upward mobility are created, little change will occur as long as the poor are convinced that they are doomed to live in poverty.

SUMMARY   Whether economic inequality is measured by income distribution or by distribution of wealth, there are wide gaps between the rich, the middle class, and the poor. Significant differences also exist in the cultural perspectives and life styles of these different groups. In cities the poor are trapped in rundown, crime-ridden neighborhoods, while the affluent have a multitude of opportunities among which to choose. Psychologically, the poor have to cope with feelings of inadequacy and inferiority because they lack the money and goods that everyone is expected to have.

There are two accepted ways of determining who is poor and who is not. The absolute approach defines poverty as the lack of a sufficient amount of money to purchase the essentials of life—food, shelter, and clothing. The relative approach holds that people are poor if they have significantly less money than the average person in their society. In either case a value judgment of some kind is necessary. The U.S. government uses the absolute approach, and federal agencies publish statistics showing the number of Americans whose incomes are so low that they are unable to buy the "necessities of life." Measured by the relative standard, the number of people living in poverty has changed very little in the past 20 or 30 years; measured by the absolute standard, the number has declined.

No matter how it is measured, poverty is not evenly distributed throughout the population. The old and the young are more likely to be poor than people in their middle years. Children from single-parent families and the members of most ethnic minority groups are also more likely to be poor. The poverty rate is highest in rural areas and lowest in the suburbs.

The ideology of individualism, which stresses personal responsibility and self-reliance, has fostered the belief that the poor are to blame for their own condition. From the beginning the welfare system was designed on the assumption that being poor was one's own fault.

Today the welfare system in the United States includes a variety of overlapping programs and jurisdictions. Included are programs that make cash payments to families with dependent children as well as to the blind, the aged, and the disabled. Other programs distribute food stamps and assist with housing and medical costs. In Canada, the federal government has emphasized programs that provide welfare services to all citizens. Among these are government-financed health care, old-age pensions, and a small family allowance for each child.

In both the United States and Canada, several government programs enlarge the incomes of businesspeople, especially those who are rich. These subsidies and tax breaks are not called welfare, but their practical effect is the same as that of cash payments.

There are many explanations of poverty. In some societies the economic base is so weak that most of the people go hungry most of the time. In modern industrial societies poverty results from unemployment, low wages, and unequal distribution of wealth. The poor do not receive a proportionate share of the wealth and often pay more than wealthy people for the same goods and services. Another explanation of poverty is based on Oscar Lewis's idea that some nations develop a "culture of poverty" with distinctive characteristics such as unstable families, female-centered homes, and weak community organization. In addition, there are political reasons for the continued existence of poverty in North America. Most important, poverty is valuable to the rich and the powerful. It ensures that dirty work gets done, prices remain low, welfare workers have jobs, and so on.

Five types of proposals for reducing poverty have been made. First, the tax system might be reformed to require the rich to pay higher taxes than the poor. Second, unemployment could be reduced by stimulating the economy, providing job training, and increasing government employment. Third, administrative waste would be cut if the welfare system were reformed by eliminating some categorical assistance programs and replacing them with welfare assistance for everyone. Fourth, the federal government could guarantee every citizen an adequate income by giving grants to all families whose annual incomes fall below a certain level. Fifth, the poor might organize themselves to influence legislation and government policies.

Functionalists see extremes of poverty and wealth as resulting from breakdowns in social organization. Conflict theorists are convinced that poverty thrives because the wealthy and powerful benefit from it. Social psychologists note that socialization practices among the poor develop attitudes and behavior patterns that make upward social mobility difficult.

KEY TERMS

absolute approach
absolute deprivation
capital gain
deduction
exclusion
income

poverty
relative approach
relative deprivation
tax shelter
wealth

7
The Ethnic Minorities

What are the sources of prejudice and discrimination?
Does education reduce discrimination?
How do prejudice and discrimination harm society?
Can political action bring ethnic equality?

The violent face of ethnic relations—riots, lynchings, and murders—is familiar to anyone who watches the evening news. From Northern Ireland to South Africa, ethnic power is a burning issue. Virtually every nation with more than one ethnic group has had to deal with ethnic clashes. Some have managed to achieve long-term stability and harmony; others have been torn apart by violence and hatred. But most have just muddled through with alternating periods of conflict and cooperation.

Exploitation and oppression of one group by another are particularly ironic in democratic nations, for these societies claim to cherish justice and equality. But attempts to create real ethnic equality meet stubborn resistance. The majority group that controls the economic and political institutions refuses to share its power. Because minorities tend to be unskilled and undereducated, they are unable to unseat the dominant group. Moreover, the fear of change causes people from all ethnic groups to hold fast to the way things are.

ETHNIC GROUPS

Members of ethnic groups share a sense of togetherness and the conviction that they form a special group, a "people." Milton M. Gordon gave the following definition:

> When I use the term "ethnic group," I shall mean by it any group which is defined or set off by race, religion, or national origin, or some combination of these categories. I do not mean to imply that these three concepts mean the same thing. They do not. . . . However, all of these categories have a common social-psychological referent, in that all of them serve to create, through historical circumstances, a sense of peoplehood.[1]

The important point is this: What sets an ethnic group off from the rest of a society is its sense of common identity, of "peoplehood."

Although a racial group is often an ethnic group as well, the two are not necessarily the same. A race is said to be based on some common set of physical characteristics, but the members of a race may or may not share the sense of unity and identity which holds an ethnic group together. Americans and Russians hardly have a sense of togetherness, even though they both believe they are members of the same race. However, when there are marked physical differences between different groups within a single society, race is likely to become an important factor in ethnic relations. Physical characteristics such as skin color are more visible than cultural characteristics, and they are much harder to change or disguise.

It is important to realize that race is more a social idea than a biological fact. Among the 4 billion people in the world, there is an incredible range of skin colors, body builds, hair types, and other physical features. Significantly, there is no agreement as to how people with these characteristics should be classified. For instance, in the United States a person who is not an Oriental or an Indian is either black or white. On the other hand, Brazilians recognize many different racial groups with varying combinations of skin color, facial features, and hair texture.[2] Even scientists who study racial types do not agree on a single classification system. Thus, physical characteristics are biological in origin, but the way they are classified and the meanings they are given are socially determined.

People from all ethnic groups see their own culture as the best and most enlightened. This is known as ethnocentrism. Briefly, it is "the tendency to view the norms and values of one's own culture as absolute and to use them as a standard against which to judge and measure all other cultures."[3] Because values and behavior patterns differ from one culture to another, one's own culture appears superior when others are judged by its standards.

Ethnocentrism seems to be universal. All cultures show prejudice toward foreigners, who may be viewed as heathens, barbarians, or savages. Such ethnocentric beliefs lead to wars and serve as justifications for foreign conquests. Similar ethnocentric attitudes are found in the various ethnic groups that make up a single society. Feelings of ethnic superiority are usually accompanied by the belief that economic and political domination by one's own group is both reasonable and natural.

Unlike ethnocentrism, racism is more closely related to physical differences than to cultural differences. Active discrimination is characteristic of racism but does not necessarily accompany ethnocentrism. Racism may be defined as "a belief in racial superiority that leads to discrimination and prejudice toward those races considered inferior."[4] Racism is common throughout the world. It can be seen in relations between African tribes with great differences in body build, in relations between the Spanish-speaking majority and the native Indians of South America, and of course in relations between whites and blacks in North America and in Western European nations.

Because racism involves active discrimination, it is usually more vicious and divisive than ethnocentrism. In most racist ideologies the subordinate group is seen as inferior but is also seen as a threat to the dominant group. Extreme racism may result in an attempt to exterminate the "inferior" group. Two chilling examples are Hitler's mass executions of European Jews and the colonists' nearly successful attempt to wipe out the Indian population of North America.

PATTERNS OF ETHNIC RELATIONS

The relationships between ethnic groups take a bewildering variety of forms. Even the relationships between North American ethnic groups can be difficult to grasp. Sociologists have helped by describing three general patterns of ethnic relations based on the distribution of economic and political power. In some cases, termed domination, one group clearly holds power and others are subordinate to it. In other cases groups are roughly equal economically, politically, and socially. One form of equality is termed pluralism and a second is termed integration.

It is important to note that these are only general patterns and that actual societies are much more complex. Conditions of domination, integration, and pluralism may exist together. Further, the exact form these characteristics take in any society is bound to differ from the one described by these general models.

Domination   When two ethnic groups come into close contact for the first time, ethnocentrism stimulates competition and conflict, and one group usually emerges as the winner. That group becomes dominant, holding most of the political and economic power and discriminating against the subordinate group.

Ethnic dominance was present in ancient civilizations and it continues to exist today. The domination of black slaves by white Americans is a good example. Politically, the displaced Africans were virtually powerless, sharing none of the basic rights of other Americans. They had no weapons or organizations with which to fight their oppressors. Their work produced riches for plantation owners, but their lowly condition was far beneath mere poverty. They were socially isolated, rejected, and considered more animal than human. Although American slavery is an extreme case of ethnic domination, the basic pattern is the same.

Segregation is a part of most systems of ethnic domination. In segregated societies, contacts between the haves and have-nots are held to an absolute minimum. When the United States had the "Jim Crow" system (segregation), it was much like South Africa today. In South Africa, it is a crime for blacks or whites to cross the barriers of segregation. Legally defined residential areas, separate public toilets, drinking fountains, and beaches, segregated sections on buses and trains, and strict prohibition of interracial sexual relations and marriage are all part of the South African

---

NINETEENTH CENTURY SOCIAL PROBLEMS

The right of colored people to attend public places of amusement under the laws of Wisconsin is to be tested. Rachel and Clara Black are the nearly white and attractive daughters of a colored barber, Alfred Black. The young women visited the Century Roller Skating Rink at Oshkosh as spectators. The next day they received a note requesting them to discontinue their visits. They went again and were invited to leave, which they did. The reason assigned by the management of the rink is that it had established a rule not to let colored people frequent the place.
February 9, 1899

system of apartheid (segregation). By keeping the subordinate group separate and isolated, the dominant group tries to keep the myth of its own superiority alive and to prevent political action to change the existing order of things.

Pluralism

In pluralistic systems ethnic groups maintain a high degree of independence. Group members make their own decisions and control their own affairs while retaining their ties to the larger society. The ethnic groups in a pluralist society control some of their own social and political affairs, and each group also keeps its own identity and cultural traditions rather than melting together in a common pot. Although different groups in a pluralist system are roughly equal, in practice some inequality exists, so that deciding whether a relationship is one of domination or pluralism becomes a matter of judgment. For instance, French Canadians are usually considered part of a pluralistic system. While they maintain a distinctive identity and have a strong cultural tradition, there are some ways in which they are dominated by English-speaking Canadians. Anglo-Canadians (and Americans) control the Canadian economy, and the English and American cultural influence is very strong throughout Canada.

When ethnic groups occupy the same geographic area, competition is usually more intense and maintaining independence more difficult.[5] In many of the most successful pluralist nations, different ethnic groups are concentrated in different parts of the country. One of the best examples is Switzerland, which has ethnic divisions between Protestants and Catholics and between French-, German-, and Italian-speaking people. Each group lives in a national district populated largely by people of the same ethnic background. The government recognizes no national language and proclaims its respect for all cultures and ethnic groups. But even in Switzerland the history of ethnic relations has not always been harmonious.

Cultural pluralism, even when it is regionally based, may result in ethnic conflicts, as in Belgium, or in warfare, as in Northern Ireland. In the extreme, separatist movements may divide the pluralist nation into two or more independent countries. This was the case in the division of India and Pakistan and of Pakistan and Bangladesh. A similar process is possible in Canada, where some French Canadians want to divide the country into separate French- and English-speaking nations.

Integration

An integrated society, like a pluralistic one, strives for ethnic equality; but the interests of one ethnic group are not balanced against those of another. Ethnic backgrounds are ignored and, ideally, all individuals are treated alike.

In a truly integrated society all people attend the same local schools, go to the same churches, and vote for political candidates on the basis of merit alone. Politicians do not try to win votes by publicly dining on spaghetti Monday, blintzes on Tuesday, and sukiyaki on Wednesday.

In America most people with northern European backgrounds have given up their ethnic identities. People with names like Seele, Soppeland, and Sutherland often are unaware that their fathers' ancestors came from Germany, Norway, and Scotland. There are also instances in which several ethnic groups have fused into one, as in the case of Jewish immigrants who came from widely different backgrounds — Spain, Germany, Russia, Poland — and now are likely to identify themselves as a single unified ethnic group.[6] A similar fusion now seems to be taking place among some immigrants from Latin America.

In the long run integration replaces domination and pluralism. Peoples who live in close contact, marry each other, watch the same TV shows, and eat at the same McDonald's hamburger stands are bound to integrate as time passes. Even racial differences may begin to fade, as they have in Mexico. However, integration is often resisted by members of ethnic groups who feel that their culture is superior, and by those who want to maintain their distinctive ethnic traditions. It is also opposed by minority citizens who are convinced that they will be at a disadvantage if they are forced to compete in a society that reflects the cultural assumptions of other ethnic groups. Although they would prefer to be treated as equals, they fear that integration would mean dominance.

PREJUDICE AND DISCRIMINATION

Prejudice and discrimination are closely associated, but they are not identical. **Prejudice** refers to attitudes, **discrimination** to actions. Prejudiced people prejudge others, but not everyone who prejudges others is prejudiced. Prejudgment becomes prejudice when the attitude is so rigidly held that it cannot be changed by new information. For example, some Americans erroneously believe that "all Mexicans are lazy." Such a belief is unreasonable, but it is not prejudiced unless the believer refuses to change his or her mind after being shown proof that Mexicans work just as hard as anyone else. Gordon Allport used the following definition in his classic study, *The Nature of Prejudice:* "Ethnic prejudice is an antipathy based upon a faulty and inflexible generalization. It may be felt or expressed. It may be directed toward a group as a whole, or toward an individual because he is a member of that group."[7] Prejudice may be expressed in terms that seem favorable to members of an ethnic group. Thus, the belief that all blacks are good athletes may be just as prejudiced as the belief that all blacks have low IQs.

Discrimination is the practice of treating some people as second-class citizens because of their ethnic status. Usually, it surfaces when a member of a dominant group denies equality to the members of a subordinate group. For instance, social clubs may discriminate against Jews by denying them admission, or the registrar of voters may discriminate against blacks by denying them the right to vote. Robert K. Merton has pointed out that some of us discriminate even if we feel no prejudice toward the person we discriminate against.[8] The reverse is also true. Sometimes we are prejudiced toward a person but reject discrimination because of moral convictions or other group influences.

The Sources of Prejudice and Discrimination

Like other types of human behavior, prejudice and discrimination are not easily accounted for. Many influences come together to create them, and their origins cannot be found entirely in individual psychology or oppressive social institutions. Psychological and social processes blend together like prejudice and discrimination themselves.

Authoritarianism

One of the most influential works on prejudice, *The Authoritarian Personality,* was based on studies done at the University of California at Berkeley shortly after World War II.[9] The researchers sought the psychological causes of the development of European fascism, and their study described a distinct type of personality believed to be associated with intolerance and prejudice. The authoritarian personality is rigid and inflexible and has a very low tolerance for uncertainty. People with this type of personality have great respect for authority figures and quickly submit to their will. They place a high value on conventional behavior and feel threatened when others don't follow their standards. Indeed, their prejudices help reduce the threat they feel when confronted by unconventional behavior. By labeling unconventional people "inferior," "immature," or "degenerate," the authoritarians avoid any need to question their own beliefs and attitudes.

The notion that authoritarian personalities are responsible for prejudice and discrimination has come under severe attack. Some critics have pointed out serious weaknesses in the methodology used in the original research. Others charge that the traits that are said to make up an authoritarian personality are not a unified whole but are merely a number of undesirable traits gathered under a single label. Some say that the concept of authoritarianism is just a political attack on conservatism. Despite these and other criticisms, the idea that some individuals show authoritarian personality traits, and that authoritarianism is expressed in prejudice and discrimination, has become extremely popular both in the scientific community and among the general public.

Scapegoating

Unpopular minority groups are often used as scapegoats for other people's problems. They are blamed for a wide variety of things that they could not possibly have caused. The term originates with a Hebrew tradition. On Yom Kippur a goat was set loose in the wilderness after the high priest had symbolically laid all the sins of the people on its head (Leviticus

16:20–22). The Jews themselves later became scapegoats. When thousands of people died in the plagues that swept through medieval Europe, rioters stormed into Jewish ghettos and burned them down, believing that Jews were somehow responsible for the epidemic. Six centuries later, when Hitler and the Nazis set up their extermination camps, Jews were still being blamed for the troubles of Europe.

One explanation of scapegoating is the frustration–aggression theory.[10] Its three basic principles are that (1) frustration produces aggression; (2) this aggression cannot be safely directed against powerful people; and (3) the aggression is therefore transfered to weaker individuals who cannot cause any harm, such as members of an unpopular minority group. Although the theory seems to make sense of scapegoating, it has some serious weaknesses. For example, frustration does not always produce aggression, and even when it does, the aggression is not necessarily directed at an ethnic scapegoat.

Learning Although prejudice and discrimination are sometimes associated with certain personality traits or with frustration, both are learned. South Africans do not need authoritarian personalities to have strong racial prejudice, because they learn such attitudes from their culture. Most prejudice is acquired early in the socialization process. Children adopt their parents' prejudices as naturally as they adopt their parents' language, and discrimination follows prejudice as regularly as night follows day.

Some of the most common prejudices are taken from ethnic stereotypes—ideas that portray all the members of a group as having similar fixed, usually unfavorable, characteristics. The "happy-go-lucky Mexican," the "lazy Negro," and the "cunning Jew" reflect elaborate ethnic stereotypes that most of us learn at one time or another. In situations of ethnic conflict, "contact conceptions" often develop. That is, people from two ethnic groups develop strong negative stereotypes about each other.[11] For instance, while white racists in the United States perpetuate vicious antiblack stereotypes, black racists have developed their own stereotypes of whites as devils bent upon subjugating the black race.

NINETEENTH CENTURY SOCIAL PROBLEMS

Some of the boys in this city have been indulging in a kind of sport of late which may soon prove to be something besides sport. They have been harassing the Chinese laundryman by tapping on his windows, throwing stones and sticks of wood against the side of the house, against the doors, and even through the windows. They have even gone so far as to open the door and throw in a dead cat. . . . We advise the boys to desist or some of them may soon be called to answer for their folly before the magistrate.
1894

While the prejudice expressed in ethnic stereotypes is usually obvious, prejudice can be quite subtle. For example, a white schoolboy living in an integrated neighborhood learns prejudice when he hears his mother explain that it is all right for him to sleep overnight at the home of a black friend, because "that house is so clean you could eat right off the floor." An unspoken but potent prejudice is at the base of the mother's praise: Blacks are crude and dirty, but this family is an exception. Social psychologists have shown, too, that as some children are taught to be "tolerant" of ethnic minorities they are quietly being taught to be bigots. If a father says to his daughter, "Some of my best friends are Jews," he is telling her that Jews are somehow bad but he is strong enough to put up with it. There even may be prejudice in the attitudes of a white employer who tries to document his lack of prejudice by bragging that in his factory "half the workers are black, and they do the job as well as anyone else."

Economics Conflict between ethnic groups fosters prejudice and discrimination. Some social scientists, particularly Marxists, are convinced that all conflict stems from economic causes. Whether one accepts this idea or not, there is ample evidence that economic competition lies beneath prejudice and discrimination. If Jews, blacks, or members of other ethnic groups cannot get into elite colleges and professional schools, they obviously will not be able to compete with members of the dominant group in occupations requiring a high degree of training. In times of high unemployment members of the dominant group can protect their jobs by making sure that members of subordinate groups are dismissed first. It has long been noted that antiblack prejudice is high among white working-class men who compete with blacks for low-paying unskilled jobs.

In other cases the practice of discrimination is so firmly entrenched that subordinate groups have practically no chance to compete. In South Africa, for example, whites see blacks as an economic threat when in fact blacks are unable to compete on equal terms. This type of discriminatory relationship is closer to exploitation than to competition. Members of the dominant group are not necessarily aware of the exploitation because their stereotypes of ethnic and racial inferiority justify their behavior. Those in subordinate groups, however, realize that they are being exploited, and their anger and resentment find expression in their own prejudices.

Politics The quest for power promotes prejudice and discrimination, just as the quest for money does. Dominant groups use discrimination as a technique for maintaining their power, appealing to popular prejudice to justify their discrimination. In some societies political discrimination is an obvious and accepted fact of life. For example, South Africa does not allow native Africans to vote, and until quite recently many American communities denied the same right to their black citizens. But most political discrimination is more subtle. Minorities who speak a language different from that of the dominant group can be excluded by a literacy test or discouraged by ballots and election information printed only in the language of the dominant group. The political participation of ethnic minorities can also be discouraged by charging a poll tax (a fee for voting) that they cannot afford, or by drawing the boundary lines of electoral districts in such a way as to dilute their influence.

Culture   Much prejudice is just another form of ethnocentrism, as when those who are reared in one moral tradition think those who are reared in a different way are their natural enemies. When members of two or more ethnic groups live side by side, such culture conflict seems to operate independently of economic and political competition. As the people of one ethnic group go about their everyday routines, they may violate the most sacred rules of their neighbors. For instance, Indian Hinduism absolutely forbids eating beef—the meat of a sacred animal—but Indian Muslims have no such objections. However, Muslims are forbidden to eat pork. To an orthodox Hindu, knowing a man who eats beef is akin to knowing a man who eats babies. To an orthodox Muslim, a man who eats pork is almost as bad. Such differences are not merely differences in food preferences. They reflect different moralities.

But cultural competition is not limited to competition between alternative sets of moral standards. In some multiethnic societies each ethnic group expects its behavior patterns to be given equal, or even special, recognition by the institutions of that society. Language is a good example. The language of the dominant group automatically becomes the language of business and government. This practice is viewed as unfair by linguistic minorities, even if they speak the national language as well as that of their ancestors. When aroused, they demand that their language be given equal status with the language of the dominant group. If these demands are successful, government activity is carried on in at least two languages, often at great expense and with some confusion. Canada, Belgium, and Southern India have all experienced this conflict. Even in Norway all schoolchildren must pass examinations in two different forms of Norwegian. Cultural competition also appears with reference to dress, the time of day at which lunch is eaten, national and religious holidays, and hundreds of other cultural traditions.

ETHNIC
MINORITIES IN
NORTH AMERICA   In North America we see all three of the patterns of ethnic relations just discussed. Non-European ethnic minorities, such as blacks and chicanos (Mexican Americans), live under a system of domination. Pluralism—the pattern in which each minority group maintains its cultural distinctiveness

and controls its own economic and political affairs—is not characteristic of North America. The closest approach to it may be seen in Canada, where French Canadians are concentrated in Quebec and are in political control of that province. On a smaller scale, there are some relatively independent towns in the southwestern United States that are predominantly chicano in culture and population. In neither of these cases, however, is it accurate to say that these groups are independent and equal.

Members of some European ethnic groups have assimilated the dominant cultures of Canada and the United States and are now completely integrated. Irish, Italian, Polish, Hungarian, and other European Catholics seem headed in that direction, but they are not as fully integrated as earlier Protestant immigrants.[12] Thus, the pattern of ethnic relations in North America is a mixture of domination and integration, with elements of pluralism thrown in to enrich the blend.

Historical Background

The Indians were the original Americans. Contrary to popular stereotypes, not all Indians were nomadic warriors. Indeed, there were many different Indian cultures. Some Indians were wandering hunters, but many others lived in stable villages and grew their own food. In some areas, principally Mexico and South America, the Indians had very advanced civilizations. American Indians spoke at least twelve major languages, and within each language group there were variations as great as the difference between English and German.[13]

Three major groups of European colonists settled in North America: French, British, and Spanish. In the beginning European–Indian relations were generally peaceful and a lucrative trade developed. But the influx of colonists disrupted this early system of pluralism. Colonists dominated the eastern tribes and then slowly moved westward, first driving Indians from their lands at gunpoint, then restricting them to isolated reserves, and finally requiring even reservation Indians to obey their law.

Conflict was not restricted to whites and Indians, for the European powers also were bitter enemies, fighting among themselves for power, money, and Indian lands. The British emerged as victors in North America, and the lands north of what is now the Mexican–American border have been dominated by English-speaking peoples ever since. The boundaries of the newly independent United States changed slowly, moving westward as Americans took over vast sections of land formerly held by Spain, France, and Mexico. This westward conquest meant, of course, that sizable European and non-European minorities were brought under the domination of the English-speaking majority.

The two new North American nations took very different approaches to the problems of their Indian minorities. Canadian treaties with Indians were usually honored, and the government attempted to minimize stealing, looting, and pillaging by the white settlers. In tragic contrast, the

Terrorism and mob violence have often been used to keep minorities "in their place" at the bottom rung of American society. The lynching of blacks who challenged the system of ethnic oppression was a common occurrence for more than a century after the abolition of slavery.

United States repeatedly signed treaties with the Indians and then broke them as soon as white settlers decided they wanted more Indian lands.[14] As a result of this policy Indians in the United States were nearly exterminated. In 1607, the Indian population of the United States was about 2 million. By 1900, only 200,000 remained.[15] After the Indian resistance was broken, they were subject to cruel domination:

> Most Indian people were denied the vote, had to obtain passes to leave the reservation and were prohibited from practicing their own religions, sometimes by force. Leadership and management of community affairs smacking of traditional forms and functions were either discouraged or ignored as proper representations of community interest. Children were dragooned off to boarding schools where they were severely punished if they were caught speaking their own language.[16]

The French minority in Canada and the Spanish minority in the United States took divergent paths. French Canada had a substantial population at the time of the English conquest, and it has maintained itself as a self-perpetuating community with little new immigration. Quebec has become an island of French in an English-speaking sea. On the other hand, the Spanish-speaking population in most of the areas taken from Spain and Mexico was quite small. With the advent of the transcontinental railroad and the California gold strikes, these people were soon overwhelmed by waves of English-speaking immigrants. However, substantial immigration from Mexico and other Latin American countries eventually led to significant increases in the Latin population of the United States.

In the first century following the American Declaration of Independence, most immigrants to the United States came from the Protestant countries of northern Europe. But from 1870 to 1920 new immigrants came increasingly from the Catholic areas of Europe—Italy, Poland, Ireland, and Eastern Europe. At first it was assumed that these immigrants would quickly assimilate into British Protestant culture, and when they failed to do so ethnic tensions and hostilities grew. In addition, nonwhite immigrants, principally from China and Japan, arrived on the West Coast to be greeted with even more prejudice and discrimination. A federal law passed in 1924 severely restricted immigration from southern Europe and stopped all immigration from Asia. In more recent times most new immigrants to the United States have come from Mexico and South America, often illegally.

The history of the Africans in North America is unique. All the early African immigrants arrived in chains. American slavery was concentrated in the southern plantation regions, and slaveholders intentionally tried to extinguish African culture. The African family system was broken up, and fathers were routinely separated from their children. Slaves who shared common cultural roots were systematically separated and forbidden to speak their own language. They were even forced to abandon their own religion and to become Christians.

After slavery had been abolished, blacks continued to be plagued by racism. Black political power blossomed briefly after the War Between the States, but this fragile flower was soon plucked. Blacks were systematically murdered, terrorized, and subjugated. Terrorist organizations such as the Ku Klux Klan and the Knights of the White Camellia drove blacks back into their subordinate status. Slavery was replaced by a system of segregation that denied blacks full rights of citizenship and isolated them from the mainstream of American society.

The rigid segregation system of the South and the more informal segregation practiced in the rest of the country thrived for 100 years. Finally, in the 1960s, the civil-rights movement broke the back of segregation. With a new sense of political awareness thousands of blacks, supported by Supreme Court decisions, organized, demonstrated, and demanded equal rights. However, despite major improvements, extensive domination continues, fueled by prejudice and discrimination.

The new sense of black pride and political awareness that developed out of this struggle had an impact on other ethnic groups. Militant chicanos and Indians organized and demanded better treatment, echoing demands for "black power" with calls for "brown power" and "red power." In Canada, the *Quebecois* (French Canadians) also began to assert their cultural identity, and some even demanded a new nation separate from Canada. "White ethnics"—especially descendants of immigrants from Italy, Poland, Ukraina, and Ireland—also intensified efforts to maintain their ethnic identity.

Institutional Discrimination

Most people think of discrimination as something one person does to another. While such personal discrimination occurs, its consequences are not as serious as the results of discrimination that are built into our economic, educational, and political institutions. North Americans are familiar with **institutional racism**, but this term is too narrow. **Institutional discrimination** is a more accurate term because unfair choices are made on the basis of ethnic group as well as race. In any case it is clear that our economic, educational, and political organizations favor some ethnic groups at the expense of others. (See Figure 7.1.) While such discrimination may be intentional, it is usually a mere byproduct of the structure and operations of these institutions.

FIGURE 7.1
SOCIOECONOMIC
CHARACTERISTICS OF
ANGLO, BLACK, AND
LATINO POPULATION, 1975

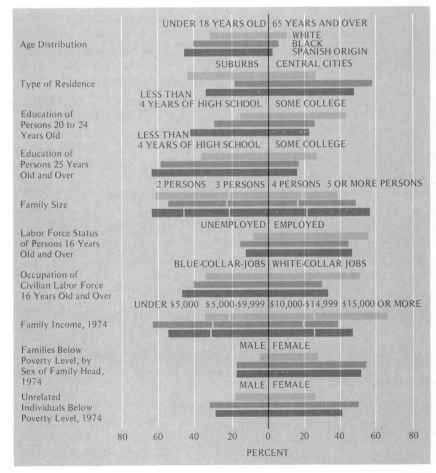

Source: U.S. Department of Commerce,
Social Indicators 1976 (Washington, D.C.:
GPO, 1976, p. xxxix.

Education   Our culture puts tremendous faith in education. Numerous studies have shown that those with the most education are likely to have higher-paying and higher-status jobs. But blacks, Latinos, and Indians receive significantly less education than others. In 1977 the average Anglo (English-speaking white) had 12.3 years of education, the average black, 11.3 years, and the average person of Spanish origin, 10.4 years.[17]

The sources of this educational inequality are rooted in the history of domination. During the period of slavery most black Americans received little schooling, and after Emancipation they were put into separate schools of decidedly inferior quality. The civil-rights movement and the Supreme Court eventually ended legal segregation. But as noted in Chapter 4, segregation has continued, largely as a result of segregated housing patterns in cities. In response to this new problem courts have ordered that schoolchildren be bused from one school to another to achieve racial balance. However, a storm of protest and conflict has made such orders difficult to carry out.

The history of Indian education is in many ways more dismal than that of black education. Many of the early Indian schools were run by missionaries who were determined to civilize and Christianize the "heathen savages." The government-run boarding schools that replaced the missionary schools were no better:

> Many of the boarding schools run by the Bureau [of Indian Affairs] operated essentially as military schools. The young Indian, torn from his family, was shipped to the school where his hair was immediately cut and where he was given a military uniform and taught close order drill. One of the prime objectives of the system was to teach him the English language as rapidly as possible. He was given demerits for speaking in his native language. Since the incoming student could speak no other language, great personal tragedies resulted, leading to high suicide rates. The policies also led to outrage among Indian parents.[18]

Many young Indians returning from boarding school were adrift: They did not fit into the white world, and they no longer fit into the traditional world of their parents.

The cultural assumptions of the white middle class are built into today's schools, and ethnic minorities have behavioral as well as learning problems as a result. For example, success in school depends largely on the student's ability to live up to middle-class standards of discipline and self-control. Students from homes that allow free emotional expression and provide few controls on behavior are therefore at a disadvantage. In addition, textbooks and other course materials are often culturally biased. Imagine an Indian boy's reaction when he reads that traitors in the natives' fight for their land are to be called "friendly" Indians. Only recently have American textbooks acknowledged the contributions of ethnic minorities to American society.

**DEBATE
Is It Fair
to Give Members
of Minority
Groups
Preference
in Hiring
and Promotion?**

PRO

Since the first European settlement of North America, minority groups have been victims of discrimination. The effects of centuries of exploitation cannot be blotted out by new laws against discrimination. Such laws are unenforceable, because employers can always find a reason why a minority applicant is less qualified than a member of their own ethnic group. Even if they were effective, such laws would do little to relieve the burden of past discrimination. Minority children whose parents received an inferior education in segregated schools are unlikely to have a home environment that is conducive to educational achievement. Children whose parents are poor because they have been denied decent jobs are themselves likely to live and die in poverty. The barriers of poverty and ignorance are just as effective as the barriers of ethnic discrimination.

These barriers can be overcome only by requiring that members of minority groups be given preference in hiring and promotion. Anything less is merely salve for the conscience of a majority that claims to favor human rights while doing nothing to end the oppression of minorities. While such preferences may work to the disadvantage of a few whites, it should be noted that their present prosperity results from past exploitation of minorities. A temporary program to give special preferences to the victims of discrimination is the only cure for the lingering effects of historical injustice. When full ethnic equality has been achieved, the system of preferences can be discarded and we will have a more stable and more just society.

CON

The economic problems of today's minorities are not unusual. Italians, Irish, Jews, Japanese, and other minorities came to North America in poverty and carried the burdens of prejudice and discrimination. Yet these groups were able to climb the economic and social ladder without the benefit of ethnic preferences. Why should blacks, Latinos, and American Indians be handed special advantages that other minorities earned by hard work? It is true that blacks are more easily identifiable as minorities than European immigrants, but they are now protected by new laws which expressly forbid ethnic discrimination.

Such antidiscrimination laws are just and proper. It is unconscionable for a democratic society to permit blatant racial or ethnic discrimination, but this is precisely the effect of affirmative-action laws. When minorities are given preference in hiring, qualified white applicants are turned away because of the color of their skin. Is it possible to imagine a more clear-cut example of racial discrimination? More shocking is the fact that our government not only permits but actually encourages this discrimination. Moreover, whites will not be the only ones to suffer if such laws are not repealed. Once we have established the legal principle that membership in a certain ethnic group is a valid criterion for employment, it may be turned against any group, including those that currently benefit from affirmative-action laws. Programs that force employers to give preference to particular ethnic groups are harmful and misguided, and must be ended now.

Cultural prejudices are also institutionalized through language. Immigrant children have always been required to do their schoolwork in English whether or not they are fluent in that language. Even though this system of instruction gave a distinct advantage to descendants of British immigrants, it seemed reasonable enough at a time when immigrants spoke dozens of different languages. But now that the United States has only two principal languages — English and Spanish — this policy is open to question. Some Spanish-speaking Americans are asking for bilingual education like the system in Canada.

It should not be concluded that differences in educational achievement among ethnic minorities stem entirely from cultural biases built into the school system. For one thing, the children of the poor are under strong economic pressure to drop out of school, and ethnic minorities are likely to be poor. Further, there are great differences in the value various ethnic groups give to education, and these differences affect achievement. For instance, Japanese Americans, who are noted for their strong family structure, have always taken great pains to see that their children are well educated. As a result, Japanese Americans have been very successful in school despite the barriers of language and racial prejudice. Studies in California indicate that Japanese Americans have an average level of educational achievement higher than any other ethnic group, including whites.[19]

Employment Most minority group members have low status and low-paying jobs, while their unemployment rate is high. "Anglos" (native English-speaking whites) are more than twice as likely as blacks or Latinos to have white-collar jobs.[20] The same pattern is evident in Canada. For instance, 12 percent of all Canadians of British descent work in managerial and professional jobs, but only 8 percent of French Canadians and 3 percent of Canadian Indians are employed in such jobs.[21] Similar patterns are found in the distribution of income. In the mid-1970s American blacks earned only 58 percent as much as whites, down from a high of 61 percent in 1969–1970.[22] People of Spanish origin earned only slightly more than the blacks, and Indians were at the bottom of the list. Canadian Indians earn only about 20 percent as much as European Canadians.[23]

Much of this inequality can be explained by educational differences already discussed. Because minorities have less education, they have fewer people who qualify for high-paying jobs. But education is not the whole story, for minorities receive less pay than Anglos with the same level of education. Racial discrimination must play an important part, given the fact that blacks have more education than chicanos but have lower average incomes. Because blacks are physically the most distinct ethnic group, they are most often the victims of job discrimination. Such racism is common in labor unions as well as businesses, resulting in the exclusion of blacks from union apprenticeship programs that pave the way to good jobs.

A related problem arises from cultural discrimination. Despite talk about job equality among people with equal ability, many people are hired and promoted because of their personal relationship with an employer or manager. And generally speaking, it is mutual understanding and a common background that promote such friendships. If the personnel manager and boss are Anglos (which is likely to be the case), the members of a minority group may be at a distinct disadvantage even if company policy prohibits job discrimination. But perhaps the biggest problem that members of minority groups must face is the fact that most of them come from lower-income families. Poor families tend to remain poor regardless of ethnic background.

Law and Justice   Discrimination in the legal system has a long history. The U.S. Constitution did not explicitly mention race or slavery, but it nonetheless provided for the return of escaped slaves and held that a slave should be counted as two-thirds of a person for congressional apportionment and tax purposes. In 1857 the Supreme Court ruled that constitutional rights and privileges did not extend to blacks:

> We think . . . that they [blacks] are not included, and were not intended to be included, under the word "citizen" in the Constitution, and can therefore claim none of the rights and privileges which that instrument provides for and secures to citizens of the United States. On the contrary, they were at that time considered as a subordinate and inferior class of beings, who had been subjugated by the dominant race, and whether emancipated or not . . . had no rights or privileges but such as those who held power and the government might choose to grant them.[24]

Even though such racist ideas are no longer part of the law, criminal-justice procedures continue to discriminate against ethnic minorities. Our legal system was built by Anglos, and it incorporates their cultural biases both in its structure and in the attitudes of those who control the system. Numerous studies have shown that blacks are more likely than whites to be arrested, indicted, convicted, and committed to an institution. Similar studies have shown that blacks have a poorer chance than whites to receive probation, a suspended sentence, parole, or a pardon.[25]

Some sociologists say that these differences appear because blacks are more often involved in serious and repeated offenses than whites, and several studies support this conclusion.[26] Others say that the differences appear because of personal and institutional biases: Police officers, prosecutors, and others tend to stereotype blacks (and some other ethnic minorities) as having a "natural tendency" to commit crimes. The idea that members of a minority group are "criminal types" becomes a self-ful-

Many members of minority groups are forced to live in cheap, rundown housing because they cannot afford anything else. But even when they can afford it, ethnic prejudice often bars minorities from better housing. Some unscrupulous landlords take advantage of this situation by charging exorbitant rents for decaying apartments in minority neighborhoods.

filling prophecy. Because blacks are expected to commit many crimes, they are watched closely and therefore are arrested more often than other people. The same stereotypes make it seem reasonable to punish blacks and other minority group members more severely than whites. In sum, prejudice and discrimination still are given much weight in our criminal-justice system.

Housing The quality of housing is another area showing the effects of ethnic discrimination, particularly for the non-European minorities. Blacks, Latinos, and Indians tend to be isolated in districts where the quality of housing is poor. In 1973 more than three times as many black families as white families lived in housing with inadequate plumbing. Black families also had less space per person.[27] The same problem exists among Mexican Americans, who are four times more likely than Anglos to live in overcrowded housing. But the worst housing conditions are found among the Indians on reservations. About half of the housing available to the Navaho Indians, for instance, is unfit for human habitation, and as much as 90 percent is below minimum health and safety standards.[28] In Canada, comparison to official standards suggests that over 80 percent of all Indian homes are overcrowded.[29] Most blacks and Latinos, and some Indians, live in segregated ghettos and barrios in rundown sections of large cities. Joan Moore's description of the Mexican barrio applies to other ethnic slums as well:

> The Mexican American *barrios* are often of a quality that reflects both the poverty of the inhabitants and the peculiar lack of institutional response to their problems. Thus when a visitor enters Mexican American *barrios* in many urban areas, ordinary urban facilities tend to disappear. Streets are unpaved; curbs and sidewalks and street lights disappear, traffic hazards go unremedied, and the general air of decay and neglect is unmistakable. Abandoned automobiles, uncollected refuse, and the hulks of burned out buildings are monuments to the inadequacy of public services in such areas.[30]

When members of minority groups try to escape to other neighborhoods, they run into a wall of prejudice. Many Anglos fear that the presence of a few minority group members in their neighborhood will depress property values. Unscrupulous realtors play on such fears through a practice known as blockbusting. Once a minority family has moved into a neighborhood, these realtors try to convince residents that property values will fall. If they are successful, the residents sell out cheaply to the realtors, who in turn sell the houses to incoming minorities at much higher prices. But not all of the blame can be placed on realtors. Most people prefer to live with neighbors from their own ethnic group. Families from one ethnic group living in a neighborhood being invaded by another are often harassed and intimidated until they pack up and move.

THE SOCIAL IMPACT OF PREJUDICE AND DISCRIMINATION

Prejudice and discrimination have many far-reaching effects on our society—some of them obvious, others hidden. The harm that prejudice and discrimination do to a minority group member who can't find a job is clear for all to see. The harm that is done to society as a whole is not so obvious, but it is no less real. Arbitrary exclusion of certain individuals from important occupations wastes badly needed talent. Minorities feel only weak allegiance to a government that permits discrimination against them, and this may become a source of political unrest and violence. Prejudice and discrimination can also have a devastating psychological impact on their victims.

The effects of oppression are reflected in death rates. (See Figure 7.2.) The life expectancy of most non-European minorities is considerably lower than the average for the entire population. For instance, the average black or Mexican American dies 6 years sooner than the average white.[31] Indians have an even more shocking death rate. In the United States Indians die about 28 years sooner than the average American, and Canadian Indians die almost 38 years earlier than the average Canadian.[32] These

FIGURE 7.2
LIFE EXPECTANCY AT
BIRTH FOR BLACKS AND
WHITES, BY SEX, 1929–1974

Source: U.S. Department of Commerce,
Social Indicators 1976 (Washington, D.C.:
GPO, 1976), p. 146.

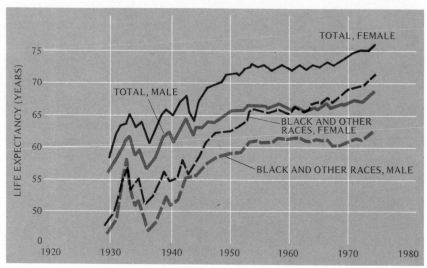

differences are due principally to higher infant mortality rates among minorities, but even at adult ages minority group members have a lower life expectancy than Anglos. The plain fact is that these people die earlier than others because they receive inferior food, shelter, and health care.

RESPONDING TO PROBLEMS OF ETHNIC MINORITIES

Until recently most people saw North America as a "melting pot"—a crucible in which people from around the world were blended to form a new and distinctive culture. The process of ethnic merging (integration) was believed to be the ultimate solution to the ethnic-relations problem. If everyone was blended into one group, ethnic prejudice and discrimination would be impossible.

But supporters of the melting-pot theory have come under increasing attack. First, it is now clear that ethnic merging has not really occurred. Indians, blacks, chicanos, French Canadians—even Irish and Italians—maintain a strong cultural and ethnic identity. Second, a rise of ethnic consciousness has led to a new determination to maintain traditional ethnic identities. More and more people are saying that they do not want to blend into the majority.

Nevertheless, all the ethnic groups in North America have undergone significant cultural changes resulting from mutual contacts. While some elements of a common culture are shared by every ethnic group, the growing emphasis on strong ethnic traditions and identity appears to work against further merging in the near future. Most recent proposals for change recommend a more pluralist system. In the long run, however, it seems likely that domination will be reduced most effectively by programs promoting integration rather than pluralism. With the exception of Indians and French Canadians, the various ethnic groups in North America are mixed together in the same towns and cities. They will therefore have to continue to share economic, education, and political institutions, and for this reason greater equality is likely to be achieved only through further integration.

The problem of balancing the ideals of pluralism and integration while moving as rapidly as possible toward full ethnic equality is one of the greatest challenges facing North America today. The responses to this problem have taken two principal forms: political activism and institutional reforms.

Political Activism

Prejudice and discrimination have been hot political issues in the United States at least since the time of the Civil War. The political issues in the bloody conflict between the North and the South went far beyond the question of freeing the slaves. Constitutionally, however, the significant outcome of the war was a political push toward integration. The Thirteenth Amendment to the Constitution (1865) prohibited slavery; the Fourteenth Amendment (1869) gave citizenship to the former slaves and granted them the "equal protection of the law"; and the Fifteenth Amendment (1870) established their right to vote on an equal basis with other citizens.

For a century these three amendments were interpreted and extended by the Supreme Court in response to pressure from political activists. One by one the features of the system of segregation and official discrimination were declared unconstitutional. Yet even after these rulings had been handed down, a tremendous political effort was necessary to force their implementation. The civil-rights movement—a coalition of liberal whites and indignant blacks—awakened poor southern blacks to the fact that they were being denied the right to vote. Civil-rights activists used demonstrations, marches, and sit-ins to call attention to many forms of unconstitutional discrimination against blacks, and they used the federal courts to do something about it.

Then the civil-rights movement was supplemented, if not replaced, by what came to be called the black-power movement. With the growth of ethnic awareness, many white liberals who had been working for the enforcement of antidiscrimination laws were eased out by black activists who demanded equality in a pluralist society rather than the blending of ethnic groups in a "melting pot." Believing integration to be just another form of domination, they pressed for separation of the races, but on an equal basis. Violence became common as black activists were increas-

Political activism has proven to be the most effective tool to win social justice for ethnic minorities. Here, the late Dr. Martin Luther King is shown leading the Selma-to-Montgomery march, which was part of the civil rights movement that finally brought an end to official racial segregation in the United States.

ingly frustrated in their attempts to realize their goals. Finally the black-power movement was repressed by force and its most militant leaders killed or jailed.

But the spirit of the black-power movement lives on. It serves as a guide for other minorities, who have formed activist groups such as the Brown Berets (Mexican Americans), the American Indian Movement, and the National Organization for Women. Political action against the system of ethnic domination also continues. But the activists, many of whom now hold powerful government offices, are increasingly working within "the system" and using conventional electoral politics. Even the Black Panthers, famous as the most militant of the black-power groups, now run their own candidates for political office.

Institutional Reforms

Political activism is a means to an end. To advance the goal of ethnic equality, there must be meaningful changes in the social structure. Some of the most commonly voiced proposals call for the expansion of bilingualism, changes in the image of minorities presented in the mass media, effective school integration, and equal employment opportunities.

Bilingualism

The most obvious way to eliminate institutional discrimination against those who do not speak English as a native language is through bilingualism, that is, giving minority languages equal status with the dominant language. This approach, which promotes equality through pluralism, has been quite successful in Switzerland but not in Canada. For most of the past century Canadian bilingualism has meant protection of the rights of English speakers in Quebec but not protection of the rights of French speakers in the rest of Canada. The Official Languages Act sponsored by Prime Minister Trudeau forced the federal government to become truly bilingual, but to many French Canadians this was too little too late. In August of 1977 the legislature of Quebec rejected bilingualism and passed the "Charter of the French Language," making French the only official language of the province and requiring its use in business and government.

It is not clear whether the recent proposals for bilingualism in the United States are a call for pluralism or for integration. While a desire for pluralism is apparent among most advocates of bilingualism, educators have tended to use the Spanish-speaking students' language as a tool for teaching them English. When this is done, the bilingual program can have the effect of heating up the melting pot, thereby promoting integration but defeating the aims of pluralism. It will be extremely difficult to achieve linguistic pluralism in the United States, for true bilingualism would require that everyone learn to speak both English and Spanish even if their native language is Italian, Chinese, or Greek. Instead of linguistic equality, this would produce domination by two language groups instead of one. And although Spanish is the second most commonly spoken language in the United States, there are dozens of others. Full equality for so many languages is clearly impossible. It therefore seems reasonable to continue the American policy of using English as the official language, but supplementing it with more sincere efforts to teach English to immigrants and their children.

The Mass Media

Before the arrival of television the mass media promoted ethnic stereotypes rather than trying to eliminate them. When black men committed crimes, newspapers were likely to run a story beginning in this way: "John Doe, a Negro, was arrested for the murder of his wife last night." Similar identifications were not made for crimes committed by whites, creating the impression that the crime rate among blacks was much higher than it was. In films and radio dramas, blacks played the roles of the inferiors that they were assumed to be in real life—janitors, maids, clowns, dancers. In the early days of television, too, there were few black roles, and the blacks who were seen on the screen were almost always depicted as inferiors.

Probably the drive for profits rather than concern with equality led to better treatment of minority groups in the mass media. It was discovered that movies with black actors in leading roles attract blacks to the box office, and television producers began using minority actors too. Soon it became standard practice to use minorities in television commercials and as announcers and newscasters.

At first these changes in the mass media seemed to be directed toward achieving integration, employing people on the basis of merit, rather than ethnicity. But a trend toward greater pluralism developed. Just as it had once seemed reasonable to have Negro and white baseball leagues and colleges, it became fashionable to have Negro and white television programs, movies, and newspapers. There was, and still is, a market for national magazines, movies, and television shows produced especially for blacks or Latinos. This new pluralism differs from the old pluralism in one highly significant respect, however: It is based on the assumption that whites, blacks, and other ethnic minorities are equals.

It is not possible to predict whether in the long run the mass media will move further in the direction of an integrated melting pot (as in sports and popular music) or whether the move will be in the direction of a pluralist equality. Both trends seem to be occurring. Whatever the outcome of these changes, it is clear that ethnic inequality in the mass media will continue to diminish. This, in turn, will help reduce prejudice among the media's millions of readers and viewers.

Schools The basic issue in the school integration controversy is not inequality per se. Of course, some people continue to believe that blacks are inferior and therefore are not entitled to an education equal to that given whites. But the vast majority of Americans now favor educational equality. The real controversy is over whether equal education is to be achieved through integration (as supporters of mandatory busing believe) or through pluralism (as supporters of "neighborhood schools" believe). (See Chapter 4.)

A side issue, but an important one, is whether the schools, like television, should be used to reduce racial and ethnic prejudice. Integrationists point to research studies showing that under the right conditions of cooperation among groups sharing common goals, integration does reduce prejudice.[33] Segregationists (pluralists) say that the same conditions of cooperation and sharing of goals can be achieved without integrating the schools. They favor equality, but they want to retain separate ethnic identities, especially their own. Some school districts with large black populations are attempting to recruit black teachers who are familiar with the culture of their students and can present positive role models. Thus, they have joined the pluralists.

Responses to proposals and programs for eliminating bigotry and cultural bias from school textbooks have been positive. As in the case of television and movies, integrationists and pluralists alike have accepted the idea that ethnic (Anglo) domination was promoted by elementary school books picturing only middle-class whites and by history books potraying blacks as happy-go-lucky "darkies" and Indians as savages who murdered innocent settlers.

Employment The idea that everyone deserves an equal opportunity to make a living has a long history and much popular support. But implementing this idea has been difficult. Until recently most proposals asked for an end to discriminatory practices in hiring and firing. For example, the Fair Employment

Practices Commission, established by executive order during World War II, aimed to end discrimination in war industries. The American Federation of Labor and the Congress of Industrial Organizations (which have since merged) both tried to organize blacks in the late 1940s and early 1950s. With the civil-rights movement of the 1960s came the 1964 Civil Rights Act, which forbids discrimination by unions, employment agencies, and businesses employing more than 25 workers. The problems in enforcing such a law have been immense. In its first year the Equal Employment Opportunity Commission received over 110,000 complaints and was quickly bogged down in paper work.[34]

Affirmative-action programs have now shifted the burden of proof to employers. They can no longer defend themselves by claiming that a decision not to hire a minority group member was based on some criterion other than ethnic group. They must prove they are not discriminating. If the percentage of minority group members in their employ is significantly lower than the percentage in the work force, companies must accept a goal for minority employment and set up timetables stating when these goals are likely to be met.

These procedures have created a powerful "white backlash." Critics charge that the ratios are not goals but quotas and that affirmative-action programs really call for "reverse discrimination" (discrimination against white males). Resolution of this conflict will be extremely difficult. It is true that some minority group members are given preferential treatment and that therefore some Anglos are discriminated against. But it is also true that minority group members still face more discrimination than Anglos do.

The Supreme Court has yet to resolve these difficult legal issues. In the Bakke decision the court upheld the general principle of affirmative action but ruled that Alan Bakke (an Anglo) had suffered illegal discrimination when he was denied admission to a medical school that reserved a fixed quota of its admissions for minority students. Thus, it is still not clear which kinds of affirmative-action programs are constitutional and which kinds are not. Because laws that merely prohibit employment discrimination against minority group members do not seem to be enforceable, some form of affirmative-action procedures will have to be continued if equality of opportunity is to be achieved. Nevertheless, the dangers of allowing, indeed requiring, employers to consider ethnic group a criterion for employment are great.

DIRECTIONS FOR THE FUTURE

While the history of the past several decades shows steady progress toward racial and ethnic equality, improvement has been slow and complete equality remains a distant goal. Elimination of the separate-but-unequal school system was a major step forward, as was the American government's official stance against ethnic discrimination in housing and employment. Illiteracy rates among minorities have dropped and levels of education have increased. Although racism and ethnic stereotypes remain, these prejudices are not publicly expressed by business and political leaders as often as they once were. In addition public-opinion surveys indicate that Anglos are less prejudiced than they were even a decade ago. Surveys by the National Opinion Research Center found that the percentage of whites agreeing with various antiblack statements dropped considerably between 1963 and 1971. For example, in 1963, 66 percent of whites agreed with the statement "Blacks have less ambition"; in 1971, 52 percent of whites agreed with this statement. Agreement that "blacks smell different" dropped from 60 percent to 48 percent; for the statement that "blacks are inferior to white people," agreement fell from 31 percent to 22 percent.[35]

Yet the picture is not without blemishes. Surveys showing a reduction in prejudice among whites also show that racism is still widespread. And other surveys show a different sort of racism to be common among blacks. A Harris poll found 68 percent of blacks agreeing that "whites have a mean and selfish streak" and 70 percent agreeing with the statement that "whites are really sorry that slavery was abolished."[36]

Economic inequality also remains a troublesome problem. Black income began to climb toward white income levels during the 1960s but fell back in the 1970s. Future economic progress for minorities probably will require another period of rapid economic growth accompanied by increased government pressure for equal opportunity.

Official records show that Spanish-speaking Americans have made considerable social and economic progress in recent years. But they now face a special problem: competition from the flood of new immigrants from Mexico and other Latin American countries. Uneducated, unable to speak English, and in the country illegally, these young immigrants are willing to work for lower wages than American-born chicanos or Puerto Ricans. These aliens, sometimes called "undocumented workers," are forcing a new examination of the problem of ethnic inequality. They often work under deplorable conditions for less than the legal minimum wage, but fear of deportation keeps them from reporting their employers to authorities. These immigrants seldom show up in census reports or unemployment figures, though they are estimated to number between 1 and 8 million persons. The United States is doing little to help them, probably because so many Americans are making profits from this supply of cheap labor. Illegal immigration would decrease considerably if the United States helped create good jobs for Mexicans in Mexico, but this kind of solution is seldom given serious consideration.

Among all the ethnic groups in North America, the original Americans —the Indians—are clearly the most deprived. They have higher unemployment rates, lower incomes, higher rates of infant mortality, and a shorter lifespan than any other ethnic group. In addition, they suffer from two special problems. First, they are the only major ethnic minority that is mostly rural. Living on reservations in remote areas, Indians are excluded from the mainstream of society as urbanized minorities are not. But the problem of cultural disruption is even more critical. The economic, political, and geographic bases of the Indian way of life were destroyed by force. The painful fact is that Indians can no longer live in their traditional ways, no matter how hard they may try. Many continue to find white culture alien and unattractive. They are trapped between two worlds and unable to make a home in either.

It is possible, however, that Indians could use their only asset—land—to shape a new future for themselves. This future might resemble that of European ethnics—immigrants from countries like Ireland, Poland, and Italy—who maintain strong ties to their native culture. But because they came with nothing and worked their way up in the face of considerable prejudice and discrimination, white ethnics generally have little sympathy for the demands of other ethnic groups, including Indians. No one helped them gain equality, and they see no reason why non-Europeans—blacks, chicanos, Indians—should get special treatment. Indeed, many of these white ethnics both fear and hate their black- or brown-skinned neighbors.[37] Long-term progress toward ethnic equality will come only when white ethnic groups are given more attention and understanding than they have received so far and when they, in turn, support demands for equality by the ethnic groups that have replaced them at the bottom of the heap.

SOCIOLOGICAL PERSPECTIVES on Problems of Ethnic Minorities

Public concern for ethnic inequality waxes and wanes with the political climate. Interest in equality is particularly intense in times of change, when old patterns of ethnic relations are breaking up and there is conflict over the direction of future change. In the United States ethnic relations raised the most public concern during the Reconstruction period after the War Between the States, and during the era of the civil-rights and black-power movements 100 years later. At both of those times ethnic inequality became a social problem because an old system of ethnic relations was deteriorating and a new pattern was taking shape.

The Functionalist Perspective

Functionalists believe that shared values and attitudes are the cement that holds a society together. The more disagreement there is over basic values, the more unstable and disorganized a society is likely to be. Although the different ethnic groups in North America have come to share many values over the years, significant differences remain, and these differences are an important source of conflict. North America lacks the unity, consensus, and organization that are essential to a harmonious society. While the efforts of the largest ethnic groups to dominate others have grown increasingly unsuccessful, neither pluralism nor integration has been achieved. Society is disorganized, unable to muster its people to work in harmony for the common good.

From the functionalist perspective ethnic discrimination is both a cause and an effect of contemporary social disorganization. The failure to give minorities full equality wastes valuable human resources and generates ethnic hostilities that reduce economic production and undermine political authority. These hostilities, in turn, contribute to prejudice and discrimination as different ethnic groups come to see each other as enemies that do not deserve equal treatment.

To functionalists, the best response to these problems is to reorganize our institutions so as to reduce ethnic discrimination. Unity is the objective, whether it is achieved through domination, pluralism, or integration. But integration is the ideal because an integrated society is likely to have the fewest conflicts. Functionalists ask for an attack on discrimination in housing, education, criminal justice, and elsewhere, arguing that an effective reform movement must increase support for "the system" among ethnic minorities while at the same time maintaining the allegiance of the majority.

The Conflict Perspective

Conflict theorists see the history of ethnic relations in North America as one of conflict and oppression. When European colonists arrived in North America, they engaged in conflicts with each other and with the Indians. Eventually the Anglos conquered most of the continent, but conflict did not end there. As new groups settled in the "promised land," some were assimilated. Those who refused to give up their ethnic identity were shunted into inferior positions—employees rather than employers, police officers rather than judges, farm hands rather than landowners, blue-collar workers rather than white-collar workers, and so on.

From the conflict perspective the history of all ethnic relations is the history of a struggle for power. When one group is more powerful than others, there develops a system of domination in which weaker groups are exploited for the political, social, and economic advantage of the dominant group. When power is more equally distributed, pluralism develops. But whether ethnic groups are in a relationship of domination or equality, there is no guarantee that the system will remain stable. Social change is primarily a process by which one group grows stronger at the expense of other groups. Those who have power want peace and stability; those who are out of power want conflict and change. Institutionalized discrimination is, thus, a technique for keeping the dominant group in power and protecting it from competition.

Conflict theorists assert that ethnic equality can be achieved only through struggle. A group that has improved its status is by definition a group that has seized some political and economic power. Conflict theorists argue that political change often is necessary to bring about economic change (jobs, education, housing, health care). The key to increased power is organization for political action. Even a small ethnic group that is unified can wield much greater power than its numbers would suggest. In a democratic society political change can be achieved by outvoting and outmaneuvering one's opponents according to the established rules of the game. Political change can also be achieved by attacking the established rules in demonstrations and protests that may provoke violence. In recent years both techniques have been used with some success.

The Social-Psychological Perspective

Social psychologists have put much effort into investigating the causes of prejudice and discrimination and their effects on individual victims. Interactionist theory, for instance, holds that individuals develop their concepts of personal identity from their interaction with the people around them. When members of a minority group are constantly treated as though they were inferior, they are bound to be affected. Some become convinced that they are truly inferior, resulting in low self-esteem and feelings of inadequacy. They are also more likely to develop other serious personal problems, such as alcoholism or drug addiction. The rate of heroin addiction is much higher than the national averages for blacks, chicanos, and Puerto Ricans, and alcoholism is a very severe problem among many Indian groups. Other minority group members reject these ethnic stereotypes, forcefully asserting their own value and importance — behavior that occasionally causes trouble with the law. Still others try to avoid the effects of prejudice and discrimination by isolating themselves in segregated ethnic communities.[38]

Proposals by social psychologists for reducing ethnic discrimination and prejudice fall into two broad categories. Those in the first category are based on the fact that whatever is learned can be unlearned. Included here are recommendations for more ethnic contact and communication and for direct attacks on ethnic stereotypes in the media and in schools. By showing people from different ethnic groups as they actually are, and not as stereotypes depict them, barriers to communication and understanding can be removed.

Proposals in the second category go to the root of the problem, recommending long-range changes that will reduce ethnic competition. More contacts and communication between ethnic groups will enable people to overcome their prejudices. But in the long run these improved contacts must be between ethnic groups of equal social status who are working together for a common goal rather than competing with each other for survival. In other words, social psychologists say that prejudice and discrimination will decrease as fear of economic competition decreases.

Unlike other social psychologists, biosocial theorists concerned themselves with the effects of biological rather than social differences between ethnic groups. The visible physical differences between people from different ethnic backgrounds, for instance, make it easier to identify members of ethnic minorities, in turn making it easier to discriminate against them. A few biosocial theorists have even claimed that heredity is the cause of important differences in the behavior of different racial groups. For instance, some argue that blacks have lower intelligence than whites. Such claims have stirred up a storm of controversy, but the overwhelming majority of social psychologists hold that the hereditary differences between people from different racial backgrounds are very slight. Indeed, social psychologists point out that the practice of grouping people into common categories on the basis of such characteristics as skin color and type of hair is simply a cultural tradition, and one that has caused enormous social problems. The only solution to the "racial problem" is to abandon those traditional attitudes and adopt the more scientifically supportable view that all people are members of a single human race.

SUMMARY

Throughout history there has been tension and conflict between ethnic groups. People with a common sense of identity and togetherness tend to be ethnocentric, believing that their ways of doing things are better than those of other groups. Ethnocentrism becomes racism when it is based on the idea that people with certain physical traits are by nature superior to others, and when it involves active discrimination.

The relationship between ethnic groups usually follows one of three general patterns. Domination exists when one ethnic group holds the power and exploits the other group or groups. When two or more ethnic groups have roughly equal power so that each controls its own affairs, a system of pluralism exists. Finally, when two or more ethnic groups blend together and share power, customs, and social institutions the relationship is known as integration.

Prejudice and discrimination are related, but they are not the same. The former refers to attitudes, the latter to actions. A prejudiced person has a strong dislike for members of a certain ethnic or racial group. Discrimination is the practice of treating people shoddily because of their ethnic status.

Social scientists have found many different causes of prejudice and discrimination. Some find their roots in rigid and inflexible authoritarian personalities; others say that frustration produces aggression, which is directed against weak scapegoats. But prejudice is learned in the process of socialization. Prejudice is used to justify discrimination, a device for preserving the economic and political dominance of a particular group. Finally, social scientists have noted that prejudice and discrimination are associated with moral and cultural conflicts as well as with economic competition.

Historically, North America has seen the conquest and domination of the Indians, French, Spanish, and Mexicans by Anglos (English-speaking peoples). Anglos also dominated black Africans and immigrants from other parts of the world, but that domination has not gone unchallenged. Some ethnic groups have retained a separate identity and added a pattern of pluralism to the pattern of dominance. There is no doubt, either, that the United States and Canada have acted as "melting pots" in which some European cultures blended together in a pattern of integration.

Discrimination is built into our economic, educational, and political institutions. Some of this institutional discrimination is intentional, designed to protect the interests of Anglos, but some of it seems to have begun accidentally. Because our basic institutions were designed and are run primarily by Anglos, they reflect the cultural values and assumptions of Anglos.

Prejudice and discrimination have many negative consequences, including the exclusion of talented people from important jobs, the weakening of overall social unity, the creation of psychological problems, and the production of unnecessary pain and suffering. There have been many responses to the problems of ethnic relations. For 100 years the goal of political activism was to secure a pattern of integration by eliminating discrimination on the part of the dominant majority. More recently, black activists and others, believing that integration is just another form of domination, pressed for pluralism. Affirmative-action programs now force employers to spend time and money to ensure that ethnic minorities are treated fairly. A variety of institutional reforms have been suggested, including bilingualism, reduction of cultural biases in the mass media and in schoolbooks, school integration, and equal employment opportunities.

According to functionalists, North American society is unable to muster its many ethnic groups to work in harmony for the common good. Social scientists who take the conflict perspective see institutionalized discrimination as a way of protecting the economic and political power of the dominant groups. The key to increasing the power of minority groups is organization for political action. Social psychologists point out that prejudice and discrimination are learned and that both are associated with fear of competition. They recommend more ethnic contacts and a reduction of economic competition between ethnic groups.

KEY TERMS		
	affirmative-action program	institutional discrimination
	authoritarian personality	institutional racism
	bilingualism	integration
	blockbusting	melting-pot theory
	discrimination	pluralism
	domination	prejudice
	ethnic group	race
	ethnocentrism	scapegoat
	frustration–aggression theory	stereotype

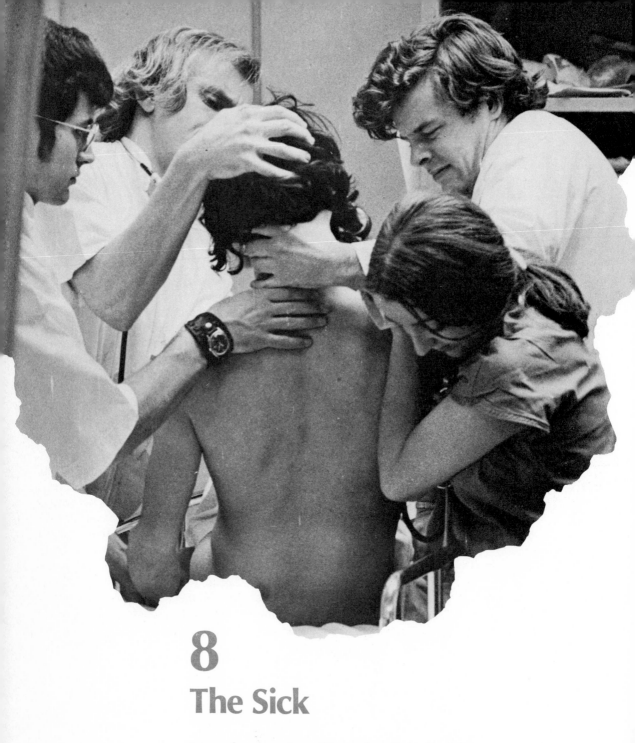

8
The Sick

How does modern life style affect health?
Why is health care so costly?
Are private insurance programs well managed?
What are the benefits of national health insurance?

Good health, like good food and water, is easy to take for granted. It is not until our health is threatened that we realize how important it is. Surveys show us that good health is strongly associated with an individual's satisfaction with life.[1] Depression and unhappiness create health problems, just as ill health often interferes with personal happiness.

The physical suffering accompanying most serious illness is obvious, but the psychological cost is often much greater. The nagging fear of death or permanent disability torments many sick people. Their inability to carry out normal social roles places burdens on their friends and relatives. Long-term illness requires a family to change its role structure — wives must go to work and husbands must care for the children. Some families even shut themselves off from outsiders and make the sick person the focus of their daily life. Too often the result is a growing sense of guilt and resentment that ends in disintegration of the family.

HEALTH AND ILLNESS

To many people, good health means simply that they have no obvious illnesses or physical problems. But some people who are depressed, lack vitality, and say they are "not feeling well" cannot be shown to have any specific illness. For this reason, the World Health Organization defines health as "a state of complete physical, mental and social well-being and not merely the absence of disease and infirmity."[2] It is clear that health is not just a biological condition but involves social and psychological factors as well. The definition of good health varies between nations and even between different classes within the same nation. The tired, listless feeling associated with poor nutrition is considered normal by poor people in most parts of the world, but seen as a sign of illness by the wealthy.

Cancer and diseases of the heart and circulatory system are the most common causes of death. But such killers are rarely the cause of our daily health problems. A 10-year study of families in Cleveland, Ohio, found that common respiratory and intestinal diseases (colds, bronchitis, flu, etc.) accounted for 76 percent of all illnesses. The average person in this study had 5.6 respiratory and 1.5 intestinal diseases a year.[3]

People who are alive today are healthier and will live longer than any other generation in history. In the eighteenth century, the average lifespan in even the most prosperous nations was no more than 35 years. Today, the lifespan in the industrialized world averages 70 years or more, largely because of a dramatic decline in infant mortality and deaths from contagious diseases.[4] As lifespan increased, the degenerative diseases of later life became the number-one killers. In 1900, the leading causes of death were pneumonia, influenza, tuberculosis, and diarrhea. In 1970, the leading causes of death were heart diseases, cancer, and strokes; influenza and pneumonia ranked fifth.[5] (See Figure 8.1.)

The great improvement in living conditions in the twentieth century is the principal reason that we are living longer. A rising standard of living

FIGURE 8.1
DEATH RATES FOR
SELECTED CAUSES,
1950-1974

Source: U.S. Department of Commerce,
Social Indicators 1976 (Washington, D.C.:
GPO, 1976), p. 153.

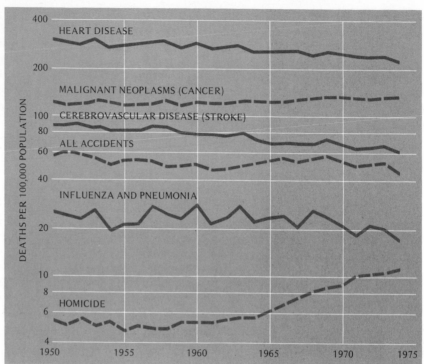

and increased agricultural production mean better food, shelter, and clothing for the average person. The installation of sewer pipes and water purification plants has sharply reduced deaths from epidemic disease.

Physicians and medical researchers have contributed to the decline in death rates in three principal ways. Most important, they discovered the causes of contagious diseases and pressed for preventive measures based on this knowledge. Without the discovery of germs, our modern sewage disposal and water treatment facilities would never have been built. Second, immunization techniques were invented to prevent such killers as diphtheria and smallpox. Third, new techniques for treating dangerous diseases were developed, the most important being antibiotics. Contrary to popular opinion, sophisticated and expensive medical procedures such as open-heart surgery have added little to the average lifespan.

HEALTH AND MODERN LIVING

Not all the changes that have transformed the twentieth-century world have been beneficial to health. Stress, pollution, and overindulgence can kill and cripple as effectively as typhoid or tuberculosis. Widespread belief in the "wonders of modern medicine" has created many unrealistic expectations. Many people eat, drink, and smoke too much, expecting that their physician will repair the damage to their bodies. But modern medicine is no substitute for a healthful life style and common sense.

Exercise, Diet, and Smoking

Most North Americans are far less active than their ancestors were. Labor-saving devices ranging from the automobile to the electric toothbrush have reduced the amount of physical effort required for daily living, and automation has created an increasing number of "thinking jobs" that demand no harder work than picking up a pencil or making a phone call.

Current medical research shows regular exercise to be essential to good health. Not only do people who exercise regularly report that they feel better, but exercise has been shown to reduce the risk of heart disease — the leading cause of death in North America. A San Francisco study found that longshoremen who did hard physical labor had fewer heart attacks than longshoremen who did only light work. In their study of Boston men, Charles Rose and his associates found the amount of exercise to be one of the best predictors of longevity.[6]

Modern technology has enabled the industralized nations to conquer the most serious dietary problem — starvation. But though most of us now get enough to eat, government surveys show that our diet is getting worse, not better. Since 1960 Americans have sharply increased their consumption of meat, fats and oils, and sugar while reducing their intake of fresh fruits and vegetables.[7] (See Figure 8.2.) While there is some disagreement over what type of diet is most conducive to good health, no nutritionist feels that the increasing consumption of foods that are high in fats and sugar is beneficial, and there is substantial evidence that such foods may cause serious health problems. A population of Canadian Eskimos who quadrupled their sugar consumption in just eight years experienced alarm-

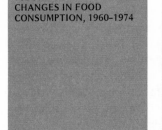

FIGURE 8.2
CHANGES IN FOOD
CONSUMPTION, 1960–1974

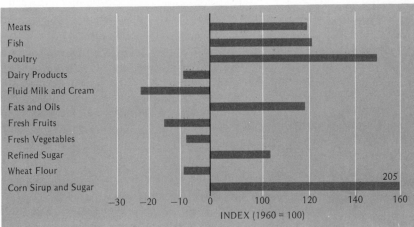

Source: U.S. Department of Commerce, *Social Indicators 1976* (Washington, D.C.: GPO, 1976), p. 179.

ing increases in diabetes, arteriosclerosis (hardening of the arteries), obesity, and gall bladder disease.[8] A study of Japanese Americans whose diets were high in fat found that they had significantly more arteriosclerosis than Japanese living in Japan, where the diet is much lower in fat.[9]

North Americans' love of high-calorie foods and their tendency to overeat have caused obesity to become a serious problem. Current research shows that heart disease, high blood pressure, and diabetes are associated with overweight. Many nutritionists are also concerned about the growing use of food additives. Some additives have been found to cause cancer or other serious ailments only after years of extensive use, as in the case of artificial sweeteners. No one knows how many of the additives now in use will later be proven dangerous.

Despite heated denials from the tobacco industry, there is no longer any doubt that smoking is a serious health hazard. It has been linked to a long list of diseases, including lung cancer, emphysema, ulcers, and heart disorders. The Surgeon General's latest report on smoking concluded that the death rate for smokers is 70 percent higher than that for nonsmokers of the same age, and the death rate for heavy smokers (two or more packs a day) is double that for nonsmokers.[10] Ironically, at the time that the American government issued this warning it was paying millions of dollars in subsidies to help tobacco farmers grow their deadly crop.

Stress

Contemporary industrial societies put enormous stress on their citizens. Workers not only work harder and longer than in agricultural societies, but more important, they are under constant pressure to meet deadlines and quality standards. Data from all over the world show that heart disease and related illnesses increase as nations industrialize.[11]

People in stressful occupations are more likely to suffer from a variety of health problems. Two-thirds of all air traffic controllers in the United States have peptic ulcers, probably as a result of the enormous pressures of a job in which a mistake may mean death for hundreds of people.[12] Stress is also associated with heart disease. A study of lawyers, dentists, and physicians found a strong correlation between the amount of stress associated with their specialty and their rates of heart disease; thus, general-practice lawyers had less heart trouble than trial lawyers, who had less heart trouble than patent lawyers.[13] The unexpected stress from sudden changes in living patterns is especially hazardous. Park's study of 4486 widowers found that their death rate was 40 percent higher than normal for the first year after the death of the spouse.[14]

Environmental Hazards

The pollutants that industries dump into the environment are more than just an ugly nuisance; they are killers. The National Cancer Institute estimates that up to 90 percent of all cancer may be environmentally induced.[15] Air pollution has been found to be related to deaths from

NINETEENTH CENTURY SOCIAL PROBLEMS

Dr. H. B. Cole, health officer, reported to the council, as a board of health, that the present year, according to the opinions of celebrated authorities, is to be a year of great danger as regards to epidemics, etc., and recommended that our citizens be required to use unusual care in the disposition of garbage and slops, that all pig stys in the thickly settled portion of the city be declared nuisances, and that none be allowed except they maintain a floor and it be cleaned twice a week during the summer, that privies be thoroughly disinfected, and that slaughter houses be not permitted to run the blood on the ground and let the hogs create as much filth as before.
May 7, 1886

bronchitis, heart disease, and emphysema as well as several types of cancer. The contamination of water with poisonous wastes, such as lead and mercury, has already taken hundreds of lives, and the list of new dangers grows daily. American industry alone creates 3,000 new chemicals every year. The government has already found 12,000 substances that are linked to serious health problems, but most of the half-million chemical compounds used by modern industry have not yet been tested.[16]

Not surprisingly, the most serious problems may be found among laborers who work directly with dangerous substances. Steelworkers are 7.5 times more likely to die of cancer of the kidney and 10 times more likely to die of lung cancer than people in other occupations. But steelworkers are lucky compared to asbestos workers. Almost half of the 500,000 workers exposed to high doses of asbestos will die as a result—100,000 are expected to die of lung cancer, 35,000 of asbestosis (another lung disease), and 35,000 of mesothelioma (an otherwise rare cancer of the linings of the lungs and stomach).[17]

Poverty   There is overwhelming evidence that poor people have more health problems than those who are better off. The effects of poverty are obvious in the overpopulated agricultural nations. Lack of clothing, housing, and food takes a frightening toll. It is estimated that 10 to 20 million people starve to death every year in the poor countries of the world. The problems of the poor in the industrialized nations are less visible, but they are no less real. They include lower life expectancies and higher rates of infant death and contagious disease. An American study found that poor families reported four times as many heart ailments, six times as much arthritis and high blood pressure, and eight times as many visual impairments as families in the highest income group.[18] Black children are three times more likely than white children to die in their first year of life, and a number of studies show that the poor and minorities are sick more days a year than are the wealthy.[19]

Poverty is the indirect cause of most of these problems. About 25 million Americans cannot afford to keep themselves adequately fed and are therefore particularly susceptible to illness and disease. Because their diet contains more cheap, starchy foods, poor people are more likely to be overweight. Goldblatt, Moore, and Stunkard found poor women six times more likely to be overweight than more wealthy women.[20] Lack of proper sanitation and protection from rain, snow, cold, and heat also take their toll. Reports of rat bites in slum areas number in the thousands each year, and contaminated water poses a severe problem for many American Indians. Moreover, the daily lives of the poor are filled with stress because they are often worried about getting the money to pay their bills and buy the groceries. Finally, the poor receive inferior care for their health problems.

HEALTH CARE

Medical science has made enormous progress in the past century. Unfortunately, however, improvements in the delivery of health care services have lagged behind advances in medical knowledge. People in poor countries seldom receive adequate health care, and millions die from easily preventable diseases like cholera and typhoid. Even the richest nations find the ballooning cost of today's sophisticated medical technology a heavy burden.

In the past, those who could not afford health care simply did without. As late as 1967, the president of the American Medical Association held medical care to be a privilege, not a right. But things have changed, even in the United States. Most people now believe that the sick have a right to health care even if they cannot afford to pay for it. As a result of these changing attitudes, most industrialized nations have adopted a system of government-supported health care available to all citizens at minimal cost. The United States has taken a different course, creating a medical-welfare system for the poor but leaving the rest of the health care system in private hands.

Health Care in the United States

The 4 million Americans who are employed in the health care industry have much to be proud of. A large portion of America's 7,000 hospitals are among the most modern and best equipped in the world. America's 360,000 physicians are rigorously trained, and its researchers have made an enormous contribution to medical science. American health care is certainly among the best that money can buy. The problem is that many people cannot afford to pay the price.

In 1976 Americans spent almost $140 billion, 8.6 percent of total national income, on health care.[21] Despite this massive expenditure, many indicators show that the health of American citizens lags far behind that of comparable industrialized nations. Infant mortality rates, for example,

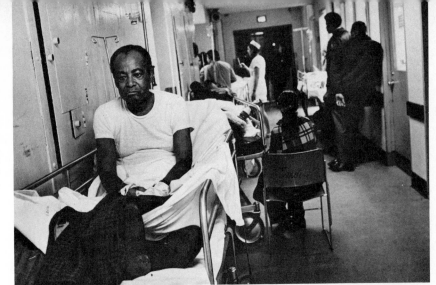

The poor must wait in long lines to see a physician and use over-crowded county hospitals, while affluent citizens receive better and more convenient care from private sources.

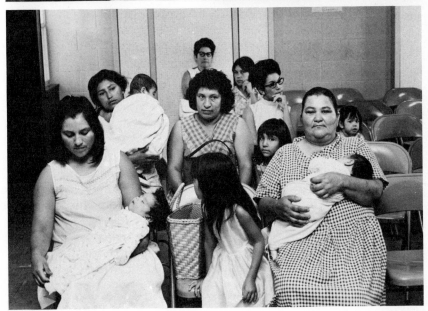

are shockingly high in the United States compared with those for Sweden or even those for much poorer countries such as Iceland and Ireland.[22] Of course, the American health care system is not entirely responsible for these differences. Variations in life style, culture, and diet are important too. Nevertheless, it appears that Americans are not getting their money's worth for their health care dollars.

In the United States health care services are provided largely on a **fee-for-service** basis, very much like other goods and services. As a result the wealthy receive excellent care while the poor receive indifferent and decidedly inferior care.

Until quite recently poor people in the United States saw physicians much less often than did wealthier people. With the coming of medicare for the aged and medicaid for the poor—two government-paid health care programs—the poor began seeing doctors more often. This does not mean, however, that equality has been reached. There is a disproportionately large number of the elderly among the poor, and they naturally require more medical attention. Also, as we have seen, the poor have more serious illnesses than other people. Thus, a poor person is still less likely to see a physician than a wealthy person with a similar health problem.

Regardless of how often poor people visit doctors, it is clear that they receive lower-quality care. For one thing, they are less likely than others to be cared for by specialists.[23] For another, many of the best physicians refuse to accept medicare and medicaid patients because of the paper work involved and because the government will not pay the high fees these physicians normally charge. Geographic distribution is a factor too—the best specialists practice only in wealthy residential areas. Even more troubling is widespread fraud and corruption in government-sponsored medical programs. A number of "medicaid mills," which process an enormous number of patients in a rather careless fashion, have sprung up in urban slums. Charges for unnecessary medical tests are common, and this cheats the taxpayers who finance medicaid. These organizations also deliver low-quality services to patients, sometimes endangering their lives.

Widespread disorganization poses another serious problem in the American health care system. Independent physicians, small medical groups, and huge hospitals all compete for the same patients. Despite a great shortage of general practitioners, new doctors flock to the overcrowded specialties such as surgery, where the money is. Isolated rural areas go begging for physicians while urban centers have many more than they need. Some patients pay their own bills, while others rely on charitable organizations and a bewildering variety of insurance plans and agencies of local, state, and federal governments. The result of this disorganization is waste and inefficiency on a grand scale.

The Doctors

Physicians command more respect and admiration than people in virtually any other profession. Books, movies, and television programs picture the physician as unselfish and dedicated, a "saint in white." As far back as the 1940s, a study of occupational prestige found that physicians were second only to members of the Supreme Court.[24] More recent studies have shown that medical doctors have maintained their high status.[25] And as is so often the case, high income accompanies high prestige. According to the American Medical Association (AMA), the average income of American physicians was $86,575 in 1976. The chief of a typical hospital department makes between $150,000 and $200,000 a year.[26]

Despite the great prestige of American doctors, there is growing discontent with their performance. Much of this dissatisfaction is related to the income figures just cited. An increasing number of "medical consumers" seem to be complaining that physicians are more concerned with their incomes than with the well-being of their patients. Certainly, some physicians try to see too many patients each day and provide depersonalized and overpriced service as a result.

Another source of dissatisfaction with the medical profession is the romanticized view of the doctor's proper role. Americans seem fascinated by the image of the old general practitioner. Whatever his medical skill, the "GP" was a family friend and adviser, not just an impersonal technician, and Americans want him back:

> Americans remember the old-time general practitioner out of a Norman Rockwell painting: driving far out to a lonely farmhouse in the middle of the night to deliver a baby, wiping the brow of a feverish child, or draining pus from the chest by lamplight on the kitchen table. The doctor was family counselor and friend, ministering angel, and miracle worker, all rolled into one. The modern physician has little hope of living up to such a romanticized picture of the old general practitioner.[27]

Since World War II the general practitioner has been largely replaced by sophisticated medical specialists. As late as 1931, general practitioners outnumbered specialists by five to one. Today that ratio is reversed—only 20 percent of American physicians are general practitioners.[28] This trend toward specialization has accompanied the rapid growth of medical knowledge, but countries that have experienced the same explosion of medical knowledge continue to produce more general practitioners than the United States. For instance, general practitioners accounted for one-third of the physicians in Sweden in 1967, and in England half of the doctors were GPs.[29] Apparently, the specialties are more attractive to American physicians than to those in other countries, perhaps because they make more money and have greater prestige within the profession.

One of the most hotly debated issues in the field of health care concerns the supply of physicians. Many studies have concluded that there is a shortage, but there is very little agreement about the number of physicians needed.[30] The most widely quoted figure is 50,000.[31] Nevertheless, America has more physicians per person than many similar countries, including Australia, Denmark, England, Japan, the Netherlands, Norway, and Sweden.[32]

Whatever the number of new doctors needed, it is clear that the physicians we have are poorly distributed. Some fields of medicine are overcrowded, while there is a serious shortage of doctors to provide basic medical care, including general practitioners, internists, and pediatricians. Greenberg reports that there is only one pediatrician for every 5185 children in the United States.[33] At the same time, prestigious specialties, such as surgery, have a surplus of physicians. A study by John Bunker, a leading anesthesiologist, found that there were twice as many surgeons and twice as many surgical operations per person in the United States as in England.[34] A study of metropolitan New York found that the workload of a typical surgeon was only one-third of what experts consider to be a reasonably full schedule.[35] The great number of surgeons has led to much unnecessary and potentially dangerous surgery. A subcommittee of the House of Representatives estimated that 2.4 million unnecessary surgical operations, costing $4 billion and 11,900 lives, were performed in one year. The AMA responded that these estimates were based on false and misleading data.[36] But the committee did not change its conclusions, and in a later report it held that widespread publicity and efforts by government and the medical community had not significantly improved the situation.[37]

The geographic distribution of physicians also is uneven. As already noted, physicians are heavily concentrated in the affluent districts of cities, leaving many rural and poverty areas with a critical shortage. About 5000 communities in the United States have no physician at all.[38] Before the start of a federally funded community health center, the black community of Watts, California, had only 8 doctors for 35,000 people.[39] Overall, it is estimated that there are three times as many physicians per person in metropolitan counties in the United States as in rural counties.[40]

At least four conditions contribute directly to this distribution of physicians. First, it is not surprising to find that doctors, like other educated Americans, prefer to live in cities, with their superior cultural and recreational facilities. Second, physicians have become dependent on the support of laboratory technologists and their sophisticated equipment, and rural areas do not have the number of patients needed to maintain such facilities. Third, physicians are overwhelmingly white and from middle-class and upper-class backgrounds (less than 3 percent of all American physicians are black),[41] and it is reasonable to believe that they feel most comfortable with patients from a similar social background. Fourth, affluent areas guarantee larger incomes than can be expected in poverty areas.

American doctors are among the most highly trained and best qualified in the world. American medical research leads the world in a number of important fields. Nevertheless, a significant number of American physicians are incompetent. A recent estimate places the number of "iatrogenic"—physician-caused—deaths at 150,000 a year.[42] A study of the Yale–New Haven Hospital showed that one-fifth of the hospital's patients were injured by their medical treatment.[43] Another study concluded that 60 percent of all patients treated in the emergency room of the Baltimore City Hospital received ineffective care.[44]

If American physicians are so well trained, why is there a serious problem of incompetence? Of course, doctors are only human, and no matter how well trained they are, some will make mistakes that cost patients' lives. But some physicians have had inferior training in questionable foreign medical schools, while others have failed to keep up with current medical techniques. Further, the medical profession refuses to weed out incompetent physicians. Neither patients nor government officials are as well qualified as other physicians to judge professional competence. For this reason the burden of protecting the public from incompetent physicians falls on the medical profession itself. Unfortunately, it has failed to shoulder this responsibility. The ethics of the profession discourage physicians from criticizing their colleagues, and as a result only the most grossly incompetent physicians are forbidden to practice medicine. In many states it is virtually impossible to remove a physician from practice for anything short of a violation of the law.[45]

Many suggestions for dealing with the problem of medical incompetence have been made. The most common proposal would require all physicians to take periodic examinations to determine whether they have kept up with current medical knowledge. Their professional record and test scores would then be examined by a medical board, and those who fail to come up to standard would have their licenses revoked. They would be forbidden to practice medicine until further examinations showed that they had improved their skills and procedures. While such proposals meet strenuous objections from physicians who oppose any interference in their profession, such a system is desperately needed. Further, the problem of medical incompetence is not limited to physicians. Any reexamination and relicensing program would have to cover nurses and laboratory technologists, who also play critical roles in modern medical care.[46]

The Hospitals Hospitals were originally *hospices,* places of refuge where the poor could die. Not until modern times did the hospital become a place where sick and injured people are given medical treatment.[47] Today hospitals are the nerve centers of the medical profession. A hospital's board determines which physicians will be allowed to use the hospital and, thus, which patients will be admitted. Hospital boards control much medical teaching and research as well.

A recent development in hospital services is the growth of "outpatient" care. From 1957 to 1972 outpatient visits to American hospitals increased by over 150 percent.[48] Some of this growth was due to demands that the hospital do a better job of meeting a community's needs. But most of the growth probably resulted from a decline in the number of general practitioners, forcing the sick to look directly to the hospital for help.

Between 1950 and 1972 the cost of hospital care rose an alarming 574 percent, and it has continued to rise in more recent years.[49] Some of the increase is due to inflation, but statistics show that hospital costs have risen more rapidly than the costs of other goods and services. One reason is that hospitals, like hotels and airplanes, are rarely filled to capacity.[50] When a hospital is operating below capacity, the cost per patient increases because there are fewer people to pay for the hospital's fixed operating expenses. Costs have also risen because all patients must pay for the purchase of expensive equipment that is used by only a few. Of 800 hospitals equipped for open-heart surgery in 1972, one-third had never performed such an operation and another third performed fewer than 12 a year.[51] Victor Fuchs argues that the introduction of medicare and medicaid encouraged waste and produced higher costs. Because government payments are based on the average cost of hospital services, inefficiency is rewarded by higher payments.[52]

The Rising Costs

Like the cost of hospitalization, the cost of all health care in America has been rising at an alarming rate. (See Figure 8.3.) In the past decade the cost has risen about 10 percent a year while overall inflation has been only 6 to 7 percent.[53] One important factor in the rise has been the development of expensive medical techniques. Such procedures as organ transplants and renal dialysis (the use of artificial kidney machines) are extremely expensive, and the practice of routinely ordering expensive laboratory tests also drives costs up. Because physicians are paid on a fee-for-service basis, there is a strong financial incentive to subject patients to as many medical procedures as possible. A study of the amount of surgery performed on government employees covered by different health insurance plans reveals some startling facts. Employees covered by Blue Shield insurance, which pays doctors on a fee-for-service basis, had more than twice as much surgery as employees with group medical plans offering doctors no financial incentives for unnecessary opera-

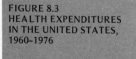

FIGURE 8.3
HEALTH EXPENDITURES
IN THE UNITED STATES,
1960–1976

Source: Chart prepared by U.S. Bureau of the Census. Data from U.S. Social Security Administration. In *Statistical Abstract of the United States, 1977* (Washington, D.C.: GPO, 1977), p. 93.

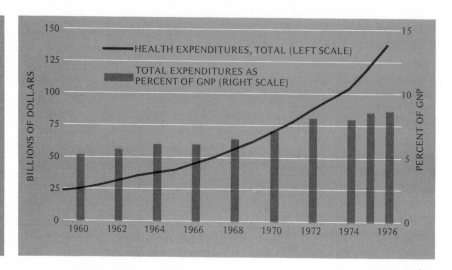

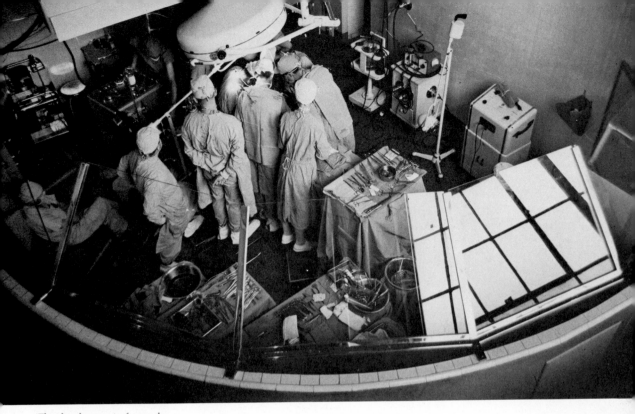

The development of complex and expensive new medical techniques has been a major factor in the rapid increase in the cost of medical care.

tions.[54] Obviously, some physicians' decisions to operate are based on the profit to be gained rather than on the needs of their patients.

Another factor in rising costs is incompetence. Patients have discovered that they can sue doctors for malpractice and win. As a result all doctors—competent or not—now must pay huge fees for malpractice insurance. This cost has been passed along to patients so that the doctors' profits remain high. Indeed, physicians' incomes have risen more than twice as fast as consumer prices since the end of World War II.[55]

Paying the Costs

Traditionally, Americans have bought medical care the way they buy beans, pork chops, and cars—purchasing the services they desire and can afford. This system has been supplemented by a variety of other programs, ranging from private charities to government grants. (See Figure 8.4.) The fastest-growing alternative has been private health insurance. Indeed, most Americans now have some kind of health insurance.[56] But although insurance schemes help distribute the cost of medical care more evenly, most policies fail to cover all health care expenses. Some policies have little or no coverage for office visits or maternity care, while others require the insured person to pay a fixed amount before receiving any benefits. Most policies also require the insured person to pay all costs above a certain amount. In 1970 about 60 percent of all medical expenses were not covered by insurance.[57] Further, many health insurance plans, being hospital oriented, actually encourage waste and inefficiency by pay-

FIGURE 8.4
PER CAPITA HEALTH CARE
EXPENDITURES, BY TYPE
OF EXPENDITURE AND
SOURCE OF FUNDS, FISCAL
YEAR 1975

Source: U.S. Department of Commerce,
Social Indicators 1976 (Washington, D.C.:
GPO, 1976), p. 171.

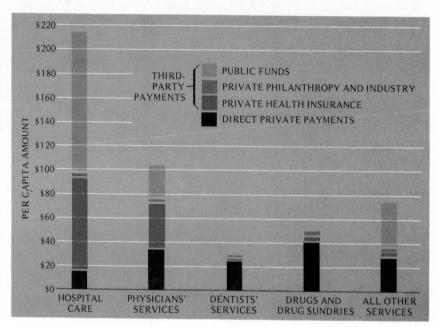

ing much higher percentages of hospital expenses than of nonhospital expenses. As a result patients are encouraged to have simple medical procedures performed in a hospital even when they could be done more easily and at much less cost in a doctor's office.

The government's contribution to the payment of medical-care expenses comes primarily from the two programs mentioned earlier—medicare and medicaid. Medicare buys medical services for people over 65 years old, while medicaid is designed to help the poor, the blind, and the disabled. The medicare program is relatively uniform throughout the nation. Medicaid, on the other hand, is administered by the states, and each state has its own standards of eligibility and levels of benefits. The benefits are extremely low in some states. Neither medicare nor medicaid pays all the costs of a patient's medical care. Both programs require patients to pay for part of the initial treatment and a percentage of all additional costs (currently 20 percent).

The medicare and medicaid programs have not overcome the fraud, waste, and inefficiency associated with some private health insurance plans. In fact, they seem to have provided a strong inducement for fraud and corruption among health care workers. Dishonest physicians and medical laboratories charge huge fees for unnecessary tests and treatments, and even bill for services that were not performed. The government pays. Some laboratories have been caught giving kickbacks to physicians who order laboratory tests for their patients. They have also been found to overcharge the government by as much as 400 percent. Medicaid mills receive 75 percent of all medicaid payments, making elderly people and poor people the victims of criminal mistreatment.[58]

Other Health Care Systems

The percentage of people served by government health care programs is smaller in the United States than in any other Western nation. Citizens of those nations pay few doctor or hospital bills; however, their taxes are higher in order to cover the costs of medical care. The British health care system is often help up both as a model of effectiveness and as an illustration of the dangers of socialism. The Canadian system, on the other hand, is in between the systems of Britain and the United States.

Great Britain

In England, Northern Ireland, Scotland, and Wales, medical care is provided at very little direct cost to the patient. The government owns all hospitals and pays all physicians. It also pays most of the costs of dental care and drugs.

Until 1965 most British physicians were paid on a straight capitation basis. That is, they received a certain amount for each patient who signed up with them, regardless of the services performed. Now physicians get extra money for treating patients over 65 and for performing special services such as night visits. Physicians working in areas that are short of doctors also get bonuses.

British citizens sign up as patients of specific doctors and may choose any physician they wish. They are expected to go to their chosen physician with all their ailments. If necessary, the physician refers them to another doctor for treatment of special problems. Citizens are free to remove their names from a doctor's list of patients and switch to another physician, but they cannot flit from doctor to doctor with each new illness. Sometimes a change of doctors is impossible because all the doctors have full quotas of patients.[59]

Signing up with a doctor in Britain is not much different from simply declaring that "Dr. Smith is our family doctor," as Americans did when general practitioners were more common. In England one out of every two physicians is a general practitioner.[60] Few British patients go to specialists unless they are referred by their family doctor. The specialists generally work directly for a government hospital, receiving a fixed salary plus bonuses. Some work only part-time, supplementing their incomes by engaging in private practice and charging fees directly to their patients.[61]

British health care seems to be more effective than the American system. For example, the death rates for most age groups are lower in Britain than in the United States. However, it is not clear how much of this difference is related to health care and how much to differences in life style.[62] For poor people the British system is obviously superior, even if it might not be superior overall. All Britishers have equal access to health care, while low-income people in the United States clearly receive inferior care.

The British also pay less for health care than Americans do. In 1970 the United States spent about 8.4 percent of its total national income on health care, while England and Wales spent only 5.6 percent.[63] Because average income is much lower in England and Wales than in the United States, this means that the cost of health care per person was much higher in the United States. Put another way, the British spend much less on health care than Americans do, but they seem to get more for each dollar they spend.

Canada

Although the Canadian and American cultures are similar, Canadians have always been more enthusiastic than Americans about government social programs. As a result Canada became involved in government-supported health care much earlier and to a much greater extent than the United States. In the late 1950s, a government hospital insurance program for all Canadians was launched. A decade later, the program was expanded to cover physicians' services and other medical needs.

The Canadian system is quite different from the British system. Most significant, it is decentralized. Each Canadian province secures health care for its citizens and pays about half the bill; the other half is paid by the federal government. As a result health care programs differ from one province to another, even though all programs are managed according to federal guidelines. Canadian governments, whether federal or provincial, do not own hospitals or employ staffs to run them. Canadian doctors are paid on a fee-for-service basis rather than on a capitation basis as in Britain. Thus, the Canadian system resembles the medicare and medicaid programs of the United States in that it encourages unnecessary tests and treatments, at great expense to taxpayers. Canadian doctors also have much higher incomes than their British counterparts.

The death rate for infants in Canada is about the same as the rate in Great Britain, and both rates are lower than that in the United States.[64] Again it is clear that low-income Canadians, like low-income Britishers, have better access to health care than low-income Americans. In terms of cost, it appears that the British system is the most efficient and the American system the least, with Canada somewhere in between. One reason Canada's costs are higher than Britain's is that Canadian physicians are paid on a fee-for-service basis. On the other hand, Canada's costs are lower than America's because fewer Canadian doctors are in private practice, charging whatever the traffic will bear.

Regular exercise is an essential component of healthy living, and growing numbers of people are making an effort to incorporate more physical activity into their life style.

RESPONDING TO PROBLEMS OF THE SICK

There are two approaches to the problems of the sick. The first is to try to prevent health problems by changing life styles and eating habits, reducing pollution, and increasing the use of preventive medicine. The second aims at improving care for people after they become sick. The latter approach includes proposals designed to create equal access to health care regardless of income and to improve the overall quality of these services at less cost.

Healthier Living

There is much that we can do as individuals to improve our health. A balanced diet is the first essential. In North America dietary problems usually stem from eating too much of the wrong kinds of food. Most of us would be better off if we ate less and avoided foods that are high in sugar, fats, and artificial additives. Regular exercise is another essential component of healthy living. The growing recognition of this fact has encouraged many people to run, swim, play tennis, and engage in other physical activities. Recent reductions in death rates from heart and circulatory disease may well be a result of such activities. Finally, it is important to avoid health hazards such as smoking and excessive stress.

There are, however, many health hazards that can be reduced only through collective action. It is easy to tell a business executive or a factory worker to avoid stressful situations, but how can one avoid stress when trying to earn a living in one of the world's most competitive economic systems? Overall levels of stress will be reduced only when changes have been made in our economic and political institutions. But there are proposals for more limited change that might bring some immediate improvements. Much stronger government action is needed to reduce occupational health hazards and make sure companies that have killed or crippled their employees at least pay for the damage they have done. Vigorous antipollution programs such as those discussed in Chapter 19 would make another major contribution to public health.

Preventive Medicine

The old saying that "an ounce of prevention is worth a pound of cure" is as true today as it was 100 years ago. As we have noted, the remarkable drop in death rates in the past century was due mainly to improvements in preventive medicine. Improvements in sanitation and nutrition have saved more lives than all hospitals combined. Yet health care systems continue to emphasize treatment rather than prevention of disease. A delicate heart operation is much more exciting than the dull business of educating people to avoid heart trouble through proper diet and regular exercise. Yet the second approach is both cheaper and more effective.

In its broadest sense preventive medicine includes a wide range of programs to encourage healthier living, including school courses in nutrition, personal hygiene, and driver training as well as campaigns against excessive use of tobacco, alcohol, and other drugs. Even efforts designed to attack poverty, racism, and discrimination can be considered part of an effective program of preventive medicine.

Medical Personnel

It has often been claimed that medical education is much too technical and that doctors are trained in useless details that are soon forgotten. Medical education is, as sociologist Eliot Freidson put it, "perhaps unparalleled by any other conventional professional training in its duration, its detail and its rigidity."[65] Students going through medical school are placed under extreme stress—physically, emotionally, and financially.

> Medical training . . . need not exact such a heavy financial and personal toll from the student. There is no reason to force medical students to go so heavily into debt and give up so many human pleasures that they begin to see themselves as a martyred sect, different from monks only in their plans to collect their heavenly reward while still on earth.[66]

Medical education must demand the highest standards if its products—doctors, nurses, and technologists—are to meet the demands of their profession. But these standards can be achieved in a much more humane and painless manner.

It is clear that American medical schools do not produce enough doctors. About one-fifth of all physicians now practicing in the United States graduated from a medical school in another country.[67] Some are Americans who went abroad for training because they could not get into an

American medical school. Others are foreigners, trained in their home countries, who came to the United States because of the opportunities here, often abandoning the people of a poor nation in desperate need of their services.

Americans also suffer because too many of their doctors are specialists. By restricting the number of students in overcrowded specialties such as surgery, medical schools could help move physicians into fields where they are badly needed, particularly general practice. Medical schools could also train a new breed of "paramedicals"—medical personnel who, while less broadly trained than M.D.'s, are qualified to perform many services that are now restricted to physicians. Such universities as Duke and Stanford now offer training for such paramedics. An innovative program at Cleveland State University allows nurses and other middle-level medical personnel to gradually build up to an M.D. degree by completing a "credit through examination" program. The wider use of such programs could greatly expand the supply of well-trained physicians in areas where they are most needed.

National Health Insurance

The United States is the only modern nation in the world that does not have some form of government-financed medical care available to its entire population. It seems to be only a matter of time until some form of comprehensive health care coverage is adopted. Such a system would certainly do much to equalize the health care received by the rich and the poor.

If hospitals remained in private hands, with doctors paid on a fee-for-service basis, the dangers of creating another oppressive government bureaucracy would be minimized. But individual corruption and profiteering are a real danger in this type of system. Without proper quality and cost controls, such a system could accelerate the already astronomical rise in the costs of health care. On the other hand, a national health insurance program with physicians paid varying salaries, as in England, would be cheaper in the long run. But American doctors oppose such a system, and the tremendous power of the AMA and other physicians' organizations makes it unlikely that it could win approval.

Health Maintenance Organizations

Some physicians have banded together to form clinics that provide health care on a prepaid insurance basis. Such health maintenance organizations are essentially group practices. A group of medical personnel, including specialists, offers a complete range of medical services. Subscribers pay a fixed monthly fee that does not, in individual cases, increase when the subscriber needs care and treatment in the clinic. Physicians are paid a fixed salary or receive a flat fee for each patient.

Health maintenance organizations remove the financial incentives for "overdoctoring." They are also more efficient than individual private practice on a fee-for-service basis. Although doctors working in health maintenance organizations have more office visits than private physicians, they hospitalize their patients less frequently and perform fewer operations. The difference in hospitalization rates is not entirely due to the greed of private physicians. In health maintenance organizations treatable conditions are detected earlier, so hospitalization is needed less often. As a result a patient's total expenses for health care are greatly reduced. The Kaiser-Permanente Medical Care Program, with over 2 million subscribers, is the largest health maintenance organization in the nation. This California corporation provides medical services for about 60 to 80 percent of the cost on a fee-for-service basis.[68]

Studies show that the subscribers of health maintenance organizations receive health care that is equal, if not superior, to that received by people with other types of insurance. Robert Robertson found that schoolteachers enrolled in a health maintenance organization health plan lost fewer days of work than those enrolled in a Blue Cross plan.[69] Another study showed that among subscribers to the New York Health Insurance Plan (a health maintenance organization) the infant death rate was significantly lower than that for the general population.[70]

Health maintenance organizations were roundly condemned by the AMA when they were first established. But now it is recognized that they provide some significant benefits for physicians as well as for patients. Among the advantages that a health maintenance organization offers the physician are retirement and sick pay, regular working hours, reduction of bookkeeping and insurance costs, and easy availability of peers for consultation and support.

It is possible that health maintenance organizations will become more wasteful and ineffective as they become more popular. They may become bureaucratic and impersonal, with physicians who are unresponsive to their patients' needs. Some may even fall into the hands of criminals who give patients just enough care to keep the money rolling in. Nevertheless, the problems of health maintenance organizations seem to be less severe than those of current fee-for-service systems.

SOCIOLOGICAL PERSPECTIVES on Problems of the Sick

Concern about the increasing gap between what modern medicine can provide and what most people receive has made modern health care a social problem. It is a problem of social organization. Social scientists of every persuasion have tried to explain why health care is not better, given the fact that it is now a multibillion-dollar business with the knowledge and technology necessary to provide excellent services for everyone.

The causes of ill health also have been a subject of great concern to social scientists. Conflict and functional theorists are concerned primarily with large-scale health problems such as environmental pollution. Their perspectives on environmental problems are discussed in Chapter 19.

The basic differences between the two perspectives are simple. Functionalists see the unhealthy conditions created by pollution as unintended (latent) dysfunctions of industrialization. Conflict theorists place the blame on industrialists who put profits ahead of the health and well-being of the people. Social psychologists are concerned with why individuals choose a healthy or an unhealthy life style.

The Functionalist Perspective

Viewed functionally, the jumbled health care system is a result of the rapid development of medical technology and the changes in public attitudes about medical care. In the nineteenth century medical knowledge was so limited that private doctors could handle almost all demands for health care. Rapid growth of medical knowledge and techniques greatly increased the kinds of services doctors had to offer. Because these services were effective, the demand for them boomed. People came to see good health care as a fundamental right, but the system of health care was unable to adapt efficiently. The idea that health care is a commodity, to be bought the way a homemaker buys a sack of potatoes or the skills of a carpenter, is still with us. The conviction that medical care should be provided by a private practitioner and not by a corporation, a group practice, or a government bureau also remains strong.

Because of this lag, functionalists say, the American health care system is not doing its job efficiently. Health care services are still sold privately. But this individualistic "free-enterprise" system has been supplemented, in patchwork fashion, by a great variety of cooperative organizations: clinics, hospitals, group practices, and health maintenance organizations. It has also been supplemented by many new sources of funding—employers, unions, insurance companies, and a host of government agencies.

In short, the American health care system is disorganized because it has grown rapidly and haphazardly, without proper planning. Obviously, the solution to this problem is reorganization. But functionalists do not agree on the form this reorganization should take. Some would have us return to free enterprise in the health care business. Others believe we should merely streamline the present system. They call for reallocating medical personnel, reducing fraud and malpractice, lowering costs, and training more medical personnel.

The Conflict Perspective

Conflict theorists see the American health care system in a different light. They argue that its problems and deficiencies stem from the fact that it is designed to serve the needs of the rich and powerful (including doctors themselves), thus neglecting the needs of low-income groups. Health care is a business dominated by businesspeople with medical degrees who try to sell their services at the highest possible price. Because physicians have a legally enforced monopoly on medical services, they are in a position to rig prices and keep the demand for their services high by preventing the training of a sufficient number of new physicians. Their services are sold at inflated prices that only the rich or well insured can pay, and programs that would reduce profits or require physicians to provide cheap health care for the poor are opposed. Further, conflict theorists claim, physicians have created an aura of mystery about their profession in order to boost their occupational prestige and cover up their shortcomings. In this atmosphere patients are not expected to judge the quality of the medical care they are receiving. ("Doctor knows best.") Incompetents and profiteers are not weeded out because patients are kept in the dark about the true nature of the medical care they are receiving.

Conflict theorists would resolve the health care problem by reducing the medical profession's control over the financing and organization of the health care system. This power would then be transferred to the government or directly to the patients themselves, and strenuous efforts would be made to ensure good medical care for all citizens regardless of their ability to pay. Most conflict theorists call for government-financed health care available without charge to individual patients. They also argue that such changes will come about only if those who receive inadequate health care organize themselves to counter the tremendous power of the health care establishment.

The Social-Psychological Perspective

Health and health care obviously are of tremendous psychological importance to every individual. Although social psychologists rarely deal directly with the organization of health care services, they have made significant contributions to the health care field. They have shown, for example, that the socialization process in medical schools often has unanticipated consequences, making doctors into something less than the humanitarians many medical students aspire to be. They have shown, further, that people learn to be "sick" (to play the role of sick people) just as they learn to be students or professors. It follows that health care services sometimes make people sick rather than well.

Social psychological research is the foundation for the popular notion that effective medical care meets patients' emotional needs as well as their physical needs. Current calls for "family medicine" and more general practitioners are based on the fact that current practice, which uses a variety of specialists and clinics, often makes the patient into an object rather than a person. ("The ulcer in room twelve." "The pregnancy in the waiting room.") Impersonal bureaucracies, whether financed publicly or privately, are poorly suited to meet an individual's emotional needs.

Social psychologists are also concerned about the causes of health problems. Personality theorists focus on the relationship between character traits and health problems. For instance, Rosenman and his colleagues found that people with "type A" personalities—hasty, impatient, restless, aggressive, and achievement oriented—are more likely to have heart disease than the easygoing "type B" personality.[71] Behaviorists and interactionists are concerned with the ways we develop unhealthy habits and life styles. Attitudes toward exercise, diet, smoking, and drinking are learned from our primary groups and reflect the attitudes of our culture as well. Social psychologists point out that unhealthful behavior is often encouraged by the media, business, and even the government. Expensive advertising campaigns designed to sell junk food, cigarettes, and alcohol are good examples. The competitive pressures of our economic system are a major factor in health problems resulting from stress and tension.

Many social psychologists believe that significant improvements can be made in public health through a concerted campaign of education and social change. First, there must be greater awareness of the damage caused by unhealthy life styles and poor diet. Second, there must be changes that will encourage everyone to follow the principles of good health. The ideal of the successful, hard-driving achiever will have to be modified to permit a new emphasis on cooperation and mutual support. It is also important that businesses take greater social responsibility for the products they sell. A new social climate must be created in which it is no longer acceptable for corporations to spend millions of dollars advertising children's breakfast cereals that are mostly sugar, developing new cigarettes with more "sex appeal," or promoting other dangerous products.

SUMMARY

In the past 100 years there has been a tremendous drop in the death rate. Improved health care and new treatments for deadly diseases contributed to this decline, but it was largely due to improvements in living conditions—better food, housing, and sanitation.

Although industrialization and modern technology have helped reduce starvation and epidemics, they have also created new health problems. The stress of modern-day living and the decline in physical exercise have increased the frequency of a variety of heart and circulatory diseases. Our diet contains too many fats, sugars, and artificial additives. Occupational hazards, smoking, and environmental pollution are major causes of death and injury.

On the average, poor people have more health problems and a shorter lifespan than others. Many factors contribute to these problems, including stress and worry, dangerous occupations, poor diet, and inadequate medical care.

The growing cost of medical care and the belief that health care is a right, not a privilege, are placing a strain on health care systems in many parts of the world. The problem is particularly acute in the United States, where health care is organized and managed like a private business.

Despite medical-welfare programs such as medicare and medicaid, poor people who cannot afford to pay for private insurance receive inferior care.

There is a shortage of physicians in the United States and Canada, and the physicians now in practice are poorly distributed. There are too many doctors in affluent urban areas and too few in rural areas and in the poverty areas of large cities. In addition, there are too many specialists and too few general practitioners. Although our doctors are among the best trained in the world, some give poor service that harms instead of heals. It is frequently suggested that medical boards should examine physicians every year or two and suspend the licenses of those who do not come up to standard.

The cost of medical care has been rising rapidly all over the world. In the United States one of the major sources of this increase is the cost of hospital care. A large number of new hospitals have been built, and many have purchased expensive new equipment that has not been used efficiently. Further, health insurance has tended to encourage excessive use of hospitals because it often fails to cover office visits. The costs of health care have also been increased by the development of expensive new medical techniques. The fee-for-service method of payment, most common in the American health care system, tends to encourage unnecessary and slipshod medical procedures. Such profiteering has raised the price of malpractice insurance for all doctors, and this new cost has been passed along to the consumers (patients). In addition, the incomes of medical personnel, many of whom were already highly paid, have been rising much faster than the average wage for other workers.

The British health care system is radically different from the American system in both funding and organization. In Great Britain almost all health care costs are paid directly by the government. Citizens are free to sign up with the general practitioner of their choice, and the physician is paid by the number of patients served, not by the number of tests or treatments performed. Hospitals are owned by the government.

In Canada most health care services are financed by taxpayers rather than by individual patients. However, the Canadian health care system is much more decentralized than the British system. Each province directs its own health care program, and the federal government underwrites half the cost. Hospitals remain in private hands. Unlike Britain, Canada pays its physicians on a fee-for-service basis.

There are two ways of dealing with the problems of the sick. One is to prevent health problems before they start through changes in life style and diet, reduced pollution, and preventive medicine. Another approach is to improve the quality of health care services. This includes proposals to increase the supply of medical personnel by increasing the output of our medical schools and restricting access to overcrowded specialties, by encouraging the formation of health maintenance organizations, and by setting up a national health insurance program in the United States.

Functionalists contend that the health care system is disorganized because the ways and means of delivering medical services have not adjusted to changes in the medical services themselves. They ask for a reorganization of this ineffective system. Conflict theorists argue that the American health care system serves the rich better than the poor because the rich are in control. The solution, they say, is to shift power away from doctors and others who benefit from the present elitist health care system. Social psychologists are concerned more with the causes of health problems than with health care. They point out that unhealthful life styles are learned from others, and call for a program of education and social change to improve our way of living.

KEY TERMS   capitation   medicaid
             fee-for-service compensation   medicare
             health   preventive medicine
             health maintenance organization

9
The Elderly

Why are the aged receiving so much attention?
Has age discrimination increased?
Should families do more for their elderly members?
How can the financial security of old people be improved?

Everyone has seen loneliness etched on the faces of elderly men and women sitting on park benches. Most Western societies give the elderly little respect or consideration. We prefer to push them out of sight where they won't trouble our conscience. But the problems of the aged are becoming harder to sweep under the rug. In the past twenty years the size of the elderly population has increased steadily, and projections show that their numbers will keep growing in the years to come. The poverty, ill health, unemployment, and despair of old people are now recognized as a serious social problem.

But the problems of the elderly are shared by people of all ages. In developing an understanding of the social and biological process of aging, we gain insight into the problems faced by everyone in our society. The transition from adolescence to adulthood, for example, poses many of the same problems as the transition from adulthood to old age. Sociologically, the problems of old age are merely the last of the many problems of aging that we face throughout our lives.

THE PROCESS OF AGING

Most people see aging as a biological process. In fact, it is a social process as well, for cultural and social conditions have a profound influence on how rapidly we age. Perhaps more important, cultural and social conditions determine what aging means to us and how we respond to it.

Aging involves a number of biological changes in the human organism. The wrinkles, poor eyesight, poor hearing, and gray hair of old people are familiar to all of us. Not so familiar are the reduction in the number of functioning cells, the decrease in hormone secretion, the drop in muscular strength, and the decrease in lung and heart capacity.[1] These changes eventually occur in all men and women, but not at the same rate. Diet, exercise, medical care, and life style all affect the aging process.

The most important social influence on the aging process is the cultural definition of what it means to grow old. Every known society is divided into what anthropologists call age grades—groups of people of similar age. As people progress through the age grades of their society, they are expected to behave in ways that are considered proper for those at their level.

Age grades and age-graded behaviors vary tremendously from one society to another, changing even within a single society over the course of history. For instance, the concept of adolescence is a recent development. Young people have always experienced the physiological changes accompanying puberty, until the industrial revolution there was no extended period during which a physically mature person was considered too young to assume adult responsibilities. Childhood ended abruptly when people became adults. Adolescence developed as a response to industrialization and the need for a prolonged period of education before entering adult life.

The "teenager" is an even more recent age grade, having been invented in the United States during the 1950s. Many of the problems of teenagers can be attributed to the roles society assigns people in that age grade. Old enough to start families of their own in most traditional societies, teenagers live in a kind of limbo between the worlds of the child and the adult. There would be no adolescent delinquency if there were no adolescents.

Aging is a series of transitions from one social role to another. From childhood to adolescence, to young adulthood, to middle age, to old age, we mark our lives by the roles we play. Each role change presents a new set of problems for individuals in transition. On the one hand, they must cope with the feeling of loss at seeing an end to a major period of their lives. On the other hand, they must face the difficult task of learning a new role. Young adults must conquer their fears and learn how to shoulder the new responsibilities expected of them. Old people must learn how to reorganize their lives after the stability given by child rearing and employment is torn away.

While any role transition is difficult and often painful, the transition to old age is perhaps the most difficult of all role changes in our society. The problems associated with the change from childhood to adolescence and then to adulthood are accepted because they are part of the process of growth and personal expansion. Each of the later roles brings greater power, prestige, and privileges than the role which preceded it. The transition to old age offers none of these attractions. For the first time individuals see their horizons contracting in an irreversible way. There is a loss of power and prestige, and of course at the end of this last transition await the inescapable mystery and finality of death.

Most cultures have what are known as rites of passage to mark transitions from one stage of life to another. These ceremonies and rituals provide individuals who are in transition with group support and symbolic confirmation of their new status. While our culture still maintains a few rites of passage such as marriage, confirmation, and bar mitzvah ceremonies, most people do not receive much social support when making critical transitions from one age grade to another.

PROBLEMS OF THE ELDERLY

In traditional societies with extended family systems, increasing age is usually accompanied by increasing prestige. For instance, in the ancient Chinese family the eldest male held the lion's share of power. He was treated with reverence and respect, and even worshiped after his death. With the breakup of the extended family in Western culture, the status of the elderly has suffered a severe decline. No longer are old men and women the respected heads of an ongoing social unit. Rather, they are increasingly isolated and alone. Youth and vigor are our cultural ideals, and there is widespread belief that older people have little or nothing left to contribute. In a common phrase, the elderly are said to be "over the hill."

The problems of the elderly have been drawing increasing attention in recent years, probably because there are more old people than ever before. Since 1900 the average life expectancy in the United States has increased by 24 years, and the percentage of the population over age 65 has more than doubled. There are now over 20 million people aged 65 or older, about 10 percent of the American population.[2] Further, the percentage of elderly people in the populations of most Western countries will continue to grow.

Health Of all the problems that trouble older people, health seems to concern them the most. There is good reason for this concern — the elderly clearly have more severe health problems than other age groups. According to a national health survey 86 percent of all Americans aged 65 or over have at least one chronic illness such as arthritis or heart disease.[3] Surprisingly, old people have fewer acute illnesses (such as colds and infectious diseases) than others, but their recovery time from such illnesses is twice that of younger adults.

Despite the prevalence of chronic illness among the elderly, only 15 percent are too sick to care for themselves. About one out of every 20 people over 65 lives in an institution, but institutionalization often has little to do with health. In many cases the elderly go into institutions because they lack the financial and family support to continue living on their own. Most elderly people say they are in reasonably good health, perhaps because they have learned to put up with illness and physical impairment as an inevitable part of the aging process.[4] (See Figure 9.1.)

The elderly have trouble getting care and treatment for their ailments. Most hospitals are designed to handle injuries and acute illnesses that are

FIGURE 9.1
(a) PREVALENCE OF CHRONIC CONDITIONS BY AGE, 1969–1973

(b) SELF-ASSESSMENT OF PERSONAL HEALTH, PERSONS AGE 65 AND OVER, BY SEX, 1973

Source: U.S. Department of Commerce, *Social Indicators 1976* (Washington, D.C.: GPO, 1976), pp. 163, 184.

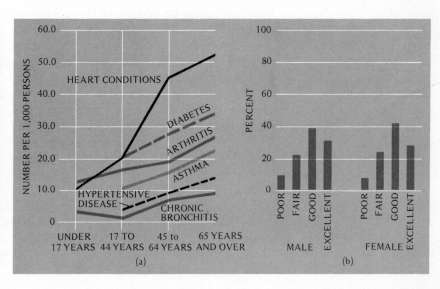

common in the young, but are inadequate to treat the chronic degenerative diseases of the elderly. Also, many doctors are ill prepared to deal with such problems. As Fred Cottrell points out, "There is a widespread feeling among the aged that most doctors are not interested in them and are reluctant to treat people who are as little likely to contribute to the future as the aged are reputed to."[5]

Old people spend twice as much money on medical care as younger people, but their incomes are only half as large.[6] Thus, even with the help of medicare, the elderly in the United States have a difficult time paying for the kind of health care they need.

Money

Most older people have good reason to worry about money. First, they are likely to be poor. In 1976 about 15 percent of all people over 65 were below the poverty line set by the U.S. government, while the poverty rate among the general population was less than 12 percent.[7] Second, because the elderly are likely to live on fixed incomes plus assets built up during their working years, they do not get cost-of-living raises to ease the burden of inflation. Ironically, as their income is reduced by inflation, their need for money increases. Medical bills increase, and if the elderly are to maintain their accustomed style of life they must hire people to cook, sweep, shop, carry out the garbage, and do many other jobs that they once did themselves.[8]

Work

As people grow older, they are less likely to be employed. While over 95 percent of middle-aged American men are in the labor force, the figure is only 21 percent for men over 65.[9] Some older people are required to retire whether they want to or not. Others find they can no longer muster the strength and stamina their jobs require. One study found that most people between 55 and 64 who stopped working did so because of sickness or disability.[10]

Another employment problem arises because technological changes suddenly make obsolete the skills that older workers have acquired over a lifetime. Old men who know only how to bake bread or build fine cabinets or repair shoes are bound to have a tough time as bakeries become bread factories, cabinets are made of plastic, and cheap shoes are imported in huge quantities. They cannot even get unskilled jobs because employers want the energy of youth. Employee training programs that might lead to new skills are closed because training directors believe that older men and women will not work long enough to repay the cost of the training.

Discrimination in hiring and promotion is a fact of life for the elderly. Employers give a variety of reasons for their reluctance to hire senior citizens. They fear that older workers will take longer to learn a new job, will not be as productive, and will be sick more often than their younger counterparts. While such fears are not groundless, they do not apply to the majority of older workers. A more realistic objection to hiring older workers stems from the fact that they probably will not stay on the job as long as younger workers. This means that expensive training procedures must be repeated more often and that the costs of pensions and retirement benefits are likely to be higher for the company employing older workers.

Pensions   Retired men and women receive income from a variety of sources, including pensions, social security, and personal savings. Most workers dream of retiring on a "fat pension," but only a minority of the retired receive any pension at all and such pensions are seldom "fat." (See Figure 9.2.) Ten years ago, 77 percent of all retired American families received no pension other than social security.[11] In 1973, the average beneficiary of a private pension plan received less than $2000 a year.[12] Further, private pension plans ordinarily do not provide for cost-of-living adjustments, so beneficiaries can look forward to seeing their retirement income slowly eaten away by inflation. Until recently most pension plans had no provision for continuing the income of a pensioner's widow or widower.

However, the picture is not all bleak. Government employees are generally covered by adequate pension plans, often including provisions for cost-of-living adjustments. In response to the demands of labor unions, more and more private companies have been setting up adequate pension

FIGURE 9.2
RETIREMENT COVERAGE
IN PRIVATE INDUSTRY,
1972

Source: U.S. Department of Commerce, *Social Indicators 1976* (Washington, D.C.: GPO, 1976), p. 122.

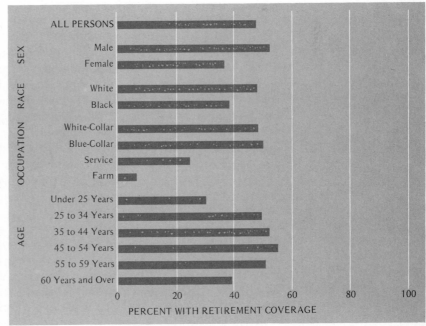

plans too. The Employee Retirement Income Security Act of 1974 brought about a number of improvements in American pension plans. This act requires most pension funds to pay survivor benefits and to make arrangements for workers who change jobs after building up years of pension benefits. It also calls for government supervision of pension funds to ensure that they will remain solvent.[13]

The single most important source of income for elderly people in the United States is payments from Old Age and Survivors' Insurance, commonly called social-security benefits. Over four-fifths of all elderly people in the United States collect social security or public assistance, and about half of the elderly have no other source of income.[14] For years fixed social-security incomes were eroded by rising prices, but now payments are adjusted to cost-of-living increases. Nevertheless, old people who have no other source of income have a hard time surviving on social security. Recent studies show that these payments provide only a fraction of the income the beneficiaries earned before retirement.[15] As Robert Atchley points out, "While Social Security pensions have the virtue of being available to almost everyone, the level of income they provide is meager at best, and for many it is significantly below the amount of income necessary to provide even the barest essentials."[16] In Canada those who receive old-age security payments fare no better. A government survey in the 1960s showed that 54 percent of elderly Canadians had annual incomes of less than $1000 and that half of those age 70 or over did not live with relatives and had no income other than their old-age security payments.[17]

Contrary to popular opinion, cash contributions from relatives make up only about 1 percent of the income of elderly people. However, this figure does not take account of the elderly people who live with relatives. Generally, old people have more assets and fewer debts than younger people. And of course a few elderly people have substantial holdings in stocks, bonds, or real estate. The problem is that those with the lowest retirement incomes also have the fewest assets to fall back on. For instance, a house that is partly or fully paid for is the most common major asset held by old people, but fewer than half have such an asset. Aside from their investment in a house, the personal wealth of more than half of the elderly amounts to less than $1000.[18]

Housing   Decent housing is especially important to the elderly because they spend so much time at home. In city centers old people living in rundown rooms must accept the risks and discomforts of life in a slum. Inexpensive housing that is within walking distance of stores and a doctor's office is likely to be substandard and within easy reach of pollution, vice, and crime. For personal comfort old people need higher room temperatures than the young require, but housing for the elderly often lacks proper heating.

Those who are physically handicaped or disabled also need wheelchair ramps, elevators, and other special facilities.

About one-third of all senior citizens live in dilapidated, substandard housing because they cannot afford anything better. They have little money to spend for housing, despite the fact that the largest share of their income must go for this purpose.[19] Even owning a home is not easy for many old people. There are mortgage payments to meet, and the costs of rising taxes and fire insurance also must be paid. Because many of the homes in which the elderly live were built before World War II, they are old by American standards. New roofs and other needed repairs may be left undone because most old people are unable to do the work themselves and cannot afford to hire outside help.

About one out of every twenty old people lives in an institution, usually a "nursing home." Most of these institutions, privately owned and managed, are profit-making businesses. Many that charge high fees give excellent service, but some of these, and most of the cheaper places, do not do much "nursing" and are in no sense "homes."

A government survey found that only 7 percent of all American nursing homes employed a full-time doctor and that only one-third arranged for visits by a doctor on a regular basis.[20] The same survey found that only about one-third of the nursing homes had rehabilitative services. Because nursing homes pay low wages, many nurses, therapists, and attendants leave for higher-paying jobs in hospitals after they have perfected their skills.

Some nursing homes are in old buildings that are overcrowded, unsanitary firetraps. There are not enough toilets, the sewers back up, and the light switches don't work because managers aim only to keep costs down and increase profits. Residents complain that they are served only the cheapest foods and do not get a balanced diet. Most old people, and many young ones, feel that entering a nursing home is a disgrace — a sign of final rejection by friends and family and proof that no one really cares.[21]

Transportation

The North American transportation system is based on the automobile. While a few cities have efficient mass transportation systems, most people without cars have limited mobility, and that includes many senior citizens. The cost of monthly payments, maintenance, and insurance places an automobile beyond their reach. Even among those who can afford a car, there are many who are refused renewal of their driver's licenses. Reasonably high levels of vision, hearing, coordination, and responsiveness are necessary for safe driving, and old age eventually reduces all three. A special problem occurs among elderly women who never learned to drive and are stranded when their husbands die. The use of taxis and buses is not a practical alternative for most old people. Even at reduced "senior-citizen" rates, taxis are too expensive, and many elderly people are unable to walk to bus stops or subway stations. Only a free taxi service will solve their problem.

Problems of Transition

Old people somehow learn to adjust to the profound role changes that are thrust upon them. But this transition can be very difficult. As pointed out earlier, role change among the elderly usually involves loss of status, while role changes for younger people are likely to involve attractive improvements. The three most significant personal transitions that the elderly must face are retirement, increasing normlessness and isolation, and death.

Retirement

The idea of retiring from work on a pension after reaching a certain age is relatively new. It developed only after the industrial system had matured enough to make retirement economically possible. Although the first retirement program was begun in 1810 for British civil servants, such programs did not become common until well into the twentieth century.[22] In 1890, almost 70 percent of American men over 65 were in the labor force. Today, only about one-fifth are working.[23]

After a person has been employed for decades, the transition to retirement can be painful. The daily routine that has given direction to the worker's life is suddenly yanked away. This change is difficult enough when it is voluntary, but it presents special problems to people who are forced to quit working when they reach a mandatory retirement age. The transition is not just a matter of finding new things to do, but requires adjustment to the idea that people who do not work are not "pulling their weight." It demands a new answer to the first question strangers are likely to ask each other: "What do you do?" Although retirees are no longer viewed as loafers, some stigma remains. An old saying held that "it is better to wear away than to rust away." People who are rusting away on park benches and shuffleboard courts are seen as a little immoral as well as useless. As Herman Loether puts it,

> The dilemma retirement presents for the American man arises from the fact that the leisurely life expected of the retired contradicts the pervasive work orientation of our society. The man who has spent 40 years or more in the labor force, devoting a major portion of his life to his job, is suddenly handed a gold watch . . . and told to go home and relax. . . . The man who has devoted his life to work frequently has nothing to substitute for it once it is denied him, for relaxation is to him an art unknown. The gist of the retirement problem is that, at least for the time being, our society does not accord retirement the positive value it accords work.[24]

In addition to these difficulties, retirees usually suffer a sharp drop in income and can no longer afford many of the things they used to buy — another sign of "failure."

Despite these problems, studies show that most retired people are satisfied with their lives. Ten years ago a Harris poll asked a sample of retired people, "Has retirement fulfilled your expectations for a good life or have you found it less than satisfactory?" Sixty-one percent of the respondents said that retirement had fulfilled their expectations, while only one-third felt that it was less than satisfactory. The two most common complaints among those who said that they were dissatisfied with retirement involved health and income. Lack of satisfying work was third on the list.[25] Other research shows that retirement does not usually affect health adversely and may even improve it. Retirement also appears to have little effect on morale, satisfaction with life, or self-esteem; so while the transition to retirement may be difficult, most people seem to be able to handle it satisfactorily.[26]

Normlessness and Isolation

More difficult than retirement is the transition to old age itself. Because elderly people do not have clear-cut roles in our society, many find themselves in an ambiguous position. As Vern L. Bengtson writes,

> [Older people] are conscious that earlier behaviors are somehow no longer appropriate, [but] there is very little evidence of clearly defined and widely shared expectations concerning what people should do during this period of life. . . . There are fewer and fewer clear-cut obligations or appropriate behavior as one passes into the socially defined stage of "old age."[27]

Such normlessness can produce a sense of alienation and even despair. Because no one seems to need their talents, many elderly people develop a growing sense of uselessness. But this normlessness can be a kind of liberating experience to some, who find that they are finally free to "be themselves" without having to worry about what others think of them.

Aimless or free, the social world of the elderly shrinks as the years accumulate. There are fewer social contacts as friends and relatives die, and moving from place to place becomes increasingly difficult. Old social roles are dropped, and even sex differences blur as a single role, that of "old people," is accepted.

Old people look and behave differently, so they are increasingly shunned by the young.[28] If they have children, or sisters and brothers, they are fortunate, for ties with surviving family members normally remain strong. When the time comes, most children take responsibility for their aged parents.[29] Those without close living relatives find their world growing smaller and smaller.

Sooner or later old people die. If one member of a married couple dies, the survivor must cope without a partner. Most survivors are women, both because most wives are younger than their husbands and because women live longer than men. The average widow is only 56 years old when her husband dies and can expect to live at least another decade

As people grow older their environment changes, old places become unfamiliar, and friends and loved ones die. Thus, many old people are isolated and lonely.

without him.[30] In widowhood normlessness, isolation, and loneliness may be particularly severe.

The older the widow, the greater the problems. There is no sex, no love, no help with daily tasks, and less income. Problems of transition begin immediately after the husband's death. The woman who depended on her husband to make the decisions and handle family affairs must, in the midst of her grief, work her way through a maze of medical bills, insurance claims, funeral expenses, and tax payments. She is likely to discover that she is eligible for little or none of her husband's pension benefits, and may have to choose among looking for a job, trying to live on social security, or remarrying. Remarriage is not likely to be easy, for there are not enough eligible older men. Moreover, after living with one man for most of a lifetime the idea of taking up with another is not likely to be attractive.

Becoming a widower has its problems too. Should the elderly widower desire to remarry, his chances of finding a mate seem brighter because there are more elderly women than men. If he does not remarry, his life may become more difficult. In most families it is the wife who keeps up contacts with friends and relatives, arranges parties, and runs the household. Consequently, a man who loses his wife is likely to lose touch with many of his friends. Further, while some widows can fall back on their maternal roles, widowers generally have weaker ties to their children and therefore are likely to be lonely and isolated.[31]

NINETEENTH CENTURY SOCIAL PROBLEMS

Died, September 20th, 1892, at his home in Sechlerville, Wisconsin, Samuel McWilliam, in the 84th year of his age. The death angel hovered over the home of Uncle Sammy for many months, threatening and retreating until gently and silently it wrapt its dark mantle around his wasted form and winged its flight to that bourn from whence no traveler returns. Born in . . . 1809, the deceased . . . was the father of 8 children, 6 of whom (2 sons and 4 daughters) remain to comfort the last days of their widowed mother. . . . His sufferings were such as only those with cancer endure. He longed for release. His eyes, closed in the darkness of here, [have] opened (we trust) in the brilliant presence of his Redeemer. September 29, 1892

Death   Death is the final personal transition. Life itself is slow death, but only old people usually think of it in that way. But however death is viewed, it is more than a biological event. It is a social event as well.

In many societies, death is an everyday occurrence celebrated by a ceremony similar to a christening, confirmation, or bar mitzvah. In North America, where death rates are low, we pretend that death is an accident. When it occurs we grieve; but we imagine that it is avoidable, like automobile collisions or flunking out of college. The dying pay the price for this denial of reality. They are avoided as deftly as our thoughts of death. About 80 percent of our people die in an institution, shut away from the familiar surroundings of home. Feelings of rejection and loneliness are common among the dying. Attempts to deceive the terminally ill about their condition only aggravate the situation. "Students of the process of dying have long emphasized the loneliness of the dying person," writes Robert S. Morrison. "Not only is he destined to go where no one wants to follow but also the people around him prefer to pretend that the journey is really not going to take place."[32]

Because death is such a mysterious event, people often respond to thoughts of death with fear and anxiety, and this may spur frantic attempts to stave off the inevitable. Modern medicine routinely prolongs the suffering of patients and their families by postponing what might have been an easy death.

Still, most old people learn to accept the inevitability of their death. Some may see it as a welcome relief. Belief in God and in life after death helps, and thus there is a tendency for people to become more religious as they age. Oddly enough, however, Herman Feifel found that the fear of death is greater among religious people than among nonreligious people.[33] Perhaps this is a reflection of the fact that some old people are attracted to religion because they fear death.

North Americans are among the healthiest and longest living people in the world, and they do not like to think about death. The dying are often lied to, avoided, and ignored because those around them do not want to face a reality they would rather forget.

RESPONDING TO PROBLEMS OF THE ELDERLY

Some of the problems of aging are personal problems. There is little that can be done to avoid physical deterioration, the loss of loved ones, the inability to work hard and long, and the other problems that come with advancing age. But even problems that are rooted in the biology of human aging are profoundly affected by our society and culture. While no one can stop biological aging, the social institutions and understandings that develop around the process of aging exert an enormous influence on the conditions under which it is experienced. Social structure and culture determine whether older citizens live out their remaining years in comfort and dignity or in loneliness and fear.

Employment

Probably the most effective way to deal with the problems of older workers is to improve the economic conditions of all workers. If the unemployment rate were not so high, employers would be required to fill their needs by turning to the many qualified and capable older workers available; and if the government supported retraining programs for all workers, there would be no need to choose between the young and the old.

The United States, like other nations, has tried to deal with the problem of age discrimination by passing laws against it. The Federal Age Discrimination in Employment Act of 1967 prohibits most types of age discrimination for workers between the ages of 40 and 65. As a result the most blatant signs of age discrimination have decreased significantly. But more subtle forms of discrimination continue. A study by the Department of Labor found that five years after passage of the Age Discrimination Act one out of every three employers was violating the law.[34] Laws of this type are difficult to enforce because it is hard to prove why an employer hired one person rather than another. Further, the law is enforced on a hit-or-miss basis because there isn't enough money to enforce it across the board.

Pension plans requiring retirement at a certain age — now usually 70 — also are discriminatory. About half of all American workers face a date on which they must stop working for their present employer.[35] Viewed in the best light, mandatory retirement plans are attempts to help workers by requiring employers to reward employees with pensions at a certain age. When the pension is high, few workers object to retiring. But many pension plans do not provide an old person with enough to live on. Because the general rule is that the lowest-paid workers get the lowest pensions, some workers who are forced to retire at age 70 are forced into poverty. Others do not wish to retire even if their pension plans are adequate. Mandatory retirement for these people is blatantly discriminatory in that it shunts them aside to make way for younger workers. There is no good ground for forcing healthy and productive individuals to give up their jobs simply because they have reached a certain age. Indeed, the state of California has already passed a law forbidding this practice, and many other legislative bodies are considering such acts.

Social Welfare

The very old, like the very young, are unable to fend for themselves. Poor health and failing personal resources eventually force most senior citizens into dependency. In some cases the needed help is provided by family members. But most families are unable to provide the needed care. Government agencies have been trying to fill the breach, and there have been numerous proposals for improving government work in this area.

Retirement Income

Social security is the only source of income for about half of all retired Americans and the major source of income for many more. Yet, as pointed out earlier, these benefits are modest and are often below the level of bare subsistence. The obvious solution to this problem is to increase the benefits. But implementing this proposal is not easy because the social-security system is in serious financial trouble.

The original idea behind the social-security system was that each worker would be required to save part of his or her income and that those contributions would be matched by the employer. When workers retired they would be entitled to regular payments from the fund that their contributions had helped build up. In practice, however, the contributions of workers have gone directly to retirees and have not been stored up in investment funds. Social security's current financial problems arise from the fact that the number of retirees is increasing much more rapidly than the number of workers. (See Figure 9.3.) Thus, today's workers must pay higher social-security taxes than in past decades. This burden is particularly heavy on low- and middle-income wage earners because the social-security tax rate does not increase as income increases (as income

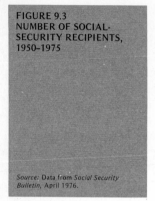

FIGURE 9.3
NUMBER OF SOCIAL-
SECURITY RECIPIENTS,
1950–1975

Source: Data from *Social Security
Bulletin,* April 1976.

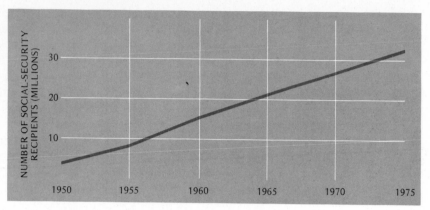

tax rates do). Those with high incomes do not pay taxes on their entire earnings but only on the portion below a fixed level.

Because of these problems, it is unlikely that social-security revenues can be increased significantly without a change in the tax base. The possibilities include making all income subject to social-security tax, instituting a progressive social-security tax that increases as income increases, and supplementing social-security funds with other tax moneys. Such changes would increase social-security revenue without placing the burden on struggling low- and middle-income wage earners.

An alternative approach is to improve private pension plans. The passage of the Employee Retirement Income Security Act of 1974, discussed earlier, was a step in this direction. Nevertheless, private pension plans are limited by the ability and willingness of the employer to support them. Many employers cannot afford to support decent pensions for their employees, and others simply refuse to do so. The benefits from most private pension plans are quite small, and many workers are not covered at all. People who run their own small shops or businesses, for example, receive no private pensions.

Housing   So-called retirement communities are one of the most successful responses to the need of the elderly for decent housing. Most of these are private and, thus, available only to people with substantial means. For example, in one Southern California retirement community there are three times as many college graduates and twice as many professionals and managers as would be expected on the basis of the California population as a whole.[36] Often built in sunny climates, these complexes of houses or apartments are designed especially for the elderly and usually include special recreational facilities. Some are run like hotels or make hotel-like arrangements for residents who can afford them. Others are hardly distinguishable from nursing homes and "old people's homes." They have been

Retirement communities with specialized recreational and social facilities are becoming an increasingly popular response to the housing problems of the elderly. However, retirement communities are expensive, and most elderly people cannot afford to live in them.

criticized because they weaken the ties between generations and give older people the feeling that their only responsibility is to kill time. Nevertheless, many old people move to retirement communities every year precisely because they seek the companionship of others who share their common interests and experiences.

The elderly poor can apply for government-subsidized housing. They may receive government help with their rent or move into low-cost government housing projects. But many eligible applicants receive nothing at all. There are not enough low-cost rooms for all the people who need them. Some cities have lists of over 30,000 elderly people who are waiting for low-income housing.[37]

Critical housing problems are also found among middle-income retirees who cannot afford expensive retirement communities and do not qualify for subsidized housing. Most of these people live in their own homes. As noted earlier, even when older citizens have paid off their mortgages they may run into financial problems ranging from soaring property taxes to the increasing costs of repairs and maintenance. One response, now in effect in a few areas, gives elderly people with financial problems some tax relief. Property taxes are deferred until death, when the state sells the house and deducts any taxes due before returning the remainder to the heirs.

Health   As noted in Chapter 8 some nations have responded to the health care problems of the elderly by making the government responsible for financing all medical care. The United States is one of the few modern industrial countries without some form of national health insurance. Medicare came into effect in 1965 as a partial response to this problem. But seven years later the elderly were paying more from their own pockets for health care than they were before the medicare program began. In 1972 medicare paid only 42.3 percent of the elderly's medical bills.[38] The elderly poor are often eligible for other welfare payments that help with medical bills, but middle-income people receive no such assistance.

Cultural Change

Most of the problems of the elderly are rooted in our cultural traditions. For example, there is a strong negative stereotype of old people. This attitude probably arises from observing the miserable conditions in which many old people must live, but eliminating poverty among the aged will not necessarily change the stereotype. A public-opinion survey sponsored by the National Council on Aging found that older people consistently describe themselves in more positive terms than those in which the general public describes them. For instance, people over 65 were almost three times as likely as those under 65 to say that the elderly are "very open-minded and adaptable." The general public also saw the elderly as much less active and more bored than the elderly saw themselves. Those under 65 were more than twice as likely to believe that the elderly spend a lot of time sleeping or doing nothing, and they were four times as likely to say that "not having enough to do" is a serious problem for the elderly.[39] Such stereotypes become self-fulfilling prophecies that lead to the exclusion of the elderly from employment opportunities and other forms of social involvement. Further, because many elderly people accept these stereotypes, they may feel that they are obliged to give up their more active pursuits.

The most effective way to change this situation is to encourage the elderly to participate in community life, putting their wealth of wisdom and experience to work for the good of others. A number of government programs are aimed toward these ends. For example, in the Foster Grandparent Program older men and women are paid to work part time at child care centers and institutions. The elderly get meaningful work and additional income, and children receive the benefits of personal attention and concern. Senior citizens' centers, which are funded by public and private sources, also employ old people in community projects. Perhaps more important, these centers provide a place where the elderly can congregate, make new friends, and get a hot meal.

The stereotype of the elderly as useless incompetents is also being challenged by old people who have organized for direct political action.

NINETEENTH CENTURY SOCIAL PROBLEMS

Alexander Gardapie, aged 90 years, died at Prairie du Chien. He walked into a salloon, drank a glass of gin, asked the time of day, sat down, and died.
January 31, 1895

Our culture stereotypes older people as useless and incompetent, but nothing could be further from the truth. The store of information and wisdom accumulated by the elderly is especially useful to the young as they are growing up.

For example, the American Association of Retired Persons has, like the Gray Panthers, shown that old people are not useless. As such organizations enlist more senior citizens and gain more political power, the aged may once again be respected, just as labor unions have made it respectable to be a manual worker. Also, better organization will bring more government programs for the aged, including increased funding for existing programs such as social security. As the percentage of old people in the population increases, their expectations also will rise. It is therefore reasonable to predict that the elderly will win the increase in status and political power they seek.

SOCIOLOGICAL PERSPECTIVES on Problems of the Elderly

To sociologists and other social scientists, it is obvious that aging, like unemployment or poverty, cannot be dismissed as an individual problem. Of course, each of us must come to terms with the realities of aging and death. But while this may seem to be an isolated, individual struggle, it is not. Cultural concepts about aging, religion, and death shape the process of growing old. Moreover, society's economic and family systems are responsible for meeting the emotional and physical needs of the elderly. If society fails to meet these needs, the elderly are bound to suffer. Even the political institution is involved, for the government now offers a host of programs that try to compensate for the failures of other social institutions.

The Functionalist Perspective

Functionalists see much confusion in the institutions and agencies that are supposed to meet the needs of the elderly. At the base of the problem are the changes that continue to transform Western culture. In the past, death came at an early age, and there were few elderly people. Those who did grow old were cared for by their families. But with the improvements in sanitation and food supplies brought about by industrialization, the percentage of elderly people in the population has increased enormously. At the same time, economic changes caused a breakdown in the traditional extended family, leaving many older people isolated, alone, and without the financial means to support themselves. Thus, both the number of elderly people and their problems have increased sharply in recent times.

From this perspective, it is necessary to reorganize the social institutions that traditionally cared for the elderly or to develop new agencies that can do so more effectively. The fact that the government has been taking increased financial responsibility for the elderly can be seen as an attempt to get the machinery of society running smoothly again. But there is a great deal of disorganization in the administration of government programs for the elderly, just as there is disorganization in poverty and health care programs. These programs are often large, cumbersome, and inefficient, and they spend far too much of their budget on administrative costs. But the most serious problem is that these agencies do not have enough money to meet the needs of our older people. However, there are signs that society is beginning to come to terms with the problems of the elderly. The old stereotypes about the elderly are beginning to change, and senior citizen's centers, retirement communities, and other organizations designed to meet the needs of the elderly are becoming increasingly common.

The Conflict Perspective

Many social scientists are convinced that the government's indifference to old people and their problems is not an accident but a product of class conflict. They argue that the wealthy and powerful have blocked efforts to help the aged because such help is not in their best interests. The wealthy do not need government assistance and do not care to pay for such assistance for others.

Value conflict also plays an important part in the problems of the elderly. Ideas about the value of competition, self-reliance, and personal responsibility clash with the effort to care for people who are no longer productive. Thus, the ideology of individualism blames the elderly for their poverty, assuming that they deserve to suffer because they have failed to provide for their future. Aging has become a social problem because increasing numbers of people are coming to believe that old people deserve a fair share of the wealth they have helped to produce.

According to conflict theory, the most effective response to the problems of the elderly is political action. Senior citizens need to organize into political groups, find support from other organizations, and use their votes to force the government to give them a better break. They must also at-

Conflict theorists feel that increasing political activism is the most effective way to solve the problems of the elderly in our society.

tack the attitudes and values that have led so many people to blame the elderly for their own poverty, instead of placing the responsibility on the social institutions that actually cause the problem. Increasing political activism among the elderly will also help to refute the old stereotypes of elderly people as feeble and incompetent.

The Social-Psychological Perspective

Social psychologists who use the biosocial perspective emphasize the importance of the physical changes we undergo as we age. Loss of strength and vitality will always be part of the process of aging, but some scientists feel that new medical breakthroughs may make it possible to slow this process of degeneration. Whatever the future may hold, it is clear that some of the physical degeneration of the elderly is due to improper diet, inadequate heating and shelter, and lack of exercise — conditions that are social rather than biological. Thus, major scientific breakthroughs are not necessary in order to improve the health of older people.

Most social psychologists are more concerned with the social process of aging than with biology. Both behaviorists and interactionists point out that social behavior is learned in interaction with other people. As people reach different age levels, their group memberships change and they play new roles. The shift from childhood to adolescence, for example, involves complex role changes. Nevertheless, most people easily learn how to move from one age grade to another. They manage these changes because their group memberships change. As they age, they are admitted to membership in a new group, one with different ideas about their rights and duties.

Most people find adjustment to the roles of old age very difficult. This occurs because old people, more than people moving into any other age group, are likely to lack group support. Children are taught to rehearse adolescent roles, and adolescents are trained how to behave as adults. But in this youth-oriented society, few of us are trained to be old people. Old age comes as a shock. And, because the roles of old people are poorly anchored in social groups, some old people literally do not know how they are supposed to behave. Previous roles disappear, along with friends and loved ones, but their new role is poorly defined. It is this lack of group support that gives so many old people a feeling of isolation and loneliness.

But the social-psychological perspective also suggests that old people are isolated and lonely because isolation and loneliness are assigned to the old-age role. Here, the idea is that there *is* a role for old people but that it is an inferior one. People in Western cultures continue to stigmatize old people and thus, to aggravate their psychological difficulties. Feelings of uselessness and inadequacy are the common result of these attitudes.

To change old people's sense of isolation and uselessness, many social psychologists recommend that the elderly be returned to the mainstream of social life. In order to reduce prejudice and stigma, the elderly need to be absorbed into communities made up of all age groups, as adolescents are, and not segregated into "old people's ghettos." However, other social psychologists disagree, arguing that the elderly are better off when they are integrated into communities specifically designed to meet their needs. These social psychologists therefore encourage the trend toward age-segregated communities and promote efforts to create better living conditions within them.

SUMMARY

Aging is a social as well as a biological process. All societies divide their members into age grades—categories of people with a common range of ages—and the members of the various age grades have different rights and duties. Sociologically, aging is a series of transitions from one social role to another, and such role transitions are difficult. The individual making such changes must adapt to a new set of expectations and leave behind the rewards and security of earlier roles.

Transition to the age grade called "old age" or "elderly" seems to be the most difficult of all the age grade transitions. Because Western culture puts high value on youth and vigor, it fails to give the elderly the prestige and respect that they receive in many other cultures.

Elderly people have more chronic diseases and poorer overall health than the general population. However, the extent of the health problems of the elderly is usually exaggerated. Most old people say that they are in reasonably good health.

Money worries are common among the aged. Most older people are not eligible for a private pension, and the private pensions that the elderly do receive are usually inadequate. About half of all the elderly people in the United States live almost entirely on social-security payments or public assistance. About one-third of America's senior citizens live in substandard housing.

The elderly must make several difficult transitions, including retirement, isolation, and death. The problems of retirement cannot be clearly separated from those of old age. Retirement as such is not bad for a person's health and does not, by itself, have devastating effects on morale. But because the elderly lose old friends and relations as well as most of the social roles they once performed, they are likely to be lonely and isolated. The death of a spouse makes matters worse. After a brief period of support and sympathy, the new widow or widower must take up a new life. Widows have some special problems of adjustment because their incomes are greatly reduced and their chances for remarriage are slim.

Many different responses to the problems of the elderly have been tried or suggested. The United States has officially outlawed age discrimination in employment. However, this legislation has not been particularly effective. A better way of dealing with the employment problems of the elderly would be to increase the overall demand for labor so that employers would need the skills the older workers have to offer.

The simplest way of improving the financial condition of old people would be to increase social-security benefits. This is complicated by the fact that the Social Security Administration collects money as though it were an insurance company but pays out money as though it were a welfare agency. The solution is to make it a welfare program in practice as well as principle, using general tax funds for pensions.

Many housing projects have been established to improve the living conditions of the elderly, both rich and poor. However, retirement communities for the rich and government-subsidized housing projects for the poor leave those in the middle with unsolved housing problems.

Two principal proposals for improving the health care of the elderly have been made. One asks the government to assume a greater share of health care costs, thereby relieving hard-pressed senior citizens. The other asks that our medical system give more attention to the illnesses of old age.

Many observers have suggested that improvement in the conditions of the elderly would come from integrating the elderly into the community. Political organization is a second way to change cultural stereotyping of old people.

Functionalists see the problems of aging as one more product of the social disorganization that follows rapid economic and social change. From this perspective it is necessary either to restore the extended family or to develop new organizations to take its place. Conflict theorists, on the other hand, are convinced that the elderly are in poor shape because the wealthy and powerful profit from their misery. They advocate more and better organization for political action by the elderly. Social psychologists study how age-graded roles are learned. They have noted that learning the role of an elderly person is especially difficult because the role is a poorly defined one that lacks group support.

KEY TERMS   age grade
aging
rite of passage
social security

10
The Sexes

How are sex roles determined?
Why do sex role stereotypes persist?
How have sex roles changed in this century?
Is sexual inequality disappearing?

Everyone has watched a motion picture hero fight his way through fire, flood, or corruption to save a defenseless heroine from disaster. But we would be amazed if the woman were shown rescuing the man while he clung helplessly to her skirts. The first plot fits our ideas about the proper behavior of men and women. The second does not.

Our ideas about differences between the sexes have deep historical roots. For generations these ideas were accepted uncritically, but things are beginning to change. New economic and social conditions are forcing us to rethink our traditional attitudes. Women are moving into the "man's world" of employment and competition, while men are beginning to explore the "woman's world" of family and children. Indeed, this redefinition of what it means to be a woman or a man may be one of the most significant developments of modern times.

At first glance these changes hardly qualify as a social problem; but sexual identity is a central part of human personality, and even minor changes have far-reaching implications. For many people, perhaps most, the new definitions are a welcome release from unreasonable social restrictions. Others, however, are experiencing confusion and anxiety. Even more important, people are becoming aware that sexual inequality is as unjust as racial, ethnic, and class inequality. Women have come to be recognized as a minority group similar in many ways to ethnic minorities.

SEX ROLES

Like veteran actors, each of us plays many roles. The list is almost endless — parent, child, student, worker, pedestrian, automobile driver, shopper, consumer. Sex roles are duties and obligations assigned on the basis of gender. There are different social expectations for males and females in countless social situations. These expectations pertain both to what people are supposed to do and to what they are not supposed to do. A male, for instance, is expected to work and support his wife and children; it is expected that he will not wear dresses and lipstick.

Sex roles are assigned early in the socialization process. Children quickly learn that they are girls or boys and act accordingly. Most keep their sexual identity for life. Nevertheless, adult sex roles are complex, involving both personality and behavioral characteristics. Women are expected to be passive, warm, and supportive. In contrast to men, who are expected to suppress their feelings, women are encouraged to express emotions openly. Women also are expected to be dependent and to need emotional support. Men, on the other hand, are expected to be active, independent, and self-controlled. An essential part of the male role is aggressiveness and dominance. The "henpecked" husband is the subject of countless jokes because he deviates from cultural expectations, but no one jokes about the woman who does her husband's bidding.

DEBATE
Should Traditional Sex Role Differences Be Abolished?

PRO

Stereotypes about the differences between men and women are relics from the past. When muscle power was the principal source of energy and breast milk the only safe food for an infant, the traditional division of labor between the sexes made some sense. But while times have changed, the old sex roles have not. Children are still trained to meet the expectations of stereotyped sex roles regardless of their psychological fitness to fill those roles. Many boys who would be happy raising children at home are pushed into the "man's world" of competition and achievement, while many bored housewives are better suited for the roles of business executive or scientist. Even those who are comfortable with the traditional role of their sex pay a heavy psychological price. Women must suppress the domineering "masculine" side of their personality, while men are often terrified of appearing submissive or "feminine." Too often the result is a one-dimensional person who is out of touch with his or her own desires and needs. The elimination of stereotyped sex roles would not, as critics have charged, force women to go to work or men to stay at home with their children. It would instead allow us to accept both sides of our personality and choose a life style that fits our own needs rather than the inflexible demands of social stereotypes.

As a result of sex role stereotypes, women receive lower wages, have less political power, and occupy an inferior position to men in our society. If there is ever to be true equality between the sexes, double standards and stereotypes must be eliminated. Only then will men and women be able to relate to each other honestly in an atmosphere of mutual respect and understanding.

CON

Traditional sex roles are essential to the survival of society. They provide a rational and efficient division of labor, allowing men to specialize in some tasks and women in others. This not only permits parents to give different training to boys and girls as they are growing up but allows for a psychological division of labor. Girls are encouraged to develop the supportive, nurturant characteristics that make them effective wives and mothers, while boys are trained to assert the aggressive side of their personality, which is needed for success in the economic world. The division of labor between the sexes minimizes competition, permitting men and women to perform different tasks that are complementary. If the reformers had their way, marital harmony would disintegrate as husbands and wives competed with each other to see who could make the biggest salary. Although reformers talk about sharing the responsibilities of child care, in most cases children would simply be shipped off to boarding schools and day care centers.

Despite arguments about the exploitation of women, traditional sex roles are fair to both sexes. While men do have advantages in the world of work, women have equal advantages in the family. The latter include rights to alimony and child custody as well as special privileges such as help with tasks that demand physical strength or mechanical expertise.

But even if the elimination of sex roles were desirable, it just isn't possible. Traditional sex roles have endured for thousands of years because they reflect biological differences between the sexes. Sex role differences are essential to our society and should be maintained.

The focus of the traditional male role is the world of work; he is the breadwinner for the family and the provider of financial security. The husband is supposed to protect and defend his family from outside dangers, make important decisions, and provide family leadership. He must show courage and strive for achievement, thus proving himself fit to "be a man."

The traditional female role centers on home and family. Most women are under strong pressure to marry and have children, and their responsibility is to run the home and rear the children. While men's prestige is derived from their own efforts in the world, women's prestige is usually derived from that of their husbands.[1]

The male sex role has greater power and privilege than the female role, but it also is more narrowly defined. A young girl is usually permitted to take on some aspect of the male role if she desires. She may wear jeans, fight, climb trees, or play competitive sports, perhaps earning the label "tomboy." But it is unheard of for a boy to wear a dress and play only with little girls. If he acts like a girl, he is condemned as a "sissy."

Similar rigidity is present in the role of the adult male. Although competition and achievement in the "male" world is discouraged by the female role, the successful businesswoman often wins great respect for her achievements without necessarily losing her identity as a woman. But even men who are most unsuited to the stresses and strains of a business career are not permitted to join the "female" world of home and family. Similarly, women can work in factories without losing their identities as women, but men who quit their factory jobs to stay at home are loafers— inferior to "real men."

Men often fear that their masculinity will be threatened if they are too passive. A study of differences between male and female fantasy patterns concluded that men are much more fearful of losing control of themselves or their situation. The men seemed to believe that "once you slip, it is all over," while the women were much more likely to believe that a person will ultimately recover from a defeat.[2]

Although the nature of sex role differences is quite clear, their origins are very much in dispute. Some hold that they are primarily a result of biological differences between the sexes, while others feel that culture is more important. Of course, no one denies that there are significant biological differences between the sexes. The issue is the extent to which these differences influence sex roles.

Biological Influences

The two most significant biological differences are the male's greater size and strength, and the female's ability to bear and nurse children. In physical contests most males have a clear advantage. Not only is the average male taller than the average female, but testosterone, a male sex hormone, promotes muscular development and strength. On the other hand, the female has a much closer biological tie with the process of reproduction. Childbearing is of course the exclusive domain of the female. And before the development of "baby bottles," only the female could feed the child for the first months of its life. Because a sexually active woman will become pregnant about every two years without the use of contraceptives, in most preindustrial societies the average woman was either pregnant or nursing a small child during most of her adult life.[3]

Despite the greater physical prowess of the male, females are clearly the healthier sex. Males are subject to a variety of sex-linked genetic defects, including hemophilia and color blindness. They are also more susceptible to some diseases, and they grow and mature more slowly than females.[4] Although more male infants are born, their rate of death is significantly greater. Females have longer lifespans in all modern societies.

Significant differences between the behavior of girls and boys can be observed soon after birth. A study of young children found that "girls were more dependent, showed less exploratory behavior, and their play behavior reflected a more quiet style. Boys were independent, showed more exploratory behavior . . . were more vigorous, and tended to run and bang in their play."[5] In the early years of school, girls score higher on tests of overall intelligence, verbal ability, and numerical computations, while boys do better on tests of spatial and analytical abilities.[6] Each of these differences can be accounted for by cultural expectations, but the fact that the differences appear so early in life suggests that there is a biological component as well.

Cultural Influences

If sex roles were determined entirely by biology, they would be similar in all cultures. In fact, there are wide variations in sex roles from culture to culture. Such variation supports the idea that culture is the dominant force in the formation of sex roles. Margaret Mead found great differences among three cultures in New Guinea. In one, males and females behaved in what we would call a "feminine fashion." In another, both sexes were "masculine." In the third, the males were "feminine" and the females "masculine."

The Arapesh, one of the cultures Mead studied, showed passivity, cooperation, and peacefulness in both sexes. Males played an important part in child rearing, and both sexes were said to "bear children." On the other hand, among the Mundugamor both sexes were highly competitive and aggressive. There was a great deal of hostility between husband and wife, and a pregnancy was often seen by both partners as a disaster. According to Mead, "In the third tribe, the Tchambuli, we found a genuine reversal of the sex-attitudes of our own culture, with the woman the dominant, impersonal, managing partner, the man the less responsible and the emotionally dependent person." In this culture the woman is the sexual aggressor and the male "holds his breath and hopes." Considering this evidence. Mead concluded:

> Human nature is almost unbelievably malleable, responding accurately and contrastingly to contrasting cultural conditions. The differences between individuals who are members of different cultures, like the differences between individuals within a culture, are almost entirely to be laid to differences in conditioning, especially during early childhood, and the form of this conditioning is culturally determined. Standardized personality differences between the sexes are of this order, cultural creations to which each generation, male and female, is trained to conform.[7]

Although sex roles show wide variation, the pattern in most societies is not so different from our own. George Murdock's study of 224 societies found clear sex differences in the types of work done by men and women. Predominantly male activities generally involve strength, cooperation, and travel. Female activities, on the other hand, are physically easier, more solitary, and less mobile. For example, Murdock found 166 societies in which hunting was always done by men and 13 in which it was usually done by men. But in no society was hunting evenly divided between the sexes or performed predominantly by women. Cooking, on the other hand, was performed exclusively by women in 158 societies and exclusively by men in only five.[8]

In a later survey of 565 societies, Murdock found that married couples were more likely to live with the husband's family than with the wife's and were more likely (by a ratio of about four to one) to trace descent through the male's family rather than the female's. Of 431 societies that permitted polygamous marriage, 427 permitted men to have more than one wife, but only four permitted women to have more than one husband.[9] After an extensive review of the literature on the subject, Roy G. D'Andrade concluded:

> the cross-cultural mode is that males are more sexually active, more dominant, more deferred to, more aggressive, less responsible, less nurturant, and less emotionally expressive than females. The extent of these differences varies by culture. And in some cultures some of these differences do not exist (or occasionally the trend is actually reversed).[10]

Two conclusions seem justified. First, sex roles are determined primarily by culture. Strong evidence for this conclusion comes from studies of people who are raised as members of the opposite sex. Investigations of babies who were mistakenly classified as members of the opposite sex by parents concluded that unless the mistake were discovered by the age of 3 or 4 the children had great difficulty adjusting to a sex role change and put up vigorous opposition to such a reversal.[11] Other studies show that men who were socialized as women act in the manner expected of women and believe themselves to be women.[12] It appears, then, that cultural socialization easily overpowers any biological tendency for males and females to behave in different ways.

Second, sex roles have a biological base. Because men are stronger and larger than women and are not destined to bear and nurse children, it is not surprising that they engage in more activities that involve strength and travel while women are more concerned with childbearing and the responsibilities of the home. The typical pattern of male dominance can be seen as a result of the physical strength of the male. The typical "family-oriented" female pattern can be seen to be a consequence of childbearing and breast feeding. Differences in temperament and personality between males and females are probably cultural creations related to biologically based social duties. The male "breadwinner" is expected to be aggressive and independent, while the female "child raiser" is expected to be expressive and nurturant. A study of 110 cultures found that the socialization practices of most of them encouraged such traits as self-reliance and desire for achievement for boys and nurturance and responsibility for girls.[13]

History Sex roles have changed over the centuries as the economic system has changed. The earliest human societies obtained food by hunting animals and gathering edible plants. Because these societies left no written records, there is little hard evidence about their culture. However, by examining contemporary hunting and gathering societies, some educated guesses can be made about the earliest human societies.

Hunting and gathering societies were small, often consisting of fewer than fifty people. There was little surplus wealth, so the differences between rich and poor were small. Politically, these societies also tended to be egalitarian, with little or no formal leadership. Leaders would emerge in response to specific problems and then dissolve back into the group when the problems were solved. Under these conditions of relative political and economic equality, the most important and lasting social division was between men and women. Ernestine Friedl has described the relationship between the sexes in present-day hunting and gathering societies as follows:

> Economic and sexual cooperation between [the sexes] is necessary, but their interdependence is full of difficulties. . . . The cleavage between men and women can be great, and relationships are sometimes hostile. Nevertheless, both men and women have considerable autonomy, and those of each sex have, in most foraging societies, the basis for acquiring self-esteem.[14]

Friedl goes on to note that the most important difference in these societies stems from the male monopoly on hunting. The meat from hunts, which is usually distributed to the entire group, gives the successful hunter a source of prestige and power that women do not share. On the whole,

There are wide variations in sex roles among the various cultures of the world. Hunting and gathering societies, such as that shown here, generally have egalitarian relationships between the sexes.

however, relationships between the sexes, like other relationships in hunting and gathering societies, tend to be egalitarian.

A major change in human society occurred with the discovery that plants could be grown specifically for human use. Horticultural societies used the hoe and the digging stick but did not have the plow or irrigation. The style of life was quite different from that in hunting and gathering societies. The development of a more dependable food supply made it unnecessary to wander from place to place in search of food. The sedentary life promoted the growth of clans and the extended family. Trade grew, and with it developed inequalities in wealth and power. Because these societies produced surplus food, they were able to support specialized economic, religious, and political roles.[15]

In contemporary horticultural societies men almost always have a monopoly on warfare and do the initial clearing of land. Typically, both men and women share in cultivation, although this is sometimes assigned exclusively to women. Child rearing is typically but not always exclusively a female task. The distribution of power between the sexes varies with economic conditions. In societies with little trade and commerce and few class distinctions, males tend to be strongly dominant. In horticultural societies in which trade is an important activity, women usually have a much better position. In many such societies women can gain prestige by displaying trading ability in the marketplace.[16]

The next major change in human societies came with the development of agriculture. Agricultural societies make use of such technological advances as the plow, irrigation, and the harnessing of domestic animals. Inventions that originated in horticultural societies were refined in agricultural societies. Economic surpluses grew, and with this growth came greater sex role specialization, a more elaborate division of labor, and more social and economic inequality. Agricultural societies created written language and the first bureaucracies. The surplus food produced by agriculture permitted the growth of the first real cities. Large centralized empires developed in many agricultural regions.[17]

Although there were many cultural variations, the growth of agriculture usually meant a decline in the status of women. Women lost the influence that came from the important contribution they made to horticulture.[18] Because of the strength required for plowing and irrigation, men did most of the agricultural labor. Men also came to monopolize the powerful political and religious bureaucracies.

The industrial revolution created more profound changes. As noted in Chapter 5, the extended family deteriorated and the nuclear family became the norm. Economic changes that made children economic liabilities led to fewer births and a smaller number of children. Together with a greatly increased lifespan, this meant that for the first time women spent most of their adult lives without dependent children.

The transformation of the family and the economic system had a particularly significant impact on sex roles. Industrialization reduced the importance of physical strength in economic production. The family was displaced as the primary unit of economic production, and women joined the labor force in increasing numbers. The qualities necessary for economic success are now related more closely to personality than to physique, and are possessed by women as well as men. More women are pursuing careers, while recent increases in divorce and a trend toward marriage at a later age have forced other women to become economically self-sufficient.

More generally, industrialization has reduced the importance of the two most socially significant biological differences between the sexes. The male's size and strength are much less important in the age of automation. At the same time, the reduction in the number of births and the development of bottle feeding have modified women's child-rearing role.

Overall, industrialization brought a significant improvement in the status of women, although cultural changes have lagged behind changes in technology. Women are no longer seen as the property of their husbands — they have equal inheritance rights — and they are generally considered equal in theory if not in practice. Although men dominate the political sphere, democratic countries now give both men and women an equal vote, and women often run for political office. Yet, the traditional pattern in which the husband works and the wife stays home to raise the children is still dominant. A new pattern in which both the wife and husband work and share family duties is developing, though the wife often carries a disproportionate share of the domestic and child-rearing duties.[19]

Sex Role Socialization

Socialization is the process by which we learn the essentials of life in our culture. Customs, behavior, mores, values, how to speak, even how to think — all these are learned in the course of socialization. Sex role

socialization is part of this process. It is the way we learn the behavior and attitudes that are expected of the members of our sex. It should not be concluded, however, that sex role socialization creates identical males and females. There is always room for interpretation and creativity. Each individual creates his or her own definition of what it means to be a woman or a man — definitions that originate in response to our unique experiences.

Sexual stereotyping starts almost from the moment of birth when boys are wrapped in blue blankets and girls in pink blankets. Girls' and boys' rooms are decorated differently and contain different kinds of toys. But the most important differences are learned as children begin to master a language. For one thing, most languages require the speaker to make frequent distinctions between the sexes. The use of the words *he* and *his* or *she* and *hers* continually draws the child's attention to the importance of sex differences. In addition, the structure of every language conveys social assumptions about the nature of the differences between the sexes. The child quickly learns that the male is given first-class status while the female takes second place. In English, for example, male pronouns and adjectives are used to describe people whose sex is unknown ("No person shall be compelled in any criminal case to be a witness against himself"). When one is referring to the entire human race, the term *man* or *mankind* is used. The male is primary in our language, the female a vaguely defined "other."[20]

The older and more aware children become, the greater the differences in the family's expectations for boys and girls. Because the male role is narrowly defined, young boys come under some particularly intense pressures. They are continually told to not be "sissies" and not to act like girls. In fact, the sex role of young boys seems to be defined primarily in terms of negatives: They are more often told what they are *not* to do than what they are supposed to do or be. A boy who playfully puts on a dress and lipstick is likely to receive a hostile and even panicky reprimand from his parents. Boys' problems are aggravated by the fact that they usually spend much more time with their mothers than with their fathers and thus lack a positive role model. They are taught to reject and even fear anything feminine, but they live in the company of women. This conflict creates anxiety in many boys:

> This situation gives us practically a perfect combination for inducing anxiety — the demand that the child do something which is not clearly defined to him, based on reasons he cannot possibly appreciate, and enforced with threats, punishments, and anger by those who are close to him. Indeed, a great many boys do give evidence of anxiety which frequently expresses itself in over-straining to be masculine, in virtual panic at being caught doing anything traditionally defined as feminine, and in hostility toward anything even hinting at "femininity," including females themselves.[21]

Sex role socialization begins almost from the moment of birth. As children grow older, boys are encouraged to develop "masculine" attitudes and skills while girls are taught "feminine" qualities. By the time most people reach adulthood, sex role socialization has produced significant differences between women and men.

Girls are not subjected to as many conflicting demands. Although passivity and dependence are encouraged, competition and achievement are at least permitted. The young girl is not continually warned against "acting like a boy" and does not have a fear of being masculine equivalent to the boy's fear of being feminine. Because girls are raised by members of their own sex, they usually have a much clearer idea than boys of what will be expected of them as adults. However, the fact that fewer demands are placed on girls in childhood may make it more difficult for them to become independent, self-sufficient adults:

From around the age of two to two and a half, when children are no longer perceived as infants but as children, more boys than girls experience more prohibitions for a wider range of behavior. In addition, and of special importance, dependent behavior, normal to all young children, is permitted for girls and prohibited for boys. Thus, girls are not encouraged to give up old techniques of relating to adults and using others to define their identity, to manipulate the physical world and to supply their emotional needs.[22]

With the coming of adolescence, it is the girls who feel pressure to restrict their behavior. As the adolescent girl becomes interested in boys and dating, "femininity" becomes increasingly important. Much of the adolescent girl's status among her peers comes from her ability to attract boys, and she learns that the competent and aggressive girl is likely to scare the boys away. As Bardwick and Douvan put it, "Until adolescence the idea of equal capacity, opportunity and life style is held out to them [girls]. But sometime in adolescence the message becomes clear that one had better not do too well, that competition is aggressive and unfeminine, that deviating threatens the heterosexual relationship."[23] Thus, the typical adolescent girl spends her time trying to be attractive, and she learns not to excel in class or in the outside world. She devotes her skill and talents to finding the mate on whom her status and much of her future life will depend.

Among the most important influences on children in the classroom are the expectations of teachers. Research shows that teachers unintentionally encourage their students to fulfill these expectations. In Chapter 4 we mentioned an experiment with a group of elementary school teachers who were led to believe that certain students would make exceptional progress in the next year. The researchers found that the "special students" actually made more progress than the others, even though they had been selected entirely at random. They concluded that the teachers must somehow have communicated their higher expectations to the students and thereby encouraged them to improve their performance.[24]

Such self-fulfilling prophecies are important in the learning of sex roles. Most teachers expect their students to live up to traditional sex role stereotypes. By the time most children enter school, they have a pretty good idea of traditional sex roles and the behaviors expected of them. The major effect of the schools is to strengthen and reinforce these sexual stereotypes. A study reported by Chafetz found that 40 percent of the elementary school teachers surveyed thought that males had an innate biological tendency to be aggressive. Males were also believed to have better abstract reasoning ability, while females were seen as more compassionate, sentimental, and intuitive.[25]

Until recently textbooks also reinforced sexual stereotypes. In children's story books girls were portrayed as passive and content. They rarely took independent action, showed little ability to follow through on their decisions, and gave up easily.[26] A study of elementary school textbooks used in California schools found that males were the main characters in 75 percent of the stories and that only 20 percent of the total story content was devoted to females.[27] Another California study found the same pattern in arithmetic books. Typical illustrations showed girls passively reading or looking on while their brothers engaged in active play. The illustrations were three times more likely to feature males than females, and problems used masculine names twice as often as feminine names.[28] For years schoolbooks tended to portray women as mothers, nurses, and secretaries rather than as people of power and influence.

As students leave elementary school, females and males are directed into different kinds of classes. Girls are encouraged to take courses that help them fulfill the traditional sex role—sewing, cooking, and typing. Boys are expected to take classes in carpentry, sheet metal work, and automobile repair. Further, counselors encourage college-bound girls to enter such "feminine" careers as nursing, social work, and teaching, while boys are urged to consider professions like business, engineering, medicine, and science. The girl who is a talented science student is likely to be encouraged to become a science teacher, while the talented boy is considered a better candidate for a career in research. Most of the careers that girls are encouraged to pursue have two things in common—low pay and restricted opportunity for advancement.

The mass media also have a profound effect on the definition of personal sex roles. A variety of research studies show that television, motion pictures, radio, books, and magazines all tend to reinforce traditional sex role stereotypes. Children's television programs are particularly important in the early socialization process, consistently depicting men and women in traditional stereotypes. Even the commercials are stereotyped. A study of 100 commercials shown on children's television programs found that 95 percent of the narrators were male. Females were three times more likely to be shown in domestic activities, and males were ten times more likely to be shown in active roles.[29]

Advertising aimed at adult audiences reveals the same bias. Typically, women are used to attract attention to a man's sales pitch—perhaps wearing a bikini while sipping a new drink, wearing a silk gown while slithering into a sports car, or staring seductively at a man who uses the right brand of shaving cream. The prime concern of the "good housewife" is the whiteness of her wash and whether she can see her face reflected in her dinner plates. Lucy Komisar notes that

> [advertising] legitimizes the idealized, stereotyped roles of woman as temptress, wife, mother, and sex object, and portrays women as less intelligent and more dependent than men. It makes women believe that their chief role is to please men and that their fulfillment will be as wives, mothers, and homemakers. It makes women feel unfeminine if they are not pretty enough and guilty if they do not spend most of their time in desperate attempts to imitate gourmet cooks and eighteenth century scullery maids. It makes

women believe that their own lives, talents, and interests ought to be secondary to the needs of their husbands and families and that they are almost totally defined by these relationships. . . . It creates false, unreal images of women that reflect males' fantasies rather than flesh and blood human beings.[30]

The same attitudes and prejudices are reflected in other media. One study of a newspaper sports page found that male athletes were typically described by such adjectives as *huge, tremendous, great, tough,* and *brilliant* while female athletes were more often described as *pretty, slim, attractive,* and *gracious.* Women's magazines such as *Ladies Home Journal* and *Better Homes and Gardens* focus heavily on traditional sex role stereotypes. Even rock music—which is supposedly sung by rebellious, antiestablishment youth—follows the stereotype. A study of the lyrics of some popular rock music found that males are the main subjects of an overwhelming majority of the songs. When females are mentioned, they are usually pictured as sensitive and sexually passive.[31]

SEXUAL INEQUALITY

In Western society the roles of females and males are not only substantially *different* but also *unequal.* As we have seen, the male is given the dominant position. In a sense he is the star actor, while the female plays only a supporting role. The male is expected to have superior strength, greater stamina, higher intelligence, and better organizing ability. Psychologically, the male is trained to play the dominant, superior role of decision maker while the female is programed to be submissive and obedient. Inequality in sex roles is reflected in our basic institutions. In education, employment, and political power, women clearly are treated as inferiors. They are victims of sexism (sexual stereotyping, prejudice, and discrimination) in much the same way that blacks are victims of racism.

Education

We have already discussed some of the subtle ways in which schools encourage achievement among males and discourage it among females. But not all sexism in education is so subtle. In the past most colleges and universities were open to men only; and until recently graduate and professional schools commonly excluded women. Such discrimination has usually been strongest at the most desirable and most prestigious schools. Harvard University excluded women from its law school until 1950 and from its graduate business program until 1963.[32] Many graduate schools still informally maintain higher admission standards for females than for males.[33] Because recent laws have forbidden sexual discrimination, women's educational opportunities have improved, but sexism remains a fact of life for most women in schools, colleges, and universities.

In the early school years girls do considerably better than boys, but the percentage of female students drops sharply as the level of education

FIGURE 10.1
HIGH SCHOOL AND
COLLEGE GRADUATION
RATES, BY SEX, 1950-1974

Source: U.S. Department of Commerce, *Social Indicators 1976* (Washington, D.C.: GPO, 1976), p. 275.

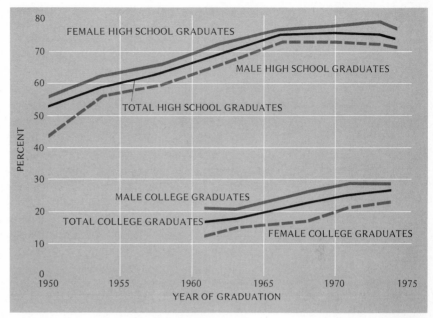

increases. Slightly more women than men graduate from high school, but the majority of college students are men. (See Figure 10.1.) In 1950, for every 100 men in their middle 20s who completed four years of college only 66 women had done so. In 1975, there were 77 women for every 100 men.[34] In graduate and professional schools the percentage of women is considerably lower than it is in undergraduate institutions, although it too has been improving. In 1970, only 8.5 percent of all M.D.s and 5.6 percent of all law degrees were awarded to women.[35] However, in 1974, 24 percent of first-year law students and 22 percent of first-year medical students were women.[36]

Why are women more likely to earn a high school diploma but also less likely to complete college? One factor is economic. If a family cannot afford education for all its children, sons are likely to be given preference over daughters. Sex role stereotypes both inside and outside the school also serve to discourage women from continuing their education. A young woman is expected to find an appropriate mate and then to shape her life—including her educational plans—to fit his needs. Attitudes toward achievement also differ significantly between the sexes. Matina Horner asked a sample of college students to make up a story centered on a student ("Anne" for the female students and "John" for the males) who was at the top of a medical school class at the end of the first term. While the stories of most of the female students showed a strong fear of success, this was not true of the males. More specifically, 65 percent of the

women's stories involved negative consequences, doubts, and fears for
the successful medical student, but only 10 percent of the males reflected
such fears. Horner also found that women with a strong fear of success
did not do as well as others academically.[37]

Employment   The role of women in the work force is undergoing remarkable changes.
Fifty years ago, fewer than one-fourth of all adult women in the United
States worked outside the home. Today, about one-half are workers and
the percentage is growing steadily.[38] In 1890, women accounted for only
17 percent of the total work force. By 1970, this figure had risen to 38 percent, and today over 40 percent of all workers are women.[39] A similar
trend has occurred in Canada, but women still account for a smaller percentage of the total work force than in the United States (34 percent in
1972).[40] Both countries are still slightly behind such European nations as
Finland, Sweden, and England.[41] (See Figure 10.2.)

FIGURE 10.2
WORKING-AGE
POPULATION IN THE
LABOR FORCE OF
SELECTED COUNTRIES,
BY SEX, 1960–1975

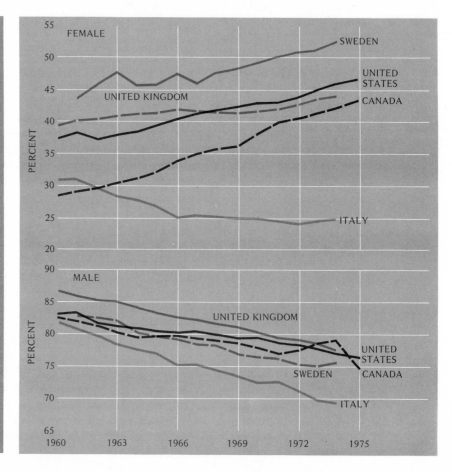

Source: U.S. Department of Commerce,
Social Indicators 1976 (Washington, D.C.:
GPO, 1976), pp. 357, 358.

FIGURE 10.3
AVERAGE WEEKLY
EARNINGS, BY SEX AND
RACE, 1967–1976

Source: U.S. Department of Commerce,
Social Indicators 1976 (Washington, D.C.:
GPO, 1976), p. 345.

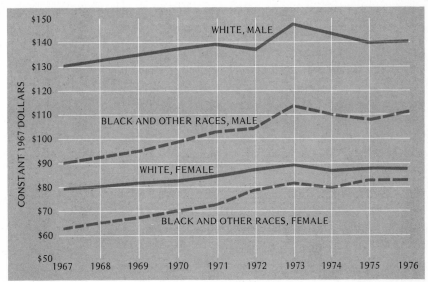

Although more and more women are working, they continue to receive substantially less pay than men. Even more disturbing is the fact that the gap between women's and men's pay has actually increased in the past 20 years, despite all the talk of sexual equality. In 1957, the average full-time woman worker was paid 64 percent of the amount received by the average male.[42] By 1970, that figure had dropped to 59 percent; and by 1974 it was 57 percent.[43] Much of this difference can be assigned to the steadily increasing numbers of women entering the work force for the first time and therefore "starting at the bottom." Nonetheless, it is doubtful that occupational discrimination against women has decreased very much. (See Figure 10.3.)

It is true that women receive lower paychecks than men because they tend to enter lower-paying jobs and hold lower-ranking jobs within their occupation. Yet there are substantial differences in pay even between men and women who do the same type of work. Women clerical workers in the United States earn less than three-fifths as much as their male counterparts. Saleswomen earn about two-fifths as much as salesmen, and women managers, officials, and proprietors earn only a little more than half the amount earned by men in similar jobs.[44] Employers often say they pay men more because men have families to support, overlooking the fact that an increasing number of women also support families. Employers also exploit women. Because lower pay for women is common, each employer knows that females are unlikely to find better pay with another company. Employers also know that unemployment is significantly higher for women and that women therefore are not as likely as men to quit low-paying jobs to seek new ones.

Most occupations are clearly "sex typed"; that is, they are considered either men's jobs or women's jobs. Two-thirds of all American artists and entertainers are men, as are 80 percent of all accountants and 99 percent of all engineers. On the other hand, 70 percent of all teachers, 87 percent of all librarians, and 99 percent of all secretaries are women.[45] "Women's jobs" usually have lower pay and status than comparable "male" positions. The nurse (usually female) is subordinate to the doctor (usually male), just as the secretary (usually female) is subordinate to the executive (usually male). Jobs that are relatively autonomous are usually typed as male, as in the case of truck drivers or traveling sales personnel. A 1972 study of independent businesses in the United States found that fewer than 5 percent were owned by women.[46] (See Figure 10.4.)

A study by Edward Gross found that the amount of sex segregation in occupations changed very little between 1900 and 1950.[47] However, the growing strength of the feminist movement and laws requiring equal employment opportunities for women appear to be causing some changes. Between 1960 and 1970 the percentage of female lawyers in the United

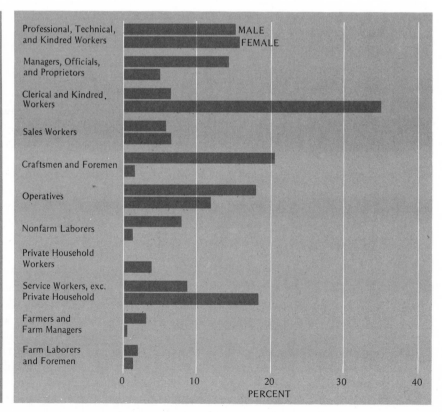

FIGURE 10.4
OCCUPATIONS OF
EMPLOYED PERSONS, BY
SEX, 1975

Source: U.S. Department of Commerce, *Social Indicators 1976* (Washington, D.C.: GPO, 1976), p. 336.

States increased from 3.5 percent to about 5 percent, and that of female physicians increased from 6.5 percent to 9.3 percent.[48] Employment advertisements are no longer divided into male and female sections, and women are entering a wide range of new fields. Many of these women are merely tokens employed to show the employer's commitment to equal employment, but such tokenism may lead to the employment of more women in the future.

Aside from low pay, most traditional "women's jobs" also offer little chance for advancement. The secretary does not become a top executive, nor the nurse a doctor. Even when a woman enters a company in a high-level job, she and the male executives are likely to be on different "tracks." Women employed in high-level corporate jobs are usually in "dead-end" positions (e.g., administering affirmative-action programs or supervising the hiring process) rather than in the production, sales, and financial posts that lead to the top corporate jobs.[49] Many companies, both large and small, are reluctant to promote young women because they believe they will become pregnant and quit their jobs. But if a woman waits until her children are in school before seeking employment, she is likely to be considered too old for the jobs that may lead to the top management positions.

Political Power

Politics has been considered a man's business in almost all societies throughout the world. Women were not even allowed to vote in most democracies until this century. The few women who have gained power have usually had the benefit of family connections to overcome objections to their sex. Indira Gandhi in India, Sirimavo Bandaranaike in Sri Lanka (Ceylon), and of course the hereditary European monarchs such as Queen Elizabeth II in England are good examples. Further, female rulers have all been advised and assisted by male staffs. Neither the United States nor Canada has ever had a woman chief of state. In 1975, only 8 percent of the state legislators in the United States were women.[50]

Despite their current lack of political power, women have enormous political potential. Most of the volunteer workers who are essential to modern political campaigns are women. Even more significant is the fact that women outnumber men and could easily outvote them at the polls. The fact that men continue to dominate the political area reflects the average woman's lack of political consciousness. Most women vote much like their husbands, showing little awareness of their own special political problems.[51] Further, women are discouraged from participating in politics by the same forces that discourage them from pursuing other professional careers. Social stereotypes tell women that it is "unfeminine" to be involved in the dirty world of politics, and the demands of home and family make it difficult for some women to devote themselves to such a demanding career.

However, there are many signs of change. Leaders of the growing feminist movement are encouraging women to get involved in politics and are attacking the stereotypes that have labeled women unfit for public office. Groups such as the National Organization for Women (NOW) are pushing for legislation to guarantee the rights of women, just as other groups have done for other minorities. Thousands of local women's groups have sprung up, aiming both to increase women's political consciousness and to support a variety of different causes. In 1974 Ella Grasso became the first woman to be elected governor of an American state without succeeding her husband. Margaret Thatcher became the first woman to head a democratic government in Europe when she was elected prime minister of Great Britain in 1979. The political climate is slowly changing, and it is likely that women soon will be accepted in the highest offices of most democratic nations. Equal political participation and power is still a long way off, however.

Social Life

Sexism in education, employment, and politics is obvious to anyone who cares to see it. But women are also victims of more subtle forms of discrimination that are woven into the fabric of our social lives. Women and girls are told in many subtle ways that they are second-class citizens who lack the abilities of their male counterparts. They are seen as emotional, unstable, and unable to direct their own lives. The "woman driver" and the "dumb blonde" are butts of countless jokes; the heroine in popular stories proves unable to solve her own problems and must be rescued by a man. Women are taught from childhood that beauty and sex appeal are most likely to lead to happiness. Success comes not from their own efforts but from the ability to appeal to the right man. Thus, women are cast in a secondary role in social life. They may be seen as wives and mothers of important people, but seldom as important individuals in their own right.

Women are routinely expected to repress their desires and ambitions in ways that are seldom demanded of men. Studies of dual-career families (in which both husband and wife work) reveal that it is the wife who must sacrifice her career if it interferes with that of her spouse. The working woman is also expected to carry most of the homemaking and child-rearing responsibilities in addition to her job.[52]

Women are expected to repress their sexuality in the same way that they are expected to repress their career ambitions. During the Victorian era women's sexuality was almost entirely denied. The "good" woman did not enjoy sex but merely endured it for her husband's sake. Recent research shows that while the double standard for sexual behavior has weakened in recent years, it is still very much with us.[53] Young men are expected to "sow their wild oats," but the "loose woman" is still condemned. And those who reject an unfaithful wife often condone a husband's infidelities with a wink.

RESPONDING TO PROBLEMS OF THE SEXES

Despite recent changes, contemporary sex roles remain rigidly defined, and women and men continue to be restricted by social expectations. The "normal" man or woman displays a certain attitude, personality traits, and sexual behavior, and plays a particular role in the larger social system as well. The restrictive nature of these roles causes severe problems for those who do not conform. Many people still find aggressive "masculine" women or passive "feminine" men unacceptable. In addition, sexual discrimination in business and politics bars many women from success in these areas.

Women have traditionally been subordinate to males and male authority, and to a large extent this remains true today. Our discussion of sexual inequality indicated that there is an established pattern of favoritism for males in employment, promotions, salary, and education. Sexual discrimination is clearly harmful not only to many women and their families but also to society as a whole. The talents of many capable women are wasted while some incompetent males reach positions of importance. Even when women reach positions of power, they are expected to perform their duties in accordance with standards that have been set by male authority and are profoundly influenced by male sex role expectations.

Although men receive the lion's share of power and authority, they too suffer from sex role stereotypes. While women are restricted by the things they are not allowed to do, men are restricted by the things they are expected to do. In discussing the complaints men and women have about their sex roles, Janet Chafetz writes,

> Thus females complain about what they can't do, males about what they must do. Females complain that they cannot be athletic, aggressive, sexually free, or successful in the worlds of work and education; in short, they complain of their passivity. Males complain that they must be aggressive and must succeed; in short, of their activity. The requirement that males be active and females passive in a variety of ways is clearly unpleasant to both.[54]

The burdens of the male sex role are often heavy, particularly for men who are not aggressive or competitive. Men, like women, are subject to many special legal restrictions based on their sex. They are required to fight in time of war regardless of their fears or objections. A man seeking custody of his children in a divorce proceeding usually faces a court that assumes that the female has superior child-rearing ability. Until recently a wife could collect her husband's social-security benefits when he died but a husband could not collect those of his wife. Many states have laws that forbid men to dress as women yet have no comparable restrictions concerning the way women dress.

The demand for equal rights and privileges for women is not new. Many of the concerns of modern feminists were first expressed by vigor-

The feminist movement has a long history in North America. Today's feminists are demanding complete equality between the sexes and an end to the discrimination against women.

ous women's movements in the nineteenth century. In the United States these movements developed out of the drive to abolish slavery as women who fought against slavery discovered that they too were oppressed. Eventually the early feminist movement narrowed its focus, moving from a wide-ranging attack on sexual discrimination to the single issue of women's suffrage. When the "suffragettes" were finally successful and women gained the right to vote, the feminist movement faded, only to be reborn in the early 1960s, when the civil-rights movement was calling attention to social injustices, just as the abolitionist movement had done earlier. Perhaps more important, the social environment of women was slowly changing. They were living longer, having fewer children, and becoming increasingly active in the world outside the home. As long-standing discrimination against women gained more publicity, sexism won increasing recognition as a social problem.

The modern feminist movement has scored some remarkable successes. Women's liberation and sexual equality are now widely discussed, and more women are entering occupations that formerly were closed to them. Through effective court and legislative actions, feminists have successfully attacked employment and promotion practices that discriminate against women. Government-sponsored affirmative-action programs now require employers to hire and promote more women and members of other minority groups. The feminists have even made some inroads on the sexual biases built into the English language. Women are increasingly identifying themselves as Ms. rather than Miss or Mrs., and new sexually neutral words such as *chairperson* and *humankind* are replacing the traditional masculine terms. Nevertheless, we are still a long way from sexual equality. Strong opposition to change has come from men who feel their power threatened, as well as from women who cherish traditional attitudes, values, and behavior patterns.

Two major responses to the problem of sexual inequality are currently being proposed, discussed, and put into action. One approach attempts to eliminate sexual discrimination, the other to restructure sex roles. While both responses are essential to an effective attack on sexism, the proposals for eliminating discrimination are less controversial than those aimed at changing familiar roles.

Few people openly support such practices as paying women less money for doing the same work as men, refusing to grant them credit, or denying them jobs and promotions simply because they are women. The values of democratic society make it very hard to justify such practices. Yet specific proposals to change these conditions often run into opposition. For instance, the proposed Equal Rights Amendment to the U.S. Constitution, which would guarantee both sexes equal rights under the law, has been attacked by some women because they fear that it will end some of the special legal rights that they have traditionally enjoyed. Government-financed child care centers would be of great assistance to working mothers, particularly those who must support dependent children without the help of the father. But opponents see such centers as an unwarranted interference of government in the private sphere. Even attempts to end the double standard for sexual activity are seen by some people as an attack on sacred values. Despite such resistance, the attack on sexual discrimination is consistent with democratic values, and feminists will probably continue to make progress as long as they continue to press for change.

Proposals for restructuring sex roles have run into much greater opposition. Attitudes and expectations about sex roles are formed early in life, and many people feel threatened when such basic assumptions are challenged. The more vicious attacks on so-called women's libbers can be seen as a response to these threats. But despite the fear and hostility produced by rapid change, sex roles in industrial societies are undergoing a revolutionary transformation. While it is impossible to say what roles will finally develop, there is no reason to suppose that sexual equality would mean that men and women would become socially identical. Some of the differences in behavior between men and women already have diminished, but the development of a "unisex" remains a prospect for the distant future, if at all.

Whatever the future may hold, it is clear that our current problems would be greatly reduced if we could learn to be more tolerant. No matter what characteristics a culture attributes to the ideal woman or the ideal man, there are many who do not conform. The nonconformist — whether an aggressive, dominating woman or a passive, dependent man — must pay an enormous personal cost for merely being a little different. There is no reason, aside from prejudice and bigotry, why traditional sex roles cannot exist side by side with a variety of other arrangements. Indeed, when we finally learn to accept our human differences we will have come a long way toward resolving many of our most perplexing social problems.

SOCIOLOGICAL PERSPECTIVES on Problems of the Sexes

Distinct roles for females and males are found in every society. These sex roles become a problem only when a significant number of people in a society object to them. Such objections are now being voiced. Functionalists, conflict theorists, and social psychologists have all noted the gap between the growing ideal of equality and the reality of male domination over females. They differ on the question of why this gap occurred and what should be done about it.

The Functionalist Perspective

Functionalists say that the problems of sex roles stem directly from the broad historical changes outlined in this chapter. Traditionally, sex roles were based on biological differences between the sexes; women were concerned primarily with child rearing and men with providing economic support. But changes brought on by the industrial revolution threw this arrangement out of balance. The decline in infant mortality and the spread of effective birth control made it possible to depart from traditional roles. It was no longer necessary for women to devote most of their adult lives to the raising of small children, and automation wiped out the importance of the male's greater strength in most types of work. However, attitudes and expectations about the proper role of women changed much more slowly than social and economic conditions. This cultural lag was itself a form of prejudice against women.

To resolve the problem, most functionalists suggest that expectations be made to conform more closely with actual conditions. Some advocate a return to the stable past, believing that too great a shift toward sexual equality is dysfunctional. They note that the traditional division of labor between men and women was highly efficient, enabling society to train people for specialized roles that meshed together in stable families. Other functionalists, however, advocate a redefinition of sex roles to bring them into line with changed economic, political, and social conditions. Although these functionalists do not agree on the exact form these changes should take, they do agree on the need for a shift toward full sexual equality and a reconstruction of women's roles to encourage economic competition and achievement. Along with this change, basic institutions would also have to be modified to eliminate sexual discrimination. For example, the current family system would have to undergo extensive changes in order to accommodate new roles for both men and women.

The Conflict Perspective

Prejudice and discrimination against women come as no surprise to conflict theorists, since they see exploitation and oppression as universal human problems. It appears that men first used their greater size and strength to force women into a subordinate position. Then, like any other dominant group, they created institutions that serve to perpetuate their power and authority. Men gain economic advantages by paying women low wages and excluding them from positions of economic control and political power. Men also benefit from women's subordinate role in the family. The "good" woman, we are told, blindly serves her husband and obeys his will like a domestic servant. According to many conflict theorists, the position of women in most societies today is similar to that of a subordinate ethnic minority such as the blacks in the United States.

There are many indications, however, that the traditional male advantages are declining in importance. The superior strength of the male means little in a highly mechanized society. The real barriers to women's liberation are now the institutions and attitudes that were established in the days of unquestioned male dominance. An increasing number of women are coming to realize this fact, and they are organizing themselves to break these final barriers. According to conflict theory, the feminist movement is both a reflection and a cause of the growing strength of women in industrial societies. Conflict theorists advise women to continue publicizing their grievances, bring all women and sympathetic men together in a unified movement, and solicit the support of other dissatisfied social groups. For the conflict theorist, social action is the road to social change and a just society.

The Social-Psychological Perspective

Social psychologists see sex roles, and the sense of identity we derive from them, as critical components of human personality. Most social psychologists are convinced that sexual identity develops in the early years of childhood in interaction with parents, peers, teachers, and the mass media. Once formed, these ideas and concepts are quite durable. Social psychologists note that prejudice and discrimination against women arise from differences in socialization. Females are conditioned to be passive and dependent and are therefore less dominant than males, who are trained to be more aggressive and independent. Thus, both sexes learn to see females as inferiors in many important ways.

Biosocial theorists, however, are yet to be convinced that sex role differences are simply a product of socialization. They argue that the personality and social differences between men and women are biological in origin. Clearly, there are differences in physical and biochemical makeup between men and women that cannot be ignored, but it is not clear how important they are in contemporary society. If sex roles are determined entirely by biology, little can be done to change them or to reduce sexual inequality.

Behaviorists, personality theorists, and symbolic interactionists are more optimistic. They are convinced that sex roles and the sexual inequality they promote can be changed if the content of the socialization process is altered. These theorists argue that girls should be encouraged to be more aggressive and boys urged to accept the passive, dependent side of their natures. Because parents have been socialized into traditional sex roles, persuading them to teach their children to behave differently is extremely difficult. Schools, which are an increasingly important influence in socialization, can be changed more easily. Feminists are already pressing to remove sexual stereotypes from schoolbooks and lectures and to promote higher educational and occupational aspirations for talented girls. The media, particularly radio, television, and films, could also promote these changes. Showing women as powerful, assertive figures, and allowing men who do not live up to the code of male dominance to be heroes equal to the "he-man" would do much to foster equality between the sexes.

SUMMARY

Sex roles, or sets of expectations about the proper behavior for each sex, are basic components both of individual personalities and of the larger social system. In Western culture the male sex role has centered on work and providing for the family. The male is expected to be more aggressive than the female and to have tighter control over emotions. The female role has centered on child rearing and the family. Females are expected to be emotionally expressive, dependent, and passive. Sex roles show a wide range of variation among cultures, and in our culture as in others, the behavior of many men and women does not fit sex role expectations.

Two important conditions seemed to have influenced the development of our sex roles—biology and culture. The fact that females bear and nurse children has had an obvious influence on the definition of sex roles, as has the fact that males are larger and stronger than females. Despite the importance of biology in the origin of sex roles, the individual's role is determined primarily by culture. Studies show that a man who is raised as a woman will think and act like a woman, and vice versa. Many cultures assign what we consider "feminine" traits to both sexes, while others assign "masculine" traits to both.

In early hunting and gathering societies the most important and lasting social division was between men and women. Horticultural societies had a wide range of sex roles, from rough egalitarianism to strong male dominance, depending chiefly on the economy. With the coming of agriculture—that is, the use of the plow, irrigation, and harnessed animals—the power of women generally declined because their contribution to agricultural production was reduced. But the economic and social conditions accompanying industrial society neutralized many male advantages. Mechanization made physical size and strength less important, and the sharp drop in infant mortality and the spread of birth control methods reduced women's child-rearing burdens.

Sex role socialization is the process by which children learn the behaviors and attitudes expected of their sex. The family plays a critical role in this process. Parents begin treating boys as boys and girls as girls almost from the moment of birth. Schools reinforce the traditional sex roles learned at home. Teachers, counselors, and textbooks encourage high aspirations in boys and discourage them in girls. Radio, television, and motion pictures also convey sexual stereotypes.

The roles we assign to each sex clearly promote sexual inequality. Men are given the dominant position, while a variety of evidence reveals a clear pattern of discrimination against women in education, employment, politics, and everyday social life.

The feminist movement emerged when women organized to protest against discrimination and to work actively for women's economic, political, and social rights. The goal of eliminating sex discrimination has gained wide acceptance, and significant legislation has been passed. However, the call for a restructuring of traditional sex roles has been met with considerable opposition and even hostility. Nevertheless, our sex roles have undergone remarkable change and will probably continue to do so. Greater tolerance and acceptance for those who do not fit into traditional stereotypes would go a long way toward reducing the problem of sex discrimination.

Functionalists see present-day sex role problems as stemming from changes in economic life that upset the traditional sex roles. They advocate a reduction in the gap between expectations and actual conditions. Conflict theorists are convinced that sex role problems arise from domination and exploitation of the weak by the strong. They advise women to organize politically and to use political power to gain equality. Most social psychologists are convinced that sex roles and sexual identity are learned in the process of socialization, but biosocial theorists cling to the idea that sex differences have biological origins. The consensus among most social psychologists is that sexual inequality can be eliminated by changing sex roles, and that sex roles will change if the content of the socialization process is changed.

KEY TERMS   double standard   sex role socialization
             sexism   sexual stereotyping
             sex role

Western culture has traditionally believed that sexual activities were unclean and that children had no interest in sex. Today, psychologists agree that sexual interests and exploration are a normal part of growing up.

Although North Americans are shocked by the thought of sexual activity among children, it is encouraged in many places. In some cultures intercourse is believed to be necessary if preadolescents are to mature sexually. The Trukese of the Caroline Islands build small huts especially for this purpose. Among the Alorese of Indonesia, mothers routinely masturbate their children in order to pacify them.[3]

Yet such liberalism is far from universal. The men of Yap Island believe that intercourse causes physical weakness and reduces resistance to disease. At one time Yap attitudes toward sex were so negative that the Yap people almost became extinct. The Manus of New Guinea consider intercourse degrading—a disgusting act that a woman must endure in order to produce children. The neighboring Dani tribe do not have sexual relations until two years after marriage, and refrain from sex for five years following the birth of each child. Closer to home, the Shakers, a Protestant sect founded in New England, banned all sexual activities, acquiring children only by adoption. Rural Ireland is also notable for its repression of sexuality. Marriages are delayed until late in life—about age 35 for men and 26 for women. Men and women are segregated in public places, and there is a strong taboo against the discussion of sexual matters. The ability of women to experience orgasm is denied by some and considered deviant by others.[4]

The sexual behavior that is considered deviant also varies widely from culture to culture. The use of force to obtain sexual favors is strictly forbidden in our culture and in most of the rest of the world. But among a tribe living in southwestern Kenya normal intercourse is a kind of ritualized rape.[5] Women are encouraged to frustrate men with sexual taunts, and the men overcome this resistance with force, often inflicting pain and humiliation in the process. Attitudes toward homosexuality also show enormous variation. Most of the societies studied by Ford and Beach disapproved of homosexuality in general, but 64 percent of them tolerated, approved, or even required homosexual acts in some circumstances for some people.

A number of societies consider homosexuality normal among adolescent males but look less favorably on it in other groups. Among many Melanesian societies homosexuality is considered a more mature form of sexual behavior than masturbation and is common among young men. However, heterosexual relations are valued more highly, and homosexuality is rare after marriage. Heterosexuality is preferred over homosexuality in practically all societies, at least in part because of its essential role in reproduction. Yet there are at least two known societies in New Guinea in which homosexuality is preferred. The Marind-anim people are so strongly homosexual that they must kidnap children from other tribes in order to maintain their population.[6] At the opposite extreme are such peoples as the Rwala Bedouins, who consider homosexuality so base that it is punishable by death. Even the incest taboo (the prohibition of sexual relations between parents and their children or between the children themselves), which is certainly the most common restriction on sexual behavior, is not universal.

There is clearly nothing innate in human beings that makes certain types of sexual behavior normal and other types abnormal. The distinction between "normal" and "deviant" sex comes from society, not biology. We are all born with a sex drive, but it is amazingly flexible and can be satisfied in a great variety of ways. We learn to satisfy our sex drive with one type of object and not another the same way we learn to satisfy our hunger drive with socially acceptable foods and not with dog meat or human flesh.

CONTEMPORARY SEXUAL BEHAVIOR

The study of sexual behavior is a difficult and confusing task. Social scientists have repeatedly found that people do not care to describe their sexual behavior to even the most objective investigators. As a result it is impossible to say how common various forms of sexual behavior actually are. North American researchers find it hard even to describe public attitudes toward sex because there are such bitter conflicts over sexual morality in Canada and the United States. At the heart of the matter is the conflict between restrictive traditional standards and the growing belief in the value of individual choice and personal freedom. Many religious groups continue to advocate the traditional values, while the media pour out an increasing stream of sexually arousing advertising and entertainment. Because of this confusion and uncertainty sex researchers have found themselves in the uncomfortable position of influencing as well as describing contemporary sexual standards. Some people evaluate their own sexual behavior by comparing it with the findings of the sex surveys, apparently assuming that unusual sexual behavior may be wrong, but that "if everyone else is doing it, it must be all right."

A Historical Sketch

Western society has lived with a very restrictive sexual morality at least since the fall of the Roman Empire. In general, sexual relations have been approved only between a husband and wife, often only for the purpose of reproduction. The origins of this attitude are to be found in the Judeo-Christian religious tradition, particularly the New Testament teachings of Saint Paul and the lectures of early Christian leaders such as Saint Augustine. These leaders held sexual abstinence to be the ideal, but allowed that "it is better to marry than to burn." Sex was seen as something evil and degrading, to be avoided as much as possible. Although such standards continued to be supported by religious and secular leaders for centuries, it is doubtful that more than a small percentage of the population adhered to them.

The Puritans of the seventeenth century reemphasized the strict moral code of the early Christians and demanded almost complete repression of sexuality. Puritan immigrants in North America helped establish this rigid code as a dominant force on the new continent. The nineteenth century also was noted for its repression of sexuality. Victorians avoided discussion of anything that could be considered even remotely sexual—legs became limbs, sweat became perspiration, and underwear became "unmentionables." Masturbation was believed to cause defects ranging from mental disorders to blindness. The double standard was so strong that fe-

---

NINETEENTH CENTURY SOCIAL PROBLEMS*

Young men who have become the victims of solitary vice, that dreadful habit that sweeps annually to an untimely grave thousands of young men of exalted talent and brilliant intellect, can call with confidence.
[Front page ad in newspaper]
August 5, 1897

---

*These "Nineteenth Century Social Problems" throughout the text are excerpts from the *Badger State Banner* published in Black River Falls, Wisconsin.

male sexuality was almost entirely denied. An American surgeon general reflected prevailing opinions when he said that "nine-tenths of the time decent women feel not the slightest pleasure in intercourse."[7] But the Victorian era is noted for its hypocrisy as well as its sexual repression. Prostitution and pornography flourished, and there appears to have been a wide gap between what people said and what they did.

In general, the history of sexual behavior in Western culture is marked by alternating periods of stern repression and quiet permissiveness. It is impossible to determine how closely the public's behavior conforms to its principles during periods of repression. But it seems clear that the Puritans were effective in enforcing their standards and that moral crusades became less effective with the passage of time.

A Sexual Revolution?

There is no doubt that sexual attitudes and practices have become much more liberal since the time of the Victorians. In reporting these changes the media often picture them as a revolutionary break with the past. Indeed, some commentators have predicted that our sudden "moral decay" will have dire consequences for Western society. But not everyone agrees that a "sexual revolution" has taken place. Some argue that today's young people are simply more open in discussing their sexual activities than their grandparents were, and that actual behavior has not changed very much.

One point about which there is no disagreement is that there have been remarkable changes in the media's use of sexual material. Magazines with pictures of scantily clad women were condemned by our grandparents but are now a fixture of supermarket magazine racks. Over the years illustrations revealed more and more of the body until nudity became the style. Further, mass circulation magazines such as *Playgirl* have broken the strong taboo against male nudity, and even relatively conservative women's magazines carry erotically oriented advertising and discussions of sex. Similar changes have occurred in movies and plays. Many writers and producers now feel that one or two sex scenes are necessary to the financial success of a new production. Even television programs feature scenes and discussions that would have been shocking just a few decades ago.

Methodological problems make it difficult to measure the extent of the actual changes in sexual behavior. Sex surveys such as the pioneering studies conducted by Alfred Kinsey and his associates in the 1940s and 1950s are the best sources of data available, but they have serious methodological weaknesses.[8] Kinsey interviewed volunteers, including people in social clubs and prisons, and it is doubtful that his subjects were representative of the overall population. Morton Hunt also ran into serious problems in his nationwide survey of sexual behavior in the 1970s. Of those approached, only about 20 percent agreed to participate in the

Kinsey's research indicates that the first wave of sexual liberation occurred in the generation that came of age in the "roaring twenties."

study, and there may have been important differences between the sexual behavior of those who were willing to cooperate and those who were not.[9] Other sex surveys have run into similar problems. In addition, the vast majority have surveyed only small, local samples of college students, neglecting the rest of the population.

When Kinsey's report on male sexual behavior was published in 1948, it shocked the nation. Kinsey concluded that 85 percent of all American men had experienced premarital intercourse, 70 percent had visited a prostitute, and over one-third had participated in at least one homosexual act. His findings were immediately subjected to numerous attacks. But despite the methodological weaknesses of such surveys, their conclusions are vastly superior to unsupported opinions and generalizations.

Kinsey's data suggest that a wave of sexual liberation occurred much earlier than is usually believed, probably in the generation that came of age after World War I. His study found that only 8 percent of white women born before 1900 had premarital intercourse by age 20, but that among those born between 1910 and 1929 the figure was 22 percent. Later surveys indicate that a second wave of liberation occurred in the second half of the 1960s and the early 1970s.[10] Kinsey found that two-thirds of the single women aged 18–25 in his sample were virgins, while Hunt's survey, conducted in the 1970s, found that only one-fourth of the single women in this age bracket were virgins.

An important part of these changes was the decay of the double standard, discussed in Chapter 10. Traditionally, both sexes were supposed to refrain from "sinful" sexual activities, but violating this taboo was considered a greater stigma for women than for men. To be a "loose woman" or an unfaithful wife was a social disgrace, but young men were expected to gain sexual experience before marriage, and a husband's carousing was passed over with a wink. A century ago the "good" woman was not supposed to enjoy sex; she was to merely tolerate it for her husband's sake.

Although the double standard has not disappeared, it certainly has been weakened. There was some increase in the amount of premarital sexual experience reported by males in the 1970s (Hunt's survey) compared with males in the 1940s (Kinsey's survey), but the change was much more dramatic for females. While one-third of all the women in Kinsey's sample reported having engaged in premarital intercourse by age 25, well over two-thirds of the women in Hunt's survey were sexually experienced by that age.[11] Hunt's survey revealed no increase in extramarital sex among male subjects or older female subjects, but it showed a large increase in extramarital sex among married women aged 25 or younger (9 percent in the Kinsey study; 24 percent in the Hunt study).[12] One should not conclude, however, that because women are enjoying more of the freedoms formerly reserved for men the double standard no longer exists. It is still with us. Rates of female participation in both premarital and extramarital sex, for instance, are still substantially lower than similar rates for men.

Comparison of the surveys also indicates that a broader range of sexual activity is now common between heterosexual couples. Particularly striking is the sharp increase in oral–genital sex. Kinsey found that 40 percent of the married males he surveyed had engaged in oral sex with their wives, while 63 percent of Hunt's male subjects said that they had done so in the past year.[13] However, not all forms of sexual behavior have become more common. There is no evidence that male or female homosexuality increased between the Kinsey and Hunt surveys, and Hunt reports that prostitution has actually decreased. As women have become more sexually active, men apparently have felt less need to use the services of prostitutes.

The increase in sexual freedom is one result of the sweeping cultural changes of the twentieth century. The weakening of the extended family and the influence of traditional religious morality have lowered the barriers that once prevented many kinds of sexual activity. There has been, as mentioned earlier, an erosion of the double standard, and as women have gained economic and political power they have gained greater equality in sexual matters as well. The development of more effective birth control techniques has reduced the fear that sexual relations will lead to an unwanted pregnancy. Growing emphasis on individual freedom and self-determination has made many people more willing to challenge traditional ideas and customs. The increasing use of erotic materials to entertain and to sell products has exerted an influence in many subtle ways. Finally, sexuality itself seems to be undergoing a basic redefinition. Sinful and degrading to Victorians, sexual activity is now a routine part of a normal life.

Predicting the future is always a hazardous business, but several pieces of information suggest that current trends toward greater liberalism are likely to continue in the years ahead. A number of studies have shown that liberal sexual attitudes are more common among the young, the better educated, and the upper classes,[14] and these groups are usually the trend setters. Further, it is not likely that the movement toward greater individual self-determination and full equality of men and women will be reversed. Both trends contribute to the new sexual attitudes.

HOMOSEXUALITY

Dozens of myths and half-truths about homosexuality are commonly accepted by the public. For instance, many people, upon encountering a male homosexual who puts on a display of femininity or a female who acts in a masculine manner, come to believe that all homosexuals behave similarly. In fact, most homosexuals appear and act like everyone else. The few who fit the popular stereotype are just more noticeable. Another common myth is that homosexuals and heterosexuals have different personality characteristics. An experiment by Evelyn Hooker, however, showed that experienced clinical psychologists were unable to identify the sexual orientation of a mixed group of subjects by examining their responses to a battery of psychological tests. Likewise, no differences were found in personal adjustment.[15] Many people believe that homosexuals endanger children, but there is no evidence to indicate that homosexuals are more likely than others to be child molesters. Finally, many people are not aware that many homosexuals form stable long-term relationships just as heterosexuals do.

A major source of confusion about homosexuality is the tendency of many people to see sexual preference in absolute terms. Most people assume that individuals either are sexually attracted to members of the opposite sex (and thus are heterosexual) or are attracted to members of the same sex (and thus are homosexual). In reality, most people have both homosexual and heterosexual urges at one time or another. The differences among homosexuals, bisexuals, and heterosexuals are a matter of degree. Kinsey found that many otherwise heterosexual males had briefly engaged in homosexual activities during their adolescent years. The choice of sexual partners may also be determined by the environment, re-

While a small percentage of homosexuals make a showy display of characteristics usually associated with the opposite sex, most homosexuals look and act like everyone else.

gardless of an individual's personal preference. Many prisoners engage in homosexual activities while they are locked up but are strictly heterosexual outside prison walls.

Causes

There are many theories about the causes of homosexuality, but little conclusive evidence. One popular explanation is that homosexuals are "born that way." The strongest evidence to support the contention that homosexuality is hereditary comes from studies of twins. For example, Kallmann found that identical (one-egg) twins are more likely to show the same sexual preference than fraternal (two-egg) twins.[16] However, the problem with this and similar studies is that identical twins are more likely to be treated alike by family and friends, and thus their similarities may be due to environment, not heredity. Biological theories of homosexuality also have difficulty explaining significant differences in the amount of homosexuality in various cultures and the reasons that some people are homosexual at some times and heterosexual at others.

Other researchers find the origins of homosexuality in the family. Irving Bieber, perhaps the most influential theorist of this school, published a widely read book about the family backgrounds of male homosexuals. He concluded that male homosexuals have domineering, possessive mothers and ineffectual or hostile fathers.[17] An important flaw in Bieber's study arose from the fact that all of his subjects were in psychiatric treatment and therefore were not likely to be typical of all homosexuals. It is clear that many homosexuals do not come from families with the characteristics that are presumed to cause homosexuality, while many heterosexuals do.

Sociologically, homosexuality is explained by examining the conditions in which it is learned. Given the enormous range of sexual behavior in the cultures of the world, it would be hard to explain the absence of homosexuality in large and diverse societies like the United States and Canada. Although strong condemnation of homosexuality discourages homosexual tendencies, homosexuality is encouraged in many other ways. For instance, when adolescents first begin to feel strong sexual urges, heterosexual intercourse is forbidden. Young males and females are not permitted to sleep or shower together, but these activities are acceptable for members of the same sex. The encouragement of specific sex role differences, combined with the pressures of mate selection, makes association with the same sex less painful and embarrassing than association with the opposite sex. Some adolescents carry on homosexual activities without arousing the suspicion of their parents, while heterosexual activities would be out of the question. Further, the widespread belief that one is either homosexual or heterosexual often causes individuals who engage in exploratory homosexual behavior to define themselves as homosexuals. And once such a self-concept takes hold it is likely to persist, perhaps for a lifetime.[18]

The Homosexual Community

There is considerable disagreement about the percentage of homosexuals in the population. Kinsey reported that 37 percent of American men and 20 percent of the women had had at least one homosexual experience, and that 4 percent of the males and about half that percentage of females were exclusively homosexual throughout their lives. Hunt's survey revealed much less homosexuality. About 1 percent of Hunt's sample of males and 0.5 percent of his sample of females considered themselves "mainly" or "totally" homosexual, with an equal number considering themselves bisexual.[19] Virtually everyone who has studied Kinsey's research methods has concluded that he overestimated the amount of homosexuality in the United States, and Hunt suggests that his own figures are low. The actual figure probably lies somewhere between these two estimates. But whatever the figure, it is clear that there are millions of homosexuals in North America.

Unlike many other minorities, homosexuals can conceal their differences from the public. So-called "closet queens" disguise their sexual preference and pass as heterosexuals. But such deception places them under great personal stress. The threat of discovery and possible blackmail is a constant danger. In the last decade a number of homosexuals

PRO

Homosexuals are the last minority group to suffer legal discrimination. They are commonly forbidden to hold government jobs in teaching or military service, and except in certain occupations, admitted homosexuals are publicly refused employment by most corporations. Because homosexuals are usually afraid to turn to the police for help, they are often the victims of vicious beatings and robberies and the targets of blackmailers who know of their sexual preference. Indeed, harsh legal penalties for homosexual behavior make the police more feared than criminals. If discrimination against women, ethnic minorities, and the handicaped is wrong, it is also wrong to discriminate against homosexuals. Only bigotry prevents us from seeing the need to protect the civil rights of gay citizens.

There is no evidence for the claim that providing homosexuals with legal protection against discrimination would encourage homosexual behavior. Although the causes of homosexuality remain in dispute, it is clear that no one simply decides to become a homosexual, just as no one decides to become a heterosexual. Centuries of legal repression did not eliminate homosexuality because the law cannot change a person's sexual preference. By the same token, legal protection for gay rights will not turn heterosexuals into homosexuals. Gay rights laws merely extend the legal protections enjoyed by other minorities to a group who has suffered centuries of abuse and exploitation, and simple justice demands that such laws be enacted.

CON

Homosexuals are not like other minority groups and should not be given the same legal protections. Unlike the case of women or blacks, the discrimination against homosexuality is not based on physical characteristics. Homosexuality is a pattern of behavior that can be altered if an individual desires to change. While it is true that some individuals are strongly attracted to members of their own sex, no one is forced to commit homosexual acts. Even if an individual feels no attraction to members of the opposite sex, celibacy remains a viable alternative. Discrimination can be avoided mereby by refraining from homosexual activity.

Legislation to protect "gay rights" would put an official stamp of approval on homosexual behavior. The passage of such legislation would give support to the claim that homosexuals' unnatural behavior is acceptable and proper. Gay rights legislation would permit homosexuals to teach in elementary and secondary schools, thus exposing children to homosexual attitudes and activities. Homosexuals in the military would create bitter antagonism between themselves and heterosexuals, destroying the effectiveness of our armed forces. The passage of such legislation would permit unrestricted homosexual propaganda and recruiting, setting off a wave of homosexual experimentation.

Homosexuality is morally wrong and socially damaging. If it were allowed to flourish, the family would collapse and birthrates would fall drastically. For its own protection society must condemn homosexuality.

"came out of the closet" and now openly participate in what might be called a homosexual community. But "coming out" means more than just admitting one's homosexuality to the public. It also means admitting it to oneself. One study of male homosexuals found an average span of six years between the subjects' first homosexual feelings and their coming out.[20] When a male homosexual accepts his sexual preference, he often goes through a "crisis of femininity," acting and dressing in an exaggeratedly feminine manner. However, this is usually a temporary phase.[21]

The homosexual community provides many services for gay men and women, including a supportive environment that rejects people who reject homosexuals. In some cities homosexuals have developed a system of mutual assistance in which preference is given to other homosexuals in business and employment, much in the manner of religious and ethnic groups. Thus, a homosexual who needs the services of a carpenter will find a homosexual carpenter; a homosexual who wants to buy a house will find a homosexual real estate agent; and so on. The homosexual community thus gives gays a sense of belonging and security as well as a way of accommodating their sexual orientation. Bars that cater to homosexuals are also important to the homosexual community. They are places for socializing and relaxing, and serve as centers for making new sexual contacts. Such bars are frequented by both men and women, but lesbians (female homosexuals) are less likely to cruise bars looking for pickups or to have a large number of sex partners. Gagnon and Simon found that most lesbians, like most other women, reject promiscuity and stress the importance of romantic love and a stable family.[22]

Homosexuality and the Law

The Judeo-Christian religious tradition condemns homosexuality as a vile sin, and Western nations have acted accordingly. During the middle ages homosexuals were commonly tortured to death. They were burned at the stake in Paris as late as 1750. In Britain homosexual activities were punishable by life imprisonment until 1956.[23]

The recent trend has been toward repeal of legal penalties for homosexuality. Britain canceled its most repressive laws in 1965, thus legalizing homosexual behavior in private between consenting adults. Other European nations followed suit, and such behavior is now legal in France, Spain, Italy, Denmark, and Finland. Canada passed a law similar to Britain's in 1969, but some official harassment of homosexuals has persisted.[24]

The trend toward legalization has developed more slowly among the individual American states. Seventeen states have legalized homosexual acts between consenting adults, but others continue to threaten homosexuals with life imprisonment. However, in the states where homosexuality remains a crime the laws are not vigorously enforced. Only a few unlucky or unwise homosexuals are arrested, prosecuted, and punished. Moreover, these enforcement efforts are directed almost exclusively against male homosexuals. Lesbian activities are ignored.

Even in states and nations where criminal penalties have been reduced or abolished, homosexuals suffer from open legal discrimination. In some places law, medicine, and teaching are closed to homosexuals. Until 1969 homosexuals were barred from U.S. government employment, and the American military still refuses to employ homosexuals. According to Williams and Weinberg, 2000 to 3000 people a year are discharged from the U.S. Army for homosexual activities.[25]

Homosexuals consider themselves a minority group. Like ethnic minorities, they have been organizing and demanding an end to discrimination and prejudice against them. Such organizations as the Mattachine Society, the Gay Liberation Front, and the Gay Activists Alliance are working for the repeal of antihomosexual legislation and for legal protection against other forms of discrimination. The American Psychiatric Association was pressured to drop homosexuality from its list of mental disorders; television stations have been persuaded to stop programs that cast homosexuals in an unfavorable light; and a number of cities—including Los Angeles, Minneapolis, and Seattle—have passed legislation protecting homosexuals from various forms of discrimination. However, the movement has had its failures as well. In 1976 the United States Supreme Court refused to ban prosecution and imprisonment of people for homosexual activities, even if those activities were conducted in private between consenting adults. Also, the gains of homosexual activists have often stirred vigorous counterattacks. In several cities "gay rights" laws have been repealed as a result of such attacks.

PROSTITUTION

Prostitution has declined dramatically in the past half-century. Kinsey's data suggested that prostitution had begun to decline in the 1940s, and Hunt concluded that prostitution had declined by over 50 percent since the time of the Kinsey report.[26] It appears that the demand for prostitution has gone down as sexual freedom has increased. Another possibility is that increasing job opportunities for women have made prostitution less attractive as an occupation. Nevertheless, it is unlikely that prostitution will disappear. For hundreds of years efforts to stamp it out have been remarkably unsuccessful.

Prostitution continues because it satisfies important needs for both prostitutes and customers. Even a moderately successful prostitute earns much more money than waitresses, store clerks, or professors:

> It is a silly question to ask a prostitute why she does it. The top salary for a teacher with a B.A. in New York City schools is $13,950; for a registered staff nurse, $13,000; for a telephone operator, about $8,000. The absolute

daily minimum a pimp expects a streetwalker to bring in is $200 a night. That comes to easily $70,000 a year. These are the highest-paid "professional" women in America.[27]

Prostitution offers its customers several advantages. Sex with a prostitute is sex without emotional ties and obligations. Customers do not have to "woo and win" the prostitute, and they have no obligation to be "nice" afterward. Prostitutes also offer to perform sexual activities that may be difficult for the customer to obtain elsewhere. Prostitutes are easily available to those who lack the time or social skills necessary for normal dating, to servicemen and others who are isolated from women, and to men with severe physical handicaps.

The Social World of the Prostitute

Prostitutes are condemned and rejected by "respectable" people, but within their own world they have a status hierarchy like those of other professions. Call girls are the best paid and the most respected. They are highly selective about their customers, charge high fees, and see the same clients again and again. Because they seldom accept unknown customers, their chances of arrest are low.

The woman who works in a house of prostitution is a step below the call girl in status. The "house girl" does not have to walk the streets in search of customers, but neither can she screen her customers. She must service a large number of clients a night and must split her fees with the operator of the house, who is usually known as a "madam."

Streetwalkers are on the bottom rung of the status ladder. They must prowl the streets in search of clients, often rob their customers, and are themselves highly vulnerable to assault, robbery, and arrest. Most streetwalkers work for a pimp who takes most or all the income. In return the pimp pays for the prostitute's apartment, buys her clothes, arranges legal services, provides protection, and gives her emotional support and affection. A pimp may have as many as twenty prostitutes in his "stable." The streetwalker's prestige among other streetwalkers is often determined by the prestige of her pimp, and the status of the pimp, in turn, is determined by how conspicuously he displays his wealth. A pink Cadillac with rabbit skin upholstery, an Omega watch, a mohair suit, and $200 alligator shoes count a lot in some circles.[28]

Most people almost automatically assume that all prostitutes are women. In fact, male prostitution is common in most big cities. A few heterosexual male prostitutes hire out to women, but most male prostitutes cater to other men. From the "call boy" to the homosexual streetwalker, male prostitutes display the same occupational distinctions as their female counterparts.

Although female prostitutes come from all walks of life, most are young, unmarried women from low socioeconomic backgrounds. Studies

Streetwalkers, both female and male, are the lowest status prostitutes. Those who work in a house of prostitution are somewhat better off, while the call girl (or call boy) has the highest status and the best working conditions.

show that many prostitutes have had severe conflicts with their families and were often considered "troublemakers" at an early age.[29] Although many people believe that female prostitutes are forced into prostitution by pimps, most prostitutes simply drift into their occupation. They begin by giving sex in exchange for favors from boyfriends, progress to occasional "tricking," and then become full-time professionals.[30]

Prostitutes use several strategies to maintain a positive self-image in the face of social condemnation and rejection. Most important, they enthusiastically reject the "straight" life. In their world view only "chumps" hold nine-to-five jobs, pay taxes, and live in tacky suburban homes. The ideal is the "player" who lives an affluent life with as little effort as possible.[31] Not all prostitutes reject middle-class values, however. Some carry on ordinary private lives, concealing their occupation as much as possible. Others fail to maintain their self-respect and sink into alcoholism or drug addiction.[32]

**Prostitution
and the Law**

In ancient civilizations prostitution was not a crime. "Temple prostitution" was common among some religious sects. During the middle ages prostitution was rarely illegal even though it was seen as a kind of necessary evil. With the coming of the Protestant Reformation, together with concern about the spread of syphilis, prostitution was outlawed. It has been widely prohibited in the Western world ever since, though antiprostitution legislation has not always been strictly enforced.

A hundred years ago prostitution was widespread in North America. It was illegal, but it was carefully ignored by most police departments. At that time most prostitutes worked in brothels (houses of prostitution) concentrated in the "red-light" districts of larger cities. Madams paid police officers to leave their girls alone, and they were not disturbed as long as they did not venture out of their district. In the early part of the twentieth century, this cozy arrangement was upset by a wave of vice crusades. The American Society of Sanitary and Moral Prophylaxis, the American Purity Alliance, the YMCA, and other organizations mounted a powerful offensive against prostitution. One by one the red-light districts were closed down and increasing numbers of prostitutes became streetwalkers instead.

Today prostitution is illegal everywhere in North America except a few counties in Nevada, where brothels are permitted. Nevertheless, prostitution seems to be practiced more openly today than it was in the 1940s and 1950s. Enforcement is sporadic, and is aimed at prostitutes while largely ignoring their clients.

Generally speaking, the laws that were intended to solve the problems of prostitution have made them worse. Closing houses of prostitution increased the number of streetwalkers, and they pose a more serious problem than "house girls." Streetwalkers solicit men who are not interested in their services, invade areas in which they are not welcome, and are often involved in criminal activities such as robbery and narcotics dealing. The prohibition of prostitution encourages organized crime to enter the business and reap enormous tax-free profits.

Prostitutes, like homosexuals, are becoming involved in political activities and in some places have organized to fight what they see as legal discrimination and harassment. Members of such organizations argue that prostitution is a voluntary business arrangement between a seller and a buyer, does no harm to society, and therefore should not be outlawed. Opponents of legalization argue that prostitution is immoral and that legalization would condone and encourage it.

PORNOGRAPHY

Strictly speaking, pornography is not a form of sexual behavior. It consists of obscene books, pictures, sights, and sounds. However, attempts to clearly define what is obscene have ended in failure and confusion.

While many people find pornography offensive, the scientific evidence indicates that it does not contribute to sex crimes or have harmful psychological effects on the viewer.

One popular definition holds that any material that is intended to be sexually arousing is obscene and, thus, pornographic. But by this definition a large percentage of all advertising, books, and movies would be pornographic. According to the Supreme Court, sexually explicit materials are not obscene unless they (1) appeal to "prurient" (lewd, lustful, indecent) interests, (2) are contrary to community standards, and (3) lack all "redeeming social value." But while these standards appear to be clear and precise, they are impossible to apply objectively. Any book, magazine, or film can be said to have some social value. In fact, the President's Commission on Obscenity and Pornography found that 60 percent of all Americans believe that exposure to erotic materials provides information about sex and entertainment, both of which appear to be of "redeeming social value." Further, the Commission found that a majority of Americans think adults should be allowed to read or see any materials they wish.[33] It is therefore doubtful that most "pornography" actually violates the standards of the majority of the people.

Critics of sexually explicit materials often charge that they lead to immorality and "moral decay." However, standards of sexual morality in contemporary society differ so widely that it is impossible to say whether pornography encourages immorality. There is considerable evidence to support the argument that looking at "dirty" books and pictures does not lead the viewer to rape women, molest girls or boys, or commit other sex crimes. Wilson found that his sample of sex offenders had less exposure to pornographic materials than the average citizen, and this finding has been confirmed by other researchers.[34] Even more telling evidence comes from Denmark, the first European nation to repeal its pornography laws. Studies revealed a substantial reduction in exhibitionism (58 percent), peeping (80 percent), and child molesting (69 percent) as erotic materials became more easily available.[35]

But while there is little evidence that erotic materials have significant harmful effects, it is clear that censorship of such materials creates serious problems. Censorship has a chilling effect on personal freedom as well as on art. Works ranging from Shakespeare's plays to *Alice in Wonderland* have been banned at one time or another. If censors are given the power to prohibit "pornography," many artistic creations may be affected as well. Because pornography is so difficult to define, there is always a danger that the decision to ban a particular book or picture will be based on political considerations. Even when the materials being censored are entirely devoid of artistic or political content, it is certainly a contradiction for a government that claims to be dedicated to the principles of freedom and liberty to tell its citizens what kinds of books they may read and what kinds of movies they may watch.

RESPONDING TO PROBLEMS OF SEXUAL BEHAVIOR

In the past there was a strong consensus about which types of sexual behavior were acceptable and which were not. Condemned sexual activities were considered a social problem, and strict laws were passed against them. Although the consensus about sexual morality has disappeared, most of the old legislation remains on the books. Adultery, "cohabitation," oral–genital intercourse, anal intercourse, prostitution, and homosexuality are criminal acts in most American states. The fact that most of the laws prohibiting such acts are seldom enforced only points up our confusion about the proper relationship between government and citizens. The heart of the conflict can be stated in a single question: Is the government justified in attempting to force people to conform to its standards of sexual morality?

Of course, not all laws restricting sexual behavior are controversial. No one objects to the fact that rape is outlawed. Laws against child molesting also fall into this category, as do laws that restrict sexual activity in public view. People no longer object to a married couple's having sexual relations in their own home, but even the most liberal will not champion the right to have intercourse on a busy sidewalk.

The controversy about the legislation of morality focuses on laws that prohibit private sexual activity between consenting adults, including homosexuality, prostitution, and viewing pornography. Some officials are convinced that these laws are necessary to preserve traditional standards and to prevent moral decay that may lead to social corruption. However, most social scientists who have studied the effects of these laws advocate their repeal. They point to the injustice of permitting one segment of society to force its personal morality on everyone else. It has also been shown that this type of legislation tends to create a wide variety of other problems. The late Herbert Packer, a Stanford law professor, made a long list of such problems, including the following:

1. Because forbidden sexual acts are hard to detect, police must rely on questionable techniques, including the use of undercover agents, decoys, spies, and paid informers.
2. Laws prohibiting these acts encourage the development of a deviant subculture as violators form links and bonds to protect themselves from the police.
3. No real harm is caused by the forbidden activities.
4. Wide-scale violation of these laws creates a climate which encourages disrespect for the law as well as police corruption.[36]

But legal changes alone cannot resolve problems of sexual behavior. Conflicts about sexual morality will persist for generations to come and management of those differences will continue to be difficult. There is an enormous difference between refusing to participate in certain sexual activities and insisting that no one else should participate in them; just as there is an enormous difference between participating in sexual activities oneself and insisting that other people watch or give their approval.

SOCIOLOGICAL PERSPECTIVES on Sexual Behavior

Because sexual behavior is deeply rooted in human biology, many people lose sight of the fact that it is socially controlled and directed. Instead, they believe that the sexual standard of their social group is a part of human nature and that those who do not follow that standard are abnormal and unnatural. Such ethnocentric attitudes help to make sexual behavior a social problem by fostering concern about "abnormal" sexual activities and by promoting campaigns to stamp out this sexual deviance. These problems are particularly severe in North America because there are so many different cultures and subcultures with contradictory standards of sexual behavior. The conflicts between moral standards and the rapid changes that have occurred in sexual attitudes have made sexual behavior a controversial social issue.

The Functionalist Perspective

Kingsley Davis's early analysis of prostitution set the pattern for most of the functionalist work on this subject.[37] Following Davis's lead, most functionalists hold that prostitution is inevitable. As long as there are sexual restrictions in a society, the argument goes, sex will be for sale. Functionalists also note that prostitution serves society by providing a sexual outlet for people who would otherwise be without one. Consequently, most functionalists, including Davis, advocate the legalization of prostitution.

At the same time, however, other restrictions on sexual expression are also considered functional. Thus, prohibition of premarital and extramarital sex is seen as a device to keep society's kinship system intact, including the system for passing property and power along from parents to children. Similarly, homosexuality should be banned because this sexual outlet does not contribute to a society's need for new members. In other words, homosexuality is dysfunctional because it does not contribute to reproduction. Considering the current overpopulation of the world, however, it can be argued that some amount of homosexuality is actually functional.

Pornography is often held to be dysfunctional because it damages an essential social institution—the family. However, the type of damage pornography is supposed to cause is seldom explicitly stated. The assumption seems to be that it encourages extramarital affairs, but there is no evidence that viewing pornography actually has that effect or that extramarital affairs are a serious threat to the stability of the family. Moreover, censorship of pornography endangers civil liberties and may therefore be more dysfunctional than pornography itself.

The Conflict Perspective

It is obvious that most problems of sexual behavior stem from conflicting ideas about sexual morality. There are many different standards of sexual behavior, but supporters of traditional standards have the power and have been able to write their convictions into law. Those whose sexual morality differs from the values of dominant groups are made into criminals and threatened with imprisonment. Conflict theorists see such actions as part of a larger effort by traditional groups to maintain their cultural dominance by controlling the criminal law. The same power struggle leads to the imprisonment of marijuana smokers, bigamists, political radicals, and others who challenge the beliefs or customs of dominant groups.

Conflict theorists see attempts to stamp out prostitution, homosexuality, and pornography as oppression of "sexual minorities," similar to the oppression of ethnic minorities by segregation laws. Aside from noting the obvious injustice of such policies, conflict theorists point out that such oppression also creates secondary problems such as the creation of an illegal market for forbidden goods and services. The huge profits to be made encourages organized criminals to move into prostitution and pornography.

Conflict theorists recommend that homosexuals, prostitutes, and other so-called sexual deviants organize and agitate for social change, as they have already begun to do. In addition, conflict theorists encourage them to form alliances with other oppressed groups such as drug users and religious and ethnic minorities. The "problem of sexual behavior" would be far less severe, according to conflict theorists, if we repealed laws prohibiting sexual acts between consenting adults and passed laws banning discrimination against homosexuals and others who engage in unpopular sexual activities.

The Social-Psychological Perspective

Biosocial theorists stress the fact that humans are the most sexually active animals on earth. The human female is unique because she is sexually receptive at all times while the females of other species are receptive only during periods of fertility. Thus, whereas other species engage in intercourse on a periodic basis, humans do so continually, a situation that creates many problems of sexual adjustment. Biosocial theory has little to say about prostitution or pornography, but some biosocial theorists argue that homosexuality is unnatural because it does not lead to reproduction. Critics of this position counter that homosexuality has often been observed in animals as well as in human beings, and therefore must be a natural adaptation to the environment.[38]

Personality theory holds sexual conduct to be a product of psychological traits and characteristics that are established early in life. Homosexuality, for instance, is usually seen to be the result of experiences in early childhood, particularly those that promote identification with the opposite sex. Behaviorists and interactionists also hold that sexual behavior and preferences are learned, but claim that one learns to engage in homosexuality or prostitution the same way one learns to engage in heterosexual activities. That is, the homosexual or prostitute simply receives more rewards and fewer punishments for such behavior than for socially acceptable alternatives.

SUMMARY

In view of the enormous range of sexual customs and beliefs found in different cultures, it is clear that sexual behavior is not biologically determined. It derives from a biological drive, but a drive that is channeled, directed, and controlled by social forces.

Traditionally, Western culture was sexually conservative. Intercourse was permissible only between a husband and wife, and then only for reproduction. But these attitudes and values have changed. Comparison of surveys by Kinsey, Hunt, and others shows that in the past four decades there has been a substantial increase in many types of sexual activity. The double standard has decayed but has not disappeared; sexual activity increased more rapidly among women than among men, but men remain more sexually active. The same surveys show no change in the amount of homosexuality, but there has been a decrease in prostitution.

A number of forces contributed to the increase in sexual activity.

These include (1) a decrease in the power of the family and traditional religious morality to control young people's sexual activities; (2) the erosion of the double standard; (3) improvements in birth control techniques; (4) growing emphasis on freedom and individual self-determination; (5) increased use of erotic materials in the mass media; and (6) a redefinition of sexuality as normal and healthy instead of as base and sinful.

In the past there was a strong consensus concerning acceptable sexual behaviors, and strict laws defined those that were not acceptable. This consensus no longer exists, and there is considerable opposition to government attempts to legislate morality. Such legislation promotes the use of questionable police techniques to uncover violators, encourages disrespect for the law, can lead to police corruption, and stimulates the development of deviant subcultures.

Homosexuality is one of the most misunderstood forms of sexual behavior. Contrary to popular belief, the differences among homosexuals, bisexuals, and heterosexuals are not absolute but are a matter of degree. Psychologists have shown that homosexuality is learned in the early years of childhood. Strong prohibitions against adolescent heterosexuality also encourage homosexual experimentation.

In the past most homosexuals concealed their sexual preference, but now they are "coming out" and admitting it. While most European countries, Canada, and seventeen American states have repealed their antihomosexual legislation, homosexuals are still subject to both occupational and social discrimination.

Prostitution has declined in this century, but it is unlikely that it will ever disappear. Prostitution offers its customers several advantages, including sex without ties or obligations, hard-to-obtain services, and sex for social isolates. Prostitutes have an occupational prestige system. The call girl has the highest rank; next is the woman who works in a house of prostitution; and at the bottom is the streetwalker, who must search out her customers in public. Legal efforts to restrict prostitution have aggravated the situation. Closing houses of prostitution created more streetwalkers, increased venereal disease, and opened the occupation to control by organized criminals.

Legally, pornographic material must be lewd, contrary to community standards, and without redeeming social value. But applying these standards is quite difficult, especially because almost any book or picture can be shown to have some redeeming value. Many believe that sexually explicit materials promote sex crimes and violations of other moral standards, but scientific evidence suggests that pornography is harmless. Opponents of censorship argue that legislation restricting pornography is more harmful than the pornography itself, since censorship threatens civil liberties and stifles artistic expression.

Two commonly suggested responses to the problems of sexual behavior are (1) more efficient repression of acts that are considered immoral by advocates of moral law and (2) legalization of all sexual behavior between consenting adults in private and cultivation of a more tolerant attitude toward those who do not agree with our own sexual morality.

Functionalists analyze the effects of homosexuality, prostitution, and pornography on society. Prostitution, for example, is said to serve society by providing sexual outlets for people who would otherwise lack them. Various restrictions on sexual expression—including homosexuality—are generally believed to be functional, since they help fulfill the need for more children. But now that the world is overpopulated, more functionalists are coming to see these restrictions as dysfunctional and advocate their abolition. Conflict theorists say that problems of sexual behavior stem from value conflicts and from efforts by powerful groups to force their morality on others. Biosocial theorists stress the fact that humans are the most sexually active of all animals and argue that problems of sexual adjustment stem from this condition. Personality theorists are concerned primarily with locating psychological traits that are acquired early in life and are believed to determine later sexual behavior. Interactionists and behaviorists have evidence that sexual behavior is learned.

KEY TERMS	bisexual	lesbian
	heterosexual	pornography
	homosexual	prostitution
	incest taboo	

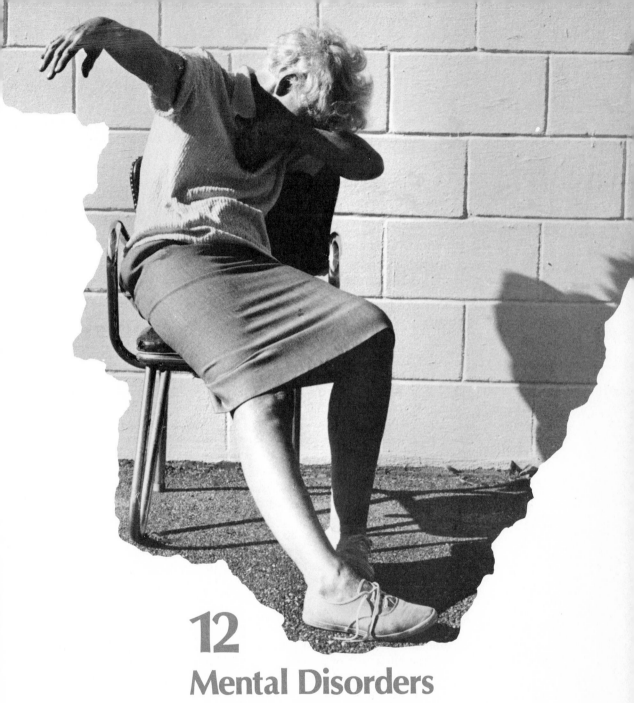

12
Mental Disorders

Is mental disorder an illness?
What are the most common mental disorders?
Do the poor have more mental problems than the rich?
Which treatment method is most effective?

Few things are more frightening than the thought of "going crazy." Literature since the time of the ancient Greeks has portrayed pathetic lunatics and madmen raging against imaginary demons. Although mental disorders are sometimes shown in a comic light, they are more commonly associated with tragic personal failure. Perhaps it is for this reason that most people react uncomfortably to any discussion of mental illness. Dark fears about how mental illness "runs in the family" make the relatives of mental patients reluctant to discuss the issue openly. Some people act as though mental disorders are contagious, fearfully avoiding any contact with the mentally disturbed.

Psychologists estimate that 20 to 25 percent of all Americans have psychological impairments that seriously interfere with their lives.[1] Millions of people, in and out of hospitals, receive treatment for mental problems every year. Almost half of all North American hospital beds are filled with mental patients.[2] Yet most people who have mental disorders never get to a hospital or receive help of any kind.

Everyone from professional therapists to the leaders of exotic religious cults claims to have a solution to the problems of mental disorder. Every year dozens of new books on "pop psychology" are published, each offering an easy cure for personal difficulties. Thousands who believe they have problems turn to such books for help. Reading a book is a private matter, but those who seek professional help are often stigmatized for admitting that they have a problem. One who was branded in this way was Senator Thomas Eagleton, who was selected to run for vice president with presidential candidate George McGovern in 1972. Senator Eagleton was warmly received until it was disclosed that he had once received treatment for depression. Many people expressed doubts about a "mental patient's" fitness to be President, and wondered whether the pressures of critical presidential decisions would cause another breakdown. The public reaction was so strong that Eagleton was dropped from the Democratic ticket.

WHAT ARE MENTAL DISORDERS?

The terms *mental illness* and *insanity* tend to create images of the most dramatic types of mental problems. A common image of the mentally disordered is that of a madman in a straitjacket, foaming at the mouth and struggling to free himself in order to attack anyone who happens to be nearby. Another is that of a dirty, disheveled woman, babbling incoherencies and engaging in random sexual relations with no regard for moral standards. But these images are misleading, for most mental disorders are neither bizarre nor dramatic; instead, they are the common experiences of anxiety or depression with which we are all familiar.

Despite years of research and study, there is no widespread agreement on the meaning of terms such as *mentally ill, insane, mentally disturbed,* and *crazy.* One person's craziness is another person's individuality. If a man says that he has talked to God and received instructions to save humanity, he may be considered crazy by most of us; but some may see him as a prophet or a saint. The difference turns not so much on what he says as on whether his audience believes him. An old woman who gives away her fortune may be considered mentally ill by her family, but those who receive the money will see her as a selfless philanthropist.

Speaking generally, a person may be said to have a mental disorder if he or she is so disturbed that coping with routine, everyday life is difficult or impossible. But this definition—and most others as well—is vague. Exactly how does one determine whether individuals can or cannot cope with their everyday affairs? There is no clear-cut answer. This does not mean that it is impossible to tell whether an individual has a psychological problem, for the behavior of some mental patients is so bizarre that few people would question their inability to cope. The catatonic schizophrenic may stand motionless for hours, even days, and must be fed through a tube. But most cases are not so obvious. People with serious physical illnesses usually are aware of their need for help. In contrast, the greater a person's mental disturbance, the more difficult it is for him or her to be conscious of the trouble.

While many psychiatrists, psychologists, and sociologists have attempted to define mental disorder precisely, none of these efforts has received widespread acceptance. Some experts see mental disorders as mental illness; others say they reflect personal maladjustment; and some simply call them deviance.

Mental Illness   The most widely accepted approach to mental disorders uses a medical model in which it is assumed that "mental illnesses" are very much like physical illnesses. Thus, the concepts and methods of modern medicine are used to diagnose and treat mental illness in the same fashion as a broken arm or measles. Mental illness is believed to be a result of a disruption in the normal functioning of the personality, just as physical illnesses are caused by some disturbance in the normal functioning of the body.

Psychiatrists who use this approach try to identify specific types of mental illnesses that, like measles and smallpox, are assumed to have specific causes. After identifying the patient's specific illness, the psychiatrist tries to cure the illness by eliminating the cause. This model is most appropriate when the mental problem can be shown to be a result of an organic condition such as an overdose of drugs, syphilis, or a biochemical condition. But because most mental disorders do not have easily defined physical causes, they are attributed to such causes as repressed hostility, frustration, and personal conflict.

In medieval times mental disorders were believed to be caused by demons and spirits. "Treatments" such as flogging, starving, and dunking the sufferer in hot water were used to drive the devils out.[3] The idea that mental disorders are a form of illness developed as part of a humanitarian reaction against these practices. The denial of supernatural influences on the mind opened the door to scientific experimentation and study. Further, the belief that mental disorders are similar to other common illnesses helped reduce the shame of disturbed people.

While the perception of mental disorder as an illness was a great advance over demonic beliefs, in recent years a growing number of critics have challenged the validity of the medical model, arguing that it has outlived its usefulness. They point out that while there is general agreement on the symptoms and causes of physical disorders such as appendicitis or pneumonia, there is little agreement about the symptoms and causes of mental illnesses. Most physicians agree that surgery is the best treatment for appendicitis and that antibiotics are most effective for pneumonia. But there is no agreement about the most effective means of treating mental illnesses. Psychiatrists prescribe psychoanalysis; psychologists ask for behavior modification; others recommend drugs or electroshock.

Pneumonia is pneumonia, regardless of the culture in which it occurs; but mental illness is different in different cultures. Thomas Szasz, a psychiatrist who is a strong critic of the medical model, argues that the whole idea of mental illness is a myth used to make the values and opinions of the psychiatric establishment resemble scientific fact.[4] He notes, first, that while everyone knows what it means to be physically healthy and agrees that being healthy is a good thing, there is no similar agreement about the nature of mental health. Second, he sees the proponents of "mental health" as mere moralists who are trying to tell others how they ought to live. Third, he argues that diagnosing people with mental problems as "mentally ill" robs them of personal responsibility for their condition and therefore undermines the moral fabric of society.

Personal Maladjustment

According to another perspective, mental disorders arise when someone is unable to deal effectively with his or her personal problems. It is assumed that disturbed behavior is caused by the same forces that govern normal behavior and that such behavior is one end of an unbroken continuum. Therapists who use this approach do not look for symptoms of a specific disease. Instead, the person's adjustment to his or her environment is examined.[5] Coleman has described this approach as follows:

> Life is a continuous process of adjusting, in which we strive to meet our own needs and maintain harmonious relations with our environment. When an individual deals with his problems effectively, he is said to be *well* adjusted —to be adapting successfully to both the inner and outer demands being made upon him. Conversely, when his problems prove too much for him—as shown by anxiety, inefficiency, unhappiness, or more serious symptoms—he is referred to as *maladjusted.*[6]

Szasz uses the personal-maladjustment approach in a modified form. Although he prefers to talk of "problems in living" rather than "personal maladjustment," the two phrases have similar implications. The basic difference is this: Szasz sees "problems in living" as universal and inescapable, whereas the personal-maladjustment approach implies that all normal men and women have a "well-adjusted" relationship to their environment.[7]

The personal-maladjustment model has three advantages over the medical model. First, it does not consider individuals in isolation from their environment, as a physician would when treating a broken leg or a "mental illness." Second, because abnormal behavior is seen to be produced by the same processes as normal behavior, it discourages the assumption that mentally disturbed people are "freaks" or "madmen." Third, it accepts the fact that any diagnosis of mental problems is a very uncertain affair and, therefore, that there are no specific "cures" for these problems.

The personal-maladjustment approach has some serious shortcomings, however. Although it does not ignore the individual's environment, as the medical model is prone to do, the basic assumption is that mental problems are personal problems. Thus, the individual—not the social order—is assumed to be responsible for the problems. But personal problems sometimes stem from an unlivable environment rather than from the individual. The healthiest individuals are not always those who are best adjusted to their environment; and refusal to accept an unjust social order is certainly not abnormal or harmful.

Social Deviance

The newest approach to mental disorders emphasizes their social aspects. Its proponents hold that there are no objective standards by which a person's mental health may be judged. Determination that someone is or is not mentally disordered is strictly a cultural matter. What is considered mental illness or maladjustment in one society is considered healthy adjustment in another. From this perspective what people call "mental illness" is merely social deviance. In other words, people are labeled "mentally ill" because they have violated rules about how they are supposed to behave, not because they have a specific disease.

Most deviants violate clearly understood rules and therefore are labeled in ways that emphasize their moral failure.[8] If a man kills another person, he is labeled "murderer"; if a woman accepts money for sexual relations, she is labeled "prostitute." According to Thomas Scheff, however, the rules that are violated by those who are labeled "mentally ill" are *residual*, meaning that they are commonly accepted and observed in a way that makes them appear to be part of human nature. There is no law against staring intently at a person's ear or foot when carrying on a conversation, but those who do so violate residual rules and are considered

The difference between being labeled a prophet and being labeled a crazy depends on the reaction of the audience. Those who agree with the man holding the sign in this picture think he is a great religious leader, while those who disagree with him are likely to feel he is mentally unbalanced.

rather strange. The same is true of a man who claims to be Jesus Christ or who smears feces on his clothing before leaving for work in the morning. Because most people cannot understand why anyone would violate commonsense customs, they perceive deviants as "sick" or "mentally ill" and label them accordingly.

The social-deviance approach places responsibility for mental disorders on the social environment rather than on the individual. The stigma of "mental illness" is thus removed. Therapists are encouraged to deal with the patient's family and personal environment rather than assuming that the patient is suffering from a personal defect or disorder. However, this approach has been severely criticized by experts who hold more traditional ideas about mental health and mental illness. These experts point out that the labeling approach neglects the disturbed individuals

NINETEENTH CENTURY SOCIAL PROBLEMS

A woman was recently found wandering about the streets of Eau Claire with a dead baby in her arms. She was from Chippewa County and had lost her husband and was destitute.
July 5, 1885

themselves. Even if no one were labeled "mentally ill," they argue, disturbed people would still have their problems. Further, labeling people "mentally ill" is the only way we can identify those who are in need of help.

Each of these theories of mental disorder has its weaknesses, but each also has something to contribute. There is no good reason for insisting that mental disorder is entirely a medical problem, entirely a problem of maladjustment, or entirely a problem of labeling. Mental problems are not simple. After centuries of study and thought we remain uncertain about their ultimate cause. We can therefore only admit the limitations of our knowledge and draw insight from any available source.

CLASSIFICATION OF MENTAL DISORDERS

Despite disagreement about the exact nature of mental disorders, psychologists and psychiatrists have attempted to classify them according to their distinctive characteristics. In 1968 the World Health Organization, in cooperation with the American Psychiatric Association, proposed a standardized classification. This international system lists dozens of different types of problems and assigns each to one of ten proposed categories. Organic disorders that have clear-cut physical causes, such as birth defects or brain damage, will not be discussed here. The major types of functional disorders (those without a proven organic cause) are neuroses, psychoses, psychosomatic disorders, and personality disorders.

Neuroses

A neurosis is a personal problem accompanied by anxiety and a chronically inappropriate response. The typical neurotic has feelings of desperate inadequacy and sees many common situations as threatening. As a result the neurotic avoids stressful situations rather than attempting to deal with them. Although neurotics may complain about their problems, they usually have little insight into the causes of those problems and are not aware of the self-defeating manner in which they attempt to deal with them. They often have feelings of guilt and are dissatisfied and unhappy with their lives, believing that they are not fulfilling their responsibilities to themselves and to others. Despite their problems, neurotics maintain contact with the people around them and rarely need to be hospitalized. There is no clear line between a normal problem and a neurotic disorder. Almost everyone has at some time displayed one or more of the symptoms of neurosis, but this does not mean that most of us are neurotic. Only if the problems are severe and persistent is someone justifiably called neurotic.

Psychoses

The psychoses are the most severe types of mental disorders. The essential difference between psychotics and neurotics is that psychotics have lost contact with "reality" while neurotics have not. Typical symptoms of a psychosis include hallucinations, delusions, severe personal disorganization, and various kinds of bizarre behavior. In many cases, however, there is no distinct difference between a psychotic and a neurotic; severe neuroses blend almost imperceptibly into mild psychoses.

There are three major types of functional psychoses: schizophrenia, paranoia, and affective disorders.

Schizophrenia

Typical symptoms of schizophrenia include extreme disorganization in personality, thought patterns, and speech. Schizophrenics tend to withdraw from social life and live in a private fantasy world. They also tend to have delusions (false beliefs that are maintained in spite of contradictory evidence) and hallucinations (apparent sensory experiences of something without an objective cause; e.g., hearing voices).

Schizophrenia is the most common and most persistent type of psychosis. Compared with people suffering from other types of mental disorders, schizophrenics tend to be admitted to mental hospitals more often, stay in the hospital longer, and return more frequently after release. Schizophrenia occurs in numerous forms, including simple schizophrenia, in which the person develops a progressive loss of interest in everyday living and withdraws into a fantasy world; paranoid schizophrenia, which is characterized by absurd delusions, irrational fears, and often vivid hallucinations; catatonic schizophrenia, which is marked by periods of stupor in which the person remains motionless for long periods; and hebephrenic schizophrenia, which is characterized by infantile behavior, giggling, silliness, and hallucinations.

Paranoia

People with paranoia suffer from overpowering, irrational fears, often believing that others are plotting against them and seeing everyday events as clear proof of these schemes. Compared with schizophrenia, paranoia generally produces less personal disorganization, and in most cases hallucinations are absent. Because victims of paranoia often can maintain themselves in the community, there are relatively few paranoids in mental hospitals. But some paranoids may attempt to harm or destroy those who they believe are plotting against them, and therefore are dangerous.

Affective Psychoses

Schizophrenia and paranoia are characterized by disturbances in thought patterns. The affective psychoses, on the other hand, involve disturbances in mood and emotion (known as *affect* in psychological terminology). The most common type of affective psychosis is manic depression. This condition is characterized by extreme swings in mood. In some cases the individual is extremely depressed, worries incessantly, withdraws from social contacts, and becomes lethargic and gloomy. Others become manic. They feel a sense of euphoria accompanied by extreme activity, have delusions of grandeur, talk all the time, or behave with excessive impulsiveness. In about 15 to 25 percent of all manic–depressive cases, the person swings back and forth between depression and mania. In other cases, the swing is between depression and "normal" or between mania and "normal."

Another common affective disorder is involutional melancholia, which is similar to other severe depressions except that it occurs during the "involutional" period (the change of life, climacteric, or menopause) and is assumed to be a reaction to the body's biochemical changes. Involutional melancholia generally occurs between age 40 and 55 in women and between age 50 and 65 in men, and it is about three times more common in women.[9]

Personality Disorders

Formerly called character disorders, the personality disorders are "deeply ingrained" maladaptive patterns of behavior that are presumed to be rooted in the individual's personality. Alcoholics and drug addicts are included in this category, as are most other types of social deviants. Also included here are the so-called sociopathic personalities, who are impulsive, self-centered, immature, and show no guilt about their deviant behavior. In many ways sociopaths are the opposite of neurotics. While the neurotic is often guilt-ridden and anxious, the typical sociopath is self-confident, aggressive, and without guilt or remorse.

Critics have been particularly harsh in their judgments about the usefulness of "personality disorders" as a category of mentally disturbed individuals. It has often been charged that it is just a convenient label for anyone involved in deviant behavior and that most of those who are diagnosed as having personality disorders have in common only their condemnation by society.

Psychosomatic Disorders

Psychosomatic disorders are physical illnesses that are caused by psychological problems. Combat soldiers sometimes develop mysterious paralyses that cannot be traced to physical causes. Similarly, writers who are under pressure to produce sometimes develop "writer's cramp," and musicians who are under pressure to perform have been known to become temporarily blind. In the past only a few physical conditions were considered to be psychological in origin. But in recent years there has been growing awareness that there is a close relationship between psychological and physical well-being. Stress and anxiety have been found to underlie physical problems ranging from ulcers to heart attacks and skin problems. Depression often produces lethargy and loss of appetite, thereby leading to severe physical consequences. In his research on the elderly, Townsend found that the "will to live" plays an important part in determining whether individuals live or die.[10]

Despite the great effort that has gone into classifying mental disorders, psychiatric diagnosis remains notoriously unreliable. Patients often have symptoms of more than one disorder, and the symptoms may change rapidly. One study found that in about 20 percent of the cases analyzed, psychiatrists disagreed as to whether a certain patient had a psychosis, and that in about half the cases studied, psychiatrists could not agree on the specific type of psychosis the patient displayed.[11] Psychiatrists in different countries also diagnose patients differently. For instance, American psychiatrists are much more likely than their English counterparts to diagnose a patient as schizophrenic. It is clear that most mental disorders cannot be diagnosed with the same degree of certainty as most physical problems.

THE DISTRIBUTION OF MENTAL DISORDERS

It is difficult to measure the incidence of mental disorders in different social classes, in urban areas compared with rural areas, or even in men compared with women. Rates of admission to mental hospitals are not accurate measures because people from one category may be more likely to seek treatment than people from another. Further, hospitals have different criteria for admission, and even out-patient treatment by a psychiatrist may be determined as much by income and attitudes toward "going to the shrink" as by need for treatment. On the other hand, surveys of communities to determine how many people are mentally ill also have serious weaknesses. Mental disturbances are so poorly defined that the results of such surveys may reflect the biases of the researchers as much as the distribution of mental disorders. As a result the following discussion necessarily relies on approximations and estimates since most of the evidence is far from conclusive.

Social Class

One of the earliest investigations of the relationship between social class and mental disorder was carried out by Robert Faris and Warren Dunham in the 1930s.[12] These researchers obtained information about the original place of residence of patients who had been admitted to Chicago's four state mental hospitals and eight private mental hospitals between 1922 and 1934. They found the highest rates of mental disorder in the central areas of the city, where the population was poor and had little living space. The lowest rates were found in the more stable, wealthy residential areas on the outskirts of Chicago. Faris and Dunham concluded that the social disorganization of the central city, with its mobility, extreme poverty, demoralization, and cultural heterogeneity, was responsible for the higher incidence of mental disorders there.

A second major study was conducted by Hollingshead and Redlich in the 1950s.[13] They obtained data on the class background of mental patients seeing private psychiatrists and those in public and private hospitals in New Haven, Connecticut. Like Faris and Dunham, they found that the psychoses, particularly schizophrenia, were much more common among lower-class people. However, the neuroses were more common among people with higher status and income. They also found that social class had a very strong influence on the type of treatment a patient received. The poor people were most likely to be treated in hospitals, while the wealthy were more likely to be treated by private psychiatrists. Lower-class men and women who were hospitalized for mental disorders remained in the hospital for much longer periods than other patients. Hollingshead and Redlich concluded that it was impossible to tell whether higher rates of psychosis for lower-class people were caused by the conditions in which they lived or by the inferior treatment they received.

A third study was conducted in Manhattan by Leo Srole and his associates.[14] Rather than using hospital admissions or other statistics pertaining to treatment, these researchers conducted a door-to-door survey of 1700 men and women, asking a variety of questions designed to determine whether the respondents had any psychological problems and what sort of treatment, if any, they had received. The startling conclusion was that over 23 percent of the respondents were significantly impaired by a mental disorder and that less than 20 percent were completely healthy. Srole and his co-workers found significant differences between social classes. In the lowest class almost half were impaired, while in the highest class only one in eight (12.5 percent) had a significant problem. The Manhattan study also found a close relationship between social class and psychiatric treatment. Only 1 percent of the impaired people in the lowest class were receiving treatment at the time of the interview, compared with 20 percent of the people in the upper-status levels.

The finding that lower-class people have more psychological problems has been confirmed by many other studies. After analyzing 44 studies, Dohrenwend and Dohrenwend concluded that "analysis of these studies shows that their most consistent result is an inverse relation between social class and reported rate of psychological disorder."[15] In other words, the lowest social classes have the highest rates of mental disorder.

Communities

The relentless growth of cities and the change in traditional life styles that has accompanied this growth have led many people to wonder about the impact of urban life on mental health. It is generally assumed that the congestion, anonymity, and stress associated with urban living cause mental problems, but the evidence for this belief is far from conclusive. It is easy to show that rates of hospitalization for mental problems are higher in urban areas, but the meaning of this fact is not clear. Because there are more hospital facilities in urban areas, it is much easier for city dwellers to get into a hospital for treatment.

The Manhattan study just discussed seems to indicate that mental problems are extremely common in that densely populated city. But it is quite possible that the high rates of mental disorder revealed by this study resulted from the kinds of questions the researchers asked, and therefore do not reflect the actual rates of mental disorder in Manhattan. A similar survey by the National Center for Health Statistics found slightly fewer reported psychiatric symptoms among residents of big cities than among those who live in small towns.[16]

A study of rural Hutterite communities in Montana, the Dakotas, and Canada did not yield the results that most students of mental disorders would expect. Hutterite communities are close knit, homogeneous, and highly integrated, and have steadfastly resisted the inroads of modern civilization. Yet Eaton and Weil found that the rate of severe mental disorder among Hutterites was roughly equal to the rate of hospitalization for mental disorders in New York State.[17] The most important difference was that the Hutterites usually cared for their disturbed people in their homes rather than in hospitals. A comparable study by Eleanor Leacock found a high rate of psychosis in some decaying rural areas and a low rate in some relatively well-off urban areas.[18] It therefore appears that the nature of an individual's immediate community has more to do with mental health than the number of people who live in it.

Other Distributions

Men and women are equally likely to receive treatment for a mental problem, but there are some important differences. Men are more often hospitalized, while women more often receive out-patient care. (See Figure 12.1.) The two sexes are very similar in their rates of diagnosed schizophrenia, but women are twice as likely to be treated for depression and men are four times as likely to be treated for alcoholism. Marital status also has a considerable bearing on the odds of being treated for a mental disorder. Married people have the lowest rates of treatment, while rates for those who have never married are considerably higher for men but

FIGURE 12.1
ADMISSION RATES TO
PSYCHIATRIC IN-PATIENT
FACILITIES, BY RACE, SEX,
AND AGE OF PATIENTS,
1971

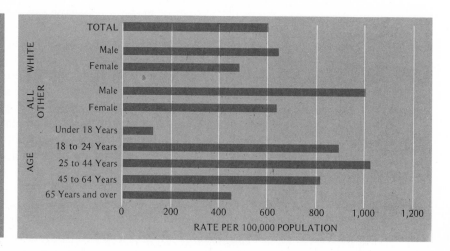

Source: U.S. Department of Commerce, *Social Indicators 1976* (Washington, D.C.: GPO, 1976), p. 168.

only slightly so for women. However, among divorced, widowed, or separated people the rates are high for both sexes. Age is significant too. While the highest rate of treatment appears in the 18–44-year-old age group, the elderly are much more likely to be treated for organic psychoses due to senility.[19] (It is important to remember that these statistics are for rates of *treatment* and do not necessarily reflect the true rates of mental disorders in these groups.)

CAUSES OF MENTAL DISORDERS

Considering the amount of disagreement over the definition and classification of mental disorders, it is not surprising that there is disagreement about their causes as well. Although the causes of mental disorders have received much scientific scrutiny, many difficult questions remain. What part does heredity play? What are the family conditions that promote emotional problems? What part do the reactions of others play in the behavior of mentally disturbed people? Do different kinds of mental disorders have different causes? Complete answers to these questions cannot be given; in fact, the principal theories about the causes of mental disorders disagree on most of the important issues.

Biosocial Theories

Because some drugs produce mental states that are very similar to psychoses, it seems reasonable to believe that psychotics may be suffering from a biochemical problem. Prolonged use of amphetamines, for instance, produces a state that is similar to paranoia. However, there are some significant differences between amphetamine abusers and psychotics. Tranquilizers seem to improve the behavior of some psychotics, but this does not prove that the causes of their behavior are biological.

Most psychologists and psychiatrists believe that there is an inherited predisposition to contract schizophrenia, but they often disagree about the relative importance of inheritance versus environment. The bulk of the evidence for the importance of heredity comes from the study of twins. Kallmann and Roth found that in 88.2 percent of the 17 pairs of identical twins (from one egg) they studied, if one twin had schizophrenia the other developed the same problem.[20] However, the rate of concordance (if one has it, both have it) was only 22.9 for the 35 pairs of fraternal twins (from two eggs). More recent studies have also concluded that close genetic relationships between twins are reflected in higher concordance rates. However, the differences found were not nearly as large as those reported by Kallman and Roth. For instance, Hoffer and Polin found a concordance rate of only 15.5 percent for identical twins and 4.4 percent for fraternal twins in a sample of almost 16,000 twins in the American armed forces.[21] Critics of these studies argue that the greater concordance between identical twins may be due to the fact that identical twins are often treated more nearly alike by their families than fraternal twins. Conclusive proof requires a study of pairs of identical and fraternal twins raised apart, but such a study has not yet been done. Another shortcoming in the research is that it focuses primarily on schizophrenia while neglecting other forms of mental disorders.

Developmental Theories

One of the most popular explanations among professionals who are engaged in treatment is that the major cause of mental disorder is a disturbance in the individual's early psychological development. Details vary from one theory to another, but all hold that the family and early social environment are critical to the individual's psychological future. Modern developmental theories borrow extensively from Sigmund Freud and his psychoanalytical school. Freud held that the unusual behavior of the mentally disturbed is merely a symptom of deeper, unresolved conflicts locked in the unconscious mind of the patient. He treated mental disorders with psychoanalysis—a slow and detailed examination of the patient's mental life. This method attempts to bring subconscious conflicts into the open, thereby permitting patients to understand and resolve them. Although critics of psychoanalysis say it is slow, costly, and ineffective, Freud's theories and methods remain part of the framework used by most clinical psychologists and psychiatrists.

Most of the early conflicts analyzed by developmental theorists occur in the family. For example, it is generally believed that parental love and affection are vital to the normal development of the child. Children who are rejected by their parents may develop a variety of psychological problems, including anxiety, insecurity, low self-esteem, and hostility. Parental standards of discipline are also important for proper development. Harsh, rigid standards may produce either a hostile and rebellious child or a passive, guilt-ridden one. Lack of discipline, on the other hand, is thought to encourage antisocial aggressive tendencies. Much has been made of the harm done by overprotective parents, whose children sometimes develop "passive–dependent personalities."[22] Such behavior is tolerated, even expected, of females. But the "mama's boy" finds it difficult to adjust to society's expectations, and psychological problems may develop as a result.

Gregory Bateson and his associates have advanced a theory of schizophrenia based on what they call the double bind.[23] This occurs when a parent gives a child two conflicting messages at the same time. For example, a boy may hear his mother say "I love you," but observe that she flinches or pulls away whenever he touches her. Children who receive such conflicting messages are in a double bind—they desperately want to believe what their parents are saying, but are constantly exposed to evidence that what is said is false. Thus, they come to mistrust and misinterpret normal communication, eventually becoming so disoriented that serious psychological problems emerge.

Many authorities believe that mental disorders are caused by problems in early socialization in the family. Lack of love, hostility, rejection, overprotection, and the conflicting messages of a double bind situation are all believed to promote mental problems.

Critics note that the developmental approach does not specify the exact conditions that produce mental disorders. Almost every family has some conditions that developmental theorists consider conducive to mental disorders, but of course most children do not develop mental problems. David Mechanic, among others, criticizes psychologists for their tendency to seize on a minor problem in an individual's life history as an explanation for mental disorder:

> For the most part, the usual variances in childrearing patterns appear to play a relatively small part in producing such profound difficulties as we are concerned with here. . . . The contexts which appear to breed pathology are those which are emotionally bizarre or deprived and in which the child experiences profound rejection, hostility, and other forms of social abuse as well as being exposed to inadequate, ineffective, and incongruous models of behavior.[24]

Learning Theories

Psychologists have been studying the process of learning for many years, and this knowledge is now being applied in the explanation and treatment of mental disorders. Learning theorists do not believe that biochemical processes or hidden inner conflicts cause mental disorders. Instead, they see such disorders merely as inappropriate behavior that has been learned as other behaviors are learned.

According to learning theorists, there are two basic mechanisms by which people learn behavior, whether normal or abnormal: classical conditioning and operant conditioning. Classical conditioning is quite passive, while operant conditioning requires the active participation of the subject. For instance, in classical conditioning it is first observed that a dog's mouth will water if the animal is shown a juicy steak. Then a neutral stimulus, such as the ringing of a bell, is presented along with the mouthwatering meat. After a few trials the dog learns to associate the two stimuli and will salivate at the ringing of the bell alone. Operant conditioning, on the other hand, involves learning by the rewards and punishments that certain behaviors produce. For instance, if a pigeon is rewarded with a kernel of corn whenever it pecks a lever, the bird will peck until it is full. However, if the pecking bird is not rewarded, the pecking will stop.

According to learning theorists, psychological disorders are little more than a series of maladaptive behaviors learned by humans the same way a dog learns to salivate or a pigeon learns to peck a lever. Critics point out that this perspective conveniently ignores everything that cannot easily be seen or measured, maintaining that abnormal behavior reflects deeper psychological problems rather than merely learned behavior.

Social-Stress Theories

Stress theory is based largely on commonsense ideas about psychological problems that are widely accepted in our society. Simply put, the theory holds that each individual has a breaking point and that if stress builds up beyond this level the individual will experience a breakdown. This theory is used by military psychiatrists to explain psychosomatic paralyses and other symptoms of "battle fatigue." But it can also be used to explain the behavior of harried parents, pressured executives, or overworked students.

The relationship between stress and mental disorder, however, is more complex than our simple illustrations suggest. A certain amount of stress is actually beneficial because it provides a challenge that motivates an individual to respond in new and creative ways. But too much stress over too long a period seems to exhaust individual resources. The problem is to determine how much stress is appropriate and how much is dangerous. Individuals have different tolerance levels, so that something that constitutes a healthy challenge for one person may bring serious psychological consequences to another.

NINETEENTH CENTURY SOCIAL PROBLEMS

The spectacle of a middle aged man rushing madly along the avenues, pursued by a mob of howling, jeering school boys who hurled tin cans, sticks, and other missiles at him, was witnessed by scores of indignant citizens at East Superior. The boisterous mob was reinforced at every corner by urchins of all sizes and descriptions . . . there were perhaps 100 in the crowd . . . the fleeing man was pelted unmercifully from all directions. Finally he rushed into a private residence and the crowd dispersed. The man was a resident of West Superior, sometimes called "Simple Joe." He had been to church at the East End, and when leaving . . . was attacked.
April 2, 1896

Social-stress theories argue that many mental disorders are the result of excessive environmental stress. Such stress is especially severe among soldiers in combat and produces a disturbance known as "battle fatigue."

Many sociologists believe that social stress is greatest among people in the lower classes. The fact that there are more serious mental problems per capita in these social groups is consistent with this theory. There is, however, another interpretation of these data. It is quite possible that people who become psychotic drift into the lower classes because they are unable to keep a job and maintain middle-class standards. Studies that have attempted to resolve this question have come to conflicting conclusions. Some say that there is a difference in social class between the parents of schizophrenics and those of nonschizophrenics,[25] while others claim that no significant class difference of this kind exists.[26] The most reasonable interpretation seems to be that the higher percentage of psychotics in the lower classes is due to both the stress of being poor and the downward mobility of the mentally disturbed.

Labeling Theory

For about a decade a school of sociologists, psychiatrists, and social psychologists has been challenging accepted ideas about mental disorders and the way they should be treated. The members of this school argue that there is nothing inherently normal or abnormal in human behavior. Whether behavior is "abnormal" or "normal" depends on the label that is attached to it. Thus, "mental illness" is just a label that is given to individuals who behave in ways that others do not like or accept. Few labeling theorists try to explain why people do things that cause them to be labeled "mentally ill." They merely note that once someone has been declared mentally ill, he or she experiences increasing pressure to behave like others who have been similarly labeled. Opportunities for labeled individuals to act out "normal" roles are steadily reduced. Others may laugh at them and shun them. Prospective employers may think of them as too unreliable and unstable to hold a responsible job. Even their efforts to shed the label are taken as evidence of their instability. Because everyone behaves as though the labeled person is sick, he or she eventually comes to believe it and to act that way.[27] Indeed, the sick role becomes attractive to some victims of labeling. It allows them to escape from responsibilities, behave as they wish, and relax their battle against the label.

Critics of labeling theory vigorously object to the idea that mental illness is just a social label. They argue that labeling theorists ignore the fact that mental disorders have clearly defined characteristics that can be seen in all cultures. Most developmental theorists and social-stress theorists now accept the idea that labeling critically affects the careers of mentally ill people. They reject the idea that the mental problem is produced by the labeling process itself. As noted earlier, even Scheff, a noted labeling theorist, acknowledges that people are labeled only after they break residual rules. Critics of labeling theory point out that the theory has nothing to say about the causes of these rule violations.

Although there are some interesting case studies showing the impact of labeling on certain individuals,[28] labeling theorists have not produced convincing evidence that labeling is as important as they claim it to be. Theorists may never be able to demonstrate that mental illness is just a myth. But even if labeling theory fails, it will have made a valuable contribution by pointing out the great harm that labeling often does to the mentally disturbed.

An extreme form of labeling theory is used by R. D. Laing, the British psychiatrist who claims that society is sick and "disturbed" individuals are well.[29] Schizophrenia, from Laing's perspective, is a normal response to a deranged society and the "normal" people are the ones who are really sick: "What we call 'normal' is a product of repression, denial, splitting, projection, introjection and other forms of destructive action on experience. It is radically estranged from the structure of being."[30] Laing sees schizophrenics as courageous explorers of "inner space and time," not as twisted and tortured individuals. In fact, he says, schizophrenia is an attempt to deal with one's "normal" consciousness as well as with the sickness of everyday life: "Can we not see that this voyage [schizophrenia] is not what we need to be cured of, but that it is itself a natural way of healing our own appalling state of alienation called normality?"[31]

Needless to say, most traditional therapists and mental-health experts reject Laing's approach. They argue that it is ridiculous to claim that normal people are sick and that mental disorder is a positive sign, not a problem to be corrected. If everyone had Laing's "healthy" condition, society would collapse and millions of people would starve to death. Some critics also charge Laing with distorting the facts and turning the study of mental illness on its head in order to attack the capitalist society that he apparently dislikes.

Many people still believe that mental disorders are caused by evil spirits and use various rituals to drive them away.

THE TREATMENT OF MENTAL DISORDERS

The treatment of mental disorders is always linked to some notion about their cause. Ancient peoples believed that mental disorders were caused by demons that had taken possession of the afflicted individual. Treatment, logically enough, consisted of driving the demons out. One of the earliest known treatments was trephining—chipping away an area of the skull to permit evil spirits to escape. Later, a common treatment was exorcism—attempting to drive out evil spirits by performing rituals. Exorcists used many techniques, including incantations, noise making, prayer, and horrible drinks made from sheep dung and urine. Medieval Christians believed that the devil could be driven off by verbal assaults, so they bombarded mentally disturbed people with a barrage of insults. But not all the techniques of exorcism were so innocent. "Madmen" were also starved, beaten, whipped, burned, and tortured in order to make their body such an unpleasant place that the demon or devil would leave.

The Greeks were the first people to ascribe mental disorders to natural causes. Hippocrates, for example, believed that mental disorders were caused by hereditary brain pathologies. Greek and Roman physicians prescribed rest, pleasant surroundings, entertainment, and exercise for individuals with mental problems. After the fall of Rome the scientific approach was carried on by the Arabs. The first mental hospital was established in Baghdad in 792 AD as a humane refuge for the mentally disordered.

The insane asylums that appeared later hardly deserved to be called hospitals. By present-day standards conditions in the early asylums were horrible. Residents were chained like dogs, some fastened in a standing position so they could not lie down to sleep. Whippings, beatings, and sexual abuse were routine.[32]

The advent of democracy brought the first humanitarian reform of the insane asylum. Philippe Pinel, who was placed in charge of a Paris mental hospital during the French Revolution, removed the chains from mental patients and began treating them like sick people rather than wild beasts. The patients responded remarkably well to this humane treatment, and Pinel's experiment was considered a great success. In North America, Dorothea Dix was an effective crusader for reform of insane asylums. In the mid-nineteenth century Dix, a former New England schoolteacher, carried on a relentless campaign to alert the public and the government to the horrors of insane asylums. She also raised millions of dollars to establish more humane hospitals in the United States and Canada.[33]

Types of Treatment

As suggested earlier, the causes of most mental disorders have not been identified. For this reason there are wide variations in the treatments recommended for these disorders. Indeed, the type of treatment a disturbed person receives depends more on the therapist than on the symptoms. Each psychological school has its own treatment methods, and new therapies come and go like clothing fashions. The three major techniques to be discussed here, however, have all been widely used and accepted.

Biological Therapies

The use of chemotherapy (drugs) has grown at an amazing pace in the past two decades. Three major types of drugs are routinely used in private practice as well as in mental hospitals. The "antipsychotics" are tranquilizers that have a very powerful calming effect on the patient. "Antianxiety" drugs, such as Valium and Miltown, are minor tranquilizers that have a milder calming effect. "Antidepressants" are stimulants used to elevate mood and counteract depression.

The use of these chemicals has revolutionized the treatment of the mentally disordered, especially in mental institutions. Since the advent of the tranquilizing drugs, hospitals have been able to abandon straitjackets and similar restraining devices. The patients seem to have benefited remarkably. Many psychotics have been able to return to a reasonably normal life when they would otherwise have been required to remain in an institution.

But chemotherapy has vigorous opponents. Among them are ex-patients who have formed organizations such as NAPA (Network Against Psychiatric Assault) to oppose what they consider excessive chemotherapy. They charge that tranquilizers are used to keep patients quiet and manageable rather than to help them. Some former hospital patients have charged that drugs are used in a punitive way to maintain the authority and power of some staff members.[34] Equally serious is the charge that chemotherapy treats symptoms, not causes. Few people deny the improvements brought about by modern drugs, but critics charge that drugs are used too often and for the wrong reasons. They argue that drugs should be employed only for the patient's benefit and in combination with other therapy.

The use of electrotherapy (electric shocks) has declined with the growing use of antidepressant drugs. However, shock therapy is still widely used. Many psychiatrists consider it one of the most effective techniques for dealing with severe depression, even though the reasons for its therapeutic effects are not known. But electroshock therapy, like chemotherapy, has come under attack in recent years. Critics charge that it causes hemorrhages, brain damage, and loss of memory. A vigorous battle to ban electrotherapy has been launched. The California legislature recently passed a law that severely restricted its use, but the law was overturned by a constitutional challenge.[35]

Behavior Modification

Based on the principles of learning theory discussed earlier, behavioral therapy aims to do exactly what the name implies — modify the behavior, not the personalities, of mentally disordered people. Behavioral therapists use a variety of specific techniques, depending on the type of problem under treatment. In all cases, however, the objective is to manipulate the patient's environment in order to modify his or her behavior. Some behaviors are modified by removing the reinforcement (reward) for them. This is called extinction. For instance, if a young girl is disruptive in class, the therapist might suggest that her parents and teachers ignore her behavior, thereby cutting off the reward (attention) she receives from the behavior. Systematic desensitization is used to treat phobias and irrational anxieties. In this form of treatment the patient is gradually exposed to the feared stimulus so that the fear is slowly overcome. Aversion therapy is old-fashioned punishment with a few modern refinements. For example, behavioral therapists have treated alcoholics by administering a mild electric shock whenever the patient takes a drink. Positive reinforcement also is widely employed to encourage appropriate behavior by using rewards rather than punishment.

Behavior modification therapies are relatively recent arrivals on the therapeutic scene, but they have had some remarkable successes. However, they — like other therapies — have not been very successful with the most severe mental disorders, such as schizophrenia and extreme depression. Therapists who focus on personality problems say that behavioral therapy, like chemotherapy, deals only with symptoms, not with causes.

Psychotherapy

There are so many different kinds of psychotherapy that it is impossible to discuss all of them here; however, most share certain common assumptions. Particularly important is the belief that mental disorders are symptoms of defective personalities. Therapy therefore consists of helping individuals first to understand and then to overcome the causes of their personality problems.

Psychoanalysis, one of the first and most influential psychotherapies, was founded by Sigmund Freud, an Austrian neurologist (1856–1939). It is a long-term procedure designed to uncover the repressed memories, motives, and conflicts that are assumed to be at the root of the client's psychological problems. Techniques used in this procedure include free association (encouraging the patient to talk at length and without restriction), dream interpretation (analyzing the patient's dreams for hidden, symbolic meanings), and analysis of resistance (close examination of thoughts or ideas that the patient is reluctant to discuss). Psychoanalytic therapy is often criticized for being too slow and too expensive, for putting too much stress on sexual conflicts, and for failure to produce experimental evidence of its effectiveness.

Carl Rogers developed another popular technique to help individuals with their psychological problems. His therapy is called client centered or nondirective.[36] Rogers saw men and women as basically rational and good. He therefore decided that, given the opportunity and a little assistance, patients could work out their own problems. Unlike Freudians, Rogerian therapists do not try to guide or direct therapy sessions. The client chooses the topic and sets the pace and direction of the session. It is not assumed that therapists know more than clients. Therapists listen as clients discuss their problems; they provide encouragement and support; and they try to help clients clarify their own feelings and attitudes.

Another recent innovation in psychotherapeutic techniques is group therapy. Some group therapy is merely individual therapy administered to a group of patients one at a time. More commonly, the group itself is the therapist. Each individual is encouraged to reveal his or her problems and experiences to the group, which then discusses and examines them. Some groups employ psychodrama, in which the members are asked to take roles and act out their problems. Others run marathon sessions, continuing around the clock for several days. Still others use "attack therapy," in which one member is criticized and "torn down" by the group.

The Modern Mental Hospital

A mental hospital is much more than just a place where patients are treated for mental problems. People who live in mental hospitals have quite different experiences from those who live at home and make periodic visits to a psychiatrist. Hospitalized patients are cut off from the outside world and are closely supervised and controlled by staff members. Their personal needs either are met by the institution or are not met at all. They live in what Erving Goffman calls a total institution, defined as "a place where a large number of like-situated individuals, cut off from the wider society for an appreciable period of time, together lead an enclosed, formally administered round of life."[37]

The mental hospital is similar to other total institutions, such as boarding schools, monasteries, and army posts. But it resembles a prison most closely. Indeed, some mentally disturbed individuals are committed to prisons and some criminals are committed to mental hospitals. Like the prison, the mental hospital must try to meet two distinct goals: custody and treatment. No matter what treatment methods are used, they must be administered within a custodial framework. Patients, like prisoners, are policed to ensure that they do not escape or injure each other. Only after these essentials have been provided for can the remaining time and money be devoted to treatment.

But the budgets of most state mental hospitals are so meager that there is not enough money for adequate custody, let alone treatment. This means that there are hundreds of patients for each nurse, psychiatrist, psychologist, and social worker. Attendants are untrained and poorly educated, and the buildings are often old, dark, and gloomy. Patients must live in wards where they have little personal privacy. Clearly, the environment of most mental hospitals is hardly designed to brighten the spirits of those who are depressed and confused.

Goffman's study of a mental hospital revealed some of the perplexing problems faced by new patients.[38] They often come into the institution with a sense of betrayal, believing that they have been tricked and manipulated by their friends and family. Upon admission, they are stripped of their clothing and personal possessions. They are poked, prodded, examined, and classified by the hospital personnel with normal medical objectivity and detachment. These "degradation rituals" strip the patient of identity, destroying personal dignity and producing a confused and demoralized individual. It is little wonder that mental hospitals often do more harm than good, regardless of the treatment programs used.

Rosenhan recently conducted a series of experiments that dramatically demonstrated the labeling effect of commitment to a mental institution.[39] He had eight normal individuals present themselves to several mental hospitals, complaining of hearing voices. After admission each of these bogus patients tried to act normally, making no further pretense at mental illness. Not one of the phonies was recognized or diagnosed as being sane. After an average stay of 19 days, they were released as schizophrenics "in remission." Rosenhan concluded that it is impossible to distinguish the "sane" from the "insane" in our mental hospitals.[40]

During the past twenty years mental-health professionals have tried to improve our mental hospitals. Most significant, they have insisted that many disturbed people remain in the community. (See Figure 12.2.) This had the effect of reducing the patient population in American mental hospitals from a high of 559,000 in 1955 to about 300,000 in the early 1970s.[41] Similar trends occurred in other Western countries. Moreover, the living conditions in mental hospitals have improved as support has grown for the idea that people who are committed for treatment have a right to such treatment and that mere custodial care is not sufficient.

FIGURE 12.2
RATES OF HOSPITALIZA-
TION AND OUT-PATIENT
TREATMENT FOR MENTAL
DISORDERS, 1955–1973

Source: U.S. Department of Commerce,
Social Indicators 1976 (Washington, D.C.:
GPO, 1976), p. 167.

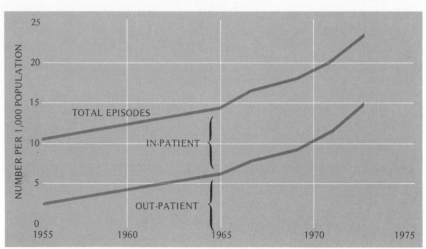

Involuntary Commitment

Depriving individuals of their freedom is a serious matter. Criminals are sent to jails and prisons because we want them to suffer. The pain stemming from loss of liberty is expected to deter them from committing further crimes. It is also assumed that when others see criminals imprisoned they will be too fearful to behave criminally. Because imprisonment is designed to be painful, careful procedures ("due process of law") are followed to ensure that only the guilty are jailed.

But none of this applies to the mentally disturbed. We do not commit people to mental hospitals because we want them to suffer. Patients suffer because their freedom is restricted, but the suffering is not imposed deliberately. Nor do we assume that loss of liberty, painful as it may be, will cure or correct the hospital patient. Likewise, we do not expect that the suffering experienced by patients will frighten others so that they will not become mentally disturbed. Unfortunately, because the mentally disturbed are committed for their own good, not as punishment, insufficient care is taken to ensure that only people who are too dangerous to be at liberty are committed.

Obviously, some people must be committed to mental hospitals as a means of protecting others from their violent outbursts, while other individuals are so disturbed that neither they nor their families can care for them. But most cases are not so obvious. Considering the inadequacies of psychiatric diagnosis, how can we be certain that an individual is so disturbed that involuntary hospitalization is necessary?

Until quite recently most American commitment proceedings were quite slipshod, giving little more than lip service to due process of law.[42] Scheff investigated involuntary commitments in both rural areas and cities. He concluded that rural courts showed some interest in determining the mental condition of those being considered for hospitalization, although questionable methods were used. However, the hearings in metropolitan courts "had no serious investigatory purpose, but were largely ceremonial in character."[43] Scheff found that in urban courts the average examination by a court psychiatrist (required by law) lasted about 10 minutes. The court hearings that he observed were hasty, the longest lasting 12 minutes, the shortest less than 2 minutes.

Court procedures have improved since the time of Scheff's study. Some states now have rigorous legal safeguards comparable to those used in criminal cases, but in most places it is still relatively easy to take away someone's freedom because he or she is suffering from a mental disorder.[44] The Soviet Union provides a chilling example of the way in which commitment proceedings without proper safeguards can be abused. Mental hospitals apparently serve as convenient prisons for political dissenters whom the state has declared insane. Several famous Soviet writers and intellectuals have been committed to mental institutions, not because they were in need of treatment but because they held unpopular beliefs. Even in democratic countries the potential for political abuse of mental hospitals is always present.

Community Treatment

As noted earlier, there has been a growing trend toward keeping disturbed people out of mental hospitals. Patients who remain in the community during treatment avoid the shock of being taken out of their normal environment. They also escape the labeling, humiliation, and feeling of powerlessness that accompany institutionalization, and the painful readjustment period that follows it.

Wealthy people have always had access to community treatment from private psychiatrists, but the poor must depend on services provided by the state, often available only in public mental hospitals. Serious efforts are now being made to provide and improve community treatment for people of all social classes. Significant change began with the Community Mental Health Centers Act of 1963, a law that sets aside federal money to assist local cities in building and operating mental-health centers. More than 400 such centers are now in operation. They provide five major services: short-term hospitalization, partial hospitalization (allowing patients to return home at night or in the evenings), therapy for patients who live in the community, emergency care for special problems, and consultation and educational services for the community at large. These centers thus provide many more services than were available previously, ranging from one-time counseling to complete hospitalization.

Many other kinds of community treatment programs have been established as well. For example, physicians, teachers, police officers, and others who are likely to come into contact with people who need mental care are being taught the best ways of handling those individuals. Many private organizations now help meet community mental-health needs. Citizens working without pay for agencies such as Hotline answer phone calls from people in need of help, refer them to appropriate agencies, try to head off suicides, or merely lend a sympathetic ear to lonely voices. "Free clinics" that attempt to meet a broad spectrum of poor people's health needs also offer counseling and therapy for mental problems.

RESPONDING TO PROBLEMS OF MENTAL DISORDERS

Scientists and researchers have given more attention to mental disorders than to any other social problem. A tremendous number of innovative approaches to prevention and treatment have been developed since World War II. One of the most promising new trends is toward the treatment of entire families in their home environment. This approach sees mental disorder as a process of interaction created by two or more people, and thus, more than one person must be included in the treatment process. For instance, the parents of a disturbed child or the husband of a woman with severe depression can be taught effective ways of interacting with the troubled individual. More significant, the entire family can be taught to develop new patterns of interaction that will benefit each member of the family.

Investigation of the biochemical basis of mental disorders is another exciting frontier. Some researchers believe that they will soon be able to identify the exact biochemical process that generates schizophrenia and related disorders. If such a discovery is made, it should be relatively easy to develop an effective treatment.

It seems unlikely, however, that any treatment—chemical, psychological, or social—will eliminate all mental disorders. We must therefore continue to learn how to interact with disturbed people and how to deal with them humanely when ordinary interaction is impossible. One giant step in this direction would be to stop using such stigmatizing labels as "insane," "crazy," or "nuts." Most people scoff at Laing's suggestion that schizophrenics are really the sanest people among us. Yet if this attitude prevailed, it would bring us much closer to removing the shame and humiliation that now go hand in hand with mental disorders.

SOCIOLOGICAL PERSPECTIVES on Mental Disorders

While human beings experience an extraordinary array of thought patterns and behaviors, all cultures limit the amount of variation that it is permissible to display. These expectations about how people should think and act give a measure of stability and permanence to people's lives. Nevertheless, in every culture there are individuals who seem unable to share in the reality experienced by others. They think and behave in ways that are bizarre and incomprehensible to most members of their society. In contemporary societies these people are considered mentally disturbed, and much scientific attention has been devoted to explaining and changing their behavior.

The Functionalist Perspective

Functionalism is a broadly based social theory that is primarily concerned with large groups and institutions. It does not attempt to account for the causes of mental disorders on the individual level. Rather, it examines the social conditions that affect the rate of mental disorder. Long ago, Emile Durkheim, the famous French sociologist, showed that suicide rates were higher among people who were not integrated into supportive social groups. Following Durkheim's lead, present day functionalists argue that social disorganization which tears people loose from their social supports is a major cause of both suicide and mental disorders. According to the functionalists, people who live in disorganized societies have higher rates of mental disturbances than others. Moreover, people who live in disorganized neighborhoods have more psychological problems than those who live in more integrated communities. Functionalists often cite the high rates of schizophrenia in urban slums and ghettos as proof of this proposition.

Considerable disorganization also can be seen in the way treatment services are delivered, or not delivered. No one wants mental hospitals to be understaffed and underfinanced, and no one wants them to give greater priority to custody than to treatment. But the people who finance and administer hospitals and community treatment programs find it impossible to be efficient. Moreover, some aspects of mental hospitals and other treatment programs are dysfunctional. The crowding, depersonalization, and rejection of mental patients makes them worse rather than better.

Functionalists argue for a twofold attack on the problems of mental disorder. First, a concerted effort must be made to reduce social disorganization and bring lonely, isolated individuals back into a supportive social network. Second, mental hospitals and other treatment facilities must be improved. More money and more effort must be invested in a serious effort to help the mentally disordered. Community treatment programs should be expanded so they can treat anyone who can benefit from their services. Mental hospitals should be reduced in size and reserved only for the most serious patients. Hospital staffs must be better trained and large enough to give the kind of personal treatment that is often impossible today.

The Conflict Perspective

Like functionalists, conflict theorists do not pretend to explain the origins of all mental disorders. Instead, they are concerned with the forces that create the high rates of mental disorder in North America. To most conflict theorists, the origins of our psychological problems are to be found in the economic system. The North American economy is the most competitive in the world. Every individual is expected to compete and achieve in a constant struggle with their competitors. The insecurity that results from this system produces constant feelings of anxiety and tension. And those pressures, in turn, produce high rates of mental disorder.

Conflict theorists are also interested in the way the incidence of mental disorder is distributed within a society. They are particularly concerned about the high rates of psychological disorders among the poor and underprivileged which they feel are the result of social, political, and economic exploitation. Because of this exploitation, the poor live under greater stress than more privileged people. Moreover, the alienation and powerlessness of most workers is itself a kind of mental disorder. Frustrations build up among people who can do little to change the conditions of their lives, and serious mental disturbances are often the final result.

The system for delivering treatment services to the mentally disturbed also favors the rich and powerful, who receive private treatment from highly skilled professionals. The poor cannot afford such help, and their troubles are ignored until they create a disturbance. Then they are locked up in underfunded mental hospitals where they receive little real help.

Conflict theorists recommend basic changes in our treatment programs. They generally believe that all funding for facilities and personnel to treat the mentally disordered should come from the government, so that everyone will receive the same high-quality care that only the rich can now afford. But in order to achieve a long-term solution to the problem of mental disorder, basic social changes will be necessary. Conflict theorists advocate a restructuring of our economic system to reduce excessive competition and eliminate exploitation of the poor and the workers.

The Social-Psychological Perspective

Because the problem of mental disorder is necessarily a social-psychological matter, we have already discussed this perspective in some detail. Each of the explanations of the causes of mental disorder described in this chapter are based on one of the major social-psychological theories. Most of the therapeutic techniques we discussed were also developed from the ideas and perspectives contained in these theories.

SUMMARY

The economic and personal costs of mental disorders are staggering. Nevertheless, there is no widespread agreement on the meaning of terms such as *mentally ill, insane, mentally disturbed,* and *crazy.* Those who support the mental-illness approach view mental problems the way they view measles and chicken pox; that is, each disordered person has a specific illness and may be helped by a specific treatment. Others advocate the personal-maladjustment approach, in which mental disorders are seen as products of the individual's inability to cope effectively with social life.

Still other experts prefer the social-deviance approach, noting that people are labeled "mentally ill," "crazy," and so on when they violate common-sense rules about how people are supposed to behave.

The World Health Organization's classification of mental disorders lists ten major categories of problems. Of these, the four most important are neuroses, psychoses, psychosomatic disorders, and personality disorders. Neuroses are personal problems accompanied by chronically inappropriate responses. Psychotics are much more severely disoriented and confused. The most common types of psychoses are schizophrenia, paranoia, and the affective disorders. Personality disorders are problems in the individual's character structure and are expressed in deviant behavior. Psychosomatic disorders are physical problems that are caused by the sufferer's mental state.

A number of studies have investigated the relationship between social class and mental disorders. The general conclusion is that people in the lower classes are more likely to have psychoses than middle-class and upper-class people. However, it has not been established that this difference is due to emotional stress caused by poverty. Some people become poor after they develop a mental disorder and can no longer hold a job or manage their money.

No single explanation of mental disorder is satisfactory. Biosocial theories contend that some mental disorders, such as schizophrenia, are caused by biochemical imbalances. Developmental theories hold that the source of each mental disorder is to be found in an individual's early psychological history. Although there are many different versions of this theory, the basic idea is that mentally disordered patients are individuals who, as children, did not develop properly. Learning theorists see mental disorders merely as inappropriate behavior that is learned the way other behavior is learned. Stress theory holds that mental disorders result from strains imposed on individuals by the environment. Labeling theory contends that "mental illness" and "abnormality" are labels attached to individuals who behave in ways that others do not like.

The type of treatment a patient receives depends a great deal on the therapist. Biological therapies use tranquilizing drugs, "mood-elevating" drugs, and electric shock. Behavior modification employs the principles of learning theory to reward appropriate behavior and extinguish inappropriate behavior. Psychotherapy applies a variety of techniques designed to give patients insight into the psychological bases of their problems, including psychoanalysis, client-centered therapy, and group therapy.

Many studies show that state mental hospitals are not good places to help mentally disordered people recover. The budgets of some hospitals are so low that little money is left for treatment once the expenses of custodial care have been met. Hospital patients experience the humiliation and degradation associated with life in "total institutions." Many patients are committed to mental hospitals by a court, but the legal procedures are often quite slipshod. Hospital populations are being reduced as more disturbed people are being assigned to community treatment centers. These programs provide more services than were previously available to poor people, and the programs are likely to expand as whole families are given help and counsel when one family member becomes disturbed.

The three principal sociological perspectives on mental disorders attempt to describe the causes of such disorders and how they should be treated. To functionalists, mental disorders are caused or aggravated by the condition of the society and the immediate social environment. Even some aspects of treatment services are dysfunctional, making patients worse instead of better. Conflict theorists attribute the high incidence of mental disorder among the poor to alienation resulting from exploitation, which leads to frustration and serious breakdowns. The social-psychological perspective consists of the biosocial theories, behavioral theories, personality theories, and interactionist theories.

KEY TERMS

affective psychosis
aversion therapy
behavioral therapy
catatonic schizophrenia
chemotherapy
classical conditioning
client-centered therapy
double bind
electrotherapy
extinction
functional disorder
group therapy
hebephrenic schizophrenia
involutional melancholia
manic depression
mental disorder

neurosis
operant conditioning
organic disorder
paranoia
paranoid schizophrenia
personality disorder
positive reinforcement
psychoanalysis
psychosis
psychosomatic disorder
psychotherapy
schizophrenia
simple schizophrenia
systematic desensitization
total institution

13
Drug Use

What drugs create the most serious social problems?
What causes drug addiction?
How has legal repression affected drug use?
Can drug use be controlled?

Drug use is part of the daily lives of most North Americans. We use drugs to ease our pain, to increase our pleasure, to keep us awake, and to help us sleep. There is a drug for every occasion—coffee in the morning, cigarettes at work, cocktails before dinner. To many people, only illegal substances like heroin or marijuana are drugs, but legal chemicals also alter the minds and moods of those who use them and can be just as dangerous as the illegal drugs. Users who claim that alcohol and tobacco aren't really drugs are deceiving themselves.

Concern about the dangers of drug use has increased in the past decade, as has drug use itself. A Gallup poll found that in 1970 the percentage of Americans who take an occasional drink reached 68 percent, the highest percentage found in the 35 years the poll has questioned Americans about their drinking. Cigarette smoking declined a bit when a 1964 report by the Surgeon General linked smoking to cancer and other health problems. But smoking has shown a steady increase in the past decade. Marijuana smoking has increased too. In San Mateo County, California, anonymous questionnaires are periodically used to survey students in junior and senior high school about drug use. The surveys have shown a steady increase in marijuana use since 1968. Between 1968 and 1971, the growth rate in marijuana use was 16 percent a year. Between 1971 and 1973, it was 5 percent a year; and between 1973 and 1974, the annual increase was 1 percent.[1]

Drug use is not confined to a few ragged deviants on the margins of society. Drugs are a big business. Americans spend $2.5 billion a year for prescription psychoactive drugs. They spend a similar amount for coffee, tea, and cocoa (which contains the stimulant theobromine), $12 billion a year for tobacco, and $25 billion for alcohol. (These estimates do not include purchases made illegally.)

The price tag for enforcing drug laws also is enormous. In 1973, 420,000 Americans were arrested for possession of marijuana, and 3 million people were arrested for alcohol-related offenses.[2] At least 40 percent of all arrests by police officers in the United States each year are made on alcohol-related charges.

Alcohol abuse costs over $25 billion each year in lost work days, medical expenses, and car accidents. According to the National Safety Council, about 60 percent of all drivers killed in automobile accidents have drunk enough alcohol to impair their driving skills. And uncounted numbers of Americans and Canadians who are unable to cope with problems stemming from use of drugs seek professional help or suffer alone.

DRUGS AND DRUG ADDICTION

While everyone uses the terms *drug addiction* and *drug addict* at one time or another, *addiction* is a technical term that is difficult to define. In the broadest sense addiction refers to an intense craving for a particular substance. But this definition can be applied to almost any desire or craving, whether it is for ice cream, potato chips, or heroin. To avoid this problem drug addiction is sometimes erroneously defined as the physiological dependence that an individual develops after heavy use of a particular drug. Most addicts, however, experience periods when they "kick" their physical dependency, yet their psychological craving continues undiminished and they return to drug use as soon as it is possible. The most accurate definition therefore is that addiction is the intense craving for a drug that develops after a period of physical dependence stemming from heavy use.

The two essential characteristics of an addictive drug are tolerance and withdrawal discomfort. Tolerance is another name for immunity to the effects of a drug that builds up after heavy use. For instance, if a person takes the same amount of heroin every day for a month, the last dose will have much less effect than the first. If the user wants the same psychological effect at the end of the month, the dosage must be increased. Withdrawal discomfort is the sickness that a habitual user experiences when the drug is not taken regularly. Addictive drugs produce both tolerance and withdrawal distress. Drugs which produce tolerance but no withdrawal discomfort, such as LSD, are not addictive.

But drug addiction is not solely a physiological matter. Psychological craving supplements biological dependence. Moreover, the behavior of those who use specific drugs is influenced by cultural expectations that are quite independent of the drug's physiological effects. For example, anyone who drinks a large quantity of alcohol will pass out—a physiological reaction. But behavior while drunk but not dead drunk varies greatly from culture to culture and even from group to group within a culture.[3] Many people believe that alcohol reduces inhibitions and generates violent behavior through its effects on body chemistry. This is not true. In our culture some people become less inhibited when drinking alcohol, but this is because they have learned to behave in a certain way when drinking, not because of changes in body chemistry. Thus, it is just as important to understand individual and group attitudes toward a drug as it is to understand its physiological effects.

Alcohol

The National Commission on Marijuana and Drug Abuse reported that alcohol dependence is without question the most serious drug problem in the United States today.[4] Alcohol, like most drugs, is rather harmless when used in moderation but is one of the most dangerous drugs when used to excess. Alcohol depresses the activity of the central nervous system and thereby interferes with coordination, reaction time, and reasoning ability. While a small amount of alcohol has a calming effect on the user, larger amounts produce disorientation, loss of consciousness, and even death. As already noted, the psychological reaction to alcohol varies from individual to individual, from group to group, and from culture to culture.

Alcohol is the most commonly used drug in North America, and it produces more personal and social problems than any other drug.

Prolonged heavy drinking may generate a number of health problems. Alcoholic beverages are high in calories but have little other food value. For this reason heavy drinkers often lose their appetite and suffer from malnutrition. The harmful effects of excessive drinking on the liver are well known; the end result may be cirrhosis, a condition in which the liver cells are destroyed by alcohol and replaced by scar tissue. Alcohol will produce addiction if used in sufficient amounts over a long period. The so-called DTs (short for *delirium tremens*) are actually symptoms of alcohol withdrawal. These symptoms commonly include nausea, vomiting, convulsions, and delirium, sometimes hallucinations and coma, and occasionally death. Aside from the 28,000 deaths attributed to drunken drivers in the United States each year, the greatest cause of alcohol-related deaths is the use of alcohol in combination with other depressant drugs. Many people have killed themselves unintentionally by taking sleeping pills (barbiturates) after an evening of heavy drinking.

While alcoholism has been drawing increasing national attention in the United States and Canada, the term is applied very loosely and is often lit-

NINETEENTH CENTURY SOCIAL PROBLEMS

The beer garden recently started on this side of the river, by permission of our town board, continues to grow offensive. The rabble from the city and the country meet there and sometimes form nothing less than drunken mobs. It is not safe for women to pass along the road near this place. Bloody fights are of a daily occurrence and drunken men may be found lying around in the bushes on all sides. Wife whipping has come into vogue since the new institution was forced upon us. . . . What it may end in need hardly be conjectured.
July 10, 1890

tle more than a derogatory label. More precisely, an alcoholic is a person whose drinking problem disrupts his or her life, interfering with the ability to hold a job, accomplish household tasks, or participate in family and social affairs. Although many people use alcohol as a means of improving their self-esteem, in the long run it often has the opposite effect.

Recent studies show that from 63 to 71 percent of all adults in the United States drink alcoholic beverages. The use of alcohol by both juveniles and adults has shown a steady increase, but the prevalence of drinking varies widely among social and ethnic groups. Most studies indicate that more men drink (75 to 90 percent) than women (55 to 65 percent); however, drinking has been increasing more rapidly among women. Catholics are more likely than Protestants to be drinkers. The prevalence of drinking is greatest among the college educated and those with high-prestige occupations.[5] But there is some evidence that excessive drinking and alcoholism are more common among those with less education and lower incomes. Estimates of the number of alcoholics in the United States range from 4.5 million to 6.8 million.[6]

Tobacco   Studies indicate that about 38 percent of American adults and about 17 percent of all juveniles smoke cigarettes.[7] More men smoke than women, but the rate has been increasing more rapidly for women, and teenaged girls are now as likely to smoke as teenaged boys. About three-fourths of all male smokers and two-thirds of all female smokers use more than 15 cigarettes a day, making tobacco one of the few drugs that addicts use practically every waking hour of every day.[8]

The principal drug in tobacco is nicotine, which is clearly addictive. Withdrawal symptoms include drowsiness, nervousness, anxiety, headaches, and loss of energy. Nicotine is a stimulant that raises blood pressure, speeds up the heartbeat, and gives the user a sense of alertness. The claim that tobacco use is relaxing probably is based on the ritual involved in smoking rather than the effects of the drug itself.

The 1964 Surgeon General's Advisory Committee on Smoking and Health concluded that smoking is unquestionably hazardous to health, and this conclusion was reaffirmed in a more comprehensive report in 1979. Cigarette smoking is linked to cancer of the larynx, mouth, and esophagus, as well as to lung cancer. Other diseases linked to smoking include bronchitis, emphysema, ulcers, and heart and circulatory disorders. It is estimated that smoking more than two packs a day reduces normal life expectancy by eight years and that light smoking (half a pack a day or less) reduces it by four years. Fire is a special danger associated with smoking, and about 75 percent of the fires in homes, apartments, and hotels are caused by careless smoking.[9]

Why, then, do so many people smoke? One explanation is that cigarette smoking is addictive, and most smokers find it difficult to stop. But what about the substantial number of young people who begin smoking for the first time every year, despite medical warnings? The answer seems to be that the tobacco industry has succeeded in establishing an association in the public mind between smoking and maturity, sophistication, and sexual attractiveness. Most young people surely have heard warnings about the health hazards of smoking, but many pay little heed. Perhaps the dangers seem too distant to be impressive.

Marijuana Marijuana use is the center of a scientific and political debate that has grown more intense during the past two decades. Marijuana is clearly the most widely used illegal drug, and its users no longer accept their legal status passively. Many efforts have been made to legalize or reduce the penalties for possession and sale of the drug. In 1972 the Canadian government removed marijuana from the Narcotic Control Act and sharply reduced penalties for possession. A number of American states have also reduced penalties for possession of the drug. Nevertheless, marijuana use is legal in only a few countries around the world.

Marijuana probably has been subjected to closer scrutiny than any other psychoactive drug. There have been at least six full-scale investigations of the drug and its effects, conducted by panels of investigators under government sponsorship. The 3000-page Indian Hemp Drugs Commission Report, published in Britain in 1894, was the first, followed by the La Guardia Committee Report in New York in 1944, two other American reports in 1967 and 1972, a second British report in 1968, and a Canadian report in 1972. Each of these reports concluded that marijuana is relatively harmless and does not pose a serious threat to society. Yet the debate about the physiological effects of marijuana continues, with emotions running so high that respected authorities on both sides are prone to publish false and misleading statements. Wesley Hall, a former president of the American Medical Association, once claimed that marijuana makes a man of 35 act like a man of 70 and that chronic use causes birth defects. He later retracted his statement, admitting that it was not based on evidence but, rather, was aimed simply at reducing marijuana use.[10]

One source of this controversy is the fact that the objectively measurable physiological effects of marijuana are very slight. Only three effects have been established conclusively: a slight increase in heart rate, dryness in the mouth, and reddening of the eyes.[11] Marijuana is also known *not* to cause the following: (1) dilation of the pupils; (2) death (there have been no proven cases of death due to overdose of marijuana), (3) growth of tolerance (repeated heavy use of marijuana does not diminish its psychological effects), (4) withdrawal discomfort (termination of marijuana after heavy and prolonged use has no known physiological effects), (5) addiction (because there is no tolerance or withdrawal discomfort, addiction does not occur).

**DEBATE
Should
Marijuana
Be Legalized?**

PRO

The prohibition of marijuana has been a complete failure. It has not stopped or even significantly discouraged marijuana use. Despite the fact that hundreds of thousands of people are arrested annually on marijuana charges, its use has steadily increased. When it was banned in the 1930s, most Americans had never heard of marijuana, but fifty years of prohibition have helped make it one of the most commonly used drugs. Marijuana prohibition also encourages other kinds of criminal activity. When otherwise law-abiding marijuana users are arrested and jailed along with hardened criminals, they are exposed to deviant attitudes and values. They are likely to return to the outside world with the stigma of a prison record and bitter resentment toward society and its legal system. Moreover, marijuana prohibition has created a large black market for the drug, depriving the government of tax revenues and generating huge profits for organized criminals and drug pushers.

Ironically, marijuana is actually less harmful than legal drugs such as nicotine or alcohol. Because the effects of marijuana are relatively mild and are not habit forming, society would benefit if alcoholics switched to marijuana. But even if marijuana were more dangerous than it is, government persecution of marijuana users would still be wrong. Marijuana prohibition violates the rights of free citizens, encourages organized crime, and has failed to discourage use of the drug. Common sense demands that it be repealed.

CON

Marijuana use is a serious social problem and should remain illegal. Year by year we have seen an erosion of the values that hold our society together. Sexual morality, the family, and the work ethic have all been affected. Legalizing another drug would aggravate an already dangerous situation. The price we now pay for alcohol use is staggering. Every year tens of thousands of deaths and untold personal suffering are caused by alcoholism. Do we really need another legal drug?

While it is true that the laws prohibiting the possession, use, and sale of marijuana have not been totally effective, it does not follow that these laws should be repealed. Laws against murder have not stopped all homicides, but no one argues that murder should be legalized. Although no one can say how much more marijuana would be used or how many more murders there would be without legal prohibition of these acts, it is certain that both would increase. If marijuana were available in local stores, many people who now do not have ready access to a supply of the drug would be encouraged to experiment with it.

Although the advocates of legalization claim that marijuana is harmless, this has yet to be proved. Researchers have uncovered evidence that marijuana may be linked to a variety of health problems. It would be foolish to legalize this drug before we are certain that such an action will not cause harm to those now living or to future generations. Legalization of marijuana would therefore be a tragic mistake.

Marijuana use, like alcohol and nicotine use, has been accused of causing a variety of health problems, from liver damage to birth defects and decreased production of male sex hormones. However, when the studies making these claims were duplicated by other researchers, the new studies did not always produce the same results. The long-range effects of marijuana use have yet to be conclusively identified.

Marijuana use is widespread and is still increasing. The National Commission on Marijuana and Drug Abuse found that 55 percent of those Americans in the 18–21 age group have used the drug. A recent nationwide survey conducted for the National Institute on Drug Abuse also found that 55 percent of the men between the ages of 20 and 30 in the United States had used marijuana at some time. Of these users, 63 percent used the drug at least once a month and 27 percent used it almost every day.[12] However, marijuana use declines rapidly in older age groups and is much less frequent than alcohol use, even among the young. For instance, the same survey of 20- to 30-year-old men found that 97 percent had used alcohol at some time and that, of these, 32 percent used alcohol almost every day. Other studies indicate that marijuana use is more common among men than among women and more common among students than among nonstudents of the same age. In the United States marijuana use is more common in the West than in the East.

The psychological effects of smoking marijuana are strongly influenced by the social environment and the expectations of the users. Becker has shown that users must learn from their peers how to identify the effects of the drug before they actually get "high."[13] Descriptions of the drug's psychological effects vary considerably from one individual to another. Typical effects include euphoria, relaxation, increased sensitivity, and hunger. While those who use marijuana occasionally tend to report more negative reactions than those who use it frequently, reactions, whether positive or negative, probably reflect the expectations of the users more than the effects of the drug itself. Orcutt has shown that the more contact a marijuana user has with the drug subculture, the less likely he or she is to have a "bad trip."[14]

Opiates

The opiates are a group of natural (opium, codeine, and morphine) and synthetic (heroin, meperideine, methadone) drugs with similar chemical compositions. The pain-relieving properties of the opiates are important to modern medicine. Although people who are under the influence of an opiate can still feel pain, it no longer seems to bother them. One widely used pharmacology textbook describes the medical importance of opiates as follows:

> If it were necessary to restrict the choice of drugs to a very few, the great majority of physicians would place the opium alkaloids, particularly morphine, at the head of the list. Morphine is unequalled as an analgesic and its indispensable uses in medicine and surgery are well defined.[15]

Other physiological effects of opiates include reduced rates of metabolism and respiration. Psychologically, the opiates tend to induce a state of tranquility, peace, or euphoria. Just as opiates relieve physical pain, they deaden psychological distress.

All opiates are highly addictive. Users rapidly develop a tolerance and must continually increase their dosage to get the same effects. Although the intensity of opiate withdrawal distress varies with the amount being taken and with the individual involved, withdrawal seldom causes the screaming agony depicted in so many books and movies. Withdrawal distress usually resembles a bad case of the flu accompanied by a feeling of severe depression. Opiate withdrawal has never been known to be a direct cause of death.[16]

Opiate addiction does have severe consequences for the health of the addict. Ironically, these problems come not from the drug itself but from the way in which it is used. When addicts receive a continuous supply of pure drugs in a normal environment, they suffer no more health problems than nonusers.[17] However, the opiate addict's life style and desperate social circumstances, as well as impure drugs and infected needles, do produce health problems:

> While there is ample evidence that the aberrant way of life followed by most heroin users has both acute and chronic consequences (i.e., tetanus, overdose, hepatitis, and endocarditis), there is insufficient scientific basis for maintaining that the long term use of opiates — in and of itself — is related to any major medical condition.[18]

Death from overdose is the most serious complication of heroin addiction. In 1970 the New York City coroner indicated that narcotics was the leading cause of death among males 15 to 35 years old. However, there is considerable debate as to what actually causes these "overdose" deaths. Some experts argue that they are caused not by too much heroin but, rather, by the drugs with which illegal heroin is cut, or by the combination of heroin and other drugs such as alcohol.[19]

Despite all the publicity, opiate use is quite rare in the United States and Canada. The National Commission on Marijuana and Drug Abuse found that only 1.3 percent of all adults in the United States had ever tried opiates, and a much lower percentage were regular users. Interviews with a sample of American men who were 20 to 30 years old in 1974 indicated that only 6 percent had ever used heroin and only 2 percent were current users.[20] In 1969 there were only about 4000 known addicts in Canada.[21] Well over half of all heroin addicts in the United States live in its three largest cities, with the heaviest concentration in New York City. Addiction is an urban phenomenon in Canada as well, with its major center in Vancouver. Despite a recent increase in heroin use among the middle classes, most addicts are young males from the poorest segments of society. Recent studies indicate that at least 80 percent of the heroin addicts

NINETEENTH CENTURY SOCIAL PROBLEMS

We are about to have a gold cure institute in this city. Dr. A. E. White and E. Krohn have purchased the right for this section to use the celebrated improved "Tri Chloride of Gold Cure" and are about to establish here an institution for the cure of the liquor, opium, morphine, and tobacco habits. . . . They guarantee a cure for a stipulated fee. The time required for treatment is 3 weeks. The patient is required to deposit the full fee in the bank, payable to the doctors when a cure is perfected, the patient agreeing to follow directions strictly. Medicine is taken internally every 2 hours, and 4 hypodermic injections are given each day. . . . We presume they will have few patients for the cure of other than the liquor habit.

June 2, 1892

in the United States are under 40 and that about 20 percent of all users are females. Addiction is more common among black and Spanish-speaking Americans than among other groups.

If opiate use is so uncommon, why is there so much concern about it? For one thing, heroin addicts project a very dramatic image that fits well into the plots of books, television shows, and movies. Almost everyone has seen or read about the skinny, haggard "junkie" prowling the streets in a desperate search for the money to buy his next "fix" (injection of heroin). Although most fictional descriptions of junkies are greatly distorted, the stories do contain a grain of truth. Most heroin addicts depend on crime to support their habits, and some will do almost anything to get a "fix."[22] However, not all heroin users fit this stereotype. There are more addicts in the medical profession than in any other occupation, yet they are seldom involved in crime or violence. There are many addicts who must buy their drugs at high black-market prices but do not commit crimes to support their habits.[23]

Psychedelics Although the physiological effects of the psychedelics are rather slight, they produce greater psychological changes in the user than other drugs. Perhaps it is for this reason that a sense of mystery surrounds the psychedelics. In the 1960s propagandists like Timothy Leary claimed that these drugs provided a shortcut to mystical experience and would revolutionize society.[24]

There are many different psychedelic drugs. LSD (lysergic acid diethylamide) and mescaline are the most popular in North America. The use of peyote cactus (from which mescaline is derived) has a long history among American Indians. It seems to have been an important element in Indian religion long before Europeans came to the continent. The use of peyote continues today as a central part of the ritual of the Native American

Church of North America, which claims 250,000 members from various Indian tribes. The members of this church have been successful in defeating government efforts to ban their use of peyote.[25]

Unlike most psychedelics, LSD is completely synthetic. It was first synthesized by a Swiss chemist, Albert Hoffmann, in 1938. However, the psychedelic effects of LSD were not discovered until 1943, when Hoffmann accidentally consumed the drug. He gave the following description of his experience:

> In the afternoon of 16 April, 1943, when I was working on this problem, I was seized by a peculiar sensation of vertigo and restlessness. Objects, as well as the shape of my associates in the laboratory appeared to undergo optical changes. I was unable to concentrate on my work. In a dreamlike state I left for home, where an irresistible urge to lie down overcame me. I drew the curtains and immediately fell into a peculiar state similar to drunkenness, characterized by an exaggerated imagination. With my eyes closed, fantastic pictures of extraordinary plasticity and intensive color seemed to surge toward me. After two hours this state gradually wore off.[26]

Colorless and tasteless, a minute dose of LSD produces a tremendous psychological effect that is highly unpredictable. While some users report an intensely beautiful experience, others find it the most frightening experience of their lives, and still others swing from one extreme to the other on the same "trip." Aside from such profound emotional changes, the psychedelics also produce hallucinations and perceptual distortions. Colors and smells often appear more intense under the influence of these drugs.

Users of the psychedelic drugs rapidly develop a tolerance. In a short period, repeated doses will produce no effect at all, regardless of the size of the dosage. Because there is no withdrawal discomfort, psychedelics are not addictive. Few people become heavy (once a week or more) psychedelic users, and those who do usually give up the drug after a few years. Although some have charged that LSD produces brain damage and birth defects, there is little evidence to support this claim.[27]

The greatest dangers of psychedelic drugs are psychological rather than physical. The so-called "bad trip"—a terrifying experience that throws the user into a paranoiac state—is an ever-present danger even for the experienced user. Some people appear to have suffered prolonged psychotic episodes as a result of such experiences. Another problem is the "flashback," or recurrence of the psychedelic state, often weeks or even months after the last use of the drug. Although some users cope with these occurrences quite easily, others find them extremely upsetting. Prolonged use of psychedelics also appears to produce psychological depression in some users.

The use of psychedelics reached its peak in the 1960s, when thousands of people experimented with the drug and the "hippie" life style with which it became associated. LSD use declined as the hippie movement faded in the 1970s. The 1974 survey of American men referred to earlier found psychedelics to be the only type of drug that showed evidence of declining use.[28]

Sedative-Hypnotics

Sedative-hypnotics such as barbiturates and tranquilizers depress the central nervous system. In moderate doses, these drugs slow down breathing and normal reflexes, interfere with coordination, and relieve anxiety and tension. Speech becomes slurred, the mind clouded. In larger doses, they produce drowsiness and sleep. Medically, these drugs are used to produce two effects: relaxation (sedation) and sleep (hypnosis).

Tranquilizers and barbiturates are widely used. One survey found that 11 percent of the people in the United States had taken a barbiturate at least once in the previous year, and 15 percent had used a tranquilizer in the same period.[29] Of the two, barbiturates are usually preferred by recreational drug users.

The psychological effects of the barbiturates are similar to those of alcohol. Indeed, the state of drunkenness that barbiturates produce is often indistinguishable from alcohol intoxication.[30] And, like alcohol, the barbiturates are addictive. Repeated doses produce a growing tolerance, and heavy use can produce withdrawal distress when terminated. Addiction to barbiturates differs from addiction to opiates in two significant respects. First, physical dependence develops much more slowly; thus, the doses required to induce sleep usually will not be addictive. Second, withdrawal symptoms are much more severe and may cause hallucinations, restlessness, disorientation, or even death. The effects are similar in many ways to the delirium tremens produced by alcohol withdrawal.[31] Heavy use of barbiturates and tranquilizers has been called the "hidden addiction" because the drugs are legally available from physicians and are not highly stigmatized.[32] In fact, patients may be unaware of their own addiction.

The combination of alcohol and barbiturates is extremely dangerous. Taken together, these two drugs have an *additive* effect. That is to say, their total combined effect is greater than the sum of their separate effects, and it is often fatal. In the United States about 3000 people die each year from barbiturate overdoses.[33] How many of these deaths are suicides and how many are accidental is not known.

Methaqualone, known under the brand names of Quaalude and Sopor, is not chemically a barbiturate. However, its effects and dangers are very similar to those of the barbiturates. Methaqualone has become very popular among young drug users in recent years, perhaps because of its reputation as a "love drug"—a sexual stimulant. Actually, all the sedative–hypnotics inhibit the sexual drive by reducing general responsiveness. However, these drugs may also reduce inhibitions that interfere with the sexual performance of some individuals.[34]

A large number of tranquilizers have been synthesized and are now on the market. Some are so strong that they are seldom used except by severely disturbed mental patients, but "minor" tranquilizers are widely used to reduce tension. Librium and Miltown are well-known brand names of minor tranquilizers, and they are sometimes used for recreational purposes. Valium has become particularly popular among drug users and is now the most frequently prescribed drug in the United States. Although many people believe this drug to be harmless, it actually has many of the same effects and dangers as the barbiturates. Valium is addictive and will produce a withdrawal syndrome when heavy use is discontinued.

One of the newest and most rapidly spreading illicit drugs is phencyclidine, often known as PCP or "angel dust." In low doses it usually produces a sleepy, dreamlike state similar to that produced by other sedatives, although the effects may vary considerably from one individual to the next. In larger doses it produces hallucinations, and therefore PCP is sometimes classified as a psychedelic drug. Still larger doses of PCP produce unconsciousness, and for this reason it has been used as a surgical anesthetic. PCP is reputed to cause fits of uncontrollable violence in some users and has been a subject of growing national concern in recent years. Unfortunately, little reliable research on the illicit use of PCP has been conducted to date.

Stimulants
A wide variety of drugs may be used to stimulate the central nervous system. One such stimulant, nicotine, has already been discussed. Other important stimulants are caffeine, the amphetamines, and cocaine, all of which increase alertness, improve mental performance, and reduce drowsiness. However, as these drugs wear off, the opposite effect often appears.

Caffeine is one of the most widely used stimulants in the world. It is found in coffee, tea, cola drinks, and even chocolate candy. Caffeine is a weak stimulant, but it produces many of the effects of stronger ones — increased alertness, restlessness, and the alleviation of fatigue. The dosages taken in coffee, tea, or other beverages produce little tolerance, and there is no evidence of withdrawal symptoms.[35] A mild psychological dependence often does develop, however. We are all familiar with people who "must" have their morning coffee in order to start their day.

Higher doses of caffeine (5 or more cups of coffee) produce mild withdrawal discomfort, including depression and a jittery, nervous feeling. These higher doses may produce agitation and insomnia, and extremely large amounts can be fatal.[36] Although serious side effects from caffeine use are rare, the growing use of this drug in pill form (e.g., No-Doz) may pose a potential hazard.

The amphetamines are a group of synthetic stimulants that include benzedrine, dexedrine, and methedrine. These drugs are widely used as "diet pills," although more and more physicians are turning to other drugs to help patients lose weight. They reduce the appetite, increase blood pressure, and increase the rate of breathing. In moderate doses they produce increased alertness, even excitement. Continuous heavy doses of an amphetamine produce a psychosis-like state that is often indistinguishable from schizophrenia. Fear and suspicion are common symptoms, and fits of violent aggression may occur. Hallucinations, delusions, and general personal confusion are also common. Amphetamines produce tolerance with repeated use, and withdrawal symptoms, mainly severe depression, also occur.

There are two distinct patterns of amphetamine use. One consists of small doses taken for medical purposes — to relieve depression or increase physical and mental endurance. As long as drugs for these purposes are obtained from a physician and not openly used for the "high" they produce, users encounter few legal complications. Those who follow this pattern often consider amphetamines to be medicine, not drugs.

The other pattern of amphetamine use involves a much higher dosage, which is usually obtained illegally. So-called speed freaks make no pretense of using amphetamines for medical purposes. They may inject the drug directly into their bloodstreams, producing a brief but extremely intense high known as a "rush." Speed freaks often compare this experience to sexual orgasm. Such heavy use takes a tremendous toll on the health of the user, and speed freaks often go on "runs" lasting several days in which they get no sleep or proper nutrition. Long-term users lose their hair, teeth, and a large portion of their normal body weight. And of course, the amphetamine-induced psychosis becomes increasingly severe.

This second pattern of amphetamine use peaked in about 1967 in the famous Haight-Ashbury section of San Francisco. However, as the huge doses of "speed" took their toll on users, more and more turned to heroin and the epidemic of amphetamine use was succeeded by an epidemic of heroin use.[37]

Cocaine is a natural stimulant derived from the leaves of the coca plant. Until 1906 it was a major ingredient of Coca-Cola and a number of patent medicines. Modern users usually sniff this white powder into the nose through a tube of paper or a straw. Because of the method of consumption, heavy users may suffer damage to the nasal passages. The effects of cocaine are similar to the effects of amphetamines, except for two differences. First, cocaine is a powerful local anesthetic; second, the effects of cocaine are not as intense and do not last as long as those of the amphetamines. This means that cocaine users often repeat their doses every hour or so as the effects wear off. Because of this difference, and because cocaine is so expensive that few can continue a "run" for more than a few hours, the psychotic reaction that occurs with the amphetamines is uncommon.

WHY USE DRUGS?   Researchers seem to be fascinated with the question of why people use drugs. A tremendous amount of effort has gone into the investigation of this topic, much of it on the assumption that if we can find out why people take drugs, we can find ways of preventing them from doing so. Most explanations are based on the social-psychological perspective.

Biological Theories   It is widely believed that addiction creates an overpowering need for drugs. In other words, physiological changes produced by the drugs eventually generate a craving that is so strong that the individual is powerless to resist. While this theory probably is most popular with the general public, some scientists support it in a modified form. For instance, Dole and Nyswander, founders of the famous methadone treatment for heroin addicts, are confident that people have different "neurological susceptibilities" to opiates.[38] If susceptible individuals use an opiate, they quickly develop a "drug hunger" that continues even when they are no longer physically dependent. Because people become addicts for physiological reasons, Dole and Nyswander argue, addicts should be given methadone to keep their drug hunger under control until such time as a chemical cure is found.

Despite Dole and Nyswander's claims, there is overwhelming evidence suggesting that addiction involves more than physiology. Culture and personal relationships are critical. For instance, patients who become habituated to opiates during a stay in the hospital but perceive the drugs as medicine seldom continue their use after discharge. On the other hand, there have been many cases of individuals who, believing themselves to be addicted, behaved like other addicts even when the drugs they were using were of such low quality that physical dependence could not have been produced.[39] Almost all drug addicts "kick the habit" from time to time, but they do not thereby kick the addiction—they often take up drugs again even though they are no longer drug dependent. Even prisoners who have been off drugs for years start looking for a "fix" as soon as they are released.

While it is clear that biological effects are not sufficient to explain the craving for drugs, it would be wrong to assume that these effects are not important. Most people take a drug because they experience its effects as pleasurable. Even though their ideas of what is pleasurable are derived from their social groups, few people would use drugs if they produced no psychological effects. Perhaps it is best to say that the psychological effects of a drug may attract the user and that withdrawal discomfort may discourage the user from quitting, but neither compel the user to become or remain addicted.

Behavioral Theory   Psychologists have done extensive studies of drug use among animals.[40] They have found that animals can be trained to use drugs and that some become habituated. Behaviorists conclude that drug use is learned through a process of conditioning. That is, use of a drug often provides a reward (positive reinforcement). When experimental animals and humans use a drug and find it rewarding, they are stimulated to use it again.

Lindesmith turns this behavioral theory on its head.[41] Rather than being attracted to a pleasant experience, he says, the addict is trying to escape the unpleasant experience of withdrawal distress (negative reinforcement). According to Lindesmith, addicts use drugs to relieve withdrawal discomfort so frequently that they begin to associate the drug with the relief it brings. They continue to use drugs even when there is no physiological dependence because they associate drug use with the relief of discomfort and pain.

The basic idea behind behavioral theory—people use drugs because they find them pleasurable, and continue to use them because doing so prevents withdrawal distress—is not new. The behaviorist contribution lies in careful examination of the learning processes that promote or discourage drug use.

Personality Theories

Many psychologists have tried to explain addiction and excessive drug use by investigating the users' personalities. However, there is no general agreement among psychologists about the exact personality characteristics of addicts and "drug abusers." The most common theory is that these people have inadequate or immature personalities. Drug addicts have thus been classified as narcissists, psychopaths, sociopaths, dependent personalities, immature, schizophrenic, neurotic, and character disordered, to list only a few of the labels used. Some years ago Ausubel gave this description of the "inadequate personality" who, he maintained, is likely to turn to drugs in order to escape responsibilities:

> The inadequate personality fails to conceive of himself as an independent adult and fails to identify with such normal adult goals as financial independence, stable employment, and the establishment of his own home and family. He is passive, dependent, unreliable, and unwilling to postpone immediate gratification of pleasurable impulses.[42]

Chein and his associates did an extensive study of heroin addicts and their families. They concluded that heroin addicts have major personality disorders originating in the addicts' early family histories.[43] Thus, 97 percent of the addicts' families were "disturbed," with histories of separation, divorce, and open hostility. The mother was usually the most important parent figure to the child, with the father cold and even hostile. Children from these homes were found to be overindulged or frustrated, and uncertain of the standards they were expected to observe. These conditions were said to produce the kind of personality traits described by Ausubel, including passivity, defensiveness, and low self-esteem.

The idea that addicts are passive, inadequate personalities has been attacked in more recent research. Preble and Casey, for instance, say that there is nothing at all passive or inadequate about heroin users. On the contarary, they note that heroin addicts are unusually aggressive and competitive. They are not escaping from life but, rather, living one of the most demanding and predatory life styles in our culture.[44] Another criticism of personality theories is that they seem to be heavily biased toward middle-class values and against drug users, artists, and bohemians. Ausubel seems to be saying that anyone who does not have stable employment, financial independence, and the desire to maintain a home and family is "inadequate."

Despite weaknesses in these theories, personality plays a critical role in an individual's decision to use a drug. The problem is that there is no single type of personality that is most likely to lead to addiction. A great number of learned behavior patterns and personality traits interact in a given environment to either promote or discourage drug use.

Interactionist Theory

Most social psychologists see drug use merely as one more behavior pattern that is learned from interaction with others in our culture. They argue, for example, that most people in our society drink alcohol not because they have some personality defect or a biological urge to drink but, rather, because drinking is a widely accepted cultural pattern. As most children grow up they see their parents and other adults use alcohol, and they learn attitudes, beliefs, and definitions that are favorable to alcohol use. When such children reach adulthood they are likely to use alcohol just as their parents did.

Interactionists hold that the use of illegal drugs is also culturally learned, although in a slightly different way. Because the dominant culture encourages negative attitudes toward illegal drugs, some contact with a drug subculture is necessary before most people start using such drugs. The longer and more intense an individual's contact with a drug subculture, the greater the likelihood that the person will accept attitudes and definitions that are favorable to drug use. Once an individual begins to actually use an illicit drug, he or she is likely to grow closer to other drug users and become more deeply committed to the values of the drug culture. In fact, some people use drugs for the companionship of other drug users as much as for the effects of the drugs themselves.

The key point in interactionist theory is that drug use is determined by individuals' attitudes toward drugs, the meaning drug use has for them, their overall world view, and their system of values—all of which are learned from interaction with people in a certain culture or subculture. Drug users, according to interactionist theory, quit only when their attitudes and values change and the drugs involved are redefined in more negative terms.[45] Labeling theory points out that such changes are much more difficult when a drug user has been discovered and publicly labeled

DRUG CONTROL IN NORTH AMERICA

"addict," "alcoholic," "junkie," or "pill head." Those who have been branded in this way often find that they are excluded from contact with groups and individuals who might support their attempts to reform.

European colonists who came to North America brought their drinking customs with them. Before 1700 most drinking was moderate and socially accepted. The most common beverages were beer and wine. Strong religious and family controls limited drunkenness and disorderly conduct. However, as expansion to the West continued, drinking patterns changed. The traditional restraints of family and religion were ineffective among rugged frontiersmen, and heavy consumption of distilled spirits became commonplace. This type of drinking, often accompanied by violent destructive behavior, was the first alcohol problem to gain social attention. At the same time, total abstinence was becoming more popular among the rural farmers of "America's heartland."[46]

By the nineteenth century there were two different drinking patterns among Americans. Rural middle-class people were largely abstainers, while the frontiersmen and the thousands of immigrants in the big cities were alcohol users. Three waves of state prohibition laws swept the United States as small-town dwellers tried to stamp out the customs of urban drinkers. The last wave resulted in passage in 1919 of the Eighteenth Amendment to the Constitution, which prohibited the manufacture, sale, and transportation of intoxicating liquors. This amendment was repealed in 1933 by the Twenty-first Amendment.

Just as the drive against alcohol intensified in the nineteenth century, so also did the drive against the use of other drugs, particularly the opiates. At that time opium was sold legally in over-the-counter patent medicines as a cure for everything from diarrhea to whooping cough. Morphine was widely used as a painkiller during the War Between the States, and veterans spread the word about its beneficial effects. After the war extensive advertising campaigns for opiated medicines also contributed to the spread of opiate use. Products such as "Mrs. Winslow's Soothing Syrup" and "McMumm's Elixer of Opium" were widely used.[47]

The nineteenth-century opiate user was quite different from today's "junkie." Most opiate users were middle-aged, middle-class females. They were no more involved in crime or deviant behavior than anyone else.[48] The critical difference between them and contemporary addicts may be seen in the way early addicts defined the drugs and themselves. Indeed, the nineteenth-century users did not define themselves as addicts at all. They perceived the drugs as medicine and therefore did not see themselves as deviant or abnormal. In contrast, twentieth-century junkies define opiates as dope and themselves as addicts.

The first opiate use to be associated with crime was opium smoking among the Chinese immigrants on the West Coast, and this negative image soon spread to other methods of opiate consumption. In 1896 the *New York Sun* coined the term *dope fiend,* and an anti-opiate drive was soon under way. Near the turn of the century some states began restricting the use of opium. Nonprescription use of opiates was prohibited in Canada in 1908 and in the United States in 1914.

This prohibition produced a sharp drop in the number of opiate users. However, users who were unwilling or unable to quit were placed in a very difficult position. They found themselves labeled "dope fiends" and were virtually forced to associate with smugglers and other criminals if they were to obtain supplies of the drug. This small group of opiate users was the beginning of the subculture of opiate addiction that has become such a problem in recent years. The price of illicit opiates rose steadily, and so did the user's need for money. The method of consumption changed from drinking opiated medicines to injecting morphine and heroin. Within a few decades after opium prohibition, the modern junkie emerged—predominantly young, predominantly male, and deeply involved in crime.[49]

Alcohol prohibition had equally negative effects on American society. While the prohibition law was in effect, Americans witnessed a wave of crime and gangsterism. The drinking public was not willing to give up alcohol, no matter what the law said. They turned to illegal sources of supply, thus creating a huge illicit market for alcohol. Organized criminals and many independent operators jumped into the alcohol business, and "speakeasies" (illegal bars) sprang up in every city.

Marijuana was the last major drug to be prohibited in this era of "temperance." As late as 1930 only 16 states had laws prohibiting marijuana use, and these laws were not vigorously enforced. Although the climate of the early 1930s was right for another antidrug campaign, a single government agency, the Federal Bureau of Narcotics, played a major role in promoting marijuana prohibition in the United States.[50] This agency was set up to enforce opium prohibition in 1930, and its director came to feel that marijuana use was an area of wrongdoing that should be under his jurisdiction. Accordingly, the Bureau began an intensive program of lobbying both state and federal governments for the prohibition of marijuana. It also circulated a number of horror stories like the following, written by the Federal Commissioner of Narcotics and published in a popular magazine of the time:

> An entire family was murdered by a youthful [marijuana] addict in Florida. When officers arrived at the home they found the youth staggering about in a human slaughterhouse. With an axe he had killed his father, mother, two brothers, and a sister. He seemed to be in a daze.... He had no recollection of having committed the multiple crime. The officers knew him ordinarily as a sane, rather quiet young man; now he was pitifully crazed. They sought the reason. The boy said he had been in the habit of smoking something which youthful friends called "muggles," a childish name for marijuana.[51]

In 1937 Congress passed the Marijuana Tax Act, which was designed to stamp out use of the drug.

THE DISTRIBUTION OF DRUGS

The history of drug use in North America points up the tremendous impact of the method of drug distribution on both the drug user and society as a whole. Drugs are distributed through three main channels: the legal over-the-counter market, the prescription market, and the illegal black market. Users of a black-market drug face an array of problems that are not experienced by others, and they, in turn, contribute to other social problems. The most critical task faced by policy makers in the drug field is that of determining the best method of distributing each psychoactive drug.

The Over-the-Counter Market

The legal over-the-counter market is by far the most popular means of distributing psychoactive drugs. Alcohol, nicotine, and caffeine are distributed in this way. A number of nonprescription medicines, such as Sominex and Sleep-Eze, are sold over the counter as well.

The Prescription Market

A wide variety of drugs are legally available only with a doctor's prescription. The minor tranquilizers are prescribed most often, followed by the sedatives and hypnotics. About 75 percent of the psychoactive drugs pre-scribed by doctors are used to produce sedation, tranquillity, and sleep, and about 25 percent are prescribed to increase energy or treat depres-sion. About two-thirds of all users of prescription drugs are women. Just as many nineteenth-century women used opium to relieve boredom and loneliness, so women today use tranquilizers, sleeping pills, and other prescription medicines for the same purpose.

The Black Market   Many of the drugs prescribed by doctors are also available on the black market. Amphetamines and barbiturates are prime examples. Holders of legitimate prescriptions for such drugs sometimes give or sell them to other users. More significant, large quantities of these drugs are diverted from the prescription market into the black market for direct sale to users. A large percentage of the illegal amphetamines and barbiturates con-sumed in North America are manufactured by legitimate pharmaceutical companies and purchased by underground drug dealers. Small Mexican drugstores have been known to purchase huge amounts of these drugs and then smuggle them back into the United States and Canada.

Among the drugs that are not available legally but are sold on the black market are marijuana, most psychedelics, and heroin. (Opiates other than heroin are available by prescription, but they are very tightly regulated.) Most marijuana used in the United States and Canada is grown on farms in Mexico and South America and smuggled across the American border by single individuals or small criminal organizations. The production and marketing of heroin and other opiates is more complex. For years opium poppies grown in Turkey and the Middle East were refined and sent to France for final processing, then smuggled into North America. Now, as a result of efforts by the U.S. government to discourage cultivation of the opium poppy in Turkey, more heroin comes from other countries, espe-cially Mexico, South America, and Southeast Asia. Organized crime dominates the distribution system, principally because the importation and wholesale distribution of opiates requires huge amounts of cash. The risks of confiscation and long prison terms are high, but the profits are enormous, and fortunes can be made with one successful shipment. It is estimated that about 20 percent of the illegal shipments of heroin are con-fiscated, so importers must have enough capital to carry them through huge but temporary losses.[52]

Once heroin reaches the United States, it moves through a chain simi-lar to that of any legitimate importing-distributing-wholesaling-retailing business. Each participant in the chain buys and then sells. Each also dilutes the heroin with milk sugar or other additives. The street-level dealer is an independent businessperson who purchases at wholesale prices and sells at retail prices. He or she may be required to buy from a specific wholesaler, but no other control is exercised by those at the top.

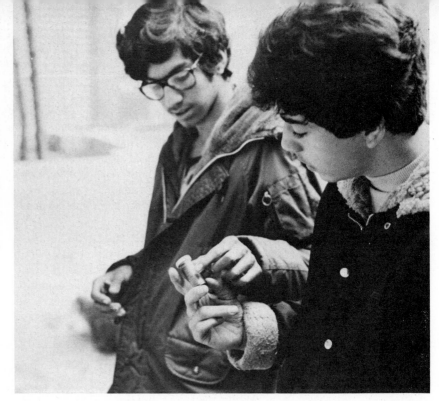

Black market drugs are readily available to North Americans of all ages. In some cases drugs originally purchased in the prescription market are diverted to the black market, but most black market drugs are produced specifically for that market.

Territory is not allocated, financial backing is not provided, and protection from arrest and imprisonment is not offered. The cost to the consumer is about five hundred times the cost at the point of importation.

RESPONDING TO THE DRUG PROBLEM

Drug use has long been considered an important social problem, at least partly because of the social costs already discussed. The Protestant ethic — which demands that individuals work hard and show self-discipline — is another major source of concern about drug use. Although these values have changed over the years, their influence remains strong. Thus, many people are disturbed by drug use itself, regardless of any damage it may do, because it is associated with laziness and self-indulgence. This attitude has aggravated the drug problem, as noted in our discussion of the history of drug use.

Proposals for dealing with drugs can be grouped into three categories: increased or continued legal repression, better treatment of individual drug users, and increased social tolerance of drug use. Repression and improved treatment aim at reducing drug use, while greater tolerance aims at reducing the social problems drug use creates.

Legal Repression

The most common response to drug use has been to make it a crime, usually by prohibiting the manufacture and sale of specific drugs and punishing users. This approach has been tried with almost all psychoactive drugs except caffeine and nicotine. In all cases legal prohibition has failed to stamp out drug use. Despite a steady increase in the amount spent on enforcement, overall use has increased. This is not to say that the prohibition approach is a failure because it has not stopped all drug use or even stopped it from increasing. Fear of the law clearly has discouraged many people from using drugs. But governmental repression has had damaging side effects. One unintended consequence has been the growth of organized crime. When a drug is prohibited by law, legitimate businesses are forced out of the market. The demand for the drug is still there, however, and criminals organize to meet it. Because such criminals have no competition from legitimate enterprise, legal prohibition guarantees them lucrative profits.

The classic example of this process is the prohibition of alcohol in the United States during the 1920s and early 1930s. As many Americans sought new sources of alcoholic beverages, gangs of criminals began to supply them. The result was widespread gangsterism and disrespect for law. Gang bosses like Al Capone, who built his illegal empire by bootlegging alcohol, virtually controlled some American cities.

Drug prohibition also has encouraged the development of deviant subcultures centered on the use of illegal drugs. The criminally oriented street addict was a direct product of opiate prohibition. Great Britain, which has pursued a somewhat less repressive policy toward opiate users, has not developed a comparable addict subculture.[53] Prohibition of widely used drugs such as marijuana brings millions of juveniles into contact with deviant subcultures, thus building antagonism toward police officers and disrespect for the law.

The enforcement of drug prohibition laws has also become a tremendous problem in itself. As drug use has increased, more attention and money have gone to drug law enforcement while other crimes have been neglected. Arrests for marijuana offenses in the United States alone increased from 7,560 in 1964 to a staggering 420,000 in 1974.[54] Moreover, civil liberties suffer as a result of the enforcement of drug laws. Because drug offenses are victimless crimes, citizens rarely call the police to report that a violation has occurred. If the laws are to be enforced, police officers must detect the violations themselves, and they soon resort to using networks of spies and informants to uncover drug law violators. The use of such secret agents not only poses a serious threat to civil liberties but also fails to catch most of the criminals. The few who are caught pay stiff penalties while the vast majority continue to operate freely.

Treatment The treatment approach, like the punitive approach, tries to discourage drug use. The difference is that the punitive approach attempts to discourage users by cutting off their supplies or sending them to jail, while the treatment approach encourages voluntary abstinence. A variety of treat-

Many different treatment programs have been developed to help those with drug problems.

ment programs have been tried, but no single program works for everyone. Many addicts go through several programs before kicking the habit.

Individual psychotherapy has proven to be one of the least successful approaches to drug problems.[55] No matter how much psychiatric care most drug users are given, strong social support is needed to motivate them to give up the drug habit. Aversive therapy is designed to associate the effects of the drug with some unpleasant sensation such as an electric shock or nausea. While aversive techniques are widely used to discourage smoking (e.g., by the Shick Centers), they have had less success with problem drugs such as alcohol and heroin.

The most successful treatment programs involve some kind of group therapy. Alcoholics Anonymous (AA) is one of the oldest such groups and is now a worldwide organization. Therapy takes the form of meetings where members give accounts of their troubles with alcohol and the help they have found in Alcoholics Anonymous. Members are encouraged to call on each other for support if their desire for a drink becomes strong.

NINETEENTH CENTURY SOCIAL PROBLEMS

Thomas Galt died at his home in this city Friday night last . . . from the effects of the Ackerman anti-dipsomania gold cure which he was taking. He was 37 . . . he contracted the drink habit and it so obtained the mastery of him that he was much of the time incapacitated for labor. He was so anxious to break the fetters that enslaved him . . . that he risked and lost his life. . . . He was a great sufferer throughout the treatment.
November 16, 1893

The AA program is religiously oriented, but its success seems to derive primarily from its system of encouraging each member to try to reform others, thus reinforcing the reformer's nondrinking behavior

Some group-oriented programs for drug addicts are adaptations of AA techniques for use in therapeutic communities where drug users live together in a house or dormitory. The first of these was the famous Synanon, founded in Santa Monica, California, in 1958. Synanon members were ex-users who maintained strict discipline, prohibited all drug use, and helped each other avoid drugs. Frequent group sessions were held in which members discussed their problems and criticized individuals who failed to live up to the expectations of the group.[56] Although Synanon has changed drastically in recent years, there are many other therapeutic communities that still follow its original principles.

Most therapeutic communities claim high rates of success. The problem is that these programs appeal only to drug users who can accept their ideology and discipline. It has been estimated that only 10 to 20 percent of those who join these communities finish the program.[57] Those who complete the program successfully often have great difficulty leaving the therapeutic community. Many who manage to leave become "professional ex-addicts" working in halfway houses or other drug programs.

Increased Social Tolerance

An alternative approach to the drug problem is to increase the tolerance for drug use. This approach includes a variety of different solutions, ranging from relatively minor reductions in penalties for some types of drug offenses to full legalization of all drugs. Advocates of these proposals claim that a less punitive reaction to drug use would reduce the negative side effects stemming from legal repression and, in the long run, reduce the need for treatment. If drugs could be obtained legally, it is argued, their attractiveness as "forbidden fruit" would decline. Further, legalization would take the profit out of drug distribution, thus taking drugs off the street. But even if this approach failed to reduce drug use, its advocates assert, it would reduce the drug problem by reducing organized crime, destigmatizing drug users, undermining drug subcultures, and promoting the growth of more effective informal controls for drugs that are currently illegal.

Legalization

Proponents of legalization believe that attempts at legal repression of drug use have been so disastrous that the problem can be solved only by taking the government out of the drug law enforcement business. In practice, regulation by government agencies probably would be maintained, as in the case of alcohol. Minors would be prohibited from purchasing drugs, and taxation and regulation of quality standards could be expected.

Most proponents of legalization do not advocate over-the-counter sales for all drugs. In fact, marijuana is the only drug for which full legalization has widespread support. Those who do advocate the legalization of all drugs often base their arguments on philosophical opposition to government interference in individual lives. Thomas Szasz, for instance, feels that the decision to use a drug is entirely an individual matter in which the government has no legitimate concern.[58]

Decriminalization

Decriminalization is a step halfway between prohibition and full legalization. Its advocates argue that the penalties for possession and use of a given drug, usually marijuana, should be dropped but that sales of the drug should continue to the illegal. The aim is to stop punishing those who use illicit drugs but to discourage such use by forbidding sales. Critics of this policy point to the contradiction between allowing legal possession and penalizing sale or purchase. Its advocates, who fear that legalization would encourage a new wave of drug use yet want to reduce the repression of users, propose decriminalization as a compromise. Decriminalization of marijuana use, or reduction of penalties for possession and use of marijuana, has been endorsed by American and Canadian commissions on drug use, the American Medical Association, and the American Bar Association.[59]

Maintenance

Maintenance programs supply addicts or habitual users with a drug while denying it to the public at large. This approach usually is advocated for the opiates, but it could also be applied to other addictive drugs. The only widely used maintenance program in the United States and Canada is the distribution of methadone (a synthetic opiate) to heroin addicts. Although methadone maintenance is often called treatment, it has little in common with real treatment programs. In essence, these programs simply provide a restricted legal supply of an opiate to people who otherwise would obtain opiates illegally.

Supporters of methadone maintenance programs believe that methadone has several advantages over heroin: Its effects last longer, it can be given orally, and it does not generate the intense high that is produced by heroin. However, many heroin addicts refuse to participate in methadone programs because they prefer heroin. Critics, including some ex-addicts, argue that methadone is just another narcotic and that dispensing it to heroin users does not solve the addiction problem.

Another issue concerns the method used to distribute methadone. In current programs the addict is supervised in a special clinic while taking a 24-hour dose. This technique is designed to minimize the diversion of methadone into the black market. Critics say that these programs throw addicts into association with each other just when they are trying to escape the culture of addiction; that they unreasonably restrict addicts' freedom to travel; and that they are demeaning because they require addicts to wait in line for their daily handout. Lindesmith has proposed that we establish a different kind of maintenance program, one that allows individual physicians, rather than government clinics, to distribute any opiate the patient needs, including heroin.[60]

SOCIOLOGICAL PERSPECTIVES on Drug Use

The problems of drug use should not be dismissed as the faults or weaknesses of individuals. Although some people seem to have more difficulty limiting their drug use than others, social psychologists have shown that anyone can become a drug addict, regardless of moral character. Sociologists have repeatedly demonstrated the enormous influence social forces have on all types of human behavior. The severe problems North American society has with drug use is the result of its culture and social structure, not the weakness of its people. Repeated claims that drug users are sick, degenerate, or abnormal are simply misguided name-calling that obscures the real source of the problem.

The Functionalist Perspective

Functionalist theory does not attempt to explain the specific reasons why individuals use or do not use drugs. It concerns itself with the social conditions that have caused the tremendous increase in drug use in recent decades. The general assumption is that drug use is a means of escaping from difficult and unpleasant social circumstances. Consequently, the current wave of drug addiction is seen as a response to social problems associated with rapid social change — poverty, racism, and alienation of the individual. Functionalists also are likely to note that inefficiency characterizes the agencies that are charged with enforcing drug laws, thus further contributing to the growing use of illegal drugs.

If drug use is indeed a secondary effect of other social problems, an effective solution certainly will not be easy to find. What is needed is a wide-ranging attack on the primary problems. While hundreds of proposals for dealing with these problems have been made, reducing these social ills to levels that would no longer motivate people to misuse drugs would be extremely difficult. A simpler response would be to devote more time and money to the enforcement of drug laws, thus attempting to cut off the supply of drugs rather than attempting to cut off the demand. However, functionalists as well as other sociologists are skeptical about such an approach, mainly because past enforcement efforts have been so unsuccessful at solving the drug problem.

The Conflict Perspective

Some conflict theorists also assume that drug users are escapists, and they agree that drug use is caused by other social problems. However, they hold that those social problems stem from exploitation and social injustice rather than from social disorganization. Like the functionalists, these conflict theorists advocate a direct attack on the primary problem (i.e., exploitation), rather than on the symptoms of the problem (i.e., drug use).

They argue that drug use will decrease only after we have created a just society that is free from exploitation and oppression.

Other conflict theorists disagree strongly, asserting that drug use itself is neither escapist nor a social problem. Rather, it is normal behavior that occurs in all societies around the world. According to these theorists, drug use becomes a problem only when groups who oppose drugs use the power of the state to force their morality on everyone else. The inevitable result of such actions is social conflict, violent repression of drug users, and a booming black market.

Most conflict theorists argue that individuals should not be jailed for using drugs if their behavior causes no harm or danger to others. Conflict theorists also say that the attempt to repress drug use creates secondary social problems such as organized crime and a seething discontent with the legal system. Those who hold this viewpoint advocate a simple solution to the drug problem: Legalize the prohibited drugs and stop jailing people who have done no harm to others.

The Social-Psychological Perspective

Most research into the causes of and solutions to the drug problem has been at the social-psychological level. As our previous discussion has suggested, each of the four major social-psychological theories has its own explanations of drug use and its preferred treatments. Biosocial theorists say that drug addiction is a physiological problem and recommend more research to develop a biochemical cure. Personality theory holds that addiction is caused by defects in the addict's personality, and recommends psychotherapy. Interactionists and behaviorists agree that drug addiction is learned behavior and recommend treatment programs designed to help addicts learn less destructive patterns of behavior.

SUMMARY

The manufacture and sale of drugs is a big business. Vast sums of money are spent on drugs and on the enforcement of drug laws. Many drugs are habit forming, meaning that continual use produces tolerance and that the user gets sick when the drug is withdrawn. Addiction is the strong craving that often develops when one uses habit-forming drugs.

Many drugs are used for recreational purposes. The most popular one, alcohol, creates the most problems for society. It is a depressant and is addictive if used in excess. Tobacco is another widely used legal drug. Cigarette smoking has been shown to cause a variety of health problems, yet large numbers of people begin or continue to smoke each year. Marijuana is one of the most heavily studied and most controversial drugs used today. Although most of the evidence indicates that it is less harmful than alcohol, there is considerable controversy concerning its legal status. The opiates are all highly addictive. Although the drugs themselves do not appear to cause great physical harm, the way they are used and the life style of most addicts make these drugs highly dangerous. Mescaline and LSD are two of the most popular psychedelic drugs, and both produce powerful psychological changes in the user, including hallucinations and alterations of mood and perception. The psychedelics produce few physical health problems but are emotionally disturbing to some users. The sedative–hypnotics depress the central nervous system and are frequently prescribed by physicians, but there is also a flourishing black market for many of these drugs. Stimulants have the opposite effects from those of the sedative-hypnotics. The most widely used stimulant is caffeine, which is not dangerous in moderate doses. The amphetamines are much stronger and more dangerous stimulants. Excessive amphetamine use produces a psychotic state as well as considerable physical damage. Cocaine is a natural stimulant with effects similar to those of the amphetamines, except that the effects of cocaine last a much shorter time.

Biological theories hold that addicts use drugs because of an overwhelming need created by the physiological effect of the drugs. Behavioral theory sees drug use and addiction as products of conditioning: People use drugs because they find the experience to be rewarding, and addicts continue to use drugs because they want to avoid painful withdrawals. Personality theorists argue that individuals who use drugs have inadequate or immature personalities, while according to interactionist theory drug use stems from attitudes, values, and definitions favorable to such behavior, often learned in drug subcultures.

The early North American colonists had few problems with drugs. Heavy drinking patterns developed among single men on the frontier, while more respectable farm families began to give up drinking. Several prohibitionist movements swept North America in the twentieth century and resulted in the banning of alcohol, opiates, and marijuana. Prohibition of these drugs fostered drug subcultures among the users, who were branded as criminals. The "junkie" or "dope fiend" subculture, which developed among heroin users, has become a particularly severe problem.

The method by which a drug is distributed has an important effect both on society and on the user. Some drugs are distributed legally in over-the-counter sales; others are available by prescription. Still others—including some prescription drugs—are distributed illegally in the black market.

Proposals for dealing with the drug problem fall into three main categories. The first is increased legal repression of drug use. This approach discourages drug use but has damaging side effects, including the growth of organized crime and drug subcultures. The second approach is treatment of drug users to help them stop using drugs. The most successful treatment programs use some form of group support, ordinarily called group therapy. Increased social tolerance of drug use is the third alternative. Included in this category are legalization, decriminalization, and maintenance clinics that supply addicts with substitutes for illegal drugs.

Functionalists generally assume that drug use is a means of escaping from unpleasant social conditions that have arisen as society has become disorganized. Some conflict theorists also assume that drug users are escapists, but they are convinced that these problems stem from exploitation rather than from social disorganization. Other conflict theorists consider drug use to be normal behavior and argue that the problem lies in the state's attempts to repress this behavior. The social-psychological perspective includes biosocial theory, personality theory, behavioral theory, and interactionist theory. Each of these social-psychological theories tries to explain why persons become drug users, and each implies a specific program of treatment.

KEY TERMS

addiction
alcoholic
decriminalization
legalization
maintenance program
opiate

psychedelic
sedative-hypnotic
stimulant
tolerance
withdrawal

WARNING
POLICE-PATROL
BY
INTER-CITY-INC
294-1848

14
Crime and Delinquency

Are official crime statistics accurate?
What causes criminal behavior?
Are juvenile delinquents criminals?
Does punishment reform criminals?
What can be done to reduce crime?

Crime is a persistent problem in all modern societies. Although it is impossible to make a precise estimate of the economic costs of all the various types of criminal activity, the total certainly runs to many billions of dollars a year in the United States alone. But even more serious are the human costs of crime—the loss of life and liberty, the physical injuries, and the nagging fear that we may be next on the long list of victims.

Public concern about the crime problem has skyrocketed since the early 1960s. As pollster Louis Harris put it, "In five short years in the 1960s, fear for one's personal safety grew from almost nonexistence to a pervasive dark shadow that followed 2 in every 3 citizens through their waking days and their troubled sleeps."[1] However, it is not clear that crime has increased nearly as much as the fear of it. Indeed, fear of crime has contributed to the growing crime rate, as measured by official crime statistics. Fear of crime leads to more reporting and recording of crime, which leads to increased fear, which leads to more official attention, and so on in a spiraling pattern. This spiral has also been fed by the growing attention the crime problem has received in the media and from politicians, who have capitalized on public concern about crime.

THE NATURE OF CRIME

A crime is a violation of the criminal law. No matter how indecent or immoral an act may be, it is not a crime unless the criminal law has listed it as a crime and provided a punishment for it.

In practice, of course, it is not always easy to tell whether a specific act is or is not a burglary, a robbery, a rape, or some other crime. It often takes a trial to determine what a particular law means. For example, the criminal law forbids the unlawful killing of human beings (murder), but is a fetus a human being? The criminal law forbids stealing (larceny), but what is stealing? The definition has changed over history as ideas about property have changed, and it continues to change today. If a factory worker takes tools home from the job, it is stealing; but is it stealing if the worker loafs on the job? If students take library books and put them on their own shelves, it is stealing; but is it stealing if they take books without properly checking them out and read and return them? Is it stealing if a student takes a library book, photocopies it, and then returns it?

Such questions must be decided by someone; and justice is the process by which such decisions are reached. It is not a mechanical process in which a precise criminal law is uniformly applied to all cases. Any fair judgment as to guilt or punishment requires wisdom, sensitivity, and a sense of balance.

Roscoe Pound, a famous American legal scholar, once pointed out that there is a great difference between "law on the books" and "law in action." What the criminal law says and what police and the courts do are often quite different. For example, some old laws—such as those outlawing certain sex acts—remain legally valid but are almost never enforced. Even more recent laws—such as those making it a crime to go nude on a beach—are sometimes ignored. In addition, police officers and courts enforce most laws selectively. This means, for example, that an act might be called burglary if it is committed by a poor person—especially one with a criminal record—but might be called trespassing or some other minor offense if it is committed by someone who is more "respectable." In the days when the Black Panthers were militant radicals, a professor at a university in Los Angeles demonstrated this point with an interesting experiment. He selected a group of forty-five students with good driving records who had not received a traffic ticket for at least a year, and placed bumper stickers supporting the Black Panther Party on their cars. In the first week four of the students received three traffic tickets apiece, and the experiment was suspended after the second week because the professor could not afford to pay for the flood of tickets his subjects were receiving.[2]

Certain types of acts, such as murder, are condemned in almost all societies. (However, the distinction between what is murder and what is "justifiable homicide" varies considerably from one culture to the next.) Other acts are illegal in some nations and legal in others. Some countries allow a man to have many wives, but in other countries a man who has more than one wife is guilty of the crime of bigamy. There are places where alcohol use is legal and marijuana use is not and places where marijuana smoking is legal but drinking is not. In America and many other large nations, there are variations from state to state and even from city to city. The point is that the creation and modification of criminal laws is a political process. When values change or political power shifts, "law in action" changes, even if "law on the books" remains the same.

IS THERE A CRIME WAVE?

In the United States, Canada, and most of the industrialized world, average citizens are convinced that a massive crime wave is threatening property and personal safety. Some experts deny that there has been a recent increase in crime, despite the fact that official statistics show great increases during the past decade. Others are convinced that the crime rate is indeed going up. These differences of opinion persist because changes in the amount of crime are very hard to measure.

The main source of statistics about the number of crimes committed is official police records. Because not all crimes are reported, these statistics underestimate the total amount of crime. But they do not necessarily distort the *trends* in crime. In the United States the FBI annually publishes statistics on arrests and on crimes known to the police in most American cities. These statistics, like those published by other Western nations, have shown a steady increase in crime until very recently. Between 1960 and 1974 the rate of all crime reported to the FBI increased 157 percent.

FIGURE 14.1
CHANGES IN REPORTED
CRIME, 1960–1977

Source: Data from Federal Bureau of
Investigation, *Uniform Crime Reports,*
1977.

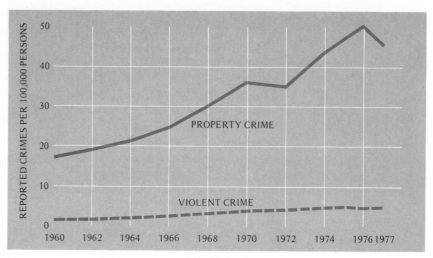

Violent crimes increased 187 percent and property crime 154 percent.[3] However, this upward trend ended in 1976, and reported crime began declining in 1977.[4] (See Figure 14.1.)

There are, however, many doubts about the accuracy of these statistics. Most police departments try to show as large an increase as possible to justify their requests for more money and personnel. On the other hand, when a city's police are criticized because the crime rate is too high, they may reverse themselves and try to show a decrease in crime. For instance, the FBI reported a 4 percent drop in total crime in 1972 — the first reduction in 17 years — and it has been charged that the figures were intentionally reduced to strengthen the Nixon administration's "law and order" image just before the presidential election.[5]

The most convincing evidence that FBI statistics have exaggerated the increase in crime comes from surveys of the victims of crime. The U.S. Bureau of the Census conducted two surveys, one in 1973 and one in 1974, asking people to report whether they had been victimized in the last year. These surveys showed no increase in violent crime between 1973 and 1974, but the FBI reported an increase of 11.3 percent. The victimization surveys showed an increase in property crime, but it was less than half of that reported by the FBI.[6]

Not all such discrepancies are due to intentional manipulation of the numbers. Greater confidence in the police, quicker and easier ways of reporting crimes, improved record keeping, and the growing popularity of theft insurance (which requires the victims to report a crime in order to collect) have all tended to boost the number of crimes reported. On the other hand, victimization surveys are not without certain shortcomings.

Some of the respondents in these surveys forget incidents in which they were victimized, while others report crimes that actually occurred years before.

It is generally agreed that murder is the most accurately reported crime. Even though some murders pass for suicides, the existence of a dead body that coroners can examine makes it difficult to conceal a murder. By the same token, it is difficult for police officers to inflate the statistics on murders. While examination of recent North American statistics indicates that murder has increased, this crime has shown the slowest growth rate of all major crimes. In the 6 years between 1965 and 1970, the Canadian murder rate increased by over 50 percent.[7] And in the 15 years between 1960 and 1974 the American murder rate increased 90 percent.[8]

THE DISTRIBUTION OF CRIME

Despite their limitations, crime statistics reveal information that is important to our understanding of crime. Overlapping information from different sources suggests that the crime rates for certain categories of people are either higher or lower than the average. Theories about crime causation try to make sense of these persistent relationships between crime and social position. The five most important relationships of this kind are those between crime and sex, age, social class, ethnic group, and residential area.

Sex

Males dominate the world of crime. If you were asked to use a single trait to predict which children in a town would become criminals, you would make the fewest mistakes if you chose sex as the trait and predicted that the boys would be criminals and the girls would not. Of course, the prediction would be wrong in many cases. Most of the boys would not become criminals and a few of the girls would. But you would be wrong in more cases if you used some other trait, such as age, ethnic group, family background, or a personality characteristic. As Sutherland and Cressey put it,

> The crime rate for men is greatly in excess of the rate for women—in all nations, all communities within a nation, all age groups, all periods of history for which organized statistics are available, and for all types of crime except those peculiar to women, such as infanticide and abortion.[9]

In the United States about 5 times as many men as women are arrested, about 10 times as many are convicted, and about 15 times as many are sent to prison. Similar ratios exist in other industrialized countries. In Canada the ratio of males to females convicted of serious offenses is about 15:1. This difference is even greater in traditional societies, where there is greater inequality between men and women. In such countries the male arrest rate may run as high as 20,000 times the female arrest rate. The ratio of men to women also varies greatly with the type of crime. Only men are arrested for forcible rape, and in general the sex differences are much greater for violent crimes than for property crimes.

Differences between the crime rates of men and women have been decreasing in recent years. The rates for women have been increasing more rapidly than those for males, bringing the two sexes closer together. Between 1960 and 1975 the male arrest rate in the United States increased 119 percent, but the female rate increased 374 percent.[10] It seems that the more women become involved in the world outside the home, the more they become involved in crime. When full sexual equality is achieved, there will be a much smaller difference between the crime rates of men and women.[11]

Age

Records of arrests and convictions from industrialized countries around the world show that criminality peaks in the teenage years. In Scandinavia, the age of maximum criminality is 13–15; in England, it is 14–17; in Australia, it is 15–18.[12] In the United States, the maximum age of criminality, as measured by arrests, is 16. After age 16 the arrest rate slowly tapers off until the middle 20s, when it begins a much more rapid decline.

But the age of maximum criminality is not the same for all crimes. In America males aged 15–19 have the highest rates for automobile theft and burglary, but young people are less likely to be involved in violent crimes than the popular stereotype of the "teenage hoodlum" would lead us to expect. In 1975 people under the age of 25 accounted for 45 percent of the arrests for homicide, 75 percent of the arrests for larceny, 77 percent of the arrests for robbery, 85 percent of the arrests for burglary, and 85 percent of the arrests for car theft.[13]

Social Class

Official statistics suggest that the largest percentage of criminals and delinquents come from the lower classes. Two-thirds to three-fourths of the men and nine-tenths of the women in prison are from the lower classes. Studies of arrests and convictions also show a disproportionate percentage of poor people. Criminologists who have compared rates of crime in the poor sections of cities with those in more affluent areas have found substantially more crime in the poor sections. Wolfgang found that 90 to 95 percent of the offenders in his homicide study were from the lower end of the occupational scale.[14]

But there are serious problems with using official records in this kind of study. The reliability of statistics on the backgrounds of criminals has been questioned even more severely than statistics on sex, age, and ethnic group. Because middle- and upper-class criminals have greater personal resources, they are better able to protect themselves from detection, arrest, conviction, and imprisonment.

To offset this bias in official statistics, unofficial measures have been used. Further support for the belief that the poor commit more crimes comes from the studies of victimization mentioned earlier. Of the six types of offenses surveyed by the National Opinion Research Center, poor people were much more often victimized in forcible rape, robbery, and burglary. Only larceny (theft) was more common among the higher income groups. While a poor person might well be expected to go into a wealthy neighborhood to commit a theft, it is highly unlikely that a wealthy person would go into a poor neighborhood to commit a burglary or robbery. So we can only conclude that more poor people are victimized because the crimes in question are committed by other poor people who live in the same neighborhood.

Another technique for determining the role of social class in crime is to ask people what kinds of crimes they have committed. A considerable number of such "self-report" studies have been done. Some have found the lower class to be the most criminal, but others have not. Because these studies have not found a consistent relationship between social class and crime, some researchers have concluded that the poor are not really more likely to break the law than anyone else.[15] One significant study using the self-report technique found that among high school students place of residence is more important to delinquency than social class in its pure form.[16] Differences among the social classes *within* the areas studied were generally insignificant. The study made clear that the "working class" that is so overrepresented in crime statistics consists of lower-class people living in the lower-class areas of large cities. Middle-class youths living in the same areas reported delinquencies in about the same measure as lower-class children.

Perhaps the gravest weakness of official statistics, victimization studies, and self-report studies is their failure to include white-collar crimes such as embezzlement, false advertising, and consumer fraud. Few people are arrested for such crimes, and most of their victims do not even know they have been victimized. But middle- and upper-class people are obviously much more heavily involved in white-collar crime than poor people. One sociologist has argued that if all crime could be counted, a U-shaped curve would emerge, indicating more crime in the lower and upper classes and less in the middle.[17] But confirmation or rejection of this hypothesis must await better measurements. The plain fact is that criminologists simply do not know whether poor people commit more crimes than others. We can say that the evidence indicates that poor people probably commit more of the crimes that are usually measured, such as murder, burglary, and theft; but that is all.

Ethnic Group

American crime statistics show considerable variation in the rates for different ethnic groups. Blacks, Latinos, Indians, and Chinese-Americans have higher-than-average rates, while Jews and Japanese have lower-than-average rates. While blacks comprise only 12 percent of the population of the United States, they account for about 25 percent of those arrested each year. In 1975 over half of the Americans arrested for murder, robbery, prostitution, or gambling were black. One study traced 9945 boys born in 1945 and living in Philadelphia from 1955 to 1962.[18] Overall, 55 percent of the boys had at least one contact with the police for something other than a traffic violation, but this percentage was 50 for nonwhites, compared with 29 for the whites. Moreover, of the offenses committed by the boys, 56 percent were committed by nonwhites, who made up 29 percent of the total number of boys. When weighted for seriousness, the nonwhite rate was 4.6 times the white rate.

However, such statistics cannot be taken as a true measure of the total amount of crime committed by either blacks or whites. Many studies have shown that blacks are more likely to be arrested, indicted, and imprisoned than whites who have committed the same offenses.[19] Thus, almost any set of official statistics is likely to inflate the rate for blacks compared with the rate for whites. It is also true that many crimes committed by blacks — especially those committed against other blacks — receive no official attention from police officers or courts. This practice of overlooking crimes is based on the prejudiced assumption that blacks are inferiors who cannot be expected to live up to the standards of a civilized society, and it offsets to some extent the bias in other recording practices.

As suggested earlier, the murder rate is the statistic that is least likely to have these shortcomings. The Wolfgang study of murder in Philadelphia found that black males were 12 times more likely to be murdered than white males and that black females were 23 times more likely to be murdered than white females. A study of criminal homicide in Chicago found higher overall rates but similar proportions between the races — the black rate was 8 times the white rate for males and 16 times the rate for females.[20]

On the basis of this and other evidence, most criminologists have concluded that there is a real, not just statistical, difference between the rates of violent crime for blacks and whites. It also appears that blacks are more likely to commit the kinds of property crimes that are usually reported in police statistics. However, whites are more likely to hold white-collar jobs, and thus probably commit many more white-collar crimes. And, given the lack of any reliable statistics on white-collar crime, it is impossible to assess black–white differences in property crime as a whole.

Residential Area For at least a century, studies from all over the world have shown more crime in big cities than in small towns and rural areas. Skeptics have wondered whether the difference is merely statistical, because more rural and small-town crime is handled informally rather than reported to a police agency. But recent studies of victimization have confirmed earlier studies using official statistics. The National Opinion Research Center's victimization study found that large metropolitan areas have about five times as many violent crimes and about twice as many property crimes as small cities and rural areas.

There are a number of reasons for the excess of crime in urban area. For one thing, the urbanite lives in a world of strangers where a criminal is not likely to be recognized. Further, the anonymity of the big city breeds alienation, and many people are isolated from supportive social groups that might prevent crime informally. Finally, the city attracts young single people, who as a group have the highest crime rate no matter where they live.

But there are crime rate differences *within* individual cities as well. The rates are highest in decaying inner-city slums, and they decrease regularly as one moves out from the central city to the better residential areas. As suggested earlier, location is more important to crime rates than social class. Even the people who live in the poor sections of small towns have higher crime rates than the other town residents. It should be noted, finally, that females have lower crime rates than males, even though they live in the same cities, in the same deteriorated areas within cities, or in the same slum areas of small towns.

THE CAUSES OF CRIME

Systematic study of crime rates and criminal behavior goes back only about two centuries. Until about the time of the American Revolution, crime was considered a product of innate depravity prompted by the devil. Because something outside the society and outside the individual was thought to be responsible for crime, the notion that crime could be reduced by modifying the conditions that produce it was entirely foreign.

The Classical School

The birth of modern criminology can be traced to 1764 and the publication of Cesare Beccaria's book *On Crimes and Punishments*. Beccaria was an Italian nobleman. The great English philosopher Jeremy Bentham applied Beccaria's ideas to legislation, and these two men became the leaders of what came to be called the classical school of criminology. They thought all people were guided by a rational desire to seek pleasure and avoid pain. According to the classical school, individuals who commit a crime choose to do so. They weigh all the options and find that a crime will give them the most pleasure for the least amount of pain. This was regarded as a complete explanation of crime, and its inventors saw no need for research on economic, personal, political, or social conditions associated with crime. Although the psychology on which the classical school was founded has since been discarded by social scientists, this approach continues to dominate Anglo-American criminal law and its administration.

The early members of the classical school were reformers who tried to soften the cruel methods used by kings and emperors to maintain social order and protect their privileged position. Bentham, for example, helped make punishments less severe and arbitrary. He contended that all laws should be clearly stated and that all people who violate a specific law should receive identical punishments regardless of age, social class, or circumstances. In other words, the punishment was to fit the crime, and the solution to the crime problem was to punish as many offenders as possible. Such punishment—which was to be severe enough to deter crime but no more severe than that—was expected to outweigh the pleasures anyone might gain from crime, thus teaching people to choose noncriminal behavior over criminality. The fact that crime has persisted through the years is evidence that this simple view of human psychology is inadequate.

The Positive School

The so-called positive school of criminology developed under the leadership of an Italian physician, Cesare Lombroso, in the last quarter of the nineteenth century. Lombroso and other positivists rejected the classical school's belief in free will and the criminal's ability to decide rationally whether or not to commit a crime. They saw crime and criminal behavior as products of natural causes.

In the past hundred years almost all criminological research has taken the positivist path, meaning that researchers assume that crime and criminality are caused rather than merely willed by individual actors. Although Lombroso's main concern was with biological causes of crime, scholars who preceded him had used the notion of natural causation in studies of the effects of culture and economic inequality on crime rates. And as the study of crime has continued, the number of social causes has increased. The classical way of thinking—which is embedded in contemporary criminal law—assumes that crime can be controlled by negative action (punishment) alone. The positivist school suggests that crime and criminality can be controlled by understanding the causal processes producing them and then intervening in those processes. Some positivists continue to believe that crime is biologically determined, but psychological and sociological theories are much more widely accepted.

Biological Theories

Lombroso thought criminals have the savage instincts of animals and are throwbacks to humanity's prehuman ancestors. According to Lombroso, these "born criminals" could easily be distinguished from normal individuals by physical traits such as sloping foreheads, small brains, large ears, overdeveloped jaws, and other apelike characteristics. Lombrosian ideas about the physical characteristics of criminals have been totally discredited, but they continue in popular thought. Many people still mistakenly believe that criminals are physically different from other people.

The Lombrosian notion that criminality is inherited remains popular too. With this idea in mind, criminologists have studied the family trees of criminals, the statistical association between the crimes of parents and children, and the crime rates of identical twins. These studies have been inconclusive, principally because some inherited traits may be related to criminal behavior by virtue of the fact that people have learned to react to them in a certain way. For example, a person's skin color affects the way they are treated in the United States and the crime rate is high among dark-skinned people. But this association tells us nothing about heredity. It is obviously impossible for criminality as such to be inherited, for crime is defined by acts of legislatures, and these vary independently of the biological traits of law violators.

Some recent research suggested that certain abnormalities in the sex chromosomes are frequently found among those in prisons and mental hospitals, and this finding led to a flurry of studies of the genetic makeup of criminals. The biological idea is that an extra Y (male) chromosome in males causes the individual to be uncontrollably aggressive. But a recent review of this research concluded that "XYY males in an institutional setting are *less* violent or aggressive when compared to matched chromosomally normal fellow inmates, and their criminal histories involve crimes against property rather than persons."[21]

Personality Theories

There is a widely held belief that many criminals, especially violent ones, are insane. After a particularly gruesome murder has occurred, we often hear the comment "A person would have to be crazy to commit a crime like that." While such statements express understandable shock and disbelief, they are misguided. In the first place, psychiatric examinations of convicted criminals show that only a small percentage are psychotic. Moreover, psychiatric records show that most psychotics are not criminals and have not attacked or harmed other people.[22] In the second place, research on the relationship between psychoses and crime is complicated by the fact that a person who is "insane" at the time that a legally forbidden act is carried out does not commit a crime. For example, a man charged with murder may defend himself in court by showing that he was insane at the time that the act occurred, just as another man may plead that his act was performed in self-defense. *Insanity* is a legal term, not a psychiatric one, and it refers to the fact that a person did not know the nature or quality of their criminal act or did not know right from wrong. "Insane" people, like infants, are legally incapable of committing crimes.

Of course, the psychoses are not the only psychological conditions that have been studied as potential causes of crime. Criminal behavior is often said to be caused by emotional disturbances or certain personality traits. But dozens of personality tests and rating scales have been used to compare criminals and noncriminals, and the general conclusion is that there are no important differences. The studies that do find differences seem to define and measure personality traits in vague ways. For example, a psychiatrist might say that a criminal has some deeply hidden personality maladjustment, but it is difficult for others to learn just what the maladjustment is or to determine how it is related to the person's criminality.

Many psychologists and psychiatrists have examined convicted criminals and concluded that most of them have "psychopathic personalities." This term is quite vague, but it refers to an inability to form close social relations, resulting in abnormal immorality. Some psychiatrists think this personality type is hereditary, but the most common explanation is that it develops in early childhood. The method of diagnosing a psychopathic personality is not at all standardized. Accordingly, the labels "psychopathic" and "psychopath" can be applied to almost anyone. It appears that this idea of causation is circular — people are labeled psychopathic because they have broken the law, and then it is claimed that people break the law because they are psychopaths. This approach has been called "neo-Lombrosian" because it continues Lombroso's search for a criminal type, with an emphasis on personality rather than anatomy.

Sociological Theories

There are dozens of sociological theories of crime and criminality. The central idea in all of them is that criminal behavior is produced by the same social processes that produce other behavior. In this sense crime is not abnormal or unusual. Analyses of the social processes and conditions producing criminality have taken two principal forms. First, sociologists have shown that variations in crime rates are associated with variations in social structure, including mobility, social class, population composition, and culture conflict. Second, sociologists have studied the processes by which a person becomes a criminal.

For generations sociologists have been trying to explain why lower-class people commit more crimes than others. As we have seen, this kind of study has been handicaped by the apparent unreliability of crime statistics. But some sociologists, convinced that there really is an excess of crime among poor people, have gone on to try to explain it. Probably the most influential sociologist doing work along these lines is Robert K. Merton, who developed what is often called strain theory.[23] Crime, according to this theory, is produced by the strain in societies that (1) tell people that wealth is available to all but also (2) restrict people's access to the means for achieving wealth. In societies where citizens are content with their lot, they do not experience such frustration. And of course, if all people "made it" in societies stressing ambition and upward mobility, there would not be much frustration either. Societies with high crime rates,

Merton said, are those that tell all people they can achieve but in fact block achievement by some people. Because poor people in such societies cannot legally obtain the things they are taught to desire, they are likely to try to reach their goals in some other way — by breaking the law. This produces a high crime rate among lower-class people.

Not all sociologists agree that lower-class people are unhappy and discontented with their lot in life. Walter B. Miller, for example, holds that American lower-class culture is distinctively different from middle-class culture and that it is much more conducive to crime.[24] Miller argues that lower-class behavior patterns might have originated in a process similar to the one described by Merton, but that strain and frustration are not the causes of the high rates of crime among the lower classes. He notes that lower-class culture is organized around six central values — trouble, toughness, smartness, excitement, fate, and autonomy — and he argues that it is allegiance to these values that produces delinquency.

Much social-psychological research has supported Miller's conclusion that criminal behavior is learned in a process of association with people who hold values that lead to trouble with the law. Indeed, a major theory of crime causation, differential association, proposes that people become delinquents or criminals when they have experienced an excess of such associations.[25] Briefly put, this theory — developed by Edwin H. Sutherland — says that people become criminals because they are exposed to more attitudes and definitions that are favorable to a certain kind of crime than attitudes and definitions that are opposed to it. Thus, a person may come into contact with an excess of behavior patterns favorable, say, to shoplifting, but an excess of behavior patterns unfavorable to burglary or robbery. However, all associations and personal contacts do not have the same influence. The longer, the more frequent, the more intense, and the more important an association is to a person, the stronger its influence. Most criminal behavior, like most noncriminal behavior, is therefore learned in intimate personal groups and not from impersonal sources such as movies and television.

A powerful source of behavior patterns favorable to crime is deviant subcultures. Some groups have developed their own perspectives, attitudes, and values, which support criminal activity. The more a boy becomes involved with members of such a deviant subculture, the more likely he is to be influenced by their opinions and join in their criminal activity. Miller considers the entire lower-class subculture to be deviant in the sense that any boy growing up in it will almost automatically violate the law. The drug subculture and the subculture of juvenile-gang members also have distinctive perspectives on the world, and both reject at least parts of the conventional morality embodied in law. For a lower-class boy who is a drug addict and a member of a juvenile gang, crime of one kind or another is almost automatic. He does not have to "choose" whether or not to commit a crime. His associations make the selection for him.

The theory of differential association is one of the most widely accepted sociological theories about crime causation, but it is far from perfect. For one thing, it is stated in quite general terms and therefore is very hard to test. The theory implies that an observer can simply add up the number of an individual's associations that favor crime, compare them to the associations that are opposed to crime, and decide whether or not that individual will become a criminal. In practice, that is impossible. Another criticism focuses on opportunities to commit crime. For example, suppose there were two people with exactly the same ratio of associations favorable to shoplifting and unfavorable to shoplifting. One might live in a large city with large stores and thus have an opportunity to commit the crime easily and safely, while the other might live in a rural area, never have such an opportunity, and never become a criminal. The differential-association principle seems to be concerned only with people who have equal opportunities to commit a crime, but this point is not clear.

The differential-association theory is considered irrelevant by some sociologists, who believe that crime is normal and natural. If all people are "born bad" or automatically commit crimes for some other reason, it is not useful to ask why they commit crimes. It is more reasonable, according to this way of thought, to ask why people do not commit crimes. Control theorists ask this question, and they answer it by saying that non-criminals are controlled and constrained by society and thus are prevented from breaking the law.

Some control theorists emphasize the importance of the internal controls that society builds up in the individual through the process of socialization. They say that a strong conscience and sense of personal morality prevents most people from breaking the law. Others say that attachment to small social groups is what keeps people in line.[26] According to this idea, most people refrain from committing crimes because they fear disapproval and rejection by the people who are important to them. Still other control theorists have abandoned positivism and returned to a basic assumption of the classical school, namely, that people do not commit crimes because they are afraid of arrest and imprisonment.[27] These different versions of control theory are not mutually exclusive. In fact, the most convincing form of control theory sees all three types of control working simultaneously.

Critics point out that control theory, like the theory of differential association, is extremely broad and virtually impossible to prove or disprove. The critics have passed particularly harsh judgment on control theory's assumption that people "naturally" commit crimes. Like the religious idea that human beings are evil by nature, it is an assumption that is almost impossible to study scientifically.

Labeling theorists, like differential-association theorists, argue that criminals learn to be criminals. As the name suggests, labeling theory is concerned with the process of branding people as criminals and with the effects of such labeling on the individual. Contrary to popular opinion and control theory, labeling theory holds that branding an individual as criminal often encourages rather than discourages criminal behavior.

For example, take the case of an adolescent boy whose "play" includes breaking windows, climbing over roofs, and stealing hubcaps. While he looks at such activities as akin to the "fun" of Halloween, to most adults his behavior is delinquent and must be curtailed. Law enforcement personnel, school officials, and his parents demand that he give up his "delinquent" activities. As he continues these activities, there is a shift away from the definition of the *acts* as delinquent to the definition of the *boy* as delinquent. The boy, of course, realizes that he is being branded as "bad" and draws closer to others who share in his "play" activities and are experiencing similar problems. Once the community is convinced that the boy is a delinquent, he is singled out for special treatment. He is threatened, punished, counseled, tested, analyzed, supervised, perhaps committed to an institution. He acquires a "record" with the police and other agencies. As the community copes with him, it crystallizes its conception of him and his conception of himself. He defines himself as he is defined, as a "delinquent" — by this time an "incorrigible" one committed to a long-term criminal career.

Labeling theory has not been as widely accepted as the differential-association or control theories. Its principal defect is its inability to explain why people commit the acts that get them labeled in the first place. It is not enough to say that "everyone breaks the law," even though that is probably true. The challenge is explaining why they do so. Another problem arises because labeling sometimes discourages delinquency and crime. Many people who are arrested and labeled as criminals are so shocked and ashamed that they never repeat the behavior that got them into trouble.

TYPES OF CRIMES

There are so many different criminal laws that it would take a massive book to describe them all. Criminal laws vary tremendously from place to place, and hundreds of new criminal laws are passed, changed, or repealed every year. Crime, then, is a rather diffuse hodgepodge of different kinds of behavior. Much effort has gone into attempts to make sense of this mess, mostly in the form of efforts to classify crimes.

In the English criminal-law system, which is used in the United States, Canada, and other former colonies, crimes are classified with respect to their seriousness, as felonies or misdemeanors. The more serious offenses are called **felonies** and are usually punishable by death or by confinement in a central prison; the less serious ones are called misdemeanors and are usually punishable by confinement in a local jail or by fines. As a sociological classification this is not very useful, and it is difficult to make a clear-cut distinction between these classes of crimes. Many crimes classified as felonies in one state or province are classified as misdemeanors in another. Moreover, the public does not always agree that some of the offenses that are legally classified as misdemeanors are really less serious than other offenses that are classified as felonies. For example, one survey found that Americans rated selling marijuana (often handled as a misdemeanor) as more serious than "killing spouse's lover after catching them," and using heroin was more strongly condemned than killing someone in a barroom brawl.[28]

The early Dutch criminologist Wilhelm Bonger classified crimes by the motives of offenders, as economic crimes, sexual crimes, political crimes, and miscellaneous crimes (with vengeance as the principal motive).[29] Many similar classifications have also been tried. But no crime can be reduced to a single motive. Robbing a bank, for example, may be motivated by a desire for vengeance, a desire for money, and a desire for political change, all at the same time. Classification according to motives is clearly inadequate.

Crimes are usually classified for statistical purposes as crimes against persons (violence), crimes against property, and crimes against public decency and order. The official statistics compiled by the FBI are classified in this way. Seven offenses are called "index crimes" or "major crimes." This category includes four violent crimes—murder, forcible rape, robbery, and aggravated assault—all of which involve the use of force or the threat of force. It also includes three property crimes—burglary, larceny-theft and automobile theft—all of which involve stealing something belonging to another. Less serious versions of these crimes are also classified as crimes against persons or crimes against property. Examples are minor assaults, arson, fraud, and sex offenses other than rape or prostitution. But the great majority of all offenses fall into the third category—crimes against public decency and order. These include prostitution, vandalism, gambling, drug offenses, drunkenness, and vagrancy.

Of all the arrests made and reported to the FBI in 1975 (excluding arrests for traffic violations), only about one-fourth were for the so-called "major" crimes.[30] Homicide arrests accounted for 0.2 percent, rape for 0.3 percent, robbery for 1.6 percent, aggravated assault for 2.5 percent, burglary for 5.6 percent, larceny for 12.0 percent, and automobile theft for 1.5 percent, for a total of 23.7 percent of all arrests. The four violent crimes accounted for only 4.6 percent of all arrests. By way of contrast, about 40 percent of all 1975 arrests were for only four of the many "public-order" crimes—drunkenness (14.7%), driving under the influence (11.3%), narcotics (6.3%), and disorderly conduct (7.9%).

Classifications of crimes for theoretical or educational purposes do not necessarily follow the schemes used for statistical purposes. Various types of crime are lumped together in ways designed to focus attention on some particular part of the total crime problem. Violent crime is one of these, and in the next chapter we will show that this category includes offenses ranging from teenage fist fights to cold-blooded murder. Other categories that shed light on the nature and extent of contemporary crime are victimless crimes, youth crimes, and white-collar crimes. The first of these categories calls attention to the fact that some offenses cause neither financial nor physical harm to any particular person other than the offender. The second notes that the majority of crimes are committed by youngsters. And the third helps make apparent the fact that crimes committed by respectable people with high social status are at least as serious as the "street crimes" committed by working-class people.

Crimes Without Victims

Crime usually involves a victim who suffers either financial or physical harm at the hands of one or more offenders. But there are a substantial number of crimes in which there is no clear-cut victim. Lawmakers have made it a crime to do certain things, even if those things do not cause harm to innocent people. The use of illegal drugs, gambling, prostitution, and homosexuality, for example, have been called victimless crimes because the harm, if any, is not suffered by anyone except the offender.

Enforcing the laws against such acts is a tremendous burden for police departments and other criminal-justice agencies. According to official statistics, almost half of all arrests in the United States are for victimless crimes. Some people argue that these arrests are taking valuable resources away from the effort to control more serious offenses. Moreover, the very fact that a crime is victimless means that few citizens call the police to complain about it. For example, the customers of prostitutes and bookmakers (takers of illegal bets on horse races and athletic events) do not report the activities of these criminals. If police officers are to make arrests for such offenses, they must seek them out on their own. In doing so they often use the services of spies and informers. Such secret police operations pose a potential threat to the civil liberties of all citizens, not just those who have committed a crime. Further, there are substantial

---

NINETEENTH CENTURY SOCIAL PROBLEMS

Victoria Hanna, a middle aged woman of Kaukauna, Outagamie County, was bound over to Commissioner Bloodgood the other day in the sum of $500 on the charge of sending obscene matter through the mails. The woman had a spite against a neighbor and mailed her a letter of the filthiest description.
May 14, 1886

portions of the population who do not think that such things as smoking marijuana and gambling are wrong, so laws against them create hostility and disrespect for the legal system. Finally, prohibition of victimless crimes often fosters the growth of deviant subcultures that may in time encourage crimes other than victimless ones.

If these laws create so many problems, why are they not abolished? The answer, of course, is that a majority or a powerful minority of the people feel that the outlawed things are wrong. They use the law enforcement machinery in an effort to reduce the incidence of what they see as sin. However, in large, complex societies, and even in some small ones, not everyone agrees on what is sinful and what is not.

Juvenile Delinquency

The difference between crime and juvenile delinquency is not simply a matter of age. It is true that adults who violate criminal laws are called criminals while juveniles who do the same things are called delinquents. But this is only part of the story. The fact is that a substantial portion of all juvenile delinquents have never even been accused of doing anything that would be against the law if they were adults. Runaways, truants, violators of curfew laws, and youngsters who get drunk, for example, are delinquents only because they have broken laws pertaining to the behavior of juveniles. Further, criminal laws must try to present clear definitions of the acts they outlaw, but juvenile codes define delinquency in vague terms. Indeed, many state codes define a delinquent child but do not define specific delinquent acts. For example, youngsters who are "incorrigible" and those who are in danger of leading an "immoral life" are often defined as delinquents. But such terms as *incorrigible, habitual,* and *immoral* are not defined clearly. The vagueness of juvenile codes gives police officers and other state officials broad power to decide what kind of behavior is delinquent and what is not.

It is no accident that juvenile courts have jurisdiction over juveniles who are considered to be in need of supervision as well as those who are accused of theft, robbery, assault, and other crimes. Juvenile-court procedures were established to *help* juveniles, whether they have committed harmful acts or not. It followed logically that neglected children as well as young criminals should be called delinquents. Doing so was a way of initiating a program to help them. Precise definitions were not needed, the argument went, because the court was to be a welfare agency. For example, deciding whether a youth had or had not stolen something — in imitation of the criminal courts — was not to be the business of juvenile courts. Instead, the judge was to decide what help should be given to juveniles whose thefts suggested that they needed help, just as the judge was to decide what help should be given to an orphan or a neglected child.

Platt has shown that the concept of delinquency was created in the latter part of the nineteenth century by middle-class reformers whom he

The juvenile courts were created to help juveniles in trouble and were given broad powers. There has been increasing concern about the violation of civil liberties. As a result, juvenile courts are becoming more and more like the criminal courts.

calls "child savers."[31] Despite the good intentions of the child savers, Platt argues, their efforts resulted in increasing governmental controls over youthful behavior which did not violate the criminal law but did violate middle-class standards of behavior. In the 1960s civil libertarians began voicing strong objections to the basic idea of juvenile court. They noted that juveniles were in fact being stigmatized and punished by the juvenile-justice process, not helped or treated. The Supreme Court consistently held that broad definitions of delinquency and the absence of criminal-law procedures violate the constitutional rights of juveniles.[32] Now juvenile courts are rapidly coming to resemble criminal courts. For instance, California has taken running away, incorrigibility, and other so-called "status offenses" (juvenile offenses that do not violate the criminal law) out of the jurisdiction of the juvenile courts; such conduct is no longer defined as delinquency. Juveniles in California and elsewhere are increasingly being prosecuted for their delinquencies in the same ways as adults are prosecuted for their crimes.

Juvenile delinquency—at least the acts of juveniles that would be crimes if committed by adults—probably has been studied more carefully than any other type of crime. The principal explanations of crime were developed from the study of delinquency as well as adult criminality, and all of them are used to explain delinquency as well as crime. Nevertheless, juveniles have special problems that make it improper to consider juvenile delinquents as nothing but small criminals. For one thing, the influence of the family is certainly greater in the lives of juvenile delinquents than in the lives of adult criminals. A number of studies show that children from homes in which one or both of the parents are criminals are much more likely to become delinquent. Discipline and training are also important. Many studies show that children from broken homes are more likely to become delinquents. However, some sociologists believe that the low income level of most single-parent families is more important than family disruption itself.[33]

Another unique problem of juvenile offenders is their youth. In traditional cultures people go directly from being a child to being an adult. But in industrialized nations there is an extended in-between period of "adolescence" in which difficult demands are placed on young people. Adolescents are not considered old enough for marriage and family responsibilities of their own, yet they are too old to remain dependent on their parents. In a sense they are between two worlds and part of neither.

Finally, the problem of juvenile gangs deserves mention. Adolescents all over the world form groups based on friendship and mutual interests. When these groups meet social approval they are called clubs, but when the community condemns them they are called gangs. Juvenile gangs of street-wise young "toughs" roam the streets of most urban slums and ghettos. The primary motivation of the "fighting gangs" is to control their "turf" (territory) and defend their honor, sometimes to the death. Some gangs have long histories, going back 30 or 40 years, and gang fights and killings have been a fact of life in some urban neighborhoods for generations.

White-Collar Crime

Sutherland invented the term white-collar crime in order to call attention to the weaknesses in theories that say crime is due to personal pathologies or poverty (such theories obviously cannot account for most criminal activities among the upper classes). He defined white-collar crime as any "crime committed by a person of respectability and high social status in the course of his occupation."[34] There are two basic types of white-collar crime—those committed *against* an organization and those committed *for* an organization. For instance, when an employee embezzles money from a bank the organization is clearly the victim. But when an executive falsely advertises that his company's mouthwash kills germs, a white-collar crime is committed on behalf of the organization. Some white-collar crimes, particularly price fixing and other violations of antitrust laws, are properly said to be committed by organizations themselves (corporations) rather than by individuals.

There are white-collar criminals in every type of occupation, from accounting to zoology, and in every type of organization, from the corner grocery store to huge government bureaucracies. Many of the victims of such criminals do not know they have been victimized and therefore do not complain to the police or anyone else. For this reason it is very difficult to figure out how much white-collar crime there really is.

Sutherland believed that the financial loss from white-collar crime is greater than the combined total of all other crimes put together. Considering the fact that a corporate crime such as price fixing can cost the public billions of dollars, Sutherland is probably right. But not all white-collar crime is committed just to make money. Government officials sometimes break the law in order to ensure their reelection or suppress their political opponents. When the FBI burglarized the offices of left-wing political organizations in the 1950s and 1960s, the objective was power, not money. The same thing can be said for the crimes of most of the participants in the Watergate burglary and cover-up. In many ways these sorts of white-collar crimes, which threaten the very foundations of our personal freedom, are more frightening than those committed merely for financial gain.

There is clearly a double standard when it comes to prosecuting crimes committed by the poor as compared with crimes committed by people with high social status. Virtually no police effort goes into the investigation of white-collar crime. Enforcement of criminal laws pertaining to offenses by high-status individuals is in the hands of the federal agencies that supposedly oversee various industries. Since the personnel of these agencies often do not consider themselves law enforcement officers, all they usually do when they uncover a crime is tell the company involved to stop the activity and threaten to sue them if they do not. The few white-collar criminals who are prosecuted and convicted receive light punishments. Former Vice President Spiro Agnew was never sentenced to a single day in jail for such crimes as bribery and income tax evasion. President Nixon received a full pardon *before* he was even charged with any crime. The same pattern of special treatment extends to less famous white-collar criminals as well.

There are several reasons why white-collar criminals receive such lenient treatment. For one thing, they have high status and can afford the best legal defense available. More important, the laws themselves are generally written to favor high-status criminals, particularly those who commit crimes that benefit, rather than harm, their companies. Children are a favored group in our society, and special juvenile-delinquency laws and procedures have been developed to deal with their offenses. By the same token, special laws and procedures have been developed to deal with the crimes of businesspeople, another favored group. Finally, the thousands of victims of white-collar crimes like false advertising and price fixing lose only a few dollars each, so there is less public resentment than there is when a criminal strikes directly at a few individual victims.

DEALING WITH CRIMINALS

The criminal-justice process reflects a conflict between two very different social goals. On the one hand, there is the need to stop crime and rid society of troublemakers. On the other hand, there is the need to protect, preserve, and nourish the rights and liberties of individuals. All societies pit these two needs against each other. Some are police states, in which the methods of crime control bulldoze citizens into submission. At the other extreme is chaos, in which individuals run wild. Democratic societies take a middle ground, tempering the need to repress crime with concern for the rights of their citizens.

But even in democratic societies few people agree on what the proper balance should be. Some North Americans favor what Packer called the crime control model of criminal justice, a program for the speedy arrest and punishment of all who commit crimes. Others advocate a due-process model, a program that softens the speedy rush to punishment with concern for human rights and dignity.[35] Speaking generally, those who fear official abuse of power favor the due-process model, while those who are more afraid of crime advocate the crime control model. But the matter is not so simple. The person who supports one model today may support the other tomorrow, depending on the merits of specific cases. For example, parents might cry for the crime control model when their daughter is raped but scream for the due-process model when their son is arrested for selling heroin to a police informer.

The matter is further complicated by the fact that criminal law itself stresses crime control while the legal rules for the administration of justice emphasize the rights of the accused to due process of law. Every criminal statute calls for strict control of criminal behavior. Each says, specifically, that whoever behaves in a certain way must be punished in a certain way. Each is thus a command issued by lawmakers to all who are paid to process suspects, defendants, and criminals. These officials are ordered to punish criminals. Legislators assume that punishment will hurt criminals so much that they will be afraid to repeat their crimes.

But other laws soften this harsh crime control procedure. They do so mostly by (1) specifying rules about arrests, court processes, and the conditions of imprisonment and (2) authorizing criminal-justice workers to adjust punishments to the circumstances of each offense and the background of each offender.

Thus, for example, the crime control model is softened by laws saying that police looking for evidence of crime cannot break into houses, that courts must give accused individuals an opportunity to cross-examine their accusers, and that punishments may not be cruel or unusual. This model is also softened by laws authorizing judges to suspend punishments and place offenders on probation and, more generally, by rules permitting officials to overlook some crimes in the name of justice. Police officers, prosecutors, judges, and others are allowed to "use their heads" and "play it by ear."

Policing

Police officers are on the cutting edge of the criminal-justice process. They are much more visible than other criminal-justice personnel, and they have more contacts with the citizenry. They have become the symbols of the whole system of justice. The kind of job they do therefore

Police officers spend more time providing public services than enforcing the law.

has an enormous influence on public confidence in the institutions of government.

In addition to their symbolic importance, police officers are the gatekeepers for the other criminal-justice agencies. They cannot possibly arrest all suspected lawbreakers. In the first place, considerations of cost and due process limit the number of officers. Police chiefs cannot put an officer at every citizen's elbow. In the second place, if the existing police force arrested all criminal suspects there would not be enough courts to process them or enough jails to house the guilty. In the third place, it is not always easy to tell whether a violation of law has in fact taken place. Criminal laws are written in general terms to cover a wide variety of behaviors, and police officers must decide whether they fit the case at hand. For example, statutes outlaw "assaults" but do not outlaw "scuffles," and officers are hard put to decide which is which. In the fourth place, police officers may not arrest a person on mere suspicion. An arrest is not legal unless the facts suggest that there is good reason to believe that the arrested person has committed a crime.

All in all, then, the work of police officers is highly discretionary. The judgment of individual officers, in turn, determines how much business there will be for the criminal-justice agencies down the line.

Of equal importance to understanding police activities is the fact that only a small part of all the work done by a police department is directly concerned with fighting crime. For example, only 10–15 percent of the calls to a police department give officers an opportunity to perform law enforcement duties. Individual officers classify as "criminal" only about 15–20 percent of the incidents they handle on any given day. Outsiders who have observed police activities confirm the idea that the terms "peace officer" or even "social worker" describe the work of police personnel more adequately than "law enforcement officer." Petersen has summarized these observations as follows:

> A prominent theme in the literature dealing with the work behavior of the police stresses that the role of the uniformed patrol officer is not a strict legalistic one. The patrol officer is routinely involved in tasks that have little relation to police work in terms of controlling crime. His activities on the beat are often centered as much on assisting citizens as upon offenses; he is frequently called upon to perform a "supportive" function as well as an enforcement function. Existing research on the uniformed police officer in field situations indicates that more than half his time is spent as an amateur social worker assisting people in various ways. Moreover, several officers have suggested that the role of the uniformed patrol officer is not sharply defined and that the mixture of enforcement and service functions creates conflict and uncertainties for individual officers.[36]

Even when performing law enforcement duties, police officers are in a difficult position. They are expected to behave in terms of the crime control model, meaning that they are supposed to apprehend lawbreakers and maintain order. But they are also expected to perform according to the due-process model, strictly meeting all the legal requirements for proper police procedures. They are criticized for not catching enough criminals, but they also are criticized if they exceed their legal authority.

There is no clear-cut solution to this dilemma. No one wants to "handcuff the police," but most citizens recognize that personal freedoms perish when legal safeguards are ignored. In the long run police officers and citizens alike will be better off as a larger percentage of the population comes to realize that police officers operate more like diplomats than like soldiers engaged in a war on crime.

The Courts   After an arrest, it is the duty of police officers to promptly take the suspect to a lower-court magistrate (judge). If it is decided that the suspect must come back to the magistrate's court at a later date, the magistrate decides the conditions under which temporary release on bail can be granted.

People accused of minor offenses are either convicted or found not guilty when they return to the lower court. But those accused of serious crimes are first given a **preliminary hearing**. At this hearing the magistrate decides whether the evidence against the accused is sufficient to justify further legal proceedings. The preliminary hearing is wholly for the benefit of the suspect. Its purpose is not to determine whether the accused is innocent or guilty. It is to determine whether the state has enough evidence to justify further court proceedings. If the evidence against the accused is insufficient, the suspect is discharged. Otherwise the accused must await further proceedings by a higher court.

Under the American bail system the accused person puts up a sum of money as security to be forfeited if he or she does not show up for trial. In most places an accused person can pay a relatively small fee to a bail bondsman, who then provides the financial security (usually called a "bail bond") necessary for release. The amount of bail varies according to the offense. The usual bail for a person charged with burglary, for example, is about $5000. Bondsmen will provide a $5000 bond for about $100 or $150.

It is a well-known fact that the bail system discriminates against the poor. The amount of money required is usually determined by the charge against the suspect rather than the person's character and responsibility. Poor people who cannot raise enough money stay in jail, while the more affluent go free on bail. At least half of all American defendants are unable to make bail. They remain in jail awaiting trial, sometimes for months.

Felony cases that are not dismissed at the preliminary hearing move up to a trial court. Each defendant is informed of the charges and asked to plead guilty or not guilty. Defendants who plead guilty are sentenced; those who plead not guilty are scheduled for trial at a later date. However, recent statistics show that the trial plays a very small part in the criminal-justice process. About 85 percent of the people convicted in the U.S. district courts are convicted on pleas of guilty, 10 percent on the findings of a jury, and 5 percent on findings of a judge.[37] Overall, in the United States about 90 percent of all convictions are convictions on pleas of guilty.

The defendant does not always plead guilty to the original charges. A single act usually involves more than one crime. For example, a person who commits burglary also commits the lesser crimes of unlawful entry and trespassing. Similarly, a grand-theft charge automatically accuses the defendant of misdemeanor petty theft as well—it is impossible to steal a lot (grand) without also stealing a little (petty). In a process that has come to be called plea bargaining, many defendants make a deal with prosecutors to plead guilty if the charge is reduced. The state is thus saved the expense of a trial, and the defendant receives a punishment lighter than the one that could be imposed if he or she went ahead with a trial on the original charge and was found guilty.

Settling cases out of court in the plea bargaining process is much faster and cheaper than taking each case to trial. Moreover, the process provides for much greater flexibility than the trial process. It permits prosecutors and defense attorneys to soften laws that call for a penalty that seems too harsh in light of what the defendant actually did. Nevertheless, plea bargaining has recently come under a torrent of criticism. Civil libertarians complain that it takes justice behind closed doors, where violations of defendants' rights are hidden from judicial and public view. They also claim that the very existence of the negotiation process coerces defendants into pleading guilty—those who exercise their right to a trial and

**DEBATE
Will Sending
More Criminals
to Prison
Solve the Crime
Problem?**

PRO

The spread of crime and lawlessness threatens the very survival of our society. Yet the criminal-justice system is hamstrung by pointless rules and regulations and obsessed with safeguarding the rights of criminals. The result is that law-abiding citizens go unprotected. The maze of legal restrictions designed to control police behavior are so complex that a legal arrest practically requires the services of a lawyer. Criminals are commonly turned loose because of minor technical errors that are not related to their guilt or innocence. Even if they are brought to court, plea bargaining arrangements allow many dangerous felons to plead guilty to minor crimes. Convicted criminals are freed by judges or parole boards after serving little or no time in prison. This leniency permits thousands of criminals to remain free, threatening the lives and property of decent citizens.

Despite the claims of liberals, putting criminals in prison is an effective way of preventing crime. Criminals obviously cannot victimize the public when they are locked up, and therefore more criminals in prison means more safety on the streets. Fear of imprisonment is a powerful deterrent to crime. If criminals were given the tough punishment they deserve, more people would be afraid to break the law. But even if strict punishment failed to reduce crime, simple justice demands that the leniency in our criminal-justice system be ended. Law-abiding citizens are cheated when criminals go free. A crackdown on crime and lawlessness would make society better for everyone.

CON

A larger portion of the population of the United States is in prison than in any other democratic nation. The proposal to solve the crime problem by imprisoning even more people is foolish and misguided. Prison actually encourages more crime. To be locked up with hundreds of criminals is to enter a school for crime in which degrading and inhuman conditions generate bitterness and resentment. The inevitable result is more crime, as is shown by the high percentage of offenders who return to prison for a second, third, or fourth time. The answer to the crime problem will be found not in severe punishment of criminals but, rather, in changing the economic and social conditions that are the primary causes of criminal activity.

Even if filling up the prisons would reduce crime, a "get tough" policy poses an unacceptable threat to civil liberties. To catch more criminals, the constitutional safeguards that regulate the criminal-justice process would need to be removed. Under such a system no one would be safe from the prying eyes of the government. Police could stop people and search them without reasonable cause; they could enter homes, tap telephones, or investigate our private lives. Can we trust the government with such unbridled power? Watergate and other government scandals prove that the answer is no. Sooner or later this enormous power would be turned to political ends. The rights of all citizens—including criminals—must be protected. We cannot surrender our freedom to an oppressive state even if it promises to solve the crime problem.

This picture was taken at President Nixon's farewell address to his White House staff. Like most other white-collar criminals, Nixon was never prosecuted and never served a single day in jail, even though there was strong evidence that he committed a number of felonies.

Prevent Crime

Proposals for punishing criminals, increasing our defenses against criminal activities, and social intervention are all concerned with preventing crime. Crime is prevented when criminals are so terrorized that they reform or at least are afraid to commit crimes. Crime also is prevented when criminals are killed or kept behind bars, and when citizens lock up their valuables and themselves, thus frustrating others who would behave criminally. Crime is prevented when the personal and social relationships of criminals are improved or when the economic, political, and social organization that generates high crime rates is modified so that it no longer does so.

Of the three methods, intervention is, or could be, the most effective procedure. We have seen that crime is rooted in the economic, political, and social order. Most social scientists realize that it is foolish to leave this organization the way it is and then try to reduce crime by punishing criminals or defending against them. But punishment and defense are easier than carrying out some of the sweeping social changes that have been proposed—eliminating poverty, unemployment, and discrimination, for example. In the long run, however, genuine crime prevention—changing the conditions that cause crime—will be both cheaper and more effective.

Better knowledge about crime and criminals does not necessarily mean that crime will be eliminated. Nevertheless, valid knowledge must be the basis of all prevention policies and programs. In the short run, we can try to reduce crime through defensive and punitive measures. In the long run, however, crime must be controlled the way diseases have been controlled — by developing valid knowledge about its causes and then using that knowledge to eliminate those causes. To put it another way, the most practical program for preventing crime is one that concentrates on criminological theory.

SOCIOLOGICAL PERSPECTIVES on Crime and Delinquency

As noted earlier, the central thesis of the sociological school of criminology is this: Criminal behavior results from the same processes as other social behavior. Studies of the ways in which these processes create crime and delinquency have taken two principal forms. First, functionalists, conflict theorists, and others have tried to relate variations in crime rates to variations in social organization such as the distribution of wealth, income, and employment and to variations in population density and composition. Second, social psychologists have studied the processes by which people become delinquents and criminals. These studies are related to general studies of social learning, and they have used such principles as frustration–aggression, differential association, and reinforcement.

The Functionalist Perspective

Functionalists study crime rates rather than individual criminal behavior. They hold, generally, that a certain amount of crime is inevitable in any society because crime makes a contribution to social order. For instance, crime is said to promote the solidarity of the group, just as war does, by providing "common enemies" (in this case criminals). It is also argued that crime is functional because it provides an "escape valve" for the pressures arising from excessive conformity. But too much crime is dysfunctional. It is a sign of disorganization.

From the functionalist perspective the recent increases in the crime rate are a product of growing social disorganization. Society has been changing so rapidly in recent years that people have lost their sense of direction. The expectations of the poor have increased much more rapidly than their actual chances for advancement, and as a result some have turned to crime. The criminal-justice system is so disorganized that it is improper to call it a "system" at all. Unable to respond quickly enough to the rapid increase in crime, criminal-justice agencies have become increasingly disorganized and case backlogs have piled up.

Functionalists call for greater social integration. For example, they ask for more legitimate opportunities for the poor and minorities to fulfill their aspirations. They also ask that criminal-justice processes be reorganized so that more criminals will be handled more efficiently and more justly.

The Conflict Perspective

Conflict theorists know that both crime and the laws defining it are products of power struggles. They argue that a few powerful groups control

Although functionalists feel that crime performs some social functions, they see our high level of crime as a sign of social disorganization and as a major social problem.

the legislative process and that these groups outlaw behavior that threatens their interests. For example, laws outlawing vagrancy, trespassing, and theft are said to be designed to protect the interests of the wealthy from attacks by the poor, since it is obvious that the wealthy have more to lose from property crimes than the poor. Although laws prohibiting such things as murder and rape are not so clearly in the interests of a single social class, the poor and powerless are still much more likely to be arrested for such crimes.

Conflict theorists believe that crime will disappear only if class inequality and the exploitation of the weak by the powerful are eliminated. But since that is obviously a very distant goal, they often advocate more limited responses to the crime problem as well. For example, they ask that the state's criminal-justice processes treat the different classes and ethnic groups more equally. Thus, they ask that more attention be given to white-collar crimes, support bail reform and programs for providing better defense lawyers for the poor, and call for elimination of class and ethnic discrimination by police officers and correctional workers.

The Social-Psychological Perspective

Most social psychologists regard criminal behavior as a product of primary-group interaction. As we have seen, however, they have developed different theories about the specific kinds of interactions that produce crime. Personality theorists focus on the personal traits and characteristics that encourage criminality and the family environments that promote the development of such characteristics. Behaviorists argue that people commit crimes because they are rewarded for doing so. A bank robber is rewarded with money, a rapist with sexual gratification, and so on. Interactionists believe that people commit crimes because they learn attitudes and motivations that are favorable to crime. A boy who associates with other boys who believe that stealing is an exciting experience is likely to adopt that attitude and start to steal.

The social-psychological perspective clearly helps us understand why one 18-year-old ends up in prison while another ends up in college. But the conditions producing criminal behavior are very hard to change. The government in a free society cannot intervene significantly in child-rearing practices and can hardly change the character of a person's associations. The social-psychological approach does have something practical to say about how to deal with criminals, however. For instance, it notes that punishment is not necessarily bad—if used sparingly and intelligently, it contributes to learning. Also, care should be taken to avoid the contagion of youngsters by confirmed criminals, as sometimes happens in prisons. Finally, offenders should be integrated into primary groups that strongly discourage criminal behavior. Ideally, this is the aim of good probation and parole programs. Social psychologists argue that the many programs that aim merely to keep tabs on probationers and parolees must be reorganized to meet this goal.

SUMMARY   A crime is a violation of the criminal law. However, it is not easy to apply this definition to actual behavior. Because of vagueness and ambiguities in statutes, unequal enforcement, and the sheer complexity of human behavior, "law in action" differs from "law on the books."

In recent years fear of crime has skyrocketed. At the same time, official criminal statistics have shown great increases in crime rates. There is reason to believe that fear of crime has increased more rapidly than crime itself. Official crime statistics are not to be trusted. It is to the advantage of law enforcement agencies to report an increasing crime rate. Politicians, too, can profit at election time by showing that crime is on the increase and calling for "law and order." Despite these statistical problems, it appears that crime has actually increased, although not as much as official records indicate.

Official arrest records and other crime statistics suggest that the crime rates for certain categories of people are higher than average. Males have higher rates than females and teenagers have higher rates than children or mature adults. Similarly, blacks, Latinos, Indians, and Chinese-Americans have higher-than-average rates, as do lower-class people and urban dwellers as compared with rural residents. There are problems with these data because the police expect people with such characteristics to be criminals and therefore watch them more closely. Nevertheless, such differences cannot readily be "explained away" by looking at defects in crime statistics.

There are many different explanations of crime. Members of the classical school of criminology argue that people simply choose to commit crime because they think they have more to gain than to lose by breaking the law. Members of the positive school, on the other hand, see crime and criminality as products of natural causes and not free will. The biological theories of Lombroso are positivistic, holding that crime is caused by hereditary factors that are independent of an individual's circumstances or environment. Psychological theories are also based on an assumption of natural causation. Some psychologists and psychiatrists argue that crime is caused by personality defects such as emotional disturbances and psychopathic traits.

Sociological theories of crime focus on the idea that crime and criminality are produced by the same social processes that produce other behavior. Two important sociological theories address the higher crime rates among the poor. According to strain theory, crime rates will be high if people are told that wealth and prestige are available to all when in fact opportunities for achieving these things are limited. The other theory holds that a distinctive lower-class culture is the cause of crime among the poor because it emphasizes values that encourage criminal behavior.

Differential-association theory holds that criminal behavior is learned in primary groups just like any other kind of behavior. Control theory, on the other hand, holds that people commit crimes because society has failed to stop them either by instilling an internal sense of morality or by threatening severe punishment. Labeling theory argues that people who are stigmatized as delinquents or criminals are unintentionally encouraged to commit further crime.

Crimes have been classified in many ways. Legally, they are classified according to their seriousness, as felonies and misdemeanors. For statistical purposes, they are classified by the character of the victim, as crimes against persons, crimes against property, and crimes against public decency and order. Crimes may also be classified as violent crimes, victimless crimes, youth crimes, and white-collar crimes.

There are two general models of how the criminal-justice process should operate. The crime control model stresses the need to get rid of troublemakers and calls for speedy arrest and punishment of all who commit crimes. The due-process model, on the other hand, stresses the need to preserve civil liberties. It calls for softening the rush to punishment and for considering human rights and the rights of accused individuals.

Police officers have come to symbolize "the law." Yet only a small percentage of the work done by a police department is directly concerned with crime. When performing as law enforcement officials, the police are expected to use the crime control model (i.e., they should catch criminals), but they are also expected to use the due-process model (i.e., they should protect the rights of the accused).

After an arrest has been made, the suspect is taken before the magistrate of a lower court. The magistrate sets bail. Accused people who cannot raise the money for a bail bond are held in prison. Thus, the bail system discriminates against the poor.

Felony cases that are not dismissed in lower-court hearings move to a higher court. There most defendants plead guilty. Only about 10 percent exercise their right to a trial before a judge or a jury. Many of the guilty pleas are pleas to reduce charges. In a process called plea bargaining a more serious charge will be reduced to a less serious one if the suspect agrees to plead guilty.

In passing sentences, judges are expected to give equal punishments, but they also are expected to order different punishments for different people, depending on the circumstances of each case. There is considerable indignation about the inconsistencies in the sentences handed down by judges, and the trend is toward more fixed sentences.

For about a century there has been a distinct movement toward correctional programs for sentenced criminals. One popular reaction to crime is hostility and punishment. Another popular reaction is an attitude of inquiry, with methods of change based on an understanding of why the criminal broke the law. Probation and parole systems, and prison rehabilitation programs as well, grew out of the effort to understand and correct criminals rather than merely punishing them.

The most common proposal for solving the crime problem is increased punishment. The United States punishes its criminals more severely than other democratic nations. Nevertheless, many people are convinced that an even more severe program would frighten citizens so much that they would not commit crime and would frighten criminals so much that they would not repeat their offenses. Other proposals for dealing with the crime problem include general programs for diverting criminals out of criminal-justice agencies, eliminating ineffective and harmless laws, promoting equal justice, and preventing crime by changing the economic, political, and social conditions that produce it.

The central theme in sociological studies of crime is that criminal behavior results from the same processes as other social behavior. Functionalists study crime rates rather than individual criminal conduct. Their main theme is that our growing crime rate is but one symptom of increasing social disorganization. Conflict theorists also are more interested in criminal law and crime rates than in the behavior of criminals. They argue that many criminal laws are designed to protect the interests of the wealthy and that legal procedures discriminate against the poor and the powerless. Social psychologists study criminal behavior rather than crime rates. Their general thesis is that criminal behavior is a product of the individual's interaction in primary groups; however, different theories stress different types of interaction.

KEY TERMS

bail
control theory
crime
crime control model
deviant subculture
differential association
diversion program
due-process model
felony
general deterrence
juvenile delinquency
labeling theory

misdemeanor
parole
plea bargaining
preliminary hearing
probation
recidivism
rehabilitation
specific deterrence
strain theory
victimization survey
victimless crime
white-collar crime

15
Personal Violence

How much violence is there?
Is violent behavior learned?
Do TV programs promote violence?
Would gun control reduce violence?

From teenage fist fights to coldblooded murder, violence is a perennial problem. Every day television, radio, and newspaper reporters tell us new horror stories. We are informed that rape, child abuse, and wife beating are on the rise. Old people are afraid to unlock their doors, and the fear of violent criminals haunts our cities and suburbs. To make matters worse, fictional violence has become the mainstay of movies and television. We are, it seems, obsessed with violence.

Presidential commissions have studied and denounced violence. So have garden societies, PTAs, and scientists. But an effective program to deal with violence has yet to be invented. When state or federal restrictions on the instruments of violence are proposed—gun control, for example—the opposition is enormous. The crux of the matter is that we like violence. We denounce and condemn it, but we are still fascinated by it. Our heroes solve their problems with blazing pistols, and acts of violence are seen as proof of manhood. Violent men are cool, sexy, and desirable. With the passage of time, frontier hoodlums like Jesse James, Davy Crockett, and Daniel Boone have become gentle Robin Hoods, shining examples of honor and dignity. The young boy who won't fight is a sissy. The man who won't fight is a coward.

This is not to say that people admire acts of wanton aggression. Only violence that is "right" is approved. But "good" acts of violence lead inevitably to "bad" acts of violence, as histories of countless dictatorships have shown.

THE NATURE OF VIOLENCE

Violence is a common enough term, and we all think we know what we are talking about when we use it. But violence is much more complex than it appears at first glance. **Violence** may be defined as behavior intended to cause bodily pain or injury to another person, but this definition can be misleading. Most people who use it are thinking only about acts that they do not like. When a criminal knocks down an old lady, it is clearly an act of violence. When a police officer knocks down a criminal, it is necessary force. Because the two acts are equally violent, the real distinction is between legitimate and illegitimate violence. Illegitimate violence is what people have in mind when they speak of "the violence problem." The catch is that there is no clear-cut distinction between legitimate and illegitimate mayhem. One person's self-defense is another person's aggression. One person's spanking is another person's child abuse.

When most people think about violence, they think about murders, stabbings, and beatings. There is nothing wrong with this view. Interpersonal violence is a serious problem. But an equally important kind of violence is collective. Riots and warfare—to be discussed in Chapter 16—are examples of collective violence. Individual violence and collective violence have different causes and therefore require different explanations and a different social response. Despite outward appearances, there is little similarity between a wife who murders her husband in a fit of anger and a terrorist who cooly assassinates a political leader.

Illegitimate violence is against the law, so it may properly be called violent crime. Only a small percentage of all crime is violent, but it is this kind of crime that worries the public most. A nationwide survey found that half of all American women and one out of five men said they were afraid to walk outdoors at night, even near their homes.[1] It seems that an atmosphere of fear hangs over many American cities like a suffocating fog.

There are four major violent crimes: murder, assault, forcible rape, and robbery. Murder is the unlawful killing of a human being with what lawyers call "malice aforethought." Thus, killing a war enemy is not murder. Neither is killing in self-defense. Murder is not the same as homicide, which is the killing of any human creature. Homicide is not necessarily a crime. It is an essential ingredient in the crimes of murder and manslaughter (the unlawful killing of another person without malice, as in a sudden quarrel or in a reckless action). But there are many cases in which homicide is committed without criminal intent. Examples are killing in time of war, in lawful execution of a judicial sentence, in self-defense, or as the only possible means of arresting an escaping felon. Homicides are classified as "justifiable," "excusable," and "felonious." Only the last of these is murder or manslaughter.

An assault occurs when one person attacks another with the intention of hurting or killing the victim. There is often little difference between murders and assaults. The fact that an armed attack took place near a hospital may spell the difference between one crime and the other. Some assaults do not involve deadly force, however. A punch in the belly is an assault. So is a slap in the face. But the essence of assault is the intention to do harm. If your professor raises his fist at you in a menacing manner, you have been assaulted. You also are assaulted by anyone who takes a swing at you and misses. "Aggravated assault" is one committed with the intention of committing some additional crime, or one that is peculiarly outrageous or atrocious, as when a deadly weapon is used. Child abuse and wife beating are special kinds of assault.

Forcible rape is sexual intercourse forced upon a person against his or her will with the use or threat of force. Most victims of forcible rape are women, but homosexual rape of men is common in prisons and not unknown on the outside. Some cases of so-called rape are not rape at all. Thus, statutory rape does not involve force or the threat of force. It is sexual intercource with a female below the legally defined "age of consent" (usually 16 to 18 years). California and other states now accurately define this crime as "unlawful sexual intercourse" rather than "statutory rape." Some states continue to call the offense "statutory rape," and it is for this reason that the violent crime is called *forcible* rape.

Robbery is the taking of someone's property by force or threat of force. Some robberies are more like theft or burglary (breaking and entering with intent to commit a serious crime) than violent crimes such as murder, assault, or rape. If a crook sneaks into your room at night and takes your billfold or purse, that is burglary. If you wake up and the crook takes your money after yelling "Keep quiet or I'll kill you," the crime is robbery. In most robberies a threat of force is enough. A masked bandit yelling "Give me the money or I'll blow your head off" is enough to intimidate most people; the robber does not even have to show a gun.

Reports from wealthy democratic countries all over the world show an alarming rise in violent crime. However, criminologists believe these figures are exaggerated by police and news media to promote their own interests. Strong support for this belief comes from the U.S. Census Bureau, which conducted broad based victimization surveys in 1973 and 1974. The conclusion was that "violent crimes — robbery, rape, and assault — showed no significant change in victimization rates from 1973 to 1974."[2] FBI statistics, however, reported an 11.3 percent increase in violent crime for the same period. Although the evidence is far from conclusive, victimization studies cast grave doubt on the almost universal belief that we are in the midst of a serious wave of violent crime.

Differences in methods of assembling criminal statistics make international comparisons risky. It appears, however, that there are wide differences in the amount of violence from one culture to the next. The best indicators of these differences are murder rates, which are highest in the poor "third world" countries, particularly in Central America. But when compared to other industrialized nations, the United States has an extremely high murder rate. It is over three times higher than the rate in Canada, which has a somewhat higher murder rate than such countries as Japan, Hungary, and West Germany. In the words of the National Commission on the Causes and Prevention of Violence, "The United States is the clear leader among modern, stable democratic nations in its rates of homicide, assault, rape, and robbery, and it is at least among the highest in incidence of group violence and assassination."[3]

Newspaper and television reports focus on dramatic and sensational crimes such as mass murders, gang fights among juveniles, and brutal

---

NINETEENTH CENTURY SOCIAL PROBLEMS

Mr. Axel, a farmer living about 6 miles east of Kiel, Manitowoc County, cut his wife's throat a few days ago so that she might not recover and then killed himself. There were various rumors as to the cause of the tragedy such as domestic infelicity etc., but a few who had dealings with Axel of late attributed the act to an aberration of mind.

May 14, 1886

rapes. But this press coverage confuses and misleads the public. The fact is that very few people are attacked or killed by demented strangers. The risk of being assaulted or raped while merely walking down the street has also been exaggerated. Over half of all assaults and murders occur in homes or other indoor locations such as taverns and bars,[4] and two-thirds to three-fourths of these crimes occur among relatives, friends, or acquaintances. Indeed, the closeness of the relationship may add to the violence of the attack when someone feels betrayed or insulted. As we pointed out in Chapter 5, beatings, slashings, stabbings, chokings, and shootings are common in many homes. The full extent of husband–wife violence is not known, but it probably is the most common form of violence in North America. Violence is often a result of attempts by a husband to dominate and control his wife. Shooting of a spouse is a common kind of murder, to which both men and women fall victim.

Wolfgang's classic study of murder in Philadelphia found that only 15 percent of the 550 murders studied occurred between strangers; almost 60 percent occurred between relatives or close friends.[5] Studies in Denmark, Italy, England, India, and Canada have arrived at similar conclusions.[6] Studies of assault also show a close relationship between victim and attacker, although it is not as close as in the case of murder. In short, the chances of being assaulted or killed depend much more on one's relationships with relatives and friends than on the whims of some predatory stranger.

The pattern of victimization in robbery is different. Most robberies are quests for financial gain. In over 80 percent of the cases, the victim and the attacker are strangers. Although the stereotyped image is that of a masked bandit holding up a bank or liquor store, most robberies occur on the street.

Forcible rape has some similarities to robbery on the one hand and to assault and murder on the other. The crime rarely is a conflict between close associates, but about half of all rape victims know their attackers. Rape victims are often attacked after a brief acquaintance with someone they met at a party or in a bar.

A disproportionate number of violent crimes are committed by young, urban, poor, black males. The victims generally have the same characteristics as the offenders. Thus, victimization rates are highest for males, blacks, poor people, and youths. While there is evidence that a disproportionate number of robbery victims are elderly, that is not true for other violent crimes. Robbery also has a high interracial character. That is, about 45 percent of all robberies involve blacks robbing whites—very often young black males robbing somewhat older white males. However, in the other violent crimes attackers and victims are usually from the same ethnic and social background.

EXPLAINING INTERPERSONAL VIOLENCE

Violence has been blamed on everything from human instincts to television. The theories are similar to those used to explain all crime—nonviolent as well as violent. But theories of violence are not restricted to illegitimate violence. They are concerned with making sense of this widespread human behavior, whether it is socially accepted or condemned.

Biological Theories

For centuries people have located the causes of violence in human instinct. Recently investigators like Konrad Lorenz and Robert Ardrey have once again popularized the notion that human beings, like other animals, have a built-in aggressive instinct.[7] According to this theory, we need only look at our genes to explain violent behavior. Ardrey, for example, argues that humans have an innate drive to conquer and control territory and that this drive is the root of our inhumanity to each other.

Behind such theories is an idea about evolution. It is said that the animals (including humans) that were most likely to survive through the years were the aggressive ones. The instinctively aggressive animals survived and reproduced while the less aggressive ones died off. Lorenz maintains that violence and aggression are useful to survival. They spread the members of a species out over a territory, thus helping to even out food supplies. They help establish a system of dominance among individual animals, thus giving structure and stability to groups. And, Lorenz holds, aggression helps ensure that the stronger males will mate with more females than the weaker males, thereby spreading superior genes.

Criticism of these instinctual theories has taken three principal forms. First, as Boelkins and Heiser point out, aggression and violence are not necessarily the same thing. Aggressive behavior may give an animal a selective advantage, but violent behavior often has the opposite effect.[8] Second, the fact that many animals appear to have aggressive or territorial instincts hardly proves that humans have them. It has repeatedly been shown that human behavior is far less instinctive than the behavior of other animals. Third, it is argued that if human beings have an aggressive instinct, all people would be violent and aggressive, but that is not the case. On the contrary, the people reared in some cultures show very little violence or aggression by our standards.[9] In sum, the instinct theory of violence is built on flimsy foundations. There is no firm evidence that an aggressive instinct provides a selective advantage for humans or that humans actually have such an instinct.

It is widely acknowledged that males are more violent and aggressive than females.[10] Some biologically oriented researchers account for this difference by theorizing that male sex hormones cause aggressive behavior. However, other researchers play down the importance of sex hormones in aggression and doubt that they have much influence on human violence. A more persuasive biological explanation of sex differences in violence argues that the important variable is the male's size and strength. Males, being stronger than females, are more effective in combat and therefore are more likely to resort to violent aggressive behavior. However, differences in socialization practices between boys and girls are probably much more important than biological differences per se. (See Chapter 10.)

Psychological Theories

Sigmund Freud, perhaps the most influential psychologist of our time, painted a very bleak picture of human nature. He saw human beings as foul creatures filled with violence, hostility, and aggression. We are, he said, engaged in a continuing struggle with our natural impulse to do evil and are barely held in check by the forces of civilization.

Psychologists of the Freudian school accept the biological idea that humans naturally have strong aggressive instincts. For them, the question is not why some people are violent; it is why most people are not. Their answer is that most people, while still children, develop a *superego* (conscience) that inhibits their destructive impulses and stops them from committing violent aggressive acts. People who do not develop normal healthy superegos cannot stop their destructive impulses. For example, it is said that the average man wants to have sexual relations with every woman he sees, with or without the woman's consent. However, the superegos of most men block these impulses, often so thoroughly that they are not even aware of them. From this perspective a rapist is simply a man with a weak superego who cannot block his natural impulses.

Freudian theories have been declining in popularity among psychologists for at least thirty years. All the criticisms of biological instinct theories apply equally well to the Freudian theories.

A more persuasive psychological theory holds that aggression and violence are caused by individual frustration. People become frustrated when they want something they can't have, and the stronger the blocked desire, the stronger the frustration. If an individual's level of frustration is high enough, the idea goes, it overcomes inhibitions, with the result that the frustrated person responds with aggression and often violence.[11] The frustrated person may lash out at the source of his or her frustration or, in the case of displaced hostility, at someone else. For example, a student who just flunked out of school might get into a fight with a roommate.

This frustration–aggression theory is one of the simplest and most popular explanations of violence, be it a family murder or a massive riot. However, like most social-science theories it has its problems. In the first place, frustration does not always produce aggression. All of us are frustrated to some degree, but only some of us are aggressive. Frustration may find an outlet in peaceful activities or may remain bottled up. In the second place, much aggression and violence seems to be unrelated to frustration. A professional killer does not have to be frustrated to carry out a job, and the same can be said of the mugger, the robber, and the soldier.

Sociological Theories

There are two principal types of sociological explanations of violence. One is *macro theory* (dealing with large groups), which sees violence as an indirect response to the social structure, whether because of the frustration of excessive social controls and inadequate opportunities or because of the chaos created by inadequate social control. The other is *micro theory* (dealing with individuals and small groups), which holds that violence is learned from other people.

Theories that blame violent behavior on the social structure are linked to the two psychological theories just discussed. The control theory used by some sociologists pictures violence as an innate human instinct that is expressed when society fails to keep tight enough restraints on its members. To control theorists, society's first line of defense is group norms that discourage violence. People who are not controlled by integrated families and other primary groups are controlled by police officers and fear of the law. When both of these controls fail, violent behavior is expressed. In many ways this theory is like Freudian theory. The difference is that violence is said to be controlled by society rather than by a mechanism within the individual. And like Freudian theory, control theory provides a reasonable explanation of why so few people are violent, but it does so by first assuming that people are naturally violent.

Sociologists also use the frustration–aggression theory on a macro level. They say that much of the frustration that leads to violence stems from the inequalities and injustices of society. They point to the statistics that show higher rates of violence in the inner-city slums and other ghet-

Sociological theories point out that children learn to be violent as they learn attitudes, values, and beliefs in the process of socialization.

tos, then argue that poverty and lack of opportunity in those areas are very frustrating to their residents. Slum dwellers want all the material goods that everyone else wants, but are unable to get them legitimately. As a result they become frustrated and lash out in bursts of violence. This social form of the frustration–aggression theory has the same weaknesses as the original. It provides a reasonable explanation for some violence but fails to explain the presence of violence among more affluent people and the lack of violence among many frustrated poor people.

Probably the most widely accepted contemporary theory is that people learn to be violent the same way they learn any other kind of behavior. The process of learning may take place in the family, in a subculture, or in an entire culture. Some individuals learn norms and values that define violence as a good thing in certain situations. Others learn a view of the world that makes violence appear to be the only way of getting what they want. Still others may learn from the experience of having been the victim of a violent attack.

There is considerable evidence that violence is learned at home. Many researchers have found that parents' attitudes toward violence are an important influence on the child. Although few parents consider violence a good thing, many consider it a necessary part of life—a behavior pattern that a child, particularly a boy, should learn. A survey conducted for the National Commission on the Causes and Prevention of Violence found that 70 percent of the respondents agreed with the statement. "When a boy is growing up it is important for him to have a few fist fights."[12] Other studies have shown that parental use of physical punishment, often

NINETEENTH CENTURY SOCIAL PROBLEMS

Lydia Berger, a 15 year old girl, is in jail having confessed to the crime of arson. Several days ago she left her home on a farm north of Milwaukee and went to town to go to . . . the carnival. . . . She was out late that night and the next day her father whipped her for staying away without his permission. She sought revenge by setting fire to the little cottage in which they lived. It was burned to the ground. A neighbor gave the family shelter and the next day the girl set fire to the house of their benefactor. Her mother ordered her to harness a team of horses which was temporarily quartered in a barn belonging to the Wisconsin Lake Ice Company. The girl went to the loft and set fire to the barn, which, with 64 tons of hay, was burned to the ground. The girl says she set fire to the places simply to have revenge on her father for whipping her.
July 19, 1898

inflicted to discourage violent behavior, is related to violent behavior in children.[13]

Children seem to learn more from the violent example set by their parents than from their nonviolent words. This is particularly true when parents go beyond the bounds of "normal" physical punishment and beat and abuse their children. Stuart Palmer compared murderers with their noncriminal brothers and found that the murderers were beaten by both their mothers and fathers more often than their brothers.[14] A number of studies also show that people who were abused as children are much more likely than others to become child abusers.[15] Moreover, as noted in Chapter 5, the usual indicators of social status—income, occupational prestige, and education—are all negatively related to child abuse. In other words, the lower the parents' social status, the more likely they are to abuse their children. It seems likely that some families pass child abuse along from one generation to the next much as they pass along speech patterns and other customs.

Sociologists have long known that attitudes toward violence differ greatly from one group to another within the same society. Wolfgang and Ferracuti presented considerable evidence along this line in their book *The Subculture of Violence*.[16] They show that in the United States there is a large subculture that has positive attitudes toward violence and that these attitudes encourage or even require violence in many circumstances. Members of this subculture admire the style of tough, aggressive masculinity, often known as machismo. Any personal slight—even the most trivial one—is seen as a direct insult, often requiring a violent reply. An accidental bump on the street or an unguarded glance that most people would hardly notice may trigger a physical attack. Wives have been severely beaten or even killed because their husbands felt insulted by a sniff or a laugh at the wrong time.

The most controversial aspect of Wolfgang and Ferracuti's work is their theory that this violent subculture is more common among minorities and the lower classes and is a principal cause of the higher crime rates for those groups. Critics argue that the poor and minorities place no higher value on violence than anyone else and that the *machismo* ideal is not typical of any single group in society. Further, they argue that people who act violently do not have any more positive attitudes toward violence than the average person but, rather, act the way they do because of the circumstances in which they find themselves.[17]

AMERICA: LAND OF THE VIOLENT?

As we have seen, the United States is clearly the most violent of all the Western democracies. American violence is often seen as a holdover from the rowdy days of frontier expansion. As an unending stream of settlers pushed westward in search of land and profit, violence became a way of life. The new Americans fought wars with Spain, England, Mexico. They practically exterminated the American Indians, and they fought among themselves. In the expansive stretches of the old West, points of law were settled with rifles, pistols, knives, and fists. Vigilante groups killed troublemakers.[18] Today movies and TV dramas still celebrate this violence.

Canada and Australia were also settled by "roughnecks," but the citizens of those countries apparently have not passed down a violent frontier tradition. Although America's violent past does not alone explain its extreme contemporary violence, the American frontier did have some unique characteristics that were not found in other areas:

> In Latin America, both the feudal values of Spain and Portugal and the difficult topography combined to blunt the frontier experience. Similarly, in Canada, the settlers of the Saint Lawrence River Valley carried prerevolutionary French cultural luggage, and the inhospitable Laurentian Shield (a range of mountains which formed a barrier to migration) deflected pioneers southward into the United States; when railroads opened the Canadian prairie provinces to British settlement in the late nineteenth century, the frontiersman came directly from the more traditional east and the process of settlement was not nearly as prolonged as was the American experience.[19]

Aside from its unique frontier tradition, America has other characteristics that seem to contribute to the violence of its people. The United States is much larger than the other Western democracies, and it contains a much broader spectrum of ethnic groups. Tensions and conflicts are to be expected in a nation with such a low level of social integration. Further, America is a wealthy nation but, compared with other Western countries, has less economic equality and inferior welfare and social programs for the poor. This condition also is a sign of low social integration and a weak sense of community.

**VIOLENCE AND
THE MASS MEDIA**

Experts disagree about the effect of television dramas on real-life violence, just as a generation ago they disagreed about the effects of movies,
radio, and comic books. These disagreements spurred an extensive study
recently published by the U.S. Surgeon General's Scientific Advisory
Committee on Television and Social Behavior.[20] The study was concerned with the characteristics of television programs and their audiences, and the potential impact of violent programs on the behavior of
viewers. But little attention was paid to criminal violence, and for that
reason the study did not settle the question of whether TV violence
causes real-life violence.

However, there is little disagreement about one of the Committee's
findings, namely, that television programs that are highly laced with violence have become part of the lives of most Americans and, for that matter, of most television viewers around the world. In the first place, the
menu offered by television features violence, including incidents of people
intentionally hurting each other. Between the ages of 5 and 14, the
average American child sees about 13,000 homicides on television. In the
second place, more and more people have ready access to television.
Youngsters 16 years of age have spent more time watching television than
they have spent in school or in any other activity except sleep. In the third
place, most people, especially poor people, consider television a believ-
able source of information about the world as it really is.

So there is no doubt that we are flooded with fictional violence. The
crucial question concerns its effects on our daily lives. In laboratory situations children imitate the violent models they are shown in special TV
programs. But laboratory studies are not necessary to show that children
impersonate television actors in play and that both children and adults imitate them in their everyday language and conduct. Among other things,
television teaches us ways of resolving interpersonal disputes, clashes,
and conflicts. It is possible that watching violence on television increases
the chances that viewers will regard it as a justifiable means of settling
disputes in everyday life. Violence is then used to resolve everyday
conflicts, as in child abuse and wife beating. Several studies have shown
that continued exposure to television violence is correlated with increased willingness to use violence, to suggest it as a solution to conflict,
and to perceive it as effective.[21]

Violent programs also seem to teach viewers that they are supposed to
"go berserk" in certain situations. Television stories show people responding to frustration with aggression—they strike out, smash, and even
kill in what looks like blind rage. They do not find or even discuss more
peaceful alternatives. The viewer learns that it is "natural" for people to
go berserk, and this increases the chances that viewers will go berserk
when frustrated or provoked. It is therefore reasonable to believe that
some of the people who go berserk in real life have *learned* that they are

supposed to act that way under certain circumstances. It also is likely that television dramas have increased the number of people who have been exposed to this message.

Television dramas may contribute to the rate of violence in an even more general way. TV creates the impression that violence is rather routine fare, so the viewing public may become indifferent to all but the most sensational crimes of violence. In this respect television dramas might have effects similar to those of sensationalistic coverage of crime in the newspapers and on radio and television. It is not so much that news stories and TV dramas describe crimes that then are imitated — as happened after the first airplane hijacking. Rather, it is that both news stories and TV dramas help create a blunting of indignation about violence, a kind of "tuning out" of real-life horrors. For instance, one study found that the physiological changes that go with emotional reactions to violence were diminished in a "high TV exposure" group of children as compared with a "low TV exposure" group.[22] A population for whom violent crime is routine has become desensitized to such crime and cannot present a consistent front against it.

It should not be concluded from these studies and observations that exposure to dramatizations of violence, even repeated exposure, will change given individuals from peaceful people into violent ones. It was shown long ago that what people see when they watch dramatizations varies with their socioeconomic, ethnic, religious, and cultural background.[23] Older studies also suggest that children living in areas where delinquency rates are high were more influenced by crime movies and radio crime dramas than those who lived in areas with low delinquency rates.[24] The same is probably true of the influence of violent television dramas.

More generally, not all experts agree that media violence has much effect on the real-life behavior of specific individuals. Some argue that children can easily distinguish between real life and the fantasies presented on television. Just because a television hero shoots someone or jumps out a ten-story window and flies away does not mean that the viewer will try to do so. In fact, some psychiatrists claim that media violence actually *reduces* real-life violence. They say that watching someone being hurt provides an outlet for the viewer's pent-up hostilities and aggressions, thus decreasing the need to let the hostility out in genuine violence. After making a comprehensive review of the literature regarding the effects of TV violence on individuals, Howitt and Cumberbatch summarized their results as follows: "Thus we conclude that, as far as is scientifically ascertained, violence in the mass media has no effect on violence in real life."[25] While this opinion is not shared by most criminologists, it does indicate the deep disagreements about this important issue. All in all, it seems reasonable to conclude that violent television dramas reinforce and support the idealization of violence and its acceptance as a "natural" part of human behavior. Its direct effects on specific individuals appear to be less significant.

FIREARMS AND VIOLENT CRIME

Americans like guns. No one knows exactly how many privately owned firearms there are in the United States, but the number is probably about 150 million.[26] Of these, one-fourth are handguns—weapons that are good for little else except target practice and killing people at close range. Guns are neither romantic nor repulsive to most Americans. They are simply a part of living, like automobiles and beer cans.

About 69 percent of all American murders are committed with firearms, as are about half of all Canadian murders.[27] To make matters worse, the total number of privately owned guns and their use in violent crime have both been increasing rapidly in recent years.[28] Gun-related homicide has become the leading cause of death among black males between the ages of 15 and 44—exceeding cancer and heart disease.

There is considerable debate about the impact of firearms on violent crime. Years ago Wolfgang argued that widespread possession of firearms has little impact on the total amount of murder.[29] His reasoning, which has been adopted by sportsmen and others, is that killers would simply substitute other weapons if guns were not available. There is considerable evidence on the other side, however. The fatality rate for attacks with a gun are four times higher than for attacks with a knife (the second most common weapon used in lethal attacks).[30] It appears that the difference between assault and murder often turns on the type of weapon involved. According to FBI figures, over two-thirds of all murders involve firearms, while guns are used in only one-quarter of all assaults. The family pistol is six times more likely to be used against a family member or an acquaintance than against a criminal intruder.

The general consensus is that a significant reduction in privately owned firearms would have little effect on the total number of personal attacks but would significantly reduce the number of deaths resulting from such attacks. However, there are those who believe that the number of attacks would decline as well. For one thing, an assault with a gun requires no physical strength and therefore gives the attacker a much wider number of potential victims. Perhaps more important, it takes only a split second to shoot a gun, while other types of assaults take longer and may provide time for second thoughts.

RESPONDING TO PROBLEMS OF VIOLENCE

Many different proposals for reducing violence have been made. Some of them, such as gun control, are fairly specific and limited, and therefore would be relatively easy to put into effect. At the other extreme are less practical, but no less important, proposals for sweeping changes in our entire social structure.

Firearms are more easily available in the United States than in any other democratic nation. Thousands of gun shops like the one shown in this picture dot the American landscape.

Gun Control

The United States has extremely loose and ineffective gun regulation. The laws vary enormously from one state to another, and the only consistent policy is that convicted felons are not allowed to own guns. And since guns are so easily available to everyone else, few felons would have any trouble getting a gun if they wanted one. In Canada all firearms must be registered, but control there is still rather loose compared to that in European countries.[31]

Despite the lack of effective legislation, Gallup polls starting as far back as 1959 have repeatedly shown that an overwhelming majority of Americans favor registration and other gun control measures.[32] Support for gun control is stronger in cities than in rural areas, but the polls show that a majority of the people in all major groups, including gun owners, favor better gun control. The major opposition consists of several organizations that are known collectively as "the gun lobby." These organizations represent sportsmen, civil libertarians, and firearms manufacturers who see their interests threatened by gun control. The desires of the people cannot seem to compete with well-financed and highly organized special-interest groups like the National Rifle Association.

Many different types of gun control programs have been proposed. None of them advocates a total ban on all firearms. Most center on the handgun or "Saturday night special," a weapon that is useless for anything except homicide. The National Commission on the Causes and Prevention of Violence recommended what seemed to be a modest control program. It asked for prohibition of the possession or ownership of handguns except by people who received a license after proving that they had a special need for such a weapon. Owners of rifles and shotguns would merely be required to obtain identification cards which would be granted to anyone over age 18 who is not a criminal or mentally incompetent. Some civil libertarians objected on the ground that this system would give the federal government too many computer records of citizen conduct, thus threatening personal freedom, and they were joined by the manufacturers and distributors of firearms, whose interests obviously were threatened by this type of proposal.

Opponents of gun control often use catchy sayings to summarize their arguments. One of them is "When guns are outlawed, only outlaws will have guns." The slogan implies that honest citizens need firearms to protect themselves from criminals. And it is indeed true that many people, especially those who live in the inner city, believe they need guns to protect themselves from robbers, burglars, and rapists. However, statistics do not bear out their fears. As we have seen, the greatest number of homicides and assaults occur between friends and relatives, not strangers.

Another slogan is "Guns don't kill; people do." The argument here is that criminals, not guns, should be controlled. If killers and other felons were all locked up, the idea goes, then there would be no need even for laws making it a crime to own a gun. A comedian has responded to the slogan with a satirical agreement: "Yeah, they throw bullets at each other."

Gun control is also opposed on the ground that citizens would need guns to fight for freedom if a dictator were to seize power. Overlooked is the fact that, should such an unlikely event take place, pistols and rifles would hardly be a match for hand grenades, tanks, jet fighters, and nuclear bombs. Certainly, no one advocates that private possession of such weapons be legalized. Consistent with this argument is the claim that government control of private firearms violates the Second Amendment of the Constitution. However, the relevant passage reads, "A well regulated Militia, being necessary to the security of a free State, the right of the people to keep and bear Arms shall not be infringed." The courts have made the reasonable interpretation that this Amendment applies to a well-regulated militia, not to individuals.

Compensation of Victims

Modern criminal justice considers the victim of a violent crime — or any other crime, for that matter — to be just another witness. Once the accused person has been convicted, the state forgets about the victim. But the victim of a violent crime may have enormous medical expenses, miss weeks or months of work, and even be blinded or crippled. Such victims, like the destitute children of murdered parents, have few legal remedies for their loss. They can sue the offender, or they can try to get the criminal court to order the offender to pay restitution. But these legal attempts to get compensation are rarely successful. For one thing, the attackers must be identified and the police must be able to find the suspect and make an arrest. For another, most violent criminals, like most victims, are penniless. Even if the victim wins a damage suit, the criminal usually has no money with which to pay. Violent criminals go off to prison for long terms, so they have no means of complying with a court order for restitution.

The only effective way of easing the tremendous financial loss of victims of violent crimes is through direct government compensation. Limited victim compensation plans have been in effect in New Zealand, England, California, and New York for some time. These programs are administered by a board that hears cases brought to it by victims. The board is limited in the amount of compensation it can award. Within this limit it awards compensation according to the amount of financial and personal loss and according to the role the victim played in the crime. (Victims who were violating the law are not likely to be compensated.) Under existing plans the compensation awarded is usually inadequate. People with medium or high incomes are often excluded because they cannot show that they were financially devastated by the injuries they received. But these shortcomings could easily be corrected.

Cultural Change

Unjustified, "bad" violence clearly is condemned in our society. At the same time, however, we lavish praise and admiration on war heroes, tough cops, and others who use "good" violence. High rates of violence arise in part from the fact that "good" as well as "bad" violence has a way of breeding more violence.[33] Further, there is no simple answer to the question of which violence is good and which is bad. The typical murder begins with a petty disagreement, escalates into a heated argument and a few slaps or blows, then ends with the use of a deadly weapon.[34] Both parties may be right in some ways and wrong in others.

Many people, especially religious leaders, have proposed that the mystique of violence, so often reflected in television and the movies, be replaced with an ethic of nonviolence. This ideal is advocated by most of the world's great religions. Nonviolence was a cornerstone of the politics of the great American civil-rights leader Martin Luther King, Jr., and of Mahatma Gandhi, the leader of the independence movement in India. Many other political leaders have called for long-range changes in violent cultural traditions. It is clear that the stronger our collective denunciation of violence and the fewer situations in which we justify its use, the more peaceful our society will be.

Criminal Justice

It is often suggested that a tougher and more efficient criminal-justice system would reduce violent crime. As we noted in Chapter 14, advocates of such policies argue that improved law enforcement will catch convicts and punish a higher percentage of those who commit violent crimes. For them, the solution to violent crime is a more violent criminal-justice system. There is considerable evidence that increased punishments for murder and assault do not prevent many people from committing these crimes, but the issue is by no means settled. Others argue for better defense rather than more severe punishment. For them, the idea is that

Many forms of legitimate violence are permitted in our society. The problem is that legitimate violence also promotes attitudes and values that produce criminal violence. In order to reduce the problem of violence, we must substitute the ideals of non-violence for the mystique of violence so common in our culture.

murderers should simply be taken off the streets and isolated in prisons, where they can do no more damage. But the fact is that very few murderers repeat their crimes, whether they are imprisoned or not. They have a much lower rate of recidivism than other criminals. Longer prison terms would affect them only slightly, if at all.

In contrast to murder rates, robbery and rape rates are more likely to go down if more robbers and rapists are punished or isolated behind bars. For this reason many states are now making it easier for courts to convict rapists. In the past defense lawyers went out of their way to try to prove that the alleged victim had consented to sexual intercourse or at least "asked for it" with provocative behavior. As a result many rape victims found that they, rather than the rapists, were being put on trial. Now police departments are increasingly using female officers to take rape complaints, and training them to minimize the victims' sense of shame and humiliation so that more victims will come forward. Also, some states now forbid defense attorneys to delve into the victim's past sexual behavior unless they have proved in advance that such inquiry is relevant to the case. These changes certainly will not stop all rapes. But they do make it easier for victims to cooperate with the police, and they ensure that fewer rapists escape unpunished. If punishment of rapists scares potential rapists so much that they are afraid to commit rape, then rape rates ought to decline significantly in the areas where conviction rates have gone up.

SOCIOLOGICAL PERSPECTIVES on Personal Violence

Violence has been a social issue ever since Cain killed Abel. For years murder and other violence were said to be prompted by evil spirits. Only 200 years ago English courts accused defendants of violating the law but also accused them of "being prompted and instigated by the devil and not having the fear of God before [their] eyes." And as late as 1862 the Supreme Court of North Carolina declared that "to know the right and still the wrong pursue proceeds from a perverse will brought about by the seductions of the evil one."

During the period when such explanations of violence were frequently used, the idea of natural causation had not developed. The notion that violence is a natural outcome of the way a society is organized, not of something outside the society, could not be imagined. Neither was it possible to imagine that violent criminals could be normal, average people—little or no attention was given to their motives or intentions, and study of the immediate circumstances in which violent acts take place was out of the question.

Sociologists have helped change all that. Functionalists and conflict theorists have shown that violence is linked to economic, political, and social organization. Social psychologists have shown that violent behavior is learned in interactions with others. None of these sociologists believes that violence can be significantly reduced by heaping torture and suffering on violent people.

The Functionalist Perspective

In huge, poorly integrated societies many people have little association with the social groups and institutions that are supposed to regulate and direct behavior. As a result, functionalists argue that many people are confused, alienated, frustrated, and alone. Some vent their hostilities in violence. Some are violent because they know no other way of life.

The functionalist solution calls for an increase in social integration. Violence would decline if alienated and frustrated people were linked into primary groups that met their psychological and social needs. Religious organizations provide this sense of belonging and personal direction, but of course in disorganized societies not everyone is attached to such groups. Social clubs, political organizations, and work groups also have that function. Generally, violence would decline if communities were better organized for peace.

The Conflict Perspective

Conflict theorists are more likely than functionalists to see a certain amount of violence as a natural part of human society. Subordinate groups do not get their fair share of the wealth and power, and they are often dominated by alien institutions and agencies that are incompatible with their own life style. As a result they are likely to have little allegiance to the legal system that tells them violence is wrong. Further, they often are unaware of the cause of their troubles, so they strike out at people who are near and dear to them instead of at their oppressors.

The conflict theorists' solution calls for giving oppressed citizens a fair share of the wealth and power so that they will not have to continue to fight for it. Such changes would also increase their respect for society and therefore would increase their willingness to abide by its laws. Most conflict theorists advocate some form of collective political action directed at bringing about change of this kind. Some even advocate collective violence as a means of reducing interpersonal violence.

The Social-Psychological Perspective

As we have already noted, biosocial theories consider violence to be a result of an "aggressive instinct" that was bred into the human race over the centuries as the timid were killed off and the violent survived. This kind of theory offers little hope for the elimination of violence—the best we can expect is a channeling of some aggression into violent sports and other "friendly" conflicts. However, few social psychologists use instinct theory of this kind. Interactionists, personality theorists, and behaviorists all see violence as a product of social learning.

Many young people clearly learn to be violent in their early socialization either from the example of their parents and friends or indirectly as they view a world that makes violence appear to be a necessary tool for survival and success. Adults continue to learn violent behavior through association with it. From this perspective, if violence is to be reduced, people must be taught to be nonviolent. Anything that is learned can be unlearned, but it is far from clear how such a change might be brought about. Programs of therapy and behavior modification may help individuals who are motivated to change, but these programs are unlikely to have a significant impact on the overall problem of violence. Large-scale cultural changes will be necessary to solve the problem. Nationwide educational programs implemented through the schools and the mass media are the most promising way to promote nonviolence. But winning the massive national commitment necessary to create effective programs will be a difficult task.

SUMMARY

Violence has been defined as behavior intended to cause bodily pain or injury to another person. But this definition causes trouble because the legitimate imposition of pain or injury is not ordinarily thought of as violence. The "violence problem," thus, is a problem of illegitimate violence, not a problem of injuries that are socially acceptable. The catch is that there is no clear distinction between legitimate and illegitimate violence.

There are four main violent crimes: murder, assault, forcible rape, and robbery. Murder is the unlawful killing of a human being with malice aforethought. It is distinct from homicide, which is any killing of a human, legally or illegally. An assault occurs when one person attacks another with the intention of hurting or killing that person. There is little behavioral difference between some assaults and some murders. In one the assault victim survives and in the other the assault victim dies. Rape is sexual intercourse with a person who consents out of fear or is unable to resist the force of the attacker. So-called statutory rape is not rape at all. It is intercourse with a female below a legally defined "age of consent." Robbery is the taking of someone's property by force or threat of force.

Violent crime is heavily concentrated in cities. Statistical problems make international comparisons difficult, but it appears that the United States is more violent than other industrialized nations.

It is unusual for someone to be assaulted or murdered by a stranger. The victims and attackers have similar economic, ethnic, and social backgrounds. The pattern of victimization in robbery is quite different, however. In over 80 percent of the cases, the victims and the attackers are strangers. Rape has some similarities to assault and murder as well as to robbery. Rape is rarely a conflict between close associates, but about half of all rape victims know their attackers.

Violent crimes are disproportionately committed by young, urban, poor, black males. Victimization rates are highest for people with the same five characteristics.

Violence has been blamed on everything from human instincts to television. Biological explanations say that violence is instinctive, and some biologists believe that an evolutionary process has made men and women more aggressive as time has passed. Among the psychological explanations, the Freudian approach is the most popular. Freud accepted the biological theory that people have an instinctive tendency to be violent and aggressive. His followers believe that most people develop a superego that blocks these aggressive instincts. Violent people, however, have a superego that is too weak to block their natural impulses. Another important psychological theory holds that aggression and violence are responses to the frustration of an individual's goals. The more frustrated people become, the more likely they are to become aggressive.

Sociological explanations of violence picture it as a product of social structure and social learning. Some sociologists argue that violence occurs when society fails to provide strong enough controls on an individual's behavior. Others say that violence is a product of the frustrations that structural inequalities cause among the poor and minorities. Still others argue that people learn to be violent the same way they learn any other kind of behavior. There is considerable evidence that violence is learned at home.

Compared with other Western democratic nations, the United States is highly violent. A tradition of violence developed as rugged frontiersmen conquered the vast continent, and this tradition continues. Further, some of our violence stems from the great size and ethnic diversity of the United States and from its relatively high level of economic inequality. Tensions and conflicts are to be expected in a society with such a low level of social integration.

Although television puts out a flood of fictional violence, there is a vigorous debate about the effects of such violence on people who watch it.

Laboratory experiments show that media violence encourages violent behavior in children. Other research, using different techniques, shows that media violence has little or no effect on specific individuals. Perhaps television's greatest effect is its popularization of a tradition of violence.

Another heated debate centers on the effects of widespread ownership of firearms. On one side is the argument that firearms have little effect on violence, that if guns were not available killers would use some other weapon. On the other side is the observation that the difference between assault and murder often turns on the kind of weapon involved. About half of all American murders are committed with handguns, 15 percent with rifles or shotguns. The family pistol is 6 times more likely to be used against a family member or acquaintance than against a criminal intruder.

Many proposals for reducing violence have been made. Among them are stricter gun control, direct compensation to victims, and cultural changes that would stop the romanticization of violence and place more emphasis on the values of nonviolence. Improved criminal-justice practices are frequently proposed as means of defending ourselves from violence.

Violence, like other social problems, is an outcome of the way a society is organized, not of something outside the society. Functionalists and conflict theorists have shown that violence is linked to economic, political, and social organization. Social psychologists have demonstrated that violent behavior is learned in interactions with others.

KEY TERMS

assault	manslaughter
control theory	murder
forcible rape	robbery
frustration–aggression theory	statutory rape
homicide	violence
machismo	

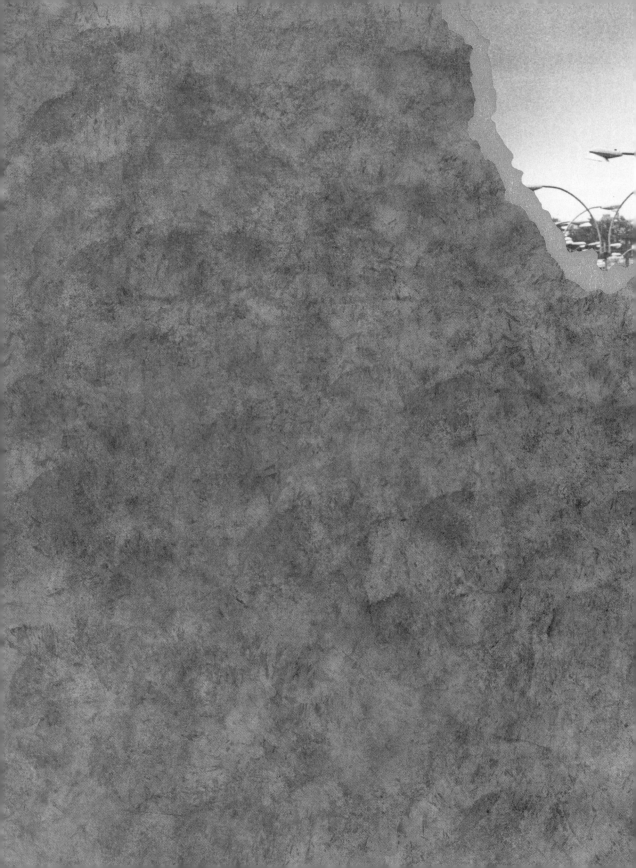

Part IV
Problems
of a Changing
World

16
Warfare

What are the causes of war?
Are there differences between international
  wars and revolutions?
Has war become unprofitable?
How can war be prevented?

The mushroom cloud that loomed over Hiroshima on August 6, 1945, permanently changed the face of warfare. Until that time, men and women certainly noticed the death and destruction left by war, but warfare was commonly considered an unavoidable evil, like droughts, famines, and plagues. The dawning of the nuclear age made the human race take warfare more seriously. The means for our own destruction was at hand, and the problem of war moved to first place on the list of human concerns.

THE NATURE OF WAR

Although warfare is an ancient custom, it is difficult to define precisely. Part of the problem is that the distinction between war and peace is a matter of degree rather than an absolute difference. Everyone will agree that World War II deserves to be called a war and that a typical murder does not. But between these two extremes are a host of riots, border incidents, armed conflicts, civil upheavals, invasions, and "policings" of one nation by another. Such conflicts are called wars if organized military forces are in conflict, and if the conflict is lengthy. War, then, is protracted military conflict between two or more organized groups. This definition helps clarify the meaning of war, but it is obviously vague. The Arab–Israeli conflict of 1967 is called "the Six-Day War," and some people still call America's lengthy participation in Vietnam a "conflict" rather than a war.

Wars are often classified on the basis of the tactics or weapons used. More significant for sociological understanding is a simple division between international wars and revolutionary wars. The former are armed conflicts between the governments of two or more sovereign nations. The latter are armed conflicts between official governments and one or more groups of national rebels. The American War Between the States or Civil War was actually a revolutionary war. The causes of international wars and revolutionary wars are quite different and will be discussed separately.

Throughout human history war has been the rule and peace the exception. Only 268 of the past 3421 years have been free from war.[1] This century alone has seen two "total" wars and dozens of lesser conflicts. Even in the most peaceful times, the next conflagration is seldom far away. There are so many international and national tensions, and the traditions of warfare are so deeply entrenched, that the world is likely to show this pattern of almost constant warfare for years to come.

THE COST OF WAR

The cost of war to human society is enormous, especially the staggering loss of life. In the 300 wars that occurred between 1820 and 1949, warfare was the direct cause of from 1 to 3 percent of all human deaths. If deaths indirectly caused by war—such as those resulting from war-related famine, disease, and economic disruption—are counted, the figure might be as high as 10 percent.[2] World War II alone took over 15 million lives. But the dead are not the only victims. Every war leaves a residue of maimed and crippled, widows, grieving parents, and orphans.

Economically, the price tag for even a small war is astronomical. Property worth $200 or $300 million has been destroyed in a single day. Modern military technology has made it possible to transform a thriving community into a pile of rubble in a matter of seconds. But even without counting the destruction of civilian or military property, the costs of war are enormous. Businesses fail; production of consumer goods slows down or stops; fields go unplanted and crops unharvested for want of labor. Many nations have plunged from affluence to starvation during a single war.

Even in times of peace we pay a price for war. The nations of the world spend three times as much for arms as for public health, and 40 percent more for arms than for education.[3] World expenditures for arms were over $400 billion in 1978. Of this amount, about 18 percent ($72 billion) was spent by underdeveloped nations that are barely able to feed their people.

These figures are so large that they are difficult to grasp. There are a number of ways of putting them in perspective. For example, a university student whose rich uncle left her $400 billion could spend about $15,000 every *minute* for the next 50 years. By the hour, that comes to $900,000; by the day, to over $21 million. With a month's spending—about $650 million—she could easily afford to buy a program that would wipe malaria off the face of the earth and still have a dollar left for each person in the United States. At $400 billion a year, the estimated cost of wiping out malaria (about $450 million) is spent every 10 hours.

Even in these relatively peaceful times, huge numbers of people devote their lives to fighting small wars and preparing for the next big war. Almost 9 million people are in the military forces of just three nations—the United States, the Soviet Union, and China. And this figure does not include the reserves, who number about 3 million in the Soviet Union alone.[4] There also are millions of civilians who work to produce the supplies and equipment used by the military.

Some economists argue that the enormous outlays for military spending are beneficial because they create jobs and stimulate the economy. This may be true. But if it is true, then it also follows that much greater benefits would be reaped if the money were spent on goods and services that are economically useful. A nation is no better off economically with 5000 nuclear missiles than it is with 1, but a nation is much better off with 5000 hydroelectric power plants than with only 1. The two developed countries with the healthiest and fastest-growing economies, West Germany and Japan, both have small armed forces and low military budgets.

THE ESCALATION OF VIOLENCE

Traditionally, most wars were limited. Their aim was a specific set of goals, not the total destruction of an enemy nation. A rather small group of military men did the fighting, and the vast majority of the population watched from the sidelines. The behavior of these military men was governed by rules of gallantry and codes of honor. The opposing armies were directed by kings and nobles who would see the modern style of total war as barbaric and uncivilized.

Modern warfare, starting with Napoleon (emperor of France, 1805–1815) and ending with World War II (1939–1945), has been marked by a steady escalation of violence. The new style is total war—an all-out national effort to kill or subdue enemy civilians and soldiers alike. Today's armies are not composed only of professional soldiers or privileged elites. They are composed mainly of average citizens, often conscripted against their will. Behind each army are many civilians, each making a contribution to the new military technology—manufacturing ball bearings, producing oil, growing food. In modern warfare the victorious nations are those with the greatest productive capacity. It follows that civilians contributing to such production are legitimate military targets. The tremendous range and destructiveness of modern weapons have moved most civilians into the combat zone.[5]

Over the years we have invented more and more efficient ways of killing our enemies at longer distances. The spear was replaced by the bow and arrow, which became the crossbow. The musket developed into the cannon, the rifle, and the machine gun. In World War I (1914–1918) the cannon and rifle were fused into the long rifle, a huge gun that enabled the Germans to shell Paris from a distance of 75 miles. The hand grenade of World War I became the bomb of World War II, dropped from high-flying airplanes a thousand miles from their base. The TNT bomb gave way to the atom bomb, and the bomber was replaced with the guided missile.

Now a modern military force can wreak destruction virtually anywhere in the world at any time. An armed missile now on the drawing boards will be so accurate that it can be fired at a single building on the other side of the world and not miss by more than 30 yards. A delicate balance of power exists between the nations that possess effective intercontinental nuclear missiles. Each knows that the others have the ability to destroy it in a few minutes.

Some people consider this tremendous destructive power an instrument of peace. At a minimum, it makes total war less appealing than it was as recently as World War II, since even the victors in a nuclear war are likely to suffer terrible devastation. Although modern nations are organized for total war, the wars that have occurred since the development of nuclear weapons have been confined to limited areas, as in Korea and Indochina. It appears that fear of a nuclear war headed off global conflict. Nevertheless, the possibility remains that such limitations will be

The frightening power of modern military technology has made it possible to wreak destruction in any part of the world on a moment's notice.

broken. The specter of all-out nuclear war remains a constant threat to human survival.

THE CAUSES OF WARFARE

Many people believe that warfare is simply part of human nature. The same "aggressive instinct" which is said to lead inevitably to personal violence is also said to lead inevitably to war. However, there is a great deal of evidence that shows that this is not the case. Most important is the fact that the people of some cultures, such as the Eskimos and the Todas of Southern India, have never gone to war. One anthropologist states the anti-instinct position as follows:

> It is clear . . . that warfare as we know it in the modern world cannot be attributed to any instinctual or other inevitable component of nature and culture. While the capacity for aggression is universal, the conditions for bringing whole groups into total mutual hostility are not.[6]

The causes of war are social, not biological. But there are great differences between wars and therefore great differences between their causes. Some are revolutions, caused by internal tensions and conflicts. Others are international, with their origins in the economic and political competition between nations. But even this distinction is too simple. Revolutionary wars are transformed into international wars when a foreign power intervenes, and the burdens of conducting an international war may stimulate a domestic revolution, as occurred in Russia during World War I.

> ### NINETEENTH CENTURY SOCIAL PROBLEMS*
>
> Waunakee was raided by tramps the other evening and nearly every business house and many residences were burglarized. The occupants of dwelling houses in many instances were driven into the street at points of revolvers while other members of the gang ransacked the buildings.
> June 22, 1893

Revolutionary Warfare

Revolutions are romantic. They have given us some of the most dramatic episodes in human history. Modern China, Cuba, Egypt, England, France, the Soviet Union, and the United States are all products of revolutionary struggles. The revolutionary theme—a small group of freedom-loving patriots fighting against overwhelming odds—has captured the imagination of countless writers and artists. Even American cowboy stories show plain and simple folk in heroic struggles against land barons and railroad tycoons. Several theories help make sense of revolutions. Nevertheless, these theories are far from perfect. All the conditions that are said to cause revolutions are sometimes present in societies where no revolutionary conflict takes place, and revolutions sometimes take place in societies that lack the important characteristics mentioned by the theorists. The cultural traditions of individual societies play an important part in revolutionary struggles, as does the influence of specific leaders.

Exploitation and Oppression

One of the earliest and most influential theories of revolution was created by Karl Marx and Friedrich Engels.[7] They believed that the injustices of capitalism would produce a worldwide revolution. As the workers in capitalist nations sank deeper and deeper into poverty and personal alienation, they would eventually come to realize that they were being exploited by the owners of the factories in which they worked. The workers would then band together, overthrow their oppressors in a violent revolution, and create a classless utopia with liberty and justice for all.

The Marxist theory of revolution is almost a century and a half old. The revolutionary movement it predicted has not occurred. The revolutions fought in the name of Marxism in China, Russia, Cuba, and elsewhere did not happen the way Marx's theory predicted and did not produce anything like the communist utopia he described. Nevertheless, many Marxists and non-Marxists alike still believe that exploitation and oppression of the lower classes eventually does produce revolutionary action. Less accepted is Marx's idea that such a revolution will necessarily destroy capitalism and create a new utopian economic system.

---

*These "Nineteenth Century Social Problems" throughout the text are excerpts from the *Badger State Banner* published in Black River Falls, Wisconsin.

Relative Deprivation Considerable research since Marx's time suggests that it is relative poverty, not absolute poverty, that sparks revolutions. According to relative-deprivation theory, revolutions are caused by differences between what people have and what they think they should have.

James C. Davies, one of the leading exponents of this theory, presents some interesting data on several major revolutions.[8] He concludes that "revolutions are most likely to occur when a prolonged period of objective economic and social development is followed by a short period of sharp reversal."[9] In other words, the people were actually better off at the start of the revolutions he studied than they had been in previous decades. Apparently, improvement in social conditions creates an expectation of even greater improvement. If a sharp downturn occurs and the people are unwilling to reduce either their standard of living or their expectations, they rise up against the government. Gurr's research shows, however, that deprivation and dissatisfaction are not enough to produce a revolution. His theory is that dissatisfaction must be "politicized" (directed toward political objects) before people will rise up against their government.[10] Many different forces affect the politicization of discontent. These include the culture and attitudes of the people, the political history and traditions of the nations involved, and the propaganda used by both sides.

Failure of Ruling Elites Studies of the world's great revolutions show that the old governments and the people who ran them were inadequate and incompetent. Brinton's study of the American, British, French, and Russian revolutions concluded that the old ruling class in all of these societies was "divided and inept."[11] The authorities seemed to make the wrong decisions and then overreact or underreact to the beginnings of revolutionary ferment. Further, Brinton shows, these prerevolutionary governments were teetering on the verge of bankruptcy, although the economies of their societies were in reasonably good shape.[12]

More generally, prerevolutionary governments seem to be characterized by a breakdown in what the Italian sociologist Vilfredo Pareto called the circulation of elites.[13] Too many capable people are excluded from positions of power by incompetent individuals of high inherited rank. As a result the ruling elite grows increasingly incompetent while powerful opposition groups appear and demand a larger share of the wealth. The longer the elite fails to "circulate" (allow effective leaders in and push incompetent leaders out), the more likely a revolutionary uprising becomes.

Partitions and Divisions Virtually all sociologists who have studied the subject agree that class conflict precedes a revolution. Before a revolution the various social classes come to view each other as hostile economic competitors. The English and French revolutions, for example, were revolts by an expanding class of merchants and traders against the feudal aristocracy.

Other major sources of revolutionary conflict are geographic partitioning and ethnic segregation. Regional differences led to the American War
Between the states or Civil War. History is full of examples of revolts by
an ethnic group in one part of a nation against its central government.
When a rebellious group controls a regional government, these conflicts
are similar to international war. Generally, if the rebels are successful, the
nation is divided up into two or more new countries. Sometimes, however, the rebellious group takes over the entire nation and reverses its relationship with the old dominant group.

**International
Warfare**

The causes of revolutionary and international wars are quite different. In
some cases the internal conditions conducive to a revolutionary uprising
may contribute to an international war. Nevertheless, the two are distinct.
For example, political leaders who are having trouble at home sometimes
stir up an international conflict in an attempt to divert the people's attention from domestic problems. It is said that "nothing makes friends like a
common enemy," so such strategy sometimes reunites a nation. But in the
long run the internal problems reemerge, often aggravated by the strains
of the international conflict.

The **great man theory of history** maintains that individual decision
makers play a key role in the creation of a war. It may be argued, for example, that if Hitler had not been born, World War II would never have
happened. But since it is impossible to rerun history there is no way of
proving or disproving such claims. It does appear that individual decisions have made the difference between war and peace in some cases.
During the Cuban missile crisis of 1962, for example, the world seemed to
be teetering on the brink of a nuclear war. American and Soviet leaders
made decisions that averted war, but one leader could well have plunged
the world into an international holocaust. Even so, the "great man"
theory can explain only the superficial causes of warfare. Certain social
conditions must be present before any international warfare is possible. If
the United States and the Soviet Union had not had enormous military
machines and been willing to fight, no conflict could have taken place, no
matter what the leaders decided.

Militarism

There are two faces of **militarism**, both of which contribute to international wars. The first is the glorification of war and combat. International
warfare is obviously more likely when a society sees it as a heroic show of
superiority or when young people see it as a path to personal fame and
fortune. Such attitudes are still common in the nuclear age, but they seem
to be on the decline. The growth of complex military technology has taken
the glory out of "man-to-man" combat, and the fear of nuclear annihilation
has quieted the cheers of civilians.

Nationalism was a major part of the motivation for Germany's attempt to conquer Europe in World War II.

The second face of militarism is strong belief in "defense." With an apparent decline in justifications of war for its own sake, there seems to have been an increase in national desires to deter and ward off aggressors. These desires are reflected in enormous military budgets and constant preparation for war. Nations that devote major parts of their economies to military purposes now claim that they are doing so merely for defensive purposes. But the line between aggression and defense is fuzzy, as is indicated by America's "defense" of itself by moving into Vietnam or by Russia's "defense" of itself by moving into Africa.

The rhetoric of defense is often used to justify aggressive military actions. It is obvious that the chances of international conflict are increased if nations stand ready to go to war at a moment's notice, whether in the name of defense or in that of conquest.

Nationalism

Like patriotism, nationalism is a sense of identification with and devotion to one's nation. In the past, growing nationalism discouraged local wars by unifying petty feudal kingdoms into larger and more stable social units.[14] In the modern world, however, unthinking nationalism all too often produces the opposite result. Many wars have been fought over some petty incident that was interpreted as an affront to "national honor." Rational settlements based on fair compromise are difficult when nationalistic feelings are involved. After all, what wise politician would dare compromise his or her nation's honor?

Nationalism is a critical part of the motivation for imperialism (the creation or expansion of an empire). As Quincey Wright points out, some wars arise "because of the tendency of a people affected by nationalism ... to acquire an attitude of superiority to some or all other peoples, to seek to extend its cultural characteristics throughout the world, and to ignore the claims of other states and of the world-community."[15] Such ethnocentrism sometimes involves religion as well as national and cultural pride. For instance, a desire to convert foreign peoples to "the true faith" was an important motive in the creation of colonial empires by Catholic Spain and Portugal, just as it was in the creation of the Islamic Empire in North Africa and the Middle East.

Economic Gain   Some wars are fought for profit. One nation may attack another in an attempt to capture valuable natural resources, attractive land, or cheap labor. Sometimes an entire nation reaps economic benefits from its conquests, but more often only a small segment of society benefits. Some people stand to gain from an outbreak of almost any sort of war, for example, high-ranking military officers and those in war-related industries such as arms manufacture. Other interest groups may also profit from a war if it gains objectives beneficial to them—exporters might profit from the conquest of a new seaport, while farmers might gain by winning access to valuable land or water.

It appears, however, that modern warfare has made it difficult for any nation as a whole to profit from an international war:

> As a general rule wars have become unprofitable in the twentieth century, at least if profitability is defined in material terms. Not only have the costs of wars increased greatly because of the vastly improved technology of devastation and the practice of total warfare, the benefits have also declined decidedly. Wars no longer gain booty, spoils, or tribute; and they infrequently gain economic concessions. Sometimes territory is gained, but the trend in the last century is one of declining territorial gains.[16]

The Vietnam War is an example of the economic burdens of modern warfare. As of 1975, it had cost the United States alone between $116 and $121 billion.[17] This figure will go higher as the nation pays veterans benefits and the interest on money borrowed during the war. Yet despite this enormous cost, the Vietnam War produced virtually no economic benefits for the United States and devastated most of Indochina.

NINETEENTH CENTURY SOCIAL PROBLEMS

The crushing of Admiral Cevera's fleet (at Santiago) has had a beneficial effect on the lumber market. . . . A large number of Eastern buyers are negotiating some large purchases at Marinette. Hayes and Company bought 2,000,000 feet of good lumber from Marinette growers.
July 21, 1898

own resources, and international trade and commerce benefit all. Multinational corporations help create common economic interests and thus tie nations together. Sooner or later international labor unions will face these international corporations. After studying international business trips, technical assistance, and foreign exchanges, Angell concluded that there have been significant increases in "transnational participation" in recent years.[22] In other words, there are growing channels for contact and interaction between nations. International peace might eventually spring from such cultural exchange and economic cooperation. Perhaps in time "world opinion" will replace the "public opinion" of nations. Even today, when world opinion is not favorable to the actions of a particular nation, the power of world opinion helps bring the nonconforming country into line.

SOCIOLOGICAL PERSPECTIVES on Warfare

In politics more time and attention are given to warfare than to any other single subject. But this is not true of sociology or of social science in general. Research on war and military matters is a minor specialty within the sociological discipline. For this reason the three principal sociological perspectives are not as sharply defined with reference to warfare as they are with reference to, say, crime or poverty. Nevertheless, each perspective provides a useful framework for understanding why warfare has existed throughout human history.

The Functionalist Perspective

Functional theory sees international warfare as an inevitable result of the way the world is organized politically. From time immemorial humanity has been creating political structures that are conducive to warfare. When there is a multitude of large and small countries with conflicting interests, there is bound to be disagreement about physical and psychological boundaries, and the international organizations set up to handle these disputes simply cannot do the job.

Given this high degree of international disorganization, war is actually functional because it is the only effective method for settling major international disputes. Warfare also provides short-term psychological and political benefits to individual nations and may function to keep a weak divided society together for a time. For these reasons, we denounce warfare but nevertheless organize ourselves to retain it. It follows that the best solutions to the problem of international war are those that seek to reorganize the world's political system. The primary need is for a program to replace our patchwork of international relations with a genuine world order.

To functionalists, revolutionary warfare arises from a different kind of disorganization. When national systems do not work smoothly and become increasingly dysfunctional, revolution is one possible result. For example, a society might exclude capable people from positions of power and distribute its wealth so unequally that "the masses" become bitter, resentful, and revolutionary. Political organization also becomes dysfunctional by championing established ways of doing things while the citizens' attitudes, values, and opinions are changing. Such rigidity is sometimes softened by revolution. Functionalists therefore believe that the best way to head off revolutionary conflict is to implement the kind of gradual reforms described in our chapters on economics, government, poverty, and ethnic minorities.

The Conflict Perspective

Conflict theorists do not usually separate economics and politics. They speak of "political economy." To conflict theorists, international and national politics are not disorganized; they are organized for economic and political exploitation. International wars stem from the efforts of national leaders to enlarge their wealth and power by expanding their economic exploitation and political domination. Revolutionary wars are generally seen as attempts by the people to free themselves from such exploitation and domination by political elites.

According to conflict theory, the best way of eliminating war is to eliminate oppression, both international and national. Some conflict theorists advocate a balance-of-power system, but one in which economic goods and the military power to protect them are distributed equally. Others call for radical economic changes that would make all government unnecessary; in this utopian state both governments and the wars they fight would vanish. Conflict theorists are not necessarily against war, at least in the short run. Their position is that conflict is basic to all human societies, and some recommend that collective violence be used to undo economic injustices that are maintained by military power. But the ultimate aim of conflict theorists is a peaceful world with full equality among all peoples.

The Social-Psychological Perspective

Social psychologists have identified both individual and cultural characteristics that are conducive to warfare. The individual traits, as we have seen, are associated with an assumed instinctual aggressiveness. The cultural traits are clearly acquired. Each culture champions a certain "ideal personality." People are encouraged in both subtle and open ways to develop personality traits consistent with this ideal. People growing up in cultures that place great importance on honor and pride are likely to encourage warlike national policies, as are people growing up in cultures that emphasize competition and individual aggressiveness. Cultures in which people learn to put a high value on humility and cooperation are much more likely to be peaceful in both national and international affairs.

One's sense of nationalism or internationalism also is learned, as is the ethnocentric belief that one's own culture and social institutions are superior to all others. Some people learn to identify so strongly with their country that any international setback is seen as a personal threat. Such people are not likely to encourage peaceful foreign policies. Even Western religions put emphasis on conquering evil in an aggressive way. War allows people to identify enemies as evil and then win honor, glory, and a sense of righteousness by conquering them.[23]

In the long run, social psychologists say, the only sure way of reducing the frequency of warfare is to emphasize cultural characteristics that favor peaceful resolution of differences. Rather than glorifying victory over evil, it would be more useful to applaud the rational compromise that heads off deadly conflict. The ideals of nonviolence must be substituted for the glorification of violence that is so common in the mass media and our everyday lives.

SUMMARY

War can be defined as protracted military conflict between two or more organized groups. Wars can be classified as international (between independent sovereign nations) or revolutionary (between groups within a single nation).

Through the years warfare has been more the rule than the exception. The cost of this warfare has been enormous. Hundreds of millions of people have been killed or injured in wars. Economically, war costs are staggering. The current arms race alone runs to over $400 billion a year.

Since the early nineteenth century there has been a steady escalation of violence in international armed conflicts. Wars once had specific, limited goals, but now they are "total." Civilians no longer sit on the sidelines watching fights between professional soldiers. They are participants and, thus, are military targets. Further, improved military technology has increased the scale and destructiveness of modern warfare.

The causes of revolutionary and international wars are overlapping but nevertheless different. There are four major theories about the causes of revolutionary wars. One says that they stem from exploitation and oppression of subordinate groups by a society's ruling elite. Another says that it is relative deprivation that stimulates the discontent essential to a revolution. The third theory says revolutions occur when ruling elites are incompetent but nevertheless exclude talented newcomers from positions of power and importance. The final theory notes that class conflict, geographic partitioning, and ethnic segregation all contribute to revolutionary conflict.

Militarism and the buildup of armaments are a major cause of international war. Ethnocentrism, when expressed in nationalism, makes conquest of "inferiors" seem reasonable. Plain greed cannot be ignored either. Some wars are fought more for profit than for anything else. But underlying all international wars is the nature of the world's political organization. The large number of heavily armed independent states all determined to advance their own interests makes warfare almost inevitable.

The most common proposal for preventing war is that the military strength of nations be neutralized by maintaining a balance of power. Because such a balance is inherently unstable, other proposals ask for disarmament—the partial or complete elimination of military forces. A third set of proposals calls for social justice—if inequality were eliminated, the chief motive for revolution would disappear and international tensions would relax. Finally, many religious, political, and intellectual leaders propose that military aggression be eliminated by the development of world government, including world law, world courts, and world law enforcement.

Functionalists see international warfare as an inevitable result of the way the world is organized politically. The world's political structures are dysfunctional, having been established to serve a bygone age. National systems do not function smoothly either, and revolution is evidence of this fact. Conflict theorists hold that international and national politics are far from disorganized. They are organized for economic exploitation—enforced by military might—of the weak by the strong. Conflict theorists usually favor a system in which economic goods and the military power to protect them are distributed equally. Social psychologists have found both personal and cultural traits that are conducive to warfare. In the long run, they say, the only sure way of preventing wars is to emphasize nonviolent cultural traits that favor peaceful resolution of differences.

KEY TERMS	balance of power	militarism
	disarmament	nationalism
	great man theory of history	relative-deprivation theory
	imperialism	revolutionary war
	international war	total war
	legitimation	war
	limited war	

17
Urbanization

Is small-town life better than living in a city?
Are the suburbs free from urban problems?
Why are cities so costly to govern?
How can the problems of urbanization be solved?

The shift from rural to urban living is one of the most significant social changes of the past two centuries. Urbanization has profoundly altered the lives of millions of people in a relatively short period. In 1790, 95 percent of the population of the United States was rural (living on farms or in villages with fewer than 2500 inhabitants). Today, only one out of four Americans lives in a rural area.[1] The same process has occurred in all the other industrialized nations. For example, Canada has about the same percentage of urban dwellers as the United States; West Germany is about 82 percent urban, and Japan about 83 percent.[2]

Although the shift to urban living is a recent development, the origins of the city are found at the very beginning of recorded history. The Sumerians, the first people to master the art of writing, are also believed to have founded the first cities, with fabled names like Eridu and Ur. Other cities soon grew in Egypt, India, and China. However, these early cities were only tiny islands in a sea of rural farmers. Their population seldom exceeded 5,000 or 10,000.[3]

The Industrial Revolution set off a tremendous burst of urbanization. As agriculture became increasingly efficient, fewer people were needed on the farms, and the surplus labor drifted to the cities. Until well into the nineteenth century the only means of ground transportation was by foot or by horse, and only the rich could afford horses. Therefore, cities rarely had a radius of more than three miles. But with the twentieth century came the advances in transportation that have allowed cities to expand both in size and in population. Small satellite cities have sprung up on the outskirts of the major cities. The area between cities has steadily been filled, until vast stretches of land are entirely covered with buildings and roads.

The term megalopolis is often used to refer to areas in which one vast city fuses with others. The largest megalopolis in North America is the unbroken stretch of cities and suburbs along the East Coast of the United States from Boston to Virginia. Another sprawling urban area is growing in California from San Diego to San Francisco. In Canada, 60 percent of the population lives in a 600-mile strip from Quebec City to Windsor, Ontario.

Transportation has become so efficient that no one is isolated from the urban influence. Today 95 percent of all Americans live within commuting distance of the nation's major metropolitan centers.[4] Further, more and more middle-income people have moved out of congested cities and into single-family dwellings in new suburbs. As a result the distinction between "urban" and "rural" has become blurred. The 1970 census revealed that for the first time more Americans lived in suburbs than in central cities themselves.[5]

As the suburbs have grown, the character of cities has changed. The middle class has moved away, leaving the central city to the working class and the poor. Many industries and small businesses have followed the middle class to the suburbs. Although cities remain the centers of business and industry, the movement to the suburbs has lowered the demand for new commercial developments in the cities. For a century residential areas near downtown commercial and industrial centers have been zones of transition. Old houses and apartment buildings were left to decay because landlords knew they would soon be replaced with business and industrial establishments. Today this transition is no longer taking place. Rather than being replaced by new stores and factories, decaying dwellings near the commercial and industrial zones continue to rot away.

THE CITIES

Civilizations have always been centered in cities. Despite the recent flight to the suburbs, modern cities are more dominant in our social life than ever before. In every Western nation huge corporations spread their influence outward from a few major cities. The large newspapers and broadcasting companies, which set our tastes and define our world, are based in cities and reflect their realities. The cities spawn and attract actors, artists, writers, and other intellectual innovators who set the cultural style of our age. Foreign visitors and immigrants stop in the great cities, rarely in country villages. In North America new immigrants first occupied the rundown sections of the cities, then moved to more affluent areas as they became acculturated. This process left the cities dotted with fragments of many different cultures—Irish, Italian, French, Chinese, Mexican, German, Russian, and more, thus adding to the diversity of city life.

Because cities have these attractions, it is surprising to find that some people dislike them and want to leave. But a Harris survey found that two-thirds of those living in big cities would prefer to live elsewhere. Similar attitudes have been uncovered in Great Britain and Holland.[6] In 1972 a Gallup poll confirmed the finding of the earlier Harris poll. When Gallup asked a representative sample of Americans "If you could live anywhere you wanted, would you prefer a city, suburban area, small town, or farm?" the answers were as follows: city, 13 percent; suburbs, 31 percent; small towns, 32 percent; and farm, 23 percent.[7]

One of the most fascinating questions confronting urban sociologists concerns the nature of life in cities. Do urban people have a unique way of thinking, a special outlook on life? One of the first people to answer this question was the famous German sociologist Georg Simmel. In a classic essay published in 1903, Simmel noted that city dwellers are continually bombarded by a tremendous amount of "nervous stimulation."[8] Noise, traffic, crowds, the rapid pace of life, and dozens of other stimuli overload the urban resident. City dwellers simply cannot pay attention to everything that goes on around them, and as a result they become indifferent to their surroundings. Because urbanites deal with so many strangers,

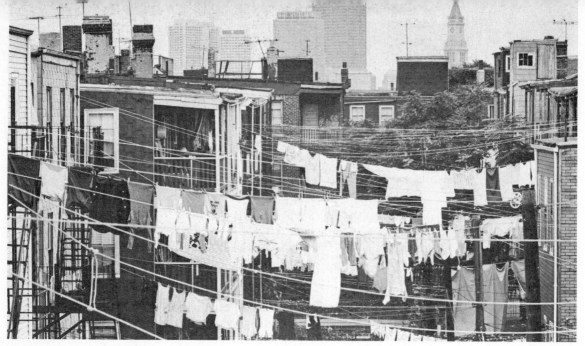

The modern city has a rich diversity of people, life styles, and architecture.

their relationships tend to be oriented toward external goals rather than direct personal satisfaction. On the whole, the city offers its people greater freedom, but it also increases the danger that they will be isolated and alone.

The most famous essay in urban sociology is Louis Wirth's "Urbanism as a Way of Life."[9] First published in 1938, this article summarized much of the thought of the "Chicago school" of urban sociology, which developed at the University of Chicago in the early twentieth century. Wirth painted with a broader brush than Simmel, but he reached similar conclusions about the psychological impact of urban life. To him, the essential characteristics of a city are its size, population, density, and social diversity: "The larger, the more densely populated, and the most heterogeneous a community, the more accentuated the characteristics associated with urbanism will be."

The diversity of social life is the most important of the city's characteristics. It springs from the size and density of the population, which create a "mosaic of social worlds." Thus, urban dwellers are specialized in the work they do and in their relationships with other people. Being highly specialized, they know each other only in superficial and impersonal ways. One person will be recognized as a bank teller, another as a co-worker, and a third as a bus driver, but they are seldom known in an intimate way. Financial interests dominate this impersonal urban world. The city becomes a complex mass of people living close together, but without deep emotional ties. The city dweller often feels lonely and isolated even in the midst of vast crowds. Urbanites learn to tolerate the attitudes and customs of other people, but they also learn to accept insecurity and instability as the normal state of the world. These characteristics work together to increase the incidence of what Wirth called "pathological conditions," including "personal disorganization, mental breakdown, suicide, delinquency, crime, corruption, and disorder."

Not all sociologists agree that city life is as dismal as Wirth pictured it. Some argue that Wirth's ideas merely reflect small-town America's dislike of cities and their rapid growth. For example, Gans notes that Wirth overlooked the many city dwellers who have a strong sense of community.[10] Gans's studies have identified five distinct types of city dwellers, only some of whom suffer from social isolation:

1. *Cosmopolites,* such as artists, writers, entertainers, intellectuals, and professionals, choose to live in the city because of its cultural activities.
2. *Unmarried or childless people* live in the city to be near its job opportunities and social life.
3. *Ethnic villagers* live in self-contained ethnic communities and therefore are able to maintain their traditional ways of life and kinship patterns.
4. *Deprived people* include the poor, the handicaped, and minority groups.
5. *Trapped people* are sliding down the social scale or are retired and living on fixed incomes and thus are unable to leave their decaying neighborhoods.

Gans argues that only the last two types of people—the deprived and the trapped—experience the urban way of life described by Wirth. The others either belong to a supportive subculture or are in the city voluntarily because of the benefits it offers. More positively, Gans found that social class and age have a greater effect on urban life styles than does city living itself. But whether the size, density, and diversity of cities or their population composition causes them to have distinctive characteristics, there is no question that such characteristics exist. Surveys have shown that cities, in contrast to rural areas, are characterized by higher levels of education and income, greater social mobility, more foreigners, smaller families, and less stable marriages. The reported rates of crime, alcoholism, drug addiction, mental illness, and suicide are all higher in cities than elsewhere.

THE SUBURBS

More Americans now live in suburbs than in cities or rural areas. The suburbs have been growing more rapidly than the cities since the turn of the century, but the biggest increase has taken place since 1950. (See Figure 17.1.) Many explanations have been advanced for the rapid growth of suburbs. Good roads were an essential ingredient, for without them the

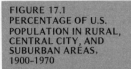

FIGURE 17.1
PERCENTAGE OF U.S.
POPULATION IN RURAL,
CENTRAL CITY, AND
SUBURBAN AREAS,
1900–1970

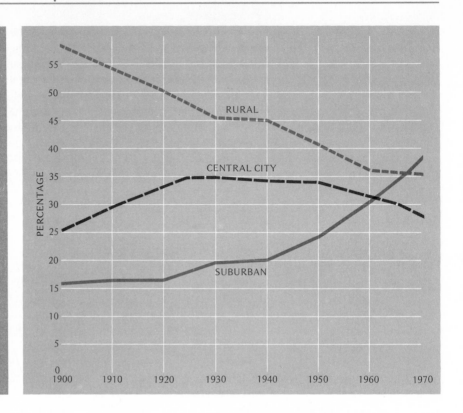

"suburban revolution" could not have taken place. The economic boom after World War II, together with the availability of government-backed loans, made suburban houses affordable for many more people than ever before.[11] But why did so many people take advantage of the opportunity? In one sense the big city, with its congestion, crime, pollution, and decay, pushed them out. But in another sense the suburbs pulled families out of the cities. Some moved to the suburbs because they were attracted to the suburban ideal of a "country home." But most had more concrete reasons — space for growing families, good schools, personal safety, and a pleasant environment at a price they could afford.[12]

North Americans have a kind of love–hate relationship with their suburbs, seeing them as both the cause of and the solution to social blight. The proponents of suburban living picture it as a refuge from the troubles of the big city. In this view mile after mile of neatly trimmed lawns and tidy, well-ordered, nuclear families greet suburbanites upon their return from their jobs in the city. Close to their new home is the symbol of modern suburbia — a huge shopping mall with dozens of stores filled with the latest consumer goods. The residents tend to be young and white. The men hold interesting white-collar jobs with promise for the future. The women are well groomed, efficient, politically aware, and deeply concerned with the welfare of their young children. In general, suburbanites are outgoing and sociable, and because they resemble each other they get along together and are active in local civic affairs.

The critics of suburbia picture it differently. They see the suburbs as an endless expanse of "crackerbox" houses that are so alike that it is difficult to tell one from the other. They say that the residents also are "ticky tacky" and that all are stamped from the same mold. Because suburbanites are mostly from the white middle class, they lack individuality and diversity and are bland and dull. The suburbanite's life centers on nothing more important than washing the car, mowing the lawn, and shopping at the supermarket. The goal of each suburban dweller is to match or surpass his or her neighbors in the collection of cars, TV sets, microwave ovens, barbecue pits, and other material things.

Neither of these views is a complete distortion, but both are faulty. Suburban life is not nearly so bland or homogeneous as many people believe, for there are many different types of suburban settlements. Some are primarily industrial regions, while others are residential areas. Some suburbs fit the image of wealth and comfort, while others are old and decaying. The idea that the suburbs are islands of safety in a sea of urban problems is increasingly outdated, for suburban life is rapidly becoming another form of urban living. As Murphy and Rehfuss point out,

> Suburbia no longer is immune from national and regional problems and no longer can escape the necessity of dealing directly with them. Criticism of urban life increasingly refers to suburban life as well. Deepseated urban problems are found in suburban areas even if they have not been recognized fully.[13]

Public opinion has failed to keep up with the changing face of the suburbs. Today's suburbs are no longer bedroom communities that are economically and culturally dependent on the central city. Almost one-third are now industrially oriented, and a wide variety of goods and services are available in suburban stores. A *New York Times* study revealed that 72 percent of the residents of America's 15 largest suburbs both live *and* work in the suburbs.[14] Another study showed that one-third of Detroit's suburbanites *never* visit the city for any purpose.[15] Suburban shopping centers have become social centers as well. For instance, Monroeville Mall, which is 12 miles from Pittsburgh, has 129 attractions, including boutiques, restaurants, department stores, professional offices, a reference library, a night club, a Roman Catholic chapel, and a counseling service headed by a Protestant minister.[16]

While the suburbs tend to be more homogeneous than the cities, the difference is minor.[17] The classic suburbanites—white middle-class families with children — are still the backbone of most suburban communities, but other groups of people now are making their home in the suburbs. These include the old, the divorced, the single, and the childless. More apartment houses than single-family dwellings are now being constructed in the suburbs. Between 1960 and 1970 the number of single-family homes increased only 17 percent while the number of multiple-unit structures almost doubled. Although the average suburbanite still makes substantially more money than the average city dweller, increasing numbers of poor people and ethnic minorities are moving into the suburbs.

Rather than producing greater social integration, these developments have made suburbs more like cities. As in the cities, the poor move into poor suburban areas, and blacks move into black neighborhoods. Indeed, it appears that some suburbs are now merely extensions of nearby cities, making it difficult to draw a distinction between urban and suburban ways of life.

Nevertheless, some differences remain. Studies show that suburbanites spend much of their leisure time at home while city dwellers make more use of public facilities such as theaters, concert halls, and ballparks. Suburbanites tend to be more interested in their neighborhood and more involved with their neighbors. The low population densities in suburbs mean that bus companies cannot show a profit, so transportation is by private car. Surveys show that suburbanites are more satisfied with their residential location than city dwellers are with theirs.[18]

RURAL TOWNS

Twentieth-century urbanization has left its mark on rural hamlets and villages. The myth of rural life as a simple, trouble-free existence shared with friends and close to nature is an alluring dream to many city dwellers looking for a peaceful life. But in reality rural communities have never been Utopias, and there have always been many kinds of rural life, ranging from the isolation of self-styled hermits to the dominance of country squires. Now the range of rural life is even broader, including the affluence of "agribusiness," the abject poverty of migratory workers, the straight-laced conservatism of small towns, the radical life styles of rural communes, and many other variations.

A key to understanding modern rural towns can be found in the census reports, which reveal that the rural population is declining not only relative to the urban population but also in absolute terms. In the United States the portion of the population living in rural areas has declined sharply, from over 50 percent at the turn of the century to 36 percent in 1950, 30 percent in 1960, and 26.5 percent in 1970. However, because of the large increase in the total population, the *number* of people who lived in rural areas actually increased until 1950, when it began a modest decline.[19] The drop in the rural population has been even more rapid in Canada in recent years. According to official figures, Canada was about

24 percent rural in 1970, a slightly smaller percentage than the United States.[20]

Not so obvious from census figures is the urbanization of rural life. Residents of open country, villages, and towns with fewer than 2500 inhabitants are becoming more and more like those of suburbs and cities. One important influence has been the decline in farming as an occupation. Traditionally, the vast majority of rural residents have been farmers, but in the 20 years from 1950 to 1970 alone farmers dropped from 15 percent to 5 percent of the population in America, while rural nonfarmers increased from about 21 percent to 22 percent. Canada has shown a similar decline: Farmers accounted for only 6.6 percent of the total population in 1971.[21]

But the way of life among those who till the soil has changed too. Farm families no longer raise their own vegetables, butcher their own hogs, milk their own cows, or cut their own wood for lumber and fuel. They buy their beans, pork, and milk at the supermarket and order building materials and fuel oil from local distributors. Gone are the days when spare time meant sitting around the stove telling tales, mending clothing, or repairing tools. Today farm families watch television or go to the movies. Some take long winter vacations in California or Florida; some go to New York for the opera season; and others jet to England to see plays, hear symphony orchestras, and visit art museums. No longer is the farm passed down to the eldest son. Instead, younger family members are given management positions in a corporation controlled by the family elders. In short, agriculture has changed from a way of life to a business. As mechanization and expensive technology moved in, farms became food and fiber factories run much like most other factories.

People born in rural areas continue to migrate to cities in search of opportunity, as they have for centuries. Not so well known is the fact that city dwellers are migrating to the country, too. A recent study by the U.S. Department of Agriculture revealed that 24 percent of the white residents of rural areas were immigrants from cities.[22] These immigrants bring the urban way of life with them, further diminishing the cultural distinctiveness of country people.

Despite all these changes, however, life on a farm or in a small town retains many special features. People know each other as people rather than as role players. The background of residents of rural communities tends to be more homogeneous than that of city dwellers, giving them a stronger sense of group identity and a clearer feeling of where they fit in as individuals. Deviant behavior is less common in rural areas than in urban ones; and though crime rates have been increasing faster in rural than in urban areas, they are still considerably lower.

But living in a small town has its drawbacks. There is less deviance in small towns because everyone watches everyone else. There is little room for dissent and none at all for groups of dissenters. The absence of anonymity reduces opportunities for many types of crime, but it also affects personal freedom, innovation, and individuality. Because individuals cannot get lost in the crowd, their neighbors often know the details of their personal lives, and small-town gossip can be malicious and spiteful. Rural communities lack much of the spice of city life because they are so small and homogeneous.[23]

PROBLEMS OF URBANIZATION

The migration from country to city, together with the migration of foreigners to North American cities, created severe problems of growth. Very little planning was involved. City officials and private developers took the migrants as they came, packing them together and straining to construct water systems, sewers, transportation systems, and other public facilities fast enough to accommodate them. As the population of cities continued to increase, boundaries were extended, placing additional demands on city services. Then came satellite cities and suburbs. As city dwellers moved to the edge of town, they established their own local governments, ignoring the effect on the cities they had just left and disregarding the need for coordination of the services provided by the old city and its new satellites.

Economically, huge metropolitan areas fused into one big unit, with the suburbs and rural areas dominated by the economy of the original city. Socially, too, the suburbs and rural villages came within the city's sphere of influence—the "urban way of life" became the life style of almost everyone. But the populations of these metropolitan areas failed to fuse politically as each tried to run its own affairs with little regard for its neighbors. In an extreme case a town would dump sewage in "its" river, polluting the drinking water of the towns downstream. Such poor coordination is at the heart of contemporary metropolitan decay. City financial crises, crumbling inner-city slums, the hidden reality of rural poverty, and a decline in the sense of community are different aspects of this process of urbanization.

Finances

A few years ago the spectacle of America's largest city teetering on the brink of bankruptcy alerted many people to the financial plight of the cities. Month after month the American public heard about New York City's inability to pay its bills. Seemingly unavoidable disasters were averted at the last minute as the city was bailed out by the state or the federal government. Some of New York City's problems were of its own making—irresponsible officials had borrowed huge sums in order to avoid raising taxes, while at the same time paying city employees handsome salaries. But most of New York's difficulties are familiar stories in other metropolitan areas as well.

Throughout the nation city residents pay more in taxes than suburbanites do. On the average, local taxes take about 7 percent of all personal income in the cities, compared with 5 percent in the suburbs.[24] The cause of this difference is the financial burden that city governments must bear. As affluent people moved to the suburbs, the cities were left with a high percentage of poor people, who need many services but are unable to pay high taxes. The central cities are older, so they need more fire protection; crime rates are higher, requiring more money for police, courts, and jails. Social services such as welfare and public assistance demand enormous chunks of public funds. Despite their needs, the cities cannot raise their taxes as high as they would like to, for doing so would accelerate the rush of people and capital to suburbs and rural areas. In fact, the suburbs actually receive indirect support from the cities in a number of ways. For instance, many suburbanites work in the city and use its recreational and cultural facilities, but pay few of its taxes.

Government

Local governments are beset by a variety of problems ranging from graft and corruption to wasteful duplication of services. The big-city political machine is the classic example of a local-government system that takes power away from the people. The public interest is ignored when city jobs and contracts are handed out as rewards for loyalty to the machine. Votes are courted in much the same way. The political organization divides up the city and appoints ward leaders and precinct captains whose job is to "deliver the vote" from their area by handing out favors in exchange for political support. Although the influence of political machines has declined greatly in the years since World War II, machine politics is still a costly problem in some cities.

But political corruption continues without the machines, and it is not limited to big cities. Suburban zoning changes have repeatedly been the focus of corruption scandals. Millions of dollars are often involved in an agency's decision to change the zoning of a piece of land. Developers and land speculators looking for a fast profit go to great lengths to convince officials to make the "right" decision. Officials in small suburban counties sometimes are influenced with cash payments, or they may be given a percentage of the developer's profits. The result is likely to be a new suburban community that turns its developers into millionaires but does not meet the needs of local residents.

Another product of urbanization is the creation of a confusing network of fragmented local governments and overlapping service districts. As the population has moved beyond the boundaries of the central cities, governmental units have multiplied like rabbits. The New York metropolitan area has about 550 governmental units, Philadelphia 876, and Chicago well over 1000. While the number of city governments has increased sharply, the largest increase has been in special-purpose districts such as those for water and sewage. In the 10 years from 1962 to 1972, the number of special-purpose districts (excluding schools) in the nation increased from 5400 to 7850.[25] Metropolitan areas often have dozens of police chiefs, fire chiefs, and department heads when only a few would be sufficient. This tremendous overlap and duplication of services is expensive and inefficient. According to the National Research Council,

> The reason for creating new governmental units often appeared self-evident to those involved: to meet the general or special needs of elements of the urban population spread over outlying areas. What in fact was accomplished, however, was a weakening and erosion of metropolitan communities' capacity to plan, finance, and execute the extension of public services through the area in an orderly and efficient manner.[26]

Many town and city governments have surprisingly little control over their own affairs because states place tight legal restrictions on their freedom to act, particularly with respect to the types and amounts of the taxes that can be levied on their citizens. Further, local governments have come to rely on federal grants, which often come with orders that specify how the money is to be spent. Powerful corporations often use their influence with federal and state governments to overpower local opposition to their plans. Finally, urban areas are underrepresented in the many legislative bodies that allocate seats on the basis of geography, without regard to the number of people living in the district.

Housing   A short walk through any decaying urban residential area will convince the visitor that something is wrong. Broken windows, peeling paint, and doors hanging by their hinges are common sights in the inner cities, The visitor who gets behind the external signs of decay will see leaking toilets, broken light fixtures, overcrowded rooms, and rats. Inadequate urban housing is a special problem for minorities and for old people, as noted in Chapters 7 and 9.

But the visitor who leaves the city and hikes through the countryside is likely to see even worse housing. Rural shacks are inferior to the urban tenements that receive so much publicity. The last census revealed that over 14 percent of all rural homes lacked adequate plumbing, while only 3.5 percent of inner-city and suburban homes had that problem. About 8 percent of all metropolitan homes had more than one person per room, but about 9 percent of all rural homes were overcrowded. The census also showed that rural housing had lower values, lower rents, and higher vacancy rates than urban housing.[27] Overall, it is clear that rural housing is more dilapidated, has fewer modern conveniences, and is more crowded.

On a national basis housing improved between 1960 and 1970 because the total supply of housing increased more rapidly than the population. As

FIGURE 17.2
(a) HOUSING UNITS
LACKING PLUMBING
FACILITIES, BY TENURE,
1940–1974

(b) HOUSING UNITS
LACKING PLUMBING
FACILITIES, BY LOCATION,
1974

Source: U.S. Department of Commerce,
Social Indicators 1976 (Washington, D.C.:
GPO 1976), p. 81.

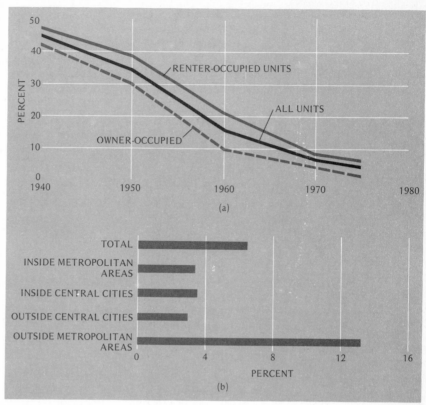

more new apartments and houses came onto the market, some people were able to move out of substandard buildings. During that period the number of overcrowded housing units decreased by almost 15 percent and the number of units with deficient plumbing decreased by over 50 percent.[28] (See Figure 17.2.) But the housing boom peaked in 1972, when housing starts (housing units on which construction was begun) reached an all-time high. Since then housing starts have declined sharply, and the outlook for the future is not bright because inflation has priced desirable apartments and houses beyond the reach of many people.

Transportation

People in industrialized nations are fascinated by cars. Some of them drive 50 or 60 miles a day to work and back, claiming that they do so because there are no buses or trains. But most of them probably would continue to drive even if the bus or train station were close to their homes and businesses. The automobile is comfortable and convenient. Even kings in their carriages did not know such speed, comfort, or convenience. But a frightful price as been paid for these advantages. More than 55,000

The automobile provides one of the fastest and most convenient forms of transportation ever devised, but we now have too much of a good thing. Traffic jams clog city streets, automobile exhaust pollutes the air, and the petroleum upon which the whole method of transportation depends is now in short supply.

Americans die violent deaths in car crashes every year—more than the total of American lives lost in the Vietnam War.

Cars are the lifeblood of suburbs, but they are destroying the cities. More than 65 percent of the land in American cities is devoted to highways, parking lots, garages, gas stations, and other uses related to the automobile. In downtown Los Angeles the figure is closer to 85 percent.[29] Construction of our huge network of freeways and turnpikes has created employment, but these ribbons of concrete have left great damage in their wake. They often run through poverty areas, where the costs of land and demolition are low, forcing residents to crowd into neighboring slums. Moreover, the highways were expected to bring shoppers to the central city, but instead they have encouraged city shoppers to move to the suburbs.[30]

The private automobile is not an efficient means of transportation, despite its convenience, for it consumes scarce energy resources much more rapidly than buses or trains. Moreover, this fuel is used in disproportionate amounts by the affluent. About 20 percent of all city dwellers have no car, and also lack friends or relatives who will drive them around. Because most cities have poor systems of public transportation, these people are cut off from employment and educational opportunities.

Crime

Crime is primarily an urban problem. Official statistics show that big cities have four times as much violent crime as their suburbs and over six times as much as rural communities. Although the differences in property crime

DEBATE
Should the Size of Cities Be Limited?

PRO

The reckless growth of our cities has created enormous problems. Greedy developers have ruined one scenic area after another, replacing trees and grass with asphalt and tract houses. The cost of providing additional services has placed a heavy burden on those who already live in the cities and has reduced the quality of the services delivered. Air, water, and land pollution have become deadly problems as more and more people have crowded together in urban areas. This crowding, combined with the anonymity of city life, has weakened the social controls that normally provide guidance and direction. Crime, delinquency, mental illness, and suicide have become serious problems as a result.

These problems are an inevitable result of the process of urbanization. They cannot be resolved as long as urban growth continues at its present rate. The reduction or elimination of urban growth would give cities time to deal with their problems without the continual demands of an increasing population; at the same time, it would reduce the problems caused by rural depopulation.

Despite loud protests by land developers and speculators, urban growth can be limited without infringing on personal liberties. Rezoning the land next to urban centers, restricting new water and sewer hookups, and creating tax breaks for businesses that locate in smaller towns would encourage a slow redistribution of the population without the use of coercive methods.

CON

Cities have always been centers of cultural change and development. The ideas that transformed the modern world all developed in cities. Today, our cities are not only the political, economic, and social nerve centers of our society; they are breeding grounds for the arts and sciences as well. The safe comforts of small-town life do not spur the kind of changes needed in the twentieth-century world. The rich diversity of city life is essential to creative development.

If the effort to limit urban growth were successful, society would grow more rigid and inflexible. The freedoms made possible by the anonymity of city life would be overwhelmed by provincial conformism. Existing cities would lose their creative spark as migration was reduced and wealthy elites gained increasing dominance.

Even if a reduction in urban growth were desirable, there is no way of achieving it without violating property rights and personal freedoms. Rezoning land so that its current owners cannot build on it effectively takes away their right to use their property as they see fit. The steady growth of urban areas is proof that people prefer to live in cities, and preventing people from living where they wish would violate their freedom of choice. Furthermore, no-growth policies would force the poor and perhaps even the middle class out of the cities, because rents and property values would be pushed upward by the limited supply of urban housing.

are not as great, it is still much more common in big cities than else-where.[31] In addition, fear of crime is much greater in the cities. Many urbanites arrange their daily lives with crime in mind, always seeking to reduce their chances of becoming victims. A recent survey showed that about half of a sample of big-city residents were afraid to walk outside at night while only about 20 percent of the suburban residents had similar fears.[32] It should be noted, however, that crime rates are increasing faster in suburbs and rural areas than in cities. Some of this increase is due to the fact that city criminals are prowling other areas in search of victims. But most of the increase stems from the fact that suburban and rural life are becoming more like city life.

Crowding There are many conflicting theories about the effects of crowding on human behavior. When studies showing the alarming effects of over-crowding on experimental animals were first published, many urban sociologists were shocked. Experiments by John Calhoun, among others, showed that the normal social patterns of rats are severely disrupted in overcrowded conditions.[33] Marauding males wander around the cage at-tacking both males and females and destroying the nests of weaker animals. Bands of "juvenile delinquents" engage in promiscuous sexual behavior and frequent fights. Some researchers concluded from these ex-periments that crowding is a major cause of urban problems. And because cities are becoming more and more crowded, they projected a very dark picture of the future of urban life.

Researchers studying animals in the wild came to similar conclusions. They noted that some animals have a "territorial instinct" to claim a cer-tain area as their own and to defend it against intruders. It was easy to conclude that humans have the same instincts and that the roots of human aggression are to be found in the violation of personal territory—which of course occurs more often in crowded conditions.[34] Again the implication appeared to be that urban problems will be solved only if population den-sity is reduced.

However, there are many reasons for doubting these conclusions. For one thing, the animals studied lack complex cultural systems. Rats and other animals have fixed patterns of behavior that are very sensitive to any disturbance. If the pattern is disrupted, the animals cannot adjust. Human flexibility, in contrast, permits almost unlimited adaptation to the environment. Further, cross-cultural studies show no consistent relation-ship between crowding and crime or between crowding and aggression. Tokyo is one of the most densely populated cities in the world, but its crime rate is very low. While this does not prove that overcrowding has no bad effects on humans, it does suggest that high population density is manageable in human cultures.[35]

Ethnic Segregation

Most large cities have a number of "ethnic villages"—areas populated mostly by members of a particular ethnic group. Whether such a residential pattern is desirable or not is open to debate. As noted in Chapter 7, those aiming for pluralism favor it and those working for integration oppose it. However, few would argue that *forced* ethnic segregation is a good thing. Yet that is exactly the position in which many members of poor minority groups find themselves, especially if their physical appearance is distinctive.

Laws that say that blacks or Hispanic peoples cannot live in certain parts of town are no longer permitted. Nevertheless, these ethnic minorities are excluded from some areas by highly prejudiced and hostile residents. In some ways, segregation has actually increased since the turn of the century as minority groups have been increasingly concentrated in the cities and more whites have moved to the suburbs. The percentage of blacks in the population of American central cities rose from about 7 percent in 1900 to 22 percent in 1970. Since 1960 there has been a slight increase in the movement of minority groups into suburban areas, but white resistance remains high. When minority group members move out of the central city, they are likely to move into segregated suburbs.[36] If this pattern of forced segregation is to be broken, vigorous action by the federal government will be required. But at present federal officials seem to be either unwilling or unable to act.

Rural Decay

The change from a predominantly agricultural economy to an urban industrial one has created some special problems for rural areas. While most of these problems are economic, the decline in agricultural employment and the cultural dominance of the city have destroyed a way of life as well.

People who live in rural areas make considerably less money than urban dwellers. In 1974 the average family income in the suburbs of a large metropolitan area was $16,320, while the average farm family income was $9,990.[37] The poverty rate is much higher in rural areas, where many pockets of poverty are found amid relatively prosperous areas.

Poverty, in turn, puts rural people at a disadvantage with respect to education and health care. Rural school districts pay their teachers less than urban districts and spend less money per student. The dropout rate is higher in rural schools, and the overall educational level is lower. There are about three times as many physicians per person in urban areas of the United States as in rural areas. Much of this difference stems from the smaller communities' inability to pay physicians as much as they can earn in cities. Studies show that rural residents see a physician less often than city residents, that more rural children die in infancy, and that there are fewer hospital beds available per person in rural areas.[38]

The migration from country to city has had the effect of increasing rural problems. When affluent people move from the city to the suburbs, they take their wealth with them, leaving the city with a financial crisis. A similar process has occurred in some rural areas, since a drop in the population of a small town means that the cost of maintaining essential services must be carried by fewer people. Stores and businesses that depend on local trade go bankrupt, reducing the tax base. As job opportunities dry up and education, health care, and other community services decline, even more people move out and the problem becomes more severe. To make matters worse, it is usually the young adults who migrate to the cities, leaving a disproportionately large dependent population of young children and elderly people who must be supported by the productive workers who remain. The eastern provinces of Canada, designated by the government as "underdeveloped economically," have dependent populations of this kind.

RESPONDING TO PROBLEMS OF URBANIZATION

Despite the complexity of metropolitan problems, there is no shortage of proposals for solving them. While some are wildly utopian and others too narrow to be worthwhile, all have one thing in common: Successful implementation would require two scarce commodities—money and motivation.

Governmental Reorganization

Most proposals for solving metropolitan political and financial problems recommend governmental reorganization. This means, generally, the creation of larger governmental units. For example, some planners suggest that cities be abolished and that county or even regional governments take their place. Others propose that only some units of government be regionalized in this way—school districts, water districts, sewage districts, airport districts, pollution control districts, and so on. Such regional government units could provide services more economically and would spread the tax burden more evenly over inner cities, suburbs, and rural areas. Some urban planners believe that these governmental units will eventually encourage a sense of regional cooperation and identity. A person would no longer be loyal to "Boston" or "San Francisco"; instead, he or she would identify with "New England" or "the Bay area."

Three different approaches to the creation of metropolitan government have been tried—expanding existing governments by annexation or merger, creating unified special-service districts, and establishing metropolitan federations of existing local governments.

Expanding City Governments

Annexation of suburbs or otherwise merging two or more governments appears to be the easiest form of reorganization. In the nineteenth century important mergers took place in New York City, Philadelphia, Boston, and New Orleans. Hundreds of cities have expanded their boundaries to take in suburbs. But there seems to be increasing resistance to mergers and annexations. Voters in suburban areas are seldom willing to merge with nearby cities. They moved to their homes to avoid the problems of the big cities, and see in proposed mergers only increased taxes and loss of autonomy. Since the turn of the century more than twenty-one proposed mergers have been rejected by American voters.[39]

Creating Consolidated Districts

Establishing a special governmental unit with its own tax base to manage a single task is by far the most popular technique of reorganization. Such units are usually called districts, as in "consolidated school district." They are usually responsible for a single service rather than many. Thus, a citizen might pay taxes to one unit for fire protection, to another for water, to another for sewer service, and to still others for an airport, a bridge, or a rapid-transit system. Such special districts have been popular with voters largely because they resolve critical areawide problems without disturbing the existing governmental structure. But the use of special districts has several drawbacks. They separate the functions being performed, making the coordination of services and planning extremely difficult by creating more new governmental agencies. They also seem to be especially vulnerable to the pressures of special-interest groups.

Establishing Federations

A federation of metropolitan governments allows existing units to continue to operate independently on some issues but joins them to coordinate their activities on other issues. For example, each city may regulate and maintain its own streets while several cities combine their efforts to handle schools or sewage. Such plans run into the same kind of opposition as proposals for annexations and mergers, and thus no large-scale federation has emerged in the United States. However, because local elections were not required, a Metropolitan Council was established in the area of Toronto, Ontario, over twenty years ago. Although this federation has its critics, it has improved water supply and sewage disposal, established an advanced rapid-transit system, improved and unified law enforcement, and constructed new public-housing and library facilities.[40]

Decentralization

Some experts on metropolitan government reject the whole idea of centralization. They argue that small governmental units are more responsive to the public will, promote a sense of community, and provide more opportunities for individual participation.[41] Some proposals for decentralization would divide existing cities into smaller units with specific functions while keeping overall control in the hands of the main city government. Other plans would shift population from overcrowded cities to rural towns beset by depopulation. A third plan would encourage cities to adopt "no-growth" policies, forcing would-be migrants to form new cities or to remain in rural areas. The Soviet Union and the People's Republic of China, for instance, allow no more immigrants into their cities than the number set by government planners. Following the end of the Vietnam War, the victorious communist forces in Cambodia used even more drastic measures, closing the capital city of Phnom Penh and driving most of its residents into the countryside to return to a life of farming. Although accurate figures are not available, there is little doubt that thousands died in this cruel attempt to reduce the urban population. Such extreme measures are unacceptable in a democratic society, but they do show the importance many countries place on maintaining a balance between their rural and urban populations.

New Cities

A degree of decentralization has been achieved in many places by erecting new cities and waiting for people to be attracted to them. Some of these cities, such as Reston, Virginia, and Columbia, Maryland, have been constructed by private developers. Although residents have found such cities quite satisfactory, few have been financially successful, and most have failed to produce the social benefits of decentralization. Indeed, they are usually "mini-cities" built within commuting distance of large metropolitan areas, thus adding to existing urban problems.[42]

Other new cities — such as Washington, D.C., Canberra, Australia, and Chandigarh, India — have been built by national governments. The most spectacular recent example is Brasilia, the new capital of Brazil, located in the jungle 600 miles from Rio de Janeiro. After the first buildings had been erected, thousands of government workers were transferred to the new capital. Many of the new residents disliked Brasilia, whose sterile efficiency stands in stark contrast to the teeming confusion of Brazil's other major cities. However, recent reports indicate that the city is becoming more popular as its residents "break it in."

National governments are the only agencies that can afford the tremendous costs of developing the full-scale cities that many urban planners dream about. Such planners believe they could build the best possible transportation system, promote the most efficient land use, and attract an equitable balance of ethnic and income groups while keeping the total size of the city at a manageable level. It seems likely that such new cities would have little trouble attracting residents from crowded inner cities. However, any decentralization program of this kind is years away. Many Americans think such large-scale planning would be totalitarian so they oppose centralization of authority even if it would decentralize city life. Corporations with huge investments in existing cities also oppose the development of new cities, and small-town residents are often convinced that a new city near them would bring with it all the urban problems they have avoided. In the long run, however, the government's role in determining where people live is likely to increase as the population grows and desirable areas become crowded.

Urban Renewal

American urban-renewal programs were begun during the Great Depression in order to improve housing and provide employment for construction workers. To this day urban renewal usually means "housing renewal." From the beginning urban-renewal projects were plagued with troubles. The original idea was simple. Government agencies were to buy up decaying central-city areas, demolish the buildings, and sell the land to private developers, who would build apartments for people with low and moderate incomes. But as it turned out, the developers were not required to build inexpensive housing. Most built office buildings, factories, and luxury apartments, which bring in higher profits. Between 1949 and 1967 urban-renewal projects in the United States demolished 383,000 housing units while providing only 107,000 new units and 75,000 reconditioned units to replace them.[43] The poor were thus forced to move from substandard homes in one area to substandard homes in another area. This caused many black leaders to say that urban renewal is just another term for "Negro removal."

Even the low-cost housing that was constructed did not overcome the poverty, unemployment, and racial discrimination of the inner cities. Generally, the new apartments were poor in design and quality. Many units quickly deteriorated through poor maintenance, and some became centers of local crime. A symbol of the failure of urban housing projects is the Pruitt-Igoe development near St. Louis, which became such a problem that large sections of the project had to be demolished.[44]

A more recent low-cost housing program was started in 1968, when Congress authorized the Federal Housing Administration (FHA) to guarantee mortgages to allow the poor to buy homes in inner-city areas. Begun with high expectations, this program ended in disaster. In many cases private real-estate speculators bought rundown houses, made superficial repairs to make them look as if they had been reconditioned, bribed or otherwise convinced FHA officials to appraise the properties at inflated values, and then sold homes to unsuspecting low-income families. No down payments were required. When the true condition of the houses became apparent or the poor families were unable to keep up payments, the new owners simply vanished and left the FHA holding the bag. Even when no corruption was involved, it was obvious that many poor people had been encouraged to take on a financial burden greater than they could bear. As a result, by 1973 the FHA was left with over 200,000 foreclosed houses.[45]

Generally, the history of governmental programs to improve housing in the United States has been one of misplaced priorities. Most federal assistance has gone to the wealthy and the middle class rather than to the poor. The largest direct housing subsidy program in the United States is the low-interest home loan program, in which mortgages are guaranteed by the Federal Housing Administration and the Veterans Administration. Over 5 million private homes for middle-class families have been built

The redevelopment of decaying urban neighborhoods has provided many cities with attractive new shopping, business, and residential areas, but it often pushes the poor from one crowded decaying neighborhood to another.

under these programs, while only 600,000 units of low-income housing have been subsidized by the federal government.[46] Federal tax policy also favors the homeowner over the renter, permitting homeowners to deduct mortgage interest payments and local property taxes from their federal income tax. Ten years ago this subsidy cost over $6 billion a year. Those who cannot afford to purchase a house receive nothing from this costly program. Even middle-class people do not receive a full share of the benefits—the greatest savings are reaped by those in the highest tax brackets.[47]

Some authorities believe that most of the defects in current housing programs could be corrected by giving direct help to the poor. Thus, a "housing allowance" in the form of a cash payment or rent voucher would enable poor families to select suitable homes from those available. This program would be effective, however, only if the prices of housing were controlled and the supply of housing kept up with demand. However, economists have noted that these two demands are contradictory in a free-market system: Developers will not risk capital on new housing if they know that government rent controls will not allow them to reap substantial profits.

SOCIOLOGICAL PERSPECTIVES on Urbanization

From the beginning urban sociology has been concerned with the sociologal differences between the village and the city. Ferdinand Tönnies concluded that these two types of communities were held together by very different kinds of social forces. Common action and cooperation in the village is motivated by a shared sense of unity, according to Tönnies, but common action in the city is motivated by mutual interdependence. Small villages are close knit because people live similar lives and have strong bonds of friendship. The community and the extended family are often identical, making the village literally "one big family." In cities, on the other hand, life styles are varied and people are held together primarily by common needs. City people need each other the way a seller needs a buyer, but there is little sense of community.

As nations have become more urban, people have lost the feeling that they are part of a community sharing common beliefs and customs. Their sense of common identity and pride in community are weak or lacking altogether. Much of the work of urban sociologists deals with problems arising from the decline in bonds of affection and identification that has accompanied urbanization.

The Functionalist Perspective

Most functionalists believe the rapid urbanization of North America has disrupted family life as well as economic, educational, political, and religious institutions. The fact that bonds of affection have weakened and people are more isolated is taken to be a symptom of more general social disorganization. When masses of people left rural villages to settle in cities, the villages became disorganized and unable to meet the needs of those who remained. Likewise, the cities were not prepared to assimilate the migrants, and to provide them with a sense of mutual identity that would encourage loyalty and contentment. The old cultural patterns that were functional for village living were abandoned, but new integrating patterns did not arise. As a consequence rates of crime, suicide, and mental illness grew, as did other symptoms of social disorganization. But before a new balance could be established, another shift in population — the flight to the suburbs — threw the social system back into chaos.

Functionalists argue that we must slow the pace of social change and allow metropolitan areas to adjust to these new conditions. They favor centralization of metropolitan government rather than decentralization, believing that a centralized administration might get metropolitan communities running smoothly again. Indeed, it is possible that such reorganization could bring order to highly disorganized areas such as urban and rural slums. In a properly functioning metropolitan system, the people in each area would develop a new sense of community, identifying with each other and with the larger metropolitan community.

The Conflict Perspective

From the conflict perspective the problems of urbanization are seen as the result of conflicts between competing interest groups. When rural land-owners were a dominant political force, they did all they could to maintain their power, using it to obtain special economic benefits. For example, in the 1930s they persuaded the federal government to build farm-to-market roads, provide electricity for farms, and pay farmers more than the free-market price for their crops. But urbanization resulted in a shift of power to the cities, where industrialists took advantage of cheap labor provided by those who could no longer make a living on the farm. Because these powerful groups placed profits ahead of social welfare, the cities began to deteriorate. The cities were used up and then abandoned the way people abandon worn-out cars.

As wealthy and influential people moved from the cities to the suburbs and corporations discovered "agribusiness," another shift in power took place. The cities were left to the poor, the weak, and the powerless. Meanwhile well-to-do suburbanites began to dominate the political scene, using their power to get special advantages for themselves. The federal government responded by favoring suburbs with freeways and express-ways, low-interest loans for single-family houses, tax advantages, and other benefits that are denied to the inner-city residents who were left behind.

Conflict theorists are convinced that the solution to urban problems lies in political organization and action. People in city slums and rural poverty areas must band together to demand fairer treatment. Such a movement should not be directed at isolated problems such as poor housing or crime but, rather, should attack inequality in every social sphere.

The Social-Psychological Perspective

Most social-psychological studies of community life have been concerned with the effects of urbanization on the psychological well-being of individuals. As noted earlier, Simmel and Wirth, among others, felt that city life has negative consequences for most people. But in a sense Simmel and Wirth were simply noting that our culture has traditionally valued the qualities of rural living above those of urban living. Thomas Jefferson warned that city life would corrupt virtue and undermine political freedom. Such antiurban values made the problems of urbanization seem like the fruits of evil living. Perhaps that is why, until quite recently, there were so few serious efforts to improve urban life styles.

Even now social psychologists seem to favor small-town life, with its sense of community and identity, over the cold impersonality of the city. Their recommendations for improving metropolitan life call for decentral-ization into smaller units so that people will have an opportunity to de-velop genuine neighborhoods. They note that many city dwellers have already rid themselves of the indifference to which Simmel and Wirth objected. Many districts in today's cities are real "communities" in the sense that they have some of the social-psychological characteristics of the village. Chinese, Italian, and Polish neighborhoods in metropolitan areas are often as tightly knit as any rural village. Similarly, some suburbs are characterized by a strong sense of neighborliness and mutual identity.

The most serious psychological problems—mental illness, alcoholism, and drug addiction—develop among those who live in the slums. Because there is little sense of community, old-fashioned social controls—gossip, ridicule, slander—are not effective. Police and other agencies of formal government try to keep order, leading slum dwellers to complain that they are treated as though they were enemies whose territory is occupied by a foreign army. Such occupation, of course, produces new problems, which in turn require more occupation forces, and thus a vicious circle develops. The decentralization of government, social psychologists say, might break this chain of events by giving slum dwellers a stake in their own affairs and their own destiny. But such decentralization is not likely to occur unless there is a shift in power along the lines suggested by conflict theorists.

SUMMARY The shift from rural to urban living in North America has profoundly altered the lives of millions of people in just a few short years. Traditionally, most families lived on farms in rural areas, but twentieth-century industrialization spurred the rapid growth of cities. In the past few decades there has been a new shift of population, this time toward the suburbs. By 1970 the population of America's suburbs was larger than that of its cities.

Pioneering sociologists such as Georg Simmel and Louis Wirth argued that city life creates certain characteristics in urban residents, including impersonal social relationships, a blasé attitude toward life, a materialistic outlook, and a feeling of indifference toward others. More recently Herbert Gans has shown that this picture exaggerates the negative aspects of city life and is true only for some types of city dwellers.

The availability of government-backed loans and the prosperity following World War II made it possible for many people to move to the suburbs, thus avoiding growing urban problems. Although the stereotype of suburbia pictures miles of well-kept houses populated by young, middle-class white professionals on the way up, there is actually a great deal of diversity in the suburbs. An increasing number of suburbs are business and industrial centers. As suburbs have aged and developed a more diverse character, they have come to resemble the cities near them. They are no longer islands in a sea of urban problems, and the suburban way of life is coming to resemble the urban way of life.

Rural towns and villages have been deeply affected by urbanization. At the turn of the century half of all Americans lived in open areas or in villages with populations of less than 2500, but now only about 25 percent are rural. Farmers now make up only 5 percent of the U.S. population. With the growth of mass transportation and communication, rural life itself has become increasingly "urban." Yet life on a farm or in a small town retains its distinctive characteristics, including more personal relationships, a sense of identify and belonging, a homogeneous culture, and intolerance of deviant behavior.

The urbanization of America was not planned. Economically and socially, the population has been fused into huge metropolitan units; politically, no such fusion has taken place. As a result many cities do not have an adequate financial base from which to draw tax money. A confusing hodgepodge of overlapping governmental units is another product of urbanization, and the resulting duplication of services is both expensive and inefficient. Other products of urbanization are crumbling inner-city slums, overdependence on the automobile, high crime rates, overcrowding and congestion, segregation of ethnic minority groups in slums and ghettos, and rural poverty.

Despite the seriousness of the problems of metropolitan areas, there is no shortage of proposals for solving them. Many urban planners recommend that local governments be reorganized into larger and more efficient units. Others have recommended decentralizing local government, moving people into new, planned cities. Urban-renewal projects have not been successful in producing adequate housing for the poor, but the backers of such projects continue to support them. Some authorities believe that most of the defects in current housing programs could be corrected by giving direct financial help to the poor.

According to functionalists, rapid urbanization has disrupted the basic social institutions—economics, education, family, government, and religion. The rates of crime, suicide, and mental illness have grown as the disorganization brought about by rapid urbanization has increased. Conflict theorists see the problems of urbanization as resulting from competition between interest groups. Each group exercises power for its own benefit and not for general welfare. Social psychologists are most concerned with the effects of urbanization on the psychological well-being of the millions of people who feel lost and lonely in large metropolitan areas. Most prefer small-town life and its sense of community and identity over the cold impersonality of the city. Their recommendations for improving metropolitan life include decentralization of metropolitan areas into small units so people will have the opportunity to live in genuine communities and neighborhoods.

KEY TERMS	district	suburb
	federation	urbanization
	megalopolis	urban renewal

18
Population

What is the cause of the population explosion?
Will population pressures cause new international conflicts?
Can food production keep up with population growth?
How can population control be made more effective?

The international decline in the death rate and the continuation of high birthrates in most parts of the world has created a population explosion.

The world's population is exploding. The number of men, women, and children on earth is now over 4 billion—twice as many people as there were only 50 years ago. If current trends continue, the world's population will double again—to 8 billion—in the next 50 years.[1]

Many scientists doubt that the earth can support 8 billion people. They note that half of our 4 billion people already have an inadequate diet and that 10 to 20 million people starve to death every year.[2] But these current problems seem minor compared to the disaster many see on the horizon. According to one expert, "The explosive growth of the human population is the most significant terrestrial event in the past million millenia. . . . No geological event in a billion years . . . has posed a threat to terrestrial life comparable to that of human overpopulation."[3]

The dangers of runaway population growth can be seen in historical perspective if we divide the present world population of 4 billion into eight equal units, each consisting of a half-billion (500 million) people. Seven of these eight units have been added in just 330 years. In 1650 there were about 500 million people (one unit) in the world—the result of all the population growth since the birth of humanity. But only 200 years (1650–1850) were required for the world to add the second unit of 500 million and reach a total of 1 billion. The third unit of 500 million was added in only 50 years (1850–1900). The next 500 million was produced in 30 years (1900–1930), another in 20 years (1930–1950), another in 15 years (1950–1965), and another in 8 years (1965–1973). The most recent unit of 500 million people was added in just *4 years* (1973–1976).[4] (See Figure 18.1.)

FIGURE 18.1
THE GROWTH OF THE
WORLD'S POPULATION

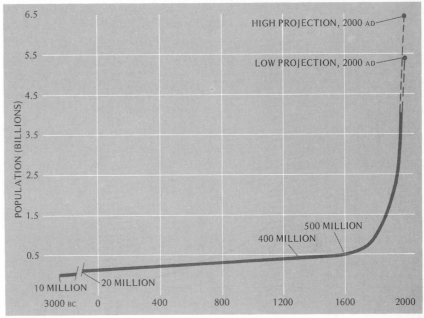

If this trend continues, the world will soon be adding 500 million people a year and eventually 500 million people a month or even a week. Obviously, the earth will not be able to support such an enormous population. The critical question is whether growth will be curbed by worldwide famine or disaster or by a rational program of population limitation.

While the long-range forecasts are ominous, the population crisis is not a thing of the future. It is here now. Next year the world must house, clothe, and feed an additional 80 million people. To make matters worse, the 220,000 who will be added tomorrow morning will not be evenly distributed throughout the world. Most will be born in the agricultural nations of Africa, Latin America, and Asia—countries that are too poor to provide for the populations they already have.

Although these poor nations may seem alike to Western eyes, there are important differences in their population problems. The most immediate crisis is in the overcrowded nations of Asia (including Bangladesh, India, Pakistan, Indonesia, and China), which already contain over half of the world's people and have few resources to deal with population growth. Between 1970 and 1974 the growth rate in Asia was 2.1 percent, much higher than those of the industrialized nations of Europe (0.6 percent) or North America (0.8 percent), but generally lower than those of poor nations in other parts of the world.[5] While current population densities are lower in Africa and Latin America than in Asia, their growth rate is higher (2.7 percent). It can therefore be expected that those areas will have

FIGURE 18.2
AVERAGE RATES OF
POPULATION GROWTH,
1970–1975

INDUSTRIALIZED NATIONS	GROWTH RATE PER YEAR
Canada	1.4%
Japan	1.2%
Soviet Union	0.9%
United States	0.8%
West Germany	0.4%
United Kingdom (Great Britain and Northern Ireland)	0.2%
East Germany	−0.2%
AGRICULTURAL NATIONS	
Mexico	3.5%
Colombia	2.8%
Nigeria	2.7%
India	2.1%
China	1.7%

Source. Data from United Nations, *Statistical Yearbook 1976* (New York, 1977), pp. 67–73.

severe population problems in years to come. Mexico, for example, has one of the highest growth rates in the world at 3.5 percent a year. At this rate the population of Mexico (now about 64 million) will double in 20 years and will reach 2 billion—half the size of the present world population—in 100 years. United Nations estimates indicate that Latin America's population, which was 283 million in 1970, will more than double by 2000 AD, while the Asian population, 2 billion in 1970, will be 1.7 times as large.[6] (See Figure 18.2.)

WHY THE
EXPLOSIVE
GROWTH?

If the population explosion is to be brought under control, it must be understood. A scientific discipline, demography, has been established to study birthrates and death rates. Its practitioners are mostly sociologists, but some biologists, economists, and statisticians are demographers as well. They agree that the population is "exploding" because high birthrates are being maintained at a time when death rates are declining.

Growth Rates

A nation's population obviously increases when the number of new arrivals exceeds the number of people leaving or dying. But the *world's* population is not affected by immigration and emigration: It is determined by birthrates and death rates alone. The birthrate is simply the number of babies born in a year divided by the total population. The death rate is the number of people who die divided by the total population. For convenience, the numbers refer to 1000 members of the population rather than to the total. For example, in 1970 the population of the United States totaled 205 million. In that year 3,690,000 births and 1,800,000 deaths occurred, for a birthrate of 18/1000 and a death rate of 9/1000. The growth rate is determined by subtracting the death rate from the birthrate. Thus, for every 1000 Americans 9 people were added in 1970. Nine is almost 1 percent of 1000, making the growth rate about 1 percent a year.

However, these are only crude rates. They are called "crude" by demographers because they do not take sex and age composition of the population into account. While national populations usually consist roughly half of men and half of women, age composition varies from time to time. Therefore, the age composition of a population must be examined in order to determine whether its growth rate is unusually high or low. One would expect a population with a large percentage of women of childbearing age (15–40) to have a higher birthrate than a population with only a small percentage of women in this age category. A birthrate that is adjusted for the age and sex of the population is called refined birthrate.

If rates of birth, death, and growth are not refined, international comparisons can be misleading. For example, rich industrialized nations have smaller percentages of young people than poor agricultural nations. Currently, about 25 percent of the population in developed nations is under the age of 15, compared with 40 percent in less developed countries. Therefore, the high birthrates of less developed countries actually are produced by populations with smaller percentages of people in their childbearing years than is the case in industrialized countries.

Data on refined birthrates, death rates, and growth rates are also essential to understanding population changes within a nation. A change in the composition of a population affects its growth rate for generations to come. Consider the "baby boom" of the late 1940s and early 1950s. At first the population was heavily weighted with babies, who of course have low birthrates and high death rates. But 20 to 25 years later these babies, now grown to adulthood, started having babies of their own, causing another baby boom that would repeat itself in the next generation. Further, at the turn of the twenty-first century the babies born during the first boom will be approaching old age, causing the death rate to rise. And in another 20 or 25 years, as the second wave of babies approaches old age, the death rate will again show an increase.

Death Rates

Many people believe that increasing birthrates are the cause of the population explosion. In fact, birthrates have either declined or stayed about the same, even in the countries with the most severe population problems. The true cause of the population explosion is the decrease in death rates resulting from the increase in the average lifespan.

In prehistoric times humans lived an average of only 20 years. Studies of the ancient Greeks and Romans show that their lifespan was 25 to 35 years.[7] In most modern industrialized countries newborn infants can expect to live about 75 years, and in poor agricultural nations life expectancy is about 50 years.[8]

The origins of the population crisis, thus, are to be found in the remarkable decline in death rates that began in Western Europe in the second half of the eighteenth century and later spread throughout most of the world. In the early years of the population explosion, the European nations and their colonies led the world in population growth. However, birthrates began declining in most of the industrialized nations in the latter part of the nineteenth century, thus reducing their rates of population growth. In agricultural nations birthrates did not begin to decline until much more recently, and they have not kept pace with the rapid drop in death rates. As a result the patterns of world population growth have been reversed. Between 1900 and 1975 Europe's population increased by 69 percent while Asia's population grew by 144 percent, Africa's by 202 percent, and Latin America's by 338 percent.[9]

It is clear that industrialization and modernization produce declining death rates. Industrial technology increases the food supply, thereby reducing the number of deaths from starvation. Industrialization also prolongs life by giving people pure water and better diets, clothing, housing, and sanitation. Insecticides prevent epidemics spread by insects and thus increase lifespans even more. In Sri Lanka (Ceylon), for example, intensive spraying with DDT wiped out malaria mosquitoes, decreasing the death rate by over 40 percent in just three years. But such important advances also create problems. Before its sharp decline in deaths, Sri Lanka was a food-exporting nation; now food must be imported.[10]

As noted in Chapter 8, the medical technology accompanying industrialization also contributes to declining death rates. Vaccinations brought smallpox and other diseases under control. The discovery of antibiotics produced cures for killer diseases such as syphilis and pneumonia. Nowadays the fruits of these medical advances are routinely available to the people of industrialized nations and are rapidly becoming available to agricultural countries as well. The result has been a further increase in the world's population.

Birthrates Why have birthrates declined in industrialized nations but remained high in agricultural nations? As pointed out in Chapter 5, industrialization produces economic changes that affect family size. Children become economic liabilities rather than assets. Children in agricultural societies make an important contribution to farm labor and usually support their parents when they grow old. In contrast, children in industrial societies make little economic contribution to the family while consuming considerably more than their counterparts in agricultural societies. Changes in traditional sex roles also have contributed to the lowering of birthrates. Bearing and

Birthrates have declined more rapidly in the industrialized nations than in the agricultural nations. One of the principal reasons is that in agricultural nations children provide farm labor and other valuable economic services, while in industrial societies children must be given years of education and economic support with little hope of any immediate financial return.

rearing children is no longer a woman's only occupation. Women in modern nations now have the option of pursuing independent careers. Some career women find it difficult to raise a large family, so they consider a small family to be one of the costs of success. Other women find working more rewarding than rearing any children at all.

New birth control techniques such as the contraceptive pill have made it easier for couples to have the number of children they want, and no more. In addition, abortions have become more widely available in recent

**DEBATE
Are Mandatory
Limits on Family
Size Needed
to Control
the Population
Explosion?**

PRO

The population explosion is the greatest problem facing humanity today. If forceful and effective action is not taken to reduce growth rates, it will soon be too late to head off an international disaster. Near-starvation diets are already common in some countries, and unchecked population growth will certainly lead to a massive international famine, disrupting the political and economic balance of the entire planet. Battles between hungry nations for control of scarce food reserves would be likely, and it is doubtful that the industrialized world could avoid the spreading conflict. Because some of the poorest nations already have nuclear weapons and others are developing the capacity to build them, it is conceivable that the population explosion could lead to a nuclear holocaust.

In the face of such dreadful prospects, it is clear that population growth must be controlled. Mandatory limits on family size are repellent, but there may be no other choice. Most voluntary programs have failed, and unless a new approach is found, strict limits may be the only solution to this menacing problem. Legal restrictions on family size would violate some of our traditional rights, but it is far better to give up a little freedom than to face the international disaster that otherwise seems certain.

CON

The world's population problem is not as serious as the alarmists claim. Many overpopulated nations are already reducing their growth rates. The claim that population growth will result in international disaster is wild speculation without scientific support. It would be foolish to invoke measures as drastic as mandatory population controls because of such fears. The world's food supply has always kept up with population growth, and it will continue to do so.

Limits on the number of children that parents could legally conceive violate basic human freedoms. It would be distasteful to send a person to prison for becoming a parent. Government has neither the right nor the wisdom to tell us how many children we may have. Trampling on individual rights may occasionally solve a problem, but democratic solutions are best in the long run.

If population problems became as serious as the doom sayers predict, parents would limit the size of their families voluntarily. Indeed, voluntary programs are already proving effective in a number of nations. Mandatory controls are therefore an unnecessary violation of our basic rights and should not be invoked.

years. In 1971, 38 percent of the world's population lived in countries where abortion was legal; but just five years later, in 1976, 64 percent of the world's population lived in such countries.[11] Yet it is easy to overestimate the impact of modern birth control techniques on the birthrate. As Westoff points out, the lowest birthrates in many European countries occurred during the Depression of the 1930s, before the invention of the pill and the intrauterine device and before the legalization of abortion.[12] Thus, it appears that limitations on family size are not dependent on modern technology.

A final condition promoting low birthrates is public awareness of the dangers of overpopulation. The availability of modern birth control techniques obviously makes no difference to those who want large families. But statistically speaking, the people of the industrialized countries want small families. Most of them want small families for reasons having to do with the personal welfare of the parents and children. But others—no one knows how many—have decided to have smaller families because they recognize the dangers of overpopulation. In particular, young educated men and women are abandoning the traditional belief that large families are desirable.

In less developed countries, where levels of education are low and mass communication is limited, the average person lives from day to day, unaware of the networks linking his or her personal fate to that of the world at large. Few people have even heard of the population explosion. Indeed, the leaders of some less developed nations are convinced that programs to reduce world birthrates are genocidal plots. At the first intergovernmental World Population Conference in 1974, delegates from China declared:

> The superpowers raise the false alarm of a "population explosion" and paint a depressing picture of the future of mankind. This reminds us of the notorious Malthus, who, more than 170 years ago, when the population of the world was less than 1 billion, raised a hue and cry about "overpopulation" and the impossibility for the growth of production ever to catch up with that of the population. . . . Today the world population has more than trebled . . . but there has been much greater increase in the material wealth of society. . . . The creative power of the people is boundless, and so is man's ability to exploit and utilize natural resources. The pessimistic views spread by the superpowers are utterly groundless and are being propagated with ulterior motives.[13]

Despite this rhetoric, at the time of this speech China was developing one of the most effective population control programs in the world.

THE IMPACT OF POPULATION GROWTH

As we have seen, environmental limitations make it impossible for the human population to keep growing at its present pace. The question obviously is not *whether* the growth rate should decrease but, rather, *how* it will decrease. Only two remedies are possible—decreasing births or increasing deaths.

One of the first people to recognize the dangers of unrestricted population growth was an English minister, Thomas Malthus. His famous book, *Essay on the Principle of Population*, raised a storm of controversy when it was published in 1798.[14] Malthus argued that the human population naturally increases much more rapidly than its food supply. While food supplies increase arithmetically (1, 2, 3, 4, 5, etc.), uncontrolled populations increase geometrically (1, 2, 4, 8, 16, etc.). The doubling effect occurs because two parents can produce four children; each of the four children can marry and produce four more children; and so on. Eventually, Malthus said, a population that keeps doubling in this way is doomed to outrun its food supply. He believed that only death-dealing disasters — famine, pestilence, and war — kept the human population within its environmental limits.

This gloomy theory was not popular in Malthus's time, when most Europeans believed in the inevitability of progress and the bright future of the human race. Indeed, until about 25 years ago most demographers were convinced that Malthus had underestimated the world's capacity to produce enough food for its people. While population was growing rapidly, new technology was increasing food production even more rapidly. The sociology textbooks of the 1940s and 1950s pointed with pride to the fact that American farm families were able to feed themselves and still have steadily increasing amounts of food left for the marketplace, making possible further urbanization. Forgotten was the fact that the amount of energy needed to produce food was beginning to exceed the energy value of the food itself. About 9 calories of energy are now required to produce 1 calorie of food.[15]

The distribution and use of energy resources helps explain why there is a shortage of food in countries like India, where most of the labor force is engaged in agriculture, and a surplus in countries like the United States and Canada, where mechanization makes it possible for a few farmers to support many urban residents. Contemporary demographers fear that as the world's supply of fossil fuel is used up Malthus will be proven right after all.

Some scientists have concluded that unrestrained population growth must eventually produce the famine — if not the pestilence and war — predicted by Malthus. But we do not have to wait for such a doomsday to see the ravages of overpopulation. The poor nations with the highest growth rates are already exhausting their natural resources. The industrialized nations have food surpluses, but they have not eliminated hunger and poverty within their own boundaries, let alone in the rest of the world.

The Agricultural Nations

Runaway population growth has meant hunger, poverty, and social instability for millions of people in the poor nations of the world.

Hunger

The histories of all of the world's agricultural nations include periodic famines. Great Britain alone has suffered more than 200 famines since the first century AD. But the worst famines occur in the nations that have the greatest population problems. Cornelius Walford's description of the Chinese famine of 1877–1878 vividly conveys the tragic results of overpopulation:

> Appalling famine raging throughout four provinces (of) North China. Nine million people reported destitute, children daily sold in the markets for food . . . The people's faces are black with hunger; they are dying by thousands upon thousands. Women and girls and boys are openly offered for sale to any chance wayfarer. When I left the country, a respectable married woman could be easily bought for six dollars, and a little girl for two. In cases, however, where it was found impossible to dispose of their children, parents have been known to kill them sooner than witness their prolonged suffering.[16]

Modern technology has enabled advanced industrialized nations to end the threat of famine for the first time in their history. But the people of the poor agricultural nations are not so fortunate. Twentieth-century famines have already claimed millions of victims. Three major famines — in China in the early 1920s, in the Soviet Union during the 1920s and 1930s, and in Eastern India in 1943 — took between 13 and 18 million lives.[17]

Since the time of World War II, the food surpluses produced by the industrialized nations have enabled them to avoid large-scale famines. However, millions of people starve to death every year in scattered pockets throughout the world. Some experts fear that large-scale famines are bound to recur as well. Despite substantial increases in world food production in the 1950s and 1960s, the safety margin of the world's food supply is declining. In 1961 the world's grain reserves were sufficient to feed the population for 69 days. But by the middle of the 1970s the reserves had dwindled to a 29-day supply.[18] Clearly, a major crop failure could have a disastrous impact on the hungry people of the poor nations.

Even though most people are able to get enough food to survive, about half of the people in the world suffer from dietary deficiencies. One-third do not get enough protein, and one-fourth do not get enough calories.[19] Malnutrition during the childhood years delays physical maturity, produces dwarfism, impairs brain development, and reduces intelligence, even if the children affected receive an adequate diet later. The undernourished adult is apathetic, listless, and unable to work as long or as hard as the healthy adult. Diseases caused directly by dietary deficiency, such as beriberi, rickets, and marasmus (a protein calorie deficiency in young children), are common in poor nations. Malnutrition also lowers resistance to disease, so the undernourished are likely to have a number of other health problems. The danger of epidemics is always high in overpopulated and underfed areas.

Poverty By North American standards the vast majority of the world's people live in grinding poverty. Differences in living costs, monetary exchange rates, and use of barter make comparisons of per capita income between different countries meaningless. But the modern industrialized nations

These people live in the streets. They have no permanent home, not even a crowded shack. Because Indians suffer poverty and overpopulation, they have little chance of improving their lot in life unless major changes are made in their society.

clearly receive the largest share of all goods and services. Poor agricultural countries account for two-thirds of the world's population but less than 15 percent of its production.[20]

The cities of these poor countries are largely slums. Millions of people live in tiny shacks made of whatever bits of cloth, metal, and wood they can find. The less fortunate have no shelter at all. They eat, sleep, and rear their children on public sidewalks, open ground, and streets. In some Latin American cities, half of the people are *paracaidistas* (parachutists), people who live on the streets without permanent housing. In India, Pakistan, and Bangladesh, millions of babies born on the streets spend their entire lives there, seldom seeing the inside of a shack, let alone living in an apartment or house.

Because populations are growing twice as fast in poor nations as in rich ones, an increasing percentage of the world's people are living in poverty. According to a United Nations report, the portion of the world's population living in less developed areas increased from 64 percent in 1920 to 70 percent in 1970, even though several areas had undergone industrialization during this period.[21] The steady growth of the populations of the poor nations makes any improvement in living conditions impossible. At present rates of growth the national incomes of most poor nations must expand more than 2 percent each year to keep the average citizen's income from falling. Egypt is a good example. Twenty-five years ago the Egyptian government, hoping to increase usable farm land and reduce poverty, began construction of the giant dam at Aswan. The completed dam increased Egypt's arable land area by over 12 percent. In the meantime, however, Egypt's population had increased by more than 71 percent.[22] The dam's economic benefits were swallowed up by the growth in population before the project had even been completed.

The age composition of the populations of nonindustrialized nations causes additional problems. In a rapidly expanding population a large percentage of people will be children, leaving a smaller percentage of adults in their working years. For example, Latin America is growing much faster than North America, and as a result only 53 percent of all Latin Americans are in their most productive years (15 to 64), compared with 62 percent of all North Americans.[23] To put it another way, adults living in poor countries with high growth rates must support more dependent children than their counterparts in wealthy nations. But that is only the beginning. As the children mature, they must find jobs, secure some other means of support, or die. The United Nations estimates that the poor nations will have to find jobs for *1 billion* new workers in the next three decades.[24] Failure to do so will mean increasing poverty. Further, these adults will soon be in the childbearing ages, and the cycle will start again if they have as many children as their parents did.

Social Instability

The expanding populations of the agricultural countries place new pressures on their traditional ways of life. Because tiny plots of family land cannot support all the family's members, young people migrate to the cities, where they join the masses of unemployed slum dwellers. The flood of immigrants from the countryside thus becomes an urban problem in an agricultural nation.

Few developing nations can industrialize fast enough to absorb the wave of new immigrants to the cities. Some have followed China's lead and put official restrictions on such migration. The majority have not done so, perhaps reasoning that it is no worse to starve in the city than to starve in the country. According to United Nations estimates, the urban population of the poor nations will triple in the next 30 years.[25] As our discussion in Chapter 16 suggests, rapid urbanization disrupts the traditions that hold agricultural societies together, thus increasing the likelihood of political upheavals.

The Industrialized Nations

Rapid population growth creates similar problems for agricultural and industrialized nations. The difference is in scale. The growth rates of industrialized countries are lower, and their great wealth makes it easier to absorb new workers. Nevertheless, until zero population growth is achieved, population changes will continue to have profound effects on the quality of life in the industrialized countries.

The Economic Burden

The cost of providing the necessities of life for a rapidly expanding population is enormous. For example, after World War II America's baby boom placed great economic strains on the nation. For a time elementary schools could not be constructed fast enough, and the quality of elementary education declined as schools were operated on half sessions. By the time the new elementary schools had been completed, the children had reached junior high school age, causing another shortage of buildings and equipment. Their next move, to high school, created similar shortages. Later, many high school graduates, some barely able to read, write, or do simple arithmetic, entered newly constructed or expanded colleges and universities, and today unemployment has become a problem as those who were born during this period compete in a job market that has little room for them. The social-security system will be strained as the "baby boom" children move on to old age.

It should be noted, however, that rapid population growth causes severe economic problems even without "booms" and declines in the birthrate. The reason is simple: Birthrates are higher among the poor than among the rich. Any nation that is determined to distribute its income more equally must face the fact that in periods of population expansion the poorest half of the population will increase more rapidly than the richest half.

Dwindling Resources

It is now widely recognized that the world is running out of energy supplies and essential raw materials. This problem will be discussed in Chapter 19. Here we merely note that the growing populations of the industrialized nations are major contributors to the problem. One American baby will use more resources in its lifetime than 30 Asian babies. Thus, even the relatively slow population growth of the industrialized nations places great burdens on the environment and on available natural resources. To make matters worse, the amount of resources consumed per person has grown even faster than the population. Between 1960 and 1975 the consumption of energy in the United States doubled while its population increased by only 19 percent.[26] If the population of the industrialized nations continues to grow and demand for consumer goods is not curtailed, there will be no energy or raw materials left for the poor nations.

The Quality of Life

The effects of the population explosion on the overall quality of life are difficult to measure. No dollar value can be placed on the loss of a beautiful lake or forest. Yet the cost of destroying nature so that more humans may live in comfort is certainly very high, and it is a cost that must be borne by all the generations to come. When the territories of birds, mammals, and reptiles are invaded and they become extinct, we are all poorer. Destruction of this kind is nothing new, but population growth has greatly accelerated this process. The more people there are in an industrialized nation, the more polluted its environment will be. Putting an end to rapid growth may not improve the quality of life, but failure to do so will surely make it worse.

RESPONDING TO POPULATION PROBLEMS

It is sometimes argued that there is no population crisis and that dire warnings about the future are the cries of doomsayers. But an increasing number of demographers, politicians, and informed citizens agree that the world faces a grave overpopulation problem. This awareness is itself a response to the population explosion. It is a first step in the direction of implementing one or both of the two basic programs for dealing with the problem: Increasing the amount of food and restricting population growth.

Advocates of each approach have strong arguments to support their proposals. Those who focus on the need to expand food supplies point to the fact that food production has outpaced population growth since the end of World War II, and they predict that it will continue to do so. Advocates of population control respond that it is unrealistic to believe that food supplies can expand indefinitely, and that unrestricted population growth will outstrip any conceivable increase in food production. Moreover, environmentalists argue that even if we could feed the huge population that present growth rates will produce, the resulting overcrowding and pollution would be completely unmanageable.

Increasing Food Production

Scientists in laboratories around the world are working night and day to invent methods for increasing food production. The greatest single advance in recent years was the creation of new strains of wheat and rice that yield much more food per acre. A "green revolution" occurred in places where these "miracle" seeds were planted. In 1968 India's wheat harvest was about 35 percent higher than ever before, largely because of these new crops.[27] But the new strains of wheat and rice require more fertilizer, insecticides, and irrigation, all of which are oil based. This means that you put oil in and take food out. This flaw in the green revolution was brought into sharp focus after the 1974 Arab oil embargo, when oil prices increased sharply. The poor nations, which are chronically short of funds, could not afford the petroleum products necessary to make the green revolution continue to work.

The American way of improving agricultural production relies heavily on mechanization—another oil-dependent technology. Just as human power gave way to animal power, animal power gave way to petroleum-burning tractors pulling ingenious sowing, cultivating, and reaping machines. The picture of the American or Canadian farmer as a ragged man with twenty acres and a mule is no longer accurate. Today's farmer is likely to drive a huge, air-conditioned tractor that costs as much as a Rolls-

Royce, and to worry about investment tax credits and the prices of commodity futures on the stock exchange.

Despite its success, the North American style of mechanization is not appropriate for poor countries with severe population problems. Few of the world's farmers can afford even the least expensive tractors. When the price of such machines is subsidized by an outside agency, they still cannot be operated economically on the small plots of land owned by most peasant farmers. It is often suggested that small farms be consolidated and worked with modern labor-saving equipment, but even if such a program were politically feasible it would create a staggering unemployment problem. Moreover, it has been calculated that feeding the world's population by means of highly mechanized technology would exhaust the supply of petroleum in only 30 years.[28]

The late English economist E. F. Schumacher, advocated an ingenious compromise. He proposed that poor nations use intermediate technology—machines that are less sophisticated than the gas-guzzling marvels of the industrialized nations but more effective than the traditional reliance on human and animal power.[29] What the world needs, Schumacher said, is simple machines that can be manufactured in poor nations at low cost and are suitable for small-scale farming. Schumacher himself helped design a small gasoline-powered plowing machine that is more efficient than a horse or an ox but much less costly than a tractor.

Another proposal for feeding the world's growing population is to cultivate more land. It has been estimated that only one-third of the world's potentially arable farm land is actually put to use in any given year.[30] Why not cultivate the other two-thirds? The answer is an economic one: It would cost too much to do so. Most of the good land is already in use. The remainder would require large amounts of oil or other energy to produce even low yields. Some arid soil could be put into production with new irrigation projects, and perhaps new hydroelectric power would come as a bonus. However, the history of Egypt's Aswan Dam casts doubt on the notion that such projects can meet the growing demand for food. The proposal that tropical jungles be cleared for farming is even less realistic. Jungle land is not farm land. Brazil's attempts to farm the Amazon Valley have shown that rain forest land has few plant nutrients and that tropical rainfall quickly washes away artificial fertilizers.[31]

As land runs out we must turn to the sea. Fish and other seafoods now contribute almost one-fifth of all the animal protein consumed by humans.[32] During the 1950s and 1960s the world's catch of fish increased dramatically because of improved technology, but the increases stopped in the 1970s. The lakes and oceans can support only a limited number of fish, and some species are nearing extinction. Nevertheless, experts believe the total catch of fish could be expanded by concentrating on smaller and less appetizing species of fish and through more careful management and control of the fishing industry.[33] The Japanese grow fish specifically for human consumption, and fish farming is bound to increase as the human population grows.

Future efforts to get more food from the sea will have to focus on plants as well as animals. Various forms of edible algae and seaweed are already being harvested in China and Japan, and marine vegetation in other parts of the world could also be exploited. However, if marine plants are to make a major contribution to the human food supply they will have to be farmed, just as they are on land. Several experimental sea farms are now in operation, but it will be some time before they are economically feasible for large-scale use.

There are other new forms of food on the horizon. Micro-organisms like yeast or blue–green algae are nutritious and can be grown rather easily. Jamaica and Taiwan already have "yeast factories" that produce a high-protein food supplement from the waste products of sugar cane production. Some population experts hope that chemists will be able to make synthetic food in time to prevent widespread starvation. Clearly, artificial food produced from something other than petroleum derivatives could solve the world's food problem for the foreseeable future. But there is little chance that scientists can reproduce nature's nutrients on a scale large enough to make a difference to a hungry world. As Georg Borgstrom writes, "To envision the future feeding of the world as removed to factories detached from fields, pastures and the sea, is simply naïve. Even a superficial examination of such an alternative reveals the impractical nature of these projects."[34]

Population Control

Gaining control over the world's explosive population growth is the most urgent task before the human race today. If we fail, we will surely have to face our ancient enemies — famine, pestilence, and war — on a new and unprecedented scale. At present the industrialized nations are much closer than their agricultural neighbors to achieving population control. The population of the industrialized nations is still growing at about 1 percent a year, but this is less than half the rate for poor nations. Moreover, most industrial nations appear to be heading toward a slower growth rate or even zero population growth. For this reason we will focus on the nations with rapid growth rates. However, should the growth rates of industrialized nations rise sharply, the proposals and programs designed for the poor nations could be applied to the industrialized nations as well.

Traditional Attitudes

The traditional attitude in most cultures is that children are economically and socially valuable: More children mean a stronger family. Such attitudes are often reinforced by religious and political doctrines. But even when they are not, the desire for children is so deeply rooted in most cultures that attempts to change such attitudes appear immoral. Yet change must come if population growth is to be controlled.

The attitudes and perspectives of the average person living in an agricultural society are very different from our own. Cultural foundations are built on rigid traditions, and little value is placed on "progress." For this reason foreign technical advisers have met strong opposition in their attempts to change agricultural methods. Peasant farming techniques are handed down from one generation to the next, and there is little desire to change time-tested methods. The same attitudes affect reproduction. Large families have always been essential to the peasants' prosperity and often to their very survival, making belief in the value of large families a deeply embedded tradition. The fact that more children are now surviving to adulthood and that population growth threatens to overtake the food supply seem to have little effect on these traditional beliefs.

Religion is a pillar of support for traditional attitudes, and most of the world's religions favor population growth. For one reason or another, it is considered moral to "be fruitful and multiply." Buddhism and Hinduism are silent on the issue of birth control, although there is an implication that humans should not deliberately interfere with the eternal process of reincarnation. Islam is rather negative toward birth control, but there is a wide range of interpretations of religious doctrine on this question. Jews and Protestants today generally accept the practice of birth control, but their faiths were not always so favorable. Of all the world's religions, Roman Catholicism is the most strongly opposed to birth control. In 1968 Pope Paul reaffirmed Church doctrine by ruling that all forms of artificial birth control block the normal "transmission of life" in marriages and thereby violate the "creative intention of God." According to Catholic doctrine, only two methods of birth control are permitted: Total abstinence from sexual relations or periodic abstinence during a woman's most fertile period (i.e., the rhythm method). However, both methods have proven unreliable since they demand a high level of self-control.

The effects of the Roman Catholic Church's opposition to birth control are not clear. An American survey found that 76 percent of all married Catholic women have used forbidden birth control techniques and that 64 percent were doing so at the time of the survey.[35] A survey of ten Latin American cities arrived at similar findings.[36] Nevertheless, Church opposition to birth control has made population control more difficult in some areas. Catholicism is the dominant religion in Latin America, which has one of the highest growth rates in the world. A study of a low-income neighborhood in Caracas, Venezuela, found that only 13 percent of the women were making any attempt to avoid pregnancy and that those who were making such an attempt had already been pregnant an average of 6.6 times.[37]

Population Programs   Some political leaders see a large population as a national asset and have used government programs to encourage population growth. As far back as the thirteenth century, a number of European nations established tax benefits for parents. Hitler's Germany enacted a variety of measures aimed at increasing its population, as have several communist countries. But the realities of the population explosion are forcing one nation after another to adopt population control programs.

Many political leaders who are interested in controlling population focus their efforts on industrialization, believing that attitudes toward the family and reproduction will change as the economy develops. As we have already shown, industrialization does bring about a demographic transition—a change in basic birthrates and death rates that ultimately results in slower overall growth. Many leaders insist that the population problem will take care of itself if we wait for this "natural" process to occur in the agricultural nations. However, such expectations are ill-founded. The export boom that fueled Japan's rapid industrialization is unlikely to occur in other nations because of slower growth and increased competition in the international marketplace. More important, the increasing scarcity of natural resources is driving the price of essential materials beyond the reach of developing nations that do not have their own domestic supplies. Thus, it seems highly unlikely that industrialization can occur rapidly enough to solve the population problems of the poor agricultural nations. According to Paul and Anne Ehrlich,

> The secret of success in reducing birth rates now appears not to be a high level of industrial development, as was previously thought. An essential factor seems to be equity. When people are given access to the basics of life — adequate food, shelter, clothing, health care, education (particularly for women), and an opportunity to improve their well-being — they seem to be more willing to limit the size of their families. Viewed in this light, it becomes clear why the family planning efforts of many "relatively advanced" less developed countries seem to get nowhere; often only the highest income groups (perhaps a quarter of the population) are benefiting from "development."[38]

Most current population control programs encourage people to limit the size of their families voluntarily. The assumption is that the birthrate will decline if couples have only the number of children they desire. Population controllers distribute information about birth control techniques and give birth control devices to the poor without charge. Such programs are called family planning, but the real objective is to cut the birthrate. Some countries support their family planning programs with publicity stressing the desirability of small families and the dangers of overpopulation. In India, for example, the symbol of population control—a red triangle with the smiling faces of two parents and two children—can be seen in every village.

Voluntary family planning programs have sprung up in nations all over the world. But unless traditional attitudes about the value of a large family are changed, such programs are doomed to failure.

Unfortunately, such programs have been ineffective. They do reduce the number of unwanted children, causing a small reduction in the number of births. But publicity campaigns have not persuaded people to want smaller families. It seems likely that even if all parents had only the number of children they desired, the world's population would continue to grow at an alarming rate. In South Korea, where a national family planning program was begun in 1964, a survey of women conducted in 1967 found no change in the ideal family size—almost every respondent said she wanted two or three sons and one or two daughters.[39] There have been similar failures in Ghana, Ethiopia, Costa Rica, India, and other nations.

Because of the weaknesses in family planning programs, some nations are now using programs that provide concrete incentives for parents to limit the size of their families—bonuses for couples with few children and penalties for those with many children. The small country of Singapore, with over 2 million people crowded into only 226 square miles, has one of the most effective incentive programs in the world. The first two children in a family are given priority for admission to school, so additional children may not receive an adequate education. Government hospital fees increase with each child. Women receive paid maternity leave for three children, but none for additional children. Small families are provided with low-rent housing, but large ones are not. Government employees with small families are viewed with favor at promotion time, as are some employees in private industry.[40] As a result of this program Singapore's birthrate fell by 8.1 percent between 1972 and 1973 and another 8.4 percent between 1973 and 1974.[41]

The most drastic proposals for population control call for mandatory limits on family size, often through compulsory sterilization of parents after the birth of their second or third child. India was one of the first countries to experiment with compulsory sterilization. The government of former Prime Minister Indira Gandhi refused to hire men with more than two children, and those who were already employed by the government were pressured to undergo vasectomy (a simple operation that makes men sterile but does not diminish their sexual interest or capacity). With encouragement from the central government, some Indian states began requiring mandatory sterilization of men after the birth of three children. The laws of the state in which Bombay is located provided for a fine of at least $250 and up to one year in prison for those who refused to undergo such sterilization. There were many reports of abuses, including charges that in some villages men were rounded up and sterilized regardless of the size of their families. This program immediately aroused intense opposition, including riots by Moslem villagers.[42] International reaction also was negative. An American law passed in 1977 prohibited the use of foreign-aid money "for the performance of involuntary sterilization as a method of family planning" and directed foreign-aid recipients not to "coerce or provide any financial incentives to any person to practice sterilization."[43] The furor over compulsory population control contributed to Prime Minister Gandhi's defeat in the 1977 elections, and India has since returned to the voluntary and largely ineffective family planning approach.

Another proposal for population control entails adding a fertility inhibitor to water supplies. Like compulsory sterilization, such an extreme measure poses an obvious threat to individual freedom and has enormous potential for abuse. D. N. Pai, who held the post of director of family planning in Bombay when the compulsory sterilization law was passed, responded to civil libertarians by pleading necessity: "If some excesses appear, don't blame me. . . . You must consider it something like a war. There could be a certain amount of misfiring out of enthusiasm. There has been pressure to show results."[44] One noted economist predicts that "iron governments" will emerge in less developed countries as a result of population pressures and that these dictatorships will be forced to use military power to cut the birthrate.[15] If runaway population growth is not checked, highly objectionable procedures of this kind might be the only way to head off an even more frightening disaster.

There are signs of hope, however. China, with one-fifth of the world's people, appears to have made amazing progress in reducing its birthrate. China's powerful and highly centralized government has convinced its people to abstain from premarital sex, delay marriages and childbearing, and use birth control techniques. Married women with two or more children carry a "paper pill" (an oral contraceptive made cheaply with dissolvable paper) with them at all times, and they are asked to share their

The People's Republic of China is one of the bright spots in the world's population picture. The Chinese population control program has apparently proven more effective than the programs in any other agricultural nation.

pills with women who have none.[46] Recent studies indicate that between 1970 and 1975 China's birthrate declined more rapidly than that of any other country—from 32 to 19 per 1000 population.[47] This has meant a decrease in the growth rate from 1.9 percent to 1.6 percent.[48] If these figures are accurate, China is one of the great success stories in the history of attempts to deal with the population explosion. However, China's population problems are not over. A growth rate of 1.6 percent means that the population will double in about 45 years. To prevent such an increase China plans to cut its birthrate still further in the next two decades.

The birthrates of industrialized nations also continue to fall. Some countries, including East and West Germany, have already reached zero population growth, and others will soon follow. The world's overall growth rate declined from a high of 2 percent in the early 1970s to 1.6 percent in the middle of the decade. This means that in 20 years there will be 5.4 billion people on the planet instead of the 6.3 billion predicted in 1970. It is not clear how the world will care for an additional 1.4 billion people in 2000 AD. What is clear is that caring for 5.4 billion people is a simpler problem than caring for 6.3 billion people. The famous demographer Frank W. Notestein presented the following optimistic assessment of the future of the population crisis:

> Optimism does not carry us to the point of forecasting that the problems will be solved without intervening tragedies. But we do have reason to believe that the problems can be solved by a world fully alert to the dangers and willing to devote serious resources and energy to attacking them. We now have a basis for expecting that a rapid decline in birth rates can be achieved in the next decades. The problems and the crisis need not be prolonged indefinitely. Much will depend on the scale of efforts both in developing the economies and in reducing birth rates in the next 20 or 30 years. We cannot argue that the solution is in sight, but we can argue that the prerequisites for a solution are at hand.[49]

SOCIOLOGICAL PERSPECTIVES on Population

Population growth is an age old social concern. But in the past the issue was how to keep population growing, not how to limit it. Plagues and famines repeatedly brought sharp reductions in population, and many people must have felt the very survival of humanity to be in doubt. For a time, the combination of strong cultural values supporting fertility and improvements in food production and public health appeared to have solved the population problem. But success in solving the old population problem, created a new one — worldwide overpopulation. Only recently has this problem received serious scientific attention, but it is now a major concern of sociologists, demographers, anthropologists, and other social scientists.

The Functionalist Perspective

Functionalists are interested in the social effects of rapid population growth. They have found that population expansion may perform several important functions. Since greater size often means greater strength, a large population provides more security during natural disasters and a stronger defense against foreign aggressors. Many economists believe that economic growth is essential to the prosperity of an industrial society, and an increasing population promotes growth by providing labor and creating new markets for consumer goods.

But population growth is also dysfunctional. An expanding population requires the construction of more houses, the cultivation of more land, and the manufacture of more clothing. All of these activities require an increase in the consumption of dwindling natural resources. Also, the competition for jobs between the growing numbers of young adults may foster alienation and even despair. Further, overcrowding contributes to urban decay and the spread of disease.

When the world's population was low and there was no shortage of natural resources, the functions of population growth far outweighed its dysfunctions. Now the social forces that promoted desirable population growth produce hunger, poverty, and social instability. For this reason, functionalists say, the population problem will be solved only when dysfunctional attitudes, values, and institutions that promote excessive birthrates are changed. Given time, society will reach a new balance. But this balance should not come about as a result of an unacceptably high death rate. It should come, instead, from massive programs that change traditional attitudes toward childbearing.

The Conflict Perspective

Conflict theory does not easily lend itself to explaining the population explosion, and a few conflict theorists even claim that there is no population problem to worry about. They argue that the rich nations' talk about the population explosion is a trick to keep poor nations from growing so large that they threaten wealthy ones.

But most conflict theorists consider population control necessary, and they have provided important insights into the forces that oppose population control. Official opposition to birth control is viewed as a reflection of a conflict between the interests of the masses and those of ruling elites. Overpopulation is harmful to most people, but an expanding population is an economic and political asset to the ruling class. Large populations mean greater international power. Population growth among a society's lower classes also helps the elite by keeping wages down and providing a large pool of laborers. Labor organization and strikes are less likely when jobs are scarce and there are many unemployed workers waiting to replace those who protest poor working conditions.

Perhaps the most significant contribution of the conflict perspective is its analysis of the problem of malnutrition and hunger. It is argued that the current "food shortage" is really a problem of distribution, not production. The world currently produces enough food to provide an adequate diet for all of its people. Starvation and malnutrition result from the unequal distribution of the food that is produced. While millions of people starve to death every year in poor countries, many people in wealthy countries are suffering from obesity. The same system of unequal distribution is found within nations as well.

The obvious solution to this problem is to redistribute the world's food so that everyone is adequately fed. But there are enormous political and economic barriers to a program for the international redistribution of food supplies. Indeed, these barriers seem insurmountable at present. Some nations, however, have dealt effectively with their domestic inequality. Sweden and Norway, for example, have guaranteed a good diet to the poor by means of welfare programs, and China has relied on rationing and careful government controls to ensure that its limited food supplies are distributed fairly.

The Social-Psychological Perspective

Biosocial theorists see human evolution as the root of the population problem. Because the most fertile individuals pass more of their genes on to the next generation, humans developed a high level of fertility. Throughout most of human history this clearly promoted the survival of the species. But now, when overpopulation is a serious threat to human survival, the evolutionary process continues to promote high fertility. Biosocial theorists see the development of more effective artificial means of birth control as the only solution to the population problem.

Other social psychologists point out that learned attitudes and beliefs must be changed before birth control measures can be effective. Peasant farmers in traditional societies have a fatalistic attitude toward life. The idea of planning a family, let alone a world population, is alien to them. Fertility is still seen as a sign of virility and competence. The "real man" is one who has fathered many sons, and the "real woman" is one who has borne and reared them. Even in industrialized nations childless couples are sometimes pitied, and the inability to bear children may be reason enough for a husband to divorce his wife.

Effective population control requires that these attitudes be changed. But social psychologists have demonstrated that attitudinal changes do not occur in a vacuum; rather, they interact with changing economic, social, and political conditions. Mere propaganda and personal appeals are not enough; they must be accompanied by concrete economic and social changes. For example, a sound social-security plan can do much to convince people that a large family is not necessary for support in their old age, and women who are provided with alternatives to the roles of wife and mother will soon learn that caring for a large family is not the only important thing in life.

SUMMARY

The world's population is growing at a fantastic rate. Demographers agree that the reason for the population explosion is that high birth rates have been maintained while death rates have been cut dramatically. Industrialization increases the average lifespan by increasing food production, improving sanitation, and controlling epidemic diseases. In industrialized nations the decline in death rates was followed by a decline in birth rates. The economic changes brought on by industrialization have made children an economic burden rather than an asset. Also, changes in traditional sex roles have made it possible for women to pursue careers instead of staying home and raising children. New birth control techniques have made family planning much easier, and public awareness of the dangers of overpopulation has increased.

Demographers agree that the human population cannot continue to grow at its present rate. Thomas Malthus was among the first to point out the dangers of unrestricted population growth. He argued that the human population naturally multiplies much faster than its food supply. Until recently most demographers were confident that Malthus was wrong and that food supplies would keep up with the population growth. This continues to be the official position of many less developed nations. But modern demographers note that agricultural production now depends on oil, and they fear that as the world's supply of fossil fuel is used up Malthus will be proven right after all.

The runaway population growth of recent years has caused problems throughout the world. Poor agricultural nations with high growth rates have already exhausted their land and other natural resources. Between 10 and 20 million people starve to death every year, and the world's grain reserves are dangerously low. At present rates of growth the national incomes of most poor nations must expand by over 2 percent a year just to keep the average citizen's income from falling. The population explosion has also generated social instability.

In agricultural nations, more and more people are migrating to cities, where unemployment is high and social integration is low, thus increasing the chances of political upheaval. And industrialized nations must spend enormous sums to provide for their increasing populations. This spending has aggravated the world's shortage of essential raw materials and severely damaged the environment.

There are two approaches to dealing with the population explosion: increasing the amount of food or restricting population growth. Proposals for increasing the world's food supply include cultivating more land, increasing the sea's food production, and inventing new forms of food, including proteins made synthetically or from micro-organisms. The drive for population control focuses on lowering the world's birthrate. The most basic approach seeks changes in traditional attitudes that make large families seem economically and socially valuable. But in many contemporary nations such attitudes are reinforced by both religion and government, making any change seem undesirable.

Family planning programs have been introduced by the governments of many countries. Such programs encourage the use of birth control devices, usually on the questionable assumption that the birthrate will decline if couples have only the number of children they desire. Because these programs have failed to reduce birthrates significantly, some nations have introduced incentive programs that give bonuses to families with few children and penalize those with many children. The most drastic proposals are for coercive population control measures. India has experimented with compulsory sterilization, but such extreme measures pose an obvious threat to individual freedom.

There are signs of hope. The birthrates of industrialized nations continue to fall. The world's overall growth rate declined between 1970 and 1975, and food production is increasing. The solution is not in sight, but growing public awareness has made the population explosion into a social problem, and that is the first step toward a solution.

Contemporary sociologists of all theoretical persuasions are observing that traditionalism in attitudes and institutions is threatening human survival. Functionalists note that as death rates have dropped, attitudes encouraging fertility have become dysfunctional. Conflict theorists point out that the current food shortage is caused by a distribution system that gives too much food to the wealthy and too little to the poor. Social psychologists have shown that the attitudes that promote high birthrates are learned, and they have made many proposals for changing people's opinions about the desirability of large families.

KEY TERMS		
	age composition	family planning
	birthrate	growth rate
	death rate	intermediate technology
	demographic transition	refined birthrate
	demography	

19
The Environment

What is the cause of the environmental crisis?
What are the long-term effects of pollution?
How can we deal with the growing shortages of natural
 resources?
Is an ecological disaster avoidable?

For centuries humans have seen their environment as a boundless store-house of wealth. Nature was to be conquered, tamed, and used in any way we saw fit. Until recently only a few people realized how fragile and limited our world really is. But the damage done by exploitive technologies and the enormous growth of the human population are forcing this realization on an increasing number of people. One by one the natural resources on which we have come to depend are dwindling away. And as they are consumed, their by-products are fouling our land, air, and water with pollution and disrupting the delicate web of life on which our very existence depends.

It is a mistake to view the current environmental crisis as a product of personal greed and extravagance. Most North Americans do seem to have an insatiable desire for higher and higher standards of living. But as social psychologists point out, all of us have acquired these desires and expectations from the culture in which we live. The environmental crisis is more accurately seen as an unintended by-product of the industrial revolution and the economics of growth. The more productive the world has become, the more resources it has consumed and the more pollution it has produced. The industrial economy is based on the assumption that there will be steady economic growth and expansion. Now, faced with a growing scarcity of essential natural resources and the buildup of dangerous pollutants, the industrialized world is trying to adjust to an era in which there will be little expansion. This will certainly be a painful transition, posing a threat not only to our economic well-being but to our personal freedoms as well.

ECOLOGY

Those who share Western culture have long seen themselves as special creatures, separate and apart from their environment. Humans are seen not as animals but as superior beings destined to rule over the planet and its lesser creatures. But there is no scientific evidence to support such beliefs. The science of ecology—the study of the interrelations among plants, animals, and their environment—has clearly shown that human beings are but one part of a complex network of living things. No human could live more than a few seconds if separated from the sheltered terrestrial environment, with just the right proportions of water, oxygen, heat, and the other essential components that support human life. These components, like our food, are entirely dependent on plants and the other animals of the earth. We could not even digest our food properly without the microorganisms in our digestive systems.

Life on this planet exists only in a thin surface layer of soil and water and the air immediately surrounding it. This region, known as the biosphere, extends only from 200 feet below sea level to 10,000 feet above it. Within the biosphere there are many ecosystems—self-sufficient communities of organisms living in an interdependent relationship with each other and their environment. Each ecosystem has its own natural balance, and human interference may set off a chain reaction with deadly consequences.

All ecosystems require energy, and virtually all energy comes from the sun. Green plants convert solar energy into food through the process known as photosynthesis. In addition to carbohydrates (food), photosynthesis produces the oxygen required for respiration in both plants and animals. Respiration, in turn, produces carbon dioxide, which is used in photosynthesis. Thus, like other aspects of an ecosystem, this process is part of a cycle that continually reuses the same basic elements. All that is needed from outside is the energy that comes from the sun.

Because animals cannot make direct use of the sun's energy for food production, all of our food ultimately comes from plants. The food produced by green plants usually goes through many transformations in what is known as a food chain before it decomposes enough for natural recycling. For example, a simple food chain may start with the grass and other green foliage eaten by a deer. The deer is then eaten by a wolf, and when the wolf dies, its decomposed body provides nutrients for further plant growth. Of course, most food chains are much more complex, involving many intricate relationships between plants and animals.

A variety of inorganic materials are, like sunlight, essential to life. Nitrogen, for example, passes through ecosystems in several cycles. The air we breathe is 80 percent nitrogen, but it can be used by plants only with the help of bacteria that convert it into more complex compounds. When food crops are planted over and over again in the same soil, the plants use up the nitrogen, thus disrupting this delicate cycle. Farmers must use fertilizer to replace the nitrogen and other nutrients taken from the soil by crops.

THE HUMAN IMPACT

Hunting and gathering peoples interfered very little with the ecosystems in which they lived. Their tools were limited, and muscle power was the main source of energy. But with the invention of agriculture humans began a trend toward destruction of their ecosystem. They attempted to replace the delicate complexity of the natural environment with the plants and animals that are best suited to supporting human life. The surplus food produced by agriculture made the development of cities possible. And with the cities came a host of new threats to the earth's ecological balance. Forests were cut down, rivers rechanneled, and tons of human waste dumped into the water and plowed into the soil. Some organisms were exterminated; others multiplied more rapidly than ever before. Humans soon became the single greatest force in the ecological balance of the planet.

Time and again the human impact on the environment has produced unexpected, unpleasant, and even dangerous consequences. Logging and overgrazing have converted hundreds of thousands of acres of fertile land into barren deserts. Improper plowing and tilling techniques have caused fertile soil to wash away in spring rains. Industrial wastes dumped into rivers and lakes have killed the fish that fed some of the humans who created the waste. The human species no longer faces danger from other predatory animals. We are our own worst enemy.

The damage created by some types of pollution, such as the release of poisons into our water supply, is obvious to any observer. But when a new substance, or an overabundance of an old one, disrupts a finely balanced ecosystem, the effects are not always obvious. Fishermen may not be aware that their declining catch is caused by a buildup of manmade chemicals in the waters they fish. Farmers may not realize that the extermination of wolves allows rabbits to multiply, thus threatening their crops. On the other hand, they may not know that wolves are eating their sheep only because humans have killed the rabbits on which the wolves formerly fed. Only recently have we begun to understand that even pollution that does no economic or physical damage makes the world a poorer place in which to live. As we scar our majestic forests with highways, hamburger stands, and litter, and drive species after species to extinction, we destroy our irreplaceable natural heritage.

Air Pollution

Few of us give a second thought to the invisible and seemly inexhaustible ocean of air in which we live. But consider the fact that a person can live for weeks without food and for days without water, but can survive for only a few minutes without air. We have been able to take our atmosphere for granted because rain and other processes naturally cleanse and renew it. But we are now dumping more pollutants into the air than can be removed by these natural processes. Air pollution is worst in the big cities, but it is rapidly becoming a global problem. Smog has already been detected as far away as the North Pole.[1]

The single greatest source of air pollution in North America is the automobile.[2] Oil and natural gas used for heating and for generating electrical power are also major contributors. Additional tons of pollutants are spewed into the air by paper mills, steel mills, oil refineries, smelters, and chemical plants. Even trash burning makes a substantial contribution to air pollution.

The amount and kinds of pollutants in the air vary greatly from one area to another. The most common pollutants are carbon monoxide, hydrocarbons, oxides of sulfur, oxides of nitrogen, and tiny particles of soot and ashes. The amounts of these pollutants vary in different industrial regions. Thus, areas that depend on oil for power have different pollution problems from those that use coal.

Air pollution is becoming an increasingly common problem in cities in all parts of the world, although the exact composition of the air pollution varies from one area to the next.

No matter which chemicals are involved, valleys and closed air basins are more likely to have air pollution problems than plains and mountains, where the air can circulate freely. When a layer of cold air moves over a layer of warm air, it acts like a lid, sealing in pollutants that ordinarily rise into the upper atmosphere. This condition, known as temperature inversion is temporary, but it may cause an acute pollution crisis. Local winds and climatic conditions affect the distribution of pollutants, carrying them from one area to another. Finally, climate also affects the kinds of pollutants that are present in different areas. For instance, sunlight acts on oxygen, hydrocarbons, and nitrogen oxides to produce new compounds collectively known as photochemical smog.

Air pollution is not merely a minor irritant that burns our eyes and clouds the skies. It is a major health problem, contributing to many chronic diseases and killing a substantial number of people each year. As long ago as 1930, a spell of acute air pollution took dozens of lives in Belgium. One of the worst attacks of air pollution in the history of North America began on October 26, 1948, when a temperature inversion developed over the small industrial town of Donora, Pennsylvania. As the pollutants in the air built up, 6,000 of Donora's 12,300 people became ill and 20 died. Similar conditions created London's famous "black fog" of 1952. Coal smoke from thousands of household and industrial chimneys combined with fog to reduce visibility to only a yard in some parts of the city. In some movie theaters audiences could not even see the screen. The intense pollution paralyzed London for two weeks and killed 4000 people.[3] In December 1962 another attack of deadly air pollution killed 300 more Londoners.

Acute attacks of air pollution are frightening and dramatic. However, widespread health problems may also grow out of prolonged exposure to lower levels of pollution. A carefully controlled comparison of geographic areas with different amounts of air pollution found a strong relationship between pollution and deaths from bronchitis.[4] The researchers concluded that reducing pollution in the worst areas to the levels present in the best areas would cut the bronchitis death rate by 40 to 70 percent. This study, like others, also found a relationship between air pollution and lung cancer, stomach cancer, heart disease, and emphysema (a serious lung disease).

The effects of specific pollutants on health are difficult to determine because the various chemicals we release into the air combine with each other to produce new pollutants. Further, all people living in a particular area are not necessarily exposed to the same amount of pollution. An executive who drives an air-conditioned car from her home to an air-conditioned office is exposed to less pollution than a traffic officer who breathes smog all day long. Other people voluntarily expose themselves to pollution, for instance, by smoking cigarettes. The smoking habit is particularly hazardous in polluted areas. Cigarette smokers in smoggy St. Louis have four times as much emphysema as smokers in relatively smog-free Winnipeg.[5]

The damaging effects of air pollution are not limited to humans, of course. Although there has been little research in this area, it appears that domesticated animals living in polluted areas suffer much the same problems as humans. It has been shown that air pollution has harmful effects on trees, shrubs, and flowers. The orange groves of California and the truck farms of New Jersey both suffer from smog damage. Chemicals sometimes combine with water in the atmosphere to produce "acid rains" that harm plant life and eat away exposed metal surfaces and buildings made of limestone or marble.

Air pollution is also creating harmful changes in the ecological balance of the earth. Recent studies suggest that the freon gas used in aerosol spray cans rises to the upper atmosphere and breaks down the chemicals that protect the earth from radiation. The chemistry of the upper atmosphere is complex, but there is a good chance that the presence of this gas is increasing the frequency of skin cancer.[6]

Air pollution also seems to be changing the world's climate. Tiny particles of solid waste screen out some of the sun's energy, causing a downward trend in the earth's temperature. However, the carbon dioxide produced by the burning of fossil fuels acts in an opposite manner. Carbon dioxide absorbs the sun's energy, tending to increase temperatures through a "greenhouse" effect.[7] The world's climate is also changed by clearing forests for agriculture or construction and by other human activities. For this reason scientists cannot yet predict what the long-term effects of air pollution will be. Even if temperatures dropped only slightly, a week or two might be cut from each end of the growing season, decreasing yields and leaving this overcrowded planet with an even more serious shortage of food. On the other hand, an increase in temperature could melt the surface of the polar icecaps, raising the level of the sea and flooding coastal lands.

Water Pollution

Over two-thirds of the world's surface is covered by water. This water is continually evaporating, forming clouds, and raining back to the earth in a cycle that provides a seemingly endless supply of clean water. Perhaps it is blind faith in the enormous reserves of water and the natural purification system that has led people to dump their garbage in lakes, rivers, and oceans. For a time the earth's water could tolerate this onslaught. But with the population explosion and the increased dumping of industrial wastes, marine animals and plants began to die in large numbers.

Organic wastes are important water pollutants. In small quantities, human feces and urine are quickly broken down by waterborne bacteria and have no harmful effects. But if too much organic material is dumped into the water, the bacteria use up available oxygen as they decompose the waste. Fish and other complex organisms suffocate, and we are left with a barren body of water. Although human sewage is a major contributor to this deadly process, industry and agriculture produce much larger amounts of organic pollutants. A single paper mill produces as much organic waste as the sewage of a good-sized city.[8]

Chemical fertilizers have the same effect as organic wastes and cause similar problems. When rains wash nitrogen fertilizers into rivers and lakes, they stimulate the growth of huge "blooms" of algae. When these blooms die they decay, using up oxygen in the same way that organic pollution does. These decaying masses of algae combine with other substances, sink to the bottom, and disrupt the ecosystem there. The layer of muck covering the bottom of Lake Erie is over 125 feet thick in some places.[9]

Pollution from such poisons as mercury and arsenic is not to be overlooked either. The concentration of these chemicals in lakes, streams, and seas is seldom high enough to cause direct harm to humans. But trouble arises because these substances build up in the tissues of the

---

NINETEENTH CENTURY SOCIAL PROBLEMS

State Chemist Daniels has furnished an analysis of Ashland's drinking water and says that it is contaminated with sewage . . . the typhoid fever epidemic from which Ashland is suffering is now directly attributed to the water supply. Efforts will be made by the Attorney General to have the water company's franchise annulled.
April 9, 1894

fish and other animals living in polluted water. When people eat the poisoned seafoods, they become ill. A Japanese chemical plant dumped so much mercury in a nearby bay that over 100 people who ate polluted seafood died or suffered severe nervous system damage.[10] The U.S. Geological Survey has estimated that the bottom of San Francisco Bay is laced with 58 tons of poisonous mercury.[11]

Heat is another dangerous pollutant. Power-generating plants, especially those using nuclear energy, greatly increase the temperature of the water they use for cooling. When this warm water is poured into a river, some species of fish and other cold-blooded animals cannot survive. Ducks, geese, and other migrating waterfowl stay on through the winter, causing additional ecological imbalances. If organic wastes are dumped in the water, thermal pollution will speed up its decomposition, thus aggravating the oxygen depletion problem.

Even the vast and seemingly indestructible oceans are threatened by an avalanche of pollution. A good share of the pollutants dumped into rivers and streams eventually find their way to the sea. There they combine with billions of tons of sewage and industrial waste pumped directly into the sea. Toxic substances such as lead, mercury, and various pesticides are common in our coastal waters and are dangerous to delicate aquatic ecosystems. The amount of mercury in Pacific Ocean swordfish recently got so high that the American government banned the sale of this fish for several months. In the ocean off New York, fish have a disease that rots their tails and fins. An increase in diseased and deformed fish has also been observed in the ocean waters off southern California.[12] Oceanographer Jacques Cousteau reports that visibility in the North Atlantic has decreased 100 to 300 feet in the past 30 years. When Thor Hyerdahl, the Norwegian adventurer, crossed the Atlantic Ocean by raft in 1970, he found the ocean surface littered with garbage.[13]

Massive spills from oil tankers and wells pose another threat to the ocean's ecology. In addition to these dramatic accidents, smaller spills and wastes intentionally flushed from the tanks of ships add significantly to the corruption of the seas. Scientists had a rare chance to study the effects of oil pollution when a relatively small spill occurred near the Wood's Hole Oceanographic Institute in Massachusetts. They found that 95 percent of the animals living within 10 feet of the surface died immediately, and many others died later. Eighteen months after the spill the oil still covered some 5500 acres of water down to a depth of 42 feet, and the original disaster area had not been repopulated.[14]

Defacing the Land

Humans have changed the face of the earth. The Bible refers to forests and jungle animals in areas that are now deserts. As recently as 1882, only about 10 percent of the earth was classified as desert or wasteland. By the middle of the twentieth century, the percentage had increased to

Strip mining and the dumping of solid wastes have already defaced millions of acres of land.

23. Large parts of the Sahara Desert, for example, were created by logging, faulty irrigation, and overgrazing. In the same period, as the deserts grew, the percentage of forest land dropped from 43 percent of the earth's total to only 21 percent.

Removal of trees and foliage exposes the soil to erosion. Then, after the absorbent layer of topsoil has been washed or blown away, rainwater quickly runs off the land. Excessive logging has caused flooding on rivers as far apart as the Eel in California and the Yang-Tse in China.[15] In addition, when forests are removed, the land absorbs less sunlight, causing temperatures to drop so that the food-producing capacity of nearby land is reduced.

Many types of agriculture also do long-term damage to the soil. Some experts estimate that as much as one-third of India's topsoil will be lost by the end of this century.[16] Modern agricultural techniques are very hard on the soil and fail to give sufficient attention to maintaining the overall ecological balance. As Georg Borgstrom writes,

> Coupled with reckless forest devastation, the agricultural methods introduced by Europeans in the course of the world-wide colonization have been among the most costly and destructive acts to which the human household has been subjected. Soil erosion reached global dimensions first in this century, and tens of millions of acres suitable for tilling were then lost in all continents. Both the Soviet Union, North America, and Europe have suffered smarting losses. More deserts have been created by man than ever new land was gained through irrigation.[17]

Another heavy burden on our beleaguered land is the huge amount of solid waste produced by industry. Each year the United States generates about a ton of trash and garbage for every person in the country.[18] Some of this refuse is burned, thus adding to air pollution, but most of it is buried in various landfills and dumps. This creates two problems. One is the increasing numbers of ravines, gullies, valleys, bays, and sloughs that are being covered as the trash mounts up. Another is the increasing disposal of plastic and other synthetic materials which, unlike organic material, never decompose. Americans dump about 100 million tires and 38 billion bottles and jars each year. Humans are the only form of life that generate wastes that are not consumed by some other plant or animal.

As if these problems were not enough, new threats to the land are looming on the horizon. Just when the population explosion demands that more and more land be used for agriculture, the growing shortage of energy and minerals is forcing us to use environmentally destructive methods to gather vital raw materials. For instance, there are enormous reserves of coal in North America, and much of it lies close to the surface. This makes it cheaper to extract, but the "strip-mining" technique that is normally used creates enormous environmental damage. Strip mines are long, shallow valleys gouged out of the earth. After the coal has been removed, the dislocated earth is dumped back into the hole. But unless the topsoil is carefully replaced (an expensive and time-consuming process), the land will not be fertile for centuries, if at all.

The growth of the cities poses yet another threat to the ecological balance of our land. Great portions of North America, Europe, and Asia are covered by expanding cities and suburbs. These vast metropolitan areas are beginning to threaten the existence of the wilderness that harbors so many different species of plants and animals. Many ecosystems have already been destroyed by urban sprawl and the outlook for the future is not bright. If population growth continues at its present rate, only the most remote mountains and deserts will remain in their natural state.

Dangerous Chemicals

The human race is dosing itself with thousands of chemicals. The air we breathe and practically everything we eat or drink contains manmade substances. Although many of these chemicals seem harmless enough, the plain fact is that we know almost nothing about their long-term effects. Recent history is full of examples of supposedly harmless food additives, drugs, and industrial wastes that were found to be serious health hazards. The U.S. Government recognizes a link between about 12,000 substances and various health problems. There undoubtedly are many more undiscovered killers among the half-million chemical compounds used in modern industry.[19] Over one-fourth of the 500,000 workers who have been exposed to high doses of asbestos fibers will die of various forms of cancer. The National Cancer Institute estimates that as many as 90 percent of all cancers may be environmentally induced.[20]

As manmade chemicals spread into the environment, the danger of secondary exposure increases. Chemicals such as DDT are stored in living tissues and increase in concentration as they move up a food chain. For example, DDT washed into a lake will be ingested by tiny microorganisms. The small fish that feed on these organisms also take in the DDT, and the chemical then concentrates in their tissues. As these small fish are eaten by larger fish, and, in turn, are eaten by humans, the DDT concentration increases. Milk from the breasts of some American women has been found to contain so much DDT that it would be banned from sale in interstate commerce.[21]

Radiation

Radiation pollution frightens people more than bad air or bad water, probably because we know so little about it. Small doses of radiation have no immediate effects. Moderate doses cause vomiting, fatigue, loss of apetite, and diarrhea. Death is practically certain for people exposed to high doses. However, no one knows much about the long-term effects of low and moderate doses of radiation. Studies of the survivors of the nuclear bombings of Hiroshima and Nagasaki show a high incidence of leukemia and other cancers, but we do not know exactly how much exposure is needed to produce cancer. There is ample proof that radiation causes genetic mutations, but again there is little information about how dangerous specific doses of radiation actually are. Some scientists fear that radi-

There is growing concern about the dangers of radiation pollution. This Washington demonstration, being addressed by Tom Hayden and Jane Fonda, is one of the many protests against our increasing dependence on nuclear energy.

ation already released into the biosphere has done genetic damage that will not become apparent for generations to come.

Most of the radiation to which humans are exposed is natural. The earth and every creature on it are continually bathed in radiation from outer space and from radioactive elements in the earth's crust. Most exposure to manmade radiation comes from the use of X-rays in medicine and dentistry. In the 1950s, fallout from the testing of nuclear weapons was becoming a major pollutant. The nuclear test ban treaty of 1963 stopped all above-ground nuclear testing by the two biggest nuclear powers—the United States and the Soviet Union. Since the time of this treaty, concern about the spread of radiation pollution has focused on the peaceful use of nuclear reactors as a source of power. Such reactors now contribute little to the overall levels of radiation in the world. But environmentalists fear that nuclear pollution will increase as the nuclear industry expands. Of even greater concern is the danger of a nuclear accident. There is little chance of a reactor erupting in a nuclear explosion, but if the cooling system of such a plant should fail, the tremendous heat of the nuclear reaction would melt the concrete and steel surrounding it, thus releasing enough radiation to wipe out an entire city. Nuclear-power plants have elaborate safeguards against such a disaster, and a major accident of this kind has never occurred. Nuclear scientists generally agree that the probability of such an accident occurring is very low, but the 1979 accident at the Three Mile Island reactor convinced many doubters that a **meltdown** is more likely than the public had been led to believe. Some scientists argue that the consequences of such an accident would be so disastrous that we dare not take the risk of allowing more nuclear-power plants to be built.

Even if no serious accident ever occurred, the radioactive wastes generated by nuclear plants are deadly pollutants and will remain so for thousands of years to come. Most of these wastes are now buried in sealed containers, but no container will last forever. Thousands of gallons of deadly radioactive liquids have already escaped.[22] Until recently there were plans to solidify these wastes and bury them in deep salt mines, but recent research has shown that leakage still occurs from such disposal sites. The plain fact is that at present there is no known way of permanently and safely disposing of nuclear wastes. And of course the more nuclear energy we use, the more deadly wastes we will have to dispose of.

Another serious hazard in the use of nuclear energy is crime. The security is high in nuclear-power plants. But the more this energy source is used, the more shipments of radioactive materials there will be and the easier it will be for a terrorist group to steal them. Although it would be extremely difficult to turn these materials into nuclear bombs, there would still be great danger. The explosion of a conventional bomb placed next to some radioactive materials could spread a deadly radioactive cloud big enough to poison a large area. A further problem might also spring from the development of "breeder reactors" that turn uranium 235, which is not usable as a nuclear fuel, into plutonium, which is. Unlike other nuclear fuels, the plutonium produced by breeder reactors can easily be made into atomic bombs. Thus, large-scale use of these reactors would create a distinct possibility that terrorists might seize some plutonium and hold entire cities for ransom, or even destroy an "enemy" city with an atomic explosion.

DWINDLING RESOURCES

Photographs of the earth taken from space have done much to further the cause of conservation. One look at a picture of that tiny blue–green globe hanging in the vast emptiness of space shows us how limited our world and its resources really are. Through most of human history we have been acting as though the world were a rich mine to be exploited. We are just beginning to realize that there are only limited amounts of oil, coal, uranium, and industrial metals. When the supply is used up, there will be no more.

The United States, with only 6 percent of the world's people, uses almost one-third of all the energy and raw materials consumed each year.[23] There is a growing feeling in poor nations that the United States and the other rich industrialized countries are using up the world's resources so rapidly that there will soon be nothing left for them. There is much talk about industrializing the poor nations so that they can stabilize their population growth and bring their level of living up to Western standards. But

The depletion of older oil fields has forced us to search for supplies in the most remote parts of the world. But no matter how much money and effort we expend, the world's supplies of petroleum will soon be exhausted.

the world's reserves of oil and minerals cannot possibly support all the world's people in the style to which the wealthy nations have become accustomed.

Energy Modern industrial society would be impossible without massive supplies of energy. If enough energy is available, most raw materials — iron, copper, aluminum — can be recycled, but this is not true of energy itself. Once a gallon of gasoline or a ton of coal has been burned up, it is gone forever. And because it took millions of years for these fuels to develop from organic materials, there is no hope that new fossil fuels (oil, coal, gas) can be created to replace the fuel we use up.

Worldwide consumption of nonrenewable energy resources has grown at a staggering pace. As recently as the nineteenth century, most of the world's power came from renewable sources. Particularly important were human and animal labor and the burning of wood and dung. But the industrialized world's appetite for power grew so rapidly that it could not be satisfied by these traditional sources. By the beginning of the twentieth century, coal was the world's principal source of power and oil was just coming into use. Now, only three generations later, the United States gets three-fourths of its energy from petroleum; Western Europe and Japan get about two-thirds of their power from that source and the communist countries about two-fifths of theirs.[24]

The increasing use of nonrenewable energy reserves has made possible an enormous growth in energy consumption. From 1950 to 1973, world energy consumption rose about 7 percent a year.[25] In the ten years between 1960 and 1970, consumption of power in the United States increased by almost two-thirds.[26] About 40 percent of this power goes directly to industrial production. The remainder is used for heating, lighting, and transportation, as well as running an array of home conveniences ranging from refrigerators and air conditioners to electric toothbrushes.

Until 1973 oil was plentiful and cheap. The price declined steadily from 1950 to 1973, and few people gave any thought to the possibility that the world would ever run out of petroleum. One prominent geophysicist did, and he published the following warning in 1949:

> The consumption of energy from fossil fuels is . . . a "pip" [on a graph] rising sharply from zero to maximum, and almost as sharply declining, representing but a moment of human history. . . . The release of this energy is a unidirectional and irreversible process. It can only happen once, and the historical events associated with this release are necessarily without precedent, and are incapable of repetition.[27]

But most people simply ignored such warnings and continued to demand more energy and a higher standard of living. In 1973 the modern world was awakened by its first great energy crisis. War broke out in the Middle East and the Arab oil producers tried to stop all shipments to nations that they believed to be supporters of their enemy, Israel. At the same time, the oil-producing countries quadrupled the price of oil. While the oil boycott was soon ended, oil prices were never reduced. In 1973–1974 energy consumption fell. For a year or two there was widespread public discussion of the need to conserve oil and the danger of using up all the world's reserves. But it soon became apparent that consumption fell in 1973–1974 only because there was not enough oil on the market to meet the demand. As soon as supplies returned to normal, energy consumption went right on climbing.[28] Between 1976 and 1977 energy use in the United States increased by 5.3 percent. Even the federal government, a strong advocate of energy conservation, increased its energy consumption by 2.2 percent.[29]

No one knows how much longer the world's supply of oil will last. The experts who have studied this question have reached conflicting conclusions. One of the most pessimistic estimates comes from a group of scientists and intellectuals known as the Club of Rome. This organization's famous 1972 report, *The Limits to Growth*, estimates that all the world's known reserves of oil and gas can last only 31 more years at the present rate of consumption.[30] That estimate is based on two unlikely assumptions—that the rate of consumption will not keep on increasing and that no new oil reserves will be found. In a second projection the Club of Rome estimated that if oil consumption keeps on increasing at its present rate, and if explorers find new reserves holding five times as much oil as we now have, the world's oil supply will still last only 50 years. A slightly more optimistic estimate puts the ultimate reserves of crude oil at 200 billion tons, or 70 years of supply at the current rate of use.[31] In a third estimate M. King Hubbert, the geophysicist quoted earlier, gives us about a century before the world's reserves of oil are depleted.[32] Whichever estimate is most accurate, the message is clear: We are quickly approaching the day when there will be no more oil. In fact, an American agency estimates that there will be a critical shortage of oil as soon as 1985, when world demand will outstrip supply.[33]

Worldwide disaster would be certain if there were no oil or natural gas tomorrow morning. Americans and Canadians, who use more energy per person than the citizens of other nations, would be hit particularly hard. Millions of people would freeze. Factories would close. Transportation would stop. Even if crops could be planted, cultivated, and reaped by hand, the land would become less productive without oil-based fertilizers, and millions would starve. Fortunately, it is unlikely that our oil supply could collapse so suddenly. It does seem likely, however, that oil prices will some day be so high that few people will be able to afford the luxuries most North Americans now take for granted. Further, there is no doubt at all that sooner or later there will be no oil available for sale at any price. The critical question is this: Will we be able to switch to other sources of power by the time that occurs?

The world's reserves of coal are much greater than its reserves of oil and natural gas. Some experts say there is enough coal in the ground to meet the world's energy needs for several hundred years.[34] But as in the case of petroleum, the actual amount of coal available for human consumption is a matter of economics. The size of the world's usable coal reserves depends on the cost of mining them. Energy trade-offs must also be considered. Thus, the size of our usable coal reserves also depends on how much energy we must use in order to dig them up. Finally, we must remember that coal, like oil, is fossilized organic matter. No matter how much we pay for it, no matter how much energy we use to mine it, and no matter how much land we destroy in the process, some day the supply will be exhausted.

Some shale rock, like other fossil fuels, contains hydrocarbons that will burn. If you heat this rock and then squeeze it hard enough, oil will drip out. There is more oil in shale than in pumpable underground pools and many nations are now gearing up to use this new source of oil. But the economies of price, energy, and environment that restrict coal mining also put practical limits on the extraction of oil from shale. And like the supplies of other fossil fuels, the supply of shale oil is limited.

Nuclear-power plants probably will supply more of the world's energy as our oil and coal are burned up. In 1976, 61 nuclear plants produced 8 percent of America's electricity, and both numbers are higher now. But it is highly unlikely that nuclear reactors, at least in their present form, can replace the energy now obtained from fossil fuels. For one thing, it takes enormous amounts of energy to build a nuclear-power plant, so a substantial portion of the energy produced by the plant merely replaces the energy used up during its construction. A second problem is that the plants produce only electricity, a form of power that is poorly suited to meet many energy needs. Third, as mentioned earlier, nuclear-power plants produce deadly radioactive wastes that are hard to dispose of. Finally, nuclear reactors depend on uranium, a nonrenewable element that is not abundant. Breeder reactors can stretch existing uranium supplies, but as we have seen, the use of such reactors will increase the danger of nuclear terrorism as well.

About one-fourth of the power now used in the United States comes from renewable sources. Hydroelectric power, generated by turbines turned by flowing water, is clean and efficient. New hydroelectric-power stations appear every year, but the cost of transporting electricity limits its use. Currently, about 30 percent of America's electricity bill pays for the production of power; the other 70 percent is for transporting the power from the generators to the consumers. Geothermal energy — the heat of the earth's inner core — can be used to generate electricity and steam and is thus a possible substitute for fossil fuels. At present, however, this energy can be harnessed only in places with very special geological conditions. Solar energy is just beginning to make a contribution to our energy supplies. The sun bathes the earth with an enormous amount of energy every day, and if that energy can be efficiently used, a clean substitute for coal and oil will be at hand.

Raw Materials

The picture of the world's reserves of minerals and other raw materials is very much like the picture of its energy reserves. At current rates of consumption the world's known supplies of zinc, tin, gold, silver, lead, and possibly copper will be mined before the end of this century. Reserves of nickel, aluminum, cobalt, and magnesium will last around 100 years, while supplies of iron and chromium may last two centuries or more.[35] But again, both the known reserves and the rates of consumption are likely to increase, although no one can say how much. It is clear, however, that as high-grade deposits of these materials are used up, we will be forced to turn to deposits of lower and lower quality, which are more difficult to collect and refine. The seas and oceans contain many minerals both in the water and on the bottom. If it were economically feasible to exploit these resources, they would greatly increase the world's supplies of raw materials. Currently, however, it costs more to mine these minerals than they are worth. Moreover, international law is so poorly developed that no one really knows who has the right to mine ocean minerals. Artificial substitutes for some minerals have been developed, but most of them, such as plastics, are produced from petroleum, which is itself in limited supply.

Unlike energy, most minerals can be recycled. A significant portion of the copper, lead, gold, silver, and aluminum being used today is at least "secondhand." Recycling of most other raw materials is not profitable at present prices. But as world stores are emptied, prices will rise and recycling will look better and better. The main problem with recycling is familiar: It requires large amounts of energy. Another problem is that industrial metals stay in use so long that only small amounts are available for recycling.[36]

ORIGINS OF THE ENVIRONMENTAL CRISIS

Many ecologists and demographers predict that an ecological disaster is on the way, most likely in the form of international starvation. While not all the specialists are so pessimistic, there is no disagreement about the fact that humans have been destroying the very ecosystems that sustain them. Such irrational behavior is not easy to explain. Its complex causes have roots stretching far back into history. Ironically, the same characteristics that have made human beings such a successful species — high intelligence and an enormous ability to manipulate the environment — have also contributed to the development of the technology and cultural orientation that are now threatening human life.

Exploitive Technology

More and more people are coming to realize that the magnificent technological advances that have made life so much more confortable have a dark side as well. As we have seen, agricultural technology has brought havoc to the biosphere; industrial technology is polluting the environment; and military technology has for the first time in history given humanity the means to destroy itself. And even if we do not destroy ourselves directly with nuclear bombs, we may do it indirectly by disrupting ecosystems, food chains, and the whole life-supporting system.

But condemning technology as though it were separate from the humans who use it is both pointless and misleading. Every group of humans from prehistoric times to the present has used some form of technology to meet its needs for food, clothing, and shelter. Only a few of those technologies, however, have caused serious damage to the environment. The real culprit is exploitive technology designed to produce the greatest immediate rewards without regard to the long-term consequences. The modern world is just beginning to discover what a heavy price future generations will have to pay for our thoughtlessness.

The people of many ancient civilizations believed their past contained some lost utopia, and they tried to rely on the "wisdom of the past" in making difficult decisions. In contrast, a radically different idea took hold in seventeenth-century Europe. To those people and to much of the modern world, the golden era lies in the future, not in the past. The promise has been that technological progress will increase human happiness by banishing tyranny, inequality, ignorance, poverty, disease, even death itself. From this notion about the future, it is logical to conclude that the more rapidly technological development takes place, the sooner a utopian world will appear. The growth of exploitive technology continues to be taken as a sign of progress in Marxist nations as well as capitalist ones.

Such optimism about the future has declined in the twentieth century, primarily because more and more people are becoming aware of the damage we have done to our fragile environment. Since the 1960s there has been a growing nostalgia for the simple technologies of our ancestors. Young people especially talk about returning to the land and living in harmony with nature. But the belief that the world could support its present population with horse-and-buggy methods is naive and unrealistic. If destructive "progress" is to be stopped, it must be done by making modern technology more compatible with the ecology of our planet.

Growth

The world's population and economy are growing faster than ever before. Not only are there more and more people, but the average individual is living at a higher standard of living and using more nonrenewable resources than at any other time in history. The environmental effects of this growth are obvious. The more people there are and the more resources each of them uses, the faster they will pollute the environment and deplete the world's reserves of natural resources.

The damage caused by reckless growth is easily seen, but our traditional belief in economic expansion and progress has blinded many people. The governments of both capitalist and communist countries pursue policies designed to increase their wealth, and there is scarcely a nation in the world today that officially opposes economic growth. Fifty years ago the same thing could have been said about population growth. In the past quarter-century, however, the harsh realities of the population explosion have forced political leaders to change their minds and introduce population control measures. The same realities are now starting to eat away at the cherished belief in the value of economic growth.

One of the strongest attacks on the values of growth came from the 1972 report of the Club of Rome, mentioned earlier. Working under the Club's direction, a team of scientists from the Massachusetts Institute of Technology constructed a computerized "world model." By programing the computer with different sets of figures, predictions about the possible outcomes of present worldwide trends were derived. The numbers included several possible rates of population growth, rates of resource consumption, levels of pollution, and levels of agricultural production. All the projections led to the same conclusion, namely, that if humanity is to survive, we must abandon the age-old idea that growth is necessarily a good thing.

Businesspeople and industrialists, as well as average workers, are likely to be skeptical about the Club of Rome's gloomy predictions and reluctant to abandon a principle that has been profitable for so long. Critics argue that the Club of Rome's predictions are wrong because by the time our resources are gone we will have found new resources and new technologies to keep the economy growing.[37] It is, of course, impossible to prove or disprove either set of claims. But it appears unwise to continue using up our resources at the present rate, thus gambling our future on possible technological advances that may never occur.

Culture

Rapid population growth and increasing use of exploitive technologies are direct causes of the environmental crisis. But underlying such growth are culturally based attitudes toward nature and humanity's place in it. As already noted, one characteristic of Western culture is the idea that humans are superior to the natural world they inhabit. According to the Book of Genesis, humans were made in the image of God, who told them, "Be fruitful, and multiply, and replenish the earth and subdue it; and have dominion over the fish of the sea, and over the birds of the sky, and over every living thing that moves upon the earth."[38] Western culture tends to see nature as a wilderness to be conquered and subdued by human effort. The art, literature, and folk tales of the West repeatedly show people in heroic struggles against the forces of nature.[39]

The attitudes of most primitive peoples and of the great civilizations of the East are quite different. In those cultures human beings are seen as part of nature. They are expected to live in harmony with their environment, not to subdue or conquer it. American Indians, Australian aborigines, and many other "primitive" peoples see all of nature as sacred—the rocks, the trees, the mountains, the animals. To them, the European's assault on the environment is not merely unwise, it is a sacrilege—the desecration of a holy place.

It is not hard to see how Western attitudes toward nature led to the current crisis. We have mastered some living things and destroyed others. We have transformed the natural world but have not conquered it. Time and again humans have paid dearly for abusing the web of life.

RESPONDING TO ENVIRONMENTAL PROBLEMS

It was not until the 1970s that the public began to realize the seriousness of the environmental problems caused by continuing growth. Dozens of different organizations, many of them with international memberships, are now working on everything from saving wild animals to developing new sources of energy. But pollution, energy consumption, and economic growth are interdependent problems. Effective programs for dealing with one of them often aggravate the others. For example, devices that clean automobile exhaust and reduce air pollution also decrease fuel economy, thereby using up our limited oil reserves more rapidly. Similarly, banning the burning of household trash reduces air pollution but increases oil consumption as trucks haul the trash to dumps. Exploiting new reserves of fossil fuel increases environmental pollution as land, animals, and scenery are sacrificed for strip mines and oil wells, and the wastes produced by the fuel are dumped into the environment. But ignoring the need for more energy stagnates the economy, thereby increasing unemployment and reducing food production.

There is a way out of this trap. In a word, it is sacrifice. The fact is, there is no way to both clean up the environment and conserve natural resources without changing the life style of the industrialized nations. The challenge is that of motivating people to make the changes that are necessary to put a lid on economic growth now, before a worldwide disaster forces much more difficult adjustments upon us.

Political Action

Criminal law, administrative law, and public education are all being used in a poorly coordinated effort to modify North America's wasteful and exploitive life style. Broad-based organizations such as the Sierra Club are concerned with a wide spectrum of environmental issues. Many smaller organizations have sprung up around specific issues—saving an endangered species, logging a forest, building a ski resort in the wilderness, constructing a nuclear-power plant, or drilling new offshore oil wells. National groups put political pressure on lawmakers and government agencies; local groups hold rallies, protest marches, demonstrations, and sit-ins. Both types of groups are also engaged in broader educational efforts. School programs teach children to conserve energy and respect wild animals, and many universities now have majors in environmental studies.

Despite these efforts, public awareness of the environmental crisis remains low. It is one thing to protest against an unsightly oil derrick that will spoil your view. It is quite another to convince Congress that it must formulate and oversee a national oil conservation policy. Moreover, it is always tempting to ease local environmental standards in order to bring in a new industry that will create employment and greater economic prosperity.

Environmental groups have already been successful in promoting a variety of environmental-protection laws. Restrictions have been placed on various forms of air and water pollution, and there is an increasing concern for the protection of rare animal species. Still, most environmental legislation is opposed by the people whose actions it tries to change. The laws that have been passed despite this opposition are seldom enforced vigorously. Exaggerated claims are often made by the opponents of environmental protection. According to their spokesmen, installing antipollution equipment in factories or strict energy-saving measures will bankrupt the nation. Voters are in effect asked to choose between jobs and clean air, between present comfort and future shortages. Given this choice, they are not likely to favor environmental conservation. Environmental groups must convince both the people and their governments to look at the long-term rather than the short-term effects of environmental-protection projects. Relentless efforts will be required merely to maintain the environmental quality we have today.

Conserving Resources

There is no doubt that our existing resources can be used more efficiently. It is possible that a large-scale, multiple-stage recycling program can be introduced in imitation of natural ecosystems. Just as the basic necessities of life are used by one organism after another in various ecological cycles, so human society could reuse many of its essential raw materials over and over. To take a simple example, garbage could be used for fuel to run mills to make recycled paper, the wastes from which could be burned as fuel. Similarly, it will not be long before community water districts become closed systems, meaning that the water is used again and again, never being discharged into an ocean or river. Some factories already have such closed systems. It is possible to envision larger closed systems designed so that no industrial product would ever be discarded as either waste or pollution.

Energy conservation can also stretch our natural resources. North Americans waste so much energy that significant amounts of oil, gas, and coal could be saved without lowering our standard of living. Sweden has a higher standard of living than Canada, but it uses almost 50 percent less energy per person.[40] Insulating homes, driving smaller cars at slower speeds, riding trains and buses, recycling the heat used in factories, and restricting the manufacture of energy-wasting gadgets are obvious ways of eliminating waste. The immediate task is not to develop technologies that are more energy efficient. The challenge is to find ways of persuading people to use the conservation measures that are already available.

New Technology

While conservation will stretch our energy supplies, new sources of energy will be needed eventually. We have already mentioned proposals for more nuclear, hydroelectric, and geothermal power stations. Some scientists are now proposing the development of power plants equipped with nuclear reactors using fusion (the merging of atoms) rather than fission (the splitting of atoms). A working fusion reactor could use common seawater as a fuel, extracting as much as 300 times more energy per gallon than is available from gasoline.[41] However, nuclear fusion generates temperatures comparable to those of the sun, and no one knows whether it is possible to control such a powerful force.

A growing number of scientists and concerned citizens are coming to see solar power as the answer to the world's energy problems. Solar-power units use the endless supply of energy from the sun, are nonpolluting, and pose no threat of radiation or explosion. Solar energy is already being used on a small scale to heat water, homes, and offices, and most ex-

Solar energy offers one of the brightest prospects for our future. It is clean, abundant, and will never run out.

perts are confident that an efficient technology for storing and using the sun's energy can be developed. Such technology will be an imitation of nature, since all the energy in natural ecosystems ultimately comes from the sun.

Limiting Growth

Technological solutions are attractive, but it is doubtful they can provide the whole answer to the environmental crisis. If the world's population keeps on doubling every 35 or 40 years, there is bound to be more and more pollution and an ever-increasing drain on natural resources. Any effective solution to the environmental crisis must include some form of population control. Restrictions on economic growth will be needed as well. It seems inescapable that more economic growth means faster depletion of resources and more pollution.

It is often argued that industrial growth is necessary to create new jobs for a growing population. But the advocates of growth ignore the obvious solutions to the problem of unemployment that do not require economic expansion, such as reducing automated technology or working fewer hours a week in order to distribute the existing jobs among more people. Indeed, anthropologists have shown that in the long run our "labor-saving" technology does not save labor at all. Most people in "primitive" societies without such devices work fewer hours a week than we do, not more. (Of course, they do not demand our luxurious standard of living.)[42] The argument that economic growth is necessary to eliminate poverty and create a more egalitarian society is also misleading. Despite decades of rapid economic growth, the industrialized nations continue to show enormous inequalities of wealth and power. The most egalitarian societies are those that depend on simple hunting and gathering technologies. This does not mean that the answer to the environmental crisis is for everyone to return to hunting and gathering. But it does seem likely that the world would be more peaceful and more secure if the people of the industrialized nations learned to accept a more leisurely life style and a lower standard of living.

SOCIOLOGICAL PERSPECTIVES on the Environment

Pollution of the air and water, degradation of the land, and wasteful use of oil and other natural resources seem to be topics for engineers, biologists, and geologists to ponder. Indeed, representatives of these disciplines, and economists as well, are making important studies of environmental problems, and it is they who have proposed most of the possible solutions. But environmental issues are also sociological issues. Sociologists take the broad view, repeatedly pointing out that social institutions are organized systems similar to the ecosystems of nature; that one must understand interacting physical, biological, economic, political, and psychological conditions if one is to understand collective human behavior; and that purposive human actions have unanticipated consequences. In short, sociologists try to teach people to understand that few human problems are as simple as they seem. The origins of the environmental crisis are not to be found in a few polluting industries, but in the basic social organization and cultural outlook of the modern world.

The Functionalist Perspective

Functionalist theory sees our environmental problems as latent dysfunctions of industrialization. Each of the technological advances that help society perform its basic functions more easily and efficiently has had negative side effects. The manufacturing, distributing, and consuming processes that make increases in our standard of living possible also produce dysfunctional by-products—pollution and resource depletion. Thus, the economic changes that helped create modern industrial society also threw the environment out of balance.

To many functionalists the answer to our environmental problems is simple. The dysfunctions of the industrial economy must be reduced through use of more efficient pollution control devices, conservation of energy and raw materials, and new technological improvements. That is, the environmental crisis is to be ended by refining and improving our present way of doing things, not by making basic changes in social and economic systems.

However, other functionalists disagree, arguing that the present industrial economy is inherently unstable because it depends on steady growth to maintain economic prosperity, yet is using up the resources that are necessary to maintain that growth. To this way of thinking, a "band-aid" approach promoting minor reforms cannot solve our environmental problems. Basic changes must be made because many of the central values of our social system have become dysfunctional. At one time the ideas about conquering nature and the importance of increasing our personal wealth inspired the effort necessary for survival. But such attitudes now threaten human existence because they ignore the long-term effects of the relentless pursuit of wealth by billions of people. The economic system is thus dysfunctional because it wastes resources and pollutes the environment in order to produce more than is necessary for the health and well-being of the people. To these functionalists, a solution to the environmental crisis will require major changes in our system of values and a reorganization of society.

The Conflict Perspective

Conflict theorists see exploitation of the environment as just one more activity of exploitive groups. Specifically, the United States and Canada are said to have economic and political systems that help wealthy and powerful people exploit the poor and the weak. This exploitive approach extends to the environment as well, because the natural wealth of "the people" is destroyed in the interests of the few.

This same pattern of exploitation also occurs internationally. According to conflict theorists, the wealthy industrialized nations are using their power to loot the poor nations of their irreplaceable natural resources, thus making the rich nations richer and the poor nations poorer. When poor nations finally try to industrialize, they find that the cheap energy and raw materials that helped develop the wealthy nations are gone.

Conflict theorists insist that the scarcity of resources is being used as an excuse to avoid doing what should have been done long ago, namely, create a world economic and political order based on equality and respect for the dignity of all humans. "In an age of slow growth, the cost of natural resources is going up and the value placed on human life is going down."[43] To stop the exploitation and destruction of our natural environment, we must reverse this trend, putting human dignity first and profits second. The competitive materialistic orientation that produced such stunning economic achievements has also degraded humans by using possessions as a measure of a person's worth. As long as this orientation and the economic system it fostered continues, conflict theorists say, we will continue to brutalize both the environment and ourselves.

The Social- Psychological Perspective

Clearly, learned attitudes, values, and ideologies are the foundation stones of the environmental crisis. One social psychologist has identified three attitudes that lead directly to environmental problems.[44] The first is an attitude of "quantitative exploitation." We assess the environment in terms of "production statistics, board feet, metric tons, gallons of liquid," not in terms of its contribution to human life, health, and peace of mind. North Americans have a particularly exploitive attitude toward nature, perhaps because of our frontier heritage. Second, attitudes favoring bigness, consumption, and individualism all lead to environmental exploitation, even though they are not necessarily exploitive in themselves. Third, an attitude that might be called "urbanism" sets humans apart from nature. City living makes the consequences of destroyed or damaged ecosystems less obvious. The attitude of urbanism is an attitude of indifference to sources of raw materials—even food—and to pollution that does not affect one's personal life.

Such attitudes are learned. According to social psychologists, if we are to deal effectively with our environmental problems these attitudes must be unlearned by an entire generation. As they are unlearned, new attitudes will take their place. Citizens of the twentieth century can learn, as "primitive" people did, that nature is to be regarded with respect and reverence, that humans are a small and dependent part of the natural environment, and that a life style that attempts to achieve harmony with nature is more pleasant than one that attempts to conquer it.

SUMMARY

As exploitive technologies have grown, the by-products of industrialization have fouled the land, air, and water, thus disrupting the delicate web of life on which human existence depends. The science of ecology—the study of the interrelationships among plants, animals, and their environment—has shown that humans are but one part of a complex network of living things.

Ecologists call the thin surface layer of air, water, and soil that supports all life on earth the biosphere. Within the biosphere there are many ecosystems—interdependent communities of living organisms. The ultimate source of the food in any ecosystem is the sun, whose energy is transformed into plant life by a process called photosynthesis.

Humans have had a tremendous impact on natural ecosystems and are now the principal source of change in the biosphere. This interference has produced unintended effects that are harmful to humanity itself. Air pollution, for example, is a severe health hazard and is causing harmful changes in the world's ecological balance.

Despite the world's enormous reserves of water, water pollution is becoming a serious problem. Organic wastes from human sewage and industry are water pollutants, as are the chemical fertilizers and pesticides used extensively in modern farming. Poisonous chemicals such as mercury and arsenic build up in the tissues of one marine animal after another, eventually reaching the humans at the top of the food chain.

Overgrazing, logging, urban sprawl, faulty irrigation, strip mining, and poor farming techniques have combined to deface the land. Over the years forests have steadily shrunk as deserts, wastelands, and cities have grown. Further, new chemicals are used in business and industry every year, and many of them are being dumped on land, in water, and in the air. Although radiation pollution is not a major problem now, there is growing concern that nuclear reactors will foul the environment with cancer-causing rays.

The modern industrial economy is rapidly using up the world's irreplaceable natural resources as well as polluting the environment. Projections show that the world's supply of oil and natural gas will run out within 100 years or less. Coal is more abundant, but even our coal reserves can supply the world's energy needs for only a few more centuries. Increasing emphasis is being placed on nuclear power, but the uranium that fuels nuclear reactors is another scarce natural substance that is not renewable.

The complex causes of the environmental crisis have roots stretching far back in human history. Technology has become highly exploitive, using large amounts of energy and natural resources and producing pollution in the process. The growth of the total human population and economic growth in the industrialized nations have severely aggravated the damage to the earth's web of life. Underlying these two conditions are culturally based attitudes toward nature and humanity's place in it. Western people look at nature as something to be conquered and exploited, and seem to show none of the reverence and respect for nature so common in nonliterate cultures.

Great concern for environmental problems developed in the 1970s. Political action met with some success, but government programs are complicated by the fact that pollution, energy consumption, and economic growth are interrelated. Programs for using existing resources more efficiently have also been introduced. Among them are recycling and education about how to avoid waste. While conservation will stretch our energy supplies, new sources of energy will be needed eventually. Scientists are at work on nuclear fusion and solar energy. Other proposals for solving the energy crisis ask for population controls, and still others call for restrictions on economic growth. It seems inevitable that more economic growth means faster depletion of resources and more pollution, but no government in the world has officially sponsored a program for restricting its own economic "progress."

Because social institutions resemble the ecosystems of nature, it is logical that sociologists should show concern for the interaction between human systems and environmental systems. Functionalists see our environmental problems as latent dysfunctions of the industrial revolution. The attitudes that inspired the industriousness necessary for survival are no longer functional. Conflict theorists see exploitation of the environment as part of a continuing war between the rich and the poor. They note that profits have been given a higher priority than human dignity, and they call for a reversal of these priorities. Social psychologists have identified several attitudes, values, and ideologies that underlie the environmental crisis. Such attitudes are learned, and if we are to deal effectively with our environmental problems they must be unlearned by an entire generation of citizens.

KEY TERMS

biosphere	hydroelectric power
ecology	meltdown
ecosystem	photochemical smog
exploitive technology	photosynthesis
food chain	solar energy
geothermal energy	temperature inversion

References

CHAPTER 1

1. See Robert K. Merton, "The Sociology of Social Problems," in Robert K. Merton and Robert Nisbet, eds., *Contemporary Social Problems*, 4th ed. (New York: Harcourt Brace Jovanovich, 1976).
2. Herbert Blumer, "Social Problems as Collective Behavior," *Social Problems* 18 (1971): 298–306; Malcolm Spector and John I. Kitsuse, "Social Problems: A Reformulation," *Social Problems* 21 (1973): 145–159.
3. See Robert H. Lauer, "Defining Social Problems: Public Opinion and Textbook Practice," *Social Problems* 24 (1976): 122–130.
4. See Howard S. Becker, *Outsiders* (Glencoe: Free Press, 1963).
5. Edward C. Wilson, *Sociobiology: The New Synthesis* (Cambridge, Mass.: Belknap Press, 1975).
6. Dorwin Cartwright, "Achieving Change in People: Some Applications of Group Dynamics Theory," *Human Relations* 4 (1951): 381–392.
7. See, *e.g.,* Herbert Blumer, *Symbolic Interactionism: Perspective and Method* (Englewood Cliffs, N.J.: Prentice-Hall, 1969), and Tamotsu Shibutani, *Society and Personality* (Englewood Cliffs, N.J.: Prentice-Hall, 1961).

CHAPTER 2

1. Adam Smith, *An Inquiry into the Nature and Causes of the Wealth of Nations* (New York: Random House, 1937).
2. *Ibid.,* p. 128.
3. Daniel Zwerdling, "The Food Monopolies," in Jerome H. Skolnick and Elliot Currie, eds., *Crisis in American Institutions*, 3d ed. (Boston: Little Brown, 1976), p. 44.
4. Max D. Stewart, "The Structure of Canadian Industry," in Lawrence H. Officer and Lawrence B. Smith, eds., *Issues in Canadian Economy* (Toronto: McGraw-Hill, 1974).
5. Daniel B. Fusfield, *Economics,* 2d ed. (Lexington, Mass.: Heath, 1976), p. 530.
6. John Kenneth Galbraith, *The New Industrial State* (New York: Signet Books, 1967).
7. Frank Ackerman *et al.,* "The Extent of Income Inequality in the United States," in Richard C. Edwards *et al.,* eds., *The Capitalist System* (Englewood Cliffs, N.J.: Prentice-Hall, 1972), p. 211.
8. *Newsweek,* December 18, 1974.
9. Morton Mintz and Jerry S. Cohen, *America, Inc.: Who Owns and Operates the United States?* (New York: Dial, 1971), p. 61.
10. Fusfield, *Economics,* p. 533.
11. C. Wright Mills, *The Power Elite* (New York: Oxford University Press, 1956).
12. For details see Richard J. Barnet and Ronald E. Muller, *Global Reach* (New York: Simon & Schuster, 1974).
13. See Anthony Sampson, *The Sovereign State of I.T.T.* (Greenwich, Conn.: Fawcett Crest, 1973).
14. *Los Angeles Times,* May 9, 1976.
15. John G. Fuller, *200,000,000 Guinea Pigs: New Dangers in Everyday Foods, Drugs, and Cosmetics* (New York: Putnam's, 1972), pp. 82–91.
16. Mark J. Green, *The Closed Enterprise System: Ralph Nader's Study-Group Report on Anti-Trust Enforcement* (New York: Grossman, 1972), pp. 147–150.
17. Richard Austin Smith, "The Incredible Electrical Conspiracy," *Fortune* 63 (1961): 132–180, 161–224.
18. These and other techniques are described in detail by Edwin H. Sutherland, *White-Collar Crime* (New York: Dryden, 1949), pp. 56–88.
19. Galbraith, *The New Industrial State,* pp. 304–305.
20. Mintz and Cohen, *America Inc.,* p. 70.
21. Robert Heilbroner, *The Economic Problem,* 3d ed. (Englewood Cliffs, N.J.: Prentice-Hall, 1972), pp. 105–108.
22. John Crispo, "Trade Unionism, Collective Bargaining, and Public Policy," in Lawrence H. Officer and Lawrence B. Smith, eds., *Canadian Economic Problems and Policies* (Toronto: McGraw-Hill, 1970).
23. Nancy C. Morse and Robert S. Weiss, "The Function and Meaning of Work," *American Sociological Review* 20 (1955): 191–198.
24. Robert S. Weiss, Edwin Harwood, and David Riesman, "The World of Work," in Robert K. Merton and Robert Nisbet, eds., *Contemporary Social Problems,* 4th ed. (New York: Harcourt Brace Jovanovich, 1976), pp. 608–609.

25. *Ibid.*, p. 611; James W. Rinehart, *The Tyranny of Work* (Don Mills, Ont.: Longman, 1975), p. 85

26. Seymour Wolfbein, *Work in American Society* (Glenview, Ill.: Scott, Foresman, 1971), pp. 21–23.

27. *Work in America: Report of a Special Task Force to the Secretary of Health, Education, and Welfare* (Cambridge, Mass.: M.I.T. Press, 1973), p. 39.

28. *Ibid.*, p. 13.

29. Melvin L. Kohn and Carmi Schooler, "Occupational Experience and Psychological Functioning: An Assessment of Reciprocal Effects," *American Sociological Review* 38 (1973): 97–118.

30. Samuel C. Florman, "The Job-Enrichment Mistake," *Harper's* 252 (1976): 18–22.

31. Stanislav V. Kasl *et al.,* "The Experience of Losing a Job: Reported Changes in Health Symptoms and Illness Behavior," *Psychosomatic Medicine* 37 (1975): 106–122.

32. Austin Scott, "Black Youth's Jobs Picture Still Bleak," *Los Angeles Times,* December 24, 1978.

33. Officer and Smith, *Canadian Economic Problems and Policies,* pp. 9–10.

34. See Government of Canada, *Agenda for Co-operation: A Discussion Paper on Decontrol and Post-Control Issues* (Ottawa, 1977).

CHAPTER 3

1. Daniel R. Fusfeld, *Economics,* 2d ed. (Lexington, Mass.: Heath, 1976), pp. 686–687.

2. Max Weber, from *Max Weber: Essay in Sociology,* trans. Hans H. Gerth and C. Wright Mills (New York: Oxford University Press, 1946), pp. 196–244.

3. Max Weber, *The Theory of Social and Economic Organization,* trans. A. M. Henderson and Talcott Parsons (New York: Free Press, 1947), p. 337.

4. Peter Blau and Marshall W. Meyer, *Bureaucracy in Modern Society,* 2d ed. (New York: Random House, 1971), pp. 100–110.

5. James Q. Wilson, "The Bureaucracy Problem," *The Public Interest* 6 (1967): 3–9.

6. Thomas Bodenheimer, "The Poverty of the State," in Alan Wells, ed., *American Society* (Pacific Palisades, Calif.: Goodyear, 1976), pp. 33–41.

7. Kenneth Prewitt and Sidney Verba, *An Introduction to American Government* (New York: Harper & Row, 1974), pp. 255–260.

8. Herbert E. Alexander, *Financing the 1968 Election* (Lexington, Mass.: Lexington Books, 1971).

9. Mark J. Green, James M. Fallows, and David R. Zwick, *Who Runs Congress? A Ralph Nader Congress Project Report* (New York: Bantam, 1972), p. 2.

10. Paul N. McCloskey, "Congressional Politics: Secrecy, Senility, and Seniority," in Alan Wells, ed., *American Society: Problems and Dilemmas* (Pacific Palisades, Calif.: Goodyear, 1976), p. 20.

11. *Ibid.*

12. For a good brief discussion of the history of the Supreme Court, see Prewitt and Verba, *An Introduction to American Government,* pp. 348–376.

13. McCloskey, "Congressional Politics." p. 18.

14. Sidney Verba and Norman H. Nie, *Participation in America: Political Democracy and Social Equality* (New York: Harper & Row, 1972).

15. Ralph Nader, "Introduction" to Morton Mintz and Jerry S. Cohen, *America, Inc.: Who Owns and Operates the United States?* (New York: Dial, 1971), p. xi.

16. David Sheridan, "The Lobbyist: Out of the Shadows," *Saturday Review* 55 (1972): 48–54.

17. C. Wright Mills, *The Power Elite* (New York: Oxford University Press, 1956).

18. C. Wright Mills, "The Structure of Power in American Society," in *Power, Politics and People: The Collected Papers of C. Wright Mills* (New York: Ballantine Books, 1963), p. 288.

19. Gabriel Kolko, *The Roots of American Foreign Policy: An Analysis of Power and Purpose* (Boston: Beacon Press, 1969), and G. William Domhoff, *The Higher Circles: The Governing Class in America* (New York: Random House, 1970), pp. 137–139.

20. David Riesman, *The Lonely Crowd* (New York: Doubleday Anchor, 1953).

21. For a good comparison of Mills and Riesman, see William Kornhauser, "Power Elite or Veto Groups?" in Seymour M. Lipset and Leo Lowenthal, eds., *Culture and Social Character* (New York: Macmillan, 1961).

22. Arnold M. Rose, *The Power Structure: Political Process in American Society* (London: Oxford University Press, 1967), p. 6.

23. Domhoff, *The Higher Circles,* p. 309.

24. Robert Michels, *Political Parties: A Sociological Study of the Oligarchical Tendencies of Modern Democracy* (New York: Free Press, 1962).

25. *Ibid.*, p. 354.

26. Vernon K. Dibble, "The Garrison Society," *New University Thought,* 1967: pp. 106–115.

27. Seymour Melman, *Pentagon Capitalism* (New York: McGraw-Hill, 1970), p. 187.

28. Fusfeld, *Economics,* p. 687.

29. See Ron Haggart and Aubrey E. Golden, *Rumors of War* (Toronto: New York Press, 1971).

30. Arthur Washow, "Watergate and Presidential Power," in Henry Etzkowitz, ed., *Is America Possible?* (St. Paul: West Publishing, 1974).

31. American Civil Liberties Union, *Congressional Digest, 1971,* from testimony given before the Senate Subcommittee on Constitutional Rights, February 23, 1971.

32. Sam J. Ervin, *Congressional Digest, 1971,* from remarks delivered on the floor of the U.S. Senate, September 8, 1970.

33. Theodore W. Adorno *et al., The Authoritarian Personality* (New York: Harper & Row, 1950).

CHAPTER 4

1. Quoted in Mavis Hiltunen Biesanz and John Biesanz, *Introduction to Sociology*, 2d ed. (Englewood Cliffs, N.J.: Prentice-Hall, 1973), p. 616.

2. U.S. Office of Education, *Digest of Educational Statistics, 1971* (Washington, D.C.: GPO, 1972), p. 27.

3. Allen Wells, "Education in America," in A. Wells, ed., *American Society: Problems and Dilemmas* (Pacific Palisades, Calif.: Goodyear, 1976), p. 256.

4. George H. Gallup, "Seventh Annual Gallup Poll of Public Attitudes Toward Education," *Phi Delta Kappan* 57 (1975): 227–241.

5. See Betty Levy and Judith Stacy, "Sexism in the Elementary Schools: A Backward and Forward Look," *Phi Delta Kappan* (1973): 105–109, 123.

6. See, *e.g.*, Jonathan Kozol, *Death at an Early Age* (Boston: Houghton Mifflin, 1967).

7. James S. Coleman, "Racial Segregation in the Schools: New Research with New Policy Implication," *Phi Delta Kappan* (1975).

8. Charles S. Bullock and Harrell R. Rodgers, *Racial Equality in America: In Search of an Unfulfilled Goal* (Pacific Palisades, Calif.: Goodyear, 1975), p. 154.

9. Diane Ravitch, "Busing: The Solution That Has Failed to Solve," *New York Times*, December 21, 1975.

10. *Ibid.*

11. James S. Coleman *et al., Equality of Education Opportunity* (Washington, D.C.: GPO, 1966).

12. See David Armor, "The Evidence on Busing," *The Public Interest* 28 (1972): 90–126; Thomas F. Pettigrew *et. al.*, "Busing: A Review of the Evidence," *The Public Interest* 30 (1973): 88–118; and Godfrey Hodgson, "Do Schools Make a Difference?" in Donald M. Levine and Mary Jo Bane, eds., *The "Inequality" Controversy: Schooling and Distributive Justice* (New York: Basic Books, 1975).

13. Nancy H. St. John, *School Desegregation: Outcomes for Children* (New York: Wiley, 1975), p. 36.

14. *Ibid.*, pp. 64–86.

15. See Harvey A. Averch *et al., How Effective Is Schooling? A Critical Synthesis and Review of Research Findings* (Englewood Cliffs, N.J.: Educational Technology Publications, 1974).

16. The Gallup Poll, *Report No. 105* (Princeton, N.J., March 1974).

17. Christopher Jencks *et al., Inequality: A Reassessment of the Effects of Family and Schooling in America* (New York: Harper & Row, 1972), p. 140

18. Basil Bernstein, *Class, Codes and Control* (London: Routledge and Kegan Paul, 1971).

19. Robert D. Reischauer and Robert W. Hartmen, *Reforming School Finance* (Washington, D.C.: Brookings 1973), pp. 5–9.

20. Victor H. Bernstein, "Educational Equality: An End to the School House Scandal," in Glenn Smith and Charles R. Kinder, eds., *Myth and Reality: A Reader in Education* (Boston: Allyn and Bacon, 1975).

21. Manley Fleischmann *et al., The Fleischmann Report on the Quality, Cost, and Financing of Elementary and Secondary Education in New York State* (New York: Viking, 1973), 1:57.

22. See Averch *et al., How Effective Is Schooling?*

23. Jencks *et al., Inequality*, p. 29.

24. Charles E. Silberman, *Crisis in the Classroom: The Remaking of American Education* (New York: Random House, 1970), pp. 79–112.

25. Robert Rosenthal and Lenore Jacobson, *Pygmalion in the Classroom* (New York: Harper & Row, 1969).

26. Aaron Cicourel and John Kitsuse, *The Educational Decision-Makers* (Indianapolis: Bobbs-Merrill, 1963), p. 51.

27. Silberman, *Crisis in the Classroom: The Remaking of American Education*, p. 128.

28. Kozol, *Death at an Early Age.*

29. *Los Angeles Times*, October 2, 1977.

30. Jack McCurdy and Don Speich, "Student Skills Decline Unequalled in History," *Los Angeles Times*, August 15, 1976; *U.S. News and World Report*, November 24, 1975.

31. *Ibid.*

32. *Ibid.*

33. Jencks *et al., Inequality*, p. 222.

34. Statistics Canada, *Income Distributions by Size in Canada, 1971.*

35. David S. Saxon, "Is It Time to Stop Learning?," *Newsweek*, June 28, 1976, p. 13.

36. J. Feldhusen, J. Thurston, and J. Benning, "A Longitudinal Study of Delinquency and Other Aspects of Children's Behavior," *International Journal of Criminology and Penology* 1 (1973): 341–351.

37. Delbert S. Elliott and Harwin L. Voss, *Delinquency and Dropout* (Lexington, Mass.: Lexington Books, 1974), p. 204.

38. Edwin H. Sutherland and Donald R. Cressey, *Criminology*, 10th ed. (New York: Harper & Row, 1978), pp. 239–240.

39. Elliott and Voss, *Delinquency and Dropout*, pp. 121, 206.

40. Coleman, "Racial Segregation in the Schools."

41. *Newsweek*, August 30, 1976, p. 77.

42. A. S. Neill, *Summerhill: A Radical Approach to Child Rearing* (New York: Hart, 1960).

43. See Reischauer and Hartman, *Reforming School Finance*, pp. 78–81.

CHAPTER 5

1. George P. Murdock, "World Ethnographic Sample," *American Anthropologist* 59 (1957): 664–687.

2. Marc J. Swartz and David K. Jordan, *Anthropology: Perspective on Humanity* (New York: Wiley, 1976), pp. 565–567.

3. See, *e.g.,* George P. Murdock, *Social Structure* (Glencoe: Free Press, 1949); William J. Goode, *The Family* (Englewood Cliffs, N.J.: Prentice-Hall, 1946); Kingsley Davis, *Human Society* (New York: Macmillan, 1949).

4. William J. Goode, *World Revolution and Family Patterns* (Glencoe: Free-Press, 1963).

5. See Ralph Linton, "The Natural History of the Family," in Ruth N. Anshen, ed., *The Family: Its Function and Destiny* (New York: Harper & Row, 1959); Louis Wirth, "Urbanism as a Way of Life," *American Journal of Sociology* 44 (1938): 1–24; Talcott Parsons, "The Kinship System of the Contemporary United States," *American Anthropologist* 45 (1943): 22–38.

6. Marvin B. Sussman and Lee Burchinal, "Kin Family Network: Unheralded Structure in Current Conceptualization of Family Functions," *Marriage and Family Living* 24 (1962): 231–240.

7. Alfred M. Mirande "The Isolated Nuclear Family Hypothesis: A Reanalysis," in Mildred W. Weil, ed., *Sociological Perspectives in Marriage and the Family* (Danville, Ill.: The Interstate, 1972), p. 40.

8. William F. Kenkel, *The Family in Perspective* (Englewood Cliffs, N.J.: Prentice-Hall, 1973).

9. U.S. Bureau of the Census, *Statistical Abstract of the United States: 1975* (Washington, D.C.: GPO, 1975), p. 51.

10. William J. Goode, "Family Disorganization," in Robert K. Merton and Robert Nisbet, eds., *Contemporary Social Problems,* 4th ed. (New York: Harcourt Brace Jovanovich, 1976), p. 527.

11. See J. Richard Udry, *The Social Contest of Marriage,* 2d ed. (New York: Harper & Row, 1971), p. 301.

12. Kenkel, *The Family in Perspective,* p. 325.

13. Roland J. Chilton and Gerald E. Markle, "Family Disruption, Delinquent Conduct, and the Effect of Subclassification," *American Sociological Review* 37 (1972): 93–99.

14. Jackson Toby, "The Differential Impact of Family Disorganization," *American Sociological Review* 22 (1957): 505–512.

15. F. Ivan Nye, "Child Adjustment in Broken and Unhappy Unbroken Homes," *Marriage and Family Living* 19 (1957): 356–361; Judson T. Landis, "A Comparison of Children from Divorced and Nondivorced Unhappy Marriages," *Family Life Coordinator* 11 (July 1962): 61–65.

16. *Statistical Abstract of the United States: 1975,* p. 57.

17. Goode, "Family Disorganization," p. 519.

18. George Levinger, "Physical Abuse Among Applicants for Divorce," *American Journal of Orthopsychiatry* 36 (1966): 804–806.

19. John E. O'Brien, "Violence in Divorce-Prone Families," *Journal of Marriage and the Family* 35 (1971): 692–698.

20. Robert N. Whitehurst, "Violence in Husband–Wife Interaction," in Suzanne K. Steinmetz and Murry A. Straus, eds., *Violence in the Family* (New York: Dodd, Mead, 1974), p. 142.

21. Rodney Stark and James McEvoy, "Middle Class Violence," *Psychology Today* 4 (1970): 52–65.

22. David G. Gil, *Violence Against Children: Physical Child Abuse in the United States* (Cambridge, Mass.: Harvard University Press, 1970), pp. 98–99.

23. David G. Gil, "Violence Against Children," *Journal of Marriage and the Family* 33 (1971): 644–648.

24. Samuel X. Radbill, "A History of Child Abuse and Infanticide," in Ray E. Helfer and C. Henry Kempe, eds., *The Battered Child,* 2d ed. (Chicago: University of Chicago Press, 1974).

25. Steinmetz and Straus, *Violence in the Family,* p. 141.

26. Richard J. Gelles, "Child Abuse as Psychopathology: A Sociological Critique and Reformulation," *American Journal of Orthopsychiatry* 43 (1973): 611–621.

27. Kenneth Eckhardt, "Deviance, Visibility and Legal Action: The Duty to Support," *Social Problems* 15 (1968): 473.

28. Thomas C. Taveggia and Ellen M. Thomas, "Latchkey Children," *Pacific Sociological Review* 17 (1974): 27–34.

29. See, *e.g.,* Lynda Lytle Holmstrom, *The Two-Career Family* (Cambridge, Mass.: Schenkman, 1972).

30. See Rustum Roy and Della Roy, "Is Monogamy Outdated?" in Jon M. Shepard and Cyrus S. Stewart, eds., *Sociology and Social Problems* (Englewood Cliffs, N.J.: Prentice-Hall, 1976), p. 255.

31. Margaret Mead, "Marriage in Two Steps," *Redbook* 127 (1966): 48–49.

32. William Masters and Virginia Johnson, *Human Sexual Inadequacy* (Boston: Little, Brown, 1970).

33. For a summary of the data on this point, see F. Ivan Nye and Felix M. Berardo, *The Family* (New York: Macmillan, 1973), pp. 514–518.

34. Nena O'Neill and George O'Neill, "Open Marriage: The Conceptual Framework," in James R. Smith and Lynn G. Smith, eds., *Beyond Monogamy* (Baltimore: Johns Hopkins Press, 1974), p. 62.

35. Larry L. Constantine and Joan M. Constantine, *Group Marriage: A Study of Contemporary Multilateral Marriage* (New York: Macmillan, 1973).

36. Rosabeth Moss Kanter, "'Getting It All Together': Some Group Issues in Communes," *American Journal of Orthopsychiatry* 42 (1972): 632–643.

CHAPTER 6

1. U.S. Bureau of the Census, *Characteristics of the Population Below the Poverty Level: 1975* (Washington, D.C.: GPO, 1977), p. 2.
2. U.S. Bureau of the Census, *Money Income and Poverty Status of Families and Persons in the United States: 1976* (Advance Report) (Washington D.C.: GPO, 1977), p. 20.
3. Economic Council of Canada, *Fifth Annual Review: The Challenge of Growth and Change* (Ottawa: Queen's Printer, 1968).
4. Ian Adams, *The Poverty Wall* (Toronto: McClelland and Stewart, 1970), p. 16.
5. *Money Income and Poverty Status*, p. 11.
6. Board of Governors of the Federal Reserve System, *Survey of Financial Characteristics of Consumers, 1962*, reported in U.S. Department of Commerce, *Social Indicators* (Washington, D.C.: GPO, 1973), p. 164.
7. Jonathan H. Turner and Charles E. Starnes, *Inequality: Privilege and Poverty in America* (Pacific Palisades, Calif.: Goodyear, 1976), p. 19.
8. Edwin Kuh, "The Robin Hood Syndrome," *New York Times*, March 5, 1973.
9. Joseph T. Howell, *Hard Living on Clay Street: Portraits of Blue Collar Families* (Garden City: Anchor, 1973), p. 8.
10. Ferdinand Lundberg, *The Rich and the Super Rich* (New York: Bantam Books, 1968), pp. 849–850.
11. John Kenneth Galbraith, *The Affluent Society* (Boston: Houghton Mifflin, 1958), p. 323.
12. Mollie Orshansky, "How Poverty Is Measured," *Monthly Labor Review* 92 (1969): 37.
13. Orshansky, "How Poverty Is Measured," p. 38.
14. Mollie Orshansky, "Counting the Poor: Another Look at the Poverty Profile," in L. Ferman, J. Kornbluh, and A. Haber, eds., *Poverty in America* (Ann Arbor: University of Michigan Press, 1965).
15. Robert J. Lampman, "Social Welfare and Poverty in America," *The Public Interest* 34 (1974): 66–82.
16. *Characteristics of the Population Below the Poverty Level: 1975*, p. 2; *Money Income and Poverty Status*, p. 20.
17. Lee Rainwater, "The Problem of Lower-Class Culture and Poverty-War Strategy," in Daniel Moynihan, ed., *On Understanding Poverty* (New York: Basic Books, 1969), p. 254.
18. Nancy Retine and Joan Huber, "The Demography of Poverty: Trends in the Sixties," in Joan Huber and Peter Chalfant, eds., *The Sociology of American Poverty* (Cambridge, Mass.: Schenkman, 1974), p. 102.
19. *Money Income and Poverty Status*, p. 25.
20. U.S. Bureau of the Census, *Characteristics of the Population Below the Poverty Level: 1974* (Washington, D.C.: GPO, 1976), p. 8.
21. *Ibid.*, p. 7.
22. *Ibid.*, p. 6.
23. *Money Income and Poverty Status*, p. 1.
24. Robert Burnett, *The Tortured Americans* (Englewood Cliffs, N.J.: Prentice-Hall, 1971).
25. *Characteristics of the Population Below the Poverty Level: 1975*, p. 23.
26. Joe R. Feagin, *Subordinating the Poor: Welfare and American Beliefs* (Englewood Cliffs, N.J.: Prentice-Hall, 1975), pp. 91–92.
27. *Ibid.*, p. 97.
28. Frances Fox Piven and Richard A. Cloward, *Regulating the Poor: The Functions of Public Welfare* (New York: Vintage Books, 1971).
29. Feagin, *Subordinating the Poor*, pp. 17–24.
30. *Ibid.*, pp. 24–28.
31. Piven and Cloward, *Regulating the Poor*, pp. 61–62.
32. *Ibid.*, pp. 184–185.
33. Daniel P. Moynihan, *The Politics of a Guaranteed Income: The Nixon Administration and the Family Assistance Plan* (New York: Random House, 1973).
34. Joan Huber, "The War on Poverty," in Huber and Chalfant, *The Sociology of American Poverty*, p. 322.
35. Lampman, "Social Welfare and Poverty in America."
36. David Matza and Henry Miller, "Poverty and Proletariat," in Robert K. Merton and Robert Nisbet, eds., *Contemporary Social Problems*, 4th ed. (New York: Harcourt Brace Jovanovich, 1976), pp. 655–656.
37. U.S. Department of Health, Education and Welfare, *Welfare Myths vs. Facts* (Washington, D.C.: GPO, 1972).
38. Matza and Miller, "Poverty and Proletariat," pp. 654–658.
39. Turner and Starnes, *Inequality*, pp. 61–64.
40. Feagin, *Subordinating the Poor*, p. 50.
41. *Los Angeles Times*, May 9, 1976.
42. Philip M. Stern, "Uncle Sam's Welfare Program for the Rich," *New York Times Magazine*, April 16, 1972.
43. *Characteristics of the Population Below the Poverty Level: 1974*, p. 4.
44. Robert L. Heilbroner, *The Economic Problem*, 3d ed. (Englewood Cliffs, N.J.: Prentice-Hall, 1972), pp. 406–407.
45. *Ibid.*, p. 9.
46. See Paul Jacobs, "Keeping the Poor Poor," in Jerome Skolnick and Elliott Currie, *Crisis in American Institutions*, 3d ed. (Boston: Little, Brown, 1976), pp. 129–139.
47. Oscar Lewis, *La Vida* (New York: Random House, 1965), pp. xlii–lii.
48. *Ibid.*
49. Charles A. Valentine, *Culture and Poverty: Critique and Counter-Proposals* (Chicago: University of Chicago Press, 1968).
50. Rainwater, "The Problem of Lower-Class Culture and Poverty-War Strategy."

51. Herbert J. Gans, "The Uses of Poverty: The Poor Pay All," *Social Policy* 2 (1971): 21–23.
52. Heilbroner, *The Economic Problem*, p. 727.
53. Richard C. Edwards, Michael Reich, and Thomas E. Weisskopf, *The Capitalist System* (Englewood Cliffs, N.J.: Prentice-Hall, 1972), p. 237.
54. Joan Huber, "Programs Against Poverty: Epilogue," in Huber and Chalfant, *The Sociology of American Poverty,* p. 336.
55. Moynihan, *The Politics of a Guaranteed Income*, p. 192.
56. Kingsley Davis and Wilbert E. Moore, "Some Principles of Stratification," *American Sociological Review* 10 (1945): 242–249.
57. See Richard A. Cloward and Lloyd E. Ohlin, *Delinquency and Opportunity: A Theory of Delinquent Gangs* (Glencoe: Free Press, 1960), pp. 19, 121, 148.

CHAPTER 7

1. Milton M, Gordon, *Assimilation in American Life: The Role of Race, Religion, and National Origins* (New York: Oxford University Press, 1964), pp. 27–28.
2. Pierre L. van den Berghe, *Race and Racism* (New York: Wiley, 1967), p. 71.
3. *Encyclopedia of Sociology* (Guilford, Conn.: Dushkin Publishing Group, 1974), p. 101.
4. *Ibid.,* p. 236.
5. Chester L. Hunt and Lewis Walker, *Ethnic Dynamics: Patterns of Intergroup Relations* (Homewood, Ill.: Dorsey Press, 1974). p. 7.
6. Milton M. Gordon, "Assimilation in America: Theory and Reality," *Daedalus* (Journal of the American Academy of Arts and Sciences) 90 (1961): 263–285.
7. Gordon W. Allport, *The Nature of Prejudice* (Garden City, N.Y.: Doubleday Anchor, 1956), p. 10.
8. Robert K. Merton, "Discrimination and the American Creed," in Robert M. MacIver, ed., *Discrimination and National Welfare* (New York: Harper & Row, 1949).
9. T. W. Adorno, E. Frenkel-Brunswik, D. J. Devinson, and R. N. Sanford, *The Authoritarian Personality* (New York: Harper & Row, 1950).
10. John Dollard, L. Doob, N. E. Miller, O. H. Mowrer, and R. R. Sears, *Frustration and Aggression* (New Haven, Conn.: Yale University Press, 1939).
11. Tamotsu Shibutani and Kian M. Kwan, *Ethnic Stratification: A Comparative Approach* (New York: Macmillan, 1965), pp. 383–391.
12. Gordon, "Assimilation in America."
13. Murray L. Wax, *Indian Americans: Unity and Diversity* (Englewood Cliffs, N.J.: Prentice-Hall, 1971), p. 3.
14. Nancy Oestreich Lurie, "The American Indian: Historical Background," in Norman Yetman and C. Hoy Steel, eds., *Minority and Majority: The Dynamics of Racial and Ethnic Relations*, 2d ed. (Boston: Allyn and Bacon, 1975), pp. 173–179.
15. S. J. Makeilski, *Beleaguered Minorities: Cultural Politics in America* (San Francisco: W. H. Freeman, 1973), p. 53.
16. Lurie, "The American Indian," p. 179.
17. U.S. Bureau of the Census, *Educational Attainment in the United States: March 1977 and 1976* (Washington, D.C.: GPO, 1977), pp. 7–9.
18. Joseph H. Cash, "Indian Education: A Bright Path or Another Dead End?" in Editors of the Winston Press, *Viewpoints: Red and Yellow, Black and Brown* (Groveland Terrace, Minn.: Winston Press, 1972), p. 14.
19. Audrey James Schwartz, "The Culturally Advantaged: A Study of the Japanese-American," *Sociology and Social Research* 55 (1971): 341–351.
20. Joan W. Moore, *Mexican Americans,* 2d ed. (Englewood Cliffs, N.J.: Prentice-Hall, 1976), p. 64.
21. J. S. Frieders, *Canada's Indians: Contemporary Conflicts* (Scarborough, Ont.: Prentice-Hall of Canada, 1974), p. 27.
22. U.S. Bureau of the Census, *The Social and Economic Status of the Black Population of the United States, 1974* (Washington, D.C.: GPO, 1975), p. 25.
23. Frieders, *Canada's Indians*, p. 24.
24. Quoted by Charles E. Reasons and Jack E. Kuykendall, eds., *Race, Crime and Justice* (Pacific Palisades, Calif.: Goodyear, 1972).
25. Many of these studies are discussed in *ibid.* and in Elton Long, James Long, Wilmer Leon, and Paul B. Weston, *American Minorities: The Justice Issue* (Englewood Cliffs, N.J.: Prentice-Hall, 1975).
26. See Edward Green, *Judicial Attitudes in Sentencing* (New York: St. Martin's, 1962), and Donald J. Black, "Production of Crime Rates," *American Sociological Review* 35 (1970): 733–748.
27. *The Social and Economic Status of the Black Population.*
28. Makielski, *Beleaguered Minorities,* p. 59.
29. Frieders, *Canada's Indians,* p. 50.
30. Moore, *Mexican Americans,* p. 75.
31. *The Social and Economic Status of the Black Population of the United States,* p. 123; Moore, *Mexican Americans,* pp. 75–76.
32. Frieders, *Canada's Indians,* p. 19; Makielski, *Beleaguered Minorities,* pp. 58–59.
33. Charles S. Bullock and Harrell R. Rodgers, *Racial Equality in America: In Search of an Unfulfilled Goal* (Pacific Palisades, Calif.: Goodyear, 1975), pp. 115–118.
34. *Ibid.,* pp. 83–93.
35. *Ibid.,* p. 155.
36. *Ibid.,* p. 152.
37. See Andrew M. Greeley, *Why Can't They Be Like Us?: America's White Ethnic Groups* (New York: E. P. Dutton, 1971).
38. See Robert Staples, *Introduction to Black Sociology* (New York: McGraw-Hill, 1976), pp. 78–84.

CHAPTER 8

1. Erdman Palmore and Clark Luikart, "Health and Social Factors Related to Life Satisfaction, *"Journal of Health and Social Behavior* 13 (1972): 68–80.

2. Quoted by John H. Dingle, "The Ills of Man," in *Life and Death and Medicine* (San Francisco: W. H. Freeman, 1973), p. 49.

3. *Ibid.,* p. 53.

4. Ansley J. Coale, "The History of the Human Population," *Scientific American* 231 (1974): 40–51.

5. Dingle, "Ills of Man," p. 54.

6. Both studies are reported in James F. Fixx, *The Complete Book of Running* (New York: Random House, 1977), p. 51; also see C. W. Frank *et al.,* "Myocardial Infarction in Men—Role of Physical Activity and Smoking in Incidence and Mortality," *Journal of American Medical Association* 198 (1966): 1241.

7. U.S. Department of Commerce, *Social Indicators 1976* (Washington, D.C.: GPO, 1977), p. 179.

8. Otto Schaefer, "Pre- and Post-Natal Growth Acceleration and Increase in Sugar Consumption in Canadian Eskimos," *Canadian Medical Association Journal* 103 (1970): 1059–1060.

9. A. Keys *et al.,* "Lessons from Serum Cholesterol Studies in Japan, Hawaii, and Los Angeles," *Annals of Internal Medicine* 48 (1958): 83.

10. *Newsweek,* January 22, 1979.

11. David L. Dodge and Walter Martin, *Social Stress and Chronic Illness: Mortality Patterns in Industrial Society* (South Bend, Ill.: University of Notre Dame Press, 1970).

12. Sidney Cobb and Robert M. Rose, "Hypertension, Peptic Ulcer, and Diabetes in Air Traffic Controllers," *Journal of American Medical Association* 224 (1973): 489–492.

13. Aubrey Kagan, "Epidemiology and Society, Stress, and Disease," in L. Levi, ed., *Society, Stress, and Disease* (London: Oxford University Press, 1971), 1:49–54.

14. C. M. Parkes, B. Benjamin, and R. G. Fitzgerald, "Broken Heart: A Statistical Study of Increased Mortality Among Widowers," *British Medical Journal* 1 (1969): 740–743.

15. Richard T. Cooper and Paul E. Steiger, "Occupational Health Hazards—A National Crisis," *Los Angeles Times,* June 17, 1976.

16. *Ibid.*

17. *Ibid.*

18. Elijah L. White, "A Graphic Presentation of Age and Income Differentials in Selected Aspects of Morbidity, Disability, and Utilization of Health Services," *Inquiry* 5 (1968): 25.

19. Daryl D. Enos, "Blacks, Chicanos, and the Health Care System," in Don H. Zimmerman, D. Lawrence Weider, and Siu Zimmerman, eds., *Understanding Social Problems* (New York: Holt, Rinehart & Winston, 1976), p. 242.

20. B. Goldblatt, Mary E. Moore, and Albert J. Stunkard, "Social Factors in Obesity," *Journal of American Medical Association* 192 (1965): 1039–1044.

21. U.S. Bureau of the Census, *Statistical Abstract of the United States: 1977* (Washington, D.C.: GPO, 1977).

22. Alan L. Sorkin, *Health Economics* (Lexington, Mass.: Heath, 1975), p. 3.

23. Nathan Glazer, "Paradoxes of Health Care," *The Public Interest* 22 (1971): 62–77.

24. National Opinion Research Center, "Jobs and Occupations: A Popular Evaluation," *Public Opinion News* 9 (1947): 3–13.

25. Robert W. Hodge, Paul M. Siegel, and Peter H. Rossi, "Occupational Prestige in the United States: 1925–1963," *American Journal of Sociology* 70 (1964): 286–302.

26. David Blumenthal and James Fallows, "Health: The Care We Want and Need," *The Washington Monthly* (October 1973). Reprinted in Duskin Publishing Co., *Group Readings in Sociology, 76/77* (Guilford, Conn.: Duskin, 1976), pp. 202–208.

27. Alex Gerber, *The Gerber Report: The Shocking State of American Medical Care and What Must Be Done About It* (New York: McKay, 1971), p. 66.

28. *Ibid.,* p. 67.

29. Odin W. Anderson, *Health Care: Can There Be Equity?* (New York: Wiley, 1972), 232.

30. See Sorkin, *Health Economics,* pp. 41–50.

31. Selig Greenberg, *The Quality of Mercy: A Report on the Critical Condition of Hospital and Medical Care in America* (New York: Atheneum, 1971), p. 126; Gerber, *The Gerber Report,* p. 121.

32. Victor R. Fuchs, *Who Shall Live?: Health, Economics, and Social Choice* (New York: Basic Books, 1974), p. 67.

33. Greenberg, *The Quality of Mercy,* p. 128.

34. Reported in Fuchs, *Who Shall Live?* p. 71.

35. *Ibid.*

36. *Los Angeles Times,* May 12, 1976.

37. *Los Angeles Times,* December 27, 1978.

38. Greenberg, *The Quality of Mercy,* p. 125.

39. Glazer, "Paradoxes of Health Care."

40. Fuchs, *Who Shall Live?,* p. 69.

41. Enos, "Blacks, Chicanos, and the Health Care System," p. 244.

42. Blumenthal and Fallows, "Health: The Care We Want and Need," p. 202.

43. *Ibid.*

44. Rich J. Carlson, "Health in America," *The Center Magazine* (November/December 1972). Reprinted in Alan Wells, ed., *American Society: Problems and Dilemmas* (Pacific Palisades, Calif.: Goodyear, 1976), p. 246.

45. See Paul B. Horton and Gerald R. Leslie, *The Sociology of Social Problems*, 5th ed. (Englewood Cliffs, N.J.: Prentice-Hall, 1974), pp. 603–605.

46. See Eliot Freidson, *Professional Dominance: The Social Structure of Medical Care* (New York: Atherton, 1970), pp. 222–225.

47. Fuchs, *Who Shall Live?*, p. 80.

48. Sorkin, *Health Economics*, p. 76.

49. *Ibid.*

50. Fuchs, *Who Shall Live?*, p. 84.

51. Blumenthal and Fallows, "Health: The Care We Want and Need."

52. Fuchs, *Who Shall Live?*, pp. 94–95.

53. *Ibid.*, p. 10.

54. Gerber, *The Gerber Report*, p. 164.

55. Fuchs, *Who Shall Live?*, p. 58.

56. Sorkin, *Health Economics*, p. 14.

57. *Social Security Bulletin* 35 (1972): 19.

58. *Los Angeles Times*, July 27, 1976, and August 30, 1976.

59. Alan Maynard, *Health Care in the European Community* (Pittsburgh: University of Pittsburgh Press, 1975), pp. 196–197.

60. Anderson, *Health Care*, p. 125.

61. Maynard, *Health Care in the European Community*, p. 203.

62. See Anderson, *Health Care*, pp. 141–160.

63. *Ibid.*, p. 217.

64. Sorkin, *Health Economics*, p. 3.

65. Freidson, *Professional Dominance*, p. 84.

66. Blumenthal and Fallows, "Health: The Care We Want and Need," p. 206.

67. Sorkin, *Health Economics*, p. 65.

68. *Ibid.*, pp. 174, 176.

69. Robert L. Robertson, "Economic Effect of Personal Health Services: Work Loss in a Public School Teacher Population," *American Journal of Public Health* 61 (1971): 35.

70. Roul Tunley, *The American Health Scandal* (New York: Harper & Row, 1966), p. 61.

71. R. H. Rosenman *et al.*, "Coronary Heart Disease in Western Collaborative Group Study—A Follow Up Experience of 4½ Years," *Journal of Chronic Disease* 23 (1970): 173.

CHAPTER 9

1. Kurt Wolff, *The Biological, Sociological, and Psychological Aspects of Aging* (Springfield, Ill.: Charles C Thomas, 1959).

2. Herman J. Loether, *Problems of Aging: Sociological and Social Psychological Perspectives*, 2d ed. (Encino, Calif.: Dickenson, 1975), p. 8.

3. U.S. Public Health Service, *Working with Older People: A Guide to Practice*, vol. 11, pub. no. 1459 (Washington, D.C.: GPO, April 1970), p. i.

4. Robert C. Atchley, *The Social Forces in Later Life: An Introduction to Social Gerontology* (Belmont, Calif.: Wadsworth, 1972), pp. 112–123.

5. Fred Cottrell, *Aging and the Aged* (Dubuque, Iowa: Wm. C. Brown, 1974), p. 19.

6. Loether, *Problems of Aging*, p. 38.

7. U.S. Bureau of the Census, *Money Income and Poverty Status of Families and Persons in the United States: 1976* (Advance Report) (Washington D.C.: GPO, 1977), p. 25.

8. See James H. Schulz, *The Economics of Aging* (Belmont, Calif.: Wadsworth, 1976), pp. 30–33.

9. U.S. Bureau of the Census, *Statistical Abstract of the United States, 1975*, 96th ed. (Washington, D.C.: GPO, 1975), p. 344.

10. U.S. Department of Labor, Bureau of Labor Statistics, *The Employment Problems of Older Workers* (Washington, D.C.: GPO, 1971), p. 3.

11. Robert C. Atchley, *The Sociology of Retirement* (New York: Schenkman, 1976), p. 79.

12. Schulz, *The Economics of Aging*, p. 114.

13. *Ibid.*, pp. 121–122.

14. Atchley, *Social Forces in Later Life*, pp. 141–142.

15. Schulz, *Economics of Aging*, p. 94.

16. Atchley, *Sociology of Retirement*, p. 78.

17. *Senate Report on Aging*, 1966 (Ottawa: Queen's Printer, 1966); excerpts reprinted in W. E. Mann, ed., *Poverty and Social Policy in Canada* (Toronto: Copp Clark, 1970), p. 292.

18. Atchley, *Social Forces in Later Life*, pp. 144–145.

19. Loether, *Problems of Aging*, pp. 46–51.

20. U.S. Public Health Service, *Services and Activities Offered to Nursing Home Residents: United States—1968* (Washington, D.C.: GPO, 1972).

21. See Gordon Moss and Walter Moss, *Growing Old* (New York: Pocket Books, 1975), pp. 61–67.

22. Atchley, *Social Forces in Later Life*, p. 156.

23. Atchley, *Sociology of Retirement*, p. 17.

24. Loether, *Problems of Aging*, p. 83.

25. *Ibid.*, p. 86.

26. See Atchley, *Sociology of Retirement*, pp. 87–108.

27. Vern L. Bengtson, *The Social Psychology of Aging* (Indianapolis, Ind.: Bobbs-Merrill, 1973), p. 25.

28. *Ibid.*, pp. 22–29.

29. See Atchley, *Social Forces in Later Life*, pp. 291–326.

30. Helena Z. Lopata, *Widowhood in an American City* (Cambridge, Mass.: Schenkman, 1973), p. 17.

31. Loether, *Problems of Aging*, pp. 105–107.

32. Robert S. Morrison, "Dying," in *Life and Death and Medicine: A Scientific American Book* (San Francisco: W. H. Freeman, 1973), p. 41.

33. Herman Feifel, "Attitudes Toward Death in Some Normal and Mentally Ill Populations," in Herman Feifel, ed., *The Meaning of Death* (New York: McGraw-Hill, 1959), p. 118.
34. See Loether, *Problems of Aging*, p. 72.
35. Schulz, *The Economics of Aging*, pp. 59–61.
36. Loether, *Problems of Aging*, p. 52.
37. *Ibid.*, pp. 50–53.
38. *Ibid.*, p. 37.
39. See Matilda White Riley and Joan Waring, "Age and Aging," in Robert K. Merton and Robert Nisbet, eds., *Contemporary Social Problems* (New York: Harcourt Brace Jovanovich, 1976), pp. 397–399.

CHAPTER 10

1. Alice S. Rossi,"The Roots of Ambivalence in American Women," in Judith M. Bardwick, ed., *Readings on the Psychology of Women* (New York: Harper & Row, 1972), pp. 125–127.
2. Robert May, "Sex Differences in Fantasy Patterns," *Journal of Projective Techniques* 20 (1966): 252–259.
3. See Jane E. Prather, "Sexism: Everyone's Social Problem," in Don H. Zimmerman, ed., *Understanding Social Problems* (New York: Holt, Rinehart & Winston, 1976), p. 189.
4. Judith E. Singer *et al.*, "Sex Difference in the Incidence of Neonatal Abnormalities and Abnormal Performance in Early Childhood," *Child Development* 39 (1968): 103–122.
5. Susan Goldberg and Michael Lewis, "Play Behavior in the Year Old Infant: Early Sex Differences," in Bardwick, *Psychology of Women*, p. 33.
6. Eleanor E. Maccoby, "Sex Differences in Intellectual Functioning," in Eleanor E. Maccoby, ed., *The Development of Sex Differences* (Stanford, Calif.: Stanford University Press, 1966).
7. Margaret Mead, *Sex and Temperament in Three Primitive Societies* (New York: Mentor Books, 1935), p. 206.
8. George P. Murdock, "Comparative Data on the Division of Labor by Sex," *Social Forces* 15 (1935): 551–553.
9. George P. Murdock, "Worth Ethnographic Sample," *American Anthropologist* 59 (1957): 664–687.
10. Roy G. D'Andrade, "Sex Differences and Cultural Institutions," in Maccoby, *Sex Differences*, p. 201.
11. John Money *et al.*, "Imprinting and the Establishment of Gender Role," *Archives of Neurology and Psychiatry* 77 (1967): 333–336.
12. See Richard Green, *Sexual Identity Conflicts in Children and Adults* (New York: Basic Books, 1974).
13. H. Barry, Margaret Bacon, and I. I. Child, "A Cross-Cultural Survey of Some Sex Differences in Socialization," *Journal of Abnormal Psychology* 55 (1957): 327–332.

14. Ernestine Friedl, *Women and Men: An Anthropologist's View* (New York: Holt, Rinehart and Winston, 1975), p. 31.
15. Betty Yorburg, *Sexual Identity: Sex Roles and Social Change* (New York: Wiley, 1974), pp. 58–61.
16. Friedl, *Women and Men*, pp. 61–64.
17. Yorburg, *Sexual Identity*, pp. 62–64.
18. Ruby R. Leavitt, "Women in Other Cultures," in Vivian Gornick and Barbara K. Moran, eds., *Woman in Sexist Society* (New York: Basic Books, 1971), pp. 276–303; D'Andrade, "Sex Differences and Cultural Institutions," pp. 182–184, 189–190.
19. Yorburg, *Sexual Identity*, p. 71.
20. See Simone de Beauvoir, *The Second Sex* (New York: Knopf, 1957).
21. Ruth E. Hartley, "Sex-Role Pressures and the Socialization of the Male Child," in Deborah S. David and Robert Brannon, eds., *The Forty-nine Percent Majority: The Male Sex Role* (Reading, Mass.: Addison-Wesley, 1976), p. 236.
22. Judith M. Bardwick and Elizabeth Douvan, "Ambivalence: The Socialization of Women," in Gornick and Moran, *Woman in Sexist Society*, p. 148.
23. *Ibid.*, p. 152.
24. Robert Rosenthal and Lenore Jacobson, *Pygmalion in the Classroom* (New York: Harper & Row, 1969).
25. Janet Saltzman Chafetz, *Masculine/Feminine or Human?* (Tasca, Ill.: F. E. Peacock, 1974), p. 89.
26. Marjorie B. U'Ren, "The Image of Woman in Textbooks," in Gornick and Moran, *Woman in Sexist Society*, p. 223.
27. *Ibid.*, p. 218.
28. Deborah J. Reid, "Sexism in Elementary School Textbooks," senior project report, Department of Social Science, California Polytechnic State University, San Luis Obispo, Calif., 1974.
29. Chafetz, *Masculine/Feminine or Human?*, pp. 82–83.
30. Lucy Komisar, "The Image of Woman in Advertising," in Gornick and Moran, *Woman in Sexist Society*, pp. 211–212.
31. Chafetz, *Masculine/Feminine or Human?*, pp. 82–83.
32. Cynthia Fuchs Epstein, "Sex Roles," in Robert Merton and Robert Nisbet, eds., *Contemporary Social Problems*, 4th ed. (New York: Harcourt Brace Jovanovich, 1976), pp. 437, 431.
33. See Chafetz, *Masculine/Feminine or Human?*, pp. 134–135.
34. *Los Angeles Times*, April 27, 1976.
35. Louise Kapp Howe, "Women in the Workplace," in *Readings in Social Problems 75/76* (Guilford, Conn.: Duskin, 1975), pp. 141–144.
36. Epstein, "Sex Roles," pp. 430–431.
37. Matina Horner, "The Motive to Avoid Success and

Changing Aspirations of College Women," in Bardwick, *Psychology of Women,* pp. 62–67.

38. Marijean Suelzle, "Women in Labor," in Jon Shepard and Cyrus Stewart, eds., *Sociology and Social Problems* (Englewood Cliffs, N.J.: Prentice-Hall, 1976), pp. 183–195.
39. Epstein, "Sex Roles," p. 442.
40. Terence H. White, "Autonomy in Work: Are Women Any Different? in Marylee Stephenson, ed., *Women in Canada* (Toronto: New Press, 1973), p. 216.
41. Judith Blake, "The Changing Status of Women in Developed Countries," *Scientific American* 231 (1974): 138–139.
42. Suelzle, "Women in Labor."
43. *Los Angeles Times,* April 27, 1976.
44. Roslyn S. Willett, "Working in 'A Man's World': The Woman Executive," in Gornick and Moran, *Woman in Sexist Society,* p. 368.
45. "The Drive to Open Up More Careers for Women," *U.S. News & World Report,* January 14, 1974.
46. *Los Angeles Times,* May 31, 1976.
47. Edward Gross, "Plus ça Change? The Sexual Structure of Occupations Over Time," *Social Problems* (1968): 198–208.
48. Epstein, "Sex Roles," p. 430.
49. *Ibid.,* p. 427.
50. *Ibid.,* p. 436.
51. See C. Safilios-Rothschild, *Women and Social Policy* (Englewood Cliffs, N.J.: Prentice-Hall, 1974).
52. See L. L. Holmstrom, *The Two-Career Family* (Cambridge, Mass.: Schenkman, 1972).
53. Morton Hunt, *Sexual Behavior in the 1970s* (New York: Dell, 1974), pp. 19–38.
54. Chafetz, *Masculine/Feminine or Human?,* p. 59.

CHAPTER 11

1. Clellan S. Ford and Frank A. Beach, *Patterns of Sexual Behavior* (New York: Ace Books, 1951), p. 14.
2. William H. Davenport, "Sex in Cross-Cultural Perspective," in Frank A. Beach, ed., *Human Sexuality in Four Perspectives* (Baltimore: Johns Hopkins, 1977), p. 124.
3. Ian Robertson, *Sociology* (New York: Worth, 1977), pp. 189–192.
4. Davenport, "Sex in Cross-Cultural Perspective," pp. 122–124.
5. *Ibid.,* p. 125.
6. Conrad Phillip Kottak, *Cultural Anthropology* (New York: Random House, 1974), pp. 83–84. For a more detailed description of the homosexual tribes of New Guinea, see V. vanBaal, *Dema: Description and Analysis of Marindamin Culture* (The Hague: M. Nivhoff, 1966).
7. Quoted in Robertson, *Sociology,* p. 196.
8. Alfred C. Kinsey, Wardell B. Pomeroy, and Clyde E. Martin, *Sexual Behavior in the Human Male* (Philadel-

phia: Saunders, 1948); Alfred C. Kinsey, Wardell B. Pomeroy, Clyde E. Martin, and Paul H. Gebhard, *Sexual Behavior in the Human Female* (Philadelphia: Saunders, 1953).

9. Morton Hunt, *Sexual Behavior in the 1970s* (New York: Dell, 1974), pp. 16–17.
10. *Ibid.,* pp. 147–149.
11. Kinsey *et al., Human Female,* p. 333; Hunt, *Sexual Behavior,* p. 150.
12. Hunt, *Sexual Behavior,* p. 261.
13. *Ibid.,* p. 34; Kinsey *et al., Human Male,* p. 386.
14. Harold T. Christensen and Christina F. Gregg, "Changing Sex Norms in America and Scandinavia," *Journal of Marriage and the Family* 32 (1970): 616–627; Winston Ehrmann, "Some Knowns and Unknowns in Research into Human Sex Behavior," *Journal of Marriage and the Family* 19 (1957): 16–22; Ira L. Reiss, "How and Why America's Sex Standards are Changing," *Trans-Action* 5 (1968): 26–32.
15. Evelyn Hooker, "The Adjustment of the Male Overt Homosexual," *Journal of Projective Techniques* 21 (1957): 18–31, and "Male Homosexuality and the Rorschach," *Journal of Projective Techniques* 22 (1958): 33–54.
16. F. J. Kallmann, "Twin and Sibling Study of Overt Male Homosexuality," *American Journal of Human Genetics* 4 (1952): 341–346.
17. Irving Beiber *et al., Homosexuality: A Psychoanalytic Study* (New York: Basic Books, 1962).
18. See Edward Sagarin, "The Good Guys, the Bad Guys, and the Gay Guys," *Contemporary Sociology* 2 (1973): 3–13.
19. Hunt, *Sexual Behavior,* p. 310.
20. Barry M. Dank, "Coming Out in the Gay World," *Psychiatry* 34 (1971): 180–197.
21. William Simon and John A. Gagnon, "Homosexuality: The Formulation of a Sociological Perspective," *Journal of Health and Social Behavior* 8 (1967): 345.
22. John H. Gagnon and William Simon, *Sexual Conduct: The Social Sources of Human Sexuality* (Chicago: Aldine-Atherton, 1973), pp. 176–216.
23. See Marshall B. Clinard, *Sociology of Deviant Behavior,* 4th ed. (New York: Holt, Rinehart & Winston, 1974), pp. 545–546.
24. Marion Foster and Kent Murry, *A Not So Gay World: Homosexuality in Canada* (Toronto: McClelland and Stewart, 1972), pp. 27–34.
25. Colin J. Williams and Martin S. Weinberg, *Homosexuals and the Military: A Study of Less Than Honorable Discharge* (New York: Harper & Row, 1971).
26. Hunt, *Sexual Behavior,* p. 145.
27. Gail Sheehy, *Hustling: Prostitution in Our Wide-Open Society* (New York: Delacorte Press, 1973), p. 104.
28. See Christina Milner and Richard Milner, *Black Players:*

The Secret World of Black Pimps (New York: Bantam Books, 1972). A detailed description of occupational status among prostitutes is presented by Donal E. J. MacNamara and Edward Sagarin, *Sex, Crime and the Law* (New York: Basic Books, 1977), pp. 101–104.

29. Norman R. Jackman, Richard O'Toole, and Gilbert Geis, "The Self-Image of the Prostitute," *The Sociological Quarterly* 4 (1963): 150–161; Nanette J. Davis, "The Prostitute: Developing a Deviant Identity," in James M. Henslin, *Studies in the Sociology of Sex* (Englewood Cliffs, N.J.: Prentice-Hall, 1971), pp. 297–322.

30. Davis, "Developing a Deviant Identity."

31. Milner and Milner, *Black Players*, pp. 211–240.

32. See Jackman *et al.*, "Self-Image of the Prostitute."

33. *Report of the President's Commission on Obscenity and Pornography* (New York: Bantam Books, 1970), p. 49.

34. W. Cody Wilson, "Facts Versus Fears: Why Should We Worry About Pornography?," *Annals of the American Academy of Political Science* 397 (1971): 105–117.

35. *Ibid.*, p. 113; Clinard, *Deviant Behavior*, p. 534.

36. Herbert L. Packer, *The Limits of Criminal Sanction* (Stanford, Calif.: Stanford University Press, 1968), p. 304.

37. Kingsley Davis, "The Sociology of Prostitution," *American Sociological Review* 2 (1937): 744–755.

38. Frank A. Beach, "Cross-Species Comparisons and the Human Heritage," in Beach, *Human Sexuality*, pp. 296–316.

CHAPTER 12

1. Theodore Millen and Renee Millen, *Abnormal Behavior and Psychology* (Philadelphia: Saunders, 1974), p. 7.

2. Benjamin Kleinmuntz, *Essentials of Abnormal Psychology* (New York: Harper & Row, 1974), p. 22.

3. James C. Coleman, *Abnormal Psychology and Modern Life*, 4th ed. (Chicago: Scott, Foresman, 1972), p. 32.

4. Thomas Szasz, "The Myth of Mental Illness," *American Psychologist* 15 (1960): 113–118.

5. David Mechanic, *Mental Health and Social Policy* (Englewood Cliffs, N.J.: Prentice-Hall, 1969), pp. 20–21.

6. James C. Coleman, *Abnormal Psychology and Modern Life*, 3d ed. (Chicago: Scott, Foresman, 1964), p. 14.

7. Szasz, "The Myth of Mental Illness."

8. See Thomas J. Scheff, *Being Mentally Ill: A Sociological Theory* (Chicago: Aldine-Atherton, 1966).

9. Coleman, *Abnormal Psychology and Modern Life*, 4th ed., p. 343.

10. Peter Townsend, "Isolation, Loneliness and the Hold on Life," in Eric and Mary Josephson, eds., *Man Alone: Alienation in Modern Society* (New York: Dell, 1962), pp. 326–339.

11. Myron Sandifer, Charles Pettus, and Dana Quade, "A Study of Psychiatric Diagnosis," *Journal of Nervous and Mental Disease* 139 (1964): 350–356.

12. Robert E. L. Faris and H. Warren Dunham, *Mental Disorders in Urban Areas* (Chicago: University of Chicago Press, 1939).

13. August B. Hollingshead and Frederick C. Redlich, *Social Class and Mental Illness: A Community Study* (New York: Wiley, 1958).

14. Leo Srole, T. S. Langner, S. T. Michael, M. K. Opler, and T. A. L. Rennie, *Mental Health in the Metropolis: The Midtown Manhattan Study* (New York: McGraw-Hill, 1962).

15. Bruce P. Dohrenwend and Barbara Snell Dohrenwend, *Social Status and Psychological Disorder: A Causal Inquiry* (New York: Wiley, 1969), p. 165.

16. Leo Srole, "Urbanization and Mental Health: Some Reformulations," *American Scientist* 60 (1972): 576–583.

17. Joseph W. Eaton and Robert J. Weil, *Culture and Mental Disorder* (Glencoe: Free Press, 1955).

18. Eleanor Leacock, "Three Variables in the Occurrence of Mental Illness," in Alexander Leighton, John Clausen, and Robert Wilson, eds., *Explorations in Social Psychiatry* (New York: Basic Books, 1957), pp. 308–340.

19. John A. Clausen, "Mental Disorders," in Robert Merton and Robert Nisbet, eds., *Contemporary Social Problems*, 4th ed. (New York: Harcourt Brace Jovanovich, 1976), pp. 113–117.

20. Franz Kallman and B. Roth, "Genetic Aspects of Pre-adolescent Schizophrenia," *American Journal of Psychiatry* 112 (1956): 599–606.

21. A. Hoffer and W. Polin, "Schizophrenia in the NAS–NRC Panel of 15,909 Twin Pairs," *Archives of General Psychiatry* 23 (1970): 469–477; see also E. Kringlen, "Hereditary and Social Factors in Schizophrenic Twins: An Epidemiological Clinical Study," in J. Romano, ed., *The Origins of Schizophrenia* (Amsterdam: Excerpta Medica, 1968), pp. 2–14.

22. Coleman, *Abnormal Psychology and Modern Life*, p. 283.

23. Gregory Bateson, Don D. Jackson, Jay Haley, and John Weakland, "Toward a Theory of Schizophrenia," *Behavioral Science* 1 (1956): 251–264.

24. Mechanic, *Mental Health and Social Policy*, p. 39.

25. See, *e.g.*, Srole, *Mental Health in the Metropolis*.

26. See, *e.g.*, H. Warren Dunham, "Social Class and Schizophrenia," *American Journal of Orthopsychiatry* 34 (1964): 634–642.

27. Scheff, *Being Mentally Ill*, p. 55–101.

28. Edwin M. Lemert, "Paranoia and the Dynamics of Exclusion," *Sociometry* 25 (1962): 162–174.

29. See R. D. Laing and A. Esterson, *Sanity, Madness, and the Family* (Middlesex: Pelican Books, 1964); R. D. Laing, *The Politics of Experience* (New York: Ballantine Books, 1967).

30. Laing, *The Politics of Experience*, p. 27.
31. *Ibid.*, p. 167 (italics in original).
32. See Coleman, *Abnormal Psychology and Modern Life*, pp. 25–39.
33. *Ibid.*, pp. 39–47.
34. *Los Angeles Times*, April 16, 1976.
35. *Los Angeles Times*, May 17, 1976.
36. Carl Rogers, *Client-Centered Therapy* (Boston: Houghton Mifflin, 1951).
37. Erving Goffman, *Asylums: Essays on the Social Situation of Mental Patients and Other Inmates* (Garden City, N.Y.: Anchor, 1961), p. xii.
38. *Ibid.*, pp. 126–169.
39. D. L. Rosenhan, "On Being Sane in Insane Places," *Science* 179 (1973): 250–258.
40. *Ibid.*, p. 257.
41. Kleinmuntz, *Abnormal Psychology*, p. 22.
42. Luis Kutner, "The Illusion of Due Process in Commitment Proceedings," *Northwestern University Law Review* 57 (1962): 383–399.
43. Thomas J. Scheff, "Social Conditions for Rationality: How Urban and Rural Courts Deal with the Mentally Ill," *American Behavioral Scientist* 7 (1964): 21–27.
44. Daniel Oran, "Judges and Psychiatrists Lock Up Too Many People," *Psychology Today* 7 (1973): 20–22, 27, 28, 93.

CHAPTER 13

1. Joel Fort and Christopher T. Cory, *American Drugstore* (Boston: Educational Associates, 1975), p. 8.
2. *Ibid.*, p. 6.
3. See Craig MacAndrew and Robert B. Edgerton, *Drunken Comportment: A Social Explanation* (Chicago: Aldine-Atherton, 1969), and Sherri Cavan, *Liquor License: An Ethnography of Bar Behavior* (Chicago: Aldine-Atherton, 1966).
4. National Commission of Marijuana and Drug Abuse, *Drug Use in America: Problem in Perspective* (Washington, D.C.: GPO, 1973), p. 143.
5. Robert Straus, "Alcoholism and Problem Drinking," in Robert K. Merton and Robert Nisbet, eds., *Contemporary Social Problems*, 4th ed. (New York: Harcourt Brace Jovanovich, 1976), pp. 189–192.
6. Richard H. Blum, "Mind-Altering Drugs and Dangerous Behavior: Alcohol," Appendix B in President's Commission on Law Enforcement and Administration of Justice, *Task Force Report: Drunkenness* (Washington, D.C.: GPO, 1967), pp. 29–49.
7. *Drug Use in America*, p. 44.
8. Fort and Cory, *American Drugstore*, p. 41.
9. *Ibid.*, p. 41.
10. Fred Leavitt, *Drugs and Behavior* (Philadelphia: Saunders, 1974), p. 74.

11. Erich Goode, *Drugs in American Society* (New York: Knopf, 1972), p. 55.
12. John O'Donnell, Harwin L. Voss, Richard R. Clayton, Gerald T. Slatin, and Robin G. W. Room, *Young Men and Drugs: A Nationwide Survey* (Rockville, Md.: National Institute on Drug Abuse, 1976), p. 24.
13. Howard S. Becker, *Outsiders* (New York: Free Press, 1963), pp. 41–58.
14. James D. Orcutt, "Normative Definitions of Intoxicated States: A Test of Several Sociological Theories," *Social Problems* 25 (1978): 385–396.
15. Louis Goodman and Alfred Gillman, *The Pharmacological Basis of Therapeutics*, quoted in Thomas Szasz, *Ceremonial Chemistry* (Garden City, N.Y.: Anchor Books, 1974), p. 121.
16. Frederick Glaser and John Ball, "Death Due to Withdrawal from Narcotics," in John Ball and Carl Chambers, eds., *The Epidemiology of Opiate Addiction in the United States* (Springfield, Ill.: Charles C Thomas, 1970).
17. Edward M. Brecher, *Licit and Illicit Drugs* (Boston: Little, Brown, 1972), pp. 21–32.
18. John Ball and John Urbaitis, "Absence of Major Complications Among Chronic Opiate Users," in John Ball and Carl Chambers, eds., *The Epidemiology of Opiate Addiction in the United States* (Springfield, Ill.: Charles C Thomas, 1970), p. 306.
19. Brecher, *Licit and Illicit Drugs*, pp. 101–114.
20. O'Donnell *et al.*, *Young Men and Drugs*, pp. 24, 39.
21. Gerald Le Dain, Chairman, *Interim Report of the Commission of Inquiry into the Non-medical Use of Drugs* (Ottawa: Information Canada, 1970), p. 148.
22. See Garrett O'Conner, Leon Wurmser, Torrey Brown, and Judith Smith, "The Economics of Heroin Addiction," in David Smith and George Gay, eds., *It's So Good Don't Even Try It Once* (Englewood Cliffs, N.J.: Prentice-Hall, 1972; Dan Waldorf, *Careers in Dope* (Englewood Cliffs, N.J.: Prentice-Hall, 1973).
23. James William Coleman, "The Myth of Addiction," *Journal of Drug Issues* 6 (1976): 135–141.
24. See Timothy Leary, Ralph Metzner, and Richard Alpert, *The Psychedelic Experience* (New York: Holt, Rinehart & Winston, 1966).
25. Robert M. Julien, *A Primer of Drug Action* (San Francisco: W. H. Freeman, 1975), pp. 147–148.
26. Quoted by Le Dain, *Interim Report*, p. 58.
27. See Julien, *Drug Action*, p. 159.
28. O'Donnell *et al.*, *Young Men and Drugs*, p. viii.
29. Brecher, *Licit and Illicit Drugs*, p. 241–253.
30. *Ibid.*, pp. 249–253.
31. Julien, *Drug Action*, pp. 54–55.
32. Arthur Moffett and Carl Chambers, "The Hidden Addiction," *Social Work* 15 (1970): 54–59.
33. Julien, *Drug Action*, p. 55.

34. *Ibid.*, pp. 60–61.

35. *Ibid.*, p. 98.

36. Brecher, *Licit and Illicit Drugs*, pp. 99–106.

37. Goode, *Drugs in American Society*, p. 134.

38. Vincent Dole and Marie Nyswander, "Heroin Addiction — A Metabolic Disease," *Archives of Internal Medicine* 120 (1967): pp. 19–24.

39. Alfred Lindesmith, *Opiate Addiction* (Bloomington, Ind.: Principia Press, 1947), pp. 67–89.

40. See Abraham Wikler, "Conditioning Factors in Opiate Addiction and Relapse," in Daniel Wilner and Gene Kassenbaum, eds., *Narcotics* (New York: McGraw-Hill, 1965); Travis Thomas and Roy Pickens, "Drug Self Administration and Conditioning," in Hannah Steinberg, ed., *The Scientific Basis of Drug Dependence* (New York: Grune & Stratton, 1969).

41. Alfred R. Lindesmith, *Addiction and Opiates* (Chicago: Aldine-Atherton, 1968), pp. 64–67.

42. David P. Ausubel, *Drug Addiction: Physiological, Psychological and Sociological Aspects* (New York: Random House, 1958), p. 42.

43. Isador Chein, Donald Gerard, Robert Lee, and Eva Rosenfeld, *The Road to H* (New York: Basic Books, 1964).

44. Edward Preble and John Casey, "Taking Care of Business: The Heroin User's Life on the Streets," *International Journal of the Addictions* 4 (1969): 1–24.

45. James William Coleman, "The Dynamics of Narcotic Abstinence: An Interactionist Theory," *Sociological Quarterly* 19 (1978): 555–564; Coleman, "The Myth of Addiction."

46. Richard H. Blum *et al.*, *Society and Drugs* (San Francisco: Jossey-Bass, 1969), pp. 24–42.

47. See Charles Terry and Mildred Pellens, *The Opium Problem* (New York: Bureau of Social Hygiene, 1928).

48. Troy Duster, *The Legislation of Morality* (New York: Free Press, 1970), pp. 3–23.

49. Coleman, "The Myth of Addiction."

50. Becker, *Outsiders*, pp. 135–146.

51. Reprinted in *ibid.*, p. 142.

52. Donald R. Cressey, *Theft of the Nation: The Structure and Operations of Organized Crime in America* (New York: Harper & Row, 1969), pp. 92–95.

53. See Edwin Schur, *Narcotic Addiction in Britain and America* (Bloomington: Indiana University Press, 1962).

54. Fort and Cory, *American Drugstore*, p. 47.

55. Roger Meyer, *Guide to Drug Rehabilitation* (Boston: Beacon Press, 1972), pp. 61–63.

56. See Rita Volkman and Donald R. Cressey, "Differential Association and the Rehabilitation of Drug Addicts," *American Journal of Sociology* 69 (1963): 129–142.

57. Meyer, *Drug Rehabilitation*, p. 72.

58. See Szasz, *Ceremonial Chemistry*.

59. Fort and Cory, *American Drugstore*, p. 49.

60. Alfred Lindesmith, *The Addict and the Law* (Bloomington: Indiana University Press, 1965), pp. 300–302.

CHAPTER 14

1. Louis Harris, *The Anguish of Change* (New York: W. W. Norton, 1973), p. 169.

2. F. K. Heuseenstamm, "Bumper Stickers and the Cops," *Transaction* 8 (1971): 23–33.

3. Federal Bureau of Investigation, *Uniform Crime Reports for the United States, 1974* (Washington, D.C.: GPO, 1975), p. 55.

4. *Criminal Justice Newsletter* 9 (March 27, 1978): 6–7.

5. Ronald J. Ostrow, "Ending FBI's Control Over Crime Statistics Proposed," *Los Angeles Times*, April 19, 1976.

6. *Criminal Victimization in the United States: A Comparison of 1973–1974 Findings*, reported in *Criminal Justice Newsletter* 7 (June 7, 1976): 1–3.

7. Gwynn Nettler, *Explaining Crime* (New York: McGraw-Hill, 1974), p. 11.

8. Federal Bureau of Investigation, *Uniform Crime Reports: 1974*, p. 55.

9. Edwin H. Sutherland and Donald R. Cressey, *Criminology*, 10th ed. (New York: Harper & Row, 1978), p. 130.

10. Rita James Simon, *The Contemporary Woman and Crime* (Washington, D.C.: GPO, 1975), p. 37.

11. See Freda Adler, *Sisters in Crime: The Rise of the New Female Criminal* (New York: McGraw-Hill, 1975).

12. Sutherland and Cressey, *Criminology*, p. 125.

13. Federal Bureau of Investigation, *Uniform Crime Reports for the United States, 1975* (Washington D.C.: GPO, 1976), p. 13.

14. Marvin E. Wolfgang, *Patterns in Criminal Homicide* (Philadelphia: University of Pennsylvania Press, 1958). p. 37.

15. For a survey of the self-report studies on this issue, see Charles R. Tittle, Wayne J. Villemez, and Douglas A. Smith, "The Myth of Social Class and Criminality," *American Sociological Review* 43 (1978): 643–656.

16. John P. Clark and Eugene P. Wenninger, "Socioeconomic Class and Area as Correlates of Illegal Behavior Among Juveniles," *American Sociological Review* 27 (1962): 826–834.

17. Walter C. Reckless, *The Crime Problem*, 4th ed. (Englewood Cliffs, N.J.: Prentice-Hall, 1967), pp. 110–112.

18. Marvin E. Wolfgang, Robert Figlio, and Thorsten Sellin, *Delinquency in a Birth Cohort* (Chicago: University of Chicago Press, 1972).

19. See Charles E. Reasons and Jack E. Kuykendall, eds., *Race, Crime, and Justice* (Pacific Palisades, Calif.: Goodyear, 1972).

20. Harwin L. Voss and John R. Hepburn, "Patterns in Criminal Homicide in Chicago," *Journal of Criminal*

Law, Criminology and Police Science 59 (1968): 499–508.

21. Richard S. Fox, "The XYY Offender: A Modern Myth," *Journal of Criminal Law, Criminology and Police Science* 62 (1971): 59–73.

22. See Sutherland and Cressey, *Criminology*, pp. 158–161.

23. Robert K. Merton, "Social Structure and Anomie," *American Sociological Review* 3 (1938): 672–682.

24. Walter B. Miller, "Lower Class Culture as a Generating Milieu of Gang Delinquency," *Journal of Social Issues* 14 (1958): 5–19.

25. Sutherland and Cressey, *Criminology*, pp. 77–98.

26. Travis Hirschi, *Causes of Delinquency* (Berkeley: University of California Press, 1969).

27. See, *e.g.*, James Q. Wilson, *Thinking About Crime* (New York: Random House, 1975).

28. Peter H. Rossi, Emily Waite, Christine E. Bose, and Richard A. Berk, "The Seriousness of Crimes: Normative Structure and Individual Differences," *American Sociological Review* 39 (1974): 224–237.

29. Wilhelm A. Bonger, *Criminality and Economic Conditions* (Boston: Little, Brown, 1916), pp. 536–537. This book was first published in French in 1905.

30. *Uniform Crime Reports, 1975*, p. 191.

31. Anthony M. Platt, *The Child Savers: The Invention of Delinquency* (Chicago: University of Chicago Press, 1969).

32. *Kent* v. *United States*, 401 F. 2d 408 (1968).

33. Roland J. Chilton and General E. Markel, "Family Disruption, Delinquent Conduct, and the Effect of Subclassification," *American Sociological Review* 37 (1972): 93–99.

34. Edwin H. Sutherland, *White Collar Crime* (New York: Dryden, 1949), p. 9.

35. Herbert L. Packer, *The Limits of Criminal Sanction* (Stanford: Stanford University Press, 1968).

36. David M. Petersen, "The Police Officer's Conception of Proper Police Work," *The Police Journal* (England) 47 (1974): 102–108.

37. *Federal Offenders in the United States District Courts, 1974* (Washington, D.C.: Administrative Office of the U.S. Courts, 1975), p. 14.

38. K. D. Harris and P. P. Lura, "The Geography of Justice — Sentencing Variations in the U.S. Judicial Districts," *Judicare* 57 (1974): 392–401.

39. *Uniform Crime Reports, 1975*, pp. 44–45.

40. See Douglas Lipton, Robert Martinson, and Judith Wilks, *The Effectiveness of Correctional Treatment: A Survey of Evaluation Studies* (New York: Holt, Rinehart & Winston, 1975), for a comprehensive review of the research on correctional treatment.

41. *Uniform Crime Reports, 1975*, p. 46.

42. Joseph E. Scott, "The Use of Discretion in Determining the Severity of Punishment," *Journal of Criminal Law and Criminology* 65 (1974): 214–224.

43. Reuben S. Horlick, "Inmate Perception of Obstacles to Readjustment in the Community," *Proceedings of the American Correctional Association*, 1961, pp. 200–205.

44. Harris, *The Anguish of Change*, pp. 183–184.

45. Eugene Doleschal, "Humane Justice" (National Council of Crime and Delinquency, Hackensack, N.J., 1976), p. 1 (mimeographed).

46. Donald R. Cressey and Robert A. McDermott, *Diversion from the Juvenile Justice System* (Washington, D.C.: GPO, 1974).

47. Edwin M. Schur, *Radical Non-Intervention: Rethinking the Delinquency Problem* (Englewood Cliffs, N.J.: Prentice-Hall, 1973).

CHAPTER 15

1. National Commission on the Causes and Prevention of Violence, *To Establish Justice, to Insure Domestic Tranquility* (New York: Holt, Rinehart & Winston, 1970), p. 16.

2. Quoted in *Criminal Justice Newsletter*, June 7, 1976, p. 1.

3. National Commission on the Causes and Prevention of Violence, *The Challenge of Crime in a Free Society* (Washington, D.C.: GPO, 1976), p. xxv.

4. *Ibid.*, p. 22.

5. Marvin E. Wolfgang, *Patterns in Criminal Homicide* (Philadelphia: University of Pennsylvania Press, 1958).

6. See Marshall B. Clinard and Richard Quinney, *Criminal Behavior Systems: A Typology*, 2d ed. (New York: Holt, Rinehart & Winston, 1973), pp. 44–45.

7. Konrad Lorenz, *On Aggression* (New York: Harcourt Brace Jovanovich, 1966); Robert Ardrey, *The Territorial Imperative* (New York: Atheneum, 1967).

8. R. Charles Boelkins and Jon F. Heiser, "Biological Bases of Aggression," in David W. Daniels, Marshall F. Gilula, and Frank M. Ochberg, *Violence and the Struggle for Existence* (Boston: Little, Brown, 1970), p. 48.

9. For an interesting example see Robert Dentan, *The Semai: A Nonviolent People of Malaya* (New York: Holt, Rinehart & Winston, 1968).

10. See, *e.g.*, Boelkins and Heiser, "Biological Bases of Aggression," p. 31.

11. See John Dollard, L. Doob, N. E. Miller, O. H. Mowrer, and R. R. Sears, *Frustration and Aggression* (New Haven, Conn.: Yale University Press, 1939).

12. See Rodney Stark and James McEvoy, III, "Middle Class Violence," *Psychology Today* 4 (1970): 52–65.

13. Robert R. Sears, Eleanor E. Maccoby, and Harry Levin *Patterns of Child Rearing* (New York: Harper & Row, 1957), pp. 262–263.

14. Stuart Palmer, *The Psychology of Murder* (New York: Harper & Row, 1960).

15. See, *e.g.,* David G. Gil, *Violence Against Children: Physical Child Abuse in the United States* (Cambridge, Mass.: Harvard University Press, 1970), pp. 113–114.

16. Marvin E. Wolfgang and Franco Ferracuti, *The Subculture of Violence* (London: Tavistock, 1967).

17. See, *e.g.,* Sandra J. Ball-Rokeach, "Values and Violence: A Test of the Subculture of Violence Thesis," *American Sociological Review* 38 (1973): 736–749. See also the discussion of "the culture of poverty" in Chapter 5.

18. See Richard Maxwell Brown, "The American Vigilante Tradition," in Hugh Davis Graham and Ted Robert Gurr, eds., *The History of Violence in America: Historical and Comparative Perspectives* (New York: Holt, Rinehart & Winston, 1969), pp. 121–180.

19. Graham and Gurr, *History of Violence,* p. 82.

20. Surgeon General's Scientific Advisory Committee on Television and Social Behavior, *Television and Growing Up: The Impact of Televised Violence* (Washington, D.C.: GPO, 1972), and George A. Comstock and Eli Rubenstein, eds., *Television and Social Behavior,* vols. 1–5 (Washington, D.C.: GPO, 1972).

21. Many of these studies are summarized in Robert M. Liebert, Emily S. Davidson, and John M. Neale, *The Early Window: Effects of Television on Children and Youth* (New York: Pergamon, 1973).

22. Victor B. Cline, Roger G. Croft, and Steven Courier, "The Desensitization of Children to Violence," in Victor B. Cline, ed., *Where Do You Draw The Line? An Exploration into Media Violence, Pornography, and Censorship* (Provo, Utah: Brigham Young University Press, 1974), pp. 147–155.

23. Theodore W. Newcomb, *Social Psychology* (New York: Dryden Press, 1950), pp. 90–160.

24. Paul G. Cressey, "The Motion Picture Experience as Modified by Social Background and Personality," *American Sociological Review* 3 (1938): 516–525.

25. Dennis Howitt and Guy Cumberbatch, *Mass Media Violence and Society* (New York: Wiley, 1975), p. 130.

26. J. Christian Gillin and Frank M. Ochberg, "Firearms Control and Violence," in Daniels *et al., Violence and the Struggle for Existence,* p. 242.

27. Lynn A. Curtis, *Criminal Violence: National Patterns and Behavior* (Lexington, Mass.: Heath, 1974), p. 111.

28. *To Establish Justice,* p. 147.

29. Wolfgang, *Patterns of Criminal Homicide.*

30. *To Establish Justice,* p. 148.

31. See Curtis, *Criminal Violence,* p. 103.

32. See David N. Daniels, Edison Trickett, Mary Shapiro, Jared Tinklenber, and Jay Jackman, "The Gun Law Controversy," in Daniels *et al., Violence and the Struggle for Existence,* pp. 250–260.

33. For example, Dane Archer and Rosemary Gartner, "Violent Acts and Violent Times: A Comparative Approach to Postwar Homicide Rates," *American Sociological Review* 41 (1978): 937–963, show that war generally contributes to higher overall homicide rates.

34. David F. Luckenbill, "Criminal Homicide as a Situated Transaction," *Social Problems* 25 (1977): 176–186, and Lonnie H. Athens, "The Self and the Violent Criminal Act," *Urban Life and Culture* 3 (1974): 98–112.

CHAPTER 16

1. David N. Daniels and Marshall F. Gilula, "Violence and the Struggles for Existence," in David N. Daniels, Marshall F. Gilula, and Frank M. Ochberg, *Violence and the Struggle for Existence* (Boston: Little, Brown, 1970), p. 428.

2. *Ibid.,* p. 428

3. Paul B. Horton and Gerald R. Leslie, *The Sociology of Social Problems,* 5th ed. (Englewood Cliffs, N.J.: Prentice-Hall, 1974), p. 674.

4. *The CBS News Almanac: 1977* (Maplewood, N.J.: Hammond Almanac, 1977), pp. 724–725, 727.

5. See Quincy Wright, *A Study of War,* abridged by L. L. Wright (Chicago: University of Chicago Press, 1964), pp. 51–87.

6. Marvin Harris, *Culture, Man and Nature* (New York: Harper & Row, 1971), p. 226.

7. Karl Marx and Friedrich Engels, *The Communist Manifesto* (Englewood Cliffs, N.J.: Prentice-Hall, 1955). This pamphlet was originally published in 1848.

8. James C. Davies, "Toward a Theory of Revolution," *American Sociological Review* 27 (1962): 5–19; James C. Davies, "The J-Curve of Rising and Declining Satisfactions as a Cause of Some Great Revolutions and a Contained Rebellion," in Hugh Davis Graham and Ted Robert Gurr, eds., *Violence in America: Histories and Comparative Perspectives* (New York: Holt, Rinehart & Winston, 1958), pp. 547–576.

9. *Ibid.,* p. 5.

10. Ted Robert Gurr, *Why Men Rebel* (Princeton, N.J.: Princeton University Press, 1970).

11. Crance Brinton, *The Anatomy of Revolution* (New York: Vintage Books, 1965), p. 51.

12. *Ibid.,* pp. 28–39.

13. See Joseph Lopreato, ed., *Vilfredo Pareto* (New York: Harper & Row, 1965), pp. 109–162.

14. Wright, *A Study of War,* p. 212.

15. *Ibid.,* pp. 213–214.

16. Kurt Finsterbusch and H. C. Greisman, "The Unprofitability of Warfare in the Twentieth Century," *Social Problems* 22 (February 1975): 451.

17. *CBS News Almanac,* p. 720.

18. Karl von Clausewitz, *On War,* trans. O. J. Matthijs Jolles (Washington, D.C.: Infantry Journal Press, 1950), p. 16.

19. Wright, *A Study of War,* p. 85.

20. Kenneth E. Boulding and Emile Benoit, *Disarmament and the Economy* (New York: Harper & Row, 1963).

21. Quoted in Wright, *A Study of War,* p. 186.

22. Robert C. Angell, "The Growth of Transnational Participation," in Amitai Etzioni and Martin Wenglinsky, eds., *War and Its Prevention* (New York: Harper & Row, 1970), pp. 75–96.

23. Walter H. Capps, "The Vietnam War and American Values," *The Center Magazine,* July–August, 1978, pp. 17–26.

CHAPTER 17

1. National Research Council, *Toward an Understanding of Metropolitan America* (San Francisco: Harper & Row, 1974), pp. 1–2.

2. Noel P. Gist and Sylvia Fleis Fava, *Urban Society,* 6th ed. (New York: Harper & Row, 1974), pp. 100–104, and C. J. Harris, ed., *The Canadian Pocket Encyclopedia,* 30th ed. (Toronto: Quick Canadian Facts, 1975), p. 73.

3. Gist and Fava, *Urban Society,* p. 23.

4. National Research Council, *Understanding Metropolitan America,* p. 41.

5. Thomas Murphy and John Rehfuss, *Urban Politics in the Suburban Era* (Homewood, Ill.: Dorsey Press, 1976), pp. 9–10.

6. Claude S. Fischer, *The Urban Experience* (New York: Harcourt Brace Jovanovich, 1976), p. 21.

7. *Ibid.*

8. Georg Simmel, "The Metropolis and Mental Life," in Robert Gutman and David Popenoe, eds., *Neighborhood, City, and Metropolis* (New York: Random House, 1970).

9. Louis Wirth, "Urbanism as a Way of Life," *American Journal of Sociology* 44 (1938): 1–24.

10. Herbert J. Gans, "Urbanism and Suburbanism as Ways of Life: A Re-evaluation of Definitions," in Gutman and Popenoe, eds., *Neighborhood, City and Metropolis.*

11. Murphy, and Rehfuss, *Urban Politics in the Suburban Era,* pp. 13–17.

12. Fischer, *The Urban Experience,* p. 209.

13. Murphy and Rehfuss, *Urban Politics in the Suburban Era,* p. 234.

14. "The Outer City: U.S. in Suburban Turmoil," *New York Times,* May 30–June 3, 1971.

15. Fischer, *The Urban Experience,* p. 207.

16. Gist and Fava, *Urban Society,* p. 299.

17. Fischer, *The Urban Experience,* p. 215.

18. *Ibid.,* pp. 212, 215–216.

19. U.S. Department of Commerce, *Statistical Abstract of the United States, 1974* (Washington, D.C.: GPO, 1975), p. 19.

20. Harris, *The Canadian Pocket Encyclopedia,* p. 73.

21. Gist and Fava, *Urban Society,* p. 66; Harris, *The Canadian Pocket Encyclopedia,* p. 73.

22. National Research Council, *Understanding Metropolitan America,* pp. 39–40.

23. See Arthur Vidich and Joseph Bensman, *Small Town in Mass Society: Class, Power, and Religion in a Rural Community,* rev. ed. (Princeton, N.J.: Princeton University Press, 1968).

24. National Research Council, *Toward an Understanding of Metropolitan America,* p. 35.

25. *Ibid.,* p. 31.

26. *Ibid.*

27. Fischer, *The Urban Experience,* pp. 55–56.

28. Gist and Fava, *Urban Society,* p. 612.

29. Bradford Snell, "American Ground Transport," in Jerome Skolnick and Elliott Currie, eds., *Crisis in American Institutions,* 3d ed. (Boston: Little, Brown, 1976), pp. 304–326.

30. See Anthony Downs, *Urban Problems and Prospects,* 2d ed. (Skokie, Ill.: Rand McNally, 1976), pp. 94–95.

31. Edwin H. Sutherland and Donald R. Cressey, *Criminology,* 10th ed. (New York: Harper & Row, 1978), pp. 182–186.

32. Fischer, *The Urban Experience,* p. 95.

33. John B. Calhoun, "Population Density and Social Pathology," *Scientific American* 206 (1962): 139–148.

34. Pierre van den Berghe, "Bringing the Beast Back In: Toward a Biosocial Theory of Aggression," *American Sociological Review* 39 (1974): 777–788.

35. See Jonathan L. Freedman, *Crowding and Behavior* (San Francisco: W. H. Freeman, 1975).

36. National Research Council, *Understanding Metropolitan America,* pp. 19–21.

37. U.S. Bureau of the Census, *Current Population Reports: Money Income in 1974 of Families and Persons in the United States,* series P-601, no. 101 (Washington, D.C.: GPO, 1976), p. 5.

38. Edward Hassinger and Robert McNamara, "Rural Health in the United States," in National Academy of Sciences, *Quality of Rural Living: Proceedings of a Workshop* (Washington, D.C.: National Academy of Sciences, 1971). pp. 8–22.

39. Murphy and Rehfuss, *Urban Politics in the Suburban Era,* pp. 236–237.

40. *Ibid.,* pp. 254–258.

41. *Ibid.,* pp. 138–141.

42. Downs, *Urban Problems and Prospects,* pp. 146–154.

43. U.S. Department of Health, Education and Welfare, *Toward a Social Report* (Washington, D.C.: GPO, 1969).

44. Gist and Fava, *Urban Society,* pp. 601–602.

45. Downs, *Urban Problems and Prospects,* p. 101.

46. Nathan Glaser, "Housing Problems and Housing Policies," *The Public Interest,* Spring 1970, p. 30.

47. Gist and Fava, *Urban Society,* pp. 616–617.

CHAPTER 18

1. Estimate based on growth rate figures in Lester R. Brown, "World Population Trends: Signs of Hope, Signs of Distress," *Worldwatch Papers* 8 (September 1976); for a slightly higher estimate see Paul R. Ehrlich and Anne H. Ehrlich, "What Happened to the Population Bomb?" *Human Nature* 2 (1979): 88–92.

2. Paul R. Ehrlich and Anne H. Ehrlich, *Population, Resources, Environment: Issues in Human Ecology,* 2d ed. (San Francisco: W. H. Freeman, 1972), p. 87, and Mihajlo Mesarovic and Eduard Pestel, *Mankind at the Turning Point: The Second Report to the Club of Rome* (New York: Dutton, 1974), p. 115.

3. Ehrlich and Ehrlich, *Population, Resources, Environment: Issues in Human Ecology,* p. 1.

4. Kingsley Davis, "The World's Population Crisis," in Robert K. Merton and Robert Nisbet, eds., *Contemporary Social Problems,* 4th ed. (New York: Harcourt Brace Jovanovich, 1976), pp. 267–268.

5. Judah Matras, *Introduction to Population: A Sociological Approach* (Englewood Cliffs, N.J.: Prentice-Hall, 1977), pp. 36–37.

6. United Nations, Department of Economic and Social Affairs, *Population Bulletin of the United Nations, 1976* (New York: United Nations, 1977), p. 98.

7. Ralph Thomlinson, *Demographic Problems: Controversy Over Population Control,* 2d ed. (Encino, Calif.: Dickenson, 1975), pp. 155–156.

8. Ansley J. Coale, "The History of the Human Population," *Scientific American* 231 (September 1974): 51.

9. Matras, *Introduction to Population,* p. 36.

10. Davis, "The World's Population Crisis," p. 272.

11. *Los Angeles Times,* October 29, 1976.

12. Charles F. Westoff, "The Populations of the Developed Countries," *Scientific American* 231 (1974): 114.

13. Quoted in Davis, "The World's Population Crisis," p. 298.

14. Thomas Robert Malthus, *Essay on the Principle of Population* (Baltimore: Penguin, 1971).

15. John S. Steinhart and Carol E. Steinhart, "Energy Use in the U.S. Food System," *Science* 184 (April 19, 1974); 310–311.

16. Quoted in Paul R. Ehrlich and Anne H. Ehrlich, *Population, Resources, Environment, Problems and Solutions* (San Francisco: W. H. Freeman, 1973), p. 15.

17. *Ibid.,* p. 13.

18. Michael T. Malloy, "The Next Crisis: Universal Famine," *Skeptic,* special issue no. 2 (1974): 19–21.

19. Ingrid Waldron and Robert E. Rickleffs, *Environment and Population: Problems and Solutions* (New York: Holt, Rinehart & Winston, 1973), p. 26.

20. United Nations, Department of Economic and Social Affairs, *The Determinants and Consequences of Population Trends* (New York: United Nations, 1973), 1:531.

21. *Ibid.,* p. 529.

22. Davis, "The World's Population Crisis," p. 274.

23. United Nations, Department of Economic and Social Affairs, *Demographic Yearbook, 1974* (New York: United Nations, 1975), p. 107.

24. United Nations, Department of Economic and Social Affairs, *Human Fertility and National Development* (New York: United Nations, 1971), p. 21.

25. *Ibid.,* p. 28.

26. Davis, "The World's Population Crisis," p. 282.

27. Ehrlich and Ehrlich, *Population, Resources, Environment: Issues in Human Ecology,* p. 113.

28. David Pimental *et al.,* "Food Production and the Energy Crisis," *Science* 182 (November 2, 1973): 447–448.

29. See E. F. Schumacher, *Small Is Beautiful: Economics as if People Mattered* (New York: Harper & Row, 1974), pp. 171–190.

30. Ehrlich and Ehrlich, *Population, Resources, Environment: Issues in Human Ecology,* p. 113.

31. *Ibid.,* pp. 113–119.

32. *Ibid.,* p. 133.

33. See Georg Borgstrom, *The Hungry Planet,* 2d ed. rev. (New York: Collier Books, 1972), pp. 432–465.

34. *Ibid.,* p. 467.

35. Norman B. Ryder and Charles F. Westoff, "The Papal Encyclical and Catholic Practice and Attitudes, 1969," *Studies in Family Planning* 1 (February 1970): 1–7.

36. See Thomlinson, *Demographic Problems,* pp. 146–148.

37. Michael Bamburger and Margaret Earle, "Factors Affecting Family Planning in a Low Income Caracas Neighborhood," *Studies in Family Planning* 2 (1971): 175–178.

38. Ehrlich and Ehrlich, "What Happened to the Population Bomb?" pp. 90–91.

39. "Korea: Trends in Four National Knowledge, Attitudes, and Practice Surveys, 1964–1967," *Studies in Family Planning* 43 (1969): 7.

40. Saw Swee-Hock, "Singapore: Resumption of Rapid Fertility Decline in 1973," *Studies in Family Planning* 6 (1975): 166–169.

41. Davis, "The World's Population Crisis," p. 300.

42. Kai Bird, "Sterilization in India: Indira Ghandi Uses Force," *The Nation* 222 (June 19, 1976): 747–749, and Sharon Rosenhause, "Killings Reported in India Protest Over Sterilization," *Los Angeles Times,* October 28, 1976.

43. Jeannie L. Rosoff, "House OKs Overseas Family Planning Authorization After Sterilization Debate," *Planned Parenthood—World Population Memorandum*, May 27, 1977, p. 2.

44. Henry Kamm, "India State Is Leader in Forced Sterilization," *New York Times*, August 13, 1976.

45. Robert Heilbroner, *An Inquiry into the Human Prospect* (New York: W. W. Norton, 1974).

46. Population Reference Bureau, "Capsules," *Intercom* 11 (1975): 7.

47. Lester R. Brown, "World Population Trends: Signs of Hope, Signs of Distress," *Worldwatch Papers* 8 (1976):7.

48. Lester R. Brown, quoted in "Population Implosion," *Newsweek*, December 6, 1976.

49. Frank W. Notestein, "The Population Crisis: Reasons for Hope," *Foreign Affairs* 46 (1967): 167–180.

CHAPTER 19

1. Paul R. Ehrlich and Anne H. Ehrlich, *Population, Resources, Environment: Issues in Human Ecology* (San Francisco: W. H. Freeman, 1972), p. 147.

2. *Environmental Quality: The First Annual Report of the Council on Environmental Quality* (Washington, D.C.: GPO, 1970).

3. Ehrlich and Ehrlich, *Population, Resources, Environment: Issues in Human Ecology*, p. 148.

4. Lester B. Lave and Eugene P. Seskin, "Air Pollution and Human Health," *Science* 169 (August 21, 1970): 723–733.

5. Ehrlich and Ehrlich, *Population, Resources, Environment: Issues in Human Ecology*, pp. 151–152.

6. Philip H. Howard and Arnold Hanchett, "Chlorofluorocarbon Sources of Environmental Contamination," *Science* (July 1975): 217–219.

7. Sterling Brubacker, *To Live on Earth: Man and His Environment in Perspective* (Baltimore: Johns Hopkins Press, 1972), pp. 59–67.

8. *Ibid.*, p. 106.

9. Ehrlich and Ehrlich, *Population, Resources, Environment: Issues in Human Ecology*, pp. 230–231.

10. *Ibid.*, p. 169.

11. *Ibid.*, p. 221.

12. Kenneth A. Wagner, Paul C. Bailey, and Glenn H. Campbell, *Under Siege: Man, Men, and Earth* (New York: Harper & Row, 1973), p. 67.

13. *Ibid.*, p. 68; Ehrlich and Ehrlich, *Population, Resources, Environment: Issues in Human Ecology*, p. 221.

14. Wagner, Bailey, and Campbell, *Under Siege*, p. 70.

15. Ehrlich and Ehrlich, *Population, Resources, Environment: Issues in Human Ecology*, pp. 202–203.

16. Georg Borgstrom, *The Hungry Planet* (New York: Macmillan, 1972), p. 510.

17. *Ibid.*, p. 510. The grammatical errors are present in the text.

18. Ehrlich and Ehrlich, *Population, Resources, Environment: Issues in Human Ecology*, p. 159.

19. Richard T. Cooper and Paul E. Steiger, "Occupational Health Hazards: A National Crisis," *Los Angeles Times*, June 27, 1976.

20. *Ibid.*

21. Ehrlich and Ehrlich, *Population, Resources, Environment: Issues in Human Ecology*, p. 160.

22. *Ibid.*, p. 173.

23. Charles H. Anderson, *The Sociology of Survival: Social Problems of Growth* (Homewood, Ill.: Dorsey Press, 1976), p. 149.

24. *Ibid.*, p. 154.

25. Kingsley Davis, "The World's Population Crisis," in Robert K. Merton and Robert Nisbet, eds., *Contemporary Social Problems*, 4th ed. (New York: Harcourt Brace Jovanovich, 1976), p. 289.

26. Anderson, *The Sociology of Survival*, p. 153.

27. M. King Hubbert, "Energy from Fossil Fuels," *Science* 109 (1949): 103–109.

28. *Newsweek*, April 18, 1977.

29. *Wall Street Journal*, August 17, 1978, p. 16.

30. Donella H. Meadows, Dennis L. Meadows, Jorgen Randers, and William W. Behrens, III, *The Limits of Growth* (New York: Universe Books, 1972).

31. See Anderson, *The Sociology of Survival*, p. 154.

32. See Ehrlich and Ehrlich, *Population, Resources, Environment: Issues in Human Ecology*, p. 64.

33. Thomas O'Toole, "Demand for Oil Will Exceed Output by '85, C.I.A. Says," *Los Angeles Times*, April 16, 1977.

34. Anderson, *The Sociology of Survival*, p. 157.

35. Meadows *et al.*, *The Limits to Growth*, pp. 56–60; Ingrid Waldron and Robert E. Rickless, *Environment and Population: Problems and Solutions* (New York: Holt, Rinehart & Winston, 1973), p. 106.

36. Waldron and Rickless, *Environment and Population*, p. 110.

37. H. S. D. Cole, Christopher Freeman, Marie Jahoda, and K. L. R. Pavitt, eds., *Models of Doom: A Critique of the Limits to Growth* (New York: Universe Books, 1973).

38. *Genesis* 1:28. A newer translation of biblical texts (the Jerusalem Bible) puts the words as follows: "Be fruitful, multiply, fill the earth and conquer it. Be masters of the fish of the sea, the birds of heaven and all living animals on the earth."

39. See Lynn White, Jr., "Historical Roots of Our Ecological Crisis," *Science* 155 (1967): 1203–1207.

40. John McHale, *World Facts and Trends*, 2d ed. (New York: Macmillan, 1972), p. 87.

41. Ehrlich and Ehrlich, *Population, Resources, Environment: Issues in Human Ecology*, p. 68.

42. For instance, Lee found that the !Kung bushmen, who live in the inhospitable Kalahari Desert, work an average of only 12 to 19 hours a week to obtain their food; Richard Borshay Lee, "The Hunter's Scarce Resources in the Kalahari," in James P. Spradley and David W. Mc-Curdy, eds., *Conformity and Conflict: Readings in Cultural Anthropology* (Boston: Little, Brown: 1977), p. 299.

43. Richard J. Barnet, "No Room in the Lifeboats," *New York Times Magazine,* April 16, 1978, p. 32ff.

44. Richard L. Means, "Public Opinion and Planned Changes in Social Behavior: The Ecological Crisis," in W. R. Burch, Jr., N. H. Cheek, Jr., and L. Taylor, eds., *Social Behavior, Natural Resources, and the Environment* (New York: Harper & Row, 1972), pp. 203–213.

Glossary

absolute approach Defining poverty by dividing the poor from the nonpoor on the basis of an objective standard (*e.g.,* income).

absolute deprivation Lack of one or more of the necessities of life.

addiction The intense craving for a drug that develops after a period of physical dependence stemming from heavy use.

affective psychosis A psychosis involving severe disturbances in mood and emotion.

affirmative-action program A program designed to make up for past discrimination by giving special assistance to members of the groups that were discriminated against.

age composition The percentage of a population in each age category.

age grade People of similar age, such as children, adolescents, and adults.

aging A set of biological and social changes that occur in all people throughout life, but at different rates.

alcoholic A person whose work or social life is disrupted by drinking.

assault An attack on a person with the intention of hurting or killing the victim.

authoritarian personality A personality that is rigid and inflexible, has a very low tolerance for uncertainty and readily accepts orders from above.

aversion therapy A form of behavioral therapy that uses punishment to discourage a particular behavior.

bail A sum of money put up as security to be forfeited if a person accused of committing a crime does not show up for trial.

balance of power The condition in which the military strength of the world's strongest nations or groups of nations is roughly equal.

behavioral therapy Modification of the special behavior that is causing a patient's problems.

behaviorist theory A theory that explains social behavior in terms of observable behavior.

bilingualism The policy of giving two languages equal legal status in a nation.

biosocial theory A theory that explains social behavior by reference to biological traits.

biosphere The life-containing region of the earth extending from about 200 feet below sea level to about 10,000 feet above it.

birthrate The number of babies born in a year divided by the total population.

bisexuality Willingness to have sexual relations with individuals of either sex.

blockbusting A practice of realtors in which residents of a neighborhood into which a minority family has moved are convinced that property values in the neighborhood will fall; the residents sell cheaply to the realtors, who resell the property to minority families at a higher price.

bourgeoisie The class of people who, according to Marx, own capital and capital-producing property.

bureaucracy A form of social organization characterized by division of labor, a hierarchy of authority, a set of formal rules, impersonal enforcement of rules, and job security.

capital gain A sum of money received from an investment and not earned as wages.

capitalism An economic system characterized by private property, exchange of commodities and capital, and free market for goods and labor.

capitation A form of compensation in which a physician is paid a certain amount for each person treated, regardless of the services rendered.

case study A detailed examination of specific individuals, groups, or situations.

catatonic schizophrenia A form of mental disorder characterized by periods of stupor in which the person remains motionless.

chemotherapy The use of drugs to treat mental disorders.

class conflict The disagreements and strife that develop between different social classes because of their different social, economic, and political interests.

classical conditioning Learning that occurs without the active participation of the subject.

client-centered therapy Psychotherapy in which the patient chooses the topic and sets the pace and direction of the therapy session while the therapist provides encouragement and support. (Also called nondirective therapy.)

commune A small self-supporting community voluntarily joined by individuals committed to living together in a family-like environment.

compensatory-education program A special program whose goal is to help disadvantaged students reach educational levels comparable to those achieved by more privileged students.

conflict theory A sociological theory that sees conflicts between different groups as a basic social process and holds that the principal source of social problems is exploitation and oppression of one group by another.

conglomerate A large firm that owns businesses in many areas of production and distribution.

control theory A criminological theory holding that people commit crimes when social norms and other social forces no longer control them.

corporate technostructure The group of technically skilled corporation managers who, according to Galbraith, make the important decisions.

crime Violation of a criminal law.

crime control model A model of criminal justice that favors speedy arrest and punishment of anyone who commits a crime.

culture The way of life of the people in a certain geographic area, particularly their ideas, beliefs, values, patterns of thought, and symbols.

cyclical unemployment Unemployment resulting from changes in the business cycle, which, in turn, cause changes in the demand for labor.

death rate The number of people who die in a year divided by the total population.

decriminalization The proposal that penalties for possession and use of a drug be abolished even if sales of the drug remain illegal.

deduction Subtracting certain expenses (*e.g.*, business and medical costs) from income for tax purposes.

de facto **segregation** Segregation of minority groups that results from existing social conditions (such as housing patterns) but is not legally required.

de jure **segregation** Segregation of minority groups that is required by law.

demographic transition A change in basic birthrates and death rates occurring after industrialization and ultimately resulting in slower overall population growth.

demography A scientific discipline dealing with the distribution, density, and vital statistics of populations.

deviant An individual who violates a social norm.

deviant subculture A set of perspectives, attitudes, and values that support criminal or other norm-violating activity.

differential association A theory holding that people become criminals because they are exposed to more behavior patterns that are favorable to a certain kind of crime than behavior patterns that are opposed to it.

disarmament Reduction of armed forces and armaments, usually by means of a treaty.

discrimination The practice of treating some people as second-class citizens because of their minority status.

displacement of goals The shifting of organizational goals away from the organization's original purpose, as when an employee does something that interferes with the achievement of the organization's goals in order to protect his or her job.

district A special governmental unit with its own tax base set up to handle a single task such as fire protection or sewer service.

diversion program A program whose goal is to keep juveniles out of courts.

domination A national system in which one (ethnic) group holds power and minority groups are subordinate to it.

double bind A situation in which a parent gives a child two conflicting messages at the same time.

double standard A code of behavior that gives men greater sexual freedom than women.

due-process model A model of criminal justice that places more emphasis on protecting human rights and dignity than on punishing criminals.

dysfunction An action of an institution that interferes with the carrying out of essential social tasks.

ecology The study of the interrelationships among plants, animals, and their environments.

ecosystem A self-sufficient community of organisms living in an interdependent relationship with each other and their environment.

ego According to Freud, the individual's conscious, reality-oriented experience.

electrotherapy The use of electric shocks to treat mental disorders.

elitist One who believes that nations should be ruled by a small elite class.

endogamy The practice of marrying within one's own social group.

ethnic group A group whose members share a sense of togetherness and the conviction that they form a distinct group or "people."

ethnocentrism The tendency to view the norms and values of one's own culture as absolute and to use them as a standard against which to measure those of other cultures.

exclusion Income received from certain sources (*e.g.*, municipal bonds) that is not counted for tax purposes.

executive branch The branch of government responsible for carrying out the laws.

experiment A research method in which the behavior of individuals or groups is studied under controlled conditions, usually in a laboratory setting.

exploitive technology Technology designed to produce immediate profits without regard to long-term consequences.

extended family Members of two or more related nuclear families living together in the same place.

extinction Modification of a behavior by removing the reinforcement (reward) for that behavior.

family planning A population control program whose objective is voluntary reduction of the birth rate.

federal system A system of government in which national affairs are handled by a central government and local affairs are left to semi-independent local governments.

federation A system of government in which each city, country, or state operates independently on some issues but fuses other activities with those of allied governments.

fee-for-service compensation A form of compensation in which a physician is paid a fixed fee for each service rendered.

felony A serious offense, usually punishable by death or by confinement in a central prison.

folkway A custom whose violators are not strongly condemned.

food chain The set of transformations beginning with production of food by green plants and ending with decomposition of the bodies of animals.

forcible rape Sexual intercourse obtained by the use or threat of force.

free school A school in which teachers encourage pupils to set their own educational goals and tempo.

frustration–aggression theory A theory holding that frustration produces aggression.

function The contribution of each part of society to the maintenance of a balanced order.

functional disorder A mental disorder that lacks a clear-cut physical cause; includes neuroses, psychoses, psychosomatic disorders, and personality disorders.

functionalist theory A sociological theory that sees society as a delicate balance of parts and holds that social problems arise when societies become disorganized.

fundamental education Education that concentrates on the teaching of reading, writing, and arithmetic.

general deterrence Punishment of criminals in order to frighten others so much that they will not violate the law.

generalized other A person's system of values and standards that, according to Mead, reflect the expectations of people in general.

geothermal energy The heat of the earth's inner core.

grade inflation The assignment of higher student grades than were formerly given for the same quality of work.

great man theory of history The theory holding that individual decision makers determine the course of history.

group A set of individuals with organized and recurrent relationships with one another.

group marriage A family that includes three or more adults as the marriage partners.

group therapy A procedure in which each member of a group is encouraged to reveal his or her problems and experiences to the group, which discusses and examines them.

growth rate The birthrate minus the death rate.

health A state of physical, mental, and social well-being.

health maintenance organization An organization in which a group of medical personnel offer a range of medical services to subscribers who pay a fixed monthly fee.

hebephrenic schizophrenia A form of mental disorder characterized by infantile behavior, giggling, silliness, and hallucinations.

heterosexuality A preference for sexual relations with individuals of the opposite sex.

homicide The killing of a human being.

homosexuality A preference for sexual relations with individuals of the same sex.

hydroelectric power Energy generated by turbines turned by flowing water.

id The instinctual drives, particularly sex, that, according to Freud, motivate all human behavior.

illegitimacy rate The number of illegitimate births divided by the number of single women of childbearing age.

imperialism The creation or expansion of an empire.

incest taboo The prohibition of sexual relations between parents and their children or between the children themselves.

income The amount of money a person earns in a given year.

industrial espionage The hiring of investigators to gain information about one's business competitors, for instance by "bugging" their offices and telephones.

institution A relatively stable pattern of thought and behavior centered on the performance of an important social task.

institutional discrimination Discrimination against minority groups that is practiced by economic, educational, and political organizations rather than by individuals.

institutional racism Prejudice and discrimination against a particular race that are built into a society's economic, educational, and political institutions.

integration A national system in which ethnic backgrounds are ignored and all individuals are treated alike.

interactionist theory A theory that explains social behavior in terms of each individual's social relationships.

interlocking directorate The situation that exists when some of the same individuals sit on the boards of directors of competing firms, or when directors of competing firms sit together on the board of directors of a firm in a different industry.

intermediate technology Machines that are less complicated than expensive energy-intensive machines but more efficient than human and animal power.

international war Prolonged armed conflict between the governments of two or more nations.

involutional melancholia A severe depression that occurs during the involutional period (change of life or menopause).

iron law of oligarchy The tendency for any large organization to be ruled, according to Michels, by a few powerful people.

judicial branch The branch of government responsible for interpreting the laws and deciding on their constitutionality.

juvenile delinquency Behavior by minors (usually defined as individuals below the age of 18) that is in violation of the law.

labeling theory A theory holding that branding a person as a criminal often encourages rather than discourages criminal behavior.

latent function A hidden function performed by a social institution or agency.

legalization The proposal that use and sale of a drug be made legal, with government regulation.

legislative branch The branch of government responsible for enacting laws.

legitimation Consent of the governed based on belief that those who govern are just and fair.

lesbian A female homosexual.

limited war A war whose goals are restricted to a set of specific objectives and in which a rather small group of military personnel do the fighting.

lobbying Activities of special-interest groups aimed at convincing lawmakers to pass the kind of legislation they desire.

machismo Tough, aggressive masculinity.

macro theory Sociological theory that is concerned with the behavior of large groups and entire societies.

maintenance program A program that supplies addicts or habitual users with a drug while denying it to the public at large.

manic depression A mental disorder characterized by extreme swings in mood.

manslaughter The unlawful killing of another person without malice.

market control Domination of a market by a few giant firms.

medicaid An American program designed to help the poor, the blind, and the disabled pay for medical care.

medicare An American program that pays for medical care of people over 65 years old.

megalopolis An area in which several large cities are fused together.

meltdown An accident in which the cooling system of a nuclear-power plant fails, allowing the heat of the nuclear reaction to melt the core, thus releasing huge amounts of radiation.

melting-pot theory The belief that North American society acts as a sort of crucible in which people from around the world are blended together to form a new and distinctive culture.

membership group A group of which an individual is a member, whether willingly or not.

mental disorder A mental condition that makes it difficult or impossible for a person to cope with routine, everyday life.

micro theory Sociological theory that is concerned with the behavior of individuals and small groups.

militarism (a) Glorification of war and combat. (b) Strong belief in "defense" combined with huge military expenditures.

misdemeanor A minor offense, usually punishable by confinement in a local jail or payment of a fine.

monogamy The practice of being married to only one person at a time.

monopoly The situation existing when a single corporation has gained complete control of a market.

moral crusader A leader who unites separate groups of dissatisfied people into an organized social movement.

mores Customs whose violators are punished or otherwise strongly condemned.

murder The unlawful killing of a human being with malice aforethought.

nationalism A form of ethnocentrism based on a sense of identification with and devotion to one's nation.

neurosis A personal problem, not as severe as psychosis, accompanied by anxiety and chronically inappropriate responses to everyday situations.

norm A social rule telling us what behavior is acceptable in a certain situation and what is not.

nuclear family A married couple and their children.

oligopoly The situation existing when an industry is dominated by a few large companies.

open marriage A marriage in which the partners are committed to their own and each other's growth.

operant conditioning Conditioned learning that requires the active participation of the subject.

opiate Any of a group of natural and synthetic drugs with pain-relieving properties including opium, codeine, morphine, heroin, meperideine, and methadone.

organic disorder A mental disorder that has a clear-cut physical cause such as brain damage.

overeducation Training more people for occupations than there are jobs available in those occupations.

paranoia A mental disorder in which the person suffers from overpowering, irrational fears.

paranoid schizophrenia A mental disorder characterized by absurd delusions, irrational fears, and hallucinations.

parliamentary system A system of government in which the executive branch is not distinctly separate from the legislative branch; the prime minister is elected by the legislature and must resign if the party in power loses its legislative majority.

parole Release of a criminal from prison after part of his or her sentence has been served.

participant observation A research method in which the researcher participates in the activities of the group under study.

personal interview A research method which asks people about their activities and attitudes.

personality The relatively stable characteristics and traits that distinguish one person from another and account for differences in individual behavior.

personality disorder A maladaptive pattern of behavior that is presumed to be rooted in the individual's personality.

personality theory A theory holding that social behavior is determined by differences in personality.

photochemical smog A group of noxious compounds produced by the action of sunlight on oxygen, hydrocarbons, and nitrogen oxides.

photosynthesis The process by which green plants convert solar energy into food.

plea bargaining A process by which a defense attorney and a prosecutor agree to let the defendant plead guilty in return for a reduction in the charge or other considerations.

pluralism A national system in which several ethnic groups maintain a high level of independence and equality.

pluralist One who believes that political decisions are made by changing coalitions of political forces.

political party A loosely organized agency whose goals are to get its members elected to political office and to influence the decisions of those who already hold office.

political socialization The process by which people learn their political values and perspectives.

polygyny The practice of being married to more than one wife at a time.

pornography Obscene books, pictures, sights, and sounds.

positive reinforcement A reward that encourages a specific behavior.

poverty (a) The state of having an income below some specified level. (b) The state of having significantly less income and wealth than the average person in the society of which one is a member.

power The ability to force other people to do something whether they want to or not.

power elite A group of wealthy and powerful Americans who, according to Mills, pursue their own interests at the expense of the average person.

prejudice Antipathy, either felt or expressed, based on a faulty and inflexible generalization and directed toward a group as a whole or toward an individual because he or she is a member of that group.

preliminary hearing A hearing at which a judge decides whether the evidence against the accused is sufficient to justify further legal proceedings.

preventive medicine The theory or practice of staying healthy by maintaining good health habits.

price fixing Collusion by several companies to cut competition and set uniformly high prices.

price leader A corporation whose prices are used as a guideline by the other firms in its industry.

probation Suspension of the sentence of a person who has been convicted but not yet imprisoned, on condition of continued good behavior and regular reporting to a probation officer.

proletariat The working class in an industrial society.

prostitution The practice of selling the services of oneself or another person for purposes of intercourse or other sexual activities.

psychedelic drugs A group of drugs that produce a significant alteration in the user's consciousness.

psychoanalysis Long-term therapy procedure designed to uncover the repressed memories, motives, and conflicts assumed to be at the root of the patient's psychological problems.

psychosis A mental disorder in which a person has lost contact with reality and may suffer hallucinations, delusions, and the like.

psychosomatic disorder A physical illness caused by psychological problems.

psychotherapy Any program for helping a patient understand and then overcome the causes of his or her personality problems.

race People who are thought to have a common set of physical characteristics but may or may not necessarily share a sense of unity and identity.

racism Stereotyping, prejudice, and discrimination based on race.

recidivism Rearrest of a person who has previously been convicted of a crime.

reference group A group with whose values and standards an individual identifies and of which he or she would like to be a member.

refined birthrate A birthrate that has been adjusted for the age and sex composition of the population.

rehabilitation The process of changing a person's criminal behavior by nonpunitive methods.

reinforcement   The reward or punishment received by an individual for a particular behavior.

relative approach   Dividing the poor from the nonpoor on the basis of the wealth and income of the average person.

relative deprivation   The situation in which persons have considerably less income, wealth, and prestige than they believe they deserve.

relative-deprivation theory   A theory holding that revolutions are caused by differences between what people have and what they think they should have.

resegregation   Ethnic segregation that results when parents remove their children from integrated schools or move to segregated suburbs.

revolutionary war   Armed conflict between an official government and one or more groups of rebels.

rite of passage   A ritual that marks the transition from one stage of life to another, especially from childhood to adulthood.

robbery   The unlawful taking of another person's property by force or threat of force.

role   A set of expectations and behaviors associated with a social position.

role strain   The feelings experienced by people when what is expected of them in one role conflicts with what is expected in another.

sample   A cross-section of subjects selected for study as representative of a larger population.

scapegoat   A person or group that is unjustly blamed for problems.

schizophrenia   A mental disorder involving extreme disorganization in personality, thought patterns, and speech.

sedative-hypnotic   A drug that depresses the central nervous system.

sexism   Stereotyping, prejudice, and discrimination based on gender.

sex role   A role assigned to a person on the basis of gender.

sex role socialization   The process by which a person learns the behaviors and attitudes that are expected of the female or male gender.

sexual stereotyping   The portrayal of all females or males as having similar fixed traits.

shock therapy   The use of electric shocks to treat mental disorders.

simple schizophrenia   A form of mental disorder in which the person progressively loses interest in everyday living and withdraws into a fantasy world.

social class   A category of people with similar shares of the things that are valued in a society, particularly life chances such as the opportunity to get a good education.

socialization   The process by which individuals learn the ways of thinking and behaving of their culture.

social movement   A social group organized to bring about or resist certain social changes.

social problem   (a) A condition that a significant number of people believe to be a problem. (b) An area in which there is a sizable difference between the ideals of a society and its actual achievements.

social-psychological theories   Micro theories dealing with the effects of individuals and groups on each other.

social security   A government-administered old-age pension program whose formal title is Old Age and Survivors' Insurance.

social stratification   The division of a society into two or more social classes (strata).

social structure   The organized patterns of human behavior in a society.

sociology   The study of social relations, organization, and change.

solar energy   The energy supplied by the sun.

special-interest group   People who have a stake in a specific area of public policy.

specific deterrence   Punishment of criminals in order to change their ways.

stagflation   Inflation that occurs during periods of economic stagnation or recession.

status   (a) A social position made up of rights and obligations. (b) Prestige inherited from one's family or derived from occupation and life style.

statutory rape   Sexual intercourse with a female below a legally defined age of consent (usually 16 or 18).

stereotype   The portrayal of all the members of a particular group as having similar fixed, usually unfavorable, traits.

stimulant   A drug that arouses the central nervous system.

strain theory   A theory holding that crime is caused by the strain produced when societies tell people that wealth is available to all but nevertheless restrict access to the means for achieving wealth.

structural unemployment   Unemployment resulting from long-term changes in the economy such as technological changes.

subculture   A culture that exists within a larger culture and is influenced by it, but has its own unique ideas and beliefs.

suburb   A district, usually residential, located on or near the outskirts of a city; often a separately incorporated city or town.

superego   According to Freud, the individual's conscience or sense of morality.

survey   A research method which asks people about their attitudes and activities, either in personal interviews or by means of questionnaires.

symbol   (a) A word or set of words. (b) Something that stands for or represents something else (*e.g.*, an object used to represent something abstract).

systematic desensitization   A form of behavioral therapy in which the patient is gradually exposed to a feared stimulus so that the fear is slowly overcome.

tax shelter   An investment bringing returns that are taxed at an unusually low rate, or which may be postponed.

temperature inversion   A condition in which a layer of cold air moves over a layer of warm air, sealing in pollutants that would otherwise rise into the upper atmosphere.

tolerance   (a) The immunity to the effects of a drug that builds up after repeated use. (b) The practice of ignoring behavior patterns that are personally objectionable.

total institution   A prison, mental hospital, monastery, or similar place where like-situated individuals lead an enclosed, formally administered round of life.

total war   A war whose goal is unconditional surrender of an enemy nation and in which both military personnel and ordinary citizens participate.

urbanization   The movement of people from rural areas to cities.

urban renewal   A program, usually financed by the government, intended to upgrade decaying city areas.

value conflict   A clash in the attitudes and beliefs held by different social groups.

victimization survey   A survey in which people are asked in personal interviews to report whether they have been the victims of various kinds of criminal offenses.

victimless crime   A crime in which the harm, if any, is not suffered by anyone except the offender.

violence   Behavior intended to cause bodily pain or injury to another; may be legitimate or illegitimate.

wage–price spiral   A repetitive inflationary circle in which prices are raised to cover the costs of higher wages, and wages are then raised to cover the increased cost of living.

war   Protracted military conflict between two or more organized groups.

wealth   A person's total economic worth (*e.g.,* real estate, stocks, cash).

white-collar crime   Crime committed by people of respectability and high social status in the course of their occupations.

withdrawal   The sickness that a habitual drug user experiences when the drug is discontinued after a period of steady use.

Author Index

Subject Index

79 80 81 82 9 8 7 6 5 4 3 2 1